AFTER BREZHNEV
Sources of Soviet Conduct
in the 1980s

CSIS PUBLICATION SERIES ON THE
SOVIET UNION IN THE 1980s

ROBERT F. BYRNES, *Editor*

AILEEN MASTERSON, *Associate Editor*

AFTER BREZHNEV

Sources of Soviet Conduct
in the 1980s

Edited by
Robert F. Byrnes

PUBLISHED IN ASSOCIATION WITH THE
CENTER FOR STRATEGIC AND INTERNATIONAL STUDIES,
GEORGETOWN UNIVERSITY, WASHINGTON, D.C.

INDIANA UNIVERSITY PRESS · BLOOMINGTON

Library of Congress Cataloging in Publication Data
Main entry under title:

After Brezhnev.

(CSIS publication series on the Soviet Union in the
1980s)
"Published in association with the Center for
Strategic and International Studies, Georgetown
University."
Bibliography: p.
Includes index.
1. Soviet Union—Foreign relations—1975–   —Ad-
dresses, essays, lectures.   2. Soviet Union—Economic
policy—1981–   —Addresses, essays, lectures.
3. Societ Union—Military policy—Addresses, essays,
lectures.   4. Soviet Union—Intellectual life—
1970–   —Addresses, essays, lectures.   I. Byrnes,
Robert Francis.   II. Georgetown University. Center for
Strategic and International Studies.   III. Series.
DK274.A5337   1983   327.47   82-48614
ISBN 0-253-35392-0
ISBN 0-253-20306-6 (pbk.)   2345   87868584

Most political decisions are a choice between
the disagreeable and the intolerable.
 —EDMUND BURKE

The most perilous moment for a bad government
is when it seeks to mend its ways.
 —ALEXIS DE TOCQUEVILLE

Participants in CSIS Project on the Soviet Union in the 1980s

Direction and Administration

Robert F. Byrnes,
*Project Director and Editor of
    Publication Series*
Indiana University

Aileen Masterson,
*Project Coordinator and Associate Editor
    of Publication Series, CSIS*

Gerrit W. Gong,
Research and Editorial Associate, CSIS

James J. Townsend,
Research Assistant, CSIS

Lee Agree,
Project Assistant, CSIS

Working Groups

The Political System

Seweryn Bialer, *Chairman*
Columbia University

George Breslauer
University of California, Berkeley

Thane Gustafson
The Rand Corporation

Myron Rush
Cornell University

Military Forces

Coit D. Blacker, *Chairman*
Stanford University

Fritz W. Ermarth
Northrop Corporation

David Holloway
University of Edinburgh

Arnold L. Horelick
The Rand Corporation

Lt. General Brent Scowcroft (ret.)
Former National Security Adviser

The Economy

Robert W. Campbell, *Chairman*
Indiana University

Morris Bornstein
University of Michigan

John Hardt
Library of Congress

D. Gale Johnson
University of Chicago

Thomas Wolf
Ohio State University

Social Trends

Gail Warshofsky Lapidus, *Chairman*
University of California, Berkeley

Walter Connor
Foreign Service Institute

Murray Feshbach
Georgetown University

Gregory Massell
Hunter College
City University of New York

Contents

Foreword

WITH GREAT pride and deep satisfaction the Center for Strategic and International Studies, in its twentieth anniversary year, has conducted the project that led to the publication of this remarkable volume. Throughout the years, CSIS has tried to emphasize anticipatory, integrated assessments of the major issues confronting America's policy makers. To us at CSIS, this study vividly illustrates the benefits of such an approach.

The issue is critical and timely because of the Soviet Union's status as one of the two global superpowers and because its combination of extraordinary military strength, external ambition, and severe internal weaknesses makes its behavior puzzling and unpredictable. Scholars disagree whether this confusing combination of qualities will make the USSR a greater or a lesser threat to Western interests over the next decade.

After Brezhnev examines the roots of Soviet conduct through a comprehensive, multidisciplinary approach. Unlike the compartmentalized analyses too often done in the government and academia, this study addresses the Soviet Union as an organic system and emphasizes how internal and external factors influence one another in shaping Soviet behavior. By analyzing the sources of Soviet conduct in the 1980s in an effort to clarify the problems and opportunities that Moscow faces in the years ahead, this volume is aimed at helping American policy makers respond effectively.

After Brezhnev represents the initial CSIS contribution to the current revitalization of Soviet studies in the United States. We hope that the present project will help reverse the downward trend in Soviet studies in America, which for more than a decade have suffered from inadequate funding, declining opportunities for graduate study, and dim career prospects. Philip Mosely, who has deservedly been called the father of Russian studies in the United States, made an immense contribution to the scholarly development of CSIS by forming its International Research Council in 1968 and chairing it until his death. I am certain that he would have been proud of this contribution to his favorite field, particularly because several of his students have participated in this analysis of the Soviet Union as a society.

This project came about through an unusual combination of circumstances. Mr. William Wood Prince of Chicago had talked to the distinguished Chairman of the Senate Foreign Relations Committee, Senator Charles Percy, about the policy makers' need for studies that would provide comprehensive factual information and a conceptual context for understanding the Soviet Union. Senator Percy and I also discussed this problem, and it was through him that I met Mr. Wood Prince. I found him to be a man of great vision and unusual wisdom who appreciated the magnitude of the task inherent in an analysis of a country as large, complex, and secretive as the Soviet Union. The Frederick Henry Prince Trusts provided a generous grant to CSIS that made this study possible. Without the interest of Mr. Wood Prince and Senator Percy, our own desires to undertake such a project would never have been realized.

Dr. Robert F. Byrnes, Distinguished Professor of History at Indiana University, led the research activities as project director and served as editor of this volume and of the related publication series. He ensured that the manuscript was completed by a strict deadline without compromising scholarly standards. My words cannot adequately praise his extraordinary leadership, sense of scholarship, and organizational ability. The project's staff in residence at CSIS played an invaluable role. Its coordinating and editorial activities and its substantive contributions have been essential in producing integrated and polished products. Special mention should be made of Aileen Masterson, coordinator of the Soviet project, whose administrative and editorial talents were crucial to the book's completion. Her unusual abilities to deal with a wide range of scholars and difficult problems won her universal respect and admiration.

This analysis helps to set a standard of the highest scholarship for Soviet studies at CSIS. We hope it will lay the basis for the national debate on the challenges that lie ahead.

Spring 1983
David M. Abshire
President, CSIS

Preface

FEW ISSUES are of graver moment for the world than maintaining peace. For Americans, both the informed citizen and the policy maker, concerns about the Soviet Union, its policies, and its relations with the United States are central. However, the problems are so numerous, they are so closely related to many other issues in other parts of the world and to American politics, and the evidence is at once so abundant and so limited, so clear and so contradictory, that few reach and maintain well-founded opinions about Soviet power and policy. Moreover, some no sooner believe they have achieved some clarity than a single event creates uncertainty.

Western policy makers and their publics have often proved tragically mistaken in their judgments of the Soviet system and of Soviet policy, whether they were ill-informed, as they were forty years ago, or whether they have mountains of information and analyses, as now. In this troubling situation, the Georgetown University Center for Strategic and International Studies, with generous financial support from the Frederick Henry Prince Trusts, has undertaken a study of the factors that will help determine Soviet policy in the next decade.

The basic purpose of this volume is to provide a framework through which the interested citizen and the policy maker can analyze and understand the Soviet Union and the elements that will most affect its policies in the 1980s. It seeks to identify the fundamental features of the Soviet system, which are as basic to it as the political processes, the religious makeup of the population, and the character of the economy are to the United States, and to provide informed and careful judgments about Soviet society as a whole. It identifies the main elements of the Soviet system, its strengths and its weaknesses, and the kinds of challenges and opportunities the outside world presents to the Soviet rulers. It describes the important internal questions and the hard choices Soviet leaders must make within the next decade to try to resolve these crucial problems. It demonstrates that these converging issues are interrelated and are inextricably intertwined with delicate international relationships and therefore with Soviet foreign policy. The concatenation of these emerging difficult choices at the same time the system must complete the transfer of authority from Brezhnev to Andropov and then to another younger generation makes the next decade an especially momentous one, a time that provides both risks and opportunities for American policy as the United States looks ahead in this long-term political struggle.

This volume does not seek to estimate or forecast particular Soviet policies. Instead, it brings together information and analyses concerning the important factors and the essential questions. Making judgments about future developments is a most hazardous enterprise, even when one does not consider the element of chance in human affairs, catastrophes of one kind or another, the emergence of especially powerful or weak leaders, and the unexpected, which seems especially common in our fluid world.

However, each chapter in this volume does describe some of the various ways in which social, intellectual, and other factors in Soviet life might develop over the next decade and the range of options the Soviet rulers have as they encounter various domestic and foreign policy issues. The final chapter concentrates on a number of the hard choices Soviet leaders face and identifies the dilemmas that the available options raise.

The list of critical questions Americans and others outside the Soviet Union have about that country, its likely development, and its policies is almost endless. What is the nature of the Soviet system and of Soviet society? Who is likely to rule in the next decade and in what ways will this affect Soviet policy? Will the system and its policies remain as immobile as they were under Brezhnev, or can the system move innovatively to meet potential threats of stagnation, instability, and decline?

What is the role of the military in Soviet policy making and in what ways is that role likely to change? Are the Soviets preparing for nuclear war? Do they expect such a war?

How strong is the Soviet economy? How long will the Soviets be able to choose guns and capital investment over butter before the economic and social strains become unbearable? What is the likelihood that the Andropov government will introduce innovations in the economy? Can the Soviet government decentralize the economy without undermining Communist control?

To what degree do religion, the revival of national consciousness among the minorities and of nationalism among the Russians, dissenters, and social malaise affect Soviet power? How significant is the stagnation of living standards?

The leveling off of the Russian rate of population growth, at a time when that of the Moslems in Central Asia continues to rise— what does it mean? The defections and the decline in civic morale evident in party programs and in pulp literature—how significant are they? And what has happened to Marxism-Leninism? Is it a vivid faith for at least the ruling few, or is it just part of the justification of the system?

Poland—can the Soviet leaders resolve the intractable economic, political, and strategic problems that mass rejection of party rule and collapse of the economy reflect? Is Poland the beginning of the end of the Soviet empire? What other countries, including the Soviet Union, will soon be affected by food shortages, widespread corruption, and visible political incompetence as Poland was, and is?

In what way can a society that seeks to borrow extensively from the outside world but at the same time to wall itself off from foreign infection manage to import effectively? Can the Soviet system cope with the information revolution? Is authoritarianism possible, or, rather, is it inevitable in the Soviet future?

When one raises one's eyes from the Soviet Union and Eastern Europe to the wider world, the questions multiply and seem even more portentous. Is Soviet foreign policy a reflection of power and confidence, an attempt to escape internal problems, or a reflection of Western weakness and of alluring opportunities? What is the likelihood that the Soviets and the Chinese can resolve their differences? What might happen if they should? What are the Soviet Union's goals in Western Europe and which policies is it likely to consider most effective there? The opportunities that abound, or may pop up, in South Africa, Southwest Asia, Central America, almost anywhere and everywhere in this anarchic and chaotic world—how attractive are these openings? What restraints and what temptations or prods help explain Soviet policies toward these developments?

What is the Soviet view of the West? What effects do restrictions on trade have upon the Soviet economy? Can the West do business with the Soviet Union? What can the United States and its allies do to affect Soviet power and policy? In short, the questions are endless and of immense importance.

Those who have helped produce this volume believe that the Soviet Union is a society in many ways different from ours, not necessarily inferior and not necessarily superior, but different, and therefore difficult to understand. They are convinced that one must try to comprehend the society as a whole, its history, the way in which it operates, the views its rulers in particular have of the world, the number and quality of the internal issues it confronts, and its strengths and weaknesses before one can begin to comprehend the Soviet system and consider the domestic and foreign policies its leaders are likely to adopt.

Many Soviet problems resemble those the United States and other countries face. The tensions of this rapidly changing age, the rivalry between the two states and systems of values, the particular set of glasses through which foreigners view the Soviet Union because of its history, and because of their history, all increase the difficulty of obtaining a clear understanding of that country. Finally, foreign analysts must overcome severe obstacles to obtain reliable information of even the most basic nature because of the controls the Soviet state exercises over access to data and over travel to and through the country.

This volume represents an intense eighteen-month effort by a group of scholars to study another society, a major world power, a competitor, and a threat, and to reach agreement concerning the basic factors or elements likely to affect the policies of that country's leaders. The group includes thirty-five men and women from seven disciplines, twenty colleges and universities in the United States and the United Kingdom, seven private research organizations, two journals, and the Library of Congress. All involved have profited from the deep knowledge of Russian and Soviet history essential for comprehending things Soviet and from extensive life and travel there. They have benefited from long-term study of the research completed in the last three decades in the Soviet Union, in Eastern and Western Europe, and in the United States, but they also recognize distinct limits to their knowledge and understanding. They have sought objectivity in their analyses. In a sense, this study represents a concise and clear summing up of the available knowledge of another country and the central questions that society faces.

The approach this group has adopted, the way in which it has defined and divided the subject, and the cooperative method effective throughout distinguish this analysis from other sets of essays on the Soviet Union. In a number of ways, it incorporates research methods often used on large and difficult problems in the natural, physical, and social sciences because it studies the Soviet Union and its empire from a number of disciplines and angles. The approach also seeks to combine the virtues of independent scholarly research with those of cooperation on problems beyond the competence of individual scholars. In short, this study of the major aspects of Soviet society—in concert, not just isolated as the political system, or economic strengths and weaknesses, or "the silence in Russian culture"—has established a multidisciplinary framework through which the participants have reached judgments about the Soviet Union and the main elements affecting its policies. It seeks to produce a synthesized, coherent view of a number of specialists concerning the principal factors, both historic and current, influencing Soviet decisions and likely to affect them over the next decade.

American academics enjoy rugged independence, although they cooperate well in many ways. Those involved in this enterprise have demonstrated both independence and recognition of the need to work together in a process that involved four stages. First, the editor, the seven authors of chapters, or chairmen, and others defined and outlined the entire project. Each chairman then chose a team of three to five able and independent scholars and in cooperation with this group defined his or her group's work, identified the important questions, divided responsibilities, and prepared draft versions of an essay, on which the team members commented. The editor, the chairmen, members of all groups, and members of the CSIS staff then together reviewed full sets of all the draft chapters. The editor, the chairmen, and a few other Center advisers subsequently reviewed the summary chapter and the entire set of papers revised after the first session. The individual authors then prepared their essays for final review and publication. At several stages, all benefited from deep and perceptive reviews by three "external readers," Professor John Armstrong of the University of Wisconsin-Madison, Mr. John Huizenga of Washington, D.C., and Professor Hugh Seton-Watson of the School of Slavonic and East European Studies of the University of London, who participated in sessions and commented on the several sets of draft papers.

In short, each chapter is the responsibility of one scholar and represents his or her views, but the writer has in every case worked closely with a small team of specialists and on occasion with a group of thirty-five. The volume as a whole reflects to a large degree the views of all participants and is therefore a unique approach to analyzing the Soviet Union.

All of us agree that there is no likelihood whatsoever that the Soviet Union will become a political democracy or that it will collapse in the foreseeable future, and very little likelihood that it will become a congenial, peaceful member of the international community for as far ahead as one can see. It will instead remain an inherently destabilizing element of the international political system. We are in full agreement concerning the framework and general theses of the volume, the characteristics of the Soviet Union as a society and as a political system, the converging problems and opportunities the Soviet Union encounters, and the difficulties its leaders face when

xviii AFTER BREZHNEV

volume, the characteristics of the Soviet Union as a society and as a political system, the converging problems and opportunities the Soviet Union encounters, and the difficulties its leaders face when considering changes of significant character in the system's structure and in its basic policies. We do not all agree on some specific details, but the general level of agreement is very high.

I should like to thank all those who have participated in this undertaking, especially the authors of the individual chapters, who contributed erudition and energy, chose effective team members, commented on each other's work and accepted suggestions with candor and grace, and above all tolerated with general forbearance my proposals and my insistence on meeting deadlines. David M. Abshire, President and Chief Executive Officer, and Amos A. Jordan, Jr., Vice Chairman and Chief Operating Officer, of the Center for Strategic and International Studies provided all possible assistance and above all allowed us the complete freedom essential for research and writing. Aileen Masterson coordinated the activities of our far-flung group with skill, tact, and good humor, and, with Gerrit Gong, also added a valuable research and editorial dimension to the project. James Townsend and Lee Agree assisted them and provided research and administrative services essential for such an undertaking. Jeanette Haxton and many other typists throughout the country transformed our scribbles and constant revisions into manageable prose. In sum, this volume is the product of a number of men and women, to all of whom I am grateful.

Robert F. Byrnes

AFTER BREZHNEV
Sources of Soviet Conduct
in the 1980s

1

★

The Political System

Seweryn Bialer

Russia is never as strong as she looks.
Russia is never as weak as she looks.
—a European statesman in the 1930s

THIS CHAPTER discusses the Soviet political system in the 1980s and the influence it may exercise on Soviet foreign policy. It will concentrate on three major areas: (1) the domestic and foreign legacy of the Brezhnev era; (2) the succession(s) to the Brezhnev government; and (3) the factors which will influence the Soviet domestic scene and their effect upon foreign policy in the 1980s.

The Politics of the Brezhnev Era

The Brezhnev era spanned a period of eighteen years, during which the general secretary was the dominant figure on the Soviet political scene.

In the highly centralized authoritarian Soviet system, the position of the leader is of central importance; this alone argues for recognizing the two decades of Brezhnev's rule as a distinctive period. This distinction also rests on important discontinuities between the period of Brezhnev's rule and that of Khrushchev or Stalin.

Brezhnev was elected by his colleagues to the position of party leader after Khrushchev's leadership had disaffected virtually all the bureaucratic hierarchies. Brezhnev received a clear mandate to revamp his predecessor's domestic policies and to stabilize the system. Khrushchev's leadership was populist and reformist; Brezhnev's was corporate and conservative. Nowhere was this distinction as noticeable as in the structure of Soviet politics and decision making.

I should like to express my appreciation to George Breslauer, Thane Gustafson, and Myron Rush for the information and critical comments they provided.

The most important feature of the Soviet political system on the leadership level has been its transformation from the personal dictatorship of Stalin and the highly personalized and confrontational leadership of Khrushchev into a relatively stable oligarchy under Brezhnev. The top leadership that developed in the Brezhnev era was collective; almost all major bureaucratic interests were represented in the leadership, but no bureaucratic group or personal machine dominated. Although the role of the first party secretary and his "loyalists" within the Politburo clearly increased from about 1972, it was still limited in the late 1970s and began to decline sharply in the last year of Brezhnev's life, parallel to the progress of his illness and his growing inability to conduct the business of the Soviet government on a day-by-day basis.

The most important differences between the Brezhnev and Khrushchev leadership cannot be described adequately by such terms as "less" or "more"; rather, they may be expressed by the question, "power for what purpose?" In this perspective, Brezhnev's power differed from Khrushchev's because the former used his authority in a different way. Khrushchev expended power most notably in efforts to change institutions and policies; alternate advances and retreats in the face of leadership and elite opposition challenged his limits visibly. Brezhnev did not test his power in those terms. He expended it primarily in ensuring the continuity of Soviet institutions and in the gradual adjustment of policies. Within that context, his position was strong and stable.

During the Brezhnev period, real politics preoccupied the Soviet elite as never before. The cult of the top leader, the centralization of the party and state, and the "planning" that supposedly permeates all aspects of Soviet life could not hide the operation of the give and take of politics. The main actors in the Soviet political process are the major bureaucratic structures and their subsections, alliances of various bureaucracies on particular issues, and, finally, territorial interests. During the Brezhnev era, these groups developed a high degree of corporate existence and identity, displayed a broad range of opinions on specific issues, and were able as never before to help resolve issues through bargaining and compromise.

During the Brezhnev era the conflicts and agreements between various bureaucracies and their subdivisions testified to the broadening of the policy-making process on the elite level, but one bureaucratic hierarchy, the party apparatus, requires particular attention. Brezhnev restored and even strengthened the central role which the party apparatus had occupied until Khrushchev tried to reorganize it radically to attain independence from any single bureaucratic constituency.

Under Brezhnev, the party apparatus on all levels, especially the central Secretariat, became the chief agency in charge of appointments to all leadership positions. In its early days the party apparatus was primarily engaged in propaganda and in checking the loyalty of state bureaucracies. In the Khrushchev period it primarily fulfilled a mobilizational function. But in the Brezhnev era its main role has been to coordinate the activities of state institutions on the regional, republican, and central level.

It would be incorrect, however, to conclude that the party apparatus acted only as a broker between various institutional interests. Most importantly, it was a power committed to representing within bureaucratic politics the all-national interests, as counterposed to particularistic interests, as the central Secretariat and the general secretary defined them. Moreover, it was in charge of agenda setting, the key element of policy making and implementation that defines the parameters within which conflicts over policies are resolved.

The role of another group, the military, also requires special consideration, not so much because of its importance in the policy process but because of the many misconceptions concerning its role. The military factor in Soviet policy making is crucial, largely because national security is the uppermost priority for the Soviet leadership. Sometimes, however, observers draw an erroneous conclusion from the role of the military *factor* in policy by assigning an exaggerated role to the military *sector* in politics. Under Brezhnev, the military broadened its powers, because it attained a high degree of professional autonomy and a great voice in matters concerning military questions at a time when military strength increased steadily. Yet, its subordination to the political leadership remains unquestioned, and its role in influencing nonmilitary matters is limited. Its success in attaining high allocations of key resources during the Brezhnev period is not a result of its independent political weight, but rather of the symbiotic view of the military and the political leadership on this matter.

The key features of the political system that Brezhnev inherited from his predecessor, and that he continued with limited changes, were subordination of the secret police to party dominance and control and abolishment of mass terror. The Soviet leadership no longer resorts to terror to control, shape, or change society, or to resolve disputes within the elite. The system is a highly repressive, pervasive authoritarian state that uses the forces of repression and the enormous police machine as safeguards against the violators of established rules of behavior and others it fears, and the punitive force is ordinarily in accord with Soviet law and commensurate to the offense perpetrated.

Yet, the influence of the KGB probably increased in the Brezhnev era. The more distant the crimes of the Stalin era have become, the greater have been the authority and political visibility of the KGB. One example is the portrayal in the Soviet media of the KGB and of its predecessors, the CHEKA, OGPU, NKVD, and MVD. Another sign of its political importance is that Yuri Andropov, then head of the KGB, became a full member of the Politburo in April 1973. Still another illustration is the inclusion under Brezhnev of all republican KGB chairmen in the Central Committee bureaus of their republics and of all KGB chairmen in the provinces (oblast) of the Russian Republic in the provincial bureaus, for the first time since Stalin's rule.

Of course the key examples are the May 1982 elevation of Andropov to the central post of Central Committee secretary in place of the late Suslov, which made Andropov a prime candidate for succession to Brezhnev's position of general secretary of the party, and finally the selection of Andropov to succeed Brezhnev as the top Soviet leader.

The stability of the composition of the Soviet leadership represents a major dimension of the conservatism of the Soviet polity. To a degree unequalled in any other period of Soviet history, the leadership and key elite groups have remained unchanged through the Brezhnev era. One index is the low turnover in membership of the Central Committee, as the following figures demonstrate:

Survival Ratio of Full Members of the
Central Committee at Consecutive Congresses

Khrushchev			Brezhnev		
XX	XXII	XXIII	XXIV	XXV	XXVI
62.4	49.6	79.4	76.5	83.4	89.0

This stability is partly a reaction to the experimentation and turmoil of the Khrushchev period and partly a secular trend representing the bureaucratization of the system. Under Brezhnev the pattern of cooptation to the central political institutions reflected the replacement of those elite members who died or retired mostly by persons from the same generation to which Brezhnev belonged. The leadership and elite are currently composed of people from the same generation who have worked together for an extraordinarily long period and who have designed rules for working relationships that are relatively benign in the light of Soviet tradition. Until recently, stability represented the basic yearnings of key Soviet elite groups, and the leadership responded positively: the Soviet Union entered the 1980s with the oldest leadership and central elites in its history.

The price of Brezhnev's conservatism has been primarily the lack of structural reform. The most striking changes in the post-Stalin era have occurred in policies, not in structures. Nowhere else is this more pronounced and remarkable than with regard to the economic system and its relations with the polity. Despite the reforms of the Khrushchev and post-Khrushchev period, discussion of improving planning and economic mechanisms, tinkering with indices of growth, and the progress achieved in modernization, the economic system today remains virtually unchanged in its basic characteristics from the model Stalin gave it: super-centralization, absence of autonomy of economic subdivisions, tight and detailed planning, stress on quantitative output, and lack of any self-regulating, self-generating mechanism.

The break between mature Stalinism and its Leninist past was more clear-cut and more profound than that between the present system and its Stalinist past. Stalin established his system through a series of deep revolutionary convulsions and transformations. The present system came into being through a process of incremental, evolutionary change. The Stalinist system acquired its shape by crushing established institutions; the present authoritarian system molded the process of adjustment.

Since as far back as the mid-1920s, when Stalin proclaimed the policy of socialism in one country, the leaders have consistently resolved the tension between an active foreign policy and the needs of the domestic system in favor of domestic priorities. In the Stalin era, the priority of domestic policies found economic expression in autarky, political expression in Soviet self-isolation in the international arena, and foreign policy expression in its focus on preventing or delaying an attack by nonsocialist powers. Foreign policy played primarily a defensive, supporting role with regard to the political system even when the Soviet Union engaged in naked expansion, as in the case of Finland, Poland, the Baltic states, and Romania in the 1939–40 period, and to a large extent when it created the Soviet empire in the 1944–48 period.

Starting in the Khrushchev period, but particularly in the Brezhnev era, active Soviet foreign policy became more visible, more important in its own right, and more independent from the domestic system. This change in the weight of foreign policy was the result partly of internal political and economic developments, partly of growing Soviet power in the international arena, and partly of the continuity of basic Soviet attitudes toward the international system.

Whatever the reasons, the Soviet Union has propelled itself into world affairs and has been drawn into world affairs more actively than before Breznhev. Attention to foreign policy has therefore increased.

Many indications reveal the greater role foreign policy has come to play. Increasingly, the domestic government devotes resources to the promotion of foreign policy. The domestic repercussions of foreign policy are more pronounced than ever. Foreign policy is more often the center of attention in plenary meetings of the Central Committee. International affairs are the subject of more speeches and articles by more leaders than before, and differences within the political elite with regard to foreign policy are more pronounced than in the past. A major expansion of formal and informal foreign policy-making channels has occurred. An advisory apparatus focused on foreign policy questions has emerged and is growing rapidly. Yet while one should recognize the greater concern of leaders and elites with foreign policy questions, the domestic preoccupation of the Soviet system's directors remains paramount.

The Politburo remains the central decisive body in all policy making, but it represents a broader range of institutions and seems a better informed decision-making body than before Brezhnev. By all accounts, the Politburo and the general secretary define the agenda for foreign policy making and select the options that will determine the directions and goals of Soviet foreign policy.

As the Soviet role in the world has grown and the foreign policy apparatus and foreign policy institutions have swollen, the process of foreign policy making has become more complex and more systematic. Under Brezhnev, partly because of his personality and the oligarchic nature of the Soviet leadership, a more regularized and routinized process has replaced the haphazard and intuitive foreign policy making of Khrushchev, which represented his personality and style.

During the Brezhnev era the number and variety of those involved in the foreign policy-making process have expanded. Many groups now participate, and their influence has increased. Those involved include individuals at the apex of the various bureaucratic hierarchies—political, military, economic, and academic—and experts attached to those hierarchies.

In addition, the input of information, explanation, and advice has increased immensely, as has the variety of views expressed, although to a lesser degree. Moreover, for the first time in Soviet history, information, explanation, and advice from within the bureaucracy are matched by input from outside the bureaucracies, especially from the academic institutes. Authorized civilian experts are now beginning to influence even military doctrine and arms control, which the military staff had monopolized until recently.

One should not exaggerate the importance of specialists. They remain occasional advisers at best. In a Soviet-type regime, the ambitious bureaucrat tries to tailor his selection of data, explanations, and advice to the perceived needs and preferences of political superiors. One has to remember also that the opinions of experts are quite heterogeneous and that the political leaders may quickly select those views that suit them best.

To some extent, political, military intelligence, and academic experts contribute to the posing of available options for the Politburo. However, their primary influence is rather in the process of implementation and adjustment of foreign policy after the Politburo has determined the "general line." Apparently, highly professional foreign ministry officials, functionaries of the foreign and information departments of the Central Committee Secretariat, and prominent members of the Academy of Sciences then have some freedom in explaining and justifying policies at home and especially abroad.

During the Brezhnev era, the Soviet Union faced a number of difficult problems. Its achievements were impressive but spotty. When the era started, Western analysts of Soviet affairs published long lists of trouble spots and potentially destructive problems that confronted the leadership. Even though Brezhnev did not solve or sometimes did not even diminish the major problems, he prevented them, singly or in their cumulative effect, from becoming a source of systemic crisis. In the domestic field the Brezhnev era, particularly from 1965 to 1976, was quite successful in combining Soviet military expansion with overall industrial growth and with a substantial rise in the standard of living of the Soviet population, particularly of the lowest paid strata. But what the Brezhnev era will be particularly remembered for is its successes in the international arena.

In military affairs the Soviet Union fulfilled its major postwar dream, achieving strategic parity with the United States and becoming a truly global power. Soviet rule over its empire was legitimized internationally at Helsinki in 1975, and the Brezhnev doctrine provided a kind of justification for secure continuation of the empire through any means. Although unable to improve its relationship with China, the Soviet Union succeeded in shifting the Sino-Soviet military balance more clearly in its favor.

While the period of Brezhnev's rule brought increased political influence for the Soviet Union in the international arena, it was a time of economic and political decline for its chief adversary, the United States. The Soviet Union was able to translate its newly won power and influence into a new relationship with members of the Western alliance, particularly the United States, called detente, that constituted a cornerstone of Soviet long-range strategy. Detente provided economic benefits but above all it permitted the expansion of Soviet global influence without danger of confrontation with the United States and its allies. It also brought about a further swing in the balance of global influence and power in favor of the Soviet Union.

From the Soviet point of view, detente meant that recognition of strategic parity by the United States would also lead to recognition of political equality with the United States. For the Soviet leaders, this meant that no major issue of international politics should be resolved without Soviet participation. It also included simultaneously entering into agreements on limitation of strategic arms while continuing a military buildup in all regions and in all systems that the agreements did not include. As former Secretary of Defense Harold Brown said, "When we are increasing our military expenditures, they are increasing their own; when we are decreasing our military expenditures, they are also increasing their own."

With regard to Europe, detente included Soviet restraint in aggressive actions, threatening signals, and bellicose statements toward Western Europe and legitimization of Soviet rule in Eastern Europe. Outside of Europe, however, the Soviet Union considered the gray, that is, the nonaligned, areas of the world open to superpower competition, which it could pursue in any form and by any means, so long as no direct military clash with the United States occurred.

In the economic field, the Soviets expected from detente unrestricted trade with the West, including importation of grain and high technology, common ventures, and easy credit. They also expected a major increase in cultural and scientific exchanges. Finally, they recognized that detente would involve some adjusting of their internal policies with regard to human rights, so as not to offend the sensibilities of Western public opinion.

Detente was meant as a long-range policy that would have slight influence upon Soviet internal political conditions but would provide important benefits to the Soviet Union and Eastern Europe and permit the pursuit of influence in the Third World, without the danger of an American-Soviet confrontation. Despite some occasional unease, the ideologues and the military supported detente, the military in part because they saw it as a major opportunity to acquire high technology from the West in order to modernize their forces.

Detente in Soviet-American relations did not survive long, largely because the leaders of the two superpowers held different perceptions of the kind of behavior detente entailed for the other side. Thus, the United States expected that detente would slow Soviet military growth, which was clearly moving beyond defensive needs; lead to

Soviet restraint and moderation in conflict areas of the Third World, especially in the use of military power; and link economic cooperation with moderate Soviet international behavior.

How can one explain American misperceptions? How can one explain the ambiguities of the early 1970s and the agreements which did not spell out explicitly the specific actions, policies, and behavior within and outside of detente-type relations?

Part of the explanation is that the United States entered detente relations from a position of weakness, as Vietnam seemed to mark the decline of American power and will just at the time the Soviet Union was on the verge of its global "take-off." The two superpowers were out of phase with each other. Under such conditions, detente could not work for the United States.

For the Soviet Union, however, detente was quite successful. Its economic gains fell short of its expectations with regard to the United States, but the European connection worked well. The Soviet military buildup continued to change the balance of power in its favor. It achieved expansion in the Third World at low risk and low cost.

A very important domestic input into Soviet foreign policy is the ideology to which the Soviet leadership and elites subscribe, the faith that is fundamental to their existence. The relationship between ideology and Soviet nationalism as the driving forces of Soviet foreign policy emerges as a major question. Some Western scholars and statesmen believe that ideology is dead in the Soviet Union and that the moving force is pragmatic Soviet nationalism. Others conclude that Marxism-Leninism is alive and well and constitutes the galvanizing mechanism in Soviet foreign policy. It seems that both answers err, that is to say, both Soviet ideology and Soviet nationalism in many of its dimensions influence and shape Soviet foreign policy.

Four major components, and their mutual interaction, determine the character of Soviet nationalism. First, the experiences of Russia and the Soviet Union characterize this nationalism as defensive in nature. Russian nationalism grew from the traumatic experiences of frequent invasion, defeat, and even near destruction. It is a nationalism for which disaster and crisis always loom large on the horizon. It stresses the separateness of Russia from other nations and the unbridgeability of the "we-they" syndrome in international relations. It is also an undiminished imperial nationalism, in all probability the last such imperialism. It is committed to the empire that Stalin built in Eastern Europe, the existence and integrity of which his successors are determined to defend at all costs. In this dimension, it expands the basically defensive preoccupation with security to include the entire East European area, as if the slogan "socialism in one country" had expanded into "socialism in one empire."

Second, Soviet nationalism is to an increasing degree the outlook of a great power attaining global stature, a power still young, dynamic, growing, ambitious, and assertive for "a place in the sun" and one that entertains hopes and illusions about the accomplishments power can achieve in the international arena. Soviet nationalism reflects the faith of an older generation of Soviet leaders who worked hard, waited long, and dreamed of achieving a dominant international position. It is also the nationalism of the post–World War II generation of Soviet leaders, who share the ambitions of their elders but not the lingering insecurities and memories of past weaknesses and who lack the maturing influence of knowing at what cost Soviet power was created.

Third, Soviet nationalism includes a universal mission. This universalist attitude was rooted in Russia long before the revolution, when it fused with the Communist world outlook. Its operational validity was dormant for a long time during periods of Soviet preoccupation with internal problems and the defensive aspects of its international relations. But it survived as an ingrained attitude even at the height of Stalin's isolationism.

Finally, the combination of ideology and nationalism gives Soviet leaders a view of the world divided into opposing systems of competing values. This combination of the dynamic of an ascending power with that of a power that represents a world outlook different from and competitive with others limits the scope of bilateral agreements and makes balance of power policies and long-range solutions inherently unstable.

To distinguish analytically between the various elements of ideology and the many dimensions of Soviet nationalism is in essence to separate artificially factors that are not separate, distinct, or counterposed to one another, but inseparable, intertwined, Soviet in form and Russian in content. They blend in the minds of those who make policy. One cannot separate them when analyzing intentions and actions.

The fundamental difficulty is that one can evaluate the relative weight of the various elements and components of ideology and nationalism only when these elements create tension in the conduct of policy and policy making. Usually, however, the components supplement and reinforce each other, as they do in the Sino-Soviet conflict, the Soviet quest for absolute security, and the Soviet commitment to an East European empire.

Moreover, the tensions that occur in Soviet foreign policy are not between nationalism and ideology but reflect differences between what the Soviet leadership and political elite expect and the risks they must take to attain them; between what Alexander Dallin aptly termed "the impulse to enjoy and the impulse to destroy."

The relationship between nationalism and Soviet ideology is especially important when considering the question of legitimacy of Soviet rule and foreign policy. The Soviet Union is one of the few political systems sustained by a universalistic doctrine that provides the prophecy of self-fulfillment on a global scale. To the extent that the doctrine of Marxism-Leninism is still accepted, the Soviet Union plays the role of the historic agent who will bring about its fulfillment. An expansionist foreign policy acts as a legitimizing factor for the system and for the regime primarily among the various Soviet elites. It also justifies the party bureaucracy's central role in the political system. There is no evidence that Soviet expansionism, particularly beyond Eastern Europe, is popular among the Soviet people.

In short, Soviet nationalism equals Russian great-power nationalism plus Soviet ideology. Ideology provides a driving force that intensifies Russian nationalism, and Russian great-power nationalism keeps ideology alive. Neither ideology nor Russian nationalism explains or determines the tactical or even the strategic zigzags of Soviet foreign policy. However, they do explain the general trend of expansionism.

Other sections of this book analyze in some detail the political, economic, military, cultural, and ideological aspects of Soviet life that affect foreign policy. Here I seek only to introduce some elements of these sources of Soviet conduct.

The political resources at the disposal of Soviet foreign policy are significant and impressive. With this foundation, the leaders have accelerated the process of Soviet political activization abroad that started under Khrushchev and ended the sectarian and isolationist approach to non-Soviet forces abroad.

Soviet policy toward change and toward revolutionary and nationalistic aspirations in the noncommunist world provides almost a blanket underwriting of any and all aspirations for change that will undermine the status quo and thus contribute to Soviet strength. This makes the Soviet Union a natural ally of nations, movements, even small groups, which harbor ambitions and aspirations, and costs the Soviet Union little.

The Soviet Union, however, displays significant weaknesses in trying to muster political resources for foreign policy goals. The repressive and deadening character of its political system is now widely understood and lacks an attractive character for most peoples. The Soviets maintain their "alliance" system almost wholly by force of arms.

The considerable difficulties the Soviet economy faces should not cloud the achievements of the Brezhnev era. The size of the economy, especially of the industrial plant, and centralized control over resources provide the Soviet Union considerable economic potential in support of foreign policy. Yet for the foreseeable future, the effect of the nonmilitary aspects of this economy will remain greatly limited. The magnitude of Soviet involvement in the world economy is not commensurate with the evolution of the Soviet state as a global power, and Soviet influence on the world economy is minimal. It has not grown during the Brezhnev era, compared with that of Western industrial nations. Except for its military power, the Soviet Union would remain an underdeveloped country.

Soviet ideological resources, at one time among the strongest components of Soviet power, are either exhausted or have become a liability. The Soviet Union has ceased to be the symbol of radical revolution. The old international Communist movement has lost most of its enthusiasm and unity and will likely continue to unravel. As model and symbol of social progress for the leftist intelligentsia in industralized societies, it has been irrevocably compromised. Among the leftist intelligentsia of the Third World, this process tends to develop in the same direction. Expediency and circumstances, not ideology, attract revolutionary regimes and groups to the Soviet Union.

The cultural assets of a country—language, educational tradition, "high culture," mass cultural patterns, and the attractiveness and impressiveness of its way of life—can be of great importance in furthering that country's influence in the international arena. Soviet cultural patterns, however, are highly formalized, rigid, stolid, intolerant, and strange to most people of various classes and national origins who are exposed to them. Far from being carriers of a culture that would enhance attempts to gain influence, the Soviet people, including the elite, are greatly attracted by Western, especially American, culture. In short, the cultural and intellectual dimensions of Soviet life do not constitute an important element of strength in the international arena.

The situation is quite different with regard to the military assets behind Soviet foreign policy. Military power is at the base of the Soviet state's authority in the world. Soviet military capabilities enable the government to offer an array of weapons covering the whole range of needs of any nation, competitive with what the United States is in a position to offer. The Soviet Union is also able to deliver all kinds of military aid, from large numbers of military advisers to the offensive deployment of the troops of a client or the offensive use of its own military forces.

Willingness to commit military assets in a growing number of areas suggests that the Soviet leaders may have partly redefined what constitutes risk. One of the principal characteristics of recent Soviet international behavior is an attempt to translate military assets into global political influence, a course that involves inherent dangers. Soviet military policy has produced some conspicuous failures, and its present successes are far from assured. Military power is not sufficient to create a Pax Sovietica, as it was not sufficient alone to create a Pax Britannica. Yet in a perverse way, the imbalance in foreign policy resources, which is rooted in the domestic system, makes the Soviet Union a much more dangerous power than would be the case otherwise. In conflict situations, the Soviets have little choice but to transform political and economic competition into military competition, supporting the weak political, commercial, or ideological structure of Soviet influence with a surplus of military power.

The growing role of the Soviet state in international politics has inevitably increased the impact of factors far beyond Soviet frontiers on Soviet domestic life and on the interrelationships between internal and external policy. This is clear in three particular areas: trade, treatment of dissenters and Jews, and scientific and cultural relationships, the latter defined in part by agreements with other countries providing for exchange.

Economic relations with the outside world provide an especially obvious connection. Increased trade with the West since the late 1960s has opened the Soviet Union to external influences, as it did in earlier centuries of Russian history. However, Western leverage through trade and credit relations with the Soviet Union can be successful only if the Western alliance develops and follows a coherent and coordinated governmental policy, which is hardly likely. The belief that by manipulating Western credits and trade one can significantly influence Soviet behavior has as little merit as the notion that the Soviets will change and become much more moderate as a result of trade and contacts with the West. Yet one should remember that political interaction involves marginal changes and adjustments. If commercial dealings between the West and the Soviet Union cease to be a private business and become rather an instrument of governmental policy, they may have a salutary effect on Soviet foreign policy, even if only a few Western industrial democracies support the United States in such long-term endeavors.

Another influence of foreign relations on the domestic system concerns the formal and therefore restricted exchange of people and ideas, which has been taking place for twenty-five years. Its first, although probably not its most important, effect has been on Western specialists on the Soviet Union and the political public in the West.

American experts on Soviet life have profited from living and working in Soviet society, thus expanding their knowledge and understanding, which they have passed on to others through publication and the educational process. In addition, the impact of Western contacts upon the Soviet elite has been considerable. Travel is the greatest privilege of all for them, and Western cultural influences of every kind have engulfed this element of Soviet society, with powerful long-term effects.

The exchanges have also "educated" Soviet experts and increased their sophistication with regard to political processes within the United States and other Western countries. Whether this is a positive or negative development depends on how the Soviet leadership will use it.

The clearest effect of the exchanges is in science and technology, where the Soviets have acquired information of considerable value for improving the quality of their military equipment and of electronic and other such industries. Some believe that these exchanges have also influenced Soviet scientists, making them a force for peace and for moderation in Soviet policies. This is doubtful, because they serve the system quietly and faithfully and in any case have little influence on policy makers, other than by providing technical expertise.

Some Western observers believed and hoped that the greatest consequences of detente and of the various exchanges would be their impact on the Soviet mass public, which they assumed would exert a major influence on Soviet dealings with the West, particularly with the United States. They underestimated the efficacy of Soviet political controls and the mobilizing force of Russian nationalism and overestimated the impact of exchanges. The Soviet mass public remains today as subordinate to the Soviet regime and as politically apathetic as it was before the age of detente arrived.

During the height of detente, Soviet participation in the international system also influenced the domestic scene in creating some sensitivity to and regard for world, particularly Western, public opinion. It is foolish to think that external public opinion could have decisive influence on Soviet behavior. However, the response of the Soviet leadership to public pressure from abroad at that time showed a clear preoccupation with its outward image on issues that were marginal to Soviet stability or goals.

In short, the Soviet leaders have learned how important Western public opinion can be at times for the success or failure of central foreign policies of the USSR, such as European detente. They have showed a willingness, as Stalin did not, to adjust marginal policies at home to foreign policy goals. The most vivid illustration of this type of accommodation was the response to Jewish and German emigration and the treatment of well-known dissenters, a "liberalism" that created precedents that may haunt the leadership in the future.

The 1980s Succession: Character and Impact

In the highly centralized and bureaucratized Soviet party-state, transfers of power from one leader to another are events of great consequence in their direct and indirect impact on structure and policies. One can predict with little risk that by far the most important domestic political event in the Soviet Union during the 1980s will be the leadership and elite successions.

The major shifts of power implied by the term "succession" constitute a severe test of the stability of the Soviet political system, as well as a major discontinuity in the process of policy making and in the substance of policies. No predetermined tenure of office attaches to the post of the leader. The terms of office, the attributes of rights and obligations and of power and influence are not standardized, nor is the protocol for relinquishing the post. Moreover, the degree of uncertainty in the procedures for selecting a new leader and for consolidating his position is much higher in the Soviet Union than in most other societies. This injects a pronounced element of unpredictability into the political process.

The consequences for the political system are profound. Probabilities of deep personal and policy conflicts within the top leadership structure increase. Possibilities for resolving the conflicts in extreme ways are maximized, and tendencies toward large-scale personnel changes within the leadership itself, and among the top elites and the bureaucratic hierarchies within which they function, grow. A period of succession offers a high potential for destroying bureaucratic inertia and for changing policies. It is conducive to structural changes, the introduction of clusters of new policies, and realignment of political coalitions. In sum, the succession, aside from its own intrinsic importance, acts as a catalyst for pressures and tendencies within society that previously had limited opportunity for expression and realization.

The succession process in the Soviet Union has been going on for quite a while. With the death of Brezhnev and his replacement by Yuri Andropov, it has entered its most dramatic and decisive stage. The present succession combines some characteristics of past successions with a number of exceptional features that give it important political implications.

From a narrow point of view, the succession concerns the replacement of the top leader and the process of the new leader's consolidation of power. The present succession might see not only the replacement of Brezhnev by another leader (Andropov), but also the failure of this leader to consolidate power, resulting in still another leader in the 1980s. From another point of view, this succession might also produce the formation of a largely new core leadership group and, as if in concentric circles, the turnover of a large part of the central elite, the advisory group who serves the Secretariat and the Politburo, and even local elites. From this point of view, the present transfer will certainly produce replacement of the majority of the core leadership group and of a large part of the central party-state elites. In all probability it will also produce major changes in the advisory group. The probable ratio of turnover among the republic and provincial leadership is more uncertain.

The age cohort structure of the leadership and elites during the final years of Brezhnev's rule is such that the replacement not only will be massive but also will occur in a relatively short time because of actuarial conditions. The greatest concentrations of holders of high offices occur in the late sixties-early seventies age group, and in the early-to-mid-fifties age group. The turnover of the political elite for reasons of health and retirement, as well as of power and policy, will lead most probably to the replacement of old officials with younger individuals. In the latter part of the succession process, particularly if the new top leader is only a transitional figure, those selected for the leadership and central elite posts will increasingly belong to a new generation, who entered political life during the post-Stalin era.

In longevity, Brezhnev's eighteen years in office were second only to Stalin's and much longer than the tenure of Roosevelt, Adenauer, Churchill, or De Gaulle. Moreover, in stability of the leadership and elite and in continuity and stability of policy, the Brezhnev period was longer than any previous one in Soviet history. Unless one believes in the Soviet institutionalization of leadership and elite relations and policies, one must expect that such a long period of stability and of petrification has led to an accumulation of unresolved animosities, conflicts, and policy initiatives likely to explode during the succession.

The single most important characteristic of the present situation is that the succession process overlaps with the need to resolve a large agenda of domestic and international issues that have accumulated over the past decade. Some of these issues, like the question of economic growth, are qualitatively different from those of the past two successions in that they require nontraditional methods of approach and new structural arrangements for effective resolution.

Many Western observers automatically associate the terms "succession" and "crisis." Looking back, it is clear that one can characterize only one of the past two successions, that after Stalin's death, as a critical period. Furthermore, the crisis which that succession created was primarily one of leadership, not of the system.

Many suggest that the replacement of Brezhnev will constitute a "crisis" not merely of leadership, but also of the system. It is probable that replacing Brezhnev will bring about a leadership crisis that will be closer in level and depth to that after Stalin's death than to that after the ouster of Khrushchev. At the same time, one should not underestimate Soviet reserves of political and social stability, and one should be skeptical concerning predictions of a systemic crisis in the Soviet Union.

Of all the positions whose incumbents change during succession, the most important is that of the top party leader, the first or general secretary. The man who occupies this position, in addition to leadership of the Secretariat, the party apparatus executive body, also chairs the top decision-making interfunctional body, the Politburo. He who acquires this position inherits the prerogatives of office, which are awesome but to a large extent potential. The occupant of the office acquires a great advantage over his colleagues in the Politburo, some of whom certainly consider themselves contenders because the office carries organizational strength, symbolism, and tradition. All three top leaders in Soviet history—Stalin, Khrushchev, and Brezhnev—held this office and the control of the party apparatus which it ensures.

Yet one should be aware that the value of the first secretaryship depends on what its incumbent wants to do, can do, and does during the process of the transfer of power. Stalin used the office as a lever to achieve unlimited personal dictatorship. Khrushchev used it to attain great power, but an overwhelming coalition of his colleagues ousted him when he tried to achieve independence from his support among the major bureaucracies without reinstating Stalin's terror. Brezhnev invested the office with great powers, which he used in a cautious and limited way, never challenging the vested interests of any major bureaucracy.

Early in the succession process, and as its result, the successful incumbent to the top leadership position gradually builds support among his colleagues in the Politburo, the Secretariat, and their constituent bureaucracies. He enlarges the prerogatives of the office and accumulates additional roles partially implied in it. In his position as chairman of the Politburo, he gains influence to the extent that he is able to set the agenda of policy making and to gain the support of the majority through new appointments. When and if his position becomes unchallenged, he may combine it with that of prime minister or the head of state. He becomes publicly recognized as commander-in-chief of the armed forces and unchallenged spokesman with foreign leaders. Finally, his position becomes personified; that is, he and the power of the office blend or merge.

Western specialists do not agree on the extent of Brezhnev's power, although all recognize that it was greater than that of any colleague. Some assert that determining its extent is crucial in evaluating the importance of the succession. Clearly, the greater Brezhnev's role, the more important his biases, idiosyncracies, and preferences were in establishing policies, the greater the potential discontinuity the appointment of Andropov will have created. Yet the magnitude of the departed general secretary's authority does not ensure that of his successor. It is sufficient to agree that Brezhnev's powers were considerable and that the vacuum his departure created is significant.

The critical questions about the new general secretary's power and policies concern other issues: the time element in the succession or successions; constraints on the general secretary's power; and elite consensus versus elite policy conflicts during the old and new general secretary's tenure.

Since the retirement and death of Alexei Kosygin, the process of succession has been underway. The elevation of Konstantin Chernenko within the Politburo, the disappearance of Andrei Kirilenko from public view, the appointment of Mikhail Gorbachev to the Politburo, the death of Mikhail Suslov, and the return of Yuri Andropov to the Secretariat of the Central Committee were all steps in an unfolding process. Equally important was the semiretirement of Brezhnev, who in his last two to three years worked only intermittently, and then for only a few hours a day. Until the summer of 1982, most observers believed that Brezhnev had ceased to direct affairs of party and state on a day-by-day basis but retained the levers of power. By the end of the summer of 1982 this no longer seemed certain, although like many old and infirm leaders he clung desperately to his powers in office. Chernenko, who relied on Brezhnev for his position, may have encouraged this.

This process, in which the succession began while the leader was still in office and his powers were declining, was different from that of the last two successions. At the same time, expectations regarding the outcome of the change and impatience to complete the succession were discernible and resembled the last years of Stalin's rule.

The longer Brezhnev stayed in office, the greater became the fragmentation of the leadership group, with various factions staking claims to succession; the greater became the accumulation of urgent unresolved issues; and the higher the likelihood of conflict after Brezhnev died in office. The timetable question has another, more important aspect: the age of the successor and the time he has to accumulate and realize the powers of office. Andropov is 68 years old, and he has had a heart attack. While his first steps in office and the appointment of his loyalists to some central positions were decisive and immediate, it is still unclear how quick and full the process of his consolidation of power will be.

The powers of the position of general secretary are nominal. The incumbent may require years of alliance building and utilization of the power of appointment to acquire unchallenged authority. Andropov may be a transitional leader, a caretaker for an interim period between two successions, who will not have time to acquire genuine authority. The important succession will be that of the successor to Andropov. Thus, after almost two decades of stability of personnel and leadership, a longer period than any other in Soviet history, we may see two successions in one decade, with destabilizing effects.

The way in which a transitional succession may influence policy making in form and substance depends on the decision-making patterns it establishes. One model suggests the succession as a "honeymoon" for the incumbent to the top position in the initial period. His colleagues assist him to initiate innovative policies concerning both process and substance. One author contends: "Numerous case studies provide strong evidence that policy change is greatest right after the succession, and those new policies are precisely the ones advocated by the new First Secretary. . . . Only later did they run into difficulties in implementation. Thus, a honeymoon, with its implied cooperative spirit, would seem to operate in Socialist contexts. It seems to be a time, in view of the results, when the new leader has the power and desire to make a change. He seems to be allowed a grace period during which he is supposed to earn his mandate. Later, of course, failure expands, political debts pile up, opposition grows, compliance fails—the honeymoon ends as it does in the West."[1]

The second model suggests that occupying the office of First Secretary only begins a long battle and that the succession is not resolved for several years. The new leader possesses sufficient power and stable political alliances to implement effectively his major policy preferences only in the later, postconsolidation phase of the succession.

If the first model should develop, potential for two successions in the 1980s would suggest periods of great uncertainty and flux in the Soviet Union and great potential ability for successors to introduce and implement major changes in decision making and in policies. If the second system should occur, the transitional succession would result not only in flux and uncertainty, but in few policy initiatives and in no major changes in substance and form of policy formulation.

I believe the second model the more likely, in part because the unfolding of the succession in the last two or three years suggests this scenario, and in part because it resembles the past successions. However, the two possibilities which seem most probable are complementary.

Andropov, a man of Brezhnev's own generation, might be able to introduce policy initiatives in economic matters and to implement those structure and policy changes about which the elite and leadership hold a general consensus. Thus, after Stalin's demise, his successors ended secret police intervention in elite conflicts and abolished mass terror, Khrushchev initiated new agricultural policies during the early phase of his dominance, and Brezhnev abolished the sovnarkhoz and administrative bifurcation system in the early phase of his rule. If a second, more permanent succession follows, the 1980s might produce major policy initiatives and marginal structural reforms upon which the entire political elite may agree, but the leadership would delay major unpopular policies until the 1990s.

The question of contraints on the general secretary's power after the period of consolidation is crucial. The institutional constraints may be partially a response to elite and leadership experience with the departed leader and may represent a secular trend in the evolution of the general secretary's powers. The powers of the leader's office and of the person who occupies this office have declined from Stalin to Khrushchev to Brezhnev, when one examines not only the abstract limits on their powers but also the question, "power for what?"

Part of this devolution is a reaction to the experience the elites have enjoyed with the last leader. The danger the elite experienced under Stalin's personal dictatorship cut short Khrushchev's quest for personal power and made him pay for his insensitivity to his colleagues' institutional interests. Brezhnev's behavior was clearly a response to the experience with Khrushchev and his inglorious end.

The decline of the general secretary's powers may also represent a secular trend reflecting the growing complexity of Soviet society and the devolution of power in an oligarchical setting. In this view, the checking and balancing powers of the oligarchical leadership and broadening of the policy-making process became institutionalized in the Brezhnev era and may survive or even widen under his successors. However, one cannot preclude the emergence of a very strong leader, especially in the second succession. The extent of the leader's powers may be a cyclical phenomenon rather than a secular trend, and the elite's need and the desire for a strong leader may not balance sufficiently their fear of the consequences.

Another question concerning the succession concerns the two different patterns of interelite and of elite-leader relations. Under Khrushchev, the pattern was primarily that of conflict; under Brezhnev it was that of compromise. Some believe that the latter pattern represents an institutionalization of broad elite participation in policy making that will probably survive the rise of a new leader. Others argue that the pattern represents a response to the Khrushchev turmoil and experimentation and may therefore change after a period of prolonged stability and immobilism. I subscribe to the latter point of view and expect a high degree of conflict about power and policies within the leadership, among the elite, and between the leader and various elites.

The Age Factor: Old Incumbents vs. New Challengers

The central Soviet leadership consists of the full and alternate members of the Politburo, the Secretariat, the Presidium of the Council of Ministers, and the Presidium of the Supreme Soviet. The most striking characteristic of this group as a whole is its advanced age, one higher than at any time in Soviet history, during any preceding succession, and in the comparable group in any industrial society. Moreover, the distribution of age groups within the leadership is such that a large proportion of its members is not simply old but very old and that the proportion of the youngest, though not young, group is relatively small.

The oldest group constitutes the core of each institution, the most important and influential members. These men and alternates have an average tenure of seventeen years in the Politburo and have experienced a long working relationship with each other in the central apparatus. The younger members are either very recent additions without much experience within the central apparatus in Moscow, or provincial and republican officials whose main responsibilities normally keep them away from the capital. In the highly centralized Soviet system, this makes them marginal, second-class members of these institutions.

No precedent exists for the advanced age of this oligarchy in Soviet history or for clustering such a high proportion in the highest age bracket, especially in the midst of succession. When Stalin died, he was 70 years old; when Khrushchev was ousted, he was 70. Yet, the oligarchies they left were much younger than the current leadership group and relatively young as individuals. The youngest full member of the Politburo today is older than the average Politburo member on the eve of Stalin's succession; the youngest alternate member of the Politburo today is older than the average alternate Politburo member on the eve of Khrushchev's ascent. These data suggest that the succession will not consist simply of replacement of the leader, but of a massive replacement and reshuffling within the highest echelons of the hierarchy.

While somewhat lower, the age configuration of the central leadership reappears in the central elite, the party and state functionaries who serve in Moscow directly below the central leadership level. This group also faces massive changes in the 1980s, even if politically dictated retirements and replacements do not occur on a broad scale.

Two additional elements underscore the incongruity of this factor and its significance. First, the Soviet Union is a very young country: according to the 1970 census, almost 50 percent of its population was 25 years old or younger. Second, the party-state leadership and elites outside of Moscow—that is to say, in the republics and provinces—are older than at any time in Soviet history, but not old by the standards of the central elite and leadership, nor considering their responsibilities.

The Central Committee already has a considerable representation of younger members, a new generation, in all levels of responsibility, especially the middle echelons of the various hierarchies, and the adviser-experts to the leaders also include a new generation. In the highly centralized Soviet system, the stability and the continuing domination of a coterie of old leaders, who are afraid of change and who stifle initiative for transforming established policies and routines, have circumscribed and dampened that younger generation's impact on policy formulation. Assuming that the influx of newcomers to positions of high and intermediate levels of power will slowly accelerate and attain a high level during the coming decade, during and partly as a result of the succession, the key question still remains: how will the newcomers differ from those they replace; how will their style of leadership, manner of behavior in office, attitudes, beliefs, and actions compare to those of their predecessors?

Answering these questions in a satisfactory manner is impossible. We do know that the younger elite members, today primarily at the republican and provincial levels, belong to a different political generation than most of their superiors in the central leadership. Therefore, in the succession, especially its later phases, we will witness a generational change among Soviet elites as well as replacement of the leader and the larger part of the highest leadership stratum.

I define political generation as an elite group whose membership is homogeneous with respect to a particular life experience at a similar point of its development. It is easy to claim excessive importance for such a concept, especially when data about elite attitudes and behavior are scarce. Yet within bounds, the indirect data concerning the new generation can be important.

The members of the new elite generation entered politics after Stalin's death. They did not experience the paralyzing and destructive process of terror that corroded and influenced the behavior of the earlier generations, despite their renunciation of mass terror, nor did they develop an appreciation of the price of Soviet achievements. Their crucial formative political experience took place during the protracted ferment and shock of Khrushchev's anti-Stalin campaign that frankly admitted some of the monstrosities no one hitherto had dared to name and that questioned authority and established truths, thereby stimulating critical thought.

The party apparatus also established supremacy among the hierarchies during this period. The entrance of this generation into politics coincided also with open recognition of the gross inadequacies of Soviet development and the backwardness of Soviet technology and with extravagant predictions of equaling Western achievements in the foreseeable future, predictions that collapsed with great embarrassment.

It is, of course, difficult to reach confident generalizations about a large group of officials about whom one's knowledge is limited and suspect. However, analysis of the information available suggests that certain qualities distinguish this amorphous cohort from those ruling today.

The new generation is clearly Soviet in its persistent adherence to the cult of the state. One cannot doubt the sincerity of its commitment to the most basic forms of Soviet political organization and its belief that the system is right and proper for the Soviet Union. However, they are skeptical about the grander claims of Soviet propaganda concerning the system's merits. In private, they do not disguise their dislike of and lack of respect for the old generation.

This new generation seems scarcely touched by populist and egalitarian traditions. Grossly materialistic in wants and expectations, it has a highly developed career orientation, a cult of professionalism and elitism. Condescending in attitudes toward compatriots and older colleagues, its members appear self-confident and insensitive to real or imagined slights. Just as one postulates strong bonds of generational solidarity for the old elite, one can suppose that members of the new generation are forming similar bonds.

Some traits of the new generation may appear contradictory. On the one hand one detects a sense of security that contrasts with the old generation's feeling of insecurity. At the same time, their attitude toward the Soviet system is defensive. If they seem stronger, more self-confident, they are also more aware of and sensitive to the failures, shortcomings, and backwardness of contemporary Soviet society and polity than their predecessors were.

The present leadership presents a specific type of modernizing mentality, thoroughly conservative insofar as it seeks to combine incremental material progress and welfare with preserving the social and political relations and the organizational framework on which material production is based. It compartmentalizes the process of modernization and tries to insulate each compartment from the others. In its most extreme form one might call it the Saudi Arabian mentality of modernization. With regard to economic development, it measures progress by how much change has occurred rather than by how much remains to create a thoroughly modernized society. It is rooted in the past and in a curious way reconciled to the fact that the Soviet Union is the most developed of underdeveloped societies or the least developed of the developed countries. This means, as T. H. Rigby has written, that "Russia's second Industrial Revolution is presided over by men who may have overlearned the task of implementing the first." It seeks progress by small steps without grand vision and grand designs. It is pragmatic in that it has respect for what is possible, but its calculus of what is possible is petty.

The modernizing mentality of the new generation is quite different. It recognized the Brezhnev administration's inability to define directions for development. It deplores the backwardness of Soviet society, the system's functional deficiencies, and the administration's inability to make progress, while at the same time it is confident of its own ability. It may be less likely to accept actual or potential international achievements as substitutes for internal development. It may be willing to pay a high price in political and social change if persuaded that this would ensure substantial improvement in the growth and efficiency of the productive and distributive processes. Above all, it would like "to see the country moving again."

I do not suggest the existence of a new generation of officials with reformist tendencies similar to those of Dubček in Czechoslovakia. Nor will it be favorably disposed to the highly ideological, frantic, and campaign-like type of innovations associated with Khrushchev. At the same time, it would be surprising if they were not reform-minded in the Soviet framework and if they were rather less than more responsible and comfortable opponents in the international arena than Brezhnev was. They may be less cautious, more prone to take risks than the Brezhnev leadership, precisely because they have not experienced the cost of building Soviet might and simply assume Soviet great-power status.

The extent to which the entrance of the post-Stalin generation will influence Soviet policies in the 1980s will depend radically on the timing of their entrance into leadership. Isolated individuals, such as Gorbachev in the Politburo, Dolgikh in the Secretariat, or Katushev in the Presidium of the Council of Ministers have had to adjust their style and preferences to those of their colleagues and superiors. If, however, the turnover during the sucession is high and the new elite enter the central leadership in great numbers, their impact on the style of leadership and policies may be substantial. One should not expect this until the end of the 1980s.

To summarize, the present succession, whatever the form and results of its initial state, will involve a replacement in the leadership and the central establishment on a scale much greater than the last two successions and will combine with a generational turnover of the political elite. This conjunction of successions in both the broad and narrow sense has no precedent in Soviet history and may have long-term duration and significance.

The Role of the Issues

The importance of the coming successions also rests on policy and structural issues that will constitute the decade's agenda. The combination of change of leadership with the significance of the numerous issues that remain unresolved makes the 1980s crucial.

Leaderships in Communist and noncommunist societies often delay and even exclude important emergent or chronic issues from their agenda or do not resolve them in any comprehensive or decisive fashion. Sometimes the leadership does not recognize the seriousness of the issues; sometimes no one possesses enough power and influence to place them on the agenda; sometimes neglecting them seems wise because any solution would endanger the political system. At times, a lack of action reflects deliberate logic, that of politics rather than of analysis.

The problems the Soviet Union faces are of such a serious and protracted nature that the price of irresolution will be high. Moreover, much evidence suggests that the leadership and elite are keenly aware of these issues and their significance. One may, therefore, expect that the new leaders will at least consider the issues, even if they do not make their resolution possible.

Are policy issues important in a succession? Are they not simply a smokescreen behind which hide the ambitions and power urges of the contenders? Clearly the succession is, if nothing else, a struggle between individuals and factions that goes through many phases. One cannot succeed in reaching a position in the Politburo if one is not ambitious and skilled in the game of power. One does not become the leader if one is not more ruthless than his opponents in manipulating power resources.

Yet policy issues, initiatives, and programs play a central role in the transfer of power. The leaders who contend have an urge to put into practice ideas that they have developed on their road to the top. Moreover, the activist Soviet ideology makes the leadership, the elite, and the political public expect from the leader or contender interven-

tionist behavior, policies that try to answer problems and provide
some vision of the future. In addition, policy initiatives are a key
resource in the struggle for position. A contender can triumph and
consolidate power not only by force, but also by manipulating coalitions grouped around institutional interests and policies and by persuasive appeals to colleagues, the strategic elite, and the party at large.
Succession, then, is a period not only of power plays, but also of policy
posturing and initiatives. He who wins is not only the one who wields
power most effectively, but also the one who best meets the party's
and elite's perception of national needs.

The contenders' policy initiatives are often an anticipatory reaction to the leadership's fear that the workers, for example, might
become disruptive and dangerous if the government did not give
sufficient consideration to their interests. Lessons of the dangers of
workers' dissatisfaction in Eastern Europe, especially in Poland, have
impressed Soviet leaders. In a system where stability is highly valued,
some dissent exists, mass terror is absent, popular expectations have
been encouraged, and the opening of Soviet society to foreigners has
made material comparison possible, the party must pay attention to
the population's material satisfactions so that it can continue to curtail
cultural and political freedoms and preserve political stability. In
short, ambition, power, and desire for change all meet in a succession,
preparing the ground for introducing innovative policy initiatives,
most likely around two poles, promises for more and better consumer
goods and promises for greater successes in the international field.

The economic agenda of the succession is the most obvious and
important. Year after year, decade after decade, the leaders poured
ever-increasing quantities of labor, capital, land, and natural resources into the economy to meet their goals. In the 1980s, the economy has reached a stage of maturity which makes rapid growth no
longer possible through the use of the traditional Soviet methods,
mobilization and extensive growth. One can compare it to an addict
who needs increasing quantities of narcotics to get a "high" but whose
supplies do not meet his needs or are even decreasing.

A number of factors discussed elsewhere explain the declining
rate of growth of the Soviet economy: the centralized system of management and planning, weakness of the Soviet industrial infrastructure, unfavorable demographic trends, exhaustion of cheap natural
resources, an unfavorable energy balance, an aged machine stock, an
enormously inefficient agricultural sector, and many other factors.

All Western observers agree that the Soviet Union faces a
difficult economic situation in the 1980s, at worst, a period of low
growth intermingled with stagnation and decline. Even the more optimistic predictions indicate that the Soviet Union will experience an

economic crunch far more severe than anything it has encountered since the 1930s.

Evidence abounds that Soviet leaders are aware of this. The difference between the optimistic and the pessimistic scenarios are important; some observers forecast a difficult situation, others a crisis. Moreover, the choice of the most likely scenario cannot depend alone on more or less precise and complex computations, but must take into account such unpredictable elements as the vagaries of nature and the seriousness and extent of countervailing policies the government adopts. Brezhnev's leadership delayed decisions necessary for improving economic performance. His successors will be denied this luxury; they must do something to ensure domestic peace. Uppermost in their minds will be tensions within the industrial working class, but making significant changes in the management of the economy would raise many other problems as well.

A major economic change in the Soviet Union would require thoroughgoing change of the pricing system and a sharp change in the workers' position in the industrial marketplace. Prices of consumer goods, particularly food and basic goods, are kept very low through immense state subsidies. Any thorough and far-reaching reform would have to abandon artificial prices and allow costs to determine prices, which workers would resent.

Can a more innovative leadership emerge during the succession? If the emergent leader, Andropov, is convinced of the necessity for far-reaching change—a large assumption—he will need time to attain sufficient strength to launch a significant program. Such a leader may emerge only during the second succession. If the past is any indication, it will take him several years to amass the necessary powers. Because of the powerful forces allied against radical reform, he could achieve this only under remarkable circumstances.

The vested political and economic interests against such a change are powerful and will remain so even when the turnover of elites and leadership is high and when the pressures to "get the country moving" again intensify. Those resistant to change are numerous and powerful: the central planners and central bureaucracies, whose amassed powers would decline; the political and economic apparatus that is afraid of the potentially negative political repercussions of reform; the medium and low-level managers and technocrats, who are trained and experienced in how to work within the system and who have benefited from it; and even the educated low-level bureaucrats and skilled workers, who profit from present arrangements. One author has remarked: "After 60 years of experience with the Socialist economy run by government agencies . . . nearly everyone seems to have found ways to turn its shortcomings to individual advantage."[2] The Soviet Union is after all a very conservative society, one which lacks the ability the Japanese have shown to assimilate and improve the work of others and to master the techniques of change.

Initiative for reform in the face of widespread and strong opposition at all levels will not come from a powerful coalition from below. Reform will require energetic initiative and constant pushing from above, especially from the First Secretary.

An oligarchic leadership, which by its nature has to act by bargaining and compromise, is ill-suited for initiating and executing major reforms of structures, procedures, or even policies. Thus, the future of reform depends to a large degree on the inclination of the top leader and on his ability to pursue and realize those inclinations.

Stalin's successors sought support from the growing and increasingly important professional and middle strata, whom it managed to insulate from the heterogeneous dissent movement. The Soviet "intelligentsia," paid off by the regime in increased material well-being and a degree of professional automony, remains career-oriented, very much part of the system.

The growing dependence of the leadership and elites on the expertise and advice of professional groups is relevant. Stephen F. Cohen is probably right when he stresses that the spirit of reform and "liberalism" is not dead but was only dormant under Brezhnev and that one would find the greatest support for radical reform among some professional groups, especially the economists. In light of their significant advisory capacity, it is important that these groups unite; this happened in Hungary and helps explain implementation of radical reforms there.

However, these groups are fragmented and divided in the Soviet Union on the kind of reforms needed, neutralizing their potential for influencing change. The various factions in the leadership, the various sectoral and functional segments of the elites manipulate them easily. Both proponents and opponents of change in the leadership will find and mobilize experts for their respective positions.

The Soviet Union has not yet experienced the explosion of expectations characteristic of the advanced industrial societies and of parts of the underdeveloped world. Soviet workers' expectations reflect their past experiences and remain low by Western standards. In the post-Stalin era they experienced a slow but steady improvement in the standard of living. Consumption, especially in durable goods, rose substantially, particularly in the 1964–76 period. Moreover, the system offered a safety valve for aspirations by providing mobility for their children into middle-class positions and occupations, partly the result of deliberate policy and partly a concomitant of rapid industrial growth.

Thus far in the 1980s, the living standard of Soviet workers has remained constant, but it may now decline, a new experience for the overwhelming majority, composed of young people who did not know the postwar years of hunger, denial, and terror. Moreover, the movement of their children into the middle and professional strata will decline, due to sagging industrial growth, stringencies in educational expenditure, and stiff competition from the children of the new middle class. Neither American observers nor Soviet leaders themselves know how the workers would respond to a period of prolonged belt-tightening.

The Soviet worker does not work hard and receives little in real terms for his work. The road to higher consumer goods incentives requires that he work harder and receive more. However, unless he starts to work harder he cannot receive more. In other words, the government must ensure greater worker productivity before wages provide the incentive to work better, a typical vicious circle. Yet, the worker will not receive more at the initial stages of a new approach to the economy but will suffer from an austerity program designed to bring basic commodity prices in line with their costs and their availability. Furthermore, change would impinge on the workers' job security, the most important workers' achievement under Communism. It is easy to organize a small-scale Shchekino experiment but quite difficult to apply it throughout the country. Therefore, thorough changes would initially have a high cost for the workers and would create combustible social and political resentment. It is likely that the political dangers inherent in such reform will prevent its initiation or implementation.

I do not suggest that the reaction would evolve into a Russian edition of the Solidarity movement in Poland. The Soviet system and the Soviet working class are quite different from their Polish counterparts and have different traditions. Yet I anticipate lower productivity, greater absenteeism, more illegal economic activity, and perhaps unrest and even sporadic violence.

Another source of social conflict may be worsening relationships between the dominant Russians and the other nations of the "internal" empire. Peace during the Brezhnev era rested not only on intimidation and coercion, but also on circumstances which may not exist for the remainder of the 1980s: the rising standard of living and permissiveness toward private economic activity in the national republics, both greater than in Russia proper. A compact between Russian decision makers and non-Russian administrators in the republics also provided career opportunities for the native elite. In the last decade, however, these elites have reached such a level of education and professionalism that they have developed a sense of identity and may question the need for Russian overseers. In any case, the change in ethnodemographic trends means increased tensions between the dominant Russians and the dominated non-Russians.

Thus, the 1980s will surely see increased pressures for change but ever greater difficulties delaying or preventing it. The system's major dilemma is how to impose new priorities effectively on old structures and processes. What is the likelihood that the pressures of necessity will produce a successful attempt to transform old structures and processes? If by transformation one means market socialism or anything even similar, for instance, to the Hungarian model, the odds overwhelmingly oppose it.

In addition to the rooted opposition of social groups, the economic and technical difficulties of change are great. A major change would most certainly involve a temporary decline in production and productivity, would significantly increase the need for real incentives, and would require reeducating the labor force and management. The difficult transition period from the old to the new system would require large reserves of capital and consumer goods, at a time when the economy will be stretched to its outer limits, and when planning is especially taut, with reserves dwindling. In short, the Soviet leaders will face a dilemma; the enormous pressures stemming from serious shortcomings do create initiative for change, but successful reform requires a cushion of economic performance to subsidize the transition. The political risks of attempting significant change during a period of economic decline must seem very great to any leadership, probably graver than the consequences of living with the old system and its shortcomings.

Another key obstacle to successful change concerns the reform mechanism, the pattern in which changes occur under conditions of post-Stalinist politics. Far-reaching reforms must be carried out extensively, without hesitation, not in a piecemeal fashion. The necessary determination and persistence for such action will most likely be lacking until the effects of such a reform are tested and recognized as effective. Judging from past Soviet experience, the response to this contradiction tends to be self-defeating. From the various possibilities, the leadership usually selects a compromise solution which will cause the least disturbance, requires the least cost and effort, and serves as an experiment on a limited scale.

Consequently, the results of change are far from conclusive and even disappointing. This outcome in turn fuels the arguments of opponents who prevent continuing change. The leadership reverts to the traditional way of doing business and continues to tinker, which absorbs and distorts well-intentioned piecemeal reforms. This piecemeal mechanism explains the inherent stability of the traditional economic system and of the instability of reform methods in the Soviet Union.

The multinational and nominally federal nature of the Soviet system also exerts a conservative influence on reformist tendencies. A radical liberalizing change would diffuse economic authority within the Soviet Union, anathema to men whose central belief is in centralized power. The leadership might tolerate such diffusion if the benefits were sufficiently high but would have to weigh carefully the effects any change would have, especially on the non-Russians. The Soviet leadership during the Brezhnev period has been able to achieve relatively peaceful relations between the dominant Russian elite and the non-Russians through a shrewd carrot and stick policy. The balance of those relations is quite precarious and is susceptible to destructive conflicts on both elite and mass levels. Instituting a liberalizing economic reform could and probably would upset that balance, tantamount to restructuring relationships among nationalities, a price they are unlikely to pay and a danger they would hardly like to face.

Thus, a major economic reorganization would constitute an overhaul of the system which would require a basic change in the working style of the leadership, elite and sub-elite, and would have a significant impact upon other spheres of Soviet life. One does not embark on such an extremely serious undertaking unless convinced that the crisis within the system is so great that fundamental changes are essential. The old leadership and the elite under Brezhnev did not reach that conclusion, and no compelling evidence exists as yet that the emerging leadership and elite under Andropov would either.

In considering a thorough or even timid reform in the Soviet Union, any Soviet leaders must anticipate also its potential impact upon Eastern Europe. Any revisions in the Soviet Union could only encourage forces for change there. Therefore, only an enormously confident or desperate Soviet leadership would initiate internal policies that would undermine its external holdings. The situation in Eastern Europe during the rest of the 1980s will be very difficult economically, explosive socially, and precarious politically. This will influence the Soviet leadership in an anti-reformist direction.

In conclusion, despite the unprecedented pressure the difficult economic situation will create for change and the rare opportunities the coming successions offer, a successful, far-reaching reform that would move in the direction of market socialism is unlikely. Changes attempted will probably be hesitant, limited in scope, and ultimately absorbed by the system. They may approach the watershed dividing this kind of reform from one which will revise the system, but they will reject the market socialism or the abolition of direct planning at the level of execution.

The most likely course is that the leadership will continue to tinker with the economic system, intensifying its "organizational" and "mobilizational" changes. Characteristically, such reforms succeed in improving one aspect of the system or in counteracting its shortcomings but do not revise the system's basic parameters. They occur at the margins of the official economy and are directed at relieving pressures on the consumer sector.

A likely marginal change of some importance may entail, as one author suggests, "a NEP type of change which retains the centrally planned economy largely intact, but allows for a flourishing small-scale private sector. Since it entails no retreat from central planning, but rather the development of a new secondary economy that offers some promise of spurring new imitation and innovation, it may be entertained seriously by the proposed successional leadership."[3]

One should not dismiss partial changes and tinkering as having no importance. Politics concerns marginal advantages and changes, and the difference between no change or some change to the political actors could constitute the distinction between a difficult situation and a deep crisis. As Hugh Heclo and Aaron Wildavsky have suggested: "In expenditures, one man's margin is another man's profit. The tiny differences which may seem unworthy of argument yield the little extras that make life worth living. Policies, as we have seen, are bargained on these margins. A few percent of hundreds of millions . . . may make the difference between sufficiency and stringency, contentment and dissatisfaction, elbow room and the straitjacket."[4]

In summary, I anticipate no fundamental changes during this decade, despite intensive and divisive discussion concerning economic reforms, a number of organizational policy initiatives, experimentation with economic structure, and significant political conflict.

It is, of course, easy to predict continuities on the basis of past experience, and some might consider this analysis of prospects for systemic change unduly rigid. The confluence of conditions necessary for an important transformation may seem too restrictive and exaggerated to those who think in terms of historical process which has to transform Communist society. The difficulty in foreseeing discontinuities lies exactly in the fact that past patterns of behavior and experience give little guidance. Yet, as Gregory Grossman has suggested, we still fail to appreciate fully the complicated conjunction of favorable circumstances necessary for a successful transition of the Soviet system beyond its traditional mold.

In each of the previous successions, the leader who acquired the top position and the leadership which he structured responded not only to his own process and policy preferences, but also to the ambitions of key segments of the elite. We do not know how this process of coincidence evolved. Most probably, at the beginning of the succession process, especially in the period of initial consolidation of power, he was responsive to a conglomeration of various interests representing his constituency as against those of his opponents. Thus, the most telling yearnings of all elites after Stalin's death were simply security of life, the lifting of the mass terror that harmed the elites as well as the masses, and the removal of the stultifying and paralyzing atmosphere of Stalinist Russia. After Khrushchev's ouster, the major goals of the elite were security of office, bureaucratic stability, an end to endless experimentation, reforms, and campaigns, and greater professional autonomy.

What were the desires of particular segments of the elite on the eve of the post-Brezhnev succession? Each specialized functional elite and each of its subsegments has its particular interests and constituency, specific fears and hopes. Yet some generalized political moods in the Soviet Union of the early 1980s cut across functional and regional lines and old and newly formed coalitions. The profile will be highly impressionistic, formed on the basis of Soviet political, economic, and military publications, Soviet fiction, talks with Soviet officials, experts, and people of various walks of life, and intuitive impressions formed by travels to the Soviet Union.

One such mood, probably the most important and widespread, is the wish "to get the country moving again" because things are not going well and the old dynamism seems lost. Many seek strong leadership which will present new programs of action, of innovation, of improvement. Still another mood is the impatience of the young and especially the middle-aged members with the old generation, which has outlived its time and is blocking advancement of the younger groups. Another discernible mood is longing for greater order and discipline, especially over the workers and the low-level bureaucrats. In past Soviet successions, a hope to get more under a new allocation of resources motivated almost all elite groups. Today the mood seems less optimistic than in the past. Almost all elite groups seem to fear getting less when the reallocation the succession produces takes place.

The economic situation in the 1980s will introduce the politics of scarcity into the Soviet system for the first time. One may argue, of course, that Soviet politics were always that of scarcity. However, the past scarcities of products, raw materials, and capital always went hand in hand with rapid growth in almost all sectors of the economy. The expectation always survived that what was scarce one year would be less scarce in absolute figures the next year, though, of course, remaining still scarce relative to the plan and market demands. Directors of the system on all levels were accustomed to operating with such a set of scarcities.

The system of scarcities of the 1980s will be quite different in that very low growth will accompany it. In the past, the relative degree of their growth differentiated the various sectors and branches of the economy. For the rest of the 1980s, the differentiation will be between decline and stagnation on the one hand and growth on the other. Thus, rapid growth will not exist to provide relative satisfaction of all diverse interests, and low growth rate will create dilemmas both economic and political in nature. Economic consequences of resolving the dilemmas in one way rather than in another will carry an appreciable political cost, and the economic logic of the selection between options may be very different from the political logic.

Economic dilemmas present in every system are resolved through political decisions. Political logic argues for the victory of short-range immediate interests of the strongest constituencies. One can expect severe political conflicts and clashes on the road to compromise. The process of the present transfer of power itself will in all likelihood produce major conflicts between contenders for power and their supporters. The complexity and gravity of social and economic issues within the framework of succession suggest that it may be closer to the post-Stalin succession process than the post-Khrushchev.

The key dilemma concerns the squeeze between consumption, investment, and military expenditures. In a situation of low growth, the pursuit of rates of growth in these three on the level of the 1960s or early 1970s is no longer possible; something has to give. Yet, the economic and political consequences of long-range decisions are enormous.

The stagnation of consumption undermines the program of increased productivity on which growth depends and may be politically dangerous. Brezhnev himself in 1981 and 1982 proclaimed that growth of consumption sectors, especially of agriculture, are "the key political tasks" of the Soviet party. Consumption can only grow from cuts in investment or military spending. The redirection of investment into the consumption sector would undermine the effort to improve drastically the productivity of labor and energy through introduction of new technology. The drastic redirection of foreign trade composition away from high technology to consumer products would have a highly detrimental effect on productivity. Cuts in military expenditures, or at least cuts in the growth of military spending, would be a decision of enormous political sensitivity.

Obviously, deciding what has to give and what will give is vastly complicated by repetitiveness within each sector. One may list here the dilemmas of expenditures between labor-productive and energy-productive investment; between oil, gas, and coal within the energy branch; between expansion of production and the overdue replacement of aging machine plant; between trying to break the bottlenecks in the economic infrastructure and expanding productive capacity; between increasing production of arms and military equipment and enlarging the base of the military-industrial complex; and between investing vast sums of money into the long-range capacity of the nonblack-soil sector of Soviet agriculture and more immediate agricultural needs.

A stronger, more tenacious competition for resources among various regions of the Soviet Union will also become involved in the increased inter- and intrasectoral competition for resources. Such competition was a normal facet of Soviet politics in the 1970s. The budgetary squabbles concerning development plans between the Ukraine and Siberia, among the other republics, and among the various provinces of the RSFSR were visible to the outside world. They are certain to increase in the decade.

The difficult political decisions in distributing available resources are complicated by another economic dilemma. The European part of the Soviet Union has a well-developed infrastructure; investments there would be relatively cheap and would provide a high return. At the same time, the European part is poor in natural resources. Those regions in the Russian republic that have natural resources are extremely poor in labor resources and lack infrastructure. Investment here will be extremely expensive and difficult to manage. Central Asia has large labor resources but is poor in natural resources and has a limited infrastructure, especially in the technological sector. In addition, the Slavic elite would fiercely debate the political role of the Central Asian elite in seeking new resources.

Regional leaders assumed the role of king makers during Khrushchev's rise to power. The regional struggle for resources will intensify during the succession period, when the influence of the provincial and the republican elite traditionally increases. The potential for playing good politics instead of good economics is therefore considerable.

After the Soviet population realizes that it will experience a prolonged decline in the growth of its living standard, the basic stability of the Brezhnev period and the compact between the elite and the workers will fray. An increase in labor unrest, growing communal dissatisfaction, work stoppages, and industrial demonstrations may occur and will affect the government's allocation policies.

When a situation becomes difficult, when no prospects for rapid improvement are available, and when tightening of the belt is required, the natural response of Soviet leadership, whether old or new, is to tighten political and social controls.

The first and foremost response of the Soviet authorities to such difficulties will almost surely strengthen the party-state's authoritarian character. Stress on law and order, social discipline, unswerving loyalty, and punitive and restrictive measures against antisocial behavior will almost certainly become more pronounced than in the 1970s. Another likely development is an increase in nationalistic and chauvinistic propaganda and an attempt to create a siege mentality. The role of the secret and not-so-secret police will increase. In short, the Soviet Union is likely to become a more repressive state, probably through a gradual process as domestic problems become less tractable.

Some Western observers, while disclaiming belief in imminent disintegration of the Soviet system, do not think that the system will survive in its present form in the next decade. Their long-range prognosis is that the Soviet Union will either return to a Stalinist autocracy or transform itself into a military regime. The first prognosis would retain the basic Soviet institutional structure and simply tighten its controls with a return to the terror of the decades under Stalin. However, the latter prognosis does not envisage a fundamental change in the structure of Soviet power, but rather a reshuffling of political actors, with the military element or militarists dominant. As one political scientist expressed it, instead of party leaders wearing marshals' uniforms, marshals would wear party leaders' civil uniforms. That is to say, military dictatorship may come to Russia disguised as party rule.

I do not believe that the succession and the major policy dilemmas and troubles of the 1980s provide sufficient cause to expect a return of the terror of Stalin's years or the establishment of a military dictatorship. The Soviet Union is almost certain to have a government more repressive in its domestic policies with regard to culture, ideology, dissent, discipline, law and order than the Brezhnev government, while at the same time it will be open to a degree of experimentation in the economic area. But unless the very existence of Soviet power is endangered, the return of Stalinism seems unlikely.

One can, of course, argue that the introduction of Stalinism could occur gradually and by stealth; yet one doubts whether history will repeat itself. The experience with Stalinism in the 1930s and 1940s is still alive within the political elite, and I believe an attempt at "creeping Stalinism" would stimulate decisive opposition from a broad coalition of leadership and elite forces and particularly the Army.

If a crisis arises that elicits a drive to change the form of government, the second scenario, with some changes in the plot, seems more

plausible. I conclude that a qualitative change in the form of government will not occur in a gradual, creeping fashion, but would require
a coup d'état, not by the military leaders themselves, but by a combination of party, state, and military leaders. I do not expect even this
more plausible scenario in the Soviet Union in the foreseeable future,
because the system's reserves of political and social stability will remain sufficient for the next decade. Moreover, I do not believe that
even such a threat as the loss of the East European empire might
spark an attempt by the military to take over the reins of government.
If such a threat in Eastern Europe occurred in the next decade, the
Soviet political leadership itself will command the armed forces to
crush such a danger to "socialism in one empire."

The last scenario in particular leads to the question of the role of
the military in the present succession and to the various elite and
leadership alliance configurations that will probably emerge in the
1980s. The role of the military in Soviet politics is the subject of a
variety of views, most of which overemphasize the military in domestic politics and policy formation and exaggerate its role in the past two
successions. In the post-Stalin succession, Khrushchev allegedly was
able to defeat the "anti-party" group only with the help and support
of the military elite led by Zhukov. As evidence, some allege that the
use of military planes which brought the members of the Central
Committee to Moscow in June 1957 was decisive in Nikita Serge-
evitch's victory.

However, the victory of Khrushchev was secure before the Central Committee meeting. Using intimidation and political bribery,
Khrushchev was able to switch the division within the Politburo from
a "mathematical" majority for his opponents to a "political" majority
for himself. Second, any First Secretary of the party is free to command military air transport for political purposes. There is no evidence that the situation in 1957 was exceptional. The military leaders
simply fulfilled an order from the head of the party. Third,
Khrushchev removed Marshal Zhukov, Minister of Defense, the most
popular war hero in the country and the epitome of professionalism
in the armed forces, with no protest, only a few months after Zhukov
had performed this great service.

With regard to the coup that ousted Khrushchev in 1964, some
allege that Khrushchev's behavior toward the armed forces, particularly the ground forces, and his behavior in the Cuban missile crisis by
pressing the deployment of intermediate-range ballistic missiles
(IRBM) in Cuba and then agreeing in humiliating circumstances to
withdraw them created enormous dissatisfaction in the Soviet armed
forces and predicated his ouster. It is moreover alleged that the
armed force leaders participated in the coup.

First, not only the armed forces but most of his Politburo colleagues were dissatisfied with Khrushchev's military policies and with his behavior in the missile crisis. Second, the coup was accomplished during Khrushchev's absence from the Politburo and later rubber-stamped by the Central Committee. The head of the Soviet military, Marshal Malinovsky was not even a candidate member of the Politburo and was not promoted to it after the coup. The acquiescence of the security police was much more important for keeping Khrushchev in the dark than the aid of the military. The head of the KGB then was Semichastny, a close protege of Shelepin, who was then a full member of the Politburo and an important partner in organizing the plot. The Central Committee then gave legitimacy to the action.

Does the present succession contain elements of such a nature that the role of the military might be greater than in the past? With the Soviet international position qualitatively different than in the past, the central role of the military in designing and implementing Soviet global plans, and the forces visible as a main achievement of Soviet power, may not the military leaders play a more significant role than in the past?

The evidence with regard to the present and future weight of the military in domestic politics is ambiguous. Party control over the military, as over every other instrument of power in the Soviet Union, seems very high. Military leaders have acquired some visibility during the Brezhnev era, but available evidence suggests party dominance is and will remain unquestioned. With the election of Marshal Grechko to full membership in the Politburo in April 1973, the Soviet professional military for the first time had a spokesman in the top leadership, if one excludes Zhukov's brief membership in 1967. Yet, one has to note that after Grechko's death Central Committee Party Secretary Ustinov, a civilian with long and close military ties (starting in 1940, he was the key civilian in the Soviet military-industrial complex), was appointed Minister of Defense and elected to full membership in the Politburo. The appointment of Ustinov was a setback for the political role of the professional military leaders: Ustinov was the first civilian in this post in the entire post-Stalin era. The appointment of Ustinov's military predecessor, Grechko, to the Politburo appears more a reward to a close companion of Brezhnev than recognition of the military's political weight. It will be very significant to see whether Marshal Ogarkov, the professional military head of the General Staff, will become Minister of Defense after Ustinov's death and, if so, whether he will receive a seat in the Politburo.

Present and future military leaders belong to the postwar generation. They do not possess the same prestige and experience as their predecessors, the legendary heroes of the Great Patriotic War. They resemble managers rather than the exciting military leaders who led the sons of Russia into battle. Their ties with party leaders of the Brezhnev, Ustinov, or even Andropov generation seem purely professional.

It is also true that the generation of war commissars is quickly disappearing, but the process of replacement inside the military is somewhat quicker than on the civilian party side. This difference will disappear in the near future, and both the professional army and the professional party leadership may again belong to the same generation. The relatively young military leaders and the relatively young party leaders will not be particularly impressed by each other's pasts and at the same time will not have special personal ties. In such a situation, the party's pride of place in the political system will be even greater than in the past. The succinct saying that "You don't ask a general if a place should be bombed, but only how" might be enforced even more strictly than in the past.

Obviously the military leadership will play an important part in the present and future successions, but so will other groups. The succession may encourage broad participation of various elite strata in politics; if this should happen, the military will presumably not be an exception. Each elite group important in the succession process may count on rewards and inducements from the contenders and from the victor, and military leaders may receive inducements and rewards either for their military branches or for themselves. The major question, however, is in the currency in which they will be paid: in favorable budgetary allocations for their branches, or in ranks, titles, and decorations for themselves?

The final point about the military's role in succession politics concerns the procedures developed after Beria's arrest and liquidation in 1953. The unwritten code of behavior for intraleadership struggle has many codicils: thou should not kill the losers or deny them a comfortable existence outside of politics, and thou should not directly involve the secret police in leadership and elite struggle. Still another unwritten rule is that the contending political leaders should not directly involve in the struggle groups over whom the political leaders have to exercise tight control, such as the military leadership.

Probable Configuration of Alliances

The last question concerns the probable configuration of alliances that may emerge in the succession. The discussion will be brief, because Western knowledge of the characters involved and the mechanism by which alliances on the leadership and elite level are formed is limited.

In Stalin's succession struggle, alliances within the leadership were continuously shifting, and the question of personal loyalty, rather than questions of institutional interest, was uppermost in Stalin's mind until the time came when he needed alliances no more.

In the Khrushchev succession struggle, the base of his claim to power rested on support within the leadership and elite of the Party apparatus. The struggle was primarily within the core leadership between Khrushchev and the apparatchiki representation in the leadership on one side, and the old Stalinist political guard, whose main resources were their own "good" name and fame and their numerous clients in almost every elite institution on the other.

The post-Khrushchev succession saw an exceptional situation: at the outset of the succession, almost the entire leadership was united, partly the result of the way Khrushchev alienated all institutions of the Soviet elite and partly the result of the manner of Khrushchev's departure: the coup required a unified core leadership group. When Brezhnev acceded, he was already a recognized leader of a broad coalition of party and state functionaries. In the process of the struggle which ensued after his nomination to the top position, his institutional base was decisively located in the party apparatus. Brezhnev was determined not to repeat Khrushchev's mistake by alienating his power base. In the course of accumulating power, Brezhnev achieved dominance over the state leadership and gradually removed those members of the Politburo who, for one reason or another, could be potential challengers. He eliminated these individuals not because of their institutional associations or major policy differences, but simply for not being his unquestioned supporters.

When Stalin died the Soviet leadership issued a communiqué asking the party members and the population not to panic. Stalin's death was met in the Soviet Union with grief by some, relief by others, and uncertainty by all. When Leonid Brezhnev died there was no need to appeal to the people not to panic, and the grief and relief at the long awaited change of the guard were muted to say the least. Yet the uncertainty surrounding Yuri Andropov's ascendency to the vacant post of general secretary of the party may be as great as it was twenty-nine years ago when Stalin died. Today, as then, the Soviet Union is confronting domestic and international problems that defy any but radical solutions.

In its sixty-five-year history the Soviet Union has had only four top leaders. Lenin, the founder of the state, led the Bolsheviks in gaining and consolidating their power. Stalin, the tyrant, used political power in an extreme manner to shape and transform society according to his own image of what it should be. Khrushchev, the innovator, shocked the party out of its Stalinist mold, instituted new policies and reshuffled the inherited structures, and activized Soviet foreign policy and ended the self-imposed Soviet autarkic isolation. Brezhnev, the administrator, tried to institutionalize the process of policy making and introduce into the Soviet political system a degree of stability unknown before; in the international arena he presided over the transformation of his country into a truly global power.

The personality, vision, and power that these leaders wielded were crucial in determining the directions of Soviet policies at home and abroad. These leaders played a role in their societies which great leaders in other industrialized nations assume to a limited extent only in emergency situations. Yet, the whole history of the Soviet Union has been one of constant emergencies that required powerful leaders. The history of the Soviet Union was that of a highly centralized party-state that produced powerful figures. The departure of these leaders therefore can be regarded as milestones of Soviet history. The present transfer of authority to the fifth leader, Yuri Andropov, may have implications for the future as great as those of the past successions.

The patterns of past Soviet successions differ from each other. Yet, some common elements with regard to both domestic and foreign policies and politics can be discerned in all the successions. In domestic politics and policies the common elements were as follows:

(1) The succession did not come to an end with the appointment of a new top leader but continued for a few years until he consolidated his position and created a lasting coalition of people loyal to him personally within the leadership group.

In the present succession, in contradistinction to the past ones, the struggle for Brezhnev's mantle started well before his death and became intensified after the death of the chief Soviet ideologue, Suslov, in the beginning of 1982. With the debilitating illness of Kirilenko, the organizational secretary of the party and by tradition the heir apparent to Brezhnev, Konstantin Chernenko, a member of the Politburo, became the key contender for the top position. Chernenko took over many of the duties of Kirilenko and, with the progressive decline of Brezhnev's health, became the man in charge of the day-to-day running of top party institutions. A crony of Brezhnev's with a very undistinguished record and career, he was clearly Brezhnev's personal choice for the top position. The transfer of Andropov from chairmanship of the KGB to the party Secretariat in May 1982 was a decision of the majority of the Politburo (only the Politburo could have made the decision to effect such a transfer) and provided evidence of the sharp decline of Brezhnev's power and of conflicts and divisions within the Politburo about policies and personal loyalties.

At the time of Andropov's transfer to the party Secretariat—and his transformation from a power behind the throne to a contender for the throne—it was, and still remains, our belief that the retirement of Brezhnev would have resulted in the victory of Chernenko, while the death of Brezhnev in office favored the candidacy of Andropov. Chernenko's basic strength and power base was his closeness to Brezhnev. His major problem was his dependence on the transfer of commitment from Brezhnev's loyalists to himself, which was no longer automatic upon the death of Brezhnev.

Andropov's key card was his prestige as a strong leader and a generalist, a combination in short supply within the present Politburo. The coalition that brought him to the top probably included a combination of some of the oldest members of the Politburo and the youngest members of the Secretariat. The men of the old generation—for example, civilian Minister of Defense Ustinov—who, because of their age, no longer aspire to the top position, feel more comfortable with a man like Andropov, who has had a distinguished career of his own and belongs to their own generation, than with Chernenko, whose entire career consisted of being Brezhnev's companion. The young secretaries of the Central Committee like Dolgikh or Gorbachev probably wanted a change rather than a continuation of Brezhnev's policies, which Chernenko's candidacy would have promised, and they wanted a strong leader from among the younger members of the old generation; these criteria fitted Andropov's credentials.

The struggle for power within the Soviet leadership has not ended, however, with Andropov's ascendency. In the near future we may see a challenge to his leadership, but it is more likely that we will see attempts to circumvent the power potentially inherent in his position as general secretary. The domestic and foreign issues and dangers facing the new leadership under Andropov would argue for a defensive unity of the collective leadership and elites, that is to say, for a repetition of the 1965 pattern of succession from Khrushchev to Brezhnev, which was characterized by compromise and conciliation. Yet, it is more likely that the issues facing the leadership today are so divisive and central to their institutional interests that the present succession process will be closer to the 1953–57 pattern of Khrushchev's ascendency, with its confrontations, sharp conflicts, and purges.

Regardless of whether the pattern is closer to the Khrushchev or the Brezhnev succession, Andropov cannot feel safe in his position until he replaces some of the present members of the Politburo, Secretariat, and Presidium of the Council of Ministers with men of his own choosing who will be loyal to him personally. This is particularly true if Andropov intends to be a leader who promotes major changes and therefore endangers many vested interests.

The first indication of change within the Politburo was the November "retirement" of the very ill Kirilenko and the promotion of the party chief of the Azerbaidzhan Republic, Gaidar Aliev, to full membership in the Politburo. In the past Aliev was the head of the KGB in Azerbaidzhan and therefore an Andropov subordinate and presumable loyalist. (Incidentally, this is the first time in Soviet history that two individuals with an extensive KGB background occupy positions within the Politburo.) Another example was the appointment of Fedorchuk, an Andropov loyalist, to replace Brezhnev's man as the minister of the interior.

(2) The key power resource of the new leader has traditionally been the support of the professional party apparatus, the representatives of which constitute the single largest bloc in the top decision-making, executive, and symbolic bodies—the Politburo, the Secretariat, and the Central Committee of the party.

Andropov's elevation to the position of general secretary is the first case in Soviet history in which an individual who had not served in the party apparatus for fifteen years assumed this position. Yet one should recognize that while Andropov was not in the party apparatus for a long time, he is clearly *of* the party apparatus. Of the forty-six years of Andropov's active political life, he was a functionary of the party for twenty-seven years and spent the last five years before assuming the KGB chairmanship in the highly influential position of secretary of the Central Committee.

Yet, the question still remains: what is Andropov's influence within the party apparatus? We will be able to judge much better when we see whether Andropov keeps intact the present composition of the party apparatus, and particularly its first provincial secretaries, or whether he changes its composition in line with his own plans for Soviet development and in the interest of his own political security.

(3) The man appointed during the succession to the top position of first or general secretary survived the later challenges of other contenders or coalitions and became an indisputable leader. The nominal power of the office is so great that a politician of even average skills finds the odds stacked decisively in his favor. His prerogatives include the chairmanship of the Politburo and the ability to decide the agenda and timing of the Politburo's deliberation; the role of chief executive of the most important bureaucracy, the party apparatus; the chairmanship of the powerful Supreme Defense Council, which oversees the Soviet military industrial complex; the supervision of the "nomenklatura," that is, the right of appointments and dismiss-

als of key office holders throughout the bureaucracies; and the symbolic legitimization from the onset of his position as the top leader.

In the present succession the odds are overwhelmingly in Andropov's favor that he will be able to consolidate his position beyond any challenge from his colleagues, that he will be able to purge personal opponents and opponents of his policies. In this respect his chairmanship of the Soviet secret police and intelligence for the last fifteen years will be very helpful. By now Andropov must certainly know where the skeletons of every member of the Central Committee are buried, and he can extract obedience, if not out of loyalty and agreement with his policy initiatives, then at least out of fear.

(4) In each succession the policies of the new leader have depended very much on the substance of policies and the pattern of politics developed during the tenure of the departed leader. To a large extent the new leader responded to the past period, whether it was Stalin's inertia of terror and petrification to which Khrushchev responded, or Khrushchev's inertia of innovation and reorganization to which Brezhnev responded with his policies of stabilization and incrementalism.

Brezhnev's leadership and policies were characterized by the abandonment of any serious attempt to change significantly the Soviet economic structure and system; by the development of a policy process which relied decisively on bargaining, compromise, and incrementalism; by the promotion of change and adaptation to new conditions by gradual and cumulative policy changes; by the stress on proven experience and seniority in the selection of the administrators who would supervise and implement his policies in the center and on the peripheries by emphasizing stable cadres and slow promotions.

While this system worked relatively well in the first decade of Brezhnev's rule, toward the end it became a major obstacle to development and it promoted petrification in domestic policies, costly delays in response to burning problems, and immobilism. In the last years of Brezhnev's rule the Soviet decision-making process began to unravel in the face of a crisis situation. If the past is any guide to the future, Andropov's leadership will react to the Brezhnev experience with strong leadership and a determined push from above to change outmoded policies and to ensure that new people will be in charge of new policies.

(5) During each succession the new leader responded at least partly to the yearnings of the political elite, and especially those groups within the elite which represented his main constituencies. Obviously, in the present succession, as in the past, the yearnings and hopes of each functional elite group are primarily concerned with the fate of the particular institution over which that elite presides. Yet,

even here one can discern a major difference between the present and the past successions. In the past each functional elite group hoped to gain stature and allocations from the new leadership. At the present juncture, each group fears that its stature will decline and its allocation will be cut, or at best that its growth will be slower than in the past.

With the present transition to power, however, there are also yearnings and hopes of the elites which seem to cut across all functional groups and which represent some form of consensus of expectations connected with the new leadership. The most visible consensus concerns a desire, undefined in terms of means, to get the country moving again, to reverse the stagnation and decline of the past years. Another consensual desire concerns the overwhelming need to strengthen social discipline, to enforce law and order more decisively, in place of the unraveling of societal and political discipline which occurred in the last years of Brezhnev's rule. Those very strong hopes and desires clearly point to the expectations that the new top leader will be strong and decisive. Clearly, there is nobody in the present Politburo who fits those elite yearnings better than Andropov, whose tenure of leadership in the security and law-and-order field is longer than that of any of his predecessors. (Of course, the law-and-order yearnings of the elites are directed toward society at large and not their own bureaucratic fiefdoms. In this respect the various bureaucracies may well be surprised when and if Andropov applies the discipline and law-and-order formula to their own behavior, as is likely.)

Finally, there is a major segment of the various elites who see their most productive middle years passing by and who feel frustrated by the seniority blockage established by Brezhnev; they hope for a quick retirement of the old generation of officials and quicker promotion for themselves. It is very likely that Andropov will respond to the expectations of those Soviet "young Turks" and will build his most effective power base on their gratitude and personal loyalty.

(6) Successions are a period in Soviet politics and policies when both the new leader and his opponents court the Soviet public and engage in old-fashioned election politics with its exaggerated promises and popular programs. We do not know how and why, but during the initial stages of the succession the popularity of the top leader or of his opponents represents a power resource even in the authoritarian Soviet system.

One may expect also in the initial state of the present succession that Andropov will present to the Soviet public a number of attractive programs which will promise more of the good things in life in exchange for greater work discipline and effort. Yet, in this succession the margin of maneuver available to the top leader is much narrower than in past successions, which took place during higher base levels of growth. Today a major effort to improve the Soviet standard of living visibly and quickly will require deep cuts in the level of growth of investments or military spending, and therefore the alienation of elite constituencies which Andropov needs in his initial period of leadership consolidation.

A long-term effort in this direction would require major structural and policy reforms, the results of which, with very few exceptions, will not be visible in the short run; moreover, reforms would probably demand initially greater austerity from the Soviet consumer. In contradistinction to the previous post-Stalin successions, there are very few economic irrationalities connected with the old regime, the abolishment of which can produce significant improvements in the Soviet standard of living while preserving the existing system. There are no quick fixes available to Andropov in this respect. His choices are either to engage in a long-range transformation of the Soviet economic system, or to strengthen the repressive features of the system, or, what is most likely, both, with the increased repressiveness of the system providing the background and condition for initiation of major economic reforms.

One has to note that while Andropov will probably court the Soviet public with attractive consumer programs, one has the impression that the expectations of the Soviet public in this respect are rather low, much lower than during the last two successions. What the man on the street expects, and even hopes for, however, is, curiously, the same thing that the elites hope for: a strong leader who will hold tightly the reins of government. Of course, the man in the street hopes that the strong leadership of Brezhnev's successor will be used not to enforce his own discipline but to control and prevent the abuses of the immense Soviet bureaucracy. It may well be that the Andropov leadership will try and partly succeed at both.

(7) The personality, the vision, and the style of the new top leader make a very major difference in Soviet politics and policies. As political scientists, we often say with regard to major political leaders that the context in which those leaders act is as important as the man who occupies the position. But as often we forget that this means that the man is as important as the context within which he acts. The new top leader is obviously restricted by the parameters of the Soviet system in which he acts, but the range of political styles and policy directions within those parameters is very broad indeed. The man occupying the top position in the Soviet leadership is, of course, molded by his bureaucratic environment, but at the same time he molds this environment in accordance with his personality, his vision, and his style.

What do we know about Yuri Andropov that would help us to anticipate the type and direction of his leadership? The biography of Andropov is quite well known and does not need a detailed recounting here. He is a Russian, born in 1914, the son of a middle-class railroad employee—the first top Soviet leader since the time of Lenin who is not of worker or peasant origin. He belongs to the Brezhnev generation of political activists for whom Stalin's great purge opened possibilities of quick advancement. From age 32 to age 37 he was a professional functionary of the Young Communist League and then the party apparatus. From 1951 till 1967 he worked in the department of the party's Central Committee concerned with East European affairs, where, after a four-year stint as the ambassador to Hungary at the time of the 1956 Hungarian revolution, he rose to the position of the secretary of the Central Committee responsible for the Soviet "external" empire. In 1967 he was appointed by Brezhnev to the all-important post of chief of the Soviet secret police and intelligence service, the KGB, a position which he held longer than any of his predecessors.

Andropov's formal education is very spotty. Aside from graduating from a vocational school of inland water transportation, he attended both a provincial university, where he studied Marxist-Leninist philosophy, and the highest party school in Moscow, but he did not finish either. Yet by all accounts he is a sophisticated individual, whose knowledge and taste have been acquired through self-education. Despite the fact that he never set foot in a noncommunist country, his preparation as the head of the secret service to guide Soviet foreign policy is impressive. His experience in managing the troubled and troublesome Soviet East European empire is second to none. His knowledge of internal Soviet policies and politics, including the politics of the non-Russian areas, is extensive. Through his experience in the KGB he is the leader most qualified to enforce law, order, and discipline in Soviet society.

Where he lacks direct experience is in the management of the Soviet economy. In this respect he will have to rely heavily on the present directors of Soviet economic specialists. Andropov is a complex individual, a strong leader with an extraordinary political sense and subtlety—a major departure from the shrewd but simple leaders who preceded him in the post-Stalin era. He is both respected and feared among the Soviet elite. This much we know about Andropov, but we do not and cannot know with certainty the direction in which he will push and pull the Soviet Union.

In a highly centralized and authoritarian state like the Soviet Union, where the views of the top leader are sacrosanct and where relations with him have to be based on highly personalized loyalties, the second-ranking leaders are safe only if they keep to themselves their ideas on how the Soviet Union should be run. Only when Andropov has been in office for a while will we gain insight into the direction of his policies. It would be just as foolish to judge him on the basis of his role in the bloody repression of the Hungarian revolution in 1956 or his position as Moscow's top enforcer of conformity as it would be to ignore these experiences altogether. Yet, only in his present and future actions and decisions will his views about how to run Russia emerge—views shaped by his present vantage point as the top leader could be quite different from those he held as chief of the KGB. We should be prepared for many surprises, which may be not long in coming.

(8) Every succession represented a major change in either domestic policies or political structures or both. Every succession provided the platform for new policy initiatives and new configurations of the major political sectors. Successions were periods of renewal and reexamination of established policies. If we consider both the strength of the man who replaced Brezhnev and the seriousness of the crisis facing the USSR and reflected in the issue agenda of the present succession, the Soviet Union may well be at a turning point comparable to that of the late 1920s, when the New Economic Policy was replaced by the Stalinist "revolution from above" with its clarity of purpose, extremist policies, and mass coercion and terror; or to that of 1953–57, when there began the hybrid system, combining Stalinist totalitarianism and traditional authoritarianism, that exists today.

That the Soviet leadership recognizes the need for change is clear, if only from the appointment of Andropov with his reputation for strong leadership. That the accumulated Soviet internal problems will exert pressure for change is certain. Yet whether a far-reaching change in the Soviet system, especially in the economy, will take place is an open question, because the political price of such changes is very high, maybe higher than the price of trying to muddle through.

In my opinion the most probable domestic changes to be expected in the next few years are the following. Andropov clearly has a mandate from his colleagues to arrest, and if possible to reverse, the rot that has set in within Soviet society, both in the center and at the periphery. It seems highly probable that he will try drastically to improve social and particularly labor discipline. One can expect a crackdown on dissent, absenteeism, alcoholism, bribery, corruption, and theft of governmental property. The policies of Andropov will be concerned with law and order in the difficult economic times which lie ahead and, far from liberalizing the system, they will lead to a strengthening of the authoritarian character of the Soviet state.

With regard to Soviet agriculture, the most important and most ailing input into the mass standard of living, there is a high probability of far-reaching structural change. Instead of throwing immense sums of money at the agricultural problem, which the Soviet economy can no longer afford, Andropov may start a transformation of Soviet agriculture very similar to that of China and to some experimental Soviet efforts in the past decade. Specifically, while preserving the collective farm as an administrative unit, Andropov may concentrate on the family unit as the basic working group responsible for a specific part of the collective farm's land, the cultivation of which will be rewarded according to its productivity; or, less likely, he may adopt the Hungarian example, which transformed the collective farm into an independent enterprise that acts as a capitalist establishment for all practical purposes. In the short run, the increase in size and investments of the private plots of the collective farmers would also bring an improvement in the food situation.

Efforts by Andropov to reform radically the industrial sectors and the entire system of planning, management, and incentives are much more dubious. We know for certain that in the last few years major economic institutes in the Soviet Union have worked on reform options to be presented to the post-Brezhnev leadership. There is no doubt also that major discussions about reform and improvement of the Soviet economy will be initiated by Andropov. Yet, I feel that while small-scale experimentation and marginal reforms will result from those discussions, no fundamental reforms will take place in the foreseeable future.

One should not minimize the effects of marginal reforms, such as the privatization all but in name of new service establishments (restaurants, repair shops, etc.) or the creation of a separate segment of industry which works solely for export, with rights and privileges reserved until now for only the military industry. Such marginal reforms, which may well be initiated by Andropov, may help to arrest for a while the declining growth of the Soviet economy.

The idea, however, that Andropov will try to transform the Soviet economic system according to the Hungarian model is highly improbable. The size of the Soviet Union, the importance of its military-industrial complex, the multinational character of the Soviet state, the lack of economic reserves for a transitional period, the devolution of political power involved in such reform and many other weighty reasons argue decisively against the *implementation* of the Hungarian reform in the Soviet Union. We have yet to meet a Soviet economist or official who believes that the Hungarian model is adaptable to Soviet conditions. To sum up then, on the domestic scene Andropov's leadership may be innovative and reformist, it may improve somewhat the Soviet economic picture, and it will almost cer-

tainly reinforce Soviet political and social stability, but it will not
radically reform the way in which the Soviets do business.

Politics and Foreign Policy in the 1980s

The Soviet leadership regards the world outside the Soviet Union
as an environment contaminated by ideas and structures inimical to
the Soviet system and hostile to the Soviet Union. It is the world of
"vashi" (yours) as compared to "nashi" (ours), a place in which the
Soviet Union can never be a full participant. What has changed and is
still changing is recognition that this outside world not only contains
dangers but also provides major opportunities.

Tradition, ideology, and nationalism reinforce each other to
create the powerful and unique Soviet concept of security. As
Thomas Wolfe suggests, Soviet rulers see the world in terms of an
inevitable systemic struggle that international agreements cannot "an-
nul" and are equally convinced that the security of the Soviet Union,
the principal Communist state, must be preserved at all costs. Wolfe
continues:

> The common denominator in both instances seems to lie in seeking to
> eliminate or reduce potential sources of threat to the Soviet Union. What
> might be called, in strategic parlance, a "damage limiting" high philoso-
> phy thus seems to permeate Soviet behavior. . . . This philosophy finds
> expression in Soviet military doctrine and policy, as well as in Soviet
> diplomacy. Whether at bottom such a philosophy owes more to ideolog-
> ical imperatives than to those of Soviet national interest remains a moot
> question. For that matter, the impulse to limit damage to one's interests is
> not peculiar to the Soviet leaders; they simply seem to carry it further
> than most, as if satisfied only with absolute security. Thus, the really
> relevant point seems to be that to the extent that negation of potential
> military and political threats to the Soviet Union involves measures that
> other states find inimical to their own vital interests, the Soviet proclivity
> to seek absolute security tends neither to promote global stability nor a
> fundamental relaxation of tensions within the international order.[5]

Ironically, the Soviet quest for total security, the Soviet ultimate
defensive policy, brings us full circle, to the question of sources of
Soviet expansionism. The inferior Soviet international situation in the
past led many to hope that the insecurities due to power inferiority
would slowly disappear with the ascendancy of international power.
This has not happened. It is ridiculous to speak today about an attack
upon the Soviet Union from the West or the East. Neither Western
nor Soviet leaders believe any longer in such an eventuality, under
any circumstances. The danger to the Soviet Union, if any, is from

within. Yet the Soviet concept of total security requires that no great power or combination of powers equal to the Soviet Union remain on the face of the globe. Only then will the Soviets feel really secure. International circumstances have provided a modifying influence on foreign policy behavior and on the intermediate-range strategies, as well as on tactics, but no one knows whether or not they have modified the far-reaching, basic Soviet view of security.

The Brezhnev era is the first in Soviet history to bring this truth home with great force, because it is the first in which the Soviet deterrent to an attack by any combination of outside forces has been more than adequate. This quest for total security, reinforced and fed by Russian messianism and Soviet belief in the "historical process," and the need to legitimize party supremacy among the elites, in their combination provide the drive for Soviet globalism.

The sources of Soviet expansionism are rooted in the domestic Soviet system, not in the international situation, which provides primarily temptations and opportunities. In the late 1950s, the marked American superiority in nuclear weapons created the Soviet Union's greatest challenge, the threat of annihilation. From the time when the Soviet Union acquired a reasonably secure second-strike capability and finally strategic parity with the United States, the nuclear balance presented the Soviet Union with its greatest opportunity for expansion. On the one hand, nuclear weapons made it imperative that the Soviet Union promote its international interests and expand its power and influence without provoking confrontations which might lead to war or to a loss of Soviet credibility, as in the Cuban crisis. In this sense, nuclear weapons exercised a restraining influence on Soviet international behavior. On the other hand, more importantly, achievement by the Soviet Union of strategic parity with the United States has provided the Soviet Union an unprecedented opportunity for extension of its power and influence on the international arena by canceling many of the West's military and nonmilitary advantages.

Nuclear weapons act as a major equalizer between the Western alliance and the Soviet empire, power coalitions not equal in terms of military potential. The conventional military potential (not mobilized military power) of the West, measured by the indices of population, industrial output, technological advancement, and scientific achievement, not only is much higher than the Soviet Union's, but may have improved in the West's favor in the last quarter century.

Though nuclear weapons do provide a deterrent against attack on the West, it is possible to argue that the Soviet Union has benefited more from nuclear weapons than have its adversaries because nuclear weapons negate the value of the superior mobilization potential of the

West. The Soviets have acquired freedom from fear of attack against their homeland and their empire. Through nuclear weapons, through the umbrella of nuclear parity, they have also acquired the ability directly and indirectly to use force in the international arena in areas the NATO defense treaty does not cover. This ability is as yet unchallenged, partly for political and historical reasons and partly because of Western fear of escalation of conflicts in the Third World into direct U.S.-Soviet warfare.

The Soviet leaders proclaim their commitment not to be the first power to use nuclear weapons, not only because their mobilized conventional forces in Europe and in the eastern hemisphere are stronger than those of the West, but also because they know that in protracted war such a commitment means nothing, especially to the losing side. Moreover, they know that the United States realizes this and therefore use the campaigns of no first use and of nuclear freeze as useful political maneuvers.

Aside from nuclear weapons, other obvious international factors exercise enormous influence on Soviet foreign policy. The turmoil in Third World countries and regional conflict connected with the post-colonial developments present the Soviet leaders with temptations and opportunities to which they often submit. The collapse of detente between the United States and the Soviet Union, but not between Western Europe and the Soviet Union, creates splendid opportunities. Yet the semi-alliance of the United States, Western Europe, Japan, and China reintroduced into Soviet thinking fear of encirclement, from which they have attempted to escape by military intervention on the south and southeastern sides of their borders. The Polish situation, for which the Soviets have yet to find an answer, creates a dilemma on how to reconcile weaknesses close at home with expansion in faraway places.

The roots of foreign policy are intertwined with domestic factors—capabilities, politics, and beliefs—all discussed in detail earlier in this chapter, or in other parts of the volume. The first group includes assessment of Soviet economic strength, the level of technological development, overall military potential, actual noncivilian expenditures, allocation of foreign assistance and its utilization, contribution of Soviet allies to Soviet strengths, and degree of Soviet dependence on international cooperative arrangements and foreign trade.

The second group of factors—politics—concerns the institutions and processes of Soviet foreign policy making; the nature and quality of the informational inputs that enter this process; the power and personalities of the key actors who participate; the identification of major pressure groups that have vested interests in foreign policy decisions, the degree of their access to the foreign policy making process, and their influence in shaping foreign policy making and its changing orders of priorities; and the more or less pronounced divisions within the Soviet leadership and elites regarding the main foreign policy line and separate foreign policy issues.

The third group of factors—beliefs—deals with the basic outlook of decision makers on international affairs; the beliefs they share in common, shaped by tradition, experience, and value system; the assumptions about themselves and other international actors with which they approach activities in the international arena; the process of learning by which they slowly adjust these assumptions; their principal concerns about foreign relations; and their fears and hopes.

The various elements which reflect Soviet strengths and weaknesses propel Soviet foreign policy in diverse directions. The economic situation, the partial loss of the system's immunity to social pressures, and concern for internal stability, together with the leadership's preoccupation with security and its recognition and fear of dangers inherent in great power confrontations, all argue against an unrestricted arms race and for increased elements of conventional and strategic arms limitation and reduction. At the same time, attainment of strategic parity with the United States and acquisition and expansion of elements of global capacity push toward a policy that will permit the translation of these capabilities into a wide-ranging influence in world affairs.

Domestic economic difficulties, present and projected, in conjunction with the leadership's unwillingness to engage in restructuring the Soviet economic system of management, controls, and incentives, press toward development of cooperative arrangements with democratic industrial societies, especially those that contribute advanced technology on advantageous terms. The intensity of these pressures varies with changes in the domestic Soviet situation and its international environment. In the final analysis, it depends on Soviet leaders' perceptions of the international environment and on the options that Western policies create, that is to say, on the opportunities and costs associated with different policies.

The indisputable compartmentalization of foreign and domestic policy issues and the attendant tendency toward greater participation and access of diverse political groups in foreign policy making seem to have produced a situation in which no institutional group, such as the defense complex, achieves preponderant influence. While the Soviet leader still possesses greater freedom of action in the foreign policy field than, say, the United States executive, his freedom of action seems more limited than in the past.

Some evidence suggests the existence of differences of opinion within the leadership and among top elite groups, if not about the general course of foreign policy, then about particular steps. Some differences derive from the particularistic interests of bureaucratic groups and some from predispositions and orientations that cut across functional and organizational lines. The evidence, however, is insufficient to identify particular leaders with specific views or to posit the existence of diverse long-range foreign policy orientations among various bureaucratic complexes.

Moreover, the streamlining of the foreign policy process has not produced a clear-cut and consistent foreign policy line. As a matter of fact inconsistencies, ambiguities, and drift characterize the policies of the late Brezhnev period. These are partly a result of the feedback into the policy-making process of the unintended consequences of foreign policy plans and actions. To some extent they also reflect the nature of policy making in the Brezhnev era, with its sensitivity to diverse internal pressures and stress on compromise solutions.

The main policy line the Soviet leadership adopted on the eve of Brezhnev's succession reflected the diverse pressures and the ambiguities and contradictions inherent in its multidirectional thrust. The result is a policy of continuing detente with Western Europe and of trying to restore detente with the United States, in which the relative weighing of constituent parts constantly changes. This policy combines commitment to SALT, avoidance of direct confrontation with the United States, and eagerness to engage in cooperative economic arrangements with a strong competitive military and political impulse toward expanding the sphere and magnitude of the Soviet influence in the international arena.

The third group of factors, beliefs, is primarily cultural in nature and consists to a large extent of ideological and nationalistic factors. I have already discussed the decisive aspect of these factors, the relationship between ideology and Soviet nationalism. One can now add only two points. The first concerns the impact of ideology on the Soviet elites and leadership; the second, the mechanism of the continuity of elite beliefs in the Soviet Union.

In Soviet ideology and leadership behavior, the choice is not between hardened, cynical politicians and doctrinaire fanatics. If that were so, in the first case one would be able to make far-reaching deals or buy off the cynical politicians; in the latter case, their actions and evaluation would be self-defeating. One should not equate ideology with doctrine. Ideology is a broader term than doctrine and is inclusive of doctrine. With regard to doctrine, present and future Soviet leaders are almost illiterate and are averse to theorizing, let alone to serious theoretical analysis. In all probability, Khrushchev was the last

Soviet leader who took doctrine seriously. But one should not conclude that ideology is unimportant in Soviet behavior.

Ideology derives from doctrine, but at a much lower level of generality, specificity, and structure or consistency, and with a different, nonintellectual mechanism of acceptance by groups or individuals. The language of ideology is that of slogans, feelings, emotive symbols, and commitments. Moreover, ideology contains the distilled historical experience of the politically dominant groups of a society. It is in a way an adaptation of the doctrinal essentials to the historically formed conditions of its adopted country.

Ideology, in other words, is a cultural phenomenon. The main channel of its adoption by groups and individuals is through cultural socialization throughout early life and careers. The ideology of Soviet elites is not what they read, but what they are and what surrounds them, the selective spectacles they use and what they derive from their reading. Ironically, the modes of behavior, discourse, and analysis of most of the emigre dissidents from the Soviet Union, individuals of great personal courage and anti-Soviet convictions who are conditioned nevertheless, by Soviet ways of thinking, best reveal the influence of Soviet ideology understood as a cultural phenomenon.

The constant reinforcing link that makes Soviet ideology the mode of thinking of the elites and leadership is its interconnection with their interests. It provides justification for the system and for the self-replicating, dominant role of the political elite. These interests make ideology viable from generation to generation, and ideology justifies and provides a higher meaning for these interests. It would be foolish, however, to think that acceptance of ideology is cynical. It is rather a process of internalization that provides the congruence between material power and status interests of the elite and their conscience and feeling of self-esteem.

The precepts of Soviet ideology concerning international relations are well known. They pronounce the long-range irreconcilability of Communist and capitalist societies; they describe an historical process which their actions serve; they accept a strategic and tactical flexibility combined with long-range commitment to historical goals and belief in power as the ultimate arbiter of historical conflicts.

This ideology, intertwined with Russian nationalism, prevents the Soviet Union from becoming a satiated or status quo power, even when it has reached a secure and exalted position in the international community. Intertwined with Russian nationalism, it ensures that relations with the Soviet Union now and for the foreseeable future will remain highly competitive, complex, difficult, and unstable. It makes a mockery of the assumption of certain Americans that the Soviet leaders "are the same people as we are." Of course, we must negotiate, and we should communicate with Soviet elite members and experts. But we must first recognize that they are not "the same people as we are"—not superior, not inferior, but greatly different. Only then can we hope to influence their outlook.

Past Soviet successions have exercised greater impact on the domestic scene than on Soviet international policy, and foreign policy has reflected most clearly the capabilities of Soviet power. The degree of continuity of Soviet foreign policy from one succession to another, from one generation to another, is more striking than its discontinuities. However, successions have had an impact on foreign policy, and the present succession will probably be no exception.

First, the key preoccupation of the new leadership is to insulate the domestic political process and the still unstable leadership configuration from challenges from abroad and from international crisis situations. In Soviet foreign policy it is the time of carrots rather than sticks. During the last two years Soviet foreign policy was already in a holding pattern and was relatively passive. The key reasons for this passivity were Soviet overextension in the international arena, the desire to preserve detente with Western Europe, the desire not to provide any ammunition to the American administration on the eve of deployment of theater nuclear forces in Europe, and, finally, the effects of the onset of succession, with the decline of Brezhnev's power and ability to rule and with the development of the struggle within the Politburo for his position.

It may be expected that the passivity of Soviet foreign policy under Andropov's leadership will not last long but that the generally defensive and rather benign direction of this policy will be initially preserved. One may expect low-cost gestures of reconciliation toward the United States, for example the release of Sakharov from his exile, or an amnesty and expulsion of some prominent Soviet dissidents. One may expect friendly speeches and expressions of desire to improve Soviet-American relations. Most of all one may expect a virtual "peace offensive," with new proposals in the arms control and reduction area with a major propaganda effort in Western Europe and the United States to sell the nuclear freeze and non-first-use proposals, reinforced by some new Soviet concessions.

Finally, one may expect for some time to come a low-profile Soviet foreign policy concerning regional danger spots where a Soviet-American confrontation is most likely, for example in the Middle East and the Persian Gulf. One may expect that the phase of retrenchment rather than expansion will continue for a while until Andropov's leadership is consolidated and a higher threshold of

Soviet resistance to engaging in foreign adventures is established when low-risk opportunities and temptations do occur.

Secondly, a major tendency of Soviet foreign policy during the internal transfer of power is to hold on to vital international positions. The new leader will want to concede as little as possible with regard to Soviet international influence and foreign holdings. In the case of Andropov, the key international holding where few compromises are possible is Poland. While martial law in Poland has be lifted sooner than previously expected and the militarization of Polish political life may begin to be reversed sooner than planned, there seems in my opinion no chance of the restoration of even a modest, limited, and truncated free "Solidarity" movement. One should also expect that in case of new troubles or explosions in Poland, the Soviet reaction, direct or indirect through their Polish viceroys, will be swift and powerful. Andropov certainly does not want and cannot afford to "lose" Poland.

Another major Soviet international position to which the new leadership will try to hold even at a high price is detente with Western Europe and particularly West Germany. With detente with the United States unraveled, and with the prospects for a new Soviet-American rapprochement apparently not promising, the preservation and strengthening of the existing detente with Western Europe are more important than ever. The minimal expectations of Soviet West European policy is to use Western Europe as the means of pressuring the United States to change its Soviet policy; the maximal role of Soviet West European policy is to tear the alliance apart on issues of military policy and on the question of attitudes toward the Soviet Union. One may expect that in the near future Andropov will try to exploit the differences within the Western alliance to the hilt and will meet with West European leaders or even travel to Western Europe while using a soft approach and stance of injured innocence as far as Soviet-American relations are concerned. Yet, the attempt to concentrate on their West European connection should not be construed as the decline of the centrality of U.S.-Soviet relations in the minds of the new leadership. The concentration on Western Europe is simply the second best policy at a time when chances for rapid improvement in U.S.-Soviet relations are very low.

Third, an important tendency of Soviet foreign policy during the period of succession is to cut their losses in the international arena and attempt seriously to reverse the unsuccessful policies and approaches of the departed leader. The succession process is a time of reevaluation and reassessment and the advancement of new initiatives. This may be especially true with regard to Andropov, whose knowledge and understanding of foreign affairs seems to be much deeper than that of his two predecessors. One may expect, therefore, that the new overtures to China to gain normalization of relations which had started in the last month of Brezhnev's rule will be intensified, that new major compromise offers will be ceded to the Chinese leadership (e.g., partial troop withdrawal from the Sino-Soviet border), and that even some dramatic moves like a trip by Andropov to Beijing can be anticipated. It seems likely that the Chinese response will be positive and that the process of normalization between the two powers will start.

Fourth, the new leader cannot afford to respond weakly and indecisively to foreign challenges to Soviet international position and prestige. During the period of consolidation of his power a show of weakness in the case of an external challenge would compromise his standing among his colleagues and provide ammunition for his opponents. The simple truth is that in the Soviet Union only a very strong and established leader can afford to respond in a conciliatory way to challenges from abroad. In this sense the temptations which some members of the Reagan administration may have to test the USSR and to push it at a time of its transition of power could be quite dangerous and miscalculated. What the Soviet leadership probably fears more than anything else is to be considered weak and irresolute; its answers to such challenges may try to overcompensate for those fears.

Of all the issues on the agenda for the new government, dilemmas of Soviet military policy remain not only the most directly meaningful for the West but also the most different in substance from these same issues in previous Soviet successions. The extraordinary Soviet buildup on the western and eastern borders, strategic parity with the United States, global reach for Soviet armed forces—these were the major accomplishments of Brezhnev's regime. Before these goals were reached, they were clear and unchanging, not subject to significant disputes. The present succession differs from the others by the extent of awesome military power which it places under the control of the new leaders. We do not know how Andropov will use those powers. In all probability in the longer range he will try, as his predecessor did, to translate military power into political power and influence in the international arena.

At the same time, and in the shorter run, one cannot deny that now, when the long-term aims have been achieved (or, as others would argue, even overachieved, clearly beyond the range of traditional defense needs), there will probably be signs of an incipient attempt to redefine national security interests, or of arguments about military policy aims under new circumstances. In the 1980s the Soviet military burden will be relatively heavier than at any time in the past twenty years, and the relative cost will increase dramatically. The Soviets must choose among their guns, their butter—and their long-term investments.

Moreover, the change in the East-West military balance has brought from the Western alliance, particularly from the United States, a major reaction, which, if countered by the Soviets, will undoubtedly start a new, major, and uncontrollable arms race spiral. This prospect could initiate a reevaluation of Soviet military policy by the new leaders and by the experts advising them. It seems to me that the inertia of Soviet military policy may be broken, and at least the question of its redefinition may enter the political agenda of the 1980s. The successor leadership, under enormous pressure from competing elite constituencies, may no longer appropriate ever-increasing funds for the military as a kind of "conditioned reflex." This may be especially true of the up-and-coming younger members of the Soviet leadership, who in the course of their advancement have developed fewer ties with the military-industrial complex than their old-guard predecessors.

The predictability of short-term Soviet foreign policy during the succession, which may provide even more dramatic Soviet peace and reconciliation moves than this, does not mean that American leaders should dismiss them as tactical maneuvers. Even if they are only maneuvers, they will probably be effective in influencing public opinion and the leadership of some West European countries, particularly West Germany.

After the initial period of succession, when and if the new leader consolidates his position and the divisions and factions within the leadership and central elite become more cohesive, a new foreign policy may emerge. Past successions do not provide help here. The new policy may be a continuation of the old, with marginal changes in targets, methods, and intensity, as was the case in Brezhnev's foreign policy after Khrushchev's ouster. It may be a policy in which changes in strategy are substantial, as was the case in Khrushchev's policies after Stalin's death. Whether one or the other will occur in the present succession depends on so many variables that it would be irresponsible to predict. One can analyze a few key factors in the present succession that may influence the formation of Soviet foreign policy.

The present succession, especially in its later stages, will involve an influx of a new post-Stalin generation of elite members into the top, particularly at the intermediate level of power positions in the party, the government, and key functional bureaucracies, which will exert some influence on the domestic style of leadership and direction of policies, especially if their entrance into the leadership is not spread through a long period of time but is massive and condensed.

However, I have the impression that their impact on the conduct and direction of Soviet foreign policy may not be decisive for a number of reasons. First, a small group of men at the apex of the hierarchy, served by a very large staff of advisers and officials, monopolize Soviet decision making with regard to foreign policy, as distinct from domestic issues. The overwhelming majority of the political elite, as represented, for example, by the Central Committee of the party, is isolated from foreign policy making. The leaders inform the large group on the policies in the foreign area they have adopted, rather than ask what the foreign policy should be. In the Secretariat of the Central Committee, the general secretary alone is involved in the overall conduct and direction of Soviet foreign policy. Among the other secretaries, none is responsible for or specializes in Soviet foreign policy proper.

Even if the Politburo or Secretariat coopts some members of the new elite generation, it will be long before they enter the inner circle of foreign policy makers, who all belong to the old generation. Advancement of the new elite generation will occur almost exclusively in the area of domestic policies, in which individuals can claim expertise. In the foreign policy area, most senior officials below the top leadership, for example, the first deputies of Foreign Minister and Politburo member Gromyko, belong to the old generation. Even if a man of the new generation replaces Gromyko when he dies or retires, there is almost no chance, considering his age and credentials, that he will be selected for Politburo membership. Finally, one should recognize that the members of the new elite generation are provincial in their outlook and knowledge. When they do participate actively in shaping foreign policy, they will have to learn about foreign policy before becoming effective.

In short, one should not overestimate the importance of the new elite generation in shaping foreign policy. Yet, for a moment, assume that this "new" group may have some indirect influence and that at some point in the future they will bear direct responsibility. What do the relevant elements of their collective makeup reveal about the direction of their probable influence? From this point of view, its most important aspect could be their apparent preoccupation with domestic problems. Their movement into the leadership circle could redirect the focus of attention from global ambitions to internal problems. One should be aware, however, that a shift will occur in the focus of their interests to balance their domestic preoccupation with foreign policy problems as these individuals rise in power. In other words, the preoccupation of this group with domestic problems is a function of the level of its activities and may change with a rise in the hierarchy.

Another important element is that members of the new elite generation were born to power and do not feel in their bones the sacrifices a generation of Soviet people made to bring the USSR to its position. They seem more arrogant and self-assured about Soviet actions and Soviet ambitions, more certain about Soviet entitlement. Ironically, this could help to make relations with the Western world more equitable if it makes them less insecure and less influenced by the subconscious inferiority complex of the older generation. It may prevent overreaction to real or imagined slights and help to moderate bluster and machismo. This depends to some degree on the policies of Western governments in denying the Soviets opportunities for low-risk expansion and, especially, in ensuring an equitable balance between Western and Soviet military capabilities. In a situation where the balance of military power between the Soviet Union and the West moves too far in the Soviet favor, the assurance of this new generation of the Soviet elite and their feelings of entitlement could lead to higher risks and a more ambitious Soviet foreign policy.

The turnover of personnel in the succession will involve not only the leadership and the political elite but also the foreign policy advisors who, along with the intelligence services, provide the leadership information, evaluations, and position papers on options. One group of those advisors, a very small one, consists of full-time assistants to the core leaders, not unlike the National Security Council staff in the White House. Little is known about this group except that they exist and that one can be reasonably sure that the new leaders will bring their own people to the new jobs. This may be very important. One can only hope that those whom they appoint will be sensible and that the West will be able to evaluate their views and tendencies.

Another group consists of the leading functionaries of the Central Committee Secretariat departments concerned with certain aspects of foreign policy, international information, Communist movements and Communist parties in power, and senior officials of the Ministry of Foreign Affairs or Foreign Trade. The views and preferences of many of these men are known. One may expect that they will remain in office when the succession unfolds and that they will provide partly the recruitment pool for the leader's personal foreign policy staff.

The third group of advisors, who are best known, consists of men in institutes of the Academy of Science which conduct research on foreign countries and international relations, such as the Institute for the USA and Canada, the Institute for Economic and International Affairs, the Far and Middle Eastern Institutes, the Latin American and African Institutes, and the Institute for the Study of Socialist Countries. The leading figures of these institutes often prepare position papers on specific request from the leadership, help write speeches, and provide evaluations of international events. There are no evident reasons why this group of advisers should change in the process of succession. Some will join the full-time staffs of the leaders or at least work in close association with these staffs. These advisers in the Foreign Office, in the Central Committee staff, and the academic institutes will provide continuity of input and judgment into foreign policy making during the process of succession and after.

A number of American experts on the Soviet Union, inside and especially outside of government, are in contact with the third, and to some extent, the second group of Soviet policy advisers. Some know, sometimes in detail, their views on policy issues and are able to trace the evolution of their ideas. Some can understand their positions with regard to the general state of Soviet-Western relations and to specific events.

At the same time, evaluating the importance of what we know and what we can judge concerning this group is most complicated. The experts on international relations represent a range of differentiated views on most issues. It is not certain whether the views of these individuals reflect those of the leadership or whether they are personal evaluations, which may or may not reach the leadership and may or may not influence the leadership's perception of international issues. Even so, knowledge of this group of experts is important, in the first case as a mirror of the range of policy opinions circulating near the top, and in the second place as an input into Soviet foreign policy making. I believe that the first case, the experts view as a reflection of views within the leadership, is probably close to the truth.

From many years of observation and contact, I have no doubt that the differences of views among Soviet academic experts reflect differences at the level of the working staff of the Ministry of Foreign Affairs and the international departments in the Central Committee Secretariat staff. Were it not for the fact that the present system of foreign policy preparation is quite broad and that a degree of professional autonomy exists for the academic experts that is higher than in the past, one should be inclined to believe that differences at the top among the patrons of the different experts sanction these differences. Today, however, this does not seem as likely as in the past.

Whatever the relationship of these experts' views to the views of the leadership, one can be fairly certain that the range of differences in the leadership is not broader than the range of differences among the academic experts and in all probability is narrower. The range of opinion among Soviet experts on international affairs may delineate the limits of views and preferences with regard to policy held by the Soviet leadership in times of such a divisive succession as that of the 1980s will be.

Should the new leaders decide not to proceed with basic reforms, they will have very little new to offer the elite and general population as far as economic, political, cultural, or social well-being is concerned. In such a situation, with its lack of domestic "quick fixes," one should ask whether the new leadership will not decide to utilize the tried method of regimes in domestic trouble, continue to strengthen the armed forces, threaten its already frightened neighbors, and engage in foreign adventurism to distract attention from domestic ills. One cannot assert with certainty that the new set of leaders will not contemplate or adopt such a course. The arguments against adventurism, however, are strong.

First, if the Soviet leaders decide to engage in a major foreign adventure for home consumption purposes, and only a major adventure would be effective, they must prepare for a confrontation with either the United States or China, or both. However, both before it gained strategic parity with the West and after, the Soviet Union has traditionally been a low-risk power even when it engaged in foreign expansion. This dominant low-risk attitude is one of the most essential characteristics which divides Soviet policy from that of Nazi Germany.

It is possible, but highly unlikely, that the new set of Soviet leaders will bring into office, or be pressured to adopt, a different set of attitudes. Yet, the individuals who will continue to occupy the core leadership positions belong to the old generation of leaders for whom caution is an ingrained characteristic. Moreover, the roots of the cautious attitude still remain in force: the leaders' knowledge of Soviet weaknesses and of the relative overall superiority of the West in the "correlation of forces," which includes economic strength, technological advancement, and reliability of alliances, in addition to military forces; fear that a gamble to gain some advantages abroad may lose all; apprehension that the leadership may lose control over events, which could then develop spontaneously, a terrible eventuality for leaders with a strong fear of spontaneity.

Second, the Soviet leadership will be preoccupied in dealing with problems in their East European empire, and a major foreign adventure would overextend them dangerously. Poland in particular should exercise a severe restraining influence for at least several years.

Third, the Soviets, especially the Russians, are very patriotic and respond quickly in defense of their country. However, they are not attracted to offensive adventures in faraway places. The difficulty that the Soviets have trying to explain their Afghanistan invasion is only one of many pieces of confirming evidence.

A major Soviet adventure would endanger the Soviet–West European connection, which is absolutely essential, even though the Soviets probably appreciate that nothing short of a major expansionist move would change the West European attitude of preserving detente with the Soviet Union at almost any price. Finally, the leadership can attain a high degree of nationalistic political mobilization without resorting to dangerous foreign adventures. The propaganda machine can whip up chauvinistic emotions to a high pitch and easily promote an aggressively nationalistic mentality in the country. One cannot be sure that the new leadership will not engage in foreign adventures. However, if it does so, strategic and foreign policy reasons, not domestic purposes, will be the cause.

Conclusions

In summary, we should ask first whether the Soviet Union finds itself at a potential turning point in its history. Will the 1980s produce a crisis of leadership or of system, or both? Will any crisis turn the system inward or outward?

A number of key ingredients for such a turning point are present in the succession, which overlaps with many critical decisions that the new leadership will have to consider. Other important ingredients are missing. Above all, the Soviet leadership and political elite clearly have the will to rule the Soviet Union and the Soviet empire by traditional means, and also to expand Soviet influence and power globally, to benefit from the decades of sacrifices and development. In the equation of foreign policies of opposing powers, the capacity to act and the will to act are partly exchangeable; the greater will to act may overcome the shortcomings of a nation's capacities.

With regard to the internal Soviet political system, one may hope for change, but one cannot expect fundamental shifts. After all, no successful political elite in history has liquidated itself.

However, one can conclude that the 1980s constitute such a critical juncture that the Soviet Union will decline politically, socially, and economically if its leaders do not implement major economic reforms. The famous "muddling through" model, applied to the Soviet future without basic reforms, should be supplemented by two options, "muddling up" and "muddling down." The latter will describe the Soviet Union in the next decade without major reforms. One should keep in mind, though, that a power such as the Soviet Union may decline internally for a long period and produce in the meantime tremendous mischief in the international arena, as long as it maintains its armed strength and its leaders and elite have not lost their nerve and possess a will to expand.

This gives rise to a second question: is the Soviet system on the verge of economic bankruptcy and political disintegration, as some Western observers believe? Everyone knows the predictions of some Westerners about "the coming revolution in Russia," the imminent "revolt of the nationalities" and the Soviet "internal" empire, and the spread of dissidence which "will engulf the Soviet intelligentsia," and of which we see only the tip of the iceberg.

Those scenarios are possible but most unlikely. What has been built through generations with much blood, sacrifice, ruthlessness, cunning, and conviction will not simply disintegrate or radically change because of critical problems. In the coming succession, the Soviet Union may face a leadership crisis and an economic crisis, but it does not now and in all probability will not in the next decade face a systemic crisis that endangers its existence. It has enormous unused reserves of political and social stability. Gigantic economies such as the Soviet Union's, presided over by intelligent and educated professionals, do not go bankrupt. They become less effective, stagnate, or experience an absolute decline for a period, but they do not disintegrate.

When analyzing the Soviet domestic and imperial situation at the beginning of the 1980s and its probable impact on foreign policy and projecting its development for the rest of the decade, I am drawn inescapably to the conclusion that we will witness the external expansion of an internally declining power.

From the Soviet point of view, the most favorable scenario over the remainder of the decade would contain the following elements. The Soviet Union will emerge from the present succession with a strong leader who will remain in office for the remainder of the decade. Any struggle within the leadership and central elite would be brief and would not involve major purges or a leadership crisis. The oligarchical nature of the Soviet leadership and the will of the leadership and political elite to rule and to expand would remain strong. Through a number of economic reforms on the margin of the system, the Soviet economy would avoid stagnation and the ratio of its growth would remain at the maximum projected levels of 2.5 percent.

Docility within the working class, the political apathy of the population, the centrifugal forces in the "internal" empire, and the career in-system orientation of the professional class would continue, though within a narrower margin of safety, safeguarded by increased authoritarianism of the domestic order and buttressed by nationalistic appeals. Within the East European empire, the population and disaffected elite groupings would remain quiescent and present Soviet power with limited challenges in only one country at a time. Finally, the leadership would be able to insulate its continuous external expansion from its domestic and imperial troubles.

From the Soviet perspective, the least favorable scenario of the domestic and imperial situation for the remainder of the decade would contain the following elements: the Soviet Union would witness in the 1980s two successions of leadership and would remain throughout the decade without a strong and secure leader; the struggle over power and policies among the leadership and central elites would resemble the post-Stalin succession in its intensity; the oligarchical nature of the leadership, rule by a committee, would be stronger and would reduce the flexibility of domestic and foreign policies; economic policy making would be of an emergency, stopgap nature and would fail to prevent virtual stagnation of economic growth; the social stability of the 1960s and 1970s would be replaced by sporadic, perhaps violent worker unrest and by the further systemic decline of the work ethic, along with an increase in corruption; irredentist pressures among the elite and the population of the non-Slavic nationalities of the "internal" empire would increase significantly; the deteriorating economic situation in the East European empire would lead to massive social and political unrest in a number of countries which military force would have to suppress; the commitment of the leadership and political elite to expansion of power and influence in the international arena would remain intact, but domestic troubles, the agony of Eastern Europe, and the leadership's fear of overextension would limit it.

In either case, the West will face an active and expansionist Soviet foreign policy. The Soviet Union is still in an ascending phase of its great power global ambitions; it still possesses an awesome and growing military machine, and its foreign policy will increasingly play a legitimizing role for rule at home. However, in either case, the domestic economic and social costs of a continuous military buildup and of an expansionist foreign policy will increase dramatically in comparison to that of the 1960s and 1970s.

Soviet foreign policies are rooted in internally determined political, economic, and cultural tendencies and sources. Yet the policies of Soviet adversaries can influence Soviet development and policies. In the late 1980s, the potential Western leverage on Soviet behavior, particularly international, and on the costs of Soviet policies will be much greater than at any time during the Brezhnev era. The Western influence on Soviet domestic policies can be, at best, marginal; but its influence on specific Soviet foreign policies may be very important.

The transformation of Western leverage from potential to actual depends partly on the revitalization of the Western alliance and on coordination of its economic and defense policies. Above all else, it depends on whether the United States, the only barrier to Soviet international appetites, will restore a domestic equilibrium shattered by the political and cultural crises of the 1960s and 1970s, regain its confidence and that of its allies, reverse the negative trends in the Soviet-American military balance, and pursue a patient and tempered long-range policy without the swings of the policy pendulum so characteristic of the 1970s.

The Soviet Union and its empire have already entered upon the road of systemic decline, but the effects of this decline on Soviet international strength and behavior may take some time to become observable. The key guideline for American policy in this period is to avoid actions that may arrest or slow this decline and to promote actively its acceleration. It is an open question whether the United States will be able to pursue such a policy, and whether, instead, the waning years of this century will witness the dangerous and unpredictable parallel process of competitive decay of the two superpowers and their alliances.

NOTES

1. Valerie Bunce, *Do New Leaders Make a Difference: Executive Succession and Public Policy under Capitalism and Socialism* (Princeton: Princeton University Press, 1981), pp. 173–74.

2. Gertrude E. Schroeder, "The Soviet Economy on a Treadmill of Reforms," in U.S. Congress, Joint Economic Committee, *Soviet Economy in a Time of Change* (Washington, D.C.: USGPO, 1979), vol. 1, p. 313.

3. Joseph S. Berliner, "Economic Prospects," in Robert G. Wesson, ed., *The Soviet Union: Looking to the 1980s* (Stanford: Hoover Institution Press, 1980), p. 108.

4. Hugh Heclo and Aaron Wildavsky, *The Private Governance of Public Money* (London: Macmillan, 1974), p. 220.

5. Thomas W. Wolfe, "Military Power and Soviet Policy," in *The Soviet Empire: Expansion and Detente*, William E. Griffith, ed. (Lexington, Mass.: D. C. Heath & Co., 1976), p. 149.

2

★

The Economy

Robert W. Campbell

Introduction

THOSE WHO would understand the Soviet economy have always had to keep in balance two startlingly contradictory aspects of its performance. It is an economy perpetually in crisis, wasteful and inefficient in the use of resources, bureaucratically musclebound in efforts to innovate technologically and institutionally, and scandalously callous and inept in meeting the Soviet population's consumption wants. Despite all this, its growth performance has been impressive. Lurching though its progress seems, it overcomes crises rather than allowing them to accumulate to the point of collapse, and year after year significant output increments become available, expanding the leadership's ability to achieve its goals. By devoting a significant share of the economy's output to investment, the leaders have continually expanded the nation's production capacity, and the Soviet Union today has achieved an aggregate output that makes it a major economic power and a military superpower. In the years after Stalin's death, consumption also began to share these output increments for growth.

The 1980s promise to bring a significant shift in the interplay between these two contradictory aspects of Soviet economic performance. The mobilizational approach that permitted growth in spite of waste has lost its efficacy. Unless the Soviet leaders can resolve the systemic weaknesses that inhibit effective use of its resources, economic stringencies will create serious pressures on foreign and domestic policy in the 1980s. Some see in this change significant constraints on the leadership's room for maneuver in the 1980s, serious tensions, vulnerability, and heightened responsiveness to initiatives on the part of the United States. One can address these issues

I would like to express my appreciation to Morris Bornstein, John Hardt, D. Gale Johnson, and Thomas Wolf for the information and critical comments they provided.

only in the context of the volume as a whole, but this chapter can set the stage for such an assessment by explaining the ways in which economic prospects represent a change from the past and by describing the economic choices and constraints facing the Soviet leaders as they confront these problems.

Growth Slowdown and Economic Constraints in the Eighties

Soviet leaders face unprecedented conditions of resource stringency in the 1980s, as growth of the economy slackens and as resource expectations and demands of the various claimants on the nation's output expand. A number of adverse trends will combine to bring the rate of economic growth well below recent experience. Soviet GNP growth has generally been decelerating in the years since the Second World War: it was 6 to 7 percent per year in the 1950s, and 5 percent in the 1960s, declining to 4 and then 3 percent in the 1970s.[1] In the 1980s, output is unlikely to grow at more than 2 percent per year.

The growth of labor supply will decelerate sharply. The civilian work force grew at a rate of about 2.3 percent per year in the 1960s and 1.4 percent per year in the 1970s, but during the 1980s will fall to probably about 0.4 percent. The Soviet economy was able to add 8.2 million persons to the work force in the Tenth Five-Year Plan (1976–80) and 17.3 million persons over the decade of the 1970s as a whole.[2] During the Eleventh Five-Year Plan period the Soviets forecast growth of the population in the working ages as only 3.3 million and for the whole decade of the 1980s as no more than 5.8 million.[3] There seems little prospect for increasing labor supply by increasing the participation rate: very few people in the working ages are not already working.

In the past, growth has depended on rapid expansion of the capital stock. However, as the rate of growth of total output slows, amounts available for investment also grow at a slower rate. With this reduced dynamism in increments to the capital stock, the growth of the latter will also decelerate. The Eleventh Five-Year Plan (1981–85) squeezes allocations of investment to maintain growth of military and consumption allocations, and this choice magnifies the effect of this reduction. The growing burden of attrition of the capital stock will also slow growth in productive capacity. In the early stages of growth, depreciation of the capital stock is relatively small compared to new additions. As the stock ages and becomes obsolete, depreciation increases as a share of increments, and net increments are squeezed further.

Growth in output takes place not only by increases in the flow of resource inputs, but also from gains in productivity. Here, too, the prospect is not encouraging. Since the Second World War the growth of GNP per unit of resource input has fallen consistently and by the end of the 1970s was apparently zero or negative. Professor Abram Bergson figured that in 1950–1958 GNP per unit of combined capital and labor grew at 1.7 percent per year, but at only 0.7 percent per year in 1958–67.[4] The CIA's calculations of combined factor productivity are methodologically close to Bergson's, though they count land inputs as well as capital and labor, and are consistent with Bergson's in showing 0.7 percent per year productivity growth in the early 1960s. The CIA figures show that productivity growth then improved somewhat in the early 1970s, but that after 1973 it was negative, declining at an average annual rate of 0.8 percent per year.[5]

The leadership indicates that it expects some kind of revolution in productivity in the 1980s and relies on acceleration of productivity growth to compensate for the slowdown in the growth of resource inputs. But a significant turnaround is unlikely. One explanation for slow growth in productivity is that the Soviet economy has reached a level of capitalization where substitution of capital for labor is difficult. If so, slow labor force growth in the 1980s cannot easily be offset by capital growth. Additions to capital too often take the form of new job slots that cannot be filled rather than labor-saving deepening of capital. Other explanations for low productivity growth include organizational slack, foot-dragging by management at lower levels, and failure to innovate. It is difficult to make a case that the Soviets can overcome these phenomena, which are deeply embedded in the system. In the 1980s, branch and regional shifts that require increases in the average amount of capital required per unit of output are also likely to reduce the effect of additional capital investment. The rail transport system has in recent years absorbed increasing loads by intensifying utilization of its capital stock but may be reaching a point where it needs large, new additions. Similarly, the energy sector operated in the 1960s and early 1970s with falling costs and low incremental capital-output ratios, as it developed new resources cheap to find, develop, produce, and transport. The Soviets must now expand output in locations where the opposite is true and shift to alternative sources for which capital costs per unit of delivered output are higher than in the previous mix. Gas with high transport costs and nuclear power with high investment costs per kilowatt of generating capacity are illustrations. Regional shifts in economic activity involve massive diversion of investment into infrastructural projects with high capital intensity and little immediate output. Examples are the Baikal-Amur railway (referred to as BAM for *Baikal-Amurskaia magis-*

tral') in Siberia, and housing, transport, and urban support facilities in the regions crucial to plans for producing energy and raw materials.

The impact of external economic relations on growth in the 1980s is unlikely to remain as favorable as it was in the 1970s. By opening their economy to more interaction with the rest of the world in the late 1960s, the Soviet leaders achieved a significant contribution to growth through importing Western technology. They also enjoyed a significant terms-of-trade bonus as prices of Soviet exports rose in relation to import prices, most spectacularly in the case of oil, for which the price revolution of 1973 generated an estimated Soviet windfall of as much as $10 billion per year in the later seventies. Foreign loans also produced a net addition to real investment resources. The USSR was able to borrow at subsidized interest rates and pressed the East Europeans for contributions to joint investment projects.

Most aspects of economic relations with the rest of the world are likely to be less favorable in the 1980s. Soviet exports face sluggish demand, price trends are unlikely to remain as favorable as in the past, and high interest rates and Western caution may limit Soviet borrowing. The USSR could face a net drain of hard currency earnings if it decides to help East European countries meet their debt service obligations.

The agricultural sector remains a critical problem. Since the mid-1960s it has consistently absorbed over a quarter of all resources allocated for investment, with relatively weak response in terms of output growth. Three consecutive years, 1979, 1980, and 1981, brought poor harvests, and 1982 was not much better. This may seem an unusual run of bad luck, but some research suggests that a trend in Soviet weather conditions makes this kind of calamity likely to recur in the coming decade. To sustain its efforts to improve the Soviet diet, the regime has had to continue massive imports of agricultural goods.

Some strong feedback mechanisms in this prospect create dilemmas for the Soviet leaders. The slower growth is, the less they have to divide among increasing consumption, defense, and investment. They might hope to stimulate growth by allocating more to either consumption (which might raise morale and incentives) or investment (to increase productive capacity), but allocating a higher share of the total output to either undercuts growth of the other.

Forecasts of the rate of growth for the 1980s depend heavily on the assumptions one makes, especially regarding the growth of productivity. Western analysts of the Soviet economy have reached a fairly well defined consensus, with few projections of GNP growth in the 1980s falling outside the range of 2 to 2.5 percent per year. The CIA has stated that the most likely rate of growth for the coming decade is not more than 2 percent per year. The most elaborate approach to forecasting Soviet growth is the model developed by Wharton Econometric Forecasting Associates, which indicates a rate of 2.3 percent per year.[6]

Pressure for Priority Choices

With supply increases thus constrained, the Soviet leaders will face hard choices as they pursue their traditional objectives: investment for economic growth, strengthening military power, and improving the lot of the consumer. When GNP was growing rapidly, each of these end uses could grow rapidly, and each of these claims generated strong demands or expectations for continued growth at customary rates. As the increment shrinks for responding to these competing demands, conflicts over allocation, always an important issue in Soviet politics, are likely to become unprecedentedly severe. Let us consider recent experience and expectations regarding each major end use.

Consumption

Consumption has traditionally been the stepchild of Soviet economic priorities. During the first half century of Soviet growth, consumption grew during most of the period at a rate well below that for GNP as a whole and trailed investment and defense. In 1970, consumption accounted for 57 percent of GNP, a smaller share than that characteristic for the industrially advanced countries. If anyone wonders how consumption can still account for 57 percent of total output when it has grown so much more slowly than the other components for half a century, the answer lies in changes in relative prices. The costs and prices of consumer goods have risen in relation to those for the investment and defense goods to which the regime has devoted its primary attention. Thus, when one measures the various components of the nation's output in 1970 costs, consumption goods bulk larger than if one valued all components in prices of some earlier period.

Even in the 1970s, when the regime declared its intention to raise its priority, consumption usually lost out to other claimants. Soviet terminology for accounting for the nation's output and its allocation among alternative uses is not especially helpful for analyzing such issues, but we can use it in this case to make the point. Within the industrial sector, Soviet statisticians distinguish Industry A, which produces the means of production, from Industry B, which produces the means of consumption. In the Ninth Five-Year Plan (1971–75), the output of Industry B was to expand faster than Industry A, but in fulfillment, Industry A grew at the planned 46 percent rate, and

Industry B grew by only 36 percent, compared to the planned 49. For all material output, the statisticians make a division into the consumption fund *(fond potrebleniia)* and the accumulation fund *(fond nakopleniia)*. The plan also projected a faster growth of the consumption fund than the accumulation fund, calling for it to rise from 74 percent of national income in 1970 to 75 percent in 1975. In fact it fell to 73 percent.[7] In the Tenth Five-Year Plan, the priority given consumption reflected in these indicators reverted to its customary low status, both in plans and in actual performance.

It is becoming increasingly difficult to postpone radical improvement in consumption levels, for both morale and incentive reasons. Indeed, it is no exaggeration to say that the stability and legitimacy of the regime depend on significant improvements. The party has traditionally justified its monopoly of political power and its right to allocate national output on the grounds that only a visionary elite could enforce the discipline needed to ensure the country's security and to divert output into accumulating capital to ensure growth and a better tomorrow. It has accomplished those purposes. The Soviet Union today supports a larger investment program and a larger expenditure of resources for each year on defense than does the United States, which has a GNP at least half again as large as Soviet GNP. Though Soviet leaders are careful not to claim military superiority over the United States, they openly assure their people that Soviet military power equals that of the capitalist world and demonstrate that change in status by increasingly bold military actions. They can make no such claim regarding the consumption component of the Soviet Union's GNP, however, because it is between a third and a half the corresponding United States aggregate.[8] Given a Soviet population of 265 million, compared to 223 million in the United States in 1980, the USSR's relative standing in per capita terms is still lower.

To an outsider, the traditional rationale for the lopsided allocation priorities of the past has lost its plausibility, and the regime's legitimacy now depends on successful efforts to raise consumption levels. In my view, this is apparent to Soviet citizens as well. Moreover, the leadership itself is coming to accept the proposition, as two recent quotations indicate. In a 1981 discussion at the Institute of Economics of the USSR Academy of Sciences, one Soviet economist asserted that the Guidelines for the Eleventh Five-Year Plan (1981–85) should acknowledge explicitly that consumption growth is a prerequisite for growth in general:

> It is necessary to underline more precisely the role of the consumption sphere. . . . Growth cannot now be adequately guaranteed if we apply the

assumptions which were widespread 15 to 20 years ago when we treated consumption as a deduction from the national income. . . . In the period of developed socialism the consumption sphere plays an active role in the process of growth, and we must take account of that circumstance.[9]

Brezhnev in his speech to the Twenty-sixth Party Congress in 1981 noted clearly the political significance of improving consumption:

As you know, comrades, the draft of the guidelines for the next five years embodies a certain acceleration of the rate of growth of Group B, to exceed the rate of growth of Group A. That is good. The problem is to create a really modern sector producing consumer goods and services for the population, which meet their demands. In concluding this point, I would like to consider it as more than a purely economic problem, and pose the question in broader terms. The things we are speaking of— food, consumer goods, services—are issues in the daily life of millions and millions of people. The store, the cafeteria, the laundry, the dry cleaners are places people visit every day. What can they buy? How are they treated? How are they spoken to? How much time do they spend on all kinds of daily cares? The people will judge our work in large measure by how these questions are solved. They will judge strictly, exactingly. And that, comrades, we must remember.[10]

Consumer needs go beyond food and other material consumer goods. Many Soviet experts believe that the regime must improve many other aspects of life as well, if only because this is crucial for improving the quality and quantity of effort the population contributes. Thus, one reads numerous expressions of worry about deteriorating health conditions, as in one author's warning that "in some regions of the country, infant mortality has risen, cardiovascular and other diseases are becoming 'younger,' the gap in life expectancy of men and women is not lessening, drunkenness among the population is not declining."[11]

One commentator on the guidelines for the Eleventh Five-Year Plan considered its goals too modest with respect to improving the populations's health. He called for amendments to commit the government to "eliminate finally the employment of women in heavy work and work dangerous for them; . . . to develop widely a network of prophylactic stations in enterprises, introduce complete provision of dispensary services for men 40 years and older and for all workers employed in heavy and dangerous lines of production; to satisfy fully the need of the population for medicines; to improve the equipping of all medical institutions with the most modern treatment and diagnostic equipment; to extend widely the struggle against alcoholism, using all means of mass information and gradually reducing the production of vodka."[12]

Many assert that the Soviet people will accept passively whatever low standard of living the regime permits and consider it a boon even to have enough to eat. But numerous observers of contemporary Soviet society suggest that the mood of the population has changed, especially that of the young, and that the people expect the regime to provide continuous improvements and a higher standard of living. Which of these views is more nearly right is impossible to settle, but the regime's actions demonstrate that it inclines toward the latter view.

Military Forces

The present Soviet leaders have demonstrated in the last fifteen years a strong commitment to increasing Soviet military strength, and they have supported a buildup of military forces at a consistently high rate of growth. As Coit D. Blacker explains in another chapter, Nikita Khrushchev sought to reduce the costs of the Soviet military establishment by developing a new strategic doctrine and by modernization. The resulting conflict with important parts of the military establishment and the humiliation of the Cuban missile crisis, when the USSR had to retreat in the face of superior United States power, no doubt played an important role in his downfall.

The present leadership came into power determined not to yield in such a confrontation and has concentrated on building Soviet military strength. According to thorough and elaborate estimates by the CIA, which are accepted by most specialists, allocations of resources to military purposes have grown in real terms since 1965 at a rate of 4–5 percent per year, and by 1980 constituted between 12 and 14 percent of the Soviet GNP. Both the growth rate and the share of GNP are figured in 1970 factor cost. CIA analysts believe that the relative costs of military goods may have risen faster in the 1970s than the costs of other elements of GNP, so that in current prices the share might be somewhat higher.

We have little information on which to base an estimate of Soviet ruble expenditures for defense, and for a large portion of the total, the CIA converts its dollar estimates to rubles, using ruble-dollar purchasing power parities. Some critics consider the resulting ruble figures too small, largely because of the way the dollar figures are converted to rubles. Others see them as too large and criticize the way the original dollar figures are generated and the way they are converted to rubles. Less controversy has emerged regarding the growth rate of these expenditures, though one critic of the CIA methodology considers 4 to 5 percent much too low, and estimates 8 percent per year growth since 1970 and an even higher figure for the fifteen years since 1965.[13] I find the CIA figures generally plausible, but one should always retain a certain skepticism regarding such a complex issue on which we possess far from full and clear information.

The experts generally agree that the resource allocation to defense in the USSR is well insulated from competing claims. On the production side a great deal of inertia protects the process by which R and D programs develop new weapons systems, which then grow into procurement and production commitments. Production facilities for military production are somewhat walled off from the civilian economy, and the sector is to a considerable degree self-sufficient. However, a significant portion of the output of the plants in industries producing military goods is for civilian use, suggesting more flexibility in reallocating resources from military to civilian production in the short run than has sometimes been claimed. Within Gosplan (the State Planning Commission, which develops both the annual and five-year plans) planning the output of military goods proceeds on its own in a separate military section rather than in direct competition with other allocations. In the very highly centralized Soviet political process, a still more restricted circle of actors makes decisions about commitments to defense. Most analysts believe that the Defense Council decides the pace and scale of weapons procurement programs, without debate in the Politburo as a whole or in the Central Committee. As Grey Hodnett says, "because of its composition and its access to highly restricted information the Defense Council probably can expect to have its decisions routinely approved by the Politburo."[14]

This separation of military-economic from general economic affairs cuts across all top-level planning and administrative bodies, with responsibility for the military sector segregated in special organs within each major central policy body: the Military Industrial Commission in the state economic structure, the Defense Council in the legislative structure, and a Military Industrial Department in the Party Secretariat. According to one expert on Soviet military affairs, "The internal environment in which major Soviet military policy decisions are made can best be described as a closed system of defense decision making within a slightly larger but also closed system of political decision making."[15] The allocation of resources to the military thus has a highly inertial character and is so insulated from the regular sources of decision making in the USSR that proponents of other interests find it difficult to advance their claims.

Investment

Soviet leaders have always considered investment the key to growth and given it a high priority. The long-run growth record shows that capital stock has grown much faster than the labor force, which is characteristic of modern economic development in general, but it has also grown faster than output, which distinguishes the experience of Soviet-type economies from other rapidly growing economies. In justifying the allocations implicit in the plans, the regime has always emphasized that building the "material-technical basis of communism" was one of the first tasks. Ideologues have generally favored a doctrinal proposition that output of the means of production (not exactly the same thing as investment goods but closely correlated) must grow faster than output of the means of consumption. This is part of the well-recognized "extensive growth pattern" of Soviet-type economies.

Against this background, it is difficult for Soviet leaders to suppress the traditional high priority for investment. In the early 1970s Abram Bergson published an article suggesting that Soviet decision makers could achieve a much higher growth of consumption over the proximate decade by accepting a lower than customary growth rate for capital stock.[16] This would reduce GNP growth somewhat but, by reducing the growth of investment, would promote faster growth. This is an intriguing application of the idea that less can be more. When one reviews what happened in the 1970s, however, one finds that the possibility did not attract Soviet planners, who persisted in seeking a rapid growth of the capital stock.

In addition to this inherent belief of decision makers in the importance of investment as the route to growth, the system in general generates excessive demands for investment. From plant managers at the bottom of the hierarchy, decision makers feel an instinctive pressure to add new facilities and capacities to improve their ability to deal with pressure from the top for increased output. In the absence of significant interest charges and market-based prices, this costless way to obtain more resources provides little motivation for project makers to economize when they design plants and when they specify and order equipment. One careful reader of Soviet discussions on this problem, Nancy Nimitz, has concluded that "goldplating" equipment and production facilities has become endemic in the Soviet investment process. An intriguing theme in current Soviet economics literature deals with an effort to introduce "passports" for machines and production facilities indicating their output capacity. Soviet managers show little enthusiasm for this campaign, and planners commonly fail to impose output assignments fully utilizing the indicated capacities even when passports are developed. Another aspect of this noneconomizing behavior is that decision makers tend to prefer expensive additions of new plants rather than modernization of old plants by replacement of obsolete equipment.

In short, out of established strategic habits of thought in pursuing growth and as a consequence of the incentive structure, the Soviet economic system has a bias toward relying on investment as the key to growth: the two have been almost synonymous in Soviet eyes.

Research and Development

Another end-use of GNP analogous to investment in its relation to growth is research and development. In recent years R and D has been given a high priority and has absorbed about 4 percent of GNP. Until recently it rose faster than GNP because of its expected contribution to growth and because of the leaders' great faith in the "scientific-technical revolution" as a way to transform Soviet society. The need for technical progress has certainly not disappeared; but a growth differential favoring R and D growth cannot continue indefinitely, and apparently the time has come to curtail its growth. Although the Eleventh Five-Year Plan does not make plans for R and D spending explicit, Minister of Finance V. F. Garbuzov subsequently cited figures indicating that R and D expenditures are to slow sharply. A decree in late 1981 provides corroboration of this by calling for reductions in 1981–85 in the number of R and D personnel from the 1980 level and for some pruning of the network of R and D establishments. Brezhnev remarked at the Twenty-sixth Party Congress earlier that year that the State Committee for Science and Technology and the USSR Academy of Sciences should arrange a "regrouping of scientific forces" and that defense industry R and D organizations should provide more help to the civilian economy. There may have been some decision to slow what must recently have been a runaway expansion of military R and D.[17]

Alternatives or Trade-offs

Obviously what is done for one claimant affects what can be done for others. A simple calculation will help assess these trade-offs. Table 2.1 presents a projection of Soviet GNP based on our knowledge of the likely growth of the labor force, the growth of capital stock under two alternative investment policies, and some assumptions about productivity growth. This calculation is less a forecast than a quantitative framework for showing the impact of the growth-decelerating forces described earlier and the implications of the trade-offs we want to consider.

The first half of the table recapitulates the kind of exercise Bergson completed for the 1970s. The projection assumes that the Soviet leaders try to maintain the growth of the capital stock at near the rate of the preceding decade, by calculating the resulting GNP growth expected for alternative productivity projections and determining the levels of investment required to achieve the postulated growth of the

Table 2.1

Soviet Growth and Allocation Alternatives
for the Eighties

High Capital Growth Strategy	1980	1985	1990
Labor supply (million persons)	136.2	139.4	141.5
Capital stock (billion rubles)	1,297	1,846	2,623
GNP (billion rubles)			
Productivity at 1%/yr	530	646 (4.0%)*	805 (4.3%)
Productivity at 0.5%/yr	530	630 (3.5%)	765 (3.7%)
Investment (billion rubles)	130	194 (8.3%)	273 (7.7%)
Defense (billion rubles)	69	84 (4.0%)	102 (4.0%)
Consumption as residual (billion rubles)	331	368 (2.1%)	430 (2.7%)
		352 (1.2%)	390 (1.7%)

Constant Investment Strategy	1980	1985	1990
Labor supply (million persons)	136.2	139.4	141.5
Capital stock (billion rubles)	1,297	1,705	2,047
GNP (billion rubles)			
Productivity at 1%/yr	530	625 (3.4%)	716 (3.1%)
Productivity at 0.5%/yr	530	610 (2.8%)	681 (2.5%)
Investment (billion rubles)	130	135	135
Defense (billion rubles)	69	84 (4.0%)	102 (4.0%)
Consumption as residual (billion rubles)	331	406 (4.2%)	479 (3.8%)
		391 (3.4%)	444 (3.0%)

*Figures in parentheses show average annual rate of growth since 1980. The 1980 base for GNP is in something close to 1970 prices, with the allocation by end use based on Soviet figures for investment (commissioned) and on the CIA assertion that defense is about 13 percent of GNP, with the residual attributed to consumption. The Soviet investment data are in a price base that I believe approximates 1970 prices. Growth of the capital stock is figured by correcting the Soviet data on undepreciated value to a depreciated basis and then moving it by investment, attrition, and depreciation. The growth rate of capital stock for the previous decade was used to project the capital stock in the high growth strategy in the growth rate of undepreciated book value in the seventies, i.e., 7.3 percent. In figuring the growth of combined factor inputs, capital receives a weight of one-third, labor a weight of two-thirds.

capital stock. Subtracting the allocation to defense on the assumption it continues its inertial growth at 4 percent per year leaves consumption in 1985 and 1990 as a residual and enables us to determine its growth rate over the period.

This strategy is quite unattractive in its implications for consumption, for consumption growth is well below GNP growth. On a per capita basis, the low productivity projection falls to about 1 percent per year. If productivity growth should fall below half a percent per year, consumption per capita would stagnate, with consequences explosive for Soviet society and for the regime. The second half of the table represents the same approach, except that it assumes that the flow of resources to investment remains constant at a level slightly above that of 1980, as is planned for 1981–85, while the allocation to defense grows as before at 4 percent per year. In this scenario, growth will indeed slow, though the rate will again depend significantly on what productivity gains the system is able to stimulate. Holding the line on investment will remove some pressure on the guns-or-butter choice and permit consumption to continue to grow at reasonable rates, even if military expenditures continue to grow at the current rate of about 4 percent per year. If productivity could be raised to 1 percent, consumption could enjoy a very respectable growth, i.e., almost 4 percent. The more likely forecast of a rise in productivity at half a percent per year brings consumption growth down by almost a percentage point. If no productivity growth at all occurs, the prospects for both GNP and consumption are much more bleak.

Competition among the three major end uses also occurs at a more disaggregated level, the most important example being the common burden which investment and military procurement put on the output of the machine-building sector. As GNP growth slows, industry and its subsectors, including the sector that produces machinery, are also likely to grow slowly. One can formulate a balance sheet for this category of output in which the supply consists of the final output of the domestic machinery sector, plus imports, with demand divided primarily into producer durables for domestic investment and for export, consumer durables such as refrigerators and autos for household consumption, and military hardware for the defense establishment. The work completed on this problem suggests that rapid growth of military spending will eat into the machinery output available for investment in the 1980s.

The impact of that competition will depend heavily upon Soviet international economic relations. Exports and imports are sufficiently large in the machinery balance that changes in the amounts of machinery imported and exported can significantly ease or exacerbate the competition between military procurement and investment. Machinery imports depend in turn on agricultural imports. In 1980 the Soviets spent a third of their hard currency earnings to import agricultural commodities, and in 1981 the share was about 45 percent. The $9 to 12 billion those imports cost would buy enough machinery and equipment to make an important contribution to easing investment bottlenecks. Soviet hard currency earnings are likely to grow little in the 1980s, which will mean little or no growth in imports of machinery unless the Soviet Union can escape the large burden of agricultural imports it has sustained in the last decade.

To sum up, the Soviet economy is confronted with a choice like the guns-butter dilemma, but with an added dimension. It is really a guns-butter-growth choice, complicated by a feedback link between the butter and growth elements. A choice about the level and division of imports that reacts on overall growth further complicates the planners' choices. Switching imports between machinery and consumer goods, mostly agricultural commodities, will influence the consumption-investment outcome.

Major Problem Areas

We have looked at the overall perspective in a very aggregative and schematic way. Before discussing implications for Soviet external policy in the 1980s, we should examine some of the major elements conditioning this perspective, consider what possibilities may exist for easing these constraints, and ponder policies the regime might adopt for that purpose. Let us consider in turn labor supply, investment, energy, agriculture, international economic relations, and possibilities for economic reform.

Labor Supply

Some general figures on the expected growth of the labor force were cited above, but I shall now explain the developments that will affect the labor force growth, examine some other dimensions of the labor problem, and consider what improvements are possible.

The starting point for labor force projections and the basis for the earlier assertion about a labor shortage is the expected additions and losses to population in the working ages over the decade. In the USSR, the working ages are considered 16 through 59 for males and 16 through 54 for females. This is based on a somewhat conventional notion of the school-leaving age and the retirement ages customary in state employment. Everyone who will move into the working ages in the 1980s is already born, and the main uncertainties concern attrition of the various cohorts over the period.

Table 2.2 shows U.S. Bureau of the Census projections of the number of people in the working ages at mid-decade and in 1990 as follows for the USSR as a whole and for the peripheral Moslem areas (millions as of January 1): The startling feature of this projection is that the entire increment between 1980 and 1985 will occur in the Moslem areas and that between 1985 and 1990 the working-age

Table 2.2

Soviet Working-Age Population

(in millions)

		All USSR	Central Asia Kazakhstan Transcaucasus
1980		154.806	29.426
1985		158.455	33.104
1990		160.796	36.423
	Increase 1980–85	3.649	3.678
	Increase 1985–90	2.341	3.319

SOURCE: U.S. Bureau of the Census, *Population Projections by Age and Sex for the Republics and Major Economic Regions of the USSR 1970 to 2000*, International Population Series, P-91, No. 26, (Washington, D.C.: USGPO, 1979), p. 128. Soviet forecasts are remarkably close to this one, with some slight differences in details. One Soviet source estimates 3.3 million as the increment in 1981–85, and 2.5 million in 1986–90. *Ekonomika i organizatsiia promyshlennogo proizvodstva-EKO* [Economics and Organization of Industrial Production], 1982, no. 3, p. 138.

population in the non-Moslem areas will actually decline. These projections have apparently been generated on the assumption of no migration, and migration could change the numbers projected for the peripheral areas. However, students of Soviet population trends conclude that there is little reason to expect migration on any significant scale, since the ethnic groups of Central Asia are reluctant even to leave the countryside where most of the increase will occur, not to mention moving from their ancestral homelands.

The number of people in the working ages is only the starting point in labor force projections. Many people outside these age groups work, and some in the relevant ages, such as students, non-working wives, and some 5 million people in the armed forces, do not participate in the civilian labor force.[18] How many people not now in the labor force could the government mobilize to add to the labor input? Are there labor policy and labor market reforms that might improve utilization of those already in the labor force? How could the government draw the new entrants in the working ages into the work force, since they are mostly non-Russians located in Central Asia, far from the places where new jobs are being created, such as Siberia and the industrialized centers?

Soviet statements suggest that there is virtually no possibility of adding to labor supplies by mobilizing nonworking members of the population. One authority says explicitly that 100 percent of the growth in the labor force must come from the growth in the number of people in the working ages in the Eleventh Five-Year Plan, with no contribution from drawing nonparticipants into the labor force.[19] Trying to reconcile population figures with the labor force figures provided in Soviet statistical sources leads more to frustration than to enlightenment, especially because of the Soviet government's reluctance to publish the results of the 1979 census. Still, some calculations with these data, too tedious to describe here, make it clear that two of the traditional sources for additions to the state labor force, nonworking women in urban areas and the overaged, juveniles, and women in rural areas engaged primarily in private plot agriculture, have so shrunk that they can provide no more recruits.

Probably the best possibility lies in persuading more pensioners to work, and the government is making significant efforts to attract people eligible for pensions into the labor force. A decree of September 11, 1979, authorized increases in pension amounts for those who postponed retirement and permitted pensioners to work and still receive all or most of their pension. I doubt that can make much difference: a decree along the same lines was issued in 1969, and the new decree only extends the provisions to some additional categories of workers.[20] Considering those who qualify for pensions on the basis of age rather than disability or other service, the fraction who work is already 30.4 percent.[21] It is difficult to suppose that share could be much increased. The most positive feature is that the cohorts most likely to continue work, men in the 60 to 65 age group and women in the 55 to 60 age group, will increase significantly in the eighties. The U.S. Census Bureau has estimated that about 30 million persons in those cohorts would reach retirement age during the 1980s. Though mortality will reduce that number appreciably over the period, the cohort it will replace in retirement contains only about 18 million persons. A Soviet source estimates that the number of working pensioners could rise by 2 to 2.5 million persons in the Eleventh Five-Year Plan.[22]

The labor problem will be greatly exacerbated by the regional and ethnic characteristics of the new entrants, almost exclusively Moslems in Central Asia and in the Transcaucasus. Unfortunately, these increments are geographically separated from the new jobs, many of which will be in Siberia, with most of the rest in the established industrial areas. Moreover, these nationality groups do not constitute good material for the work force, since they tend not to know Russian and to be relatively low in modern industrial skills. As one Soviet authority says, as a result of historically formed traditions the native inhabitants of these republics have lower social mobility (readiness to improve their skills, to change occupations, to move from the countryside to the city, and so on) than the population of other regions.[23]

In the report of a conference held in Dushanbe in 1981 all local spokesmen asserted that these people will not move and that it is important to create jobs locally, while the Moscow representatives essentially ignored the issue whether jobs should be created locally or migration could solve the problem.[24] I conclude that the drafters of the Eleventh Five-Year Plan have not reconciled forecasts they have made for additional labor supply with the ethnic and regional composition of those additions.

Another geographic imbalance occurs because many new jobs are being created in big cities, where official policy seeks to slow population growth. Studies of Moscow, Leningrad, and other cities show that the number of new jobs created far exceeds the addition to the work force expected, a corollary of failure to make the investment plan consistent with labor supply. Apparently enterprise and ministerial officials often use the official campaign favoring modernization and reequipment of old factories to circumvent prohibitions on creating new capacity and jobs in existing centers.

A traditional source for expanding labor supply has been shifting people from low productivity employment in agriculture to nonagricultural employment. The group working on collective farms in collective and private plot production has released about 5 million people to the rest of the economy in the last decade. As it still numbers about 14 million people, it may contain some slack. But most investigators conclude that the age and sex composition of the group precludes its providing much help.

Another possibility might be to reduce the size of the armed forces. A reduction of a million persons would be significant in relation to the less than 3 million increment in civilian employment the current five-year plan envisages or even in relation to the 5 million increment for the decade as a whole, but it would represent a great sacrifice for the military. In any case the current leaders have demonstrated the high priority they assign to raw manpower for the armed forces by a decision in December 1980 to eliminate most higher education deferments for cohorts reaching conscription age.

Better utilization of the existing labor force through enhanced mobility is an alternative to adding more bodies. The labor market is one of the freer markets in the Soviet economy but still suffers from administrative interference. Although employers have some room for maneuver in the wages they offer by juggling job classifications and piece rate systems, the centrally imposed wage pattern probably offers too little differentiation to move and motivate workers. Employers face excessive restrictions in trying to fire workers. Moreover, many features of the incentive system, such as salary and bonus formulas that relate managers' rewards to the size of a unit's labor force and the knowledge that managers are expected to supply labor to help with harvest campaigns, motivate them to keep more workers on the payroll than they need. A great potential exists for reforms that would create a freer market allowing labor to move where needed and giving employers the freedom to bid for it. Some Soviet labor policy measures in recent years move in that direction, e.g., by removing barriers that inhibit part-time work by women and pensioners.[25] For the most part, however, recent labor legislation has introduced more administrative controls on the labor market, such as ceilings for each enterprise and ministry, organized placement of graduates from vocational-technical education, and increased penalties for workers who quit. Soviet planners have an instinctive fear of labor mobility and assert that excessive turnover (20 million people change jobs each year) leads to large losses, since the average time lost in a job change is one month. But losses from keeping workers in the wrong jobs far outweigh the time lost in job changes. One of the major recent changes in planning, a shift to value-added measures of output, as it lessens the incentive to overemphasize material-intensive outputs, may induce a bias toward labor-intensive production mixes that enterprise labor ceilings only loosely control.

In short, the Soviet economy must cope with an unprecedented labor problem in the Eleventh Five-Year Plan. A consistent feature of past plans has been failure to achieve targets for growth of labor productivity, compensated by above-plan increases in labor force growth. That solution will not be possible during the approaching period. In fact, a number of comments in Soviet discussions of the plan have suggested that the plan may presume a larger growth of the labor force than is possible, considering the geographic and ethnic problems just described. One author notes that the plan does not explain how labor productivity growth can account for only 90 percent of the increment, since he sees no growth in the labor supply. N. K. Baibakov, chairman of Gosplan, in one of his formulations suggests that the labor force will grow at a much lower rate than even that suggested above.[26]

Growing Investment Needs

The character and growth of the economy during the 1980s will depend very much on how the Soviet planners allocate investment among the major sectors, shown in Table 2.3 for 1980. This distribution is for the broadest Soviet concept of investment, which includes cooperative investment and private investment in housing as well as state investment. This breakdown shows investment in housing on collective farms as investment not in agriculture, but in housing. The reader should be alerted that Soviet planners and statisticians frequently mention an agricultural investment figure "for the whole

Table 2.3

Sectoral Allocation of Soviet Investment, 1980

	Billion Rubles	Percent of Total
All investment from all sources	133.5	100.0
Industry	47.3	35.4
Agriculture	26.8	20.1
Transport and communication	16.1	12.1
Construction	5.3	4.0
Housing	17.9	13.4
Other (mostly municipal, commercial, and service sectors)	20.0	15.0

SOURCE: Tsentral'noe statisticheskoe upravlenie [Central Statistical Administration], *Narodnoe khoziaistvo SSSR v 1980 godu* [The National Economy of the USSR in 1980] (Moscow: TsSU, 1981), pp. 336–37.

complex" accounting for 27 percent of all investment. In addition to agriculture proper, this includes agricultural research, some agricultural processing, firms in the agricultural sector engaged in construction and the production of construction materials, and others. A still broader concept referring to investment in the "agro-industrial complex" includes investment in industrial branches supplying inputs to agriculture and processing agricultural produce. Brezhnev's 1982 description of the food program and other references cite this concept. That aggregate is to account for about one-third of all investment in the Eleventh Five-Year Plan.

Quantitatively the most important sector absorbing investment resources is industry. Apart from the traditional reliance on investment as a growth factor, a number of trends underway in this sector will raise the amount of capital above the amount needed in the past. It seems impossible that the Kremlin can meet the needs for energy investment, development of territorial production complexes, investment to replace labor-, fuel-, and material-wasting equipment, more workplaces in Central Asia, and so on without increasing the dominance of industry as a claimant on the investment pool. Indeed, in the Eleventh Five-Year Plan, the share of industry is expected to rise by 4 percentage points over the share in 1976–80.[27]

Within the industrial sector, energy investment will be especially demanding. The amount of capital tied up per unit of productive capacity is rising dramatically across the whole range of energy producing, transforming, and transport activities. Nuclear and hydro power, which will be the fastest growing components in the electric power sector, have much higher investment costs per kilowatt of capacity than other types of power generation. The investment required to transport a given output of gas to the consumer will increase sharply because of the rapid rise in the average distance it must be transported. The best summary indicator of the significance of these trends is that the energy sector's share in all investment was only about 16 percent in the late 1970s but rises to 21 percent in the Eleventh Five-Year Plan. This trend will undoubtedly continue during the second half of the decade in the Twelfth Five-Year Plan (1986–90).

The transportation sector has long-delayed needs for new capacities. Transport is inherently a sector characterized by investment lumpiness: once capacity is built, intensifying utilization of the plant can increase the amount of transport work done. But eventually the capacity of a given link or network is reached. Then the network requires large new additions of capital to accommodate more traffic. One of the central elements in current strategy is to develop territorial production complexes in Siberia in areas which have virtually no infrastructure. Expensive investments in transport, housing, and power must therefore accompany creation of new production capacity.

A distinctive feature of Soviet investment distribution is the high share of agricultural investment. In the United States this amounts to 7 to 8 percent of all investment, compared to the 20 percent for the USSR shown above or the 27 percent figure cited "for the whole complex" which has been constant for a number of years. The annual Central Statistical Administration reports invariably cite this share, suggesting that the leaders adhere to this commitment to agriculture. Although this share is planned at 27 percent for the Eleventh Five-Year Plan and the food program envisages a further rise in 1986–90, that decision will surely be a subject of intense discussion during political succession.

As the table shows, housing has been a significant drain on investment resources as the leaders have tried to relieve the crowded conditions of Soviet cities and to cope with the large increase in the urban population accompanying economic growth. They have managed a notable improvement, raising the urban housing stock from an average of 10 square meters per person in 1965 to about 13 square meters in 1980 (this refers to the total space in dwellings and exceeds by one-half the "living space" for which the Soviet planners have proclaimed a long-standing norm of 9 square meters, still not attained). The USSR has a large backlog of housing needs for people who share apartments with others and would like housing of their own. It is difficult to estimate the magnitude of that backlog, since the Central Statistical Administration does not publish information on the stock of housing units which we could compare with the number of households. But figures on new family formation, together with information on the number of new dwelling units made available in the last five years, suggest that they may be falling behind, rather than catching up: 13.8 million marriages have taken place in the last five years, while the system created only 10.3 million new dwelling units. This is an imprecise comparison, since deaths diminish the total number of households, and the destruction of existing units reduces the net growth of dwelling units. Divorces create even more complications by adding to the demand for housing units and offsetting somewhat the demand from new marriages. But imprecise as the comparison may be, reasonable allowance for these factors suggests that the backlog of unmet need is rising. The demographic changes described earlier in which the cohorts entering the labor force will be unprecedentedly small should reduce somewhat the rate of family formation and ease the pressure. Since Soviet economic literature provides virtually no systematic data on rural housing, the situation in the countryside is less easy to document, but it is certainly much worse than in the urban areas.

The demand for housing has a high income elasticity. That is, as incomes rise Soviet citizens want this element to increase more than their consumption in general. Moreover, some policies discussed earlier involve locational shifts that will expand the need for housing. Housing is one of the major infrastructural requirements for the development of Siberia. As efforts continue to develop the agro-industrial complex, many new jobs will be in rural areas, and the government must provide housing to attract people. Other elements of the agricultural program, such as the effort to reclaim and improve the low fertility soils of the nonblack earth regions, also require significant housing construction. Apparently one reason that program has achieved so little is that too few have moved in to work the newly reclaimed areas. In connection with the food program the party has stipulated in the Eleventh Five-Year Plan that 176 million square meters of housing be built at collective and state farms and other agricultural enterprises.[28] Total housing construction in rural areas, which is a much broader category than state and collective farms and other agricultural enterprises, was only 149.1 million square meters in 1976–80. This significantly higher amount within a total housing target that has not been increased over the Tenth Five-Year Plan (1976–80) suggests that urban dwellers are not going to note any improvement.

The Soviet government could encourage more private construction, aided by government credit and more cooperative construction. This was a feature of housing policy for a number of years, but apparently nonstate forms of housing construction have been cut back, especially in rural areas. The share of private housing fell from

25.2 percent of all housing construction in the Ninth Five-Year Plan to 21.4 percent in the Tenth. The same retreat took place in cooperative housing. Discussion of housing policies for the Eleventh Five-Year Plan indicates no shift toward private and cooperative housing. This is a puzzle, since nonstate forms of housing construction would seem an attractive method of absorbing excess cash held by the population and help to correct the erosion of incentives this overhang causes. Thus, both in terms of production objectives and as part of any effort to provide incentive-enhancing consumption increases to the population, investment in housing remains vital.

The same argument applies to the final category of distribution, investment in health facilities and in municipal, commercial, and other services. Though in Soviet parlance these are "nonproductive" investments, they are important for achieving production increases and for providing facilities essential for improvement in consumption levels and variety. Important among the things Soviet citizens want as their incomes increase are better services, more amenities, and better health care, but apparently the government will sacrifice these services along with housing in the current investment crunch. Gosplan Chairman Baibakov says that the share of nonproductive investment will fall by 4 percentage points in the Eleventh Five-Year Plan, i.e., just offsetting the rise in the share of industrial investment. In about the only direct reference to the kind of investments sacrificed, Baibakov says: "We must have a certain reduction of the construction in cities of theaters, places of culture, swimming pools, and stadiums."[29]

There seems to be a contradiction here. On the one hand, the planners would like to restrain investment spending somewhat to permit greater growth of consumption, but to some extent they can make growth in consumption possible only by first investing in the capital facilities to produce consumption goods and services. The emerging investment priorities sacrifice investment in the nonproductive sectors producing housing and other services to cover the growth in the share of industry. Moreover, it seems that the reallocation taking place within industry is away from the sectors producing consumer goods and toward the fuel and energy sectors. As execution of the investment plan begins, hints are emerging that it is too tight. As the informal priority system works to accommodate this, further shifts are taking place toward the high priority sectors of industry and away from those a consumption-oriented policy would need to emphasize. For example, Brezhnev in his speech to the May 1982 plenum of the Party's Central Committee on the food program said that investment targets for the nonagricultural components of the food program are not being met satisfactorily.[30]

Are there any possibilities for ameliorating this investment crunch? The Soviet leaders do have a strategy. First, they consider it possible to get more for less by reducing the stock of unfinished investment. Investment in the USSR has a long gestation period, with dispersion of resources over a large list of projects, some of which progress almost imperceptibly. This stock of unfinished construction and uninstalled equipment at project sites seems to grow inexorably. The Soviet planners, eternal optimists, expect they can reverse that pattern in the Eleventh Five-Year Plan, with new commissionings planned to exceed investment by about 9 billion rubles.[31] I consider this impossible and see in this another factor working against fulfillment of Soviet growth plans in the Eleventh Five-Year Plan period. A second argument says much investment requested by producers is not really needed and cannot be absorbed, so that starving investment may force some salutary improvements in the use of investment funds.

Some argue that investment too often creates jobs that cannot be filled. A number of articles in the economic press have suggested this is one reason additional capital investment pays off so poorly in extra output. The directives for the Eleventh Five-Year Plan noted that it is necessary "to adopt measures to achieve balance between existing and incremental jobs and labor resources," but a number of interesting commentaries on what is happening are much more informative on the seriousness of the problem than on measures taken to deal with it. The "shift coefficient" in industry, which measures the intensity of multishift working, is falling because it is impossible to staff the intended second and third shifts. The Soviet shift coefficient is now below that of any industrial developed country. At the level of equipment design rather than factory design, one Soviet economist has asserted that it is impossible to train enough operators for the scheduled output of machine tools, given their type and number.[32]

Another long-standing bias in Soviet investment decisions favors new investment over replacement and a corresponding emphasis on structures over equipment. Some U.S. specialists on Soviet agriculture believe this is one reason large investments in agriculture have been so unsuccessful in raising output. The Soviets are now making efforts to discourage new construction and to encourage replacement of obsolete equipment: in the Eleventh Five-Year Plan the share of investment for reequipment and reconstruction is supposed to rise to 32.5 percent, compared to 29.2 percent in the last quinquennium, and the share of equipment in the total (as contrasted with construction) is to rise by several percentage points.[33] Undoubtedly large wastes occur in investment, and it is not difficult to identify ways to save. But it is not clear whether stinting the supply will overcome long-standing habits and biases and force project planners and designers to make savings.

Energy

Developments in the energy sector in the 1980s will have a very important influence on the economy as a whole, especially because of its investment requirements and because of the crucial role energy exports play in Soviet ability to earn hard currency. During the sixties and seventies, the energy sector has had a favorable impact on Soviet and East European economic growth. The investment cost per unit of incremental fuel output has fallen until recently, and the average production cost per BTU of energy produced has behaved similarly. The ease with which supply could be increased has been such that the Soviet Union could not only meet its own growing needs for energy at low cost, but also export oil to meet the needs of Eastern Europe and of the market economies. The latter made it possible to finance large increments in modern capital goods and grain imports.

The major causes of this favorable situation have been intensive exploitation of rich oil reserves and the sharp rise in oil prices after 1973. Oil output rose from 3 million barrels per day at the beginning of the 1960s to over 12 million barrels per day in 1980. More recently, availability of cheap and easily producible oil resources has declined, and natural gas has begun to take the place of oil in the expansion of energy production. During the past two decades, growth of oil and gas output covered 85 percent of the total increment in Soviet primary energy production, and oil accounted for about 60 percent of the growth in hard currency earnings from the industrialized market economies. More recently, between 1975 and 1980, oil accounted for only 44 percent of the increment in energy output and gas for 47 percent. On the trade side, in the same period, oil accounted for 66 percent of the increment in hard currency earnings and gas for 14 percent.

One of the most striking indicators of the favorable impact of energy on development is that while the energy sector took about 37 percent of all industrial investment in the Fourth and Fifth Five-Year Plans, that share fell to only about 28 percent after 1965.

In the eighties, the energy situation will be much less favorable. The Soviet Union will be able to expand output to meet its energy needs, but investment requirements will rise very sharply, both per unit of energy output and as a share of all industrial investment. During the Tenth Five-Year Plan, investment in the energy sector was 88 billion rubles, which amounted to 16 percent of all state investment, or about 40 percent of all state investment in industry. In the Eleventh Five-Year Plan period, the share in all state investment will rise to 21 percent and the share of the energy sector in all state investment in industry will approach one-half, 47.5 percent to be exact.[34] I see no reason to expect that the increased burden of energy investment will ease in the second half of the decade. With the costs of producing, transforming, and utilizing energy resources rising to a much higher level, the total gains from exporting energy will appreciably decline.

Table 2.4 sets out a framework for quantitative evaluation of alternative scenarios for the supply of primary energy and its disposition among alternative uses in the 1980s. Aggregate domestic energy consumption is likely to grow about as fast as GNP in the USSR. The GNP elasticity of energy demand in the USSR has had a value of 1 or higher. That is, each percent increase in GNP has required more than a one percent increase in energy consumption. Although Soviet planners will give much attention to promoting conservation, I am skepti-

Table 2.4

Estimated Energy Production and Consumption in the USSR in the 1980s

Production		1980	1985	1990
Oil	MTnat	603	630	500
	MTst	863	901	715
Gas	Bm3	435	630	716–804
	MTst	516	747	852–957
Coal	MTnat	716	775	892
	MTst	484	514[a]	580[a]
Nuclear	BKwH	251	450[b]	—
and				
Hydro	MTst	82	149	175
Hydro	BKwH	184	—	—
only	MTst	60	—	85
Shale, wood, peat, incl.				
decentralized	MTst	70	65	65
Total	MTst	2015	2376	2387–2402
Net Exports	MTst	303	300	300
Domestic consumption	MTst	1712	(2,076)	2,087–2,192

NOTE: 1980 outputs are from Tsentral'noe statisticheskoe upravlenie, *Narodnoe khoziaistvo SSSR v 1980 godu* [The National Economy of the USSR in 1980] (Moscow: TsSU, 1981), except for nuclear power from *Elektricheskie stantsii* [Electric Power Stations], 1981, no. 1, p. 2, and decentralized fuel, which is my estimate.

MTst means million tons of "standard fuel," the unit used as a common denominator in Soviet energy accounting. A ton of standard fuel is 7 giga-calories. To convert million tons of standard fuel to quads divide by 36, to convert to million tons of oil equivalent divide by 1.43. MTnat is million tons in natural measure. To convert oil output from tons in natural measure per year to barrels per day divide by 50.

[a] Assuming that all increments over 1980 will consist of kansk-Achinsk and Ekibastuz coal, which if they are given equal weights would have an average heat content of 3955 kilocalories per kg. (Robert Campbell, "Energy in the USSR to the Year 2000," in Abram Bergson and Herbert Levine, eds., *The Soviet Economy to the Year 2000* (London: Allen & Unwin, 1982).

[b] The draft plan indicated 220–225 BKwH of nuclear power and 230–235 BKwH of hydro power, but I am not sure we can interpret 450 as consisting of 220 BKwH of nuclear and 230 BKwH of hydro power.

cal these efforts will be effective. GNP growth at 2 to 2.5 percent per year, with energy demand elasticity at 1 would imply an increase in domestic consumption by 1990 of 375 to 480 million tons of standard fuel. How can these requirements be covered?

A great deal of controversy has taken place over Soviet petroleum prospects, too complicated to evaluate in detail here. My position is pessimistic about the growth of oil output, which I believe must fall from 603 million tons in 1980 to perhaps 500 million tons (i.e., 10 million barrels/day) by 1990.

Even if oil output drops significantly, the Soviet Union will be able to meet nonsubstitutable domestic demands for oil. The USSR produces more petroleum than any other country in the world. With total output of crude petroleum and condensate of 603 million tons in 1980, domestic consumption was only about 388 million tons. Of that, approximately 175 million tons was fuel oil burned in boilers and furnaces, where other kinds of primary energy can replace oil. At the end of the 1970s, the requirements of the Soviet economy for such nonsubstitutable uses of petroleum as motor fuel and petrochemicals were only about 200 million tons, compared to United States consumption of over 700 million tons. The Soviet Union should be able to resolve a tightening oil supply situation by improving the way it uses oil, i.e., by deeper refining to produce more motor fuel and petrochemical feedstocks. There are alternative energy sources whose output can grow to substitute for the lost residual fuel oil.

Nuclear power, a new and growing source, can probably make a significant contribution. In the Tenth Five-Year Plan capacity increases averaged about 2 gigawatts per year, but the new Atommash plant at Volgodonsk, when fully in operation, is supposed to produce one of the two types of reactors which the USSR has developed, the pressurized, water-cooled and moderated VVER, at a level of 8 gigawatts per year. Other plants will produce the second major type of reactor, the graphite moderated, boiling water RBMK. Plans will surely be underfulfilled, but if we assume that it is possible to add five to six 1 gigawatt reactors per year for the 1981–90 decade, capacity could grow at 13.5–15.7 percent per year and the fuel equivalent of additional nuclear power output (assuming utilization of 5,000 hours per year and a heat rate of 330 grams of standard fuel per kilowatt hour) would be 82.5–99 million tons of standard fuel by 1990. Nuclear power can probably contribute 90 million tons of standard fuel by 1990, an increment of 67 million tons of standard fuel.

The hydropower resources of the USSR are still far from full development. If we assume that the rate of growth can continue at the 1970–80 rates, an incremental contribution of about 25 million tons of standard fuel by 1990 could occur.

Coal output stagnated in the Tenth Five-Year Plan, actually falling in 1979 and 1980, but may grow appreciably in the 1980s. Quality will deteriorate, so that even large increments in physical quantities will be unimpressive in terms of energy content. An additional 100 million tons of standard fuel may be possible by 1990. Minor sources (firewood, oil shale, and peat) are unlikely to grow and could actually shrink. I show them at 65 million tons of standard fuel in both 1985 and 1990.

Gas is the energy source least constrained by production problems, and its output can expand significantly. Reserves exist to support output levels double or more current levels. The significant bottleneck will be putting transmission and distribution capacity into operation. Gas will play the role of gap filler in the Soviet energy balance, and the most useful approach is not to forecast an output, but to ask how much the Soviet gas industry must increase output to be consistent with various possible scenarios. If the question is whether it can produce the output necessary to maintain aggregate energy exports in standard fuel at the 1980 level, the increase in gas output necessary to cover the gap is 281–369 billion cubic meters by 1990. The gas increments would have to come completely from Western Siberia. Indeed, West Siberian output will have to increase by more than the increment in total consumption to make up for declines in the European areas. This creates a tremendous transport problem. To ship an additional 350 billion cubic meters of gas from Western Siberia to the center in 1520 mm lines operating at 75 atmospheres pressure would require 12 additional lines.[35] Apart from transport feasibility, two additional questions are relevant, i.e., whether that much gas can be absorbed domestically in replacing oil, and whether it is a feasible substitute for oil exports. The answer to both is probably yes. The energy balance surely ought to be able to cope with a drop in oil output of 100 million tons, by substituting gas for 60–70 million tons of oil to maintain hard currency earnings and by replacing 100 million tons of residual fuel oil now being burned in boilers and furnaces. Substitutions of those magnitudes would cover the decline in crude oil output and provide an increment in the output of light products.

The balance could end up a little tighter than this forecast. It is possible that GNP could grow at 2.5 percent per year rather than 2. It is quite possible that oil output will drop to less than 500 million tons, and the forecasts in Table 2.4 for nuclear and hydro power are probably at the outer limits of feasibility. The investment requirements to build the necessary pipelines, especially for pipe and compressor capacity, will severely strain the economy, whether inputs are produced domestically or are purchased abroad for hard currency. Indeed, the importation from Western Europe of large diameter pipe and of high-quality compressors was and remains critical for the Soviet Union. Overall, I believe that the USSR will probably have to reduce energy exports in the 1980s.

The Soviet planners' forecast for the first five years of the decade is now available in the targets of the Eleventh Five-Year Plan. Column (2) of Table 2.4, which summarizes this forecast, is basically consistent with our longer range forecast for the decade as a whole. The production targets imply a total primary energy output of 2,375 million tons of standard fuel in 1985. If exports remain constant at 300 million tons of standard fuel, the implied amount available for domestic consumption in 1985 would be 2,076 million tons of standard fuel, for an annual average rate of growth of energy consumption of 3.9 percent. That is well above the GNP growth even if the energy plan is seriously underfulfilled, as I believe will be the case. It seems doubtful that oil output can grow appreciably: the target figure of 630 million tons is probably more a political pronouncement than a realistic target. The industry will be fortunate even to keep output constant, and this change alone would drop the growth in domestic availability to 3.5 percent per year, assuming constant exports. The nuclear power target is demanding, and the coal target represents a very sharp turnaround in performance compared to the Tenth Five-Year Plan. The gas target is no doubt attainable in terms of the availability of reserves, but whether gas can fill the gap is again a question of putting the transport capacity in place fast enough.

Despite these uncertainties, it seems most unlikely that the situation could become so tight either in the first five years of the 1980s or over the decade as a whole that the Soviet Union would need to import energy. However, energy exports will probably fall below the present level, which would have important implications for external economic policy. The Soviets need growth in hard currency imports proportioned to growth in GNP, and it is also in their interest to expand exports to Eastern Europe. That region cannot pay for energy imports from hard currency sources to keep growing.

All these judgments about growth of energy supply, both for the immediate five-year period and for the longer perspective, assume large Soviet imports of technology and energy-related equipment from the developed market economies. It has been possible to achieve the current levels of oil output only by extensive import of several kinds of oil production equipment, especially submersible pumps and gas lift equipment. The USSR was able to expand gas output at the achieved rate only by importing very large amounts of wide diameter pipe and compressor equipment. Meeting the oil targets for the Eleventh Five-Year Plan and beyond will require a continuation of these imports, as well as considerable expansion of technology transfer in exploration, offshore work, drilling, and for the first time, refining. Pipe imports are indispensable for meeting the gas output plans, and there will still be a great need for compressor equipment. The gas industry will obtain most of the compressors needed from domestic production of several new, large capacity models of turbine-powered units, and there are also hints that much more use will be made of electric powered units. But reasonable estimates of how much compressor capacity will be needed so far exceed past performance in developing and producing large compressor units that one can only conclude large imports will be necessary.[36] This situation explains why purchases of gas line pipe, compressors, and rotors from the West is such a critical matter for the Soviet Union.

Agriculture: The Problem Sector

It may be misleading to consider the problem of trade-offs purely at the level of such end-use aggregates as consumption, investment, and defense. In order to improve the consumer's lot the Soviet economy will have first to expand particular kinds of output, and second to master tasks that have always been poorly done, such as servicing consumers. These changes may encounter institutional obstacles or very high marginal costs. One of the major consumer demands is an improved diet, especially increased availability of most vegetables and fruit. The increment of GNP involved may constitute an imperfect measure of the institutional and resource costs. It is therefore worth reviewing closely the problems of agriculture, the sector that plays the major role in fulfilling the goals of the "food program."

The dominant feature of the agricultural problem is that Soviet agriculture is a very high cost activity. During its fifteen-year tenure the Brezhnev regime succeeded in expanding agricultural output at a rate of about 2 percent per year, which compares favorably with overall growth of GNP.[37] However, it attained this result at very high incremental cost, reflected in the high share of agriculture in all investment, in the very high costs of animal products output, in a huge subsidy bill, and in the need to import large quantities of animal feed from hard currency areas.

As indicated earlier, agriculture proper takes 20 percent of all Soviet investment, compared to approximately 7 or 8 percent in the United States. Much of this investment goes into equipment, land improvements, and facilities for animal husbandry: in the Eleventh Five-Year Plan (1981–85) almost 80 percent of the "productive" investment will be for these three purposes.[38] The investment in equipment produces discouragingly low results because the equipment tends to have short service lives. The unavailability of repair parts and poor repair practices keep much of it unavailable to help increase output.

Why the other kinds of investment are so unproductive is not clear, though it is partly because the investment in land improvement is offset each year by large attrition. In the last ten years new land has been prepared for irrigation amounting to 8.346 million hectares, but the total reported in use has risen by only about 6 million, with the rest probably abandoned because it has become salinized or was unsuitable in the first place. An even greater gap exists between the amounts of land with drainage facilities added over this fifteen-year period, 11.9 million hectares, and the growth in the amount of such land reported in use, only 3.7 million hectares. I conclude that much of the investment in melioration, canals, and other facilities for draining land is very poorly managed. Many of these projects were probably never completed or involved land never put into production because no one wanted it or because there was no population. A recent Soviet statement says explicitly that much work was poorly done and that extensive reconstruction will have to be carried out in the Eleventh Five-Year Plan.[39]

A major reason for high costs in agriculture is low productivity, a high ratio of input to output at each stage of production. In crop production, seeding rates are much higher than in the United States: for wheat the Soviet seeding rate is 240 kilograms per hectare compared to 85 kilograms in the United States. In combination with relatively low yields, this means that an unusually high share of the output goes back to seed. Animal production makes inefficient use of feed, in part because rations are not balanced nutritionally. A very large share of output is wasted along the way from field to user because of poor storage facilities and unreliable transportation. One Soviet author declared that as much as one-fourth of the output of vegetables and fruits spoil on the way to the consumer. Another wrote: "We are the largest producers of potatoes in the world, with an output 6.5 times larger than the United States. But can it be said that in the consumption of potatoes we are on the same level? I think not, since the mass of *marketed* potatoes is no more than half the output and the volume of retail sales is below the American level. The use of potatoes for seed, the amount fed to livestock (a completely uneconomical use), and especially the losses at all stages of the post-harvest cycle from transport to the kitchen table are excessively high."[40]

The payoff of expensive outlays on fertilizer is smaller than it should be because of losses in transport and storage. In addition, fertilizer is not produced in the most advantageous mixes and forms and is wastefully applied. The state heavily subsidizes fertilizer and other industrial inputs into agriculture, weakening incentives for their careful use. Much Soviet territory has too little moisture to make fully effective use of fertilizer.

The high marginal cost of coaxing more output from the agricultural sector, together with unchanging retail prices for the major food items, has led to a large and rapidly growing subsidy bill. In 1980 the state procurement and trade organs paid agricultural producers 81 billion rubles for the commodities they bought. These goods were then sold to final consumers at a price level such that procurement agencies and processors incurred large losses, over 30 billion rubles in 1980, which the state reimbursed. The state also subsidizes agriculture by preferential prices for some production inputs it purchases, such as machinery, fuel, and fertilizer. In a number of cases collective farms also have the privilege of buying back processed agricultural products from procurement organizations at lower-than-standard prices, depending on the amount of raw products delivered. Together, these elements of the subsidy bill reached an estimated 37 billion rubles (more than $50 billion) by 1980, so that the price covered less than half the cost of agricultural produce sold to the population.[41] The proper formulation is not that "agriculture is heavily subsidized," but that "the level of prices of agricultural output the consumer is charged is set well below costs." This distorts decision making (it is cheaper to feed bread to animals than to feed grain), creates disequilibrium in many consumer goods markets leading to lines, black markets, and general dissatisfaction, and requires that the state budget raise large funds from other activities to cover the difference. These costs are the more difficult to justify because the subsidy program has been only moderately successful in inducing agricultural producers to expand output and improve productivity.

In short, Soviet agriculture remains a most critical problem for the Soviet system and its leaders. Supplying ample amounts of satisfying food is among the most elementary requirements any system faces: the Soviet Union has not been successful in meeting this rising challenge as it grows in seriousness and conflicts with economic growth, and this inability has become ever more visible and restrictive. Massive, expensive imports of grain, which violate the highly valued goal of economic independence and to which the Soviet Union has had to devote increasing billions of dollars annually, reflect the clear failure of Soviet agriculture even to approach meeting the food requirements of its population. This dependency weakens the bases of Soviet foreign policy by making the country turn to the United States and other Western states for a Soviet necessity and demolishes the myth that the Soviet system can serve as a model for other rapidly developing countries.

Solutions to this problem and reduced reliance upon imports to meet consumer expectations are quite unlikely as long as the Soviet leaders remain committed to the collective farm system and to centralized decisions, aimed at detailed control of agriculture. The changes that the Brezhnev era introduced, from huge investments to price and wage policies favoring the peasant, have been and will remain ineffective. This problem is probably not one which money can solve, but it is probably reasonable to expect that impressive results could be obtained by abandoning bureaucratic control of agricultural operations and guiding agriculture mostly by price signals. This would be a wrenching break with all traditions, but without some change of this nature, agriculture will remain a constant drain upon financial and human resources, especially hard currency, and will restrain Soviet foreign policy by reducing Soviet independence.

International Economic Relations:
Importing Western Technology

Trade involves one of the closest links between Soviet domestic economic development and external behavior. The purpose of this section is to ask how international economic relations will interact with Soviet growth prospects in the eighties. How critical is the Soviet need for Western grain and technology? Can trade policy offer significant amelioration of otherwise dismal growth prospects? What effect will trade policy have upon foreign policy?

In spite of Soviet respect and even reverence for science since Lenin, its possession of perhaps 40 percent more scientists than the United States, and the emphasis given to expansion of scientific research and development over the past two decades, the Soviet Union has been unable to narrow the gap between its technological level and that of the West. In fact, the gap is widening as the West moves dramatically ahead and comes to terms with the implications of the information revolution, which may have consequences as significant in transforming societies and international politics as the steam engine or the telephone have had. The Soviet Union is hardly on the brink of this great change and is in danger of falling very far behind in the next decade or two.

The causes of Soviet weakness in scientific creativity and innovation include overly centralized planning and control, which tend to stifle initiative; the limits bureaucracy places upon creativity; the separation of research and development from the production processes; the insulation of producers from the suppliers and consumers who might push them to innovate; a price and incentive system which discourages innovation. The apparent separation of most of the industries producing for the armed forces from the less well equipped and staffed concerns working for other sectors of the economy inhibits diffusion of the innovations made. Above all, Soviet concentration on control rather than opportunity and the restrictions imposed upon information from abroad and upon the free flow of information within the Soviet Union greatly hamper activity.

The principal consequence of these shortcomings is that as the

Soviet Union seeks to absorb each new wave of progress made abroad, it is once again left behind and continues to trail the West in many if not most fields of research and technology. The massive Soviet purchases of energy equipment are one illustration of this shortcoming. The Soviets lack adequate domestic equipment and techniques for exploration and exploitation of oil fields, for offshore operations, deep drilling, and construction of efficient pipelines to move Urengoi gas westward. The turn to the West and the shift in Soviet trading patterns in the past twenty years paradoxically may have delayed a Soviet effort to close the gap by inhibiting reforms that would release the entrepreneurial spirit and creativity within the Soviet Union itself.

The Soviet Union has not demonstrated the capability to absorb new technologies and then to innovate independently that has propelled the Japanese into the forefront of scientific, technical, and industrial progress. Soviet productivity suffers as a consequence, and the Soviet Union is likely to continue to need technology imported from the West. This need is likely to grow and will affect Soviet conduct.

During the 1960s and even more in the 1970s, the Soviet Union moved away from its traditional autarkic stance in international economic policy to a more open one toward the nonsocialist world. After the Second World War, the USSR's international trade expanded faster than GNP, so that trade became ever more important in relation to total economic activity. The disparity was especially great in the first half of the 1970s, when trade grew in real terms at 7.8 percent per year and GNP at 3.7 percent. In the early years most Soviet trade was with Eastern Europe, and much was not helpful for economic growth. Most observers would say that the flows involved had little relation to comparative advantage and did little to boost growth of any of the partners by technology transfer. Beginning in the mid-1960s, however, Soviet policy makers redirected more of the USSR's trade toward the industrialized market economies. This trend was especially strong between the mid-1960s and the mid-1970s, when the share of the industrialized market economies in Soviet trade turnover rose from 19 percent to 31 percent. The share has since drifted up a bit and now seems stabilized at about one-third.

This shift to Western trading partners concentrated on imports of equipment embodying a higher level of technology than that achieved in the Soviet economy. Imports of machinery and equipment from industrialized market economies (as represented by the OECD) rose from $462 million in 1965 to about $4,576 million in 1975 at a rate of about 25 percent per year. For comparison, Soviet statistics show that the machinery and equipment element in capital investment (in 1973 prices) rose during the same period from 16.9

billion rubles to 37.1 billion rubles—a rate of 8.2 percent per year. As a result, imported equipment rose from a negligible element in all investment in machinery in 1965 (about 2.2 percent) to a palpable share of 6 percent or more in the mid-1970s. A recent investigation of how foreign machinery is priced when absorbed in the domestic economy concludes that earlier conversion rates for calculating the domestic value of Soviet machinery imports were mistaken and that the share is today actually 10 to 12 percent.[42]

Imports of Western equipment were part of a deliberate strategy to stimulate productivity growth, accelerate structural change, and break bottlenecks in domestic supply, as in production of fertilizers and automobiles. Most Western studies of the impact on the Soviet economy of Western machinery imports have concluded that they made a significant difference to economic expansion. British economist Philip Hanson asserts in his study *Trade and Technology in Soviet-Western Relations* that they may have raised industrial growth by as much as half a percentage point over what it would otherwise have been. The USSR, unlike most smaller East European countries, based its expansion of hard currency imports to only a small extent on borrowing and paid for them mostly by expanding its exports of primary products, especially oil, and by gold sales.

The question for the 1980s is what will happen to the current orientation of Soviet trade policy toward the nonsocialist world in response to the economic pressures described earlier. The Soviet leaders might push technology transfer even more vigorously than in the past in the hope that productivity gains from such an expansion would offset other growth-inhibiting trends. I believe this is unlikely to happen. The energy supply situation will make expanding hard currency export earnings difficult. Indeed, hard currency earnings from oil exports are likely to fall, the drop depending on the trend in Soviet oil output and Soviet success in substituting gas for oil domestically and in pushing the East Europeans to make the same substitution. The major offset to declining oil exports will consist of exports of natural gas to Western Europe. The best guess is that the USSR can perhaps keep hard currency earnings constant at the level of the early 1980s.

The price of gold has fallen sharply, and the USSR has drawn down its stocks in the early 1980s to acquire foreign currency. Expansion of Soviet borrowing is a possible additional source for financing imports. At the beginning of the 1980s, the Soviet hard currency debt was quite small, less than $10 billion, and the debt service burden was much more manageable than in the case of the smaller East European countries. The hard-currency debt service ratio for the USSR in 1980, figured as interest and repayments in relation to hard currency earnings, was less than 10 percent, quite unlike Poland's 100 percent. Nevertheless, both the traditional conservatism of the Soviet leaders regarding foreign indebtedness and the likelihood that Western lenders will become extremely cautious in lending to any Communist country make significant growth in Soviet indebtedness an unlikely source for financing technology imports.

The attitude of Soviet leaders may change regarding external economic relations. Extensive evidence suggests disenchantment with the technology import policy, in part because parochial calculations by Soviet officials often lead to requests for imported equipment that could be met equally satisfactorily from internal R and D efforts, without burdening the balance of payments. Brezhnev probably articulated a fairly widely held view in his report to the Twenty-sixth Party Congress in March 1981 when he said, "We must look into the reasons why we sometimes overlook our leading position in technology and spend large amounts of money to buy abroad such equipment and processes as we are fully able to produce ourselves, and moreover often of higher quality."[43]

A second reason is that some foreign equipment imports have been poorly utilized and some projects based on foreign technology unsuccessful. Further analysis of the crisis in Poland can only strengthen the position of those making that argument. Moreover, Western disenchantment with lending to the socialist countries and United States efforts to reduce the flow of trade with the USSR will narrow the possibilities for continuation of the recent policy of technology transfer. On the other hand, scientific and technical progress will continue apace in the West, especially in fields important in military and political competition. In short, the Soviet leaders face a critical problem when determining their technology import policies and finding the hard currency necessary for payment.

The triangular relationship among the USSR, the East European members of the Council for Mutual Economic Assistance (CMEA) (Poland, Czechoslovakia, East Germany, Romania, Hungary, and Bulgaria), and the industrialized market economies also raises questions concerning technology import policies and hard currency for payments. The six East European states face very difficult times in the coming decade, of a kind which the Polish debacle illustrates in the most extreme form. All these countries (some, like Czechoslovakia, much less than others) have followed a policy of borrowing, but, because the Eastern Europeans often invested these borrowed resources in inefficient projects or spent them to support higher consumption levels, and because the hoped-for export expansion has foundered in the face of world economic recession, opportunities for obtaining additional capital are drying up. Aggregate net hard currency debt of these six countries reached about $60 billion by 1980. For some, the debt accumulated is already beyond their capacity to service. While Western governments and banks will accept some postponement of interest and repayments of principal, they are unlikely to extend new credit. With heavy debt service obligations and with the cessation of new net inflows, the East European six accordingly face a period of austerity in which they must adjust consumption and investment levels downward to live within their means.

Fundamentally, the only way the USSR could help the East Europeans solve the hard currency problem is to earn a surplus in its own hard currency trade and transfer it in the form of a loan or in exchange for goods for use in servicing the latter's debt. The Soviet Union could help in a more general way by running export surpluses with the East European partners: the extra supplies acquired from the USSR might contribute to reducing Eastern Europe's hard currency import needs. The Western countries can do little to persuade the Soviet Union to follow such a course by putting pressure either on the USSR or on the East European countries themselves. The harder the West makes it for the Soviets to earn or borrow hard currency the less likely they are to help Eastern Europe with its hard currency problem. On the other hand, extending Western credit to the USSR to lend to East European countries to pay their debts to Western creditors is neither likely nor wise. Our control over the situation is essentially limited to making sure Eastern Europe does not sink further into debt to the West.

Eastern Europe will have to adjust its investment and consumption downward and adjust the composition and direction of its trade. Poland is the prototypical case. It will have to reduce the imports it has been receiving from the industrialized countries, replace them insofar as possible with substitutes from within the bloc, and divert some exports away from the market economies to the bloc to pay for them. All the East European countries will need to adopt the same short-circuiting of the triangular trade, with the USSR and Eastern Europe sending to and getting from each other what they now exchange with the market economies, at least as far as increments are concerned. If Soviet trade is not going to increase with the market economies, growth requires directing any increments in trade mostly to Eastern Europe. Unfortunately, such short-circuiting of either existing flows or possible increments is difficult because of the *structure* of the respective trade flows.

As Table 2.5 shows, the East European countries as a group and the USSR each carry on about the same volume of trade with the market economies. The arrows in Table 2.5 show the direction of the indicated flows. For example, the USSR in 1980 exported to the

Table 2.5

The Bloc's Trade Flows and Balances with Market Economies

(1980 Exports and Imports, Millions of Dollars)

Products	USSR	OECD*	Eastern Europe
Food & other agricultural products	258→		→3,887
		+6,564	
	5,169←		←2,234
Crude materials	2,739→		→1,708
		−1,647	
	845←		←1,461
Mineral fuels	16,818→		→493
		−20,392	
	131←		←4,198
Chemicals	1,310→		→3,393
		+3,258	
	2,548←		←1,373
Manufactures	1,996→		→5,652
		+4,657	
	7,505←		←6,504
Machinery & equipment	666→		→5,566
		+7,948	
	5,388←		←2,340
Total	23,788→		→20,697
		+387	
	21,587←		←18,109

*Balance of trade with the USSR and Eastern Europe as a whole. A plus sign indicates an OECD export surplus, a minus sign a net import. Arrows indicate direction of trade flows.

SOURCE: OECD, *Statistics of Foreign Trade,* Series C, January-December 1980.

OECD countries $258 million worth of food and other agricultural products and imported $5,169 million worth of food from them. Considering that a similar imbalance occurred in trade with the six East European countries, the net export surplus of food and other agricultural products from the OECD to both areas together was $6,564 million, shown with a plus sign in the OECD column. Examination of individual categories, even at this high level of aggregation, suggests it would be impossible for the USSR and Eastern Europe to trade with each other what they now buy and sell in the industrially developed market economies. Taken together, they have a huge deficit in machinery, food, manufactured goods, and chemicals. Eastern Europe cannot supply to the USSR, or the USSR to Eastern Europe, what the other needs in any of those categories. The socialist world pays for the goods it must have from the industrialized market economies with raw materials and fuels, only part of which it could absorb within its own markets. At a more disaggregated level, this analysis would reveal some possible switches. Eastern Europe could no doubt use more energy, raw materials, and semifabricates, which the USSR would find difficult to supply. The USSR probably has little to gain by shifting its imports of investment goods from the market economies to Eastern Europe but could probably use agricultural products, which would reduce its external vulnerability, and manufactured consumer goods from East Europe could probably make an important contribution to Soviet efforts to improve consumption, especially in providing variety, modernity, and quality in consumer goods. East European countries, in varying degrees, could supply manufactured consumer goods, especially as their own consumption levels stagnate, except that little of their capacity for expansion in the recent growth phase has been in those branches.

I believe that the total East-West flow of machinery will not grow and may even decline somewhat as the bloc-wide source for paying for it, Soviet and Polish energy exports, stagnates or declines. The impact on the Soviet economy will be to depress prospects for increasing productivity and growth.

Other Possible Strategies

Another possible strategy for the USSR would be to expand technology imports, financing them by a reduction in food imports. This might be possible if the resources being poured into agriculture bear fruit soon. Such a policy would emphasize Western Europe over the United States as the source of hard currency imports. This policy might preserve for the USSR the economic gains from technology transfer and at the same time split the Western alliance by exacerbating the conflict between an American administration pressing Western Europe to curtail trade and the West European view of such trade as greatly in its interest.

Room also exists for shifting trade somewhat in the direction of the less developed countries. As the example of Argentine wheat shows, these countries can probably supply some food and agricultural goods the USSR needs. So far the USSR has found it difficult to align itself with these countries in opposition to the industrialized market economies in the North-South argument over trade issues. It has been suggested, however, that the USSR could move to expand its trade with them, and by implication, its influence by a kind of bifurcated trade policy. Even as it seeks to maintain an exchange of raw materials and fuel for modern equipment with the Western market economies, the Soviet Union could expand an exchange of arms and less sophisticated machinery for food and selected raw materials with the developing countries. Such a policy might avoid the heavy development costs for domestic production of particular kinds of raw materials, reduce dependence on its greatest adversaries for food, and exploit one of its major comparative advantages. Success would depend to an important degree on ability to expand arms exports, which today account for about half of Soviet exports to the developing countries and are paid for largely in hard currency. The Soviet leaders could probably increase that trade if they were willing to accept payment in goods. Though the share of developing countries in Soviet foreign trade turnover remained essentially constant in the 1970s, dramatic increases occurred in 1981 to 15 percent, compared to 12.8 percent in 1980. Since Argentina accounted for only a fourth of the increase, something more general than the reaction to the grain embargo may be at work here.

Economic Reform

A recovery or acceleration in productivity growth could considerably ameliorate the bleak forecast for growth. As Table 2.1 showed, even under a constant investment strategy, productivity growth at 1 percent rather than one-half percent per year would raise GNP growth from 2.5 to 3.1 percent per year. Alternatively, one could consider the tremendous resource wastes that occur in the Soviet economy as "reserves" that could be turned into additional output. Indeed, Soviet planners often describe them in this way. How likely is it that the pressure of the resource crunch will induce Soviet leaders to institute reforms that will significantly improve economic efficiency and hence productivity growth? This is probably the most uncertain aspect of any forecast of changes that could affect economic growth.

Stagnating productivity seems to characterize most major industrialized nations at the present juncture, but the causes in the Soviet economy are different from those in other countries. We think stagnant productivity in the industrialized market economies may be a temporary phenomenon associated with cyclical problems, diversion of resources into environmental protection efforts, and substitutions required by the revolution in energy prices.

In the USSR the slowdown in productivity improvement seems the result of exacerbation of a number of fundamental weaknesses that become more serious as the economy matures. Many explanations have been offered for low productivity in the Soviet economy: misallocation of resources, uneconomic choices concerning technology, perverse incentives, a general disinclination to act in an economizing way, refusal to exercise initiative, unwillingness to accept the challenge of innovative or risky behavior, and little sense of dedication on the part of the worker. In my view it is helpful to divide these sources of inefficiency into two broad types.

One source of inefficiency is the waste from bad decisions about allocation. On the basis of faulty data or wrong criteria, planners locate a plant in the wrong place, choose its size unwisely, or give it a technology less then optimal. The Gosplan may fail to achieve equilibrium in the supply and demand of some commodity, so that production in related sectors is disrupted, or may misallocate some resource so that its contribution to output or cost reduction is unequal at the margin in different uses. Enterprises may find that the prices and bonus systems destroy their interest in producing the products assigned or in meeting quality standards specified in their plans. These mistakes often flow from ideological constraints imposed by Marxist dogma, clumsy payoff formulas, misleading information fed to decision makers, or simple irrationality in allocation. Most of these defects could be ameliorated by better prices, by refining bonus formulae, and by improved capacity to transmit and process data into sensible decisions as computers become more widespread. The Soviet Union in the last decade has made a great deal of progress along these lines.

In my view, a second kind of waste flowing from the hierarchical character of the system itself is more serious and more intractable. In the Soviet planned economy, a system of vertical links between enterprises and superiors rather than interactions between enterprises themselves define communication, influence, power, and attention. Enterprises are not responsive to the needs of their consumers and have little power to influence their suppliers. One may argue at one level that this should not present any fundamental problem: with the growth in the capacity to communicate and process information, with more sophisticated and economically rational models for processing information into decisions, the gap between what the center induces a plant to do and what its consumers might want it to do will disappear, so that the vertical channels of influence and communication will generate outcomes as good as a market system. But that view overlooks a more fundamental difficulty with the administrative approach.

The greatest wastes in the Soviet system take the form of generally unresponsive and even noncompliant behavior on the part of management at lower levels, which flows from a defect in the bargaining relationship between superiors and inferiors in the hierarchically organized administrative structure of the economy. In this system the top levels try to direct the behavior of lower level decision makers by the classic administrative paradigm of assigning responsibilities, basically in the form of assigning an annual plan, checking on performance, and offering rewards for good performance. As this periodic process moves from one cycle to the next, the terms of the relationship are frequently renegotiated unilaterally from above. An enterprise that responds to the bait of rewards for improving performance beyond the plan is likely to encounter the famous "ratchet effect," the tendency for superior organs to renegotiate the terms of the bargain against it. In this situation the manager quickly learns that it is important to manipulate the upward flow of information, to conceal reserves, to understate real potential, and to seek an easy plan, pleading weakness and demonstrating it by as poor a performance as is manageable. Managers shun initiative, avoid risks, and hoard reserves to protect themselves against extraordinary demands. They do not fight to correct the mistakes of higher level planners: their goal is to survive rather than to make improvements. They are likely to use the little room for initiative they have defensively against their superiors rather than aggressively to expand output, to best their competitors, or to win new customers. A Soviet economist has summed up the situation by saying that "the existing system of incentives has a number of powerful defects. It puts in an advantageous position those collectives which set a plan low in output and high in inputs. That is, it does not create conditions for developing ambitious plans, gives no advantage to the best enterprises, validates the worst, and leads to egalitarianism."[44]

In my view the regime must make a determined effort to reform this system and improve productivity by changing the relationship between the center and the managerial class. The experience of the last decade in the Soviet Union and in Eastern Europe suggests that reform efforts will have no significant effect in improving performance unless the problem is attacked in these fundamental terms. Tinkering with details will not suffice; it is necessary to "constitutionalize" or "propertify" the position of the managerial class. Enterprise management needs more responsibility for its success or failure, and at the same time more security and independence in exercising that responsibility. The system needs a clear statement of the terms on which the central administrative bodies will do business with the managers and a retreat by the regime from its present arbitrariness in changing the rules, from its day-to-day oversight of managerial behavior, and from its willingness to rescue poor management and to impose added burdens on the successful. The rulers must convince managers and the enterprises they control that they must perform or perish under clearly stated conditions.

This can happen only if the terms on which they will succeed or fail are made more stable and immune from arbitrary manipulation by the superior organ, whether in the form of arbitrary hardening or of relaxation in response to pleas of special conditions and weaknesses. Only this kind of change will shift managerial attention from trying to manipulate their superiors toward trying to elicit cooperative behavior from their suppliers and to satisfy their customers. Most Western experts who have specialized in studying the Soviet-type economy share this view, as do many Soviet economists. A recent round-table discussion of the reasons Soviet machine tools trail those in other countries in quality and why producers pay so little attention to the users' needs described the situation accurately. One discussant said, without demur from others, that the system forces the director to decide whether to sacrifice plan fulfillment or the reputation of his plant. Few managers are quixotic enough to sacrifice the plan to satisfy their customers' interests.[45]

The problem is not that the Soviet leaders have not tried to "reform" the system. They have launched an unending set of experiments, rule changes, and institutional realignments, in what Gertrude Schroeder has perceptively called a veritable "treadmill of reforms."[46] The difficulty is that the long history of "reform" in the Soviet Union has never produced a direct attack on the central problem. The present regime has an acute sense of defects in performance but a very limited comprehension of what it must do to solve the problem and has shunned radical economic reform. It has not hesitated to change many traditional features of the system: there has been significant price reform; full-cycle planning and financing of R and D programs has been introduced; normative net value has replaced gross output as the measure of output. The leaders have changed the formula for rewarding output increases in agriculture from overfulfillment of planned deliveries to increases above annual average deliveries of the preceding period as the basis for premia. They have amalgamated enterprises to combine related activities under one boss. Among the many changes and experiments carried out in the Brezhnev period, some have helped to make the enterprise more independent, stabilize expectations, and enhance the power of lateral interactions as a disciplining force to supplement control from above.

Nancy Nimitz has suggested that a number of changes one might describe under the heading of "self-financing" may help shift the enterprise focus from manipulating its superiors to influencing the enterprises with which it interacts.[47] These changes force ministries to finance investment out of their own profits rather than from state grants and so motivate them to control cost and to demand cost-cutting improvements from suppliers of capital goods so they can live within investment budgets. The literature on reform in the small East European economies has a constant theme that tightened budget constraints such as would come with self-financing could greatly strengthen economizing behavior on the part of enterprises. The Soviet economy is a seller's market. Buyers have little power to act in a discriminating way, effectively articulating demands for quality, product improvements, and timeliness in performance, because excess demand gives sellers the upper hand. From the other side they do not need to, because everyone works under loose financial constraints. Financial penalties to deter bad performance are weak; buyers wink at defects that raise their costs because cost and profit are not crucial issues for them; directors of investment projects accept cost overruns, poor design, and obsolete equipment because they can avoid the budget limit for investment projects.

Some specialists on Soviet economic affairs find corroboration of the "self-financing" idea in the way the military sector operates. The Ministry of Defense is a demanding customer because it must meet the test of foreign competition and because, as a single buyer in relation to many suppliers, it has the upper hand in deciding whether or not to accept a product. The same principle appears in the civilian economy in one case where the buyer has a stronger than usual position vis-à-vis its suppliers, i.e., the Ministry of Power and Electrification in buying equipment for power stations. This is one reason this ministry has a better than average record of innovation and technical change.[48]

The central issue for all who have pondered the question of "economic reform" in the Soviet-style planning system is whether piecemeal changes can help significantly, whether numerous small changes can ever constitute a revision of the fundamental character of the system, and if so how much is enough to achieve a transition from quantitative to qualitative change. There is no consensus on these matters. Nevertheless, I believe that no significant improvement in the behavior of managerial decision makers will occur until some bold regime is willing to cross the threshold of abandoning the physical allocation system, specification of output plans, and monthly, quarterly, and annual evaluation of plan fulfillment.

The discussion so far has concerned the behavior of management personnel in their relations with superior organs and with the firms which they serve and on whom they depend. An analogous problem exists at a lower level, i.e., eliciting dedicated and intelligent effort from workers. The worker's behavior is determined not so much by the administrative or planning system as by his employment relation to the firm, i.e., job security, conditions of pay, and so on, and his ability to convert money earnings into real income by exchanging them easily for goods and services that are strongly desired, such as housing, travel, consumer durables, and various amenities that enhance the quality of life.

The Soviet system makes heavy use of pay incentives to encourage worker effort. In practice, however, over-full employment and the inability of workers to turn monetary returns from effort into an improvement in real consumption seriously weaken the motivating power of the wage system. To deal with this problem, the Soviet Union requires more than a quantitative increase in the resources allocated to consumption. Improvements in quality and variety of goods, better pricing to equate supply and demand, and institutional changes that make the sector producing consumer goods more responsive to the desires of consumers are also crucial. The incentive effect of the resources the regime allocates to consumption is seriously diluted by the fact that purchases require huge investments of time as well as money, that the quality and mix of goods are poor, and that durables break down and cannot be repaired. This is partly a systemic problem in that the dominance of vertical over horizontal ties reduces producers' motivation to please consumers, but in part it is a policy problem. Soviet planning has always been biased toward overfull employment planning. Plans are overambitious, and informal priorities and adjustment mechanisms in their execution lead to imbalance in consumer goods markets and repressed inflation. Weak financial controls and pressure to fulfill plans lead enterprises to pay out more money to households than planned. At the same time, overoptimistic goals for output are not met, especially output of consumer goods, leaving the population with excess cash. In the Tenth Five-Year Plan this phenomenon apparently grew completely out of control.

Deposits of the population in savings banks rose from 91.2 billion to 156.7 billion rubles during the Tenth Five-Year Plan. Since there is little advantage and probably some disadvantages in keeping one's savings in the bank, given the low interest rates, significant accumulations in the form of cash held by households probably also occurred. Gregory Grossman has made calculations indicating that cash holdings of households may have increased by about as much as their savings in savings banks.[49] Some savings are desired to accumulate funds for such expenditures as consumer durables, but most must be unwanted. This overhang erodes incentives and facilitates the growth of the "second economy" of illegal and semilegal production and speculation outside government control. Evidence is accumulating that this economy is significant in size, and a powerful influence for corruption and diversion of resources from the regular economy.

Inept pricing in individual markets compounds the problem.

Some goods are particularly underpriced; meat, housing, and durables are notorious cases. The current Soviet regime is unwilling to meet this problem by adjusting the general price level and the prices of goods most in demand. Soviet politicians seem to believe that the social contract requires that prices for consumer goods not change, but Soviet economists certainly understand the deleterious effects of this policy and criticized it strongly in the discussion of the Eleventh Five-Year Plan draft. As S. S. Shatalin said, "guaranteeing balance in the consumption sector of our economy is the most important condition for steady growth of the people's welfare, for the creation of an effective system of material incentives, and for a transition to a primarily intensive, balanced, development of the national economy as a whole."[50] But the leadership does not accept this argument. An official of the State Committee on Prices expressed their position:

> Continuation of the strategic course of the CPSU to hold retail prices stable once more affirms the inadequacy of the views of those economists who think that in our economy it is necessary actively to use the price mechanism for equating supply and demand for certain consumer goods. Raising the prices on products of mass consumption, demand for which is still not fully satisfied, cannot in my opinion be considered a cardinal solution of the problem of balance and is fraught with negative social consequences. The solution of the problem is in the increase by all possible measures of the output of consumer goods, especially those that are today in short supply.[51]

Official spokesmen say that the Eleventh Five-Year Plan corrects the macro-imbalance of the Tenth and that goods supply will match the money incomes of the population. But one can rightly be suspicious that they are as overoptimistic on this occasion as they have been in the past.

Prospects for Change

The greatly increased pressure to seek improvements in performance and the possible shift from immobility to fluidity accompanying a leadership succession may open the way for significant institutional and policy changes. A new leadership which has grown up in different circumstances might be willing to try something bold and radical. Certainly many specialists—economists, planners, and managers—understand what is needed and support radical changes. On balance, however, I am skeptical of significant change in the system.

The increasingly radical tone of the analysis and policy prescriptions Soviet economists now offer is impressive. They do not hesitate

to suggest substituting enterprise choice of supplier for central allocation, raising housing rents to reflect costs, and taking lessons from the
second economy to overcome the clumsiness of central allocation.
Many recommended overhauling the whole complex of wage structure, consumer goods pricing, fiscal planning, and allocations to collective consumption in order to make rewards proportionate to
effort. Some even apparently attack the burden of military expenditures in an Aesopian mode by describing the high cost of weapons
systems in the United States. Abel Aganbegian and the economists
associated with his Institute for Economics and Organization of Industrial Production in the Siberian Branch of the USSR Academy of
Sciences are most outspoken; some Western observers interpret this
as a reflection of their distance from Moscow geographically and in
terms of influence. But equally venturesome ideas appear in many
other places much closer to the center, such as the Scientific Research
Center for Economics attached to Gosplan and the Research Institute
for Systems Studies. Even in older and more traditional institutes,
such as the Institute of Economics of the USSR Academy of Sciences,
criticisms and advice seem more forthrightly novel than in the past.

Nor are these people on the fringes of the economics establishment. Two of the most critical economists were elected corresponding
members of the USSR Academy of Sciences in the 1982 elections.
When the new leadership turns to the economics fraternity for recommendations for "perfecting administration and the whole economic mechanism" and "accelerating the shift of the economy onto
the path of intensive growth" (a meeting of the Central Committee in
July 1982 did precisely this), they will probably hear a much narrower
range of opinion with an overall tone more radical in recommendations than happened on previous occasions when they consulted the
economists.[52]

Nonetheless, great obstacles to significant change still exist. First,
any serious attack on the problem of managerial behavior described
above would undermine the role of the party, which is bound to see
any move to "propertify" or "constitutionalize" the status of the managerial group as a threat to its role. Second, institutional reform
would threaten many vested interests in the economic system, especially for those who have a stake in continuing in a way that is familiar
and for those groups whose livelihood is tied to continuation of misal-
locations made in the past. It is difficult to imagine the kind of coalition that could push change through against all opposing interests.
Policy reform aimed at realistic and balanced planning has not been
attainable in the past: it inevitably suggests lowering aspirations, and
many would attack those who would propose this on that ground.
Ideologically, on the other hand, such a shift to less ambitious, more

realistic plans is certainly conceivable. If Stalin held that "there are no fortresses Bolsheviks cannot storm," Lenin had earlier sanctioned the idea of "less but better."

Worker opposition would be a formidable obstacle to the policy and institutional changes most observers consider vital to enhance motivations, raise productivity, and unfreeze the labor market. Such fundamental changes must include some reduction in job security, sharper differentiation in the reward structure, price increases for goods of high income elasticity such as meat, quality clothing, housing, and durables for which market disequilibria are greatest, and an attack on the cash asset positions of households. The historical analogy that comes to mind is Stolypin's "wager on the strong" as a policy to encourage initiative and productivity growth in tsarist agriculture and to win the loyalty of the strongest elements among the peasantry.

Our reading of the social contract as the Soviet working class understands it, the experience of Polish leaders in trying to impose such changes, and the history of Stolypin himself combine to convince us, and no doubt the Soviet leaders as well, of the riskiness of such a policy. My summary judgment is that only a very solidly entrenched leadership group or one desperate to the point of adventurism would contemplate undertaking so radical a course.

All this does not rule out innovation, but does suggest that change will require a sense of desperation among the leadership, combined with determination that it is difficult to believe any faction fighting to capture power could sustain long enough to achieve radical change. The Polish experience is relevant here in revealing how the leadership of a socialist society can adamantly refuse to adapt, even when the situation is desperate.

The dilemmas economic stringency forces on the Soviet leaders offer no easy escape. The Brezhnev regime clearly revealed its resolution of these conflicts in the Eleventh Five-Year Plan, which sacrifices investment in favor of the claims of the military establishment and of consumption. The plan is full of verbiage about improving planning and the economic mechanism and increasing discipline, but the leaders clearly have sidestepped significant efforts at economic change. They approach the centerpiece of the consumption effort, the food program and agricultural policy, primarily by an extraordinary commitment of resources rather than by significant reforms that would enhance the prospects of making this investment pay. When the price reform of January 1, 1982, raised prices on many important commodities, the government exempted agriculture from having to pay higher prices. A continued inflow of investment resources is backed up by a new increase in agricultural procurement prices. The incentive payments of the previous five-year period have been absorbed into a new higher guaranteed level of agricultural prices, topped with the promise of a new 50 percent price premium for deliveries exceeding the levels realized during the Tenth Five-Year Plan. The food program continues a policy of forgiving debts incurred by collective farms, converting those loans in retrospect to a free gift.

In confronting its agricultural sector the Soviet regime seems to feel the same impotence Western creditors feel toward Poland. The program promises higher incomes to collective farm management and offers concessionary terms to those collectives whose inefficiency and high cost put them at a disadvantage even under the new generous terms. An indigent imagination has limited institutional revisions to support this infusion of resources into agriculture to adding another new layer of bureaucrats in the form of regional production administrations, with only a slight offset in the form of some increased freedom for private plot agriculture.[53] An American cannot help but recall our own disillusioning experiences with trying to solve complex problems by throwing money at them.

One cannot call current policy an imaginative response, but one can appreciate that it flows from the inherent conservatism of an aging leadership with a short planning horizon, a vivid memory of recent events in Poland, and values that make them susceptible to the argument they must not now let themselves fall behind after persistent efforts to catch up. Current strategy contains some internal contradictions, but overall its weakest feature is its unattractiveness as a long-run policy, since it mortgages future growth prospects to short-run exigencies.

One might argue that the consumption emphasis may stimulate growth by increasing incentives and productivity, but that argument is not persuasive. Food alone will not make the population content with their government and give them incentive to work harder: the government is doing too little to support the increased allocation of resources to consumption with appropriate institutional and policy changes. Without changes in pricing, without reform of the decision making system on the production side that produces wrong assortments, low quality, and bad distribution of consumer goods, without changes in the labor markets, the incentive and productivity effects of the resources devoted to producing consumer goods will be minor. One suspects that even within the constraints the planners have accepted, the plan for 1981–85 is still too ambitious and that investment bottlenecks will develop that undercut growth, including the intended growth in consumption if investment retains its low priority. I see nothing being done to reform agricultural decision making to make it possible to attain output increments that match the huge resources invested in agriculture.

If the agricultural program and some improvement in the weather enable the Soviet Union to avoid agricultural imports, the Kremlin can reserve hard currency earnings for financing technology imports which could help growth. On the whole, however, the current strategy does not seem to embody a clear line on international economic relations. Technology imports will certainly continue on a large scale, but current policy seems irresolute in adopting either of two policies needed to expand their contribution to growth, i.e., developing a supporting export program or revising arrangements for absorbing imported technology to maximize its growth enhancing properties.

It is true that gas development plans are specifically shaped to ensure an export surplus, according to Brezhnev, for many years to come. But this is primarily a replacement for oil rather than an incremental program, and a multitude of problems endangers its long-run prospects. On the absorption side, the planners seem neither to have identified strategic sectors where the Soviet Union might achieve critical breakthroughs, as was done with fertilizer, nor to have moved toward an economic reform that would create flexibility to direct imports toward highly productive, small-scale, bottleneck areas.

Longer-Range Perspectives

I am doubtful that the current economic strategy can survive the turmoil of succession. Certain parts of it, such as the food program, carry Brezhnev's name. The current strategy undoubtedly represents a consensus within the Politburo, but some significant groups no doubt are less than wholehearted supporters, and even within the Politburo itself doubts may arise. The agricultural policy, in particular, must seem to many misguided and excessively costly. In my view, the measures the food program embodies must have stretched the tolerance of other groups to the breaking point. In his justification of the food program at the May 1982 Central Committee plenum, Brezhnev spoke of the commitments it implies beyond 1985, but his expectation of extracting such commitments sounds somewhat far-fetched. In attempting to cope with what appears will be severe underfulfillment of the plan, the new leadership may be tempted to blame Brezhnev and retreat from some of his policies. The precedent of Khrushchev's scrapping the Sixth Five-Year Plan (1956–60) in mid-course in favor of a new start under a Seven-Year Plan is perhaps apropos here.

What kind of changes might the new leadership make, in terms of possible resource reallocations and policy innovations to support them? One possible program would be a complex of shifts in a "progressive" direction. I suspect that the investment problem will emerge as a dominant concern. I have already noted the long-range implications of slow investment growth, but investment shortages are likely also to cause serious short-run implications before 1985. Renovating the capital stock to adjust to the scarcity of labor and the high cost of materials and energy poses investment needs on a scale the planners' calculations have probably not yet absorbed. Numerous bottlenecks are likely to emerge, both in individual sectors starved for capital and in the infrastructural investments supporting regional shifts. Pressure is likely to grow to reduce agricultural investment, perhaps even military procurement, and to expand the share of investment and redirect it more to producers goods industries. As the new leadership responds, it might formulate the question: "Given that we are still fully committed to the triple aims of growth, defense, and welfare, can't we find a more effective set of policies for getting there?"—a question it could ask each of the major claimants.

National security will remain a paramount goal, but the external situation may change enough to justify reassessment of many aspects of military policy. The United States administration may suffer serious disappointments in its efforts to rearm, the Soviet leaders may absorb lessons from Poland, Afghanistan, and the Falklands. Cheap opportunities may emerge for making significant gains by political and diplomatic means. The new leadership could reopen the question of its resource commitment to defense, asking that the military rethink the national security task, including the force structure and appropriate rate of buildup. We do not understand the nature of the regime's commitment to the military very well. We have tended to express it as a promise of continued growth in the allocation to the military at the current rate, basically because that is the historical record we see. It seems more logical to suppose that the military may formulate its expectations in terms of individual weapons programs, rate of buildup of the forces, and so on, and that the government may grant much that the military wants without committing itself to a fixed rate of growth in the allocation to defense. Even if the allocation to defense were frozen or reduced from the current rate, Soviet military capacities will still grow at an impressive rate.

The possibility of arms limitation or reduction agreements with the United States is obviously relevant to the leader's position on the defense allocation. Force expansion matched by the opposition adds little to national security, and resource stringency should stimulate a rethinking of the goals the USSR might seek in arms agreements as a resource-saving and security-enhancing move. Issues of strategic doctrine and defense decision making are discussed in other chapters of this study, but the economic aspects of this issue merit mention here.

The important point is that the outlays on strategic arms are only one component of Soviet military expenditures. The CIA estimates that Soviet expenditure on strategic forces in 1980 accounted for about 17 percent of all military spending when all elements are valued in 1979 dollars.[54] The share in rubles is likely to be higher, since strategic forces are rich in inputs with high ruble-dollar ratios. They are also especially demanding in some of the inputs that compete with investment. The CIA's calculations show that construction and procurement of hardware for strategic forces cumulatively accounted for 37 percent of all military construction and procurement for 1971–80. Both these share calculations omit research and development from both halves of the ratio. Since strategic systems are probably R and D intensive, these ratios may understate their importance in the overall military burden on the economy. Despite all the uncertainties and possible errors in this kind of comparison, the point remains that limitations in strategic arms with the United States affect only part of the Soviet military burden.

Military expenditures could be reduced for programs other than strategic forces. Such reductions or limitations depend on many other considerations besides the general strategic relationship with the United States, i.e., the perception of the Chinese threat, possible diplomatic and political approaches as an alternative to military force in dealing with Western Europe, problems and opportunities in the Middle East, and so on. The possibility of constraining military outlays should not be linked solely with arms limitation agreements.

A final caution is that experts dispute how transferable resources now devoted to military production are to production of civilian goods. Some branches of military production are so specialized and the working conditions so special that the resources involved would contribute little to civilian lines of production. But many Soviet production lines are intentionally designed for dual use. I believe that resources used for producing military hardware could be transferred within the limits of conceivable reductions, especially when the shift would be to production of investment goods. And of course many components of military expenditure are for items such as manpower, fuel, and other inputs easily transferred into operations.

Such a renegotiation has already taken place regarding investment. Brezhnev and his colleagues adopted toward producers somewhat the same line that Khrushchev took toward the "metaleaters," asserting that the resources available were adequate to the tasks for which they were responsible, and that they had the responsibility to find ways to expand production capacity by utilizing the current level of investment allocations more effectively. It is true that such institutional change as has occurred seems inadequate to validate this message and policy, but the message and policy are unambiguous. The current strategy has identified correctly many of the tactical elements, such as replacement, user pressure for improved equipment quality, and so on, but has thus far done little to create the relevant instruments and incentives to alter decisions in this direction.

One might ask a similar question regarding consumption. Recent Soviet economic commentary indicates that a real change in Soviet priorities has occurred. The belief that the time has come to deal with consumption is widely shared in Soviet society, and the leadership has acknowledged and even roused popular expectations in this regard. Without calling into question the leadership's priority for meeting consumer aspirations, the new regime could argue that the present complex of measures is ineffective. It could reconsider the degree of autarky sought in agriculture and in manufactured consumer goods and contemplate institutional and policy changes that would elicit more output from agriculture at a lower cost. A new approach to consumption would have to include some decentralization for the nonagricultural sector as well, especially in the form of giving managers incentives to economize on labor and more realistic pricing in relations with households. One United States student of agriculture argues that the Soviet citizen is not badly undersupplied with meat even today. At 52 kilograms per capita per year, Soviet consumers are well below the United States level of 108 kg, and appreciably behind rich, traditionally meat-eating societies such as France and Germany, with annual per capita consumption between 80 and 90 kg. But in relation to a number of other European countries, especially those at income levels more comparable to the USSR, such as Italy, Spain, and the United Kingdom, the gap is about 10 kg. and is only 9 kilograms compared to the Swedish level.[55] Part of the problem concerning meat is that inflexibility of the distribution system and underpricing of meat create extraordinary frustrations and extract huge welfare losses from the population as they acquire and consume it.

In a very perceptive piece in a 1982 issue of the journal of the Institute for Economics and Organization of Industrial Production, S. S. Shatalin develops persuasively the idea that the regime has achieved a "dialectical unity of ends and means" in linking the growth of the welfare of the people with a shift of the economy to the path of intensive development.[56] Whether that unity can be achieved in practice is the real issue.

The problem with any such "progressive" scenario is obvious. We are discussing the central authorities' renegotiating their contract with major constituencies, the population in general, the military, the industrial workers, the state economic bureaucracy, and the managers. The leaders may see less possibility for maneuver in each of these areas than this discussion suggests. Precisely because the regime has never allowed popular participation in discussion of the priority given consumption, it is likely to receive a bloody-minded response to any suggestions of retreat from what are considered tacit agreements, such as the policy of keeping retail prices unchanged. The Polish case certainly supports such an interpretation.

An individual or clique aspiring to consolidate a power position in the succession might consider such a progressive approach too risky even to try. Anyone proposing it would be vulnerable to ideological criticism and would also alienate groups whose support a rival could mobilize in the struggle to capture the dominant role in the power structure. The succession could, however, be a kind of controlled shift toward a new consensus rather than a factional struggle for power. In view of the tension attendant on economic stringency, the leadership may unite behind an effort to carry out such a renegotiation.

If the new leadership is rebuffed in an effort to renegotiate these various implicit contracts, the alternative is likely to be a retrogressive set of policies, shifting resources back to investment, substituting discipline and repression for satisfaction and incentives through consumption increases, preserving the primacy of the military allocation, and so on.

I believe it foolhardy to predict which of these courses the USSR will follow. Much depends on one's view of how the succession will evolve and on the nature of Soviet politics, especially the interplay between the "clientelistic" processes that make state policy a compromise between various power groups, and the "elitist" processes that permit the party core to use the instruments of state power to impose its will on groups within society.

The economic prospects for the USSR, examined in isolation, suggest both great pressure for systemic change and great potential for improvement through change, if the leaders are sufficiently radical in attacking the causes of the monumental waste, inflexibility, and nonenterprising character of the economic actors in the system. The causes of these defects are so intimately wrapped up with the political system that they probably preclude evolutionary change of the economy in the coming decade. In my view, discouraging as economic prospects are, they are unlikely to create such overwhelming pressure as to topple the system or threaten its rulers' hold over society.

After all, we expect growth to continue, even if at reduced rates. If output grows at 2 to 2.5 percent each year for the decade, it creates an easier situation in which to maneuver than the United States has faced during the years 1978–82, when GNP grew only 2.5 percent over four years. It is true that many problems urgently demand attention, but the situation is not beyond repair, even if the leaders are not willing to turn in their creaky old model for a radically new economic system. It is possible to attack particular problems by introducing changes in policy, without undertaking radically to revise core institutions. Some problems are more serious than others, and a leadership freed of the Brezhnev presence can begin to work on them one at a time. It should be able to restore the motivating power of the ruble by changes in consumer goods prices and in wage policy without raising implacable opposition. Since agriculture is a more or less separate sector, it is feasible to reduce the degree of central administrative control in favor of more market direction without scrapping centralization for the rest of the economy. I believe this would result in a striking improvement in agricultural performance. For the doubters, a working example is at hand in Hungary. Policy changes in those two areas alone could result in enough savings in resources and enough extra output to make a significant difference.

I do not anticipate a radical reorientation of priorities, except for some reallocation to investment. If some relatively straightforward policy changes can indeed produce more satisfaction and effort from the resources already devoted to consumption, and if agriculture can be weaned of its investment habit, that will free some resources for increasing investment and reallocating it to crucial needs. It will no doubt be some time before we understand what Brezhnev told the military leaders in his speech shortly before his death, but it is not implausible to conclude that part of the message was that some restrictions must be placed on military requirements, justified in part by easing tensions with China.

This, after all, is what is meant by "muddling through"—little adjustments here, some trimming of aspirations there, palliative measures to defuse a few of the most threatening situations. What all this would mean for external conduct is risky to forecast. Considering the problem from the perspective of economic considerations alone, these tendencies would suggest a turning inward of the leaders' attention, more concern and effort devoted to urgent domestic problems, and some temporary retrenchment in foreign efforts. This process is likely to last several years. I do not foresee complete withdrawal from international economic relations with the West, however, since the Soviets will still need grain imports, and they will rely on technology imports as the cheapest and fastest way to solve certain domestic tasks.

NOTES

1. Stanley Cohn, *Economic Development in the Soviet Union* (Lexington, Mass.: D. C. Heath, 1970), p. 28; CIA, Net Foreign Assessment Center, *Handbook of Economic Statistics 1980* (Washington, D.C.: USGPO, 1980), p. 56.
2. The work force consists of state employment (described in Soviet sources as *rabochie i sluzhashchie*), collective farm members engaged in socialized production, and the members of families of workers and employees

and collective farmers working only in private plot agriculture. The Soviet statistical yearbook, *Narodnoe khoziaistvo SSSR* [National Economy of the USSR] (Moscow: Tsentral'noe statisticheskoe upravlenie), for the respective years, routinely reports these figures.

3. *Ekonomika i organizatsiia promyshlennogo proizvodstva-EKO* [Economics and Organization of Industrial Production], 1982, no. 3, p. 138.

4. Abram Bergson, "Toward a New Growth Model," *Productivity and the Social System: The USSR and the West* (Cambridge: Harvard University Press, 1978), p. 27.

5. CIA, *Handbook of Economic Statistics 1980*, p. 59.

6. Five-year forecast through 1986, released in April 1982.

7. N. K. Baibakov, *Gosudarstvennyi piatiletnyi plan razvitiia narodnogo khoziaistva SSSR na 1971–75 gody* [The State Five-Year Plan for the Development of the National Economy of the USSR in 1971–75] (Moscow, 1972), and *Narodnoe khoziaistvo SSSR za 60 let* [National Economy of the USSR for Sixty Years], p. 168.

8. U.S. Congress, Joint Economic Committee, *Consumption in the USSR: An International Comparison* (Washington, D.C.: USGPO, 1981), p. 6.

9. E. P. Gorbunov, in a round-table discussion of the Eleventh Five-Year Plan guidelines, in *Voprosy ekonomiki* [Problems of Economics], 1981, no. 1, p. 64.

10. *Ekonomicheskaia gazeta* [The Economic Newspaper], 1981, no. 9, pp. 10–11.

11. *Ekonomika i organizatsiia promyshlennogo proizvodstva-EKO*, 1981, no. 5, p. 15.

12. *Voprosy ekonomiki*, 1981, no. 1, p. 7.

13. An informative survey of the variety of opinion and the relevant arguments on this matter is available in *CIA Estimates of Soviet Defense Spending*, hearings before the Subcommittee on Oversight of the Permanent Select Committee on Intelligence, U.S. House of Representatives, September 3, 1980 (Washington, D.C.: USGPO, 1980).

14. Grey Hodnett, "The Pattern of Leadership Politics," in Seweryn Bialer, ed., *The Domestic Context of Soviet Foreign Policy* (Boulder, Colo.: Westview Press, 1981), p. 103.

15. Thomas Wolfe, *Military Power and Soviet Policy*, Rand P-5388 (Santa Monica, Calif.: The Rand Corporation, 1975), p. 15.

16. Bergson, *Productivity and the Social System*, pp. 24–37.

17. The Garbuzov statement is in *Finansy SSSR* [Finances of the USSR], 1982, no. 1, p. 20; the decree on personnel reductions, in *Izvestiia*, November 24, 1981; and the Brezhnev statement, in *Ekonomicheskaia gazeta*, 1981, no. 9, p. 10.

18. According to U.S. Arms Control and Disarmament Agency, *World Military Expenditures and Arms Transfers, 1970–79*, (Washington, D.C.: USGPO, 1982), p. 76, the number of persons in the Soviet armed forces was 4.8 million in 1979. Other sources suggest somewhat higher figures. I use 5 million as an approximation.

19. *Ekonomika i organizatsiia promyshlennogo proizvodstva-EKO*, 1982, no. 3, p. 141.

20. The two decrees are available in *Resheniia partii i pravitel'stva po khoziaistvennym voprosam* [Party and Government Decisions on Economic Questions], vol. 7 (Moscow, 1970), pp. 677–79, and vol. 13 (Moscow, 1981), pp. 136–45.

21. *Sotsialisticheskii trud* [Socialist Labor], 1981, no. 10, p. 4.

22. U.S. Bureau of the Census, *Population Projections by Age and Sex for the Republics and Major Economic Regions of the USSR, 1970 to 2000,* International Population Series, P-91, No. 26 (Washington, D.C.: USGPO, 1979), p. 91. The Soviet estimate is in *Sotsialisticheskii trud,* 1981, no. 3, p. 52.

23. *Ekonomika i organizatsiia promyshlennogo proizvodstva-EKO,* 1982, no. 3, p. 138.

24. *Sotsialisticheskii trud,* 1982, no. 3, pp. 64–71.

25. An excellent survey of recent changes may be found in Ann Goodman and Geoffrey Schleifer, "The Soviet Labor Market in the 1980s," in U.S. Congress Joint Economic Committee, *The Soviet Economy in the 1980s: Problems and Prospects,* (Washington, D.C.: USGPO, 1982).

26. *Planovoe khoziaistvo* [Planned Economy], 1982, no. 1, p. 6.

27. Ibid., no. 3, p. 30.

28. For the decree on housing for agriculture, see *Pravda,* May 30, 1982, p. 1.

29. *Planovoe khoziaistvo,* 1982, no. 1, p. 11.

30. *Ekonomicheskaia gazeta,* 1982, no. 22, p. 5.

31. N. K. Baibakov in ibid., 1981, no. 4, p. 6 of insert.

32. Three interesting recent pieces on the excessive creation of work places are: V. Cherevan', "Soglasovanie vosproizvodstva rabochikh mest s trudovymi resursami" [Coordination of Creation of Work Places with Labor Resources], *Voprosy ekonomiki,* 1982, no. 2, pp. 51–61; R. Tikhidzhiev, "Voprosy sbalansirovannosti vosproizvodstva osnovnykh fondov i trudovykh resursov" [Questions of Balanced Growth of Fixed Assets and Labor Resources], *Planovoe khoziaistvo,* 1981, no. 12, pp. 44–53; and N. Gorelov et al., "Organizatsiia ucheta rabochikh mest i obespechenie ikh sbalansirovannosti s trudovymi resursami" [Organizing the Accounting of Work Places and Guaranteeing Their Balance with Labor Resources], *Planovoe khoziaistvo,* 1982, no. 3, pp. 82–87. The discussion of machine tool design is by S. A. Kheinman in *Ekonomika i organizatsiia promyshlennogo proizvodstva-EKO,* 1982, no. 1, p. 49.

33. *Planovoe khoziaistvo,* 1982, no. 1, p. 11.

34. In his speech on the Five-Year Plan in *Ekonomicheskaia gazeta,* 1981, no. 4, p. 4 of insert, Gosplan Chairman N. K. Baibakov says that in 1981–85 about 132 billion rubles will be invested in the branches of the fuel and energy complex as compared to 88 billion rubles in 1976–80. He also provides a figure of 618.4 billion rubles for all state investment. Industrial investment of 277.9 billion rubles in 1981–85 is implied in a statement in *Planovoe khoziaistvo,* 1982, no. 3, p. 2, that its share in all investment will rise by 4.4 percentage points in the Eleventh compared to the Tenth Five-Year Plan. Baibakov's figures for energy sector investment clearly refer to a broader concept than is used in the figures on the distribution of investment by branch in the Central Statistical Administration's statistical yearbook, cited above, which show investment in the big four energy branches for 1976–80 as only 65.638 billion rubles. There are a number of other statements on the changing share of fuel and energy of investment shares but they are not mutually reconcilable, probably because of differences in concept.

35. *Ekonomika gazovoi promyshlennosti* [Economics of the Gas Industry], 1977, no. 9, p. 18, gives the capacity of such lines as 28–30 billion cubic meters per year.

36. For a discussion of the equipment import dependence of the Soviet gas industry and the prospect for meeting the Eleventh Five-Year Plan goals, see Robert Campbell, "Soviet Technology Imports: The Gas Pipeline Case," Cali-

fornia Seminar on International Security and Foreign Policy, Discussion paper no. 91 (Santa Monica, Calif.: 1981), and Edward Hewett, "Near-term Prospects for the Soviet Natural Gas Industry, and the Implications for East-West Trade," in U.S. Congress, *Soviet Economy in the 1980s.*

37. David Schoonover, "Soviet Agricultural Policies," in U.S. Congress, Joint Economic Committee, *Soviet Economy in a Time of Change* (Washington, D.C.: USGPO, 1979), vol. 2, p. 83.

38. *Planovoe khoziaistvo,* 1982, no. 4, pp. 100–105.

39. Data on land improved and prepared for irrigation are regularly reported in the statistical yearbooks. The statement on the need for reconstruction is in *Planovoe khoziaistvo,* 1982, no. 4, p. 104.

40. *Voprosy ekonomiki,* 1981, no. 1, p. 89.

41. Vladimir G. Treml, "Subsidies in Soviet Agriculture: Record and Prospects," in U.S. Congress, *Soviet Economy in the 1980s.*

42. Sources for this and the preceding paragraph are Eugene Zaleski and Helgard Weinert, *Technology Transfer between East and West* (Paris: OECD, 1980), p. 321; Philip Hanson, *Trade and Technology in Soviet-Western Relations* (New York: Columbia University Press, 1981), p. 129; Vladimir Treml and Barry Kostinsky, *The Domestic Value of Soviet Foreign Trade: Exports and Imports in the 1972 Input-Output Table,* Foreign Economic Report no. 20, U.S. Dept. of Commerce, Bureau of the Census (Washington, D.C.: USGPO, 1982).

43. *Ekonomicheskaia gazeta,* 1981, no. 9, p. 10.

44. *Planovoe khoziaistvo,* 1982, no. 5, p. 73.

45. *Ekonomika i organizatsiia promyshlennogo proizvodstva-EKO,* 1982, no. 1, p. 66.

46. Gertrude Schroeder, "The Soviet Economy on a Treadmill of Reforms," in U.S. Congress, *Soviet Economy in a Time of Change,* vol. 1, pp. 312–40.

47. Nancy Nimitz, *The July 1979 Decree and Soviet Economic Reform,* Rand Corporation Series, *The Burden of Soviet Defense: A Political, Economic Essay* (Santa Monica, Calif.: The Rand Corporation, 1981).

48. Robert W. Campbell, *Soviet Energy Technologies: Planning, Policy, Research and Development* (Bloomington: Indiana University Press, 1980), pp. 246–47.

49. Gregory Grossman, "A Note on Soviet Inflation," in U.S. Congress, *The Soviet Economy in the 1980s.*

50. *Voprosy ekonomiki,* 1981, no. 1, p. 63.

51. Ibid., p. 102.

52. *Ekonomicheskaia gazeta,* 1981, no. 28, p. 3.

53. The description of the food program and Brezhnev's explanation of it are available, among other places, in ibid., 1982, nos. 22 and 23.

54. CIA, *Soviet and U.S. Defense Activities, 1971–80: A Dollar Cost Comparison* (Washington, D.C.: USGPO, 1981), p. 48.

55. Kenneth Gray, "Soviet Livestock: Stymied Growth, Increased Cost and Search for Balance," in U.S. Congress, *Soviet Economy in the 1980s;* Economic Commission for Europe, *Review of the Agricultural Situation in Europe at the End of 1980* (New York: United Nations, 1981); U.S. Department of Agriculture, *Agricultural Statistics, 1981* (Washington, D.C.: USGPO, 1982).

56. S. S. Shatalin, "Narodnoe blagosostoianie i sovershenstvovanie raspredelitel'nykh otnoshenii" [National Welfare and Improvement of Distribution Relationships], *Ekonomika i organizatsiia promyshlennogo proizvodstva-EKO,* 1982, no. 1, p. 3.

3
★

Military Forces

Coit D. Blacker

Introduction

THIS CHAPTER, which is divided into four parts, seeks to answer the following sets of questions: (1) What are the major elements of Soviet military power? (2) What is the nature of the relationship between the Soviet military, as an institution, and the political, economic, and social system of which it is a part? How might these relationships change over the course of this decade? (3) How has Soviet military doctrine evolved since the early 1950s, and what has been the role of new weapons technologies in the development of Soviet military strategy? How do Soviet leaders view the problems of general and limited war in the nuclear age? (4) How is the growth of Soviet military power likely to affect both the character and the conduct of the country's foreign policy in the 1980s? Will the Soviet Union become more assertive in pursuit of its foreign policy goals as a result of the military buildup, and if so, to what extent and in what areas of the world?

It is the central premise of this essay that the current leadership regards the country's military power, and the further development of that power, as a prerequisite for the attainment of future foreign policy objectives. This conviction will have important implications for the conduct of Soviet foreign policy in the 1980s. Specifically, Soviet leaders appear to believe that the continuous expansion of military capabilities will enable them and their successors to improve Moscow's international position, and that of the "socialist community" generally, with fewer risks and greater rewards than in the past. The Soviets seem notably sanguine about the political utility of military power in such proximate environments as Western Europe and Southwest Asia

I should like to express my appreciation to Fritz Ermarth, David Holloway, Arnold Horelick, and Lt. General Brent Scowcroft (Ret.) for the information and critical comments they provided.

and about prospective gains in so-called third areas, including parts of
the less developed world. Much of the Kremlin's optimism derives
from its estimate that the "worldwide correlation of forces" has
shifted to the advantage of the socialist countries; this includes favorable trends in the overall balance of military power between the
superpowers, although Moscow realizes that this particular relationship may not be a permanent condition of international politics.

There is little evidence to suggest, however, that Kremlin authorities will be significantly more inclined than in previous years to
engage in "high-risk" diplomacy or foreign policy behavior that might
precipitate serious military confrontations with the United States and
its major allies, even as Soviet leaders seek to enhance their global
position. The Soviets will continue to attach a high priority to avoidance of war with the West, especially general nuclear war; on the
other hand, should a new world war become "inevitable" in the Kremlin's view, the objective of Soviet leaders will be to prevail in such a
conflict (whatever its intensity), a goal necessitating the early and effective use of nuclear weapons, among other military measures.

Finally, for reasons explored in the second part of this essay, it is
unlikely that Moscow's increasing reliance on military power as an
instrument of foreign policy will result in an enlarged political role
for the armed forces within the Soviet system, despite their critical
contribution to regime authority, their professional competence, and
their obvious and substantial material and economic resources.

Soviet Military Power: Capabilities, Command, and Prospects

The attentive public in the West has become accustomed to analyses of the Soviet Union that begin by describing the country's formidable military strength. Observers usually describe the Soviet
Union as a "superpower," denoting military capabilities roughly equal
to those of the United States. Less often but with increasing frequency, analysts employ the term "global superpower" to convey what
they regard as the more precise image of the Soviet Union as a country with enormous military resources and the power to project those
resources worldwide. Some describe the Soviet Union as the ascendant military power in the world, allegedly because it overtook the
United States with respect to overall military capabilities at some point
toward the end of the last decade. Others note its great strengths but
indicate that Soviet forces suffer from significant shortcomings, that
numbers alone are not an adequate measure of strength, and that
their operational effectiveness may be much less impressive than their
apparent capabilities.

Although important differences separate these Western analysts, all would agree that Kremlin leaders since the end of the Second World War have transformed the Soviet Union from essentially a regional or "continental" military actor to one of the two most powerful countries in the world, complete with global commitments, global responsibilities, and, in the opinion of some, a global appetite. Indeed, more so than at any time in the past, Soviet military forces are now able to perform their four principal and interrelated missions: deterrence against nuclear attack; defense of the homeland against conventional military assaults; protection of the "socialist commonwealth" in Eastern Europe; and the projection of military power, especially into areas contiguous to Soviet borders, such as Southwest Asia.

Capabilities

Much Western anxiety rests upon Soviet military capabilities and an awareness that the East-West balance of power has shifted in the last ten years in ways disadvantageous to the United States and its allies.[1] This, in turn, has led to a kind of amorphous fear regarding Soviet "intentions." For students of the Soviet military, however, the source of anxiety is more specific: for the first time in Soviet history, Kremlin leaders have at their disposal a modern and balanced military force for possible use across the full spectrum of conflict, from intercontinental nuclear war with the United States to limited interventions in the Third World. Moreover, appreciation of this in the Western world has given the Kremlin a degree of political and psychological leverage, which it has used on occasion with considerable skill.

At 3.67 million, Soviet armed forces, the most basic component of the Kremlin's military power, are more numerous than those of any other country except China, which maintains a total of 4.75 million men and women under arms. An additional 560,000 forces—border patrol, internal security, construction and railroad troops—bring the Soviet total to well over 4 million. U.S. armed forces, by contrast, number approximately 2 million.[2]

The Soviets have been able to achieve this modern and balanced military posture through a vigorous and sustained weapons procurement policy, extensive integration of their forces (especially at the theater level), and centralized command and control. With respect to the strategic mission, the Kremlin has created a large force of intercontinental-range, land-based missiles, equipped with highly accurate warheads for "counterforce" missions, as well as a strategic "reserve" of modern ballistic missile submarines and long-range bombers. Soviet strategic defensive programs include both "active" and "passive" measures. These and the preemptive use of the strategic offensive forces are designed to reduce the level of destruction that the USSR would suffer in the event of a nuclear war and enable the country to prevail in such a conflict.

To discharge the theater mission, Soviet strategy calls for the coordinated use of ground, air, and naval forces, utilizing conventional, chemical, and/or nuclear weapons across "theaters of military operations." To implement this strategy in Europe, the Kremlin maintains approximately 500,000 troops in East Germany, Poland, Czechoslovakia, and Hungary (backed by additional divisions in the western military districts of the USSR) and exercises tight control over the armed forces of most of its Warsaw Pact allies through a command structure directly under the Soviet General Staff.[3] Frequent Warsaw Pact field exercises provide Soviet commanders the opportunity to simulate (and evaluate) military operations at the theater level.

Trends in Soviet power projection capabilities suggest a willingness to extend greater protection to clients and friends in the Third World during the 1980s than in the past and to assume additional political and military obligations in distant areas. In this effort, the Soviets can expect to receive important assistance from several principal allies, including Cuba, East Germany, Czechoslovakia, and Vietnam, as they have since the mid-1970s. The Soviet Union's higher profile in the less developed world will enlarge its political and military influence in areas once beyond its reach, thereby underscoring its status as the "other superpower" and diminishing U.S. power and influence in many parts of the world American policy makers deem important. Distinguishing current Soviet military activities in "third areas" from those of previous years is not simply the magnitude of these efforts but also the capability and the will to sustain them over time.

Soviet military capabilities, while impressive, are offset to a degree by a number of persistent problems, several of which deserve special mention. First, much of the Kremlin's more advanced military equipment, such as tactical aircraft, sea-launched ballistic missiles, and ballistic missile submarines, tends to be inferior in quality and performance to the high technology systems produced by the United States. In such critical technologies as weapons miniaturization, very high speed integrated circuitry, and terminal guidance, all of which are essential, for example, to the production of American-type cruise missiles, the Soviets lag behind the United States by as much as 5 to 7 years, depending on the specific technology. There is little evidence to suggest that the Soviets have the capacity to close that gap entirely within the foreseeable future, although they may succeed in pulling abreast of the Americans in certain technologies.[4] In addition, Soviet military equipment, with the notable exception of armored vehicles and artillery, is often less reliable and less capable than comparable U.S. weapons.

Second, not all Soviet forces receive the high level of combat training characteristic of elite Soviet or of American troops more generally. Soviet airmen, for example, on the average fly fewer hours per month and engage in fewer exercises than U.S. pilots. Third, Soviet air force and naval personnel lack extensive combat experience, which calls into question the ability of these forces to discharge their assigned missions in a hostile environment or against enemy forces (such as those of NATO countries) who specialize in air and naval military operations. The Soviets may in particular lack the equipment, bases, and experience to do more than attempt to deny the West control of sea lanes it considers essential. Doubts that Soviet leaders must have about the operational effectiveness of their commanders, troops, and weapons in combat situations constitute an important untested element of Soviet military capabilities. Finally, there is at least some reason to suspect that Soviet armed forces, specifically the army, may be less reliable than commonly assumed in the West.[5]

These shortcomings, all of which could have important implications for the actual performance of the Soviet armed forces, are central when evaluating the Kremlin's military potential.

The strategic rocket forces. Constituted as a separate military service by Nikita Khrushchev in 1959, the strategic rocket forces include all land-based, nuclear ballistic missiles with ranges greater than 1,000 kilometers. The inventory totals nearly 1,400 intercontinental ballistic missiles (ICBMs), deployed across the Soviet Union in reinforced underground silos, and 700 intermediate-range systems (IRBMs), based in the western and central regions of the country and to the north of the Sino-Soviet frontier. Of the 1,400 ICBMs, roughly 750 are the so-called fourth generation systems, the SS17s, SS18s, and SS19s, first deployed in 1975. Most of these are equipped with multiple independently targetable reentry vehicles (or MIRVs) of high accuracy and reliability. The remainder of the ICBM force comprises 640 older, single warhead SS11 and SS13 missiles. At least two new missiles are under development as possible replacements for the SS11; a storable liquid-fuel, medium-sized missile and a "lighter" solid-fuel system which could be deployed in a mobile mode; neither had yet been flight-tested in 1982. The total Soviet inventory of land-based, long-range ballistic missile warheads is approximately 5,500. By comparison, the United States maintains a force of 1,052 ICBMs, of which 550 are MIRVed. American ICBM warheads number approximately 2,150.

In addition to the intercontinental-range missile systems, the

Soviets have deployed roughly 350 launchers for the intermediate-range SS20 missile, targeted against Western Europe and China. The road-mobile SS20, introduced in 1975, is a highly accurate system, equipped with three independently targetable warheads. Each SS20 launcher is also equipped with additional "refire" missiles. The 400 SS4 and SS5 missiles, deployed in the late 1950s and early 1960s, round out the Soviet IRBM force. The Soviets are gradually with-drawing these from service as the SS20s enter the inventory.

The fourth generation of Soviet ICBMs generate special alarm in the United States because of their potential capacity to destroy such "hardened" or protected military targets as ICBM installations through a combination of numbers, accuracy, and yield. The SS20 has the same capability against targets located in Europe and Asia. For example, the Soviets could devote 3,000 to 4,000 SS17, SS18, and SS19 warheads to a "counterforce" strike against U.S. strategic assets, including, most importantly, the 1,052 Minuteman and Titan missiles. By conservative estimates, such an attack could disable 90 percent of the American ICBM force (assuming the U.S. missiles were not launched on warning or under attack). The development of this Soviet option deeply disturbs some Western military and political leaders, because they believe it makes the prospect of a Soviet preemptive strike more likely. As such, they argue, it enhances the Kremlin's ability to "intimidate" or to "coerce" the United States and its allies during times of severe tension or crisis.

The ground forces. The development of Soviet ground forces in the eighteen years since the ouster of Khrushchev has been less evident than that of the strategic rocket forces but no less thorough. The size of the Soviet army, at 1,800,000, has risen modestly since 1964, with the number of combat divisions increasing from 150 to approximately 180. The Soviets maintain slightly fewer than half the divisions at either full or three-quarter combat strength.

The Soviet Union currently deploys 31 divisions in Eastern Europe (a figure unchanged since the 1968 invasion of Czechoslova-kia) under Marshal Viktor Kulikov, commander-in-chief of the United Forces of the Warsaw Pact. All are nearly full strength and equipped with the most modern armaments. Forty-six divisions are stationed in Soviet Asia, including 3 in Mongolia, with a concentration of 27 to 28 divisions in the vicinity of the Manchurian border. Krem-lin forces in Afghanistan now total 6 divisions, and the number of Soviet troops and military advisers deployed abroad exceeds 100,000 (excluding Warsaw Pact forces). The balance of the Soviet army is based in the European and Central Asian military districts of the

USSR. Perhaps one-quarter of these divisions are near combat-ready at any given time.

Soviet ground forces are extremely well armed. The total Soviet inventory of heavy and medium tanks exceeds 50,000, divided between 47 armored and 126 motorized rifle divisions. Approximately 62,000 armored fighting vehicles are deployed with the ground forces, including the BMP and BMD mechanized infantry combat vehicles, able to transport troops in nuclear and chemically contaminated environments. The Soviet army is equipped with more than 20,000 medium to heavy artillery pieces, ranging from 240-mm mortars to 122-mm self-propelled guns. Thirteen hundred nuclear-capable, surface-to-surface missile launchers of short to medium range (10 to 600 miles) are deployed with Soviet ground forces in both the USSR and Eastern Europe. The newest tactical and theater range systems, the SS21, SS22, and SS23, are just now entering production.

In recent years, the Soviets have emphasized the development of an airborne assault capability for the projection of power beyond their borders and to that end have earmarked 7 divisions, along with an appropriate number of aircraft and helicopters from military transport aviation. They used elements of an airborne division to seize critical facilities in and around Kabul in advance of regular Soviet forces during the 1979 invasion of Afghanistan, as they had used such troops in seizing the airport in Prague in 1968.

No simple comparison between Soviet ground forces and the United States Army is possible. Comparisons that focus on such static indicators as troop strength and the number of tanks can be misleading; an evaluation that includes a mix of quantitative and qualitative factors is more useful but beyond the scope of this chapter. The numerical balance (or imbalance) is revealing nonetheless. For example, the size of the Soviet army is more than twice that of the American. The Kremlin produces and deploys at least three times as many tanks, armored fighting vehicles, and artillery pieces as the United States. In addition, the Pentagon must recruit and maintain the U.S. Army by offering financial and other material incentives, placing a heavy burden on limited defense resources. The Soviet army is largely a conscript force. An American enlisted man's salary begins at $700 per month; his Soviet counterpart receives the equivalent of $6 per month.

The air forces. Soviet air forces consist of three elements: frontal aviation, long-range aviation (the assets of which are being transferred to "air armies"), and military transport aviation. Frontal aviation (comparable to the U.S. Tactical Air Force) has primary responsibility for the ground attack, interdiction, and reconnaissance missions at the theater level. In the event of war, its operations would be closely coordinated with those of the ground forces. The Kremlin maintains 16 tactical air armies, 12 within the Soviet Union and 1 with each of the four Groups of Soviet Forces in Eastern Europe.

Frontal aviation controls roughly 4,800 fixed wing aircraft, as well as 2,000 armed helicopters. Within the last ten years, frontal aviation has been transformed from essentially a defensive-postured force to one with significant offensive capabilities for theater warfare, especially in Europe. One-third of Soviet tactical aircraft, including the MiG27 Flogger D, the Su17 Fitter, and the Su24 Fencer, are designed for ground attack and interdiction bombing, an important shift in mission emphasis from the late 1960s. The counter-air (or air superiority) mission is assigned to the 1,300 MiG23 Flogger B aircraft, introduced in the mid-1970s, which are replacing the older and less versatile force of MiG21s. Both the MiG23 Flogger B and the MiG21 Fishbed D have all-weather capabilities.

Long-range aviation, with approximately 800 strike and support aircraft, is responsible for nuclear and conventional bombing strikes against adversaries at intercontinental range (primarily as a "reserve" force) and within the theater. The 150 Tu95 Bear and 45 Mya4 Bison long-range bombers are products of early postwar technology, travel at subsonic speeds, and are vulnerable to interception. No new aircraft of either type has entered the Soviet inventory since the mid-1960s. Some evidence suggests, however, that Soviet leaders may be reassessing the utility of strategic bombers; a new aircraft, codenamed Ram-P, similar in many ways to the U.S. B1, is under development and may be ready for deployment during the second half of this decade. A small tanker force provides a limited in-flight refueling capability.

The Kremlin devotes considerable resources to the maintenance of a large theater-range bomber force. In addition to the 600 Tu16 Badger and Tu22 Blinder aircraft, the Soviets have also assigned 70 Tu22M Backfire bombers to long-range aviation for use primarily against targets in NATO Europe, the Far East, and the Middle East/ Persian Gulf regions. The Backfire, with its large weapons load, high speed, and extended range (about 4,000 miles), represents a qualitative improvement in the Kremlin's ability to deliver nuclear and conventional ordnance to areas deep behind enemy lines, including NATO countries from Norway to Spain, and all of China. Backfire production, which began in 1974, is currently estimated at 30 per year.

Military transport aviation includes 750 short-range An12 Cub,

130 Il76 Candid long-range jet transports, and 50 An22 Cock aircraft. The An22 is the only heavy lift aircraft in the Soviet inventory; its payload is 80 percent of the American C5A. The Il76, though smaller than the An22, has greater range and is of advanced design. The Il76 can lift twice the payload over five times the distance of the An12s they are replacing. Since 1965, the Soviets have more than doubled their total lift capability, although the United States retains more than a two-to-one advantage. Aircraft from military transport aviation played prominent roles in four recent Soviet military operations: the 1973 Middle East conflict; the Angolan Civil War (1974–75); the war between Ethiopia and Somalia (1977–78); and the 1979 invasion of Afghanistan. In the course of the Ethiopian-Somali campaign, it has been estimated that up to 15 percent of the Soviet airtransport fleet—180 planes—flew resupply missions from the USSR to facilities in Ethiopia.

The air defense forces. Since 1948, the Soviet Union has maintained a separate service, the air defense forces (Voyska PVO; formerly PVO Strany) to protect the USSR from all air- and space-borne assaults. In addition to the antiaircraft mission, this includes defense against ballistic missile attack and against whatever weapons may be deployed in space. Voyska PVO are also responsible for operating the country's early warning systems, both ground-based (radars) and exo-atmospheric (satellites).

The Soviets commit roughly 2,500 interceptor aircraft to the air defense mission, of which two-thirds are the latest generation MiG23 Flogger B, MiG25 Foxbat, and Su15 Flagon. They have also deployed over 10,000 low- to high-altitude surface-to-air missiles (SAMs) in 1,200 fixed sites for long-range "strategic" interception, as well as a large complement of mobile SAM launchers for use against tactical and/or theater aircraft. Improvements in both fighter aircraft and SAM installations are continuous; for example, within the next several years, the Soviets are expected to introduce a sophisticated "look down, shoot down" radar for deployment with air defense interceptors to assist in detection and destruction of low-flying enemy aircraft and possibly cruise missiles.

Soviet anti–ballistic missile (ABM) efforts are currently limited in scope and effectiveness, in conformity with the restrictive provisions of the 1972 Anti–Ballistic Missile Treaty. The "Galosh" system, deployed around Moscow, is fully operational with 32 interceptor missile launchers, as well as battle management and missile engagement radars. The Treaty prohibits the deployment of more than 100 launchers, although it permits modernization of the existing facility. The Department of Defense has expressed concern over the scope and intensity of the Soviet ABM research and development program, especially the concentration on more rapidly deployable and transportable launchers and radars which could be used to modernize the Moscow-based "Galosh" installations. The air defense forces have also tested in space a rudimentary antisatellite device, for possible attacks against low-orbiting American reconnaissance and communications satellites. To date, the results of the program have not been impressive. Testing continues, but at a slower pace than in previous years.

Clearly, the Kremlin seeks to limit damage to the Soviet homeland in the event of war, even strategic nuclear war, through the coordinated use of interceptor aircraft, anti–ballistic missiles, antisatellite weapons, and early warning facilities.* American policy makers, who concluded that defense against a determined adversary is not possible in the nuclear age, decided long ago to allocate minimal resources to the air defense mission. There is nothing to indicate that the Soviet leadership finds or will find the U.S. position worthy of emulation; it is more likely, in fact, that the Americans will reexamine their policies in this area.

The navy. Of all the Soviet military services, the navy, under the determined leadership of Admiral of the Fleet (and Commander-in-Chief) S. G. Gorshkov, has undergone the most extensive modernization in the last twenty years. From a glorified coastal patrol force under Stalin and Khrushchev, the navy has become an important vehicle for the worldwide display of Soviet military power and political purpose. The Soviets maintain more large surface combatants than the United States (294 to 201) and more attack submarines (190 to 84). Soviet combat ships are also newer on the average than those of the United States and more heavily armed. Over the last ten years, the rate of Soviet ship construction has been the highest in the world. To this point in time, Soviet naval strategy remains more defensive than offensive in character. However, the Soviets are enhancing their limited capabilities for underway replenishment and gaining access to an increasing number of distant ports, which will improve their ability to project naval power in the 1980s.

In conjunction with the strategic rocket forces and long-range aviation, the Soviet navy has important strategic nuclear responsibilities. Under navy command are 62 modern ballistic missile submarines (SSBNs) of the Yankee and Delta classes (five variants in all), armed with 950 missiles. Roughly half the submarine-launched bal-

---

*I discuss later in this chapter other means available to the Soviets to limit the extent of damage during wartime, such as surprise attack against the offensive forces of the adversary and civil defense measures.

listic missiles (SLBMs) are of the 4,000 mile range and, as of early 1982, approximately 200 are MIRVed. The Soviets have begun sea trials of a new missile-carrying submarine, the 25,000-ton Typhoon (larger than the American Trident), which is to be equipped with 20 extended-range SSN20 missiles. It, too, will be MIRVed, with as many as 12 independently targetable warheads.

The Soviets have the ability to increase significantly the number of warheads deployed on submarine-based missiles through extensive application of MIRV technologies. Soviet SLBM warheads are of a higher average yield than comparable American systems but relatively inaccurate. Moreover, for a number of complex technical reasons, Soviet SLBMs are assumed to be less reliable than their U.S. counterparts. As such, they do not pose the same "counterforce" threat to U.S. land-based missiles as the latest generation Soviet ICBMs. Only about 20 percent of the Soviet SSBN fleet—12 to 13 boats—is on station at any given time, compared to more than half the American force. There are 190 Soviet attack submarines of which 54 are nuclear-powered (SSN). Most are deployed to protect ballistic missile submarines and surface ships from potentially hostile forces, primarily U.S. attack submarines and carrier task forces. The remainder seek to track American ballistic missile submarines on patrol. The extremely fast and deep diving Alpha is the newest class Soviet SSN. One has been deployed and more are anticipated. The Kremlin has also constructed a sizable force of cruise missile submarines, including the new Oscar-class boat, which can fire its 24 long-range antiship cruise missiles while submerged.

The Soviet surface navy is made up largely of guided missile cruisers, destroyers, and frigates, many of which have been commissioned within the last decade. The 23,000-ton nuclear-powered Kirov cruiser, which joined the fleet in 1979, is the largest surface combatant constructed since 1945, excepting aircraft carriers. Since 1975, the Soviets have also commissioned two 40,000-ton Kiev-class carriers, equipped with vertical takeoff and landing (VTOL) aircraft and helicopters; two more are under construction. There are substantiated reports that the Kremlin is building at least one and perhaps several large carriers (60,000 tons), comparable in terms of size to the U.S. Midway-class, which will provide the Soviets their first sea-based platforms for tactical aircraft on the American model. The rate at which new ships join the Soviet navy is likely to remain constant or diminish slightly over the next ten years.

Attached to Soviet naval aviation are 70 Backfire B bombers, based mostly in the area of the Kola peninsula for deployment with the Northern Fleet, and 300 older Tu16 and Tu22 aircraft. The majority are antiship platforms, a role for which the fast and heavily armed Backfire is especially well suited. Antisubmarine warfare operations are carried out by a large force of converted heavy bombers and several hundred helicopters. The utility of Soviet naval aviation against U.S. and allied navies remains limited at this stage, as all the above-mentioned aircraft must operate from air bases in Eastern Europe, European Russia, and the Soviet Far East. This will change within the coming decade, however, as the Soviet Union begins to procure large deck carriers, which will reduce the dependence of the navy on shore-based aircraft.

Civil defense. One of the most interesting and disturbing aspects of the Soviet military effort is the country's civil defense program, headed by a deputy minister of defense, Army General A. T. Altunin, who oversees the expenditure of nearly $2 billion per year (were a comparable effort to be undertaken by the United States) and directs a peacetime force of 115,000.

The purpose of the civil defense program is to reduce the level of Soviet casualties in the event of nuclear war. The effort has two quite separate dimensions and is hierarchical: first, protection of essential cadres; second, provision for the general population. U.S. intelligence estimates that the civil defense program could adequately shelter up to 110,000 key Soviet personnel from the political, military, industrial, and scientific sectors should a nuclear war erupt between the superpowers. Thus, seventy-five command centers have been built in and around Moscow to increase the likelihood Soviet leaders would survive a nuclear attack and to provide them the physical infrastructure from which to direct Soviet wartime operations. Additionally, shelters at important economic installations could accommodate a small percentage of the total work force.

The government has made no significant efforts to shelter the population at large. Instead, Soviet civil defense plans call for evacuation of the country's approximately 100 million urban dwellers to more sparsely populated outlying areas, where they would then construct makeshift shelters and await the outcome of the nuclear exchange. The obvious shortcomings of such a system—its dependence on timely warning, an orderly exodus, pre-positioned food stocks, adequate medical facilities, and rudimentary construction materials, to mention only a few—suggest that Soviet leaders do not believe it possible to hold civilian casualties to 5 to 10 percent of the population, as several Western analysts have claimed. Soviet authorities have never attempted a practice evacuation from any large urban area, nor have they directed the transport of food and medical supplies to so-called host areas. Moreover, Soviet leaders recognize that American nuclear weapons could be retargeted against the evacuated populations within a matter of days, if not hours, should the United States decide to maximize civilian casualties. The evacuation plans may simply reflect a perceived need on the part of the Kremlin to take some action to protect Soviet citizens from the most direct and immediate effects of nuclear weapons, such as blast and intense heat.

The utility of the Soviet civil defense program, therefore, is difficult to assess. It is of obvious importance to the 110,000 preselected Soviet elites, and suggests that Soviet leaders hope, perhaps even believe, the substance of a government would survive to carry on a general war. Its value to the average Soviet citizen is problematic. Its utility is further diminished by the failure of the leadership either to "harden" significantly the country's industrial base against the effects of nuclear weapons or to disperse key installations and facilities.

Paramilitary forces and intelligence services. Two additional kinds of forces, KGB units and special security troops of the Ministry of the Interior (MVD), contribute in important ways to the Soviet military effort. These forces exercise critical control functions both within the USSR, monitoring dissident activities, for example, and along the entire Soviet frontier (preventing unauthorized entry and exit); active duty KGB and MVD border patrol forces number 460,000. In addition to their surveillance and patrol duties, these troops perform vital internal security functions, from guarding forced labor camps (MVD) to protecting nuclear weapons stockpiles and communications facilities (KGB). The Thirteenth Directorate of the KGB is charged with security control of the armed forces and military intelligence (GRU). KGB officers also oversee the political attitudes of the country's militia and the MVD. In wartime, KGB and MVD units would supplement regular Soviet military forces, especially at the outset of hostilities in "forward areas."[6]

The KGB's security and intelligence activities extend far beyond the borders of the Soviet state.[7] KGB units are deployed in every Warsaw Pact member country (except Romania), where they "cooperate" with local security forces and monitor the political and military reliability of the host regime. KGB personnel are also regularly assigned to the Kremlin's diplomatic missions abroad, from which they seek to gather sensitive information through electronic surveillance and human contact, engage in espionage, and occasionally undertake more direct forms of subversion. The number of Soviet "diplomats" who carry out security and intelligence duties in the major Western countries is especially high. It is difficult to overestimate the importance of the KGB in assisting Soviet foreign and military policy objectives because of the range of its activities and the sophistication of its methods.

The Warsaw Pact. Finally, note must be taken of the role of allied forces in Soviet military strategy. Although the Soviet Union has acquired several allies in the Third World, the Warsaw Treaty Organization (WTO) or Warsaw Pact remains the Soviets' most important military alliance. The Warsaw Pact dates from a 1955 agreement signed by the governments of the Soviet Union, Albania, Bulgaria, Czechoslovakia, East Germany, Hungary, Poland, and Romania (Albania withdrew from the alliance in 1968). In addition to its military importance, the Warsaw Pact, along with related economic and political organizations, fulfills important political roles in the maintenance of Soviet hegemony in Eastern Europe, as Andrzej Korbonski explains in chapter 6. Indeed, the Soviets have called upon their allies to help enforce discipline within the bloc, as in the 1968 invasion of Czechoslovakia.

Eastern Europe provides a geographical buffer between the Soviet homeland and Western Europe and extends the Soviet air defense network. Equally important, non-Soviet Warsaw Pact forces contribute significantly to Soviet military strength in Europe. Of the 85 Warsaw Pact divisions in Europe, 54 are non-Soviet. A numerical count alone, however, does not directly measure the combat effectiveness of these forces. The quality of the East European military establishments varies widely from country to country, from the well trained and equipped East German forces to the less capable Czech military.

The reliability of non-Soviet Warsaw Pact forces depends to a large extent on specific scenarios. Soviet doctrine calls for a rapid advance into Western Europe along multiple axes with as little warning time for NATO as possible. This offensive would use combined conventional, chemical, and/or nuclear weapons. To be successful, such a strategy would require active contributions from all the Warsaw Pact military forces and assumes that the non-Soviet Warsaw Pact armies would be reliable and capable of discharging the missions they are assigned by their Soviet commanders. The Soviets have taken certain steps to ensure the loyalty of their allies in a military conflict. Soviet units, for example, would fight alongside and between East European units. Although a lightning offensive by Warsaw Pact forces depends heavily on East European participation, it is also the most likely scenario to ensure their cooperation. It is plausible that the East European armies would remain loyal in an attack against NATO as long as their side prevailed. In this sense, time would work against the Soviets in a military operation because it would give the Western allies a chance to break their momentum and to disrupt Eastern European morale.

In sum, the East European military establishments provide a greater adjunct to Soviet military power than at any time in the past, although the quality of East European troops varies greatly from country to country and their reliability in time of war cannot be predicted with certainty.

The Soviet Defense Budget

The modernization and expansion of Soviet military forces has placed a heavy demand on Soviet economic resources. Precisely how onerous a burden is a matter of some dispute. All Western analysts regard expenditures on defense as officially stated in the budget (17 billion rubles, or 2.8 percent of the Soviet gross national product) as absurdly low and conclude that it includes only the operating and some military construction costs of the armed forces. If expenditures for military R and D, procurement, stockpiling, and all support services are included, as they are in the United States, the cost to Soviet society of the total defense effort is far greater than the official figures indicate.[8]

The Central Intelligence Agency estimates that the Soviet Union spends 12 to 14 percent of its GNP on defense. This remains the most widely quoted and accepted estimate. U.S. intelligence also calculates a 4 percent annual growth rate for Soviet military expenditures for every year since 1970 (adjusted for inflation). Other estimates range as high as 7 to 8 percent per annum.

Whatever the exact level of spending, the evidence is overwhelming that as a percentage of GNP, the Soviet Union (at 12 to 14 percent) consistently spends more on defense than the United States (at approximately 6 percent). From an economic base half the size of the American, the Kremlin maintains at least a quantitative edge in almost all indices of military power, from the number of men under arms to the number of strategic nuclear delivery vehicles.

Command of the Armed Forces

Soviet leaders have established a highly centralized system of military command and control, characterized by an extraordinary degree of coordinated effort between and among the political, military, and economic sectors of society. The extent of this centralization, which reflects Communist emphasis on control, sets the Soviet system apart from all others. From the Kremlin's perspective, the system is necessary because of two related problems: the persistence of a powerful external threat in the form of U.S., allied, and Chinese military power; and the size, complexity, and resource demands of the Soviet armed forces.

U.S. AND SOVIET DEFENSE ACTIVITIES*

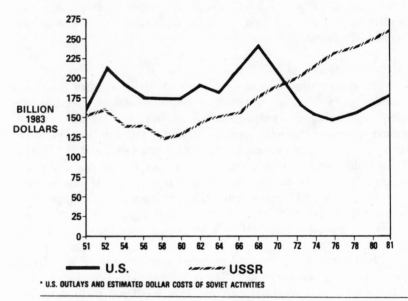

—— U.S.   ⟋⟋⟋ USSR

* U.S. OUTLAYS AND ESTIMATED DOLLAR COSTS OF SOVIET ACTIVITIES

SOURCE: Organization of the Joint Chiefs of Staff, *United States Military Posture for FY 1983* (Washington D.C.: U.S. GPO, 1982), p. 16.

Control and direction of the Soviet military are the explicit responsibility of three institutions which together comprise the high command: the Politburo, the Defense Council, and the General Staff. Subordinate to the high command are the five combat services, the Warsaw Pact and Far Eastern military commands, the four Groups of Soviet Forces in Eastern Europe, the country's 16 military districts, and all departments, bureaus, and special agencies of the Ministry of Defense. Because of the priority the government gives the military forces and the military's demand for goods and services, the high command also plays a direct role in the allocation of resources, determination of economic priorities, and formulation of the Five-Year economic plans.

In theory, ultimate authority in military matters rests with the party Politburo. In actuality, the Defense Council, a subgroup of the Politburo, determines military policy and commands the armed forces. The Defense Council, whose existence the Kremlin acknowledged only in 1976, is presumably chaired by Yuri Andropov in his capacity as general secretary of the Communist party. The Council's permanent members after the death of Brezhnev in 1982 probably include Prime Minister N. A. Tikhonov, Defense Minister D. F. Us-

tinov, Chief of the General Staff N. V. Ogarkov, and Chairman of the
State Planning Commission (Gosplan) N. K. Baibakov. It is the highest source of authority on "Soviet military doctrine," which one Western analyst has described as the intellectual and policy framework
which informs war planning and guides force acquisition.[9] The Defense Council makes most important military policy decisions, such as
the size of the armed forces, the development and deployment of
weapon systems, and the determination of the defense budget. Participation of the prime minister and the chairman of Gosplan suggests
that the Council may also play a role in Soviet economic planning; for
example, it may have the authority to review and revise the assignment of resources to Group A (Heavy Industry) and Group B (Consumer Goods) industries. Finally, it monitors plans for economic
mobilization in the event of war.

The largest and most professionally competent institution of the
Soviet high command is the General Staff, under the direction of
General Ogarkov. According to U.S. government sources, the General Staff functions as the executive arm of the Defense Council,
coordinating the activities of the five services, the Groups of Soviet
Forces, the Rear Services, and Civil Defense. Unlike the U.S. Joint
Chiefs of Staff, General Ogarkov and his deputies enjoy considerable
administrative as well as operational control over most Soviet armed
forces.

In addition to its command authority, the General Staff is responsible for the development and formulation of Soviet "military
science," defined as "the system of knowledge concerning the nature,
essence and content of armed conflict. . . ."[10] Officers assigned to the
General Staff also study "military art," the principal component of
military science, under whose heading fall such recognizable terms as
military strategy, operations, and tactics. In short, the General Staff
has the duty to define and then to provide, in an operational sense,
the means to achieve in war the political-military objectives outlined
by the Politburo and the Defense Council.

The General Staff's Military Science Directorate oversees the development of military strategy. For example, it played an important
part in the decade-long debate (1954–64) within the military on the
significance of nuclear weapons in war, and it has published the most
important statements concerning strategy. It also produces the
classified monthly journal, *Military Thought,* a vehicle for the country's
military theorists to present new and sometimes controversial ideas
for discussion and peer review.

Responsible to the General Staff are the eight commanders-in-
chief of the Soviet armed forces: the chiefs of the five Soviet combat
services and the commanders-in-chief of the Warsaw Pact, the Group

of Soviet Forces in Germany, and Soviet forces in the East. None of
the eight, however, is assigned directly to the General Staff, given
their extensive functional and operational responsibilities.

Administratively, the Soviet military is divided into 20 geographic commands: 16 military districts and the four Groups of
Soviet Forces in Eastern Europe (Germany, Poland, Czechoslovakia
and Hungary). Each military district is under the effective command
of a single senior officer, a ground forces general, who also controls
regionally deployed units of frontal aviation, but not local elements of
the air defense and strategic rocket forces, which report directly to
their respective service chiefs. Soviet authorities believe that the infrastructure of the military district facilitates rapid mobilization of both
human and material resources and ensures a high degree of combat
readiness. The Groups of Soviet Forces are organized along similar
lines, with the exception that the GSF commanders report directly to
the General Staff.

During wartime, what the Soviets term "theaters of military operations" or TVDs would eclipse the military districts in importance.
The Soviets have divided the world into 13 TVDs, of which 5 would
be along the borders of the USSR: Northwestern, Western, and
Southwestern Europe, Central Asia, and the Far East (in addition to 4
intercontinental and 4 maritime TVDs). Forces deployed in each military district would be subsumed within the appropriate TVD, as the
General Staff decides. The High Command would also appoint a
theater commander-in-chief, who would be granted extensive authority to direct military operations throughout the region and within its
"strategic sectors." Only within the last several years have senior
Soviet military theorists begun to discuss the TVD concept, and public
discussions have been cursory, at best. As a result, Western analysts
have only begun to understand the precise meaning of the term and
its full implications.

The designation of Generals M. M. Zaytsev (GSF Germany) and
V. L. Govorov (Soviet Far East) as commanders-in-chief indicates that
Soviet leaders anticipate the need for large theater commands in both
regions at the outset of hostilities with NATO countries and/or
China. The lack of a comparable command structure for Soviet forces
deployed in Central Asia and in Southwestern and Northwestern
Europe suggests that the Kremlin regards conflict in these three areas
as both less probable and likely less intense than in the center of
Europe and along the Chinese frontier.

Future Development of Soviet Military Power
Within whatever economic and budgetary constraints may exist
during the 1980s—and they are likely to be considerable—and with or

without arms limitation agreements, the Soviet leadership will almost certainly continue to expand its military forces and to improve their performance characteristics, with particular reference to strategic capabilities and forces for the projection of power. The reasons for this are numerous and compelling. Reducing military forces even in open societies where large numbers seek this goal is difficult. Even the most wise and sensitive policies on the part of the United States, China, and other powers and the most benign developments in international relations throughout the world during the 1980s would not be likely to reduce tensions sufficiently that the Soviet rulers, whoever they may be, could feel secure with reduced armaments. In addition, the Soviet Union faces a difficult territorial problem because of its size and location, particularly as it now faces hostile Communist states on its periphery. The fear that the United States will again widen the technological imbalance enlivens a pervasive historical concern for security, even survival. Soviet pathological fear of China will remain strong, even should Soviet-Chinese relations become cordial, and will escalate irrationally if the Chinese should attain a rapid rate of economic growth and develop increasingly close ties with Japan and/or the United States. Russian and Soviet history, the role Soviet military forces have played in making the Soviet Union such a respected power, and the Soviet political system add to these barriers.

With regard to strategic capabilities, by the middle of this decade the Kremlin will no doubt deploy a replacement system for the aging SS11 ICBM, most probably a "medium" weight missile, armed with a single warhead and deployed in a mobile mode. By the end of the 1980s, a larger, multiple warhead system could begin to replace the 150 SS17 missiles. Should the Kremlin decide to exceed the warhead "fractionation" (or MIRV) limits contained in the SALT II Treaty, the total number of Soviet ICBM warheads could double within five to seven years, from approximately 5,500 to over 10,000. The accuracy and reliability of Soviet strategic weapons, both land- and sea-based, will continue to improve. Toward the end of this decade, the Soviets may also begin to produce advanced air-, sea-, and ground-launched cruise missiles, comparable in terms of sophistication to the current generation of American systems, for possible use in both strategic and theater missions. It is extremely unlikely, however, that the Kremlin will be able to match, much less surpass, U.S. achievements in this critical area of weaponry before the mid-1990s at the earliest, given the extent of the American technological lead. In addition, the leadership will accelerate the development of antisatellite capabilities for use against American space-based communications and early warning facilities, with the objective of reducing the U.S. capacity to detect and to respond to a nuclear attack. It will maintain Moscow's ABM and ballistic missile defense efforts, both as a hedge against American technological breakthroughs and to enable rapid expansion of the existing network should either side abrogate the 1972 ABM Treaty. It appears that the Soviets will continue to emphasize nuclear and conventional means of ballistic missile interception, although the development of more exotic techniques (such as directed energy weapons) is feasible.

The Soviet Union will also attempt to enhance its ability to intervene quickly in regional crises at such a level as to deter Western, especially American, military action. This suggests special Soviet attention to airborne and perhaps amphibious assault forces, through the procurement of additional military transport aircraft and naval assault vessels. It could also enlarge its naval infantry, the Kremlin's equivalent of the U.S. Marine Corps, from its current strength of 12,000. As noted, Moscow will enhance its sea-based tactical airpower during the 1980s by construction of at least several large-deck aircraft carriers.

The direction of Soviet theater military developments is more difficult to anticipate. Presumably the Soviets will continue to focus on the development of more capable tactical aircraft, especially for the ground attack and close air support missions, on improvements in theater nuclear forces, and on better antiarmor capabilities. A new Soviet tank, the T80 (essentially an advanced version of the T72), is expected to enter serial production within the next several years.

Given the projected decline of the service-age population, however, Soviet leaders may find it necessary to reduce the size of the army at some point during this decade. Should they take such a decision, they will attempt to maintain the military's combat readiness through introducing new and more capable weapons systems. However, such a substitution of technology for people is expensive, as American experience has demonstrated, and would place additional strains on an already overburdened economy. Nonetheless, demographic realities and the Soviet government's determination to increase its military power could dictate this action, despite the cost. Alternatively, Soviet authorities could sanction a gradual reduction in army manpower over a number of years without undertaking extensive new investments in weaponry. The state of the economy and Soviet perceptions of the future international political environment will heavily influence this decision.

The Military in the Soviet System

Any treatment of the Soviet military must analyze the position of the armed forces in the system of which they are a part. The purpose of this section is to investigate how the military, as an institution, connects to the Soviet system at three critical junctures: its relationship to the political structure, its effect on the economy, and its social or sociopolitical role. All three sets of relationships have obvious implications for the ability of the armed forces to discharge their principal mission, to defend the country against potential adversaries. This discussion also suggests under what conditions and in what directions the existing pattern of relations might evolve during the remainder of this decade.

Party-Military Relations

The enormous weight of the military within Soviet society has led to considerable debate in the West about the ability of the country's political leaders to exercise effective control over their subordinates in the armed forces. For the most part, the conclusions of those who study Soviet civil-military relations are remarkably similar: the military has never seriously challenged the party's "leading role," its capacity to dictate policy on all important issues and at all levels, nor is there reason to suspect that such a challenge will occur. The reasons for party hegemony are several: party policy, Russian and Soviet traditions, institutional features of the system, the organizational and managerial skills of the party, and the compatibility of political and military interests.

The tradition of civilian control over the military predates the October Revolution. William Odom, for example, has described the tsarist armies as "executants" rather than initiators of policy.[11] Throughout its history, the Soviet military has fulfilled essentially the same function, under vigilant party supervision. The principal Bolshevik innovation was to formalize and extend tsarist practice through the introduction of political commissars it attached to military units, from the company to the divisional level, from the outset of the new regime. With certain modifications and adjustments, Soviet authorities have retained that system.

Political stewardship of the armed forces is the direct responsibility of the Main Political Administration (MPA), whose chief since 1962, General A. A. Yepishev, ranks fourth in the Soviet military hierarchy, behind the defense minister and the three first deputy ministers. Yepishev and his deputies occupy unique positions within the Soviet military establishment, as they are directly accountable to both the party Central Committee, to whom they owe their appointments, and to the Defense Ministry. The MPA's dual allegiance may be more apparent than real, however. While the political nature of the MPA's role within the military requires that it maintain a direct connection to the Central Committee apparatus, its intimate involvement in the ministry's daily affairs demands close and continuous interaction with senior military officials. A number of Western analysts contend, in fact, that the relationship between the MPA and the Defense Ministry, despite the potential for conflict, is essentially cooperative and supportive in nature rather than antagonistic.

The two major functions of the MPA are to provide ideological guidance and instruction to the armed forces and to ensure the military's loyalty to the regime. To discharge its second responsibility, political oversight, the MPA has created a command structure which essentially parallels that of the regular military. MPA officers serve in all five services and in every principal command. Officers of the Main Political Administration receive the same training, commissions, and privileges as their colleagues in the army, the air forces, and the navy. This system affords the MPA a degree of institutionalized access to all levels of the Soviet military hierarchy which the party regards as indispensable to maintenance of its preeminent position within society. The MPA's educational responsibilities are straightforward. Political officers teach compulsory courses in Marxism-Leninism to all military personnel, commissioned officers as well as enlisted men and women, and control the development and content of curricular materials for use throughout the military's educational system.

In contrast to the Stalinist period, the contemporary MPA seems to operate within comparatively narrow jurisdictional parameters laid out by the party in consultation with the armed forces. The relatively limited power of today's MPA may explain the generally cooperative tenor of its relationship with the military. It is unlikely, for example, that the MPA interferes directly in military decision making of an operational or expert character, although it exercises important powers in such personnel-related matters as promotions and assignments.

A second mechanism through which the Soviet party exercises control over the armed forces is military membership in the Communist party and the Young Communist League (Komsomol). Eighty percent of enlisted personnel and an even higher percentage of commissioned officers belong to one or both organizations. Party units function at the regimental level, Komsomol groups within companies. The party formally empowers the MPA to direct all party work within the armed forces, although the Central Committee and the Secretariat maintain several independent channels for supervision and development of party military relations. The fact that virtually all Soviet officers above the rank of lieutenant are either candidate or full members of the CPSU suggests the nature of the relationship. This reflects the reality that membership in the CPSU is a requirement for career advancement in the services and an explicit recognition of the party's supremacy.

To enhance its capacity to oversee the activities and ensure the loyalty of the military bureaucracy, the party also promotes within rather rigid limits participation of selected members of the armed forces in governmental and political affairs. Defense Minister Ustinov, for example, is a voting member of the Politburo, as was his predecessor, Marshal Andrei Grechko, a career military officer. Ustinov and his senior deputies from the ministry are also full members of the Central Committee. The number of uniformed military personnel elected to the Central Committee has remained relatively constant over the last twenty-five years (about thirty), although as a percentage of the total membership, its representation has declined from a high of 9 percent in 1961 to 7 percent in 1981. However, the most striking feature of the military's formal role within party and government institutions is its peripheral character. At all key levels of the national political apparatus, the Politburo, the Central Committee, the party Secretariat and the Council of Ministers, the professional Soviet military is either underrepresented or denied all but cosmetic access to principal decision makers.

Much early Western scholarship on Soviet civil-military relations focused on the roles of such institutions as the MPA and the Central Committee in explaining the party's predominant position. These and other organizations, it was alleged, maintained effective control over the military bureaucracy through coercion, both actual and implied. The relationship between party officials and military commanders was believed tense, characterized by frequent and profound conflict and pervasive mutual distrust.[12]

More recent work has revised this assessment, suggesting that the apolitical character of the Soviet military is less a function of coercion than of cooption. In addition, this research indicates that the party and the military leaders are in fundamental agreement on the nature of the system and on Soviet policies, more generally, and share a number of critical sociopolitical values, such as the utility of compulsory military service, the importance of nationwide defense preparedness and the need for public discipline and social regimentation.

In addition to the party's conscious attempt to inculcate a system of popular values which the military endorses and supports, the Politburo's routine allocation of 12 to 14 percent of the country's GNP to defense purposes also helps ensure the political passivity of the armed forces. The determination of the Soviet military budget reflects carefully calibrated judgments about the nature of the external threat and the forces required to defend against it. Nonetheless, the party cannot be insensitive to the fact that providing the military bureaucracy with ample resources helps retain its confidence and goodwill. The political leadership understands, in other words, the importance of satisfying the material requirements as well as the social and psychological needs of those within society pledged to defend it.

Relations between party and military authority in the Soviet Union are multidimensional. Doubtless conflicts, both personal and institutional, do arise. The critical point to bear in mind, however, is that the competition takes place among party members and within limits set by the party, which defines the rules, monitors compliance, adjudicates differences, and enforces outcomes. No evidence indicates that the military has ever challenged the authority of the political leadership to direct the affairs of state or that the military, as an institution, has ever taken a position opposed to that of the party on any critical policy issue. The existing pattern of relations seems destined to continue, at least throughout the course of this decade, barring a sudden and dramatic shift in policy, such as a leadership decision to reduce significantly the allocation of resources to the defense sector.[13]

The Military and the Economy

The Politburo, of course, determines Soviet economic policy, including the level of defense spending. Economic management, on the other hand, is the responsibility of government ministries and ultimately of the Council of Ministers. The government's Military-Industrial Commission coordinates the activities of the Defense Industry Ministry with those of the eight other ministries directly involved in the manufacture of defense-related equipment. The Central Committee's Defense Industry Department ensures compliance with party directives and monitors both the quality and output of the production ministries. The Defense Ministry and the General Staff outline the military requirements of the services and specify weapons characteristics and capabilities. They, along with the Defense Industry Department, also exercise critical supervisory functions at the production stage, with special authority in the areas of quality control and testing.

The most distinct features of the Soviet defense sector are its priority claim to national economic resources and the caliber of its managerial, technical, and skilled personnel, both of which presumably make that sector more rational and efficient than other parts of the Soviet economy. The magnitude of Soviet defense production has demanded of the political leadership an unambiguous decision to commit the requisite material and human resources over the long term. Without question the party has made that commitment: the economy gives the highest priority to the efficient production of large numbers of military goods. The benefits of such favored status and higher standards are apparent and concrete: high-quality equipment, consistency of effort, a willingness to innovate, and a well-motivated and well-compensated work force. The consequences for the other sectors of the economy are adverse, however. Nondefense enterprises receive those resources, goods, and services for which the defense industries have no use. As a result, the craftmanship of consumer items is usually shabby, production inefficient, and the rate of output uneven.

A number of U.S. analysts allege that the Defense Ministry's "penetration" of the economy is virtually complete, that the entire system of production has been mobilized and that the country has been placed on what amounts to a "war footing." Others disagree, citing the relatively gradual growth of Soviet military capabilities and the regime's identification of and support for other, nonmilitary economic priorities. All are in accord, however, that the defense sector enjoys a privileged status within the system, relative to the other sectors. The size of the Soviet military and the quantity and sophistication of its equipment and weaponry have placed and will continue to place severe demands on the country's economic infrastructure. Millions are engaged in production; thousands more manage the effort. Both the party and state bureaucracies assign significant numbers of officials to oversee the performance of the relevant ministries and bureaus.

The most accurate image of the Soviet economy is that of two parallel systems, military and civilian, connected at certain key junctures, but essentially separate in form and function. Moreover, little indicates that Soviet authorities have sought or are seeking to reform the structure in the direction of greater integration. They are unwilling, it seems, to run the risk that extensive penetration of the military industries by their "civilian" counterparts might compromise the standards and performance of the defense sector; for this reason, the latter's "privileged" status within the economy seems assured for the foreseeable future.

From the perspective of Soviet decision makers, the economy performs well enough to satisfy one of the regime's most important objectives: the steady development of the country's military capabilities. According to David Holloway, the Soviet economic system, despite its obvious and serious shortcomings, ". . . remains a relatively effective mechanism for extracting resources from the economy and directing them to goals set by the political leaders and one of the most important of these goals has been the creation of military power."[14]

The Military and Society

In addition to the military's relationship to the political structure and its impact on the economy, Soviet armed forces also fulfill a number of crucial social functions. They provide a convenient if not irreplaceable mechanism for the inculcation of important national and patriotic values, helping to foster identification with and loyalty to the regime. At least in theory, the military is a "Soviet" rather than a Russian (or a Lithuanian or a Kirgiz) institution, in which the individual national identities of the conscripts assume secondary importance. Thus, the armed forces play a critical and necessary integrative function, bringing together for a time the highly heterogeneous populations of the multinational Soviet state. No other institution within the system fulfills this role to the same degree.

The reality, however, falls considerably short of the ideal. Perhaps the most serious social problem within the armed forces is the persistence of strong racial, ethnic, and religious tensions, both among enlisted personnel and between the officer corps (which is overwhelmingly Slavic) and the non-Russian soldiers who make up an increasing proportion of total military manpower. The problem seems certain to become more acute over time, as the share of non-Slavic groups in the draft-age cohort rises all through the 1980s.

This shift in the racial and ethnic composition of the armed forces raises important questions about the reliability of the army under certain conditions, such as possible combat operations against neighboring Moslem and Asian countries or the use of military force to suppress ethnic-based domestic unrest. As the authors of a recent Rand Corporation study on this subject note, "We can envisage combat-related scenarios in which ethnic or racial riots, minority conflicts with local populations or even military mutiny based on ethnic grievances could become real possibilities."[15]

To compound the problem, non-Slav recruits tend to be less educated than their Russian colleagues and to enter military service with fewer technical and/or professional skills. Moreover, many Moslem and Central Asian conscripts either cannot speak Russian or are barely fluent in it, posing potentially serious difficulties of communication and command. It seems reasonable to assume that these educational and linguistic deficiencies will continue to have negative implications for the effectiveness of Soviet armed forces.

It is difficult to know how extensive or profound these problems are or will become or the extent to which they might undermine the leadership's confidence in the loyalty of the armed forces. On balance, it appears that Soviet authorities do not consider the problem unmanageable. The government routinely assigns non-Slavic military personnel to areas within the Soviet Union far from their ethnic homelands. It details Moslem and Central Asian soldiers to support and nonessential operations to the fullest extent possible. These and other solutions provide short-term answers to what promises to become an issue of much greater salience to the leadership in the coming decades, as the number of national "minorities" serving in the Soviet military continues to increase and as the rate of Russian entry declines.[16] In response to this problem, the armed forces could intensify remedial efforts, such as special language and technical training programs for non-Slavs. They could also implement more radical measures, including the imposition of ethnic quotas or a policy of selective induction, but probably not without a modest reduction in military manpower, a step the regime may, or may not, be prepared to entertain.

The Development of Soviet Doctrine and Military Capabilities: 1953–82

In the attempt to understand the connection in Soviet thinking between military capabilities and how and under what conditions those forces would be put to use in the event of war, Western observers have studied the Kremlin's extensive pronouncements on military doctrine and, to a lesser extent, military science. Most of these analyses reflect careful reading of the same source materials, but in many cases the conclusions differ significantly.

Some experts argue, for example, that contemporary Soviet doctrine is essentially a blueprint for military "victory" over the United States and the West, to be achieved through a combination of crippling offensive nuclear strikes against U.S. and allied military installations and passive and active defensive measures to limit damage to the Soviet homeland. Others contend that Soviet leaders recognize the futility of such a "war-winning" strategy in light of the manifest ability of the United States to absorb such a preemptive strike against its nuclear retaliatory forces and to respond with devastating counterblows against Soviet military, industrial, and urban targets. These analysts assert that Soviet views on nuclear war approximate traditional Western thinking on the subject, which tends to dismiss the idea of victory as absurd. They acknowledge, however, that Soviet and American planners define their strategic military requirements in different ways, which has not only produced dissimilar forces, but also given rise to considerable anxiety in the West over Soviet military "intentions."[17]

In fact, the evidence is ambiguous. It is impossible to resolve the dispute by reference to what Soviet authorities have said and written on the subject of war in the nuclear age. To illustrate the problem, senior party leaders since the mid-1970s have repeatedly dismissed the notion of victory in nuclear war as an illusion, a dangerous fantasy of the West, while representatives of the military high command emphasize the premium of a well-orchestrated surprise attack against the "nuclear means" of the adversary, in order to destroy his military capacity and thus defeat him at the very outset of conflict.

By strict definition, it is not the purpose of Soviet military doctrine to set the mission requirements of the armed forces. As defined in 1975 by the late Soviet minister of defense, Andrei Grechko, military doctrine "is a system of views on the nature of war and methods of waging it, and on the preparation of the country and army for war, officially adopted in a given state and its armed forces."[18] Once the architects of doctrine have established both the probable character of a future world war and the types of weapons likely to dominate its conduct, military science has the responsibility to determine how best to achieve the designated political-military objectives. Therefore, the interaction between military doctrine and the "science of war" is of critical importance in assessing Soviet intentions.

It is a central premise of this chapter that senior Soviet leaders, political as well as military, have sought to develop a strategic military posture that would allow the USSR to prevail over the United States in the event of a general nuclear war, in conformity with doctrinal precepts first formulated in the mid to late 1950s. This analysis traces the evolution of Soviet military doctrine and development of the country's military capabilities over a thirty-year period, from the death of Stalin in 1953 to the present.

The Revolution in Doctrine, 1953–59

Within months of Stalin's death in March 1953, Soviet military theorists began a comprehensive review of military doctrine, largely unchanged since the conclusion of the Second World War. At issue was the continuing validity of Stalin's "five permanently operating principles" of modern war, defined as the stability of the rear; the morale of the army; the quantity and quality of divisions; the level of armaments; and the organizing ability of the military commanders.

In the opinion of some prominent military theorists, including General N. A. Talensky, editor of the General Staff's *Military Thought*, the introduction of nuclear weapons constituted a virtual revolution in the art and science of war, in effect rendering Stalin's five precepts obsolete. Publication of Talensky's views in late 1953 provoked an intense and acrimonious debate within Soviet military circles, which eventually led to the general's dismissal as editor of the journal. Conservative factions within the armed forces, especially disgruntled ground forces commanders, sought to reaffirm the primacy of the Red Army and to defend the need for large conventional forces-in-being in the wake of Talensky's removal.

Several of Stalin's would-be successors seized on Talensky's critique to distinguish themselves from their political rivals and to garner the support of elements within the military who sought change.

Prime Minister Georgi Malenkov, for example, declared in August 1954 that nuclear war between the Soviet Union and the United States would be an unparalleled disaster for mankind that could spell the end of civilization. Malenkov's pronouncements proved too "defeatist" for many of his more orthodox colleagues on the Politburo and contributed to his downfall six months later. Party Secretary Khrushchev led the attack against Malenkov, citing the incompatibility of Malenkov's views on nuclear war with the tenets of Marxism-Leninism, which held that in the inevitable global military confrontation between the world's two leading social systems, socialism would emerge victorious over capitalism.

One year after the removal of Malenkov, at the Twentieth CPSU Congress in February 1956, Khrushchev essentially renounced his earlier position on the relationship between nuclear weapons and Marxist-Leninist ideology by calling for a vigorous reexamination of military science. Khrushchev went on to imply the revolutionary nature of nuclear weaponry when he declared that a future world war was no longer "fatalistically inevitable" but could be postponed indefinitely through adequate defense preparedness by the socialist countries. Khrushchev's formulation, with its accent on the "positive" value of nuclear weapons as a deterrent to war, differed from the earlier statement of Malenkov, but only in degree; both recognized the implications of a U.S.-Soviet military relationship based on the reciprocal ability to inflict intolerable levels of death and destruction on the adversary.

In May 1957, a conference convened by the General Staff and restricted to senior officers of the armed forces began a comprehensive review of military strategy. In 1958, a series of seminars followed the conference to consider, in operational terms, the implications of a major interstate or intersystemic conflict conducted largely with nuclear weapons. By the end of the year Soviet military theorists had reached a consensus that the development of fission and especially fusion devices, along with the advent of long-range ballistic missiles as their primary means of delivery, had altered fundamentally the nature of modern war. This, in turn, required thorough and immediate revision of doctrine and strategy. In accordance with this conclusion, Khrushchev authorized the creation in 1959 of strategic rocket forces, a new and separate military command for the intercontinental (and theater) delivery of ballistic missiles. Reflecting an important shift in emphasis, authoritative Soviet sources began to describe strategic rocket forces as the "leading branch" of the armed forces, in effect displacing the ground forces command from its traditional dominant position in the military.

By 1960, the first phase of the debate over a new military doctrine had come to an end, with the elements seeking change scoring an impressive victory. As Khrushchev revealed in a January 1960 speech to the Supreme Soviet, the substance of which other high-ranking political and military leaders of the time reiterated, seven central precepts characterized the revised doctrine: first, a new world war, while likely, was no longer inevitable; second, if world war should occur, it would "inevitably" take the form of a nuclear rocket war, "that is, the kind of war in which the main means of striking will be nuclear weapons and the basic means of delivering it to the target will be the rocket"; third, the use of strategic nuclear weapons will produce "decisive military results" in the opening phase of the conflict; fourth, Soviet nuclear forces must have the capacity to "repulse an enemy surprise attack" and "to frustrate his criminal plans," presumably by preemptive strikes; fifth, war involving the Soviet Union and the United States will "inevitably" escalate to general nuclear war; sixth, while the initial phase of the conflict may prove decisive, final victory can be secured only through joint actions of all military services;* and seventh, while a world nuclear war will result in extensive physical destruction and massive civilian casualties, socialism's superior political, social, and economic system will ensure its eventual triumph over capitalism.[19]

The new doctrine left unresolved a number of important issues. For example, Soviet theorists seemed uncertain about the truly "decisive" character of nuclear weapons in war and left open the possibility that conventional military power would be required to guarantee a favorable outcome after the initial nuclear exchange. They reserved judgment whether a global conflict would be a relatively brief engagement or a protracted struggle, and they failed to articulate precisely how the Soviet Union could ensure victory in the aftermath of a nuclear holocaust. In some cases, Soviet analysts did not address these and other troublesome questions until the mid- to late 1970s, following maturation of the country's strategic capabilities. It is striking, nonetheless, that with several important modifications the essentials of Soviet military doctrine formulated under Khrushchev have remained unchanged since their promulgation in the early 1960s.

Changes in Force Structure, 1960–64

As early as 1956–57, changes in military doctrine began to affect the character and composition of Soviet military forces. Deployment of first generation medium-range ballistic missiles, targeted against

---

*This caveat to the revised doctrine probably reflected a compromise between the Khrushchev-led faction and more traditional elements within the Soviet military establishment. It also suggested a Soviet conviction that large conventional forces would be required to exploit the initial military gains obtained through the use of nuclear weapons, especially in the European theater.

Western Europe, began in the months preceding the October-November 1956 crises in Hungary and the Middle East. The launch of Sputnik I in October 1957 signaled attainment of a long-range missile capability, provoking widespread anxiety in the United States. In retrospect, the alarm proved somewhat premature, as the Soviets never deployed more than a handful of these crude systems, preferring to concentrate upon development of a less vulnerable and more reliable "second generation" of missiles.

It was only after Khrushchev's address to the Supreme Soviet in January 1960, however, that Soviet planners began in a consistent way to restructure the armed forces in line with revisions in doctrine. In that speech, Khrushchev underscored the primacy of nuclear-armed ballistic missiles as the foundation of Soviet military power and claimed that the Kremlin's lead over the West in ICBM technology was both real and destined to continue. He argued that development of Soviet nuclear weapons capabilities effectively deterred imperialist aggression; at the same time, he promised to use Moscow's nuclear arsenal should the United States and its allies seem poised to unleash a new world war. Khrushchev announced that Moscow's spectacular achievements in ballistic missile technology (both theater and long-range) enabled a one-third reduction in the size of the Soviet army, to be implemented over the following several years.

Khrushchev's ambitious plans to reconstitute Soviet armed forces, outlined in 1960 and again at the Twenty-first CPSU Congress in 1961, were never realized in their entirety. The poor performance of the economy, resistance from within the military, and the general "deterioration" of the international political environment made extensive reform difficult and prevented the kind of shift in resources to the strategic rocket forces that the first secretary had anticipated. The large-scale reduction in Soviet army strength did not occur, although the Kremlin did curtail expenditures for the air forces, PVO Strany, and the navy to provide additional funding for the ballistic missile and nuclear weapons programs. As a result, by the time of the Cuban missile crisis in October 1962, Soviet intercontinental nuclear capabilities were inferior to those of the United States and only marginally better than they had been in the late 1950s.[20] That Khrushchev was aware of the true nature of the strategic balance in 1962 is beyond doubt; the installation of Soviet intermediate-range missiles in Cuba was, in part, designed to provide nuclear equality with the United States. The failure of the Cuban adventure demolished Khrushchev's claim to military superiority over the West and contributed directly to his ouster in October 1964.

Throughout the early 1960s, a discontinuity existed between the military doctrine to which the Soviet Union allegedly subscribed and

the forces-in-being necessary to implement it, a problem the country's
senior political leadership understood. On the one hand, the evolution and refinement of doctrine continued under the auspices of the
General Staff. In 1962, the first edition of *Military Strategy*, a lengthy
study prepared by the prominent military theoretician Marshal V. D.
Sokolovsky and several of his colleagues appeared. The analysis discussed in considerable detail both the development of doctrine in the
postwar period and the profound changes in Soviet military art and
science the advent of nuclear weapons had caused. Most of Sokolovsky's conclusions faithfully reflected the convictions of Khrushchev
and the military "modernists"; a second edition, released shortly after
the Cuban missile crisis, struck a more cautious note, endorsing a
number of precepts long associated with the "traditionalist" wing of
the armed forces, such as the continuing importance of the ground
forces and the overarching need for a diversified and well-balanced
military posture.[21]

On the other hand, Soviet long-range missile deployments, made
up almost exclusively of the highly vulnerable SS7 and SS8 ICBMs,
numbered perhaps 200 in 1964 and, from the Kremlin's standpoint,
must have seemed barely adequate for purposes of minimum deterrence. Most of these systems could be destroyed by a determined
American preemptive attack, at least in theory, severely limiting the
Kremlin's ability to deliver "crushing nuclear strikes" against "groupings of the enemy's armed forces, industrial and vital centers [and]
communications junctions," as Defense Minister R. Y. Malinovsky
stipulated in 1961.[22] In addition, Soviet leaders had decided not to
build a large force of intercontinental bombers on the American
model to compensate for the slow rate of ICBM production. At the
time of Khrushchev's fall, the total inventory of Tu95 Bear and Mya4
Bison bombers probably did not exceed 150. The first Soviet ballistic
missile submarines, the Hotel-class SSBN, armed with several 600-
mile-range SSN5 systems, did not enter service until late 1964, by
which time the United States had commissioned over 26 Polaris boats,
each equipped with 16 SLBMs. It now appears that as late as 1965, the
United States enjoyed as much as a 4 to 1 advantage over the Soviet
Union in numbers of intercontinental-range nuclear delivery vehicles, including ICBMs, SLBMs, and bombers. The American lead in
strategic nuclear weapons (bombs and warheads) was even greater.

In an irony that could not have escaped Soviet military planners,
ten years after the first doctrinal stirrings, the Kremlin's basic ability
to deter general war with the United States continued to reside in its
capacity to destroy Western Europe, albeit with nuclear weapons. In
reality, since the mid-1950s the mere possibility that a fraction of the
Soviet ICBM and long-range bomber force might survive a first strike

had been sufficient to forestall any American resort to nuclear weapons against the USSR, except in retaliation to direct attack against the United States or its principal allies. From the Soviet perspective, however, a surprise American attack must have seemed at times more than an abstract possibility. Whatever the reality, the obvious inability of Soviet strategic forces to accomplish many of the military missions Marshal Sokolovsky and others of the General Staff deemed essential, as well as the failure of Moscow's nuclear weapons program to reap the significant international political benefits Khrushchev had promised, precipitated a thorough reassessment of the country's military programs.

The Early Brezhnev Era: 1965–72

Shortly after their assumption to power in 1964, the new collective leadership moved to improve Soviet military capabilities across a broad spectrum, largely within the doctrinal framework first elaborated in 1960. They sanctioned several interesting modifications and refinements, however, which were to prove of lasting significance. First, the country's military theorists began to argue, tentatively at first, that conflict involving the armed forces of the two superpowers need not escalate immediately to general nuclear war, although pressures to do so would remain enormous. Second, while underscoring that the use of nuclear weapons would almost certainly characterize any major war, they held out the possibility that such a conflict might begin with conventional weapons. Third, they emphasized the utility of large, modern, and well-equipped ground, air, and naval forces to increase the number of options available to and the flexibility of Soviet military commanders. This new accent on theater capabilities, nuclear as well as conventional, was designed to supplement the regime's heavy investment in ICBMs and SLBMs; it did not mean that the Soviet Union should in any way diminish its commitment of resources to the strategic rocket forces.

To obtain larger and more capable theater and strategic nuclear forces, the new leadership increased the level of defense spending by a steady 4 to 5 percent every year after 1964.[23] This decision constituted a clear rejection of Khrushchev's policies which, his successors concluded, had enabled the United States to maintain measurable military superiority with respect to strategic weapons. They considered this American advantage both dangerous to the Soviet Union and a powerful impediment to realization of important foreign policy goals. To enhance the country's international political position relative to that of the West, Soviet leaders sanctioned a comprehensive buildup in military power, focusing in particular on expansion of the strategic nuclear arsenal, improvements in theater warfare capabilities, and the development of naval as well as sea- and air-lift forces. The Soviets also began during this period to reinforce their military position along the Chinese frontier.

The Kremlin's primary military objective in the immediate post-Khrushchev period was the rapid growth of strategic offensive forces to attain approximate nuclear equality with the United States. To this end, the Soviets constructed over 1,300 new ICBM launchers between 1966 and the signing of the first SALT agreements in May 1972. Almost 1,000 SS11 missiles were deployed, as well as 300 large SS9 systems, many equipped with warheads of enormous yields. Total Soviet ICBM deployments numbered 1,527 by mid-1972. By contrast, the U.S. land-based missile force had remained constant at 1,054 since 1967. The new Soviet ICBMs were also housed in "hardened" underground silos, making them substantially more "survivable" against preemptive attack than the SS7 and SS8 systems built under Khrushchev. The Soviet SLBM program advanced more slowly. Construction of the Yankee-class ballistic missile submarine did not begin until 1965; seven years later only 28 Yankees with 448 launch tubes were operational. Eventually, the Soviets would deploy 62 modern SSBNs with 950 missiles, the number permitted under the 1972 Interim Agreement on Offensive Forces, although they were not to reach that figure until 1981. No effort was made to expand the size of the strategic bomber force, which had leveled off at roughly 190 by 1968.

In addition, Soviet authorities devoted considerable resources in the mid- and late 1960s to development of an anti–ballistic missile system for the defense of Moscow. The ABM Treaty, the most important of the SALT I agreements, prevented the United States and the Soviet Union from constructing a nationwide anti–ballistic missile network. Under the terms of that treaty, however, the Soviets were permitted to retain and improve the Moscow-based "Galosh" system. The leadership also authorized an expanded civil defense effort, centered upon plans to shelter government elites and to evacuate the urban population to less heavily targeted areas outside the cities, as a way to enhance the country's ability to withstand the effects of nuclear war.

As a result of these several and related steps, Brezhnev and his Politburo colleagues had attained by the early 1970s their initial military objective: rough equality with the United States in strategic nuclear forces. Moreover, the United States formally recognized and confirmed this new relationship through signing the SALT I accords.

By the early 1970s, the Soviets had achieved, in operational terms, the ability to inflict catastrophic destruction on their principal adversary, even after absorbing an American first strike. Through the agreement to ban nationwide ABM deployments, SALT I essentially guaranteed the Kremlin's nuclear deterrent for the foreseeable future. The second part of SALT I, the Interim Agreement on Offensive Forces, ensured a relationship of rough equality in strategic forces between the two superpowers. From the Kremlin's perspective, this meant that Washington was no longer in a position to resort to "nuclear blackmail" as it had allegedly done in previous years, most graphically during the Cuban missile crisis. For obvious reasons, Soviet leaders regarded this as a major achievement.

With the expansion and modernization of their strategic nuclear forces well underway by 1966–67, Soviet leaders turned their attention to the special problems associated with theater warfare, first in Europe and later in the Far East. Beginning in 1967–68, they made extensive improvements in Soviet ground force divisions and tactical air armies deployed in Eastern Europe. They outfitted Soviet forces in East Germany, Poland, Hungary, and Czechoslovakia (after 1968) with advanced versions of the T-64 and T-72 (from 1974) medium tanks; deployed new and more effective mobile surface-to-air missile systems to upgrade Warsaw Pact air defenses; and also increased the frequency of training exercise and combat maneuvers. During 1970–71, they assigned the first units of MiG21 Fishbed J/K, MiG23 Flogger B, and MiG27 Flogger D tactical aircraft to the Soviet air forces (frontal aviation and PVO Strany) in Warsaw Pact countries. They also made significant attempts to improve the reliability and endurance of the Kremlin's command, control, and communications facilities in the European theater.[24]

In the 1965–70 period, Soviet planners sought to provide their forces deployed in Eastern Europe with better all-around military capabilities. Increasingly, however, the introduction of new "dual capable" weapons, especially aircraft, became Moscow's principal military focus in that theater, in part because the Soviets hoped to forestall the early use of nuclear weapons in any military confrontation with the NATO countries and to prolong the conventional phase of conflict. While continuing to modernize their already robust theater nuclear forces in the event their use became unavoidable, the Soviets attempted as a matter of policy to keep the nuclear threshold in Europe as high as possible. This new accent on conventional military operations between NATO and the Warsaw Pact, within the context of parity at the strategic level, also served to undercut the American pledge to defend its Atlantic allies with tactical and theater nuclear weapons. In essence, the Soviet ambition throughout this period, and beyond, was to achieve effective nullification of Washington's commitment to regard the security of NATO Europe as indistinguishable from that of the United States by making the cost of such a commitment too high to bear.

In the Far East, the Kremlin's military strategy in the first seven years after Khrushchev was to intimidate the Chinese through deployment of 46 divisions within striking distance of the Sino-Soviet frontier. Between 1964 and 1970, total Soviet ground force manpower in the Siberian, Transbaikal, and Far Eastern military districts increased fourfold; "dual capable" aircraft and theater-range nuclear missile systems also increased significantly, with additional deployments to follow in the mid-1970s.[25] As in Europe, the Soviets sought to acquire a conventional military option should large-scale hostilities erupt with the Chinese, although it is doubtful that they had much confidence, either then or later, that a war in the Far East could remain nonnuclear for long.

In sum, Soviet capabilities for the conduct of theater military operations in both Europe and Asia improved so substantially between 1965 and 1972 as to assure the country's political leaders and military commanders greater operational flexibility than ever before. The Kremlin's investment in new weapons technologies, conventional and nuclear, specifically designed to meet the special requirements of theater warfare, not only continued after 1972 but in fact accelerated.

The development of Soviet naval power lagged behind expansion of strategic nuclear and theater forces. From 1965 to 1972, the number of major Soviet surface combatants increased only marginally. The rate of ship construction, on the other hand, more than doubled, with heavy emphasis on antisubmarine warfare platforms, such as the VTOL aircraft and helicopter carriers Moskva and Leningrad, guided missile cruisers and destroyers, and nuclear-powered attack submarines.* Most of the new vessels had greater firepower and "sustainability" than their predecessors. During this period, units from the four Soviet fleets began regular courtesy visits to friendly regimes in Africa and Asia, and a large Soviet naval squadron first entered the Mediterranean, a presence that has endured.

In the late 1960s, future Soviet maritime strategy became a topic of intense debate within senior military circles. Despite initial misgivings on the part of the political leadership, Admiral Gorshkov's forceful arguments in favor of a large, ocean-going Soviet navy as an essential prerequisite for global military reach proved persuasive. By 1972, however, the exact content of the Kremlin's maritime strategy and the full dimensions of the Soviet naval buildup remained somewhat of a mystery to Western analysts and policy makers. Gorshkov's writings notwithstanding, the largely defensive character of the Soviet navy persisted.

---

*This was in addition to the construction of 3 to 4 ballistic missile submarines every year between 1967 and 1980.

As with the Kremlin's naval forces, the expansion of Soviet sea- and air-lift capabilities proceeded slowly during the first seven years of Brezhnev's tenure. While some modest improvements occurred, the ability of the Soviet Union to ferry large numbers of men and significant quantities of materiel across great distances remained quite limited well into the 1970s. Serial production of the An22 "Cock" heavy transport aircraft, for example, began only in mid-1967, while the smaller and more versatile I176 Candid did not enter regular production until several years later.

The development of Soviet military power in the years 1965–72 was well-conceived, comprehensive, and continual. Directed in the first instance at erasing the American strategic advantage, the buildup was also intended to liberate Soviet leaders from the heavy reliance on nuclear weapons that had marked Khrushchev's defense policies. While not losing sight of the importance of nuclear weapons in establishing and enforcing their claim to superpower status, Soviet policy makers also sought to focus on the development of nonnuclear theater military capabilities, which they perceived as important as strategic forces in influencing the behavior of neighboring as well as more distant countries. After all, conventional forces could actually be used to resolve international political differences in a way nuclear weapons could not, except at great risk. This capacity to impose through the use of limited force favorable outcomes at the regional and subregional levels of conflict while at the same time deterring nuclear war with the United States constituted the essence of Soviet military strategy from the mid-1960s to the early 1970s.

Contemporary Doctrine and Strategy

The major propositions of Soviet military doctrine have remained largely unchanged since the revisions of the early Brezhnev era. Soviet theorists continue to argue that nuclear weapons will probably be used from the very outset of hostilities in any future world war involving the United States and the Soviet Union. As before, the side that strikes first with the appropriate kind and number of nuclear weapons will achieve "decisive" military advantage. The war will be global in character and enormously destructive to all belligerents. Worldwide conflict is not inevitable, but the imperialists may unleash it at any time. Vigilance and defense preparedness are the best guarantees of peace and as necessary as at any point in the past. What has changed, in the view of Soviet leaders, is the aggregate balance of military power between East and West, which over the last ten years has moved in a direction favorable to the socialist countries. From Moscow's perspective, this shift in the military relationship is the direct result of the sustained investment in all five Soviet combat services, although the single most important development has been the attainment of a strategic nuclear arsenal numerically superior to that of the United States.

The development of Soviet power since the mid-1970s has had a pronounced impact on the country's military strategy, however. The revisions are critical, as they represent important modifications of previous Soviet thought on the probable conduct of general and theater warfare.

For much of the postwar period, the principal purpose of Soviet nuclear forces was simply to deter war with the United States. Any more ambitious objectives, such as "disarming" the United States in a surprise attack or limiting damage to the Soviet homeland, were effectively ruled out by the limited number and technical crudity of the Kremlin's offensive systems, as well as inability to defend against an American retaliatory strike. In practical terms, Soviet leaders, military and political, accepted the logic of what American analysts termed "mutual assured destruction."

Unlike their counterparts in the United States, however, the Soviet leadership has never embraced the notion of mutual societal vulnerability as a viable strategic doctrine. In the Kremlin's view, deterrence based on the ability to inflict "unacceptable" retaliatory damage on one's opponent constitutes a formula for defeat rather than a strategy for conflict resolution. Deterrence has been and remains an objective condition of international politics and not a doctrine for war or for the design of military forces. Implicit rejection of the assured destruction model, evident in Soviet military writings as early as the 1950s, does not constitute renunciation of deterrence per se. Cognizant of the profound destructive capacity of nuclear weapons, the Soviets have consistently underscored the need, by political as well as military means, to prevent general war with the United States and its allies. That emphasis continues.

Since the middle of the 1970s, however, important advances in strategic nuclear weaponry have permitted Soviet authorities to imagine conditions under which the USSR could avoid defeat, should a nuclear war erupt between the superpowers despite their best efforts. Two developments, significant improvements in the accuracy of land-based missiles and the application of MIRV technologies to the fourth generation of Soviet ICBMs, have made it theoretically possible for the first time to mount a successful attack against high-value American military assets, including "hardened" underground ICBM silos and critical command, control, and communications facilities. Such a preemptive strike could seriously weaken the ability of the United States to respond in a timely and proportionate manner. Attacks against American early warning, damage assessment, and communications satellites could further reduce U.S. capabilities. Less accurate Soviet land- and sea-based missiles could destroy "softer" and less time-urgent targets, such as ballistic missile submarines not on patrol, bombers on nonalert status, key industrial installations, and important political centers. The Soviets harbor no illusions that an attack of this kind would eliminate all American strategic nuclear systems; much of the U.S. submarine force would survive intact, with the capacity to inflict large-scale devastation on the Soviet urban-industrial base. Because of their relative inaccuracy, however, SLBMs would be of limited use against secure military targets.

Moreover, Soviet military planners apparently believe that the effects of an American retaliatory attack could be mitigated, at least in part, by various damage limitation measures already in place. They conclude that protection of more than 100,000 leaders, plans to shelter at least a portion of the industrial work force, and limited "hardening" of certain key Soviet industries could reduce the extent of economic destruction to a level not inconsistent with the goal of recovery.

As a consequence of these related developments, Soviet military rhetoric on nuclear war, which has long identified "victory" as both desirable and achievable, has assumed greater relevance in recent years. Increasingly, the architects of the Kremlin's military strategy have apparently reached the conclusion that in the event deterrence fails, the Soviet Union can survive as a coherent political-economic entity through a combination of crippling "counterforce" nuclear strikes against the United States and its allies, the thorough reduction of American, West European, and even Chinese military potential, and a large-scale civil and industrial defense program. At the same time, the Soviets have the capability to shatter for decades, and perhaps longer, the foundations of American power, political, economic, and military, which sustain the anti-Soviet coalition. What makes these military objectives noteworthy is not their identification by Soviet theorists, which predates the contemporary period, but the Kremlin's potential capacity to realize them.

Beyond this new and tentative conclusion that the USSR, given adequate preparation and warning, may be in a better position than the United States to wage a nuclear conflict, Soviet military strategy has changed in other important ways. In contrast to the ambiguity of the earlier years, the Soviets now anticipate that general war could be a protracted affair, involving extensive use of conventional and naval forces, in addition to nuclear weapons. They anticipate complex and multifaceted military campaigns, described as "combined arms operations" and have sought to provide their theater commanders with the full range of military resources necessary to wage war on this scale.

War between the superpowers would probably begin (following a period of extreme tension) with intercontinental and theater-range nuclear strikes; eventually, however, it would expand to include the simultaneous conduct of military operations in a number of geographic areas, including Europe, the Middle East, Northeast Asia, and adjacent oceans. Under such conditions, a Sino-Soviet conflict would be unavoidable. Regional wars, in which Soviet and American forces are directly engaged, could remain limited in scope, however, as long as nuclear weapons were not employed by either side.

For the political leadership, of course, the technical or theoretical capacity of the Soviet Union to disable a significant number of American strategic nuclear systems and to shelter a fraction of the population does not constitute a convincing rationale to initiate nuclear war. The possibility, indeed, the virtual certainty that a surprise attack would not proceed as intended, that industrial "hardening" would prove ineffective, and that plans to evacuate cities would be more difficult to implement than expected, deters Soviet policy makers from the unprovoked use of nuclear weapons. Western analysts who contend that Soviet leaders believe it possible to fight and win a general nuclear war have, at best, a partial understanding of what the Soviets have said and written on the subject. They seem to confuse at times the Kremlin's determination to acquire the means to wage a nuclear war with the intention to start one. On this point, the Soviets can be taken at their word: the essential function of nuclear weapons is to prevent their use by the other side. A viable "war-fighting" strategy, the Soviets seem to believe, is the most effective way to guarantee this central objective.

The proponents of the "fight and win" school are correct, however, in pointing out that the Soviet Union and the United States differ in their assessments of the purpose of these weapons once war begins and the nuclear threshold has been crossed. Although important changes have taken place recently in American strategic thought, traditional U.S. doctrine has tended to underplay their utility except as agents of revenge; American strategic planning until quite recently focused rather narrowly on the initial stages of conflict, paying relatively less attention to the probable character of the political and military environment following the first exchange of nuclear weapons. The Soviets view the role of nuclear weapons from what has been described as a "Clausewitzean" perspective, focusing on the political as well as the military implications of their use. For Moscow, the purpose of nuclear weapons, from the point at which general war erupts, is to conclude the conflict, regardless of its intensity or duration, on terms favorable to the Soviet Union.

The evolution of Soviet military doctrine between 1953 and the present represents an organized attempt to understand the effect of nuclear weapons on both the art and the science of modern warfare. On balance, those responsible for the formulation of Soviet military strategy have apparently concluded that nuclear weapons, despite their immense destructiveness, have not invalidated the historic justification for armed conflict between sovereign states, the resolution through violent means of intractable political differences. Soviet civilian leaders, in their public statements at least, seem less confident on this point.

It is difficult to determine which of these two assessments is more representative of Soviet elite thinking. Given the extraordinary risks that would attend any use of nuclear weapons, however, it is likely that the more cautious position associated with the political authorities will dominate in the Soviet decision-making process over the course of this decade.

Military Power and Foreign Policy

If it is a central concern of those who study Soviet military affairs that the Kremlin aspires to the capability to wage and prevail in a nuclear war, these analysts are only slightly less preoccupied with the way in which Soviet leaders envision the relationship between military power and the conduct of foreign policy. In its most abbreviated form, the question most often posed relates to future Soviet behavior: how will the relative and absolute growth of Soviet military power affect both the character and the conduct of the country's foreign policy in the 1980s and beyond? More precisely framed, the issue has to do with the intentions of the Soviet leadership: is the Kremlin likely to become more assertive in pursuit of its foreign policy objectives as a result of the dramatic increase in Soviet military capability and if so, to what extent and in what areas of the world?

As the debate over the significance of Soviet military power has intensified, many Western observers have attempted to divine Soviet thinking by reference to such factors as the role of Russian history, the importance of geography, the impact of ideology, the character of Soviet culture and society, and the influence of domestic politics. They have also examined instances in which Soviet leaders have resorted to the use of force in order to achieve their foreign policy objectives. As might be anticipated, this methodology has given rise to a number of competing interpretations. Among American and other noncommunist analysts there is not, nor has there ever been, anything approaching an agreed interpretation of the connection in Soviet thinking between military power and political purpose.

Soviet scholars are of little assistance to their Western colleagues, as their analyses tend to be intellectually sterile and rigidly self-serving. Kremlin sources seldom advance beyond the simple assertion that the sole purpose of Soviet armed forces is to defend the territorial and political integrity of the USSR against all adversaries and to protect the entire "socialist camp" from imperialist aggression, regardless of the form in which it appears. Only occasionally do Soviet commentators write analytically about the political utility of military power; when they do, it is most often to criticize American concepts and policies.

A useful way to underscore the intensity of the Western debate on this issue is to compare the major contentions of the two most distinct and opposed schools of thought, recognizing in advance that few observers would identify completely with either position. At one end of the spectrum are those who argue that the principal goals of Soviet foreign policy are to increase the number of areas under direct Soviet control, to extend the Kremlin's political, military, and economic influence to all regions of the world, and to compel the retreat of American power to the Western hemisphere, implying military force in pursuit of these objectives, if necessary.[26] In seeking to extend the frontiers of the state and to eliminate all potential rivals for hegemony, they see Soviet leaders acting in a manner consistent with Russian historical tradition. Just as Peter the Great sought to "militarize" Russian society in order to realize his imperial aspirations, so have his Communist heirs continued that process. From Stalin's absorption of the Baltic republics in 1940 to Brezhnev's invasion of Afghanistan forty years later, this analysis holds, the dominant thrust of Soviet foreign policy has been expansion through military means. They interpret the Kremlin's more recent assistance to various left-leaning Asian, African, and Latin American regimes, as well as its support for national liberation movements on a worldwide scale, as a logical and predictable extension of Moscow's international political ambitions, merely denoting a shift in emphasis, away from continental expansion and toward acquisition of a global empire.

These analysts ascribe the Kremlin's "expansionist" tendencies to the fundamental internal weaknesses of the Soviet system, which compel the leadership to confirm its legitimacy and to justify its existence by demonstrating the regime's military prowess. They argue that, in much the same way as several of the tsar's advisers urged initiation of a limited war with Japan in 1904 to distract the Russian people from their misery, the current leadership seeks to compensate for the system's failures by creating military capabilities greater than those of its nearest rival and by using those resources in the interests of the "international class struggle." As a consequence, therefore, of Russian historical tradition, more recent Soviet practices, and the domestic shortcomings of the regime, they consider the Kremlin's "expansion-ist" activities a function of the system and as such, resistant to any-thing other than the most profound internal and external developments.

The second school also looks to Russian history to explain the regime's heavy reliance on coercion in the conduct of foreign policy but contends that the dependence derives less from aggressive intent or the dynamics of the political system than from the leadership's pervasive sense of vulnerability and insecurity.[27] From the invasion of the Mongols to the Napoleonic assault in 1812, from the Allied inter-vention against the Bolsheviks in 1919–20 to Hitler's Operation Bar-barossa, they see the Russian and Soviet national experience as one of war and attempted subjugation. According to this interpretation, much of the Kremlin's diplomacy after 1945, beginning with Stalin's installation of Communist regimes in Eastern Europe, was designed to reverse this pattern and ensure the country's security through the creation of a system of dominated states along its borders. The essen-tial character of Soviet foreign policy, especially in the first twenty years after the Second World War, was thus defensive: to safeguard the "gains of socialism," if necessary by recourse to force. They ex-plain the rapid increase of Soviet military power in the period follow-ing the ouster of Khrushchev in much the same way, as a response in part to the continuing threat to Soviet security that the United States and its NATO allies pose.

Analysts drawn to this view of Soviet behavior also tend to ascribe different motives to the Kremlin's assumption of more global political and military responsibilities than those identified with the "expan-sionist" school.[28] While not denying that this phase of Soviet policy represents a clear break with past practice, they tend to explain its emergence not by reference to long-standing imperial Soviet ambi-tions but to extensive changes in the international political environ-ment, such as the explosion of nationalist and anticolonialist sentiment in the Third World, which have presented Kremlin policy makers with an abundance of low-cost and relatively low-risk oppor-tunities to expand Soviet influence at the expense of the West. Moreover, they believe that the Soviets avoid serious military involve-ments in those areas deemed "immature" in revolutionary terms, areas in which political and economic conditions are not sufficiently advanced to guarantee Soviet success. Consistent with this analysis, they see the conditions that give rise to turmoil and instability in Third World regions, rather than Soviet activities per se, as the princi-pal threat to Western security.

Those who subscribe to this interpretation often characterize Soviet policy in such "third areas" as cautious, prudent, and restrained. Likewise, they consider Soviet objectives relatively modest in scope: to preserve the "gains of socialism" in those countries already embarked on the Marxist-Leninist path of development; to assist such progressive forces as may exist; and, in pursuing these goals, to avoid direct military confrontation with the United States.

As most Western analysts will readily admit, neither the "expansionist" nor the "defensive" model provides an adequate framework within which to assess Soviet attitudes toward the use of military power in foreign policy. Both interpretations capture elements of reality and identify important aspects of Soviet behavior. Ultimately, however, their attempt at universality and their failure to recognize that both tendencies can and do exist simultaneously in Soviet policy limit their analytical utility. Moreover, it is extremely unlikely that those responsible for the conduct of the Kremlin's foreign policy view the connection between force and diplomacy in such simple and unambiguous terms.

The willingness of Soviet leaders to consider the use of military power to achieve desired political outcomes probably turns less on preconceived notions regarding expansion or defense than on a complicated set of ever-changing variables, such as the salience of the issue (political and economic), the utility of a military response, perceptions of risk, political and military, and the possible implications of a decision not to act. It seems reasonable to assume that such pragmatic considerations rather than more abstract concepts of historical experience, national character, and ideology condition Soviet attitudes, although these factors provide a frame of reference or a context within which Kremlin leaders consider their options. With the steady growth in Soviet military capabilities, the critical issue then becomes how the Kremlin's assessment of these variables is likely to change over time and in what direction and thus affect the Soviet definition of "pragmatic."

While it is not possible to determine the precise degree to which Soviet leaders may rely more heavily in future years than in the past on military power as an instrument of foreign policy, one can make a number of appropriately tentative observations and predictions based on an analysis of the growth of Soviet power and of recent Soviet behavior in three quite different contexts: actions taken in defense of the "socialist commonwealth"; relations with the West; and policies in the Third World.

In reference to the first dimension, the Kremlin's relations with proximate Communist allies, Soviet leaders will continue to rely on their enormous and usable military power both to prevent the erosion of Communist Party control and to preserve within these countries their special and privileged position as security guarantor. In the second dimension, relations with the West, Soviet attitudes and policies seem likely to retain much of their present form and content. The Soviets do not anticipate that the prospective strategic nuclear balance of power will afford them the opportunity for dramatic gains at the expense of their principal adversary. However, the leadership does seem to expect a further, albeit gradual and uneven, decline in Western Europe's commitment to the Atlantic Alliance and a concomitant reduction in American influence on the continent, as a result of the Soviet military buildup. With respect to the third dimension, Soviet policies in so-called third areas, the growth of Soviet military power, specifically the expansion of the country's power projection capabilities, is almost certain to result in more assertive Soviet behavior in many areas of the less developed world, including a greater willingness than in the past to lend military assistance to "revolutionary" and "progressive" forces and to protect, again through military means, these newly won "gains of socialism."

"In Defense of Socialism"

Maintenance of political control over the Eastern European regimes remains an essential prerequisite of the Kremlin's security, second in importance only to defense of the Soviet homeland itself. Soviet efforts to forge more "organic" links with Eastern Europe notwithstanding, the ultimate source of Soviet authority in the region is the leadership's actual and perceived willingness to maintain political and social discipline, if necessary by force. The Kremlin has made it abundantly clear that it is prepared to take whatever steps may be necessary, including the use of military power, to guarantee orthodox Communist Party rule in Warsaw Pact member countries. On this critical issue, Soviet thinking has not changed since the establishment of these regimes.

In the immediate aftermath of the Polish military coup in 1981, some Western observers speculated that Soviet failure to employ overt military force to restore the authority of the Polish Workers' Party and to eliminate the challenge posed by Solidarity signaled an important shift in Kremlin policy toward its Eastern European *glacis*.[29] They concluded that Soviet leaders found it difficult to resort to explicit forms of coercion against Warsaw because of their desire to preserve the detente relationship with Western Europe, to avoid the deleterious consequences of open Soviet repression, and to escape the profound effect Soviet invasion would have produced everywhere in the world. In this sense, detente probably helped postpone more direct Soviet action. It would be misleading, however, to extrapolate from this very special case. Had there been no General Jaruzelski or had Polish security forces proved unable to arrest what the Kremlin regarded as Poland's slide toward "anarchy," the Soviet Union would have intervened directly.

Precisely how direct Soviet intervention would have been accomplished, had the Jaruzelski coup failed to achieve its objectives, is difficult to judge. It is probable that the first Soviet step would have been to dispatch specially trained army and KGB units to Poland to seize control of key political, economic, military, and communications centers, either alone, with Polish security forces, or in anticipation of the arrival of regular Soviet armed forces. Given the sensitivity of Poland's relations with its East European neighbors, especially East Germany and Czechoslovakia, I conclude that the least likely form of military coercion would have been a multinational Warsaw Pact invasion, on the model of the 1968 Czech occupation.

The Polish case has demonstrated both the disinclination of Soviet leaders to rely exclusively, or in the first instance, on overt military instrumentalities when more subtle forms of persuasion are available, and the skill with which they and their Polish executants can act. In part, however, the availability of these other instruments, such as political pressure and "native forces" loyal to the Soviet Union, is an outgrowth of the overwhelming military power which the Kremlin can bring to bear against recalcitrant allies, should the situation warrant. The expansion and modernization of Soviet armed forces, especially the development of such readily usable capabilities as airborne assault and improved communications, serve to underscore the credibility of that threat and the utility of Moscow's military option.

If the situation in Poland provoked some discussion in the West about the relative "restraint," patience, and skill the Soviet Union had demonstrated, the Kremlin's 1979 invasion of Afghanistan had exactly the opposite effect. For the Soviets, however, the two crises had much in common; in both countries, "counter-revolutionary forces" were threatening to topple Marxist-Leninist governments with strong links to Moscow. A principal difference between the crises in Poland and Afghanistan was that in the latter case the Kremlin's reliance on nonmilitary forms of pressure had proved ineffective, necessitating more overt action. In justifying the invasion, Kremlin sources stressed Soviet security interests, the impermissibility of political chaos in proximate areas, and the irreversibility of Communist revolutions, three arguments that were also used to warn Poland of its extreme danger barely one year later. From the Soviet perspective, developments in the two countries were linked in a conceptual sense as different manifestations of the same process, the potential collapse of Communist regimes in areas the Kremlin defined as critical to its own security.

This is not to suggest that the crises were of equal magnitude or importance from the Soviet perspective. Clearly, the threat to Soviet security from events in Poland was far greater than the danger the collapse of Communist authority in Afghanistan posed. Ironically, Afghanistan's remoteness from the central axes of world politics made the Soviet decision to intervene less difficult. The situation in Poland, on the other hand, required particularly deft handling on the Kremlin's part, precisely because of Poland's political centrality and the probable impact of developments in that country on Soviet relations with the outside world, especially the countries of Western Europe.

It is extremely unlikely that in defense of their position in Eastern Europe, and in Afghanistan and Mongolia, as well, Soviet leaders will be any less willing to employ military power in future years than they have been in the past. It is rather more likely, in fact, that they would use coercive methods with even less hesitation than previously, should additional crises develop, as the leadership seeks to convey an image of strength and solidarity to the outside world during what promises to be a long struggle over political succession.

The more interesting issue is the extent to which Soviet authorities may be prepared in the future to adopt a similar policy with respect to "new" Communist regimes in areas more distant from the borders of the USSR. In other words, will the Kremlin seek to enforce the doctrine of the irreversibility of socialist revolutions in such volatile client states as Ethiopia and South Yemen? In light of the importance that the Kremlin attaches to the creation of a worldwide "socialist community," and its increasing capacity to provide significant levels of military support to friendly Third World regimes, we must assume that Soviet leaders will be more concerned than in the past to protect their hard-won gains outside the Eurasian "heartland." In practical terms, of course, those countries located within easy reach of Soviet military power will be more likely to enjoy the Kremlin's "protection" than those not so well situated. This suggests special Soviet attention in the 1980s to at least four "progressive" Asian and African countries with which the Kremlin has concluded treaties of friendship: Ethiopia, Iraq, Syria, and South Yemen. Iran, too, could qualify for such special Soviet treatment, in the event a leftist regime should emerge in that country. Cuba and Vietnam, although hardly "new" Communist states, already enjoy favored status, despite their more distant location.

The Political Uses of Military Power:
The West

In the East-West dimension, the most important implications of the Soviet military buildup are more political than military in nature.

A direct military engagement between the superpowers or between NATO and Warsaw Pact countries remains a remote possibility, given the enormous risks that would attend such conflict and the potential for escalation. Soviet policy makers are unlikely deliberately to provoke a confrontation with the United States or its major allies that they believe might precipitate a nuclear exchange, despite their increasing confidence that they could bring a general war to an end on terms favorable to the USSR. The Soviets do not rule out the possibility, however, that a nuclear exchange might erupt, brought on by political miscalculation or an accidental launch of nuclear weapons. In short, Kremlin leaders appear to accept the fact that for the foreseeable future mutual deterrence will continue to define the strategic military relationship between the United States and the Soviet Union.

The Soviets do anticipate, however, that their success in pulling abreast of the United States in strategic nuclear forces and in some forms of general military power is a continuing base for tangible political benefits. As early as 1972, senior Soviet analysts cited the growth in the country's military strength, specifically the buildup in strategic forces, as the principal reason for the advent of a more "realistic" and accommodating United States foreign policy. They argued that detente was an outgrowth of the realization, especially in Washington, that "objective conditions" governing relations between the two sides had changed in fundamental ways because of the historic shift in the worldwide "correlation of forces." The Soviets believe this new and more equal relationship of forces not only serves to inhibit the "aggressive" instincts of imperialism, but also wins the respect of states throughout the world, especially near neighbors, and enables the Soviet Union to chart a more assertive course in foreign policy and in international diplomacy more generally.

In essence, Soviet leaders assume, as they have since the early 1970s, that attainment of parity at the strategic military level will compel Washington to acknowledge the essential *political* as well as military equality of the Soviet Union, guaranteeing Moscow the same superpower rights and privileges long accorded its principal rival, and enabling Soviet leaders to make politically effective use of their military power beyond "the socialist world," while denying outside forces any role in areas under Moscow's control.

For Moscow, this new relationship of strategic forces has a kind of paralytic effect on American diplomacy, making it much more difficult for the United States to influence the character and conduct of Soviet foreign policy through the largely implicit threat to invoke nuclear weapons in a crisis or to engage in what Soviet analysts once referred to as "nuclear blackmail." The attainment of strategic equality, the Soviets believe, deprives Washington of the ability to intimidate the USSR, as the United States no longer enjoys demonstrable military superiority or the capability to dominate the ladder of military escalation. Equality at the strategic level thus enables the Soviet Union to assert truly global political and military aspirations. In the Soviet calculus, parity has especially important consequences for the superpower competition in western Europe and in "third areas"; its impact on Japan and the People's Republic of China is more problematic. The pattern of political outcomes over the last decade has largely confirmed Soviet suspicions that the most effective way to advance the Kremlin's diplomatic fortunes is through expansion of its armed forces.

Their success notwithstanding, the Soviets have also found it in their interest to underplay the military significance of changes in the balance of power and, in their public statements, to characterize the strategic relationship as one of essential equality or equilibrium. To assert Soviet military superiority, they fear, would only encourage a new round in the superpower arms competition; given American industrial and technological resources, such a prospect can hardly appeal to Kremlin policy makers. Thus, Soviet observers argue that it was the American inability to accept the loss of its preeminent military position, and its "frenzied" attempts to regain that status, rather than any Soviet quest for "strategic superiority," that precipitated the collapse of detente. Later, high-ranking Soviet authorities sought to reassure Western governments by renouncing any ambition to obtain measurable military advantage. In a 1977 address, for example, Brezhnev declared that the USSR "will not seek military superiority over the other side. We do not want to upset the approximate equilibrium of military strength that now exists . . . between the USSR and the U.S." Ten months after the Reagan administration's assumption to office, the Soviet president returned to this theme in a carefully worded statement, asserting that it would be "dangerous madness" for either superpower to count on victory in a nuclear war. He dismissed the concept of a first strike by arguing that anyone starting such a war "has thereby decided to commit suicide."[30] The dilemma for the Soviet leaders is that while a strategic nuclear relationship with the United States based on rough equality may not provide spectacular political gains at Washington's expense, neither will a clear-cut bid for superiority if such an effort serves to activate a determined American response.

The Soviets recognize that the existing balance is not immutable; it could shift to their disadvantage. Moreover, they sense that the Reagan administration is determined to erase any real or perceived strategic advantage that the Kremlin currently enjoys. As a consequence, one of Moscow's central objectives in the coming decade must be to maintain whatever margin of superiority has been achieved, while denying its existence, at least in public fora. A more explicit claim to superiority might yield substantial short-term benefits; over a longer time frame, however, it could erode the relationship they seek to preserve. The Kremlin, therefore, frames its pronouncements on the military balance with considerable precision. To friends and allies it boasts that the growth of Soviet military power has brought about a virtual revolution in international relations; to its principal opponent, it claims that the military equation remains as before. For this reason, in part, Soviet spokesmen tend to avoid the fine points of the military relationship between the two sides, preferring to discuss the broader trends in the global "correlation of forces."

This desire to preserve the existing military relationship suggests a continuing Soviet interest in strategic arms control negotiations with the United States through the 1980s. For the Kremlin, arms control agreements, such as the 1972 SALT I accords and the 1979 SALT II Treaty, signed but not ratified by either country, have proved a useful way to reduce the danger of war, stabilize and regulate the strategic arms competition, improve or at least maintain its relative military position, and limit development of new American nuclear weapons systems. In addition, arms control agreements have served to under-score Moscow's claim to political equality with the United States.

Soviet statements in the early 1980s reveal an increasing level of concern about the dimensions of the American military buildup and prospects for a new strategic arms control agreement. Senior Soviet authorities, including General Ogarkov and Defense Minister Us-tinov, warn that the USSR will take whatever steps may be necessary to maintain essential military equality and to frustrate any American bid for "strategic superiority." The Soviets seem to anticipate a difficult and threatening period ahead, marked by renewed and per-haps intense competition between the two countries. To compound the problem, Soviet leaders detect a greater American willingness than in the recent past to rely on military power as a central instru-ment of foreign policy; this, they write, only serves to increase the probability of general war.

For both political and economic reasons, therefore, the Soviets are likely to persist in their advocacy of negotiated arms control agreements, whatever the political climate, even as they continue to build new and more capable strategic nuclear weapons systems and to improve the overall strength of their armed forces.

The Soviets also believe that strategic equality with the United States facilitates a larger and more effective Soviet political role in Western Europe, where the Kremlin already enjoys a degree of con-ventional military and theater nuclear superiority. Throughout the last decade, Soviet authorities have consistently linked the emergence and durability of detente on the continent to the more equal relationship of strategic nuclear forces between the superpowers. For the Kremlin, the declining credibility of the American commitment to defend NATO Europe with nuclear weapons, brought about through strategic parity and Soviet theater nuclear superiority, compels the West Europeans to conduct their relations with the USSR from a position of relative weakness, thereby helping to produce policies often consistent with Soviet political and economic interests.

This change in the military relationship between the Soviet Union and Western Europe has permitted the Kremlin to realize a number of important objectives in the region unimaginable twenty years earlier. In essence, the growth of Soviet military capabilities and NATO's failure to keep pace with that buildup have enabled Moscow to transform the character of its relations with Western Europe, particularly by playing upon the fear of war and using this stimulated fear to increase West European suspicion of the United States.

The Kremlin's arms control policies have been especially important in this regard. The fact that the United States and the Western European countries view arms control negotiations as necessary affirms in a subtle way the objective character of the Soviet military threat. At the same time, Moscow's participation in both the Central European force reduction negotiations between NATO and the Warsaw Pact and the intermediate-range nuclear forces talks serves to enhance its political status in Europe by permitting the Soviets to pose as the leading advocates of the "relaxation of international tensions" and "military detente." This ability to play on the political, military, and moral vulnerability of Europe while holding out the prospect of reduction in tensions has been a source of Soviet diplomatic strength and a hallmark of the Kremlin's European security policy since the early 1970s. The collapse of detente with the United States and the particular sensitivity of the Western Europeans to the growth of Soviet military capabilities strongly suggests that Moscow's two-track approach toward NATO Europe, perhaps the best contemporary example of "carrot-and-stick" diplomacy, will become even more than today a centerpiece of Soviet foreign policy in the 1980s. Soviet skill in playing upon Western European hopes and anxieties constitutes a most important element of Soviet conduct.

The Soviets have also sought, with considerably less success, to achieve a similar relationship with Japan, Washington's principal Pacific ally. However, in this case the steady expansion of Soviet military forces in the Far East has strengthened rather than undermined U.S.-Japanese cooperation on security issues, in part because of Moscow's heavy-handed policies toward Tokyo, which have intensified the

level of anti-Soviet sentiment among Japanese elites and the population at large. Moscow's assignment of ground and air units to the
southernmost Kurile Islands, which it acquired in 1945 and which the
Japanese seek to regain, is perhaps the best known example of the
Kremlin's tendency to rely on military instruments rather than diplomacy to accomplish its political objectives vis-à-vis Japan.

Soviet leaders seem of two minds with respect to Japan. On the
one hand, they are determined to retain territories acquired in 1945
and to preserve their regional military preeminence. On the other
hand, they recognize that their extensive reliance on military power
has had profoundly negative implications, preventing the development of more cordial political and economic ties. They seem
unable to fashion policies which would permit them to retain their
military position and pursue detente with Tokyo. Moreover, given the
historical record, it is unlikely that the Kremlin will be able at any
point during this decade to attain with Japan anything like the relationship it enjoys with Western Europe.

Soviet difficulties with Japan notwithstanding, it is the political
significance of changes in the military balance to which the Kremlin
assigns special importance in its relations with Western countries.
Through their military power, the Soviets expect to preserve what
they describe as the "essential achievements of detente," such as
greater Western sensitivity to Moscow's security interests and economic preferences, if not for the time being with Washington, then
with the major capitalist countries of Europe; Japan, for the reasons
indicated, represents a paradox for Soviet policy makers. Given the
new strategic relationship and the Kremlin's theater military
capabilities, Soviet analysts argue that detente, or some amended version of that concept, must ultimately prevail as the sole model for
East-West relations.

Within this context, it is unlikely that coercion, per se, will play
any direct part in East-West relations. It is virtually inconceivable, for
example, that at any point during this decade the Soviet Union will
resort to the explicit use of military force against Western countries
for any reason, short of a deliberate decision to go to war or in response to an attack on its vital interests. In all probability, the Kremlin
will be content to allow the reality of its military power to shape
Western policies in more subtle ways and to advance whatever foreign
policy and security goals it defines as appropriate.

The Third World

Doubtless, the most interesting shift in recent Soviet security policy has been the Kremlin's more extensive and visible involvement in a
number of Third World conflicts, most notably in Africa and parts of

Southwest Asia, where Soviet policy has entered a new and more active phase. Representatives of the Soviet military, both combat forces and advisers, are currently deployed in fourteen Asian and African countries. Small contingents of Soviet military advisers serve in Angola, Mali, Mauritania, Mozambique, the Seychelles, and Kampuchea; more substantial forces are present in Ethiopia, North and South Yemen, Libya, Syria, Iraq, and Vietnam. The number of Soviet troops stationed outside Warsaw Pact countries totaled 17,000 in 1982, excluding Afghanistan.[31] Military and paramilitary personnel from Cuba, East Germany, and Czechoslovakia have also been deployed abroad. The provision of Soviet and East European military equipment, from small arms and artillery to armored infantry vehicles and tanks, made possible the victory of pro-Communist forces in Angola (1975) and the Ethiopian defeat of the Somalis (1978).

The recent success of the Soviet Union in establishing a military presence in the Third World and in providing valuable military assistance to both revolutionary regimes and national liberation movements stands in marked contrast to the Kremlin's policies of the early 1960s, which not only failed to produce long-term gains but served to emphasize the relative weakness of Soviet power-projection capabilities. Perhaps the best known, although hardly the only, Soviet failure during this period was the defeat of pro-Moscow forces in the Congo by the better-equipped faction supported by the United States and other Western countries. Until the early 1970s, the Soviet Union was simply not in a position to compete militarily with the United States on global terms. The twin effort to obtain a more equal relationship of strategic forces and to improve its relative position in the European theater consumed most of its military resources.

Several developments within the last decade have enabled Soviet leaders to adopt a much higher military profile in distant areas. The first has been the marked rise of political and economic instability throughout the Third World, which has created for Moscow a greater number of opportunities for both political and military penetration. The second was Moscow's achievement of essential nuclear equivalence. By helping to induce a degree of paralysis at the strategic level, and thereby make less credible an escalatory American response to any Soviet use of force in third areas, parity has allowed Soviet policy makers to intensify the level of their military activities in those regions the United States did not identify as critical to its national security. In other words, parity has enabled Moscow to compete with the United States for access and influence in the Third World on more equal terms and, in the view of Soviet leaders, with substantially fewer risks. In the Soviet view, among its other consequences parity in strategic nuclear forces has compelled American policy makers to abandon their "diplomacy of force," through which Washington had prevented unwelcome change in many areas of the world by the threat or the actual use of force.[32]

The third development has been the Kremlin's acquisition of substantial air- and sea-lift capabilities for the transport of military equipment and personnel to any country with port facilities and/or an airstrip of requisite length. Over the past decade, the military utility of these forces has been demonstrated repeatedly. In addition to such well-known instances as the Soviet resupply effort to the Arab countries during and after the October 1973 war in the Middle East and the assistance to Angola's MPLA and Ethiopia's Dergue, the Kremlin has also supported and financed Libya's bid for regional military hegemony and South Yemen's attempt to subjugate its western neighbor by force. This capacity to lend substantial military assistance to Third World governments and to "progressive" forces sympathetic to Soviet interests has provided the Kremlin a new and invaluable mechanism for enhancing its influence and diminishing that of the West. The Soviets have also demonstrated, in contrast to the situation that prevailed twenty years ago, that they have the ability as well as the intention to sustain their military presence over time.

It is in these third areas, the less developed countries of Asia and Africa, that the growth of Soviet power has created resources for profoundly different Soviet policies. The application of limited military power can produce spectacular gains in such regions, the Soviets appear to believe, given a favorable "correlation of forces" at the local level, good prospects for military victory and an American decision not to oppose directly Kremlin policy in the region. Obviously, the Soviet incentive to become heavily involved in regional military conflicts weakens considerably when any of these three conditions, especially the last, does not obtain.

Two factors are likely to be especially influential in any Soviet decision to assume additional political and military responsibilities in the less developed world during the 1980s. The first is the attitude and behavior of the United States. American passivity during the Soviet and Cuban interventions in Angola and Ethiopia essentially assured the Kremlin military carte blanche in these conflicts. In light of the Kremlin's weak political claims in the region, it is unlikely Soviet leaders would have been prepared to run the risk of a major military confrontation with the United States in an area so far removed from their central interests, whatever the probable outcome of an actual military engagement. Had the United States provided substantial military assistance to the forces opposing Moscow's clients, UNITA in the former case, the Somalis in the latter, Soviet-supported factions could have secured victory only at great cost, if at all. How the

Americans will behave in some future crisis will, therefore, have an important bearing on Soviet policy. While a greater American willingness to commit military forces in defense of its interests in such contested "third areas" would not under all conditions deter Soviet involvement, it would compel the Kremlin to assess the potential costs of involvement with considerably greater care than has been evident in recent years.

A second factor that will condition Soviet behavior is geography. Clearly, Moscow will be more tempted to take advantage of these opportunities that lie within easy reach of its armed forces than it will those less conveniently located. Increasingly, for example, the Soviets contend that they cannot remain "indifferent" to political and military developments in areas near their southern borders, implying a willingness to use military power first to create and then to maintain what they regard as a consonant regional environment. As in the past, however, the leadership will distinguish sharply between turmoil in adjacent areas, such as Iran, where the full weight of their military power could be brought to bear in a crisis, and conflict in other, more distant areas, where the odds favoring the success of such an operation would be less attractive. This suggests that a Soviet-American military confrontation is far more likely as a result of events in and around the Persian Gulf than in any other part of the world, given the West's enormous economic stake in the area and the proximity of sizable Soviet ground and air forces.

In sum, Soviet attitudes toward the utility of force are complex, reflecting the diversity of the Kremlin's political, military, and economic interests in different parts of the world. Moreover, Moscow's attitudes have changed over time and will continue to change as a result of developments both within and beyond the borders of the Soviet Union. Ultimately, the readiness of the leadership either to threaten the use of or to commit its military power in pursuit of Soviet foreign policy interests will be determined by two factors: the ability of the armed forces to accomplish the assigned mission in operational terms and the perceived *costs* of such operations, measured against probable *gains*. How Soviet leaders define what constitutes acceptable risk will depend heavily on the context and/or the environment in which it will use its military forces; this must include estimates of such abstract concepts as the political will of the adversary, as well as more easily quantifiable indicators, such as the military balance of power.

In the first of the three dimensions discussed above, Soviet relations with proximate Communist allies, the Warsaw Pact states, Afghanistan, and Mongolia, Moscow will continue to rely heavily on coercion (either explicit or implied) to maintain its privileged position and to prevent unwelcome change. Given the importance the Soviets attach to the maintenance of these "friendly" regimes, they will be prepared to bear whatever costs may arise in connection with the exercise of their imperial prerogative. In addition, the Kremlin's military capabilities are more than adequate to defeat any conceivable challenge to Soviet authority that may develop in these areas, now and for the foreseeable future. As indicated, the Soviets may also seek to extend their "protection" to a number of nonadjacent client states bound to Moscow through bilateral political and military agreements, depending on the level of effort necessary to safeguard the local leadership and the perceived importance of the investment.

In the second dimension, Soviet relations with Western countries, Kremlin policies are likely to retain much of their existing character. There is little to suggest, for example, that Soviet leaders anticipate a significant change in the pattern of superpower relations that has prevailed since the early 1970s, as a consequence of projected developments in the strategic military balance. They do not, in other words, seem to have much faith that they can translate their "advantages" at the strategic level into direct political gains at Washington's expense. They do expect, however, that Soviet military power will continue to erode the resolution of the Western alliance and to impose rather severe constraints on American policy, depriving the United States of the flexibility that characterized its behavior before the advent of parity.

From the Soviet perspective, this development has had and will continue to have especially important implications for U.S. alliance relations in Europe and Asia, undercutting the credibility of Washington's military guarantees and exacerbating the already intense differences over security related issues that separate the Americans from their European allies. Moreover, the Soviets seem increasingly confident that they can exploit these differences through maintenance of theater military superiority and the use of differentiated diplomacy. At a minimum, the leadership foresees a continuation of NATO Europe's sensitivity to Moscow's political and economic preferences in the region, commensurate with the growth of Soviet power. In their more optimistic moments, they probably believe that they can eventually transform Western Europe's current "sensitivity" to Soviet interests into a form of outright deference, leading to what some analysts have called "Finlandization." At the same time, the Kremlin recognizes that such an evolution is by no means inevitable and will come about, if at all, only as the result of a gradual, uneven, and lengthy process over which the Soviet Union will exercise only limited influence. This would seem to indicate that Soviet leaders will refrain from any direct use of force against Western Europe in the 1980s, lest it endanger what has already been achieved and undermine future prospects.

It is in the third dimension, in "third areas," that the shift in the strategic and conventional military balances (including the ability to project power across great distances) will have the most discernible impact on the foreign policy behavior of the Soviet Union in coming years. The expansion of Soviet capabilities virtually assures a more active and assertive Kremlin posture in many less developed regions of the world, including several areas, such as Southwest Asia, in which the United States has evident and long-standing security and economic interests. This combination of greater Soviet military power, willingness to employ those resources under favorable conditions, and established American interests suggests that the management of East-West relations in connection with conflict in "third areas" will become a permanent and potentially explosive item on the super-power agenda, even if, as seems probable, the essential character of the central strategic balance does not change in future years except in cosmetic ways. How to regulate this competition is perhaps the most difficult challenge awaiting Soviet and American policy makers.

Conclusion

The purpose of this essay has been to examine contemporary and probable future Soviet military forces, focusing in particular on the growth and character of the Kremlin's military capabilities and the connection in Soviet thinking between military power and the conduct of foreign policy. Four major conclusions emerge from this analysis.

First, for the first time in Soviet history, Kremlin leaders have at their disposal a modern and balanced military force for possible use across a large spectrum of conflict, from intercontinental nuclear war with the United States to limited interventions in the Third World. Moreover, the current leadership regards further development of Soviet military power as a necessary precondition for the attainment of future foreign policy objectives. Military power has become the main Soviet instrument in the long-term political struggle they foresee with the West and with China.

Second, the role of the military within the Soviet system is unlikely to change significantly during the 1980s, given the party's determination to retain its preeminent political position and the pattern of party-military relations. The military will continue to enjoy a privileged status within the economy, despite the anticipated downturn in economic performance, and to perform a number of critically important sociopolitical functions.

Third, the architects of Soviet military strategy appear to believe that in the event deterrence fails and a nuclear war erupts between the superpowers, the survival of the Soviet Union as a coherent political-military entity can best be ensured through a combination of counterforce nuclear strikes against the United States, the thorough reduction of American, West European, and even Chinese military potential, and civil defense measures. Soviet civilian leaders seem less confident than their military counterparts that the Soviet Union could achieve such an outcome.

Fourth, Soviet attitudes toward the political utility of military power have undergone an important change in recent years, which will have significant implications for the country's foreign policy in the 1980s. In particular, as a consequence of the apparent shift in the East-West balance of military power, Soviet leaders anticipate the "institutionalization" of detente with Western Europe and increasing sensitivity to Soviet policy preferences on the part of noncommunist countries near or adjacent to the borders of the USSR, especially in Southwest Asia. In addition, the Kremlin now has the resources to intensify its efforts to enlarge the international "socialist community" of states through the provision of economic and military assistance to selected Third World revolutionary groups and regimes in which they believe investments are likely to produce long-term gains. In this connection, Moscow will probably strengthen its existing security commitments to some Third World governments and undertake such new commitments as it feels consistent with Soviet interests and resources. At the same time, Kremlin leaders will seek, as in the past, to avoid direct military confrontations with the United States, although in light of greater Soviet activism the likelihood of such confrontations will increase in coming years.

NOTES

1. All factual data on Soviet military capabilities are drawn from recent, unclassified Western sources. See especially *The Military Balance 1981–82* (London: International Institute for Strategic Studies, 1981), pp. 10–15, 121–29; and U.S. Department of Defense, *Soviet Military Power* (Washington, D.C.: USGPO, 1981).

2. *The Military Balance 1981–82*, pp. 5, 10, 73.

3. The relationship between the Soviet and Eastern European militaries is the subject of a number of excellent recent studies. Among the most detailed and informative are Robert W. Clawson and Lawrence S. Kaplan, eds., *The Warsaw Pact: Political Purpose and Military Means* (Wilmington, Del.: Scholarly Resources, Inc., 1982); A. Ross Johnson, Robert W. Dean, and Alexander Alexiev, *East European Military Establishments: The Warsaw Pact Northern Tier* (New York: Crane, Russak, 1982); and Christopher Jones, *Soviet Influence in Eastern Europe* (New York: Praeger, 1981). See also Lawrence T. Caldwell, "The Warsaw Pact: Directions of Change," *Problems of Communism*, September-October 1975, pp. 1–19.

4. See William Perry, "The Nature of the Defense Problem in the 1980s

and the Role of Defense Technologies in Meeting the Challenge," *The Role of Technology in Meeting the Defense Challenges of the 1980s,* A Special Report of the Arms Control and Disarmament Program (Stanford, Calif.: Arms Control and Disarmament Program, 1981), pp. 1–18.

5. See pp. 41–43, below.

6. John M. Collins, *U.S.-Soviet Military Balance* (New York: McGraw-Hill, 1981), p. 214; and Defense Intelligence Agency, *Handbook of the Soviet Armed Forces* (Washington, D.C.: USGPO, 1978), pp. 13-2 to 13-5.

7. For a concise discussion of Soviet intelligence-related activities abroad, see *Soviet Military Power*, p. 90. Also see Harry Rositzke, *The KGB: The Eyes of Russia* (Garden City, N.J.: Doubleday, 1981).

8. See the chapter by Robert W. Campbell in this book for a more detailed analysis of the economics of Soviet defense spending.

9. John J. Dziak, *Soviet Perceptions of Military Power: The Interaction of Theory and Practice* (New York: Crane, Russak, 1981), p. 23.

10. *Dictionary of Basic Military Terms (A Soviet View)*, U.S. Air Force translation (Washington, D.C.: USGPO, 1976), p. 38.

11. William E. Odom, "The Party Connection," *Problems of Communism*, September-October 1973, p. 25; idem, "Who Controls Whom in Moscow," *Foreign Policy*, Summer 1975, pp. 109–23.

12. See for example Roman Kolkowicz, *The Soviet Military and the Communist Party*, (Princeton, N.J.: Princeton University Press, 1967); and idem, "Interest Groups in Soviet Politics: The Case of the Military," in Dale R. Herspring and Ivan Volgyes, eds., *Civil-Military Relations in Communist Systems* (Boulder, Colo.: Westview Press, 1978), pp. 9–25.

13. Timothy Colton has written that for the immediate future "no major change in civil-military relations in the Soviet Union is to be anticipated. The determinants of military quiescence are deeply rooted and not susceptible to disturbance in the short run. . . . In comparative perspective, the party-army relationship has been remarkably free of direct conflict, and the safest prediction is that such confrontation will be avoided in the future. The relationship presumably has enough resilience and slack to withstand even quite substantial shocks." From Timothy Colton, *Commissars, Commanders and Civilian Authority: The Structure of Soviet Military Politics* (Cambridge, Mass.: Harvard University Press, 1979), p. 285.

14. David Holloway, *War, Militarism and the Soviet State,* Working Paper Number 17, World Order Models Project (New York: World Order Inc., 1981), p. 19.

15. As quoted in the *Washington Post,* July 18, 1982.

16. See ch. 4 for a more thorough discussion of Soviet demographic trends.

17. Richard Pipes is perhaps the most forceful and articulate exponent of the view that despite the advent of nuclear weapons, the principal objective of the Soviet Union, in the event of general war, is military "victory" over the United States. See his "Why the Soviet Union Thinks It Can Fight and Win a Nuclear War," *Commentary,* July 1977, pp. 21–34; see also Joseph D. Douglass and Amoretta M. Hoeber, *Soviet Strategy for Nuclear War* (Stanford, Calif.: Hoover Institution Press, 1979). For a competing interpretation, see Raymond L. Garthoff, "Mutual Deterrence and Strategic Arms Limitation in Soviet Policy," *International Security*, III, no. 1 (Summer 1978), pp. 112–47; and Robert L. Arnett, "Soviet Attitudes Toward Nuclear War: Do They Really Think They Can Win?" *Journal of Strategic Studies*, September 1979, pp. 172–91.

18. A. A. Grechko, *Vooruzhennye sily sovetskogo gosudarstva* [*Armed Forces of the Soviet State*] (Moscow: Voenizdat, 1975), p. 340.

19. Harriet Fast Scott and William F. Scott, *The Armed Forces of the USSR* (Boulder, Colo.: Westview Press, 1979), pp. 41–44.

20. Raymond L. Garthoff, "The Meaning of the Missiles," *Washington Quarterly*, Fall 1982, p. 77.

21. Harriet Fast Scott analyses the differences among the three editions of Sokolovsky, in Harriet Fast Scott, ed., *Soviet Military Strategy*, third edition (New York: Crane, Russak, 1975).

22. R. Y. Malinovsky, "Report to the Twenty-second Congress of the CPSU," as quoted in Scott and Scott, *The Armed Forces of the USSR*, p. 43.

23. Central Intelligence Agency, *Soviet and U.S. Defense Activities, 1970–79* (Washington, D.C.: USGPO, 1980). W. T. Lee, "Soviet Defense Expenditures," in William Schneider and Francis P. Hoeber, eds., *Arms, Men, and Military Budgets: Issues for Fiscal Year 1977* (New York: Crane, Russak, 1976), advances a figure of 8 to 10 percent for the annual growth of Soviet defense spending for the years 1970–76.

24. Thomas W. Wolfe, *Soviet Power and Europe, 1945–1970* (Baltimore: Johns Hopkins University Press, 1970), pp. 460–76; and *The Military Balance 1971–72* and *1972–73* (London: International Institute for Strategic Studies, 1971, 1972).

25. See especially *Defense of Japan 1978* (Tokyo: Defense Agency, Japan; translated by Mainichi Daily News, 1978), pp. 31–34; *Defense of Japan 1980* (Tokyo: Defense Agency, Japan; translated by Japan Times, 1980), pp. 49–60; *Asian Security 1979* (Tokyo: Research Institute for Peace and Security, 1979), pp. 45–48; and *Asian Security 1980* (Tokyo: Research Institute for Peace and Security, 1980), pp. 29–38.

26. Elements of this interpretation are contained in Richard Pipes, "Militarism and the Soviet State," *Daedalus*, Fall 1980, pp. 1–12; and Colin S. Gray and Rebecca Strode, "The Imperial Dimension of Soviet Military Power," *Problems of Communism*, November-December 1981, pp. 1–15.

27. A number of "revisionist" and "post-revisionist" Western scholars have been drawn to this view of Soviet foreign policy, including Gabriel Kolko, *The Politics of War* (New York: Random House, 1968); Walter Lafeber, *America, Russia and the Cold War 1945–1980* (New York: Wiley, 1980); and John Lewis Gaddis, *The United States and the Origins of the Cold War* (New York: Columbia University Press, 1972). See also Marshall Shulman, *Stalin's Foreign Policy Reappraised* (Cambridge, Mass.: Harvard University Press, 1963); and Shulman, *Beyond the Cold War* (New Haven: Yale University Press, 1966).

28. Several contemporary analysts of Soviet affairs have argued in ways that are generally supportive of this hypothesis. See, for example, Marshall Shulman's testimony in Hearings before the House International Relations Committee of the 95th Congress, First Session, October 26, 1977, "Soviet Union: Internal Dynamics of Foreign Policy, Present and Future" (Washington, USGPO, 1978); Robert Legvold, "The Nature of Soviet Power," *Foreign Affairs*, Fall 1977, pp. 49–71; and idem, "The Concept of Power and Security in Soviet History," in Christoph Bertram, ed., *The Prospects of Soviet Power in the 1980s* (London: Archon Books, 1980), pp. 5–12.

29. Many Western and especially American foreign affairs journalists seemed drawn to this interpretation of Soviet behavior during the initial fifteen months of the Polish crisis, from August 1980 to November 1981. See especially the *New York Times* coverage throughout this period.

30. Leonid I. Brezhnev, "Great October and the Progress of Mankind," *Pravda*, November 3, 1977, pp. 2–3 (quoted in *Current Digest of the Soviet Press*, XXIX, no. 44, November 30, 1977, p. 11) and "L. I. Brezhnev Answers a Question from a Pravda Correspondent," *Pravda*, October 21, 1981, p. 1 (quoted in *Current Digest of the Soviet Press*, XXXIII, no. 42, November 18, 1981, p. 13).

31. *The Military Balance 1981–82*, p. 14.

32. See especially Georgy Arbatov, "Soviet-American Relations at a New Stage," *Pravda*, July 22, 1973.

4

★

Social Trends

Gail Warshofsky Lapidus

Introduction

As THE Soviet system enters the last two decades of the twentieth century, it faces an array of economic, political, and social problems whose scope, complexity, and cumulative impact are unprecedented in the postwar period. At a minimum they portend a widening gap between the expectations of the Soviet population and the capacity of the system to meet them and growing strains over the conduct of economic policy, management of political affairs, and allocation of status and rewards among different social and ethnic groups. At a maximum they could precipitate real manifestations of sociopolitical instability.

In comparison with the situation likely to prevail in the years ahead, the decades following Stalin's death were characterized by a high degree of social and political stability. The relaxation of terror diminished what had been a major source of popular alienation from the regime, while the combination of rapid economic growth and expanding educational and occupational opportunities helped strengthen the system's popular support and legitimacy and eased the task of allocating wealth, status, and power among rival social claimants. By ensuring political continuity and stability, by meeting the population's modest expectations for improved living standards, and by enhancing the power and status of the Soviet Union on the global scene, the post-Stalin leadership was able to tap substantial reservoirs of popular approval and support.

By the time of Brezhnev's death, the Soviet system had already entered a new era. Andropov and his successors face a considerably

I should like to express my appreciation to Walter Connor, Murray Feshbach, and Gregory Massell for their contributions and critical comments, and to thank Amy Saldinger for her research assistance.

bleaker economic and social environment, as well as the prospects of increased political uncertainty both at home and abroad. Declining economic prospects and the crystallization and hardening of social structure are likely to create intensified competition over shrinking increments of material goods and social opportunities. Growing social malaise and increasing manifestations of social strain are already visible. In the absence of an overriding external threat, these internal problems are far more likely to divide than to unite the Soviet population. They are also more likely to constrain than to propel the Soviet leadership in its pursuit of expanded influence abroad.

This essay will examine the evolution of Soviet society in the 1980s and beyond, focusing on five key trends which have direct bearing on the prospects for sociopolitical stability and implications for the conduct of Soviet foreign policy. The task is a daunting one. The Soviet political system, economic system, and military establishment are subject matters relatively well defined, if vast; Soviet "society," however, is all too often a kind of residual category. Its substance is amorphous, its boundaries ill defined, its independence of political and economic forces problematic, and its impact on foreign policy exceptionally difficult to conceptualize. Moreover, to assess the role and significance of social issues on the conduct of any state's policies is complicated, even when active and organized groups working in an open democratic environment are able easily to express their policy preferences. Making such judgments about a society which places sharp constraints on public discussion of social issues, and for which observers cannot readily obtain objective data on social conditions, is more difficult still.

This paper will nonetheless attempt to identify and assess points of real or potential strain in the Soviet social fabric which evoke leadership concern, as well as effort toward amelioration. However, connecting these in any precise manner with present and future trends in Soviet external behavior is complicated by several factors: (1) The traditional tendency of all governments and the considerable ability of the Soviet government to insulate the process of foreign policy formulation and execution from domestic pressures; (2) The fact that domestic conditions affect Soviet foreign policy not directly but through the filters of leadership perceptions, filters about which we know little, because of our limited access to the governing elite; (3) The coming replacement of one generation of Soviet leaders by another that may have different perceptions and orientations; (4) The extraordinary juxtaposition of contradictory elements on the contemporary Soviet scene: enormous military power combined with great insecurity, vast economic resources combined with slowing economic growth, considerable social resiliency alongside serious social problems, and institutional rigidity in the face of rising pressures for change. These factors make it exceptionally difficult to offer a balanced assessment of the strengths and vulnerabilities of the Soviet social system and to relate them, however loosely, to the pressures and constraints present and future Soviet leaderships will experience in formulating and pursuing foreign policy objectives.

The Bases of Social and Political Stability after Stalin

The high degree of sociopolitical stability that characterized the post-Stalin era reflected a broad congruence of societal expectations and regime performance in several crucial areas. It depended, first and foremost, on the ability of the leadership to deliver substantial improvements in mass consumption and the level of economic welfare. Despite continuing shortcomings in the level and quality of consumer goods and services, these decades were marked by significant growth in real per-capita consumption. The gains were substantially greater in the 1950s and 1960s than in the 1970s, and they varied considerably among republics, but over the period through 1978 per-capita consumption for the USSR as a whole grew, on the average, 3.2 percent per year. Soviet families, particularly urban families, acquired more and better housing, enjoyed improved diets, and gained access to a wider supply of goods and services, especially consumer durables.

The economic policies pursued by the leadership after Stalin also entailed a substantial reduction of wage differentials while preserving security of employment and relative price stability, especially for basic commodities. The collective farmers, neglected for so long, enjoyed rising incomes and gained access to social programs and benefits from which they had previously been excluded, while the process of "leveling up" wages also brought substantial gains to the poorer-paid segments of the industrial labor force. Increasing equality in the distribution of official incomes was supplemented by two additional policies: a continuing commitment to job security, and the maintenance of stable prices for basic commodities. Taken together, these constituted the central ingredients of a tacit "social compact" between the leadership and its population, in which the latter was expected to support the regime and its policies. This compact, in turn, established the foundation for the special benefits enjoyed by key elites, whom the Brezhnev regime accorded enhanced personal and political security, increased material rewards, and a broad array of privileges.

For substantial segments of the Soviet population, a rising standard of living was also a function of substantial upward social mobility. The expansion of educational opportunities and attainments provided a major channel for social advancement, while rapid growth of white-collar and technical occupations offered new employment opportunities and enhanced social status to the offspring of peasants and workers. This process was especially dramatic in the less developed republics of the USSR and contributed significantly to the regime's success in coopting native elites in non-Russian areas. The leadership was thus in a position to expand and consolidate its social base by supplementing material rewards with social recognition and status.

A third factor contributing to stability was the substantial congruence of elite and popular values. As the refugee interviews of the Harvard Project on the Soviet Social System demonstrated in the 1950s, and as more recent emigre interviews reaffirm, even those Soviet citizens who reject many aspects of the system reveal great attachment to the dominant values of its political culture: order, discipline, paternalism, and social conservatism. They highly value security and stability in social and political life and appear to assign relatively low importance to political and civil liberties. Moreover, the experience of past decades suggests that the average Soviet citizen holds relatively modest material as well as political expectations and is rather passive in the face of disappointment. Finally, the leadership has been able to capitalize on a considerable reservoir of nationalist and patriotic feeling, not only on the part of the Russian majority but extending to the population as a whole. Soviet victory in the Second World War, the emergence of the Soviet Union as a major military and industrial power, the achievement of strategic parity in the 1970s, and its status and recognition as a global actor on the international arena all evoke considerable pride and satisfaction. These attitudes constitute a major political asset and contribute to the stability and perceived legitimacy of the Soviet system.

This combination of material and normative incentives was sustained by a residual system of coercion employing a wide and subtle range of instruments to maintain social control and deter sociopolitical deviance but far less central, visible, and unpredictable than during the Stalin period. All these factors help explain the ability of the post-Stalin Soviet leadership to deal successfully with significant challenges to its rule, including an unprecedented level of intelligentsia dissent.

Potential Constraints on Regime Performance

A number of domestic factors will affect the capacity of the Soviet leaders to meet societal demands and expectations in the 1980s and beyond.

First and foremost among the potential constraints on regime performance are declining rates of economic growth. Because economic performance has been so central to the stability and perceived legitimacy of the system, within the elite as well as for the population itself, the prospect of low-growth introduces new uncertainties. It will compel difficult choices about the allocation of resources in a system which until now has enjoyed the luxury of being able to afford guns, butter, and growth simultaneously. Where high rates of growth permitted the leadership to satisfy the demands of key interest groups, bureaucracies, and regional elites, low-growth will intensify the competition among rival claimants and reduce the resources available for managing conflicts. It is already constraining the leadership's ability to sustain steady improvements in consumer welfare. Moreover, to the extent that current problems compel new initiatives in economic policy, they are likely to entail relatively high social costs. Thus, measures which might alleviate current economic difficulties, such as freeing the labor market at the expense of job security or reforming the price structure to reduce the state subsidy of basic commodities, would jeopardize key elements of the existing social compact and generate significant working-class discontent.

Economic constraints will be compounded in coming decades by broad changes in social structure which reduce opportunities for upward social mobility. A sequence of major upheavals and social transformations—from the revolution itself to the rapid industrialization and urbanization created by the Five-Year plans, to the impact of the purges and of World War II—generated opportunities for rapid upward movement. Sons and daughters of peasants left the countryside to join the urban working class, while the offspring of urban workers moved into rapidly expanding white-collar and administrative jobs. Education increasingly became the major channel of upward social mobility, especially for movement across the manual-nonmanual line. While the drama of transition from rural to urban, from peasant to industrial society is largely over, the ambitions and aspirations it generated linger to create a set of major social problems for the Soviet leadership.

Moreover, as prospects for further improvement in living standards decline, the stakes in the mobility competition increase. The relative costs or benefits associated with different social statuses become more salient, and the visibility of the stratification system is enhanced. A growing social potential for disaffection and alienation is therefore a likely consequence of current trends.

Unfavorable demographic trends constitute a third source of constraints demanding the Soviet leadership's attention. Declining birthrates among the Slavic and Baltic populations, coupled with high rates of reproduction among the Moslem populations of Soviet Central Asia, will intensify competition for resources among different regions and republics and for access to higher education and valued jobs within them. Moreover, differential birthrates will also compound the problems posed by a labor shortage and by an economically irrational distribution of labor resources among the major regions of the country, as well as the problems posed by rising ethnonationalism among Russians and non-Russians alike.

Fourth, the process of political succession is likely to complicate the management of current problems further. The Brezhnev era was characterized by elite consensus around the rules of the political game and a tacit understanding to confine conflicts within a circumscribed milieu; the Andropov era offers the likelihood of intensified political competition. The immobilism of the Brezhnev leadership served to intensify the pressures for new initiatives, while the imminence of a massive turnover of an entire political generation provides an element of additional high unpredictability. Major conflicts over policy and power, articulation of alternative programs, and even appeals to domestic constituencies are likely to be more frequent in the years ahead, given the considerable temptations to aspiring contenders to expand their social and political base. Thus, the political climate carries the potential for significant shifts in orientations of the political elite, which could affect such major social issues as the relative priority of consumer welfare, the scope and limits of egalitarianism in economic and social policy, and the balance between the claims of Russian nationalism and the demands of the non-Russian nationalities.

Finally, the Soviet leadership faces a less benign international environment than has prevailed during much of the post-Stalin era. The demise of Soviet-American detente and the confrontational foreign policy stance of the Reagan administration in its dealings with the USSR necessarily impinge on domestic priorities, concerns, and policy debates. Pressures for increased military outlays, greater economic autarky, heightened internal vigilance, and reduced exposure of the Soviet population to foreign influences are more easily sustained in an atmosphere of siege and confrontation than in the more benign environment associated with detente. Increased repression of dissidents, renewed jamming of foreign radio broadcasts after a seven-year lull, major cutbacks in telephone communications between the USSR and the West, the decline in the number of exit visas for Israel granted by Soviet authorities (from 51,000 in 1979 to 10,000 in 1981 to 2600 in 1982), and renewed attacks on Western lifestyles and on contacts between Soviet citizens and foreigners are but a few examples of the tightening of internal controls which have accompanied the deterioration of Soviet-American relations.

Political legitimacy can be eroded by unfavorable changes in objective social and economic conditions or by subjective changes in expectations and demands which alter the terms of the implicit social

compact between leaders and led. The potential for such a development is greater than at any time in postwar Soviet history as the
Soviet leadership faces a series of unprecedented social problems.

Stagnation in Living Standards

The most critical social problem with which the Soviet leadership
of the 1980s will have to contend, one with direct bearing on the
prospects for sociopolitical stability, is the impact of resource constraints on the leadership's ability to sustain its commitment to improve living conditions. For the first time in the last thirty years,
economic performance will be insufficient to provide more than a
marginal increase in per-capita consumption unless productivity increases dramatically or resources are reallocated from investment or
military spending. In their absence, improvements in the standard of
living could come to a halt.

Progress since Stalin
From the late 1920s until 1953, the Soviet population was victim
of a strategy of economic growth that accelerated the development of
heavy industrial and military capabilities at the expense of mass welfare. At the time of Stalin's death, the Soviet living standard was only
slightly above that of 1928; the Soviet people were "ill-fed, ill-housed,
and ill-clothed by any modern standard."[1] Their diet was worse, and
the scarcity of consumer goods and personal services reflected the low
priority Stalin's investment strategy assigned to consumer needs. Only
education and health care, treated as investments in human capital,
had experienced real advances.

The quarter century which followed Stalin's death saw a major
reordering of priorities to redress the gross imbalance of the Stalinist
strategy, and the Soviet consumer benefited from allocation of a
higher share of annual increments from rising GNP to consumption.
Rising living standards, reflected in improved diet, housing, supplies
of consumer durables, and clothing, resulted from an increase in per-
capita consumption averaging roughly 4 percent annually from 1951
to 1975. The greatest gains were made in the 1950s and in the late
1960s; during the 1970s growth rates slowed to roughly 2.5 percent
per year and fell below 2 percent in 1981 (Table 4.1).

For the Soviet consumer, these broad trends translate into concrete improvements in everyday welfare. A sharp increase in per-
capita food consumption has meant improvements for the average
diet, which now contains higher proportions of meat, milk, and vegetables and less bread and potatoes than previously. Even so, the Soviet
consumer still obtains half his or her calories from bread and potatoes

Table 4.1

*Average Annual Rates of Growth in Consumption
per Capita in the USSR, 1965–81*

	1966–70	1971–75	1976–80	1981
Total consumption	5.1	2.9	2.2	1.8
Goods	5.4	2.8	2.1	1.8
Food	4.3	1.6	1.0	1.4
Soft goods	7.1	3.0	3.1	2.1
Durables	9.1	10.0	5.4	2.7
Services	4.3	3.0	2.5	1.9
Personal	5.8	4.6	3.4	2.1
Education	2.9	1.5	1.6	1.3
Health	3.2	1.4	1.4	−0.2

SOURCE: Gertrude E. Schroeder, "Soviet Living Standards: Achievements and Prospects," U.S. Congress, Joint Economic Commitee, *The Soviet Economy in the 1980s: Problems and Prospects* (Washington: U.S. Government Printing Office, 1982), p. 5.

and eats less than half as much meat as his or her Western counterpart.

An improvement in housing conditions has been another benefit of the "new deal" for Soviet consumers. As a result of a massive building program, a majority of urban families now have their own apartments, although an estimated 30 percent still live in dormitories or share kitchen and bathroom facilities with neighbors. Virtually all urban housing now has electricity, indoor plumbing, hot water, gas, and central heating; in rural areas only electricity is widely available. Cramped conditions and poor quality remain a subject of widespread complaints. Despite a virtual doubling from 4.7 square meters in 1950 to 8.4 square meters in 1978, urban living space still remains below the norm for minimum "health and decency" of 9 square meters per capita that the Soviet government set in 1929.

The availability of other consumer goods, from clothing to consumer durables, has increased sharply in recent decades. A high proportion of Soviet families are reported to own radios (85 percent), televisions (83 percent), refrigerators (86 percent), and washing machines (70 percent), all virtually nonexistent in the 1950s, although automobiles remain the exception rather than the rule, with 9 cars for every 100 families in 1980.

International Comparisons

By international standards, the growth in consumption from the mid-1950s to 1978 was substantial but far from unique: Soviet rates of growth were exceeded by those registered in Japan, West Germany, and France, equalled those of Italy, and remained ahead of the United States and the United Kingdom. During the 1970s, however, the slowing Soviet rate left only Italy, the United Kingdom, and Czechoslovakia behind. Although the gap between Soviet living standards and those of Western industrial societies narrowed during the 1960s, in the 1970s it began to widen.

A Soviet citizen in a position to make the comparison would have discovered that per-capita consumption in the Soviet Union in the late 1970s was roughly one-third that of the United States. He or she would also have observed striking variations among categories. Expenditures on education, for example, were relatively high compared to American levels, reaching almost four-fifths of the American level, while those on food and clothing were half the American level, on medical care one-third, on consumer durables one-fifth, on housing one-seventh, and on private transportation one-twenty-fifth of the American level. The structure of Soviet consumption more closely resembles that of less developed countries than it does patterns prevailing in other industrial societies, with relatively high expenditures devoted to goods, and relatively low expenditures to the poorly developed service sector. Thus, food, beverages, and tobacco represent almost half of total Soviet consumption, compared with one-fifth of American and 25–40 percent of European totals. The share of consumption devoted to hard liquor is exceptionally high, 17 percent, while the shares for housing, health, and education are lowest of all. The low expenditures on health, 4 percent, may appear surprising, but they reflect the low wages, sparse use of materials, price differentials, and relatively inferior quality of Soviet health services in comparison with European and American standards.

Another way of placing Soviet consumption into a broader comparative perspective is by comparing the relationship between average wages and the prices of basic commodities in different countries. As Table 4.2 indicates, to purchase the contents of a typical weekly shopping basket for a Soviet family of four, an industrial worker in Washington, D.C. would have to work 18.6 hours, in Munich 23.3, in Paris 22.2, in London 25.7, and in Moscow 53.5. Combining monthly rent with the shopping basket reduces the disparities because of the heavy state subsidization of housing costs in the Soviet Union. The most extreme differences occur with respect to certain consumer durables, particularly automobiles, where a Moscow worker would have to devote five times as many months of work for its purchase as his London counterpart, and ten times as long as a worker in Washington, D.C.

Table 4.2

Retail Prices of Goods and Services in Units of Work-Time,
March 1982 (Weekly Basket of Consumer Goods for Four
Persons at Soviet Level of Consumption in March 1982,
Expressed as Work-Time Units)

(Minutes of Work-Time)

Item	Kilograms	Washington	Munich	Paris	London	Moscow
Flour	1.0	5	9	6	6	28
Bread	7.0	112	189	126	175	119
Noodles	2.0	28	32	22	28	68
Beef	1.0	69	150	119	115	123
Pork	1.5	63	150	108	117	176
Minced Beef	1.0	37	70	80	63	123
Sausages	1.0	33	75	75	51	160
Cod	1.0	61	45	118	72	47
Sugar	3.3	30	33	30	36	191
Butter	0.5	28	26	24	25	111
Margarine	2.0	46	34	36	64	222
Milk (liters)	12.0	72	84	96	108	264
Cheese	2.0	200	130	118	130	370
Eggs, cheapest (units)	18.0	14	22	23	29	99
Potatoes	9.0	63	36	36	27	63
Cabbage	3.0	27	21	27	30	36
Carrots	1.0	11	10	7	13	19
Tomatoes	1.0	23	28	25	32	62
Apples	1.0	10	15	15	23	92
Tea	.1	10	10	17	5	53
Beer	3.0	33	24	21	54	48
Gin/Vodka (liters)	1.0	87	106	153	187	646
Cigarettes (units)	120	54	96	48	150	90

(Hours of Work-Time)

Weekly basket, as above		18.6	23.3	22.2	25.7	53.5
Monthly basket, as above		74.2	93.2	88.8	102.8	214.0
Monthly rent		51.0	24.0	39.0	28.0	12.0
Total of monthly basket and rent		125.2	117.2	127.8	130.8	226.0
TV, black and white		38	49	44	35	299
TV, color		65	143	106	132	701

(Months of Work-Time)

Small car		5	6	8	11	53
Large car		8	9	12	18	88

SOURCE: Keith Bush, "Retail Prices in Moscow and Four Western Cities in March 1982," *Radio Liberty Research Supplement*, June 4, 1982, p. 7.

The 1980s

In the 1980s, declining allocations to consumption are likely to compound serious shortcomings in the provision of consumer goods and services and to further intensify a serious imbalance between the supply of desired goods and services and effective demand. Acute shortages of food products and other prized consumer goods develop side by side with rising inventories of unsalable products. As rising incomes outstrip the production of wanted goods and services, a thriving private "second economy" flourishes to bridge the gap. Mounting cash deposits in savings banks exceeded half of total disposable money incomes in 1979, while Soviet and Western economists alike can only guess at the size of cash hoards in private hands. This combination of slowing growth in material welfare and a growing overhang of purchasing power poses difficult economic and social problems, while available remedies carry high social costs.

Food. The food supply has become an especially serious economic and political problem in the last few years. Chronic agricultural problems, compounded by a succession of poor harvests, have created near-stagnation in agricultural output and widespread shortages of meat, dairy products, fruits, and vegetables, especially in smaller cities. The state has imposed rationing of a number of food products, and has relied increasingly on special distribution channels to supplement distribution through retail trade outlets. The widening gap in prices between state stores and collective farm markets further reflects growing shortages; official Soviet writings confirm unofficial reports that indicate price differentials ranging from 1.5 to 4 times higher. According to one Soviet economist, prices on collective farm markets exceeded state prices by 37 percent in 1965, 55 percent in 1970, 75 percent in 1975, and 100 percent in 1979.[2]

The willingness of the Soviet leadership to import large quantities of grain and food products—which now account for one-third of all hard currency imports—is clear evidence of the high priority assigned the food program and the real concern about its social and political consequences. Indeed, by the final year of Brezhnev's rule it had become the central domestic issue, "not only a paramount economic task but also an urgent social and political task," as Brezhnev himself put it in convening a special session of the Central Committee in 1982 to address it.[3]

Consumer goods. Although the food supply has taken on particular urgency, the limited availability and poor quality of consumer goods and services more generally are an important source of dissatisfaction. Rising incomes and living standards have increased the demands and expectations of consumers, who fill Soviet publications with complaints about the poor quality, durability, and style of Soviet products. According to one source, the proportion of goods either rejected or lowered in grade when received by trade organizations has increased in recent years to the point that "trade refuses to accept one of every 10 garments, one of every 8 pairs of shoes, and one of every 10 meters of fabric."[4] Repairs were needed on 227,000 refrigerators from enterprises of one ministry alone and on over 1.5 million television sets of another. Greater consumer leverage has also resulted in growing accumulations of unsalable goods. In 1978 alone some 4.6 billion rubles worth of goods had accumulated in unsold inventories, and the state budget allocated about $1 billion annually to cover losses on such goods.

The underdevelopment of the retail trade network and the inadequate development of consumer and personal services create further problems for the Soviet consumer. In the mid-1960s housework consumed close to 1 billion man- and woman-hours. The average Soviet woman walked 12 to 13 km/day in the course of four hours of domestic chores. He, or more usually, she, devoted enormous time and energy to the tasks of "hunting and gathering." The word "to shop" is *"dostat'*,*"* meaning "to procure," with a broad spectrum of connotations: locating desired goods at suitable prices, queuing, bartering, bribing, and exchanging favors. In a recent article devoted entirely to the problem of shortages, a Soviet economist lamented that "a large part of the population is preoccupied with the search for scarce goods."[5]

The social consequences of declining rates of economic growth will depend on both the severity of the slowdown itself and on the policy choices which the leadership makes in attempting to cope with it. If productivity remains flat in the 1980s, if the share of defense spending remains constant, and if investment continues to rise at 3.5 percent per annum, a growth rate of GNP of roughly 3 percent per year would permit per-capita consumption to rise approximately 2 percent per year, a level that would allow a slow but nonetheless continuing improvement in living conditions. Under more pessimistic and likely assumptions of growth rates at or below 2 percent per year, or of rising defense expenditures, the growth of consumption would fall below 1 percent per year, bringing the improvement of mass welfare to a virtual standstill.

While initial economies are likely to touch those categories of socially marginal expenditures least visible in the short run, such as health and education, a severe slowdown over a protracted period would force retrenchment in higher-priority and more visible areas. While the expectations of the Soviet population remain modest by Western standards, they have nonetheless been shaped by the promises and achievements of the past three decades, as well as by exposure to the world outside Soviet borders.

Social consequences. Because economic performance has been so central to sociopolitical stability, the consequences of this stagnation are potentially serious. First, a slowdown in the rate of improvement of living standards will disappoint the expectations which past promises and performance have generated. While Khrushchev's promise that by 1980 the Soviet population would enjoy "the highest living standard in the world" has long been discounted, the Soviet leadership has repeatedly declared raising the level of material welfare its major goal. The large investments of recent years in agriculture, including grain imports, housing, consumer goods, and automobiles offer evidence of the degree to which it bases its own sense of legitimacy on improvements in mass welfare. A standstill or reversal of these trends would clearly weaken its popular support as well.

Second, these problems erode the effectiveness of the material incentives so critical to the leadership's efforts to improve labor productivity and to maximize labor force participation. An increasingly educated and sophisticated labor force cannot be coerced into increased efficiency; only a developed and flexible incentive system is likely to elicit the needed results. At this stage in Soviet history these incentives depend above all on the availability of desired goods and services; if increased effort cannot be translated into improved living standards, worker motivation is eroded.

Third, shortcomings in the supply and distribution of goods and services in official channels not only divert increasing shares of time and energy into procurement but also encourage the expansion of unofficial or illegal networks. The imbalance between effective demand and the supply of goods and services provides a powerful impetus to the development of the "second economy," which in turn leads to an unofficial and uncontrollable redistribution of resources and income. While this may have its functional aspects and provide a safety valve for consumer discontent, it does so at the price of severe distortions of economic relations and the erosion of public norms. Ultimately, reduced availability of resources for material incentives and the growing difficulties of controlling and directing their use may contribute to increased authoritarianism and greater reliance on coercive instruments for dealing with labor problems, however counterproductive they might prove to be.

Soviet options. While there are a number of possible remedies to this situation, each of them carries high costs. A price reform that would attempt to bring supply and demand into balance, possibly combined with a currency revaluation to capture large cash hoards, would require sharp increases in the prices of basic commodities, particularly food. While this would make possible a substantial reduction in government subsidies as well, now covering virtually half the cost of meat, to take one example, the Soviet leadership has been fearful of such an approach because of its potential for social unrest. Events in Poland have a double edge: they demonstrate not only the urgency of economic reform but also its extraordinary risk. Moreover, because the Soviet elite is itself deeply enmeshed in economic corruption, as was its Polish counterpart, the potential for instability exists at every level of the system. Under these circumstances, the costs of fundamental reform may continue to outweigh the perceived costs of the status quo.

A second option would attempt to increase labor productivity and make more efficient use of labor resources by encouraging the dismissal and transfer of redundant workers. While the Shchekino experiment, which attempted this on a small scale, demonstrated its possible rewards, it also raised the specter of unemployed workers. The potential threat to the job security that is so central to the tacit social compact between the regime and the population and central also to the ideological contrast of socialist and capitalist systems has thus far prevented a broader application of this approach.

A third option would allot an increased role to the private sector for providing not only food supplies but other consumer goods and services. Some steps in this direction have already been taken in agriculture, both by expanding private plots and by encouraging industrial enterprises to develop auxiliary agricultural activities. The possibilities in retail trade are especially great. But both ideological and practical concerns place obstacles in the path of such developments and discussion has not been followed by action.

Finally, the leadership could contemplate a more radical expansion of the private sector, a reform along the lines of the New Economic Policy of the 1920s, which would encourage small-scale private entrepreneurship in retail trade and the services while maintaining central control over the "commanding heights" of the economy. But a major reform of the economic system in the direction of decentralizing would be so far-reaching in its consequences for virtually every aspect of economic, political, and social life that it would require a unique combination of economic and political conditions to make it appear both essential and feasible. Consequently, a continuing but unofficial expansion of private economic activity and a continuing growth of the second economy—punctuated by periodic official campaigns against corruption—are the most likely short-term responses to the declining prospects of the state sector.

Declining Opportunities for Upward Social Mobility

One of the Soviet system's major political assets has been its association with greatly expanded opportunities for educational and professional advancement. The Stalin regime enjoyed immense success in persuading the population that it provided significantly greater chances for upward social mobility than had a tsarism few remembered or a capitalism none had experienced. The rhetorical exaltation of workers as the "leading" social class and of collectivized peasants as their close ally combined, paradoxically, with periodic reminders that Soviet conditions made it easy for the talented to ascend from these classes and become members of the intelligentsia. Membership in the "leading class" and upward mobility out of it were taken, simultaneously, as evidence of the justice of the new social order. In a period of slowing growth and growing crystalization of the social structure, this particular political asset is nearly spent.

Moreover, the conjunction of diminishing economic growth with slowing social mobility creates a distinctively new set of problems. An economy in straitened circumstances can moderate public dissatisfaction if it can nonetheless offer large numbers the prospect of improving their individual positions by some combination of effort, acquisition of credentials, and expertise. Career success, the ability to claim a larger share of a stable or shrinking economic pie, and enhanced social status can serve to offset or compensate for a slowdown in mass consumption. However, the Soviet economy is no longer expanding in ways that hold out that prospect, and the comparatively fluid social structure of earlier times has frozen in ways that tend to maintain existing social groups in their places.

Social Mobility under Stalin

A succession of historical developments were responsible for the high rates of social mobility which characterized Soviet society under Stalin: the revolution, with its violent attack on traditional social elites and the distribution of wealth, status, and power; the process of rapid industrialization, collectivization of agriculture, and urbanization launched by the Five-Year Plans which precipitated an exodus from the countryside and created an insatiable demand for industrial workers and a larger intelligentsia and administrative apparatus; the swelling of the state and Party bureaucracies, which gave further impetus to expansion of the intelligentsia; and the casualties of the purges and then of World War II, which created a growing deficit of males and fueled the massive entry of women into the labor force. These developments sustained a fluidity of social structure and expanding opportunities for social mobility until well into the post-Stalin period. The pressures from above were complemented by a "demand" from below, as the sons and daughters of peasants left the countryside in pursuit of urban employment, while the offspring of workers sought to move into prestigious and better-rewarded white-collar jobs. Their desires were nourished by and largely coincided with the needs of the regime itself.

Increasingly, education became the key to social mobility, especially for movement across the manual-nonmanual line. Demand and desire, plus basic literacy, sufficed to move a peasant to worker status. For ambitious urban workers and their children, workers' facilities (*rabfaki*) were created to prepare, in rapidfire fashion, talented "proletarians" with the equivalent of secondary schooling necessary to go on to higher education, while *vydvizhenie*, direct promotion, based largely on political and social criteria, propelled former workers into management positions. The network of formal educational institutions also expanded rapidly, with growing numbers of children entering primary and secondary institutions as well as trade schools, and growing numbers continuing to universities or more specialized higher educational institutions.

Stalin's social policies in the 1930s began to stabilize and consolidate an increasingly hierarchical social system, which offered extraordinary rewards for political loyalty and technical skill but still retained a high degree of fluidity. The removal of political impediments to access to higher education for children of formerly privileged strata and the institution of fees for later years of secondary (and higher) education in 1940 altered the class composition of student bodies. Worker and peasant students made up 72 percent of higher education enrollment in 1932, but only 56 percent, a vast underrepresentation of their "weight" in the society at large, in 1938. A new Stalinist elite began to emerge, for whom personal insecurity was the price of social advantage. Even so, these were still years of educational expansion and upward mobility. More children of humble birth, year by year, completed secondary education (though still a minority), more in absolute numbers moved on to higher education. The upper reaches of the system retained room for both privileged and underprivileged. The system offered a stake to those who took advantage of the opportunities it offered, while rapid social mobility helped to compensate for the decline in real incomes and mass welfare which accompanied Stalinist industrialization.

The Social Hierarchy

The drama of transition from rural to urban, from peasant to industrial society is a tale once told. But the desires it fostered and the aspirations for mobility with which it suffused many sectors of society remain and create a major problem for the Soviet leadership in the years ahead. The problems became visible in the early 1960s, when the Soviet social system reflected many features associated with modern industrial societies everywhere. It was a hierarchical social system composed of five major groups. At the bottom of the social ladder were the collective farm peasants, disadvantaged on virtually all social indicators and excluded until the mid-1960s from state pensions and other welfare benefits. Next in the hierarchy stood workers, varying in their educational level, skills, and incomes, depending on whether they worked in favored branches of heavy industry or in lower-paid light and consumer industries. The white-collar stratum, largely female in composition, ranked somewhere in the middle in terms of education, income, and prestige. At the apex of the social pyramid stood the intelligentsia and the *nachalniks* or governing political elite, sharing comparable life styles and incomes but distinguished by the fact that the power of the ruling elite derived from its positions, while that of the intelligentsia stemmed from the authority and prestige inherent in the functions it performed.

These broad social groups differed significantly not only in such objective indicators as education, income, prestige, political participation, and access to scarce goods and services, but also in attitudes, life styles, and behavior, as a proliferation of Soviet sociological studies has made abundantly clear. Indeed, while some Soviet sociologists deny the applicability of Western stratification theory to the USSR, insisting that the concept of "lower" and "higher" social strata is fundamentally inapplicable to a socialist society, others maintain that differentiation among socio-occupational groups is even more significant under socialism than under capitalism precisely because property recedes in importance as a determinant of social status.

This social structure, like that of other modern industrial societies, is based on socio-occupational groupings, but it differs in one significant respect. In the West, market forces are decisive in shaping the stratification system, and the class position an individual occupies is the crucial determinant of his or her life chances. In the Soviet Union, by contrast, political decisions shape social stratification and political or administrative roles create access to resources or opportunities that are quite independent of market forces. Because the distribution of rewards reflects political regulation rather than the operation of market forces, the policy choices of different groups of leaders have considerable influence on both individual incomes and the position of social groups.

To the extent that the party consciously attempted to prevent social strata from consolidating and transmitting their privileges, as was the case under Khrushchev, the system preserved elements of its earlier social fluidity. In more recent years, however, the combination of enhanced personal security, reduced political turnover, and consolidation of the elite's prerogatives has promoted the emergence of a privileged stratum which enjoys not merely high incomes but access to goods and services not available on the "market" or accessible to the ordinary Soviet citizen; from high-quality housing to restricted stores carrying deficit or imported goods at nominal prices to special medical and vacation facilities and to travel abroad.

Access to Higher Education

The crystalization of a new social hierarchy has also meant the growing ability of new elites to transmit their advantaged position to offspring. Here the evolution of the Soviet educational system played a crucial role. While a "sorting" process still occurs at the transition from eight- to ten-year education (with the social profile of those who continue for the ninth and tenth years more "elite"), a growing share of the age cohort completes the ten years of education necessary for subsequent admission to a higher educational institution. However, admissions to such institutions are restricted, and as their rate of growth slowed—from 10 percent between 1961 and 1965 to 3.5 percent from 1966 to 1970 to only 1.2 percent from 1971 to 1975—only a progressively smaller share of growing cohort of secondary school graduates could continue to higher education. Where over half could go on in the early 1950s, today only one in seven enjoys that opportunity (Table 4.3). This situation is responsible for a growing gap between the aspirations of young people for higher education and the possibilities of their realization. Khrushchev's ill-fated educational reforms of 1958, though largely prompted by a growing labor shortage, were also an effort to address the consequences of this problem: a society increasingly overeducated for its occupational structure, a generation of young people aspiring to be engineers and disdainful of manual jobs, and a privileged elite attempting to use the educational system to pass its advantaged position to its offspring.

By the 1960s Soviet sociologists were openly expressing concern about the lack of "fit" between the educational and career aspirations of young people and the possibilities open to them. The disparity was evident in a succession of studies that revealed that over three-quarters of graduating secondary school students hoped to continue their studies at a time when far fewer were actually able to do so (Table 4.4). In the heightened competition for access, different social strata differed markedly in their prospects for success, with the off-spring of peasant background uniquely disadvantaged: nine out of ten children of urban nonmanuals who desired to continue their education full-time were able to do so, compared to only one out of ten peasant offspring.

Less systematic but more humorous testimony to the disparity between young people's aspirations and societal needs was offered by a 1973 account of the results of a Young Communist League survey:

> Let us transport ourselves magically to a desert island where each of the pupils has become what he wanted to be. We find many designers, but only seven construction workers and one work superintendent. Every tenth person is a doctor, but there are only five nurses. Manufacturing is hopelessly bad, with only eighty factory workers. There are hundreds of journalists and writers, but no printers to publish their work. We find one restaurant director, twenty-three cooks and no waiter—but with only seven livestock specialists, one tractor driver and one fisherman it is hard to feed all the scientists, actors and coaches at work on the island.[6]

In the view of many Soviet sociologists, the combination of exces-sively high aspirations on the one hand and disdain for blue-collar jobs on the other has resulted in serious demoralization when expec-tations were disappointed. The "shattering" of career plans contrib-utes to "attitudes of skepticism" and "a weakening of belief in ideals,"

Table 4.3

Number of Students Admitted to Daytime Study
in Higher Educational Institutions (VUZy)

	Daytime VUZ Admissions	
Years	*In % of Daytime Secondary School Graduates*	*In % of Total Secondary School Graduates*
1950–53	77	61
1960–63	57	32
1970–73	24	19
1975	22	17
1976	21	16
1977	20	15

SOURCE Murray Yanowitch, "Schooling and Inequalities," in Leonard Schapiro and Joseph Godson, eds., *The Soviet Worker: Illusions and Realities* (London: Macmillan, 1981), p. 134.

Table 4.4

*Educational Aspirations of Secondary School Graduates
and Their Realization, by Social Group,
Novosibirsk Region, 1963 (%)*

| | Aspirations | | Outcomes | |
Parents' Occupation	Work with or without part-time study	Study only	Work with or without part-time study	Study only
Urban intelligentsia	7	93	18	82
Rural intelligentsia	24	76	42	58
Workers (industry & construction)	17	83	39	61
Workers (transport & communication)	18	82	55	45
Workers (service industry)	24	76	41	59
Agricultural workers	24	76	90	10
Other occupations	50	50	75	25
Average for the sample	17	83	39	61

SOURCE: V. N. Shubkin, "Molodezh' vstupaet v zhizn'," *Voprosy filosofii*, 1965, no. 5, p. 65.

according to one leading Soviet specialist.[7] High labor turnover reflects the unhealthy tendency for young people to "roam" from one low-level and unsatisfying job to another, jobs they view as "temporary evils" until they succeed in gaining admission to a higher educational institution, which usually fails to happen.

Some Soviet scholars maintain that the problem has begun to ease in the last few years as students reduce their aspirations to correspond with a realistic assessment of their chances. Supporting his contention that "the career plans of graduating students are moving into greater conformity with the objective requirements of Soviet society," one well-known Soviet sociologist, F. R. Filippov, maintains that 80 to 90 percent of secondary school students in the mid-1960s were inclined to continue their studies, but that the figure had dropped to about 46 percent in 1973–75.[8] Fragmentary evidence of a decline in applications to higher educational institutions, from 269 per 100 vacancies in 1970 to 245 in 1977, would support his view. However, it is children of workers and collective farmers who are more likely to scale down their aspirations than the offspring of employees and specialists. The increasing competitiveness over access in the past two decades has therefore tended to strengthen the position of children from advantaged families.

Numerous studies conducted by Soviet sociologists since the early 1960s document that children from higher status families tend to begin formal schooling with better preparation, achieve higher levels of academic performance, have higher educational aspirations, and experience greater success in fulfilling those aspirations than their less advantaged counterparts. They dominate the specialized secondary schools for talented children that offer advanced training in the sciences, mathematics, and foreign languages. Moreover, not only do they make up a disproportionate share of the applicant pool at higher educational institutions, but they are more successful in winning admission. In short, the Soviet system experiences the same contradiction between a commitment to equality and a commitment to rapid social and economic development that other societies confront. As two leading sociologists put it:

> Socialist society is interested in selecting those individuals who will yield maximum benefits in the future as skilled specialists. Competitive examinations for higher educational institutions, generally speaking, enable us to choose those who are best prepared to master a given specialty. But it is well known that the degree of preparation of an applicant depends not only on his natural abilities, but also on the material and cultural level of the family in which he was raised, on the quality of teaching in the secondary school that he attended, and on many other factors that promote the early development of abilities and the acquisition of greater knowledge by the time of the examination. . . . In ignoring the conditions under which applicants are trained, and in making judgments based only on the applicants' knowledge, admissions committees in effect sanction inequality of opportunity.[9]

Family position affects educational opportunities in more direct and material ways as well. Children of higher status families are more successful in passing the entrance examinations because of their ability to utilize private tutoring. The rector of Moscow University himself announced in 1969 that 85 percent of the students admitted to the Faculty of Mechanics and Mathematics that year had received private instruction prior to taking the entrance examinations.[10] A 1975 article in *Komsomol'skaia pravda* testified to the widespread social acceptance of this phenomenon:

> "The contest of tutors"—do you remember how at first this sounded like a joke? But only at first. Just listen to your acquaintances, sit in on the entrance examinations for the higher schools, where the parents of secondary school graduates nervously await the results—it is a surprising fact that people are no longer ashamed of having tutors, they are proud of them. They call them by their titles and, among circles of friends, by the posts they hold. The costlier the tutor, the more prestige he has. This

means that our system of free education, equally available to everyone and based on competition in knowledge, has been invaded by the ruble.[11]

Financial circumstances also affect the ability of young people to defer employment in order to continue their studies. Although the state heavily subsidizes higher education, providing stipends for almost three-fourths of full-time students and subsidized dormitory accommodations for roughly half, students still depend in varying degrees upon family support.

Finally, the meritocratic features of educational access are tempered by informal practices which discriminate against or offer preferential treatment to particular individuals or members of social groups. Accumulating evidence makes it clear that examination procedures are manipulated to exclude Jewish applications or to promote "affirmative action" on behalf of non-Russian nationalities and that well-placed or well-endowed parents are frequently in a position to influence the selection process on behalf of their offspring.[12] Although the use of influence or bribery by elite families has come under attack in recent years, the selection process itself invites such corruption.

As a consequence, higher educational institutions have taken on an increasingly elitist profile, with the most prestigious institutions drawing a larger share of students from intelligentsia families, while those of lower quality or those offering training in less prestigious fields attract higher proportions of students of working class or peasant background. The emergence of a hierarchically stratified system of higher educational institutions thus corresponds to the crystalization of status within the population more broadly and to a decline in opportunities for upward social mobility via formal education for worker and particularly for peasant youth.

Increasingly competitive access to higher education does not completely close off the opportunity for upward mobility to working class or peasant offspring. Extensive programs of continuing, adult, and on-the-job education are available to the Soviet worker; although their quality is low, formal certification of new skills is an almost automatic guarantee of job promotion. More important still, the party itself continues to represent an alternative channel for upward movement, as do careers in the KGB and the military, although these too demand increasing qualifications. Ambitious and talented young people rising within these channels have access to separate educational and training institutions at various stages of their careers; the party in particular maintains a broad network of schools and programs for this purpose.

Nonetheless, the Soviet leadership has been sufficiently concerned about the problem to have attempted to diminish or defuse the frustration of aspirations inherent in this situation in a number of ways. Not wishing to expand enrollments in higher education, and thereby create an even greater imbalance between educational enrollments and occupational needs, it has sought simultaneously to expand opportunities for lower social strata and to lower aspirations.

First, it established highly visible, if limited, opportunities for more disadvantaged young people to enter higher educational institutions. In 1969, it created preparatory divisions, reminiscent of the *rabfaks* of an earlier era, to alter the social composition of higher educational institutions by offering college preparatory programs to young people employed as workers or collective farmers for at least a year. At the same time, the leadership has promoted a major expansion and upgrading of the network of vocational-technical schools to attract larger numbers of young people into programs training skilled workers. Thirdly, it has sought to increase the attractiveness of blue-collar occupations by increasing their rewards. The narrowing of wage differentials between blue-collar, white-collar, and engineering occupations during the past two decades represents just such an effort, although it appears to have reached its limits. Finally, it has launched a highly visible if selective attack on bribery and other forms of corruption in the competition for access to higher education. Indeed, the head of the Azerbaidzhan party organization and recently elected full member of the Politburo, Gaidar Aliev, specifically described such efforts in a recent article, mentioning a decree that specifically forbade family members of the republic's administrative elite from even applying for admission to medical schools, an implicit admission that only Draconian measures could forestall corrupt practices.

It is too early to evaluate the success of these efforts. Yet even if aspirations, expressed by application to higher education, are moderating, this does not resolve the problem; much expressed willingness to settle for less than an intelligentsia career may mask serious disgruntlement. Were this not the case, young men and women would make more use of specialized secondary or vocational-technical "trade" schools. While enrollment in the latter increased in the 1970s for those deciding not to complete academic secondary school (from 6.4 percent of those completing eighth year in schools in the Russian Republic in 1973 to 14.0 percent in 1977), so also did the percentage of eighth graders moving into complete academic secondary education: 54 percent in 1973, 61 in 1977.

Moreover, even if a larger cohort moves from secondary education directly into employment, the gap between aspirations and job content will not necessarily diminish. Rising educational attainments tend to increase the demand for more satisfying and nonroutine jobs, but educational attainment in the USSR is actually outrunning the increase of such jobs. Indeed, a number of Soviet analysts are concerned that job dissatisfaction will be a growing rather than a diminishing problem in the years ahead. V. Churbanov, writing in 1973, formulated the problem of "educated youth and uninteresting work" in these terms:

> The higher a young person's educational level, the greater his need for interesting work. Yet most industrial work presently requires no more than a sixth to eighth grade education, and the scientific and technical revolution is not expected to keep pace with the spread of education in the next few years. The transition to universal secondary education, otherwise so desirable, will only exacerbate this problem.[13]

Thus, Soviet social policy faces in the 1980s and 1990s a situation which calls for considerable finesse. Ideally, in the face of labor and capital shortages the state should divert teenagers from general secondary training and expand instead specialized secondary or vocational-technical education which will lead them to jobs as skilled and more productive workers. Morale should rise, productivity should increase (insofar as this is an outcome of workers' skill and morale), and this generation of new workers should in turn raise a generation of offspring ready in large numbers to duplicate their parental status, in line with a realistic appreciation of the "needs" of the economy in the years to come.

This is not likely to happen. As the prospects for significant further improvement of living standards grow distant in a low-growth economy, stakes in the mobility competition increase. Except in the unlikely event that the structure of wages is radically transformed, the relative costs of being a worker and the advantages of being a professional will increase. A highly stratified society may be able to "block" from higher education those who desire to rise through it to higher status, but to "cool out" the desires themselves is a far more difficult undertaking.

Thus, declining opportunities for upward social mobility are likely to intensify the efforts of privileged families to defend and transmit their social status to offspring and to increase the resentment of those who perceive themselves to be excluded. The erosion of an official ideology which seeks to prevent the development of class consciousness, combined with the scarcity of resources to compensate in part for status differences, points to increasing visibility of social differentiation and increasing tension between social strata.

Compounding this problem is the growing gap between educational qualifications and job content. Under ideal conditions, a high degree of job satisfaction in the workplace itself might well offset other sources of alienation or discontent. Although numerous experiments with work organization are underway, Soviet writings are rather pessimistic about their prospects and do not anticipate that dissatisfaction will be substantially reduced in the years ahead. High rates of labor turnover, low productivity, and problems of worker morale are therefore likely to be a source of continuing problems in the years ahead.

Unfavorable Demographic Trends

Declining Rates of Population Growth

Declining rates of population growth, compounded by other unfavorable demographic trends, present Soviet policy makers with an additional set of dilemmas in the 1980s. Stemming in part from broader transformations universally associated with urbanization and rising educational levels and in part from conditions specific to Soviet society, these demographic trends have provoked considerable alarm in Soviet scholarly and policy circles in recent years and have prompted a number of policy initiatives seeking to reverse them.

First among these problems is the slowdown in the rate of population growth. Throughout Soviet history until the 1960s, the tendency for successive cohorts of women to bear fewer and fewer children was partially offset by declining mortality. More recently, however, the combination of declining birthrates and rising mortality rates have resulted in a sharp drop in net population increase, from 18 per thousand in 1969 to 9 per thousand in 1970 to 8 per thousand in 1980 and to a projected 7.5 per thousand in 1990 and possibly under 4 per thousand in the year 2000.

As a result of the combined effects of declining birthrates and rising mortality rates, by the year 2000 the size of the Soviet population will have increased to about 300 million, rather than the 340–350 million anticipated earlier by Soviet analysts (Table 4.5). The disparity between a rate of reproduction a number of Soviet demographers would consider optimal and the actual rate, which in some regions falls below the replacement rate, is in their view sufficiently alarming to require that the government give highest priority to eliminating the possibility of a future decline in population "regardless of any considerations that may be advanced from an economic, ecological, sociological, or any other point of view."[14] Debate over the causes of and remedies for declining fertility has become a national pastime.

Reasons for Concern

That declining fertility rates should be a source of anxiety in a world where some view zero population growth as the only solution to resource constraints reflects a concern with their implications for

Soviet economic and political development. First is the potential effect a stable or shrinking population exercises on future economic growth. In the face of a mounting labor shortage and of male and female participation rates that already approach the demographic maximum, a continuing supply of new entrants to the labor force seems essential to continuing economic growth. By 1984 the entire labor force for the rest of the century will already have been born. That virtually no net increases in labor resources can be expected from this source for the remainder of the century is sobering news. Although efforts are underway to shift from an extensive to an intensive pattern of economic development and to compensate for labor shortages by encouraging technological innovation, increased labor productivity, and continued employment of the pension-aged population, the record holds little promise of significant gains. In the past few years the USSR has even resorted to importing labor from Eastern Europe and more recently Vietnam to overcome specific shortages. Labor constraints in the prime industrial regions of the USSR, especially Russia and Siberia, are likely to become especially acute because a growing proportion of new labor supplies will be located in regions such as Central Asia, where relatively low levels of industrialization and low rates of outmigration have already produced a labor surplus. The prospects of shifting large supplies of Central Asian labor to regions of labor scarcity are exceedingly dim in the near future, given the lack of "fit" in skills and lifestyles and the comfortable living conditions and relative immobility of the Central Asian population. On the other hand, the acceleration of industrial development in Central Asia would demand enormous investments for river diversion and irrigation, expansion of small-scale light industry in small towns and massive development of day care institutions to make most effective use of rural labor surpluses, including women. No easy resolution of current dilemmas is, therefore, in sight.

In addition to its contribution to future labor resources, expanding population is also considered necessary to maintain an optimal balance between the productive and the dependent segments of the population. The growing weight of the pension-aged in the total Soviet population, from 10 percent in 1950 to 15 percent in 1970 and possibly 20 percent by the year 2000, places increasing strains on the system of social services. In 1978 they consumed more than 7 percent of national income and 72 percent of the 40.3 billion ruble welfare budget. Thus, the combined effects of a growing population of aged and the urgently needed liberalization of pension benefits will constitute an increasing drain on resources in coming decades.

A further source of concern less openly discussed is the effect of current demographic trends on military and political power. The

Table 4.5

Estimates and Projections of the Age Distribution of the Population
USSR and by Republic, Both Sexes: 1970 and 2000

(in Thousands)

1970	USSR	RSFSR	Ukraine	Belorussia	Moldavia	Estonia	Latvia	Lithuania	Armenia	Azerbaidzhan	Georgia	Kazakhstan	Kirgizia	Tadzhikistan	Turkmenistan	Uzbekistan
0– 4	20,526	9,323	3,444	742	338	96	160	268	289	744	433	1,520	413	494	348	1,886
5– 9	24,495	11,974	4,094	911	397	102	177	297	356	812	514	1,741	431	479	341	1,869
10–14	25,008	13,179	4,197	952	412	100	174	281	334	699	486	1,592	378	378	279	1,565
15–19	22,017	12,311	3,866	772	345	101	166	236	252	466	402	1,265	278	264	205	1,090
20–24	17,119	9,797	3,123	600	233	95	164	217	169	295	300	947	178	165	139	688
25–29	13,781	7,148	2,980	511	230	95	178	229	127	234	278	769	143	149	112	600
30–34	21,161	11,748	4,346	734	274	111	196	241	210	401	403	1,160	209	193	144	790
35–39	16,606	9,350	3,108	691	244	105	181	238	167	333	343	738	177	166	120	649
40–44	19,018	10,946	3,885	687	239	104	182	226	169	290	366	851	180	154	116	624
45–49	12,265	6,711	2,800	491	208	81	142	177	87	163	226	501	113	96	76	391
50–54	9,085	5,260	1,941	302	134	58	100	112	52	113	176	373	78	68	55	274
55–59	12,023	6,862	2,758	421	167	75	133	138	74	154	213	450	93	78	67	341
60–64	9,783	5,347	2,247	388	122	72	131	157	69	132	178	368	86	74	55	355
65–69	7,825	4,304	1,793	309	96	57	103	123	54	105	141	294	69	58	43	279
70 and over	10,929	5,775	2,529	485	129	99	174	187	82	174	236	410	109	85	57	395
Total	241,640	130,036	47,111	8,999	3,568	1,356	2,363	3,127	2,491	5,115	4,685	13,004	2,932	2,899	2,158	11,796

0– 4	23,995	9,746	3,527	746	370	102	166	267	332	913	469	1,804	644	858	604	3,448
5– 9	24,044	9,715	3,537	777	377	100	165	275	347	972	482	1,874	640	840	591	3,351
10–14	25,008	10,493	3,701	832	402	100	167	281	379	980	507	1,962	624	807	565	3,209
15–19	25,127	11,093	3,823	844	414	103	170	276	382	880	502	1,920	586	725	509	2,901
20–24	22,960	10,392	3,632	754	385	103	167	257	332	728	456	1,720	507	631	436	2,458
25–29	20,776	9,363	3,508	710	348	105	169	263	290	669	429	1,515	447	524	374	2,062
30–34	19,774	8,902	3,364	722	322	97	161	265	292	708	421	1,484	394	470	334	1,840
35–39	23,390	11,330	3,971	881	375	102	177	293	358	765	497	1,655	407	451	323	1,806
40–44	23,455	12,229	4,011	911	382	99	172	274	333	647	465	1,488	349	348	260	1,488
45–49	20,154	11,128	3,618	726	313	96	159	226	248	422	377	1,153	251	237	185	1,014
50–54	15,206	8,571	2,847	551	215	94	153	203	164	260	276	839	156	144	122	623
55–59	11,630	5,918	2,581	448	192	84	157	204	117	195	245	645	118	121	92	512
60–64	16,826	9,169	3,557	612	215	92	164	204	184	316	336	916	162	149	111	636
65–69	11,899	6,569	2,295	524	172	79	136	183	133	234	259	524	123	116	83	470
70 and over	23,805	13,216	4,778	971	308	151	267	335	210	324	481	1,005	206	170	133	753
Total	308,050	147,834	53,248	11,010	4,777	1,507	2,549	3,804	4,101	9,014	6,202	20,507	5,614	6,590	4,722	26,572

SOURCE: Godfrey Baldwin, *Population Projects by Age and Sex: For the Republics and Major Economic Regions of the USSR: 1970–2000*. Series P-91, No. 26, International Population Reports, Washington, D.C., September 1979, Table 1, pp. 25–90 and TsSU SSSR. *Narodnoye khozyaystvo SSSR v 1979 godu, statisticheskiy yezhegodnik*, Moscow, Statistika, 1981, p. 10.

view that "a country's position in the world, all other things being equal, is determined by the size of the population" is not confined to demographers. Frequent comparisons of Soviet population trends with those of the United States, Japan, and China indicate that Soviet analysts are sensitive to the strategic implications of population dynamics, a sensitivity that undoubtedly prompted a recent suggestion that the Soviet leadership adopt as its goal the maintenance of a constant ratio between the size of the world's population and that of the USSR.[15]

Ethnic Differentials

Declining rates of population growth, however, are only part of the demographic problem: ethnic differentials in birthrates and mortality rates complicate it further. The national data tend to obscure the fact that the more industrialized Western regions of the USSR, including the Russian, Ukrainian, and Baltic republics, are experiencing sharp declines in birthrates, while the rates of population growth remain high and have even been increasing in other parts of the country, particularly in the Moslem areas of Central Asia. While the single-child family is now the norm in the Slavic and Baltic republics, large families are widespread among many of the non-Slavic populations. For example, only one percent of all families in the urban areas of the Russian republic have four or more children, compared with 25 percent of all urban families in Turkmenistan. The proportion of large families is greater still in rural areas, constituting almost half the total in Uzbekistan, Tadzhikistan, and Turkmenistan and even more in Azerbaidzhan. Regional variations in marriage and divorce rates and in the age structure of the population further compound demographic disparities resulting from economic and cultural patterns that affect desired family size. Thus, the rate of births per 1000 population in the Central Asian republics is roughly two and a half times greater than in the Baltic and Slavic republics. Since the age structure of the latter republics also generates higher mortality rates, the net differences in population growth are even greater than differences in birthrates alone.

As a consequence of these variations, the Moslem populations of the Central Asian and Transcaucasian republics will provide an increasing share of future net population growth. In 1959, these republics accounted for just over 12 percent of all births in the USSR; by 1970, their share had risen to 20 percent. The disparity is even more dramatic with respect to the natural increase of population overall because of the smaller proportion of aged with high mortality rates. In 1959, these republics accounted for 15 percent of the total, and eleven years later for 30 percent. Thus, by the beginning of the twenty-first century, the Russian Republic's share of the total Soviet population will decline from its present 52 percent to 46 percent, while Central Asia's share will rise from 14 percent to 21 percent of the total.

The profound implications of these trends for the supply and quality of military manpower, as well as for the nature and availability of future labor resources, are of particular concern to Soviet analysts and policy makers. As Table 4.6 suggests, ethnic differentials in birthrates will have major consequences for the ethnic composition of the Soviet armed forces by the end of the century. Because of the poorer quality of their educational background and more limited command of the Russian language, as well as more generalized distrust, Central Asian conscripts have traditionally been relegated in disproportionate numbers to lower-status services or those branches of service demanding fewest technical skills. They tend to concentrate in noncombat units, such as construction battalions, or in noncombat capacities in combat units, and often receive no systematic military instruction beyond basic training. While levels of educational attainment and Russian language competence have been steadily rising in recent years, and while these issues are now receiving serious attention from the leadership, the prospect that Central Asian conscripts will constitute a growing share of the total is clearly a source of concern. Thus, while the high fertility rates in these regions are in some respects a welcome compensation for the low rates prevailing elsewhere, they create additional and delicate problems of their own.

Increases in Mortality Rates

Yet a third demographic problem contributing to the slowdown in population growth and troubling Soviet scholars and policy makers alike is the sharp and puzzling increase in mortality rates. Until the mid-1960s, crude death rates had steadily declined, but since then they have risen sharply. While rising mortality rates partly reflect changes in the age structure of the population, more specifically its general "aging," the rates show the same trend even when age is eliminated as a factor. This is in turn the product of two alarming developments: an apparent increase in infant mortality, and a rise in the overall level of mortality among Soviet males, especially pronounced among the cohort of males between the ages of 40 and 50.

A recent study of Soviet infant mortality by two Western specialists argues that after a long period of decline in infant mortality rates, which by 1971 reached a low of 22.9 deaths per thousand live births, infant mortality began to rise again, making the Soviet Union the first and only developed country to experience a sustained reversal of the normal downward trend.[16] Moreover, this reversal was astonishingly

Table 4.6

Estimates and Projections, Male Population 16, 18, and 20
Years of Age, USSR and by Republic: 1970 to 2000
(as of July 1, in Thousands)

Place and Age Cohort	1970	1980	1990	2000	Place and Age Cohort	1970	1980	1990	2000
USSR					**Armenia**				
16	2,297	2,316	2,174	2,585	16	28	36	30	40
18	2,238	2,542	2,135	2,544	18	26	38	30	39
20	2,132	2,636	2,024	2,456	20	21	40	29	37
RSFSR					**Azerbaidzhan**				
16	1,283	1,084	984	1,122	16	52	83	67	94
18	1,261	1,251	959	1,124	18	47	80	68	88
20	1,224	1,336	900	1,098	20	38	78	70	82
Ukraine					**Georgia**				
16	395	394	358	390	16	42	50	44	52
18	393	427	365	389	18	40	52	43	51
20	382	450	348	381	20	37	52	43	49
Belorussia					**Kazakhstan**				
16	80	84	72	87	16	134	165	159	199
18	79	95	73	86	18	129	180	154	193
20	77	99	71	82	20	120	176	148	184
Moldavia					**Kirgiziia**				
16	34	38	37	43	16	30	43	48	61
18	32	41	37	43	18	26	43	46	59
20	30	44	33	42	20	23	41	43	56
Estonia					**Tadzhikistan**				
16	10	11	11	10	16	26	53	58	78
18	11	11	11	10	18	25	47	54	73
20	12	11	11	10	20	21	42	50	70
Latvia					**Turkmenistan**				
16	17	18	17	17	16	22	35	41	54
18	18	19	18	17	18	22	35	39	51
20	19	19	17	17	20	18	32	36	48
Lithuania					**Uzbekistan**				
16	24	29	26	28	16	117	193	223	309
18	24	31	28	28	18	105	190	211	292
20	26	32	27	27	20	86	183	198	273

Source: Unpublished estimates and projections prepared by Godfrey Baldwin, Foreign Demographic Analysis Division, U.S. Bureau of the Census, March 1980.

sharp; it rose to 27.9 in 1974, at which point the Soviets stopped publishing the figures, to an estimated 31.1 per thousand in 1976, an increase of over one-third in just five years, and to a possible figure of 39 to 40 per thousand in 1979. These statistics are particularly striking when compared to the U.S. figure of 12.9 deaths per thousand live births in 1979; the Soviet rate would appear to be virtually triple.

This same period also witnessed a startling rise in mortality rates among males, especially those in the prime working and military age bracket of 20 to 44. The death rate for this category increased to a level roughly three times that of the comparable female group, to the point that premature deaths of males now exceed divorce as the main cause of the increase of female-headed households. As a consequence of this trend, the life expectancy of Soviet males, which had reached 66 years in 1965–66, declined to 64 years in 1971–72 and may in 1982 be as low as 62, compared to female life expectancy of roughly 73 years.

The dimension of these trends and their causes and implications have been a subject of considerable controversy among Western specialists,[17] exacerbated by confusion among Soviet officials and scholars themselves. While a substantial part of the problem in the case of infant mortality is attributable to the unreliability of Soviet statistics, especially for earlier periods when infant deaths were underreported, particularly in Central Asia, and Soviet achievements thereby exaggerated, the evidence suggests that at least part of the apparent increase in infant mortality may be more than a statistical artifact and that the Soviets themselves believe that they face a real problem. If indeed a part of the apparent increase is due to better reporting, then past levels of infant mortality have been much higher than was hitherto believed to be the case and the impact of improvements in health care was correspondingly lower.

In the case of infant mortality, rising rates appear to be associated with several factors whose importance differs in different regions of the country. They include more extensive reliance on day care facilities as rates of female employment rose; underutilization of existing health care facilities and their failure to keep pace with new needs; replacement of breast feeding by the use of formula in conditions where adequate nutrition and sanitation were not assured; the widespread reliance on abortion as the major method of birth control; rising female alcoholism; and the effects of several virulent strains of influenza in the 1970s with which the Soviet health system was unable to deal adequately.

In the case of male mortality, increased alcohol consumption appears to bear a large share of the responsibility. Alcohol abuse is an important contributing factor in coronary heart disease, which accounted for two-thirds of the total mortality change. The residual change was largely attributable to the combined effects of accidents, poisonings, traumas, and to a lesser extent respiratory system diseases, with alcohol abuse the underlying cause of roughly half the total. Alcohol poisoning alone was responsible for 40,000 deaths in a single year, 1976, compared to 400 such deaths in the United States.[18]

While it would be an exaggeration to conclude that the Soviet health care system is experiencing a "crisis," there is mounting evidence that it is not responding adequately to growing demands upon it and that existing problems are exacerbated by the reduced investments in health care in the 1970s. In his report to the Twenty-sixth Party Congress in 1981 Brezhnev himself drew attention to continuing shortcomings in the delivery of health care:

> The work of polyclinics, dispensaries, and out-patient clinics which handle 80 percent of all the sick must substantially improve. Unfortunately, in a number of places they lag behind the possibilities of medicine, there is a shortage of personnel, especially middle and junior, equipment is obsolete, and modern medicines are in short supply. Plans for the construction of hospitals and health facilities fall behind schedule.[19]

A health care system that places a heart clinic in its capital city on the fifth floor of a building without an elevator offers substantial room for improvement.

A number of Soviet scholars have begun to explore the negative impact of the "scientific-technical revolution" on working and living conditions. Occupational hazards, environmental changes, high mobility, information overload, and increased stress, among other factors, are adversely affecting health. These changes expand both the need and the demand for health services, including preventive medical care. Improvements in the health of the Soviet population, in their view, as well as a reduction in mortality rates, require major improvements in the quality of health care as well as increases in the expenditures devoted to it.[20]

The Pro-Natalist Program and Its Problems

The 1959 census first alerted both Soviet and Western observers to these demographic trends and inaugurated an increasingly public discussion of their causes and consequences. The revival of sociology and then demography, both suppressed under Stalin, provided the scholarly underpinning for public debates. The results of the 1970 census confirmed the urgency of the problem and gave impetus to Brezhnev's call at the Twenty-fifth Party Congress in 1975 for formulation of an "effective demographic policy." While many specialists were skeptical of the need for or desirability of such an effort, their reservations were overshadowed by the arguments of a vocal group of demographers, economists, and sociologists who had long urged the adoption of pro-natalist measures to mitigate the effects of declining fertility in the European areas of the USSR, if not to reverse the trend altogether. Despite precedents in Romania, Czechoslovakia, Hungary, and Bulgaria, or perhaps mindful of the Soviet precedent of

1936–55, the advocates of such pro-natalist measures refrained by and large from recommending restrictions on abortion, insisting that such measures were inadmissible in principle, ineffective in practice, and potentially harmful in their effects. They urged instead a series of measures that would alter the social and economic context of reproductive behavior.

The recommendations included measures designed to enhance fertility potential by enlarging the pool of married females in the prime reproductive age cohort and by providing additional incentives to marriage. Second, they urged policies designed to alter social values in favor of large families. Placing the blame for low birthrates on social trends that raised the cost and reduced the benefits of children and that devalued reproduction in favor of other social and personal goals, they advocated a national effort to stimulate the desire for children. In order to achieve an optimal 2.65 children per family, they launched a campaign to persuade young couples to have at least two and preferably three children as a patriotic duty as well as a guarantee of family happiness.

A third group of recommendations stemmed from the view that living conditions rather than reproductive motivation constituted the major obstacles to increased family size, a view buttressed by extensive demographic surveys which indicated that an overwhelming majority of Soviet families had fewer children than they desired. These measures sought to reduce the material burden of child-rearing by offsetting its cost.

Whether pro-natalist measures should be uniformly applied nationwide or whether demographic policy should be regionally, and by implication ethnically, differentiated has become the subject of serious if muted controversy. Any uniform policy would in any case have a different impact on different regions of the country, given the socioeconomic and cultural diversity of Soviet society. Advocates of a differentiated approach urge that demographic policy explicitly attempt to depress the birthrate in high-fertility regions as well as to increase birthrates in the more developed regions where they are especially low. Implicitly criticizing the existing system of uniform child payments, which inevitably directed the bulk of these resources to the "heroine-mothers" of Central Asia, they urged anti-natalist measures in this region designed to "liberate" women from large families and improve the quality of life. In a discreetly worded passage, a leading Soviet demographer suggested the contours of such a differentiated approach:

For the USSR, where there exist large regional differences in the processes of reproduction of the population, from approximately stationary to greatly expanding, and where, moreover, these differences are largely determined by different levels of fertility, it is an important question whether demographic policy should vary by region of the country. If one proceeds from the view that demographic policy should primarily be directed at the creation of a single optimum type of population reproduction in the nation, then there should exist a single general direction of demographic policy for the entire country. For example, if we consider the optimal type of reproduction of population which is characterized by a net coefficient of 1.0–1.2 . . . with such parameters . . . it is necessary to stimulate by various measures the birth of first, second, and third children in the family . . . but beginning with the fourth child all measures of an encouraging nature should cease, or at a minimum significantly weaken. Such a system might stimulate fertility in areas where it is low and at the same time further the lowering of fertility in areas where it is very high.[21]

The implications of such an approach were not lost on Central Asian demographers, who in turn defended large families as a legitimate "national tradition" altogether compatible with full participation of women in social life.

The debate sharpened in the late 1970s, with proponents of a differentiated approach arguing that a concern with quantitative population growth must be accompanied by concern with "quality" and that the Soviet state could not be "indifferent to what kind of population increase occurs, whether it is highly mobile or, owing to a variety of circumstances (including large families and language barriers), bound to one specific region." Criticizing this view, a prominent Kazakh demographer bluntly asserted that a "differentiated population policy is by its nature and intent the same thing as a discriminatory policy."[22]

The Twenty-sixth Party Congress in 1981 brought the debate to a close: the Soviet leadership opted for a compromise that sought to stimulate fertility in the European regions without rescinding the existing system of child allowances. New initiatives announced at the Congress and additional decrees which followed outlined a two-pronged effort: first, introduction of partially paid maternity leave for working mothers (initially promised in 1976) at the very modest rate of 35 rubles a month for the first year (and 50 rubles in Siberia, the Soviet Far East and certain northern regions) to be introduced in unspecified stages; second, a new system of child allowances paying 50 rubles on the birth of a first child, 100 rubles each for the second and third, and nothing for subsequent children. This plan was superimposed on the existing system of state family benefits, so that resources flowing to poor families and to the large families of Central Asia would not be cut off, but the clear intent of the new measure is to encourage single-child couples of the low-fertility regions to have second and third children.

Taken by themselves, these measures are too limited and the scale of payments too small to have significant effect on demographic behavior; they are far more limited, for example, than those adopted in Hungary. The preferential assignment of new housing to young families would probably have a more potent effect. Nonetheless, these measures indicate the high priority which the Soviet leadership has begun to assign to demographic and family policy, the pro-natalist direction that future policies are likely to take, and the increasingly influential role of social scientists in shaping the contours of such measures. The nature of current demographic trends, however, makes them relatively resistant to small-scale tinkering. Without a far-reaching effort to reduce significantly the costs of children to working mothers of the European urban regions and to create economic opportunities that would significantly raise their cost in Central Asia, current demographic trends are not likely to alter greatly in the foreseeable future, nor will the problems they raise be easily resolved.

The Rise of Ethnonationalism

The multinational character of the Soviet state is the source of still further problems in the decades ahead. Although the resurgence of ethnic self-assertion has been a worldwide phenomenon in this century, and a major source of political instability from Canada to India, the Soviet system has thus far proven comparatively immune to its disruptive effects. It is unlikely that a future Soviet leadership will continue to enjoy this luxury; the "nationality problem," in the view of Western and Soviet analysts alike, is likely to become one of the most difficult in the years ahead.

As the largest multinational state in the world, dominated by its Russian core but comprising over 100 distinct nationalities of which 22 number over one million people each, the USSR has had to grapple from the beginning with the problem of combining centralized economic and political control with some degree of cultural pluralism. The result has been a nationality policy marked by a fundamental tension. On the one hand, the system proclaims a commitment to the development and flourishing of all nationalities, with the major groups given political and administrative recognition in their own republics or autonomous regions and social recognition in a partially pluralist educational and cultural system. At the same time, the expectation that modernization will promote the ultimate withering away of national identities and the emergence of a homogeneous and unified "Soviet" nation undercuts this very commitment. The very effort to promote integration and convergence, connoting as it does increasing Russification, provokes intensified ethnic consciousness and self-assertion among the non-Russian minorities, which elicits increased Russian nationalism in response.

The Problem of Nationalism Appears

The experience of the past three decades, beginning with the self-assertion which Khrushchev's thaw facilitated, has provided evidence that the repressive policies of the Stalin era had temporarily silenced the quest for collective identity but hardly obliterated it. The appearance of the dissident movement, which included an important national and religious component, focused new attention on the sources of alienation in the Soviet system. A rising tide of protests in the Baltic and Ukraine, among the Crimean Tartars, and in Georgia, coupled with the large-scale emigration of Germans, Armenians, and Jews, demonstrated the degree to which ethnic identity might form an independent basis of political action. More recently, the rise of Islamic fundamentalism in the Middle East, with its growing salience for Soviet policy, coupled with the astonishing demographic vitality of Soviet Central Asia revealed in the 1959 and 1970 censuses, has brought this region to the forefront of both scholarly and policy concern.

These developments have generated a major reassessment of Soviet perceptions and expectations. Until two decades ago, Soviet scholars routinely asserted that the nationality problem had largely been solved. The convergence of socioeconomic systems among the various republics and nationalities of the USSR had produced a gradual rapprochement *(sblizhenie)* of values and behavior among the nation's varied ethnic groups, which would in turn result in their full assimilation and their ultimate merging *(sliianie)* into a new identity, the Soviet *narod.* These views have undergone profound alteration in recent years. *Sliianie* has virtually disappeared from the official vocabulary, and scholars castigate the emphasis on merging as "one-sided."

The Soviet leadership has come to appreciate that the rapprochement of Soviet nationalities is a far more problematic and long-term process than was anticipated under Khrushchev and one demanding patient and delicate social engineering. It now encourages Soviet scholars to devote serious study to ethnonational processes and in 1969 created a Scientific Council for Nationality Problems under the Academy of Sciences to coordinate research, plan future projects, and prepare "scientifically based" proposals for resolution of nationality problems. Khrushchev's optimistic assertion at the Twenty-second Party Congress that "the Party has solved one of the most complex of problems, which has plagued mankind for ages and remains acute in the world of capitalism to this day—the problem of relations between nations," has been superseded by Brezhnev's more somber recognition at the Twenty-sixth Party Congress that "the dynamics of the development of a large multinational state like ours gives rise to many problems requiring the Party's tactful attention."

The increased assertiveness of the non-Russian nationalities, given impetus by de-Stalinization, by reopening discussion of the nationality question, and by the successes of national groups in other parts of the world, and reinforced by demographic trends which appear to give biological reinforcement to new political demands, have contributed in turn to an upsurge of Russian national consciousness. While some of this resurgence reflects a broader search for roots or has taken the form of movements for the restoration of historical and cultural monuments, some of it carries chauvinistic overtones which in turn stimulate the counternationalism of the non-Russian nationalities.

Several distinct issues bearing directly on the resources, power, and status of both Russian and non-Russian nationalities have come to the forefront of recent debates and provide a focus for the crystalization of ethnic identifications and cleavages. The first of these involves the nature of the federal system and the balance between a unitary and centralized, as opposed to a federal or pluralist, definition of its structure. A protracted controversy over the autonomy, power, and status of the Union Republics long delayed promulgation of the Soviet Constitution of 1977. Advocates of reducing the formal status and role of the republics urged their case both on grounds of economic rationality, namely, that the present system is an impediment to the optimal planning of economic development overall, and presumably on grounds of political expediency as well, that retention of the republican structure constituted an impediment to rapid political and cultural integration and ultimate assimilation. Defenders of the intrinsic legitimacy of the original autonomist arrangement cited Lenin and other Russian leaders on its behalf. In the end, the existing structure was preserved, although with some diminution of republic autonomy. In subsequent comments about these discussions, however, Brezhnev did not challenge the principle of a unitary system but indicated only that a change in that direction was inexpedient at the present time.

The pace and pattern of economic development constitute a second source of controversy bearing directly on regional and ethnic concerns. Within the framework of a unified national economy based on regional specialization and a "fraternal division of labor," considerable controversy remains over the degree to which the allocation of investments should encourage, or at a minimum permit, a balanced pattern of economic growth within republics. The narrow concentration on cotton cultivation in Uzbekistan, for example, has created a virtual "plantation economy," while much recent development in Central Asia is based on extractive industries similarly dependent on external processing and oriented toward external markets. Low productivity, increasing underemployment, disadvantageous terms of trade, and intimations of the perpetuation of underdevelopment, all stemming from the absence of a sufficiently diversified pattern of industrial development capable of drawing on indigenous labor, have been the object of concern and criticism by local elites, who have in turn been accused of "national narrow-mindedness" and "localism."

Closely linked to issues of the pace and pattern of economic development are questions concerning the criteria for economic investment. The emphasis on Siberian development characteristic of recent Soviet economic policy, both because of its vast reserves of natural resources, including energy, and its strategic geopolitical position, has been challenged by advocates of a "European" strategy who insist that the higher productivity of investments in the more developed regions of European Russia, with skilled labor forces, excellent transportation network, and nearby markets should attract the bulk of investment. The advocates of increased investment in Central Asia urge yet a third strategy, based on availability of labor and commitment to equalization of development levels among republics. Implicitly challenging Brezhnev's 1972 statement that "the problem of the leveling of development of the national republics has on the whole been solved," a position he reaffirmed most recently at the Twenty-sixth Party Congress in 1981, Central Asian authors insist that equalization is far from achieved and press for increased allocation of resources to their region to achieve this goal.[23] Their efforts are unlikely to succeed because such a strategy would have less immediate economic payoffs and would not provide the same cultural and symbolic rewards to Russian-dominated elites as investments in the heartland. Nonetheless, the growing labor surplus in Central Asia will compel some new investment initiatives, however modest, and will sustain a continuing debate over this issue.

The allocation of opportunities, or "life chances" more broadly, constitutes yet another focus of interethnic tensions. The commitment to rapid socioeconomic modernization facilitated the creation of indigenous scientific, cultural, and administrative elites endowed with the skills and resources as well as the aspiration to fill the new positions which rapid industrialization, urbanization, and cultural development have generated. Widespread opportunities for upward mobility, particularly in cultural and scientific domains, have in turn facilitated cooptation of local elites and given them a substantial stake in the system.

At the same time, the process of modernization brought with it a major influx of Russian and other Slavic settlers into urban centers who provided needed technical and political-administrative skills and enjoyed, in turn, career opportunities and living conditions beyond what they might have attained in the provincial capitals of the Russian Republic. Expanded contacts between indigenous and settler communities heightened the ethnic self-awareness of each and generated a significant degree of tension over competition for elite positions. Language and cultural policies have become especially sensitive; long-term upward mobility, especially in political and scientific or technical arenas, depends upon the mastery by local elites of Russian language and cultural norms. The Slavic settler communities, however, faced little pressure to master the indigenous languages of the republics in which they lived and worked, a source of widespread resentment among indigenous elites.

The competition for access to higher education and desirable professional positions, and for upward social mobility generally, thus pits indigenous aspirations against those of the settler communities, leading to demands by local elites for further compensatory efforts and complaints by the settlers that members of the indigenous nationalities receive preferential treatment in their own republics, a policy justified during earlier stages of Soviet development but now in need of change.

Cadres policy constitutes yet another highly sensitive area of conflict within the party itself, involving closely controlled access to positions of political power. The *nomenklatura* system has preserved the dominance of Slavic elites in the most sensitive positions of the political hierarchy, not merely in central state and party organs but in the non-Russian republics as well. For example, while the first secretary of the Union Republic's Communist Party is now customarily a member of the titular nationality, the second secretary, who controls all-important cadres policy, is usually a Russian or other Slav, in effect an agent of central control. A rather explicit hierarchy has emerged in which a number of republics—Georgia, Azerbaidzhan, and Armenia among them—have received a substantial degree of responsibility for management of their political affairs, while Slavic cadres dominate the political elites of other republics, including those of Central Asia. This is increasingly less true at the local level, where "indigenization" has proceeded quite far and where the Slavic cadres are themselves "locals" rather than agents deployed from the center.

Moreover, despite slight variations in the pattern, local members of the non-Russian nationalities play a significant political role only in their own republics, except for Ukrainians and Armenians; upward mobility does not extend to responsible positions in other republics or at the all-Union level. Thus, of some 123 non-Russians serving in leading political roles, all but one was a member of the titular nationality of the republic in which he served. While the resentment this generates seldom reaches public expression, substantial evidence exists of dissatisfaction and of efforts for increased, even proportional, representations of indigenous cadres in republic-level organs. Brezhnev was undoubtedly alluding to this problem in his speech at the Twenty-sixth Congress when he tactfully stated:

> The population of the Soviet republics is multinational. All nations, of course, have the right to be adequately represented in their party and government organs. Needless to say, the competence and ideological and moral make-up of each candidate must be carefully scrutinized.

Others have opposed such demands with less tact and greater force:

> In the past, when actual equality among peoples had not yet been established, when there still existed significant residues of the former backwardness of the indigenous nation in this or that republic, it was necessary to conduct a policy of indigenization of the apparatus. . . . But under present-day conditions . . . where there are no longer any backward national districts the need for such advantages no longer exists.[24]

Purges of republican officials of the local nationality are often accompanied by charges that they attempted to substitute ascriptive criteria for merit in appointments and promotions to responsible positions.

The sociocultural status and recognition accorded various Soviet nationalities amount to a further source of interethnic tension. Changing interpretations of national history and cultural evolution, of the relationship between the minority nationality and the Russian "elder brother," and the development of national languages all involve, in the broadest sense, both an assertion of developing cultural identities and an effort by Russian and non-Russian elites alike to convert cultural traditions into a political resource. Exploration and glorification of a group past, resurrection of folk heroes, including those previously under opprobrium, purification of national languages and exclusion of foreign borrowings, evocation of group achievements, and concern with preserving the group's environment, both cultural and natural, all represent efforts at national self-assertion typically led by local cultural elites and directed against Russian cultural domination.

Language policy has been an especially sensitive barometer of nationalist attitudes. A large-scale effort has been under way since the

1970s to expand and improve mastery of Russian language not only as a *lingua franca* in government, economic, military, and scholarly domains but also as a vehicle for the acculturation of the non-Russian nationalities into a "Soviet" people. The elevation and glorification of the Russian language has in turn provoked resistance, subtly in reminders that Lenin had opposed a compulsory official language or in calls for Russians to master the local languages of the republics in which they work, and more dramatically in public demonstrations in Georgia opposing changes in language policy.

Finally, interethnic relations, particularly at the personal level, continue to reveal elements of tension. While the Soviet regime has been remarkably successful in maintaining outward order and respect in relations among ethnic groups, ethnic antagonisms continue to simmer below the surface. These latent tensions appear especially sharp in the armed services. While some dissident nationalist writings have depicted military service as a "denationalizing" experience, indirectly supporting the official view that the armed forces are an integrative mechanism, other evidence suggests that barracks life may in fact heighten ethnic self-awareness. Emigre sources report that conscripts of different nationalities tend to form their own groups, partly because of linguistic and cultural affinity and partly out of self-defense; that racist attitudes and ethnic discrimination directed against Central Asians, and occasionally also Georgians and Armenians, are widespread; and that numerous episodes of ethnic-related conflict and violence take place.

While it is impossible to assess the frequency and intensity of such conflicts or to place them in a comparative context, Soviet writings testify to their presence. A major 1980 article in the military journal *Krasnaia zvezda* complained that "national prejudices" in the military are "extremely tenacious" and that frictions between various ethnic groups would not disappear spontaneously, and warned that the elimination of discrimination and of national tensions was a matter of "decisive importance" for the Soviet armed forces.[25]

The 1980s

The dangers a rise in ethnonationalism pose are self-evident: they threaten the unifying force of Soviet patriotism, provide a social base for the organization of group activity directed against official values and policies, infinitely complicate the resolution of other issues, virtually ruling out reforms that entail some degree of decentralization, challenge the unitary structure of such major organs of social control as the party and the military, and strengthen ties of affinity and loyalty with regions outside Soviet borders, with serious consequences. It is no wonder that such leading Soviet figures as the late

Mikhail Suslov have identified ethnic antagonism as one of the three major conflicts standing in the way of building Communism.

There are three conditions under which ethnic tensions might grow and their control become more tenuous in the years ahead: changes in the expectations and demands of either Russian or non-Russian nationalities that increase dissatisfaction with the status quo; change in the system, or in its performance, which these groups perceive disadvantageous to their interests; and loss of effectiveness on the part of dominant elites which increases the capacity of subelites to mobilize challenges to the prevailing distribution of power and benefits. Several emerging trends in Soviet political life increase the likelihood for such developments.

The process of replacement of an entire political generation, which promises heightened competition and instability at the apex of the political system, and the likelihood of important shifts in orientations and policies, could well impinge upon nationality policy. The present pattern of ethnogeographical representation within the Politburo is not immune to challenge, and the growing weight of Central Asia in the Soviet system lends itself to demands for increased political representation. The promotion of Aliev to the Politburo may well have symbolic importance in this respect. On the other hand, the reemergence of nationalist and imperial themes in Russian political culture in recent years and the predominant role of Russians in the Soviet "selectorate," the key apparatuses of the party, the military, the security police, and the central state bureaucracy, all arenas in which non-Russians have limited leverage, make appeals to Great Russian patriotism a more likely scenario. Such a "tilt" in the delicate balance of official ideology, however, would jeopardize the integration of the non-Russian nationalities into a larger Soviet nationhood.

Declining rates of economic growth are also likely to make more difficult the management of ethnic relations, intensifying competition over allocation of limited resources among the union republics as well as within them. An expanding economic base has mitigated both the costs of empire on the one hand and resentment at exploitation on the other. In straitened economic circumstances, rival groups are more likely to directly and bitterly voice their perceptions and claims. A recent article in the prominent journal *Soviet State and Law,* for example, expresses a widespread sense of grievance among Russians by cataloguing a succession of policies, from family allowances to state procurement prices, which transfer resources from the Russian heartland to unspecified "outlying regions." "As for budget policy," it concludes, "not once in the entire existence of the Soviet state has the Russian republic benefited by a subsidy from the all-Union budget, as several other republics have."[26]

Major shifts in the relative "weight" of different regions resulting from new technological and resource constraints and from current demographic trends further compound problems of low growth. The increasingly critical role of energy resources and of labor will have an important impact on development strategies. At the same time, making optimal use of these resources and accommodating the necessary shifts in relative priorities demand a more flexible deployment of resources between the older industrial regions and the emerging "sun belt" than the Soviet system has attained in recent years. Recent efforts to address the problems of differential birthrates and immobile labor are far too limited both in scope and in financing to offer promise of substantial success, while newly introduced demographic policies, which implicitly discriminate against the large families of Central Asia, may breed local resentment.

The prospect of reduced social mobility in the decades ahead is especially likely to exacerbate ethnic tensions. In the absence of major investments in the industrialization of Central Asia, particularly the Siberian river diversion project, which would result in massive expansion of urban employment and which regional elites so ardently advocate, the competition for educational and professional advancement is likely to sharpen. Differential birthrates intensify the difficulties: a rapidly expanding cohort of young people of indigenous nationalities will compete with a small and relatively stable cohort of their Slavic counterparts. Graduates of Central Asian educational institutions are encouraged to accept jobs outside their republic, with limited success. In the West as well as in the Third World, activists in nationalist movements have been recruited largely from among white-collar strata facing limited career opportunities. In the Soviet Union, where survey data repeatedly demonstrate the importance of educational opportunity and professional advancement for levels of personal satisfaction, and where a high level of social mobility has been an important factor in reducing ethnic prejudice among intellectuals and professionals, disappointed expectations pose serious future dilemmas.[27]

The increasing salience of foreign policy in Soviet domestic affairs may also interact with ethnic assertiveness. The greater involvement of the Soviet Union in the outside world during the past two decades has exposed the Soviet population to a wider variety of influences, values, and experiences than when official media held an unchallenged monopoly. Both the forms of interaction and their impact are highly differentiated for different regions of the country. In the case of Central Asia, for example, the orientation of Soviet policy toward the Third World, in particular the Middle East, has accelerated emergence of Tashkent and of Soviet Central Asia generally as a showcase of Soviet achievement: proliferation of officially sponsored technical, cultural, and even religious delegations; increasing reliance on Central Asian cadres in technical and diplomatic roles; and, most recently, dispatch of Soviet armed forces and administrative personnel into Afghanistan have created both opportunities and problems for Soviet policy. The gains from using members of different nationalities to expand Soviet influence abroad are undeniable, but recent developments have also rekindled traditional anxieties about divided loyalties, anxieties amply evident in recent Soviet writings.

The consequences of increased interaction with the outside world on popular attitudes are extremely difficult to assess. At a maximum, they may well introduce a new frame of reference for evaluating Soviet accomplishments and failures. Whether or not comparisons of Tashkent with Kabul or Tehran are as unfavorable to the Soviet Union as comparisons of Moscow with New York, renewed campaigns against religious organizations and activities, now embracing "foreign Moslem reactionaries," testify to official sensitivities. Recent Soviet publications issue sharp warnings against efforts to bring the "flame of the Islamic revival" to the USSR in order to destabilize Central Asia, inflame nationalist prejudices in these regions, and "arouse discontent among believers with the policies of the Communist Party and the Soviet state.[28]

The greater visibility and impact of linkages between foreign policy and regional domestic needs also help explain the growing attention to foreign policy issues on the part of Soviet regional elites. Finally, the Sino-Soviet conflict may also intersect with the Soviet nationality problem, both in providing impetus for better treatment of the indigenous nationalities of Soviet Central Asia and in prompting Soviet appeals to fellow nationals across the Chinese frontier.

The combination of the ethnic problems with these long-term trends creates mutually reinforcing dilemmas. Ethnic cleavages intensify many functional problems and complicate their solution, as in the case of decentralizing economic reforms, while certain functional problems in turn sharpen ethnic cleavages and create additional bases for ethnic solidarity. The potential for political instability is greatest precisely where socioeconomic and cultural cleavages converge. However, the presence of ethnic cleavages and the potential for growing competition and even conflict are a necessary but not sufficient condition of future political instability. To threaten stability, additional ingredients are essential. One is the availability of an organizational infrastructure and local leadership in a position to capitalize on popular grievances (i.e., able to build political or religious careers on exploitation of ethnic issues) and having an interest in doing so. A second is the possibility of mobilizing popular support on the basis of a single major cleavage along ethnic lines that would overcome all other bases of identification. The capacity of the system to forestall or manage such developments then becomes critical.

Constraints on the Political Mobilization of Ethnicity

Here, the Soviet system possesses important assets as well as liabilities. First, significant intrinsic constraints restrict the political mobilization of ethnicity in the Soviet Union as elsewhere. The repertoire of potential ethnic identities is relatively broad, and their salience varies among individuals and in different situations. In the case of Central Asia any individual may identify himself/herself as Soviet, Central Asian, Turkic, Uzbek, or Muslim or some combination of these, depending on the context or role at any given moment. It is difficult to imagine circumstances in which a politically significant grass roots movement might crystalize around a single one of these. Furthermore, individuals have multiple and overlapping identities and roles, of which ethnicity is only one and not necessarily the most salient. The limited evidence of Soviet sociological surveys suggests that educational level and professional role are often more critical determinants of attitudes and behavior than ethnicity.

An additional constraint on the political mobilization of ethnicity in the USSR is the absence of a single overriding cleavage around which mobilization might take place. The issues which pit the interests of Russians against those of the non-Russian nationalities form only a small part of a large spectrum. This spectrum includes points of competition and conflict among the non-Russian nationalities themselves, for some of whom the Russians represent allies or protectors against traditional enemies; competition among republics over allocation of resources; and conflicts internal to each republic which divide its ethnic communities within themselves. The existence of multiple cross-cutting cleavages which are not cumulative and mutually reinforcing constitutes a major regime asset in the management of ethnic relations.

Another Soviet system asset turns on matters of comparative size, "consciousness," integration, and demand on the system among national groups. The most "advanced" of the Soviet nationalities, the peoples of the Baltic states of Latvia, Lithuania, and Estonia brought into the Soviet Union after World War II, who are likely to make the greatest demands and are potentially least "digestible," are also numerically smallest. The potential demographic weight of the Central Asian republics is offset in the short run by their more parochial, underdeveloped, and self-sufficient way of life, which makes comparatively few demands on the system.

Apart from the intrinsic obstacles to the political mobilization of ethnicity, members of non-Russian nationalities derive substantial benefits from working within the system. Unlike classical colonial systems, the Soviet Union proffers full and equal citizenship, providing symbolic recognition and genuine opportunities for participation and advancement to the non-Russian nationalities in exchange for loyalty and partial assimilation. Having initially destroyed traditional local elites and eliminated the economic and political bases of alternative centers of power, the Soviet system has gone on to train, promote, and coopt new indigenous subelites and to reward them for collaboration and loyalty. These elites are more likely to direct their energies toward within-system demands than toward secessionism.

In addition, a potential nationalist movement faces a political system which has exceptionally highly developed control mechanisms. Repression and the threat of repression have been and remain a central component of Soviet nationality policy. The official monopoly over all forms of organization and association as well as over all means of public communication is a further impediment to expression of demands outside official channels, while the assignment of soldiers outside their own regions ensures the loyalty of the armed forces in possible use in local disturbances.

Displacement and depoliticization are further instruments for management of ethnic tensions: the enormous expansion of cultural and scientific elites in Central Asia channels ethnic aspirations away from more sensitive political and administrative domains, while the creation of societies for the preservation of cultural monuments is a comparatively harmless alternative to other forms of ethnic self-assertion. The regime has also employed a strategy of avoidance in certain areas. By concentrating control on the "commanding heights" and avoiding direct assaults on local customs and norms, the regime has prevented counterproductive confrontations. The treatment of Islam in Soviet Central Asia is an illustration. Thanks to its control of the recruitment, training, and activities of official religious elites, and to an active campaign of antireligious propaganda, the regime can afford to tolerate some private religious practice.

Another major device in the management of non-Russian nationalisms is exploitation of alternative lines of cleavage and solidarity. By emphasizing class rather than ethnicity as a fundamental social division, by promoting contacts across ethnic boundaries among different professional groups, from writers and artists to natural and social scientists, and by exploiting conflict between ethnic groups, as well as conflicting tendencies within groups (like pitting traditionalists against modernizers), the Soviet leadership has sought to create and reinforce solidarities that transcend ethnic boundaries and to exploit lines of cleavage that cut across them. It has also sought to avoid situations which activate ethnic identities in politically destabilizing ways.

Finally, the leadership has motivated ethnic elites to participate in and benefit from the system, rather than to exacerbate ethnic conflict. By exploiting external threats, particularly from China directed at Soviet Central Asia, by pressing the view that any conflict would detract from the economic well-being of the whole, and by making clear that the acquisition or retention of political power depends upon collaboration with central elites, the Soviet leadership has emphasized the benefits the present system confers as well as the dangers of fragmentation. Under these circumstances, while the political salience of ethnicity will probably increase significantly over the next decade, it is difficult to imagine a scenario, short of major war, in which ethnonationalism would seriously threaten the stability of the regime.

The Decline of Civic Morale

Possibly the most dramatic change of recent years, and one with profound implications for the legitimacy and stability of the Soviet system, has been a shift in attitudes within the Soviet population during the past two decades. Most visible within the middle class and intelligentsia but extending to the working class as well, it involves growing pessimism about the Soviet future, increasing disillusionment with official values, and an accompanying decline in civic morale.

This judgment necessarily rests on fragmentary data. Soviet studies of public opinion are, with a few exceptions, rudimentary, uninformative, and methodologically flawed. Investigations of public attitudes on politically sensitive issues are pursued in closed institutes, and their results circulate only among a small group of party officials. Moreover, Soviet political indoctrination over several decades has reinforced a political vocabulary so lacking in complexity and nuance that broad and unbiased studies would not be very revealing, even if they were conducted.

The Soviet press is another possible source of information about popular attitudes because it offers a forum for criticism of public institutions and for debate over domestic policy and implementation. It is more useful in identifying problems than in assessing the scope or intensity of attitudes, however, and it is far from comprehensive in its coverage. Soviet literature is a potentially rich source of insights into popular attitudes, but one that social scientists have barely tapped. We are thus obliged to rely, for the most part, on fragmentary and impressionistic accounts of Westerners who have some familiarity with Soviet society, though a familiarity confined largely to limited contact with an educated urban milieu in Moscow and Leningrad, and of emigres whose attitudes may not be typical of a large part of the Soviet population.

The accumulating evidence from these varied sources, however, indicates that a major shift in attitudes among the Soviet population is indeed taking place, a shift far-reaching in its scope and profound in its implications.

The Basic Consensus:
Discipline, Authority, Welfare

In order to comprehend fully the nature and implications of this change, it will be useful to look backward briefly to the most extensive body of evidence concerning popular attitudes and expectations and their bearing on Soviet political culture: that of the Harvard Project on the Soviet Social System, conducted in 1950–51 and based on a survey of almost 2,500 refugees. The findings of this survey, which Alex Inkeles and Raymond Bauer summarized in *The Soviet Citizen*, were extraordinarily revealing, for they called into question beliefs then widely held about the fragility of the Soviet system. The project found that the system had acquired a high degree of legitimacy in the eyes of its people and conformed in such important respects to their fundamental expectations and values that even refugees not favorably disposed to many specific features of the system nonetheless expressed a high degree of attachment to many core values and institutions. This study did not anticipate the emergence of serious intelligentsia dissent, nor of nationalist disaffection in subsequent years, for a number of reasons. But its findings with respect to core political culture were reinforced some twenty-five years later when a new wave of Soviet emigration enabled scholars to compare the attitudes of a new Soviet generation with those of their predecessors. The continuity of the two proved striking, lending confidence to the results summarized here.

Both surveys demonstrated a substantial degree of consensus around basic elements of Soviet political culture. Respondents in both groups attached high value to order, discipline, and strong leadership. While they saluted the principle of civil liberties, they were willing to tolerate a high degree of governmental intervention so long as it was exercised benevolently and on behalf of the national interest. Tolerance for a high degree of government paternalism was reinforced by strong support for the welfare-oriented features of the system. The refugees highly valued free public education, socialized health care, job security, and other social benefits and considered them the most attractive features of the Soviet system. Its basic political and economic arrangements were also widely accepted, except for the terror, which all resented. Public ownership of heavy industry was more solidly supported than of light industry and the services, but on the whole respondents were proud of Soviet accomplishments and criticized regime performance rather than institutional arrangements. Little evidence indicated they saw any alternatives to the system, or that they viewed "capitalism" as preferable. Political freedom had attractions, but they associated it with anarchy, lack of control, and insecurity.

Moreover, the study carried potential implications for future social trends. While all respondents were relatively modest in their material and political aspirations, a positive correlation emerged between social status and approval of the system. Workers and collective farmers, the two groups experiencing the greatest degree of material deprivation, tended to express greater dissatisfaction and alienation, while those with higher levels of education and social status expressed greater approval. Thus, although higher educational level was also associated with greater "liberalism," economic and social opportunity had greater impact on political attitudes than did political conditions in and of themselves. Finally, acceptance of the Soviet system appeared to increase with each successive generation, with younger cohorts expressing more favorable views than their parents or grandparents.

The findings of their research prompted Inkeles and Bauer to predict that a post-Stalin political leadership seeking to increase social support would likely focus on diminution of terror and improvement in living conditions and would particularly concern itself with the material welfare of collective farm and working-class strata. Were it to do so, in their view, it would find a broad and welcome response and would tap substantial reservoirs of popular support and approval.

The Old Optimism

Had the Khrushchev leadership read *The Soviet Citizen,* it could not have responded more directly and astutely to the sources of alienation the study identified. By reducing the terror, identifying improved material welfare—particularly among workers and collective farmers—as a high regime priority, and promising the Soviet population a standard of living which would overtake that of the West within a short period of time, Khrushchev's reforms tapped those reservoirs of popular approval and support.

They also created an atmosphere of optimism and heightened expectations about the future. A small illustration of the exaggerated expectations Khrushchev's utopianism stimulated comes from an account by Jerzy Kosinski of a poll he took among Moscow University students in the late 1950s which John Bushnell has cited in a stimulating essay.[29] Of 85 fifth-year students he asked about their chances of acquiring an automobile, 52 said they expected to be able to purchase one within two or three years, another 28 estimated four to six years, while only 5 believed they would never have an opportunity to own one. Of 85 workers polled at the same time, 23 saw purchase as a likely prospect in two to three years, 31 in four to six years, and 31 believed they would never own one. While the differences in expectations reflected realistic perceptions of differences in the opportunities of different social classes, at a time when the system was producing virtually no passenger cars for private purchase such expectations were unrealistic in the extreme.

Bushnell has described in some detail the optimism that extended from this student milieu throughout the middle class. Despite economic difficulties in the mid-1960s that provoked working-class demonstrations and compelled the leadership's partial retreat from unrealistic promises, the optimism persisted. If anything, the sobriety of the Kosygin-Brezhnev leadership offered greater assurances that the future was in good hands. Opinion surveys not only within the USSR but among emigres who had recently departed testify to the widespread view that material conditions had improved considerably, that the people believed the regime had their interests at heart, and that conditions were likely to continue to improve.

Growing Pessimism

The intellectuals were among the first to experience a shift in attitude. The reversal of de-Stalinization, trials of dissident writers, the invasion of Czechoslovakia, and general tightening of political controls played a major role in their increased malaise. But it was not until prospects of economic slowdown reinforced political concerns that this mood spread to the middle class more widely and to the working class as well. The 1975 crop failure provided the final shock; growing food shortages and disruptions of supply in subsequent years simply compounded the growing conviction that the economy was unable to deliver further improvements in living standards and that the economic system itself was at fault. Shortcomings which were viewed in the early 1960s as deviations from the overall upward movement had by the 1970s come to be viewed as the norm.

The decline in optimism was strikingly captured by two Soviet surveys, the first, taken in 1971, to ascertain the social expectations of working people in Leningrad and the second, taken four years later, to determine whether anticipated improvements had occurred. In the case of both earnings and education, improvements had exceeded expectations. In other categories, however, including living conditions, service industries, and medical services, achievements fell short of what correspondents had anticipated. Moreover, the expectations themselves appeared quite modest: while 57 percent of those surveyed expected improvements in the quantity and quality of the Tenth Five-Year Plan, only 45 percent were convinced their incomes would rise during this period and only 35 percent expected their housing conditions to improve.[30]

Rising pessimism reflected a shift in the standards by which the population evaluated regime performance. The traditional explanations of failure—the survival of capitalist remnants, growing pains, the aftermath of war, the machinations of unseen enemies—were no longer compelling to a generation raised to expect that the USSR was on the verge of overtaking the West. The distant past no longer formed the standard against which to measure present achievements; rather, it was the recent past and expectations of the future. Moreover, the comparative reference was no longer the peasant or worker household of the 1930s but the living standard of the Soviet or, increasingly, foreign elite.

The growing exposure of the Soviet population to the world outside its borders, one of the major consequences of the changes after Stalin and of detente, had an incalculable impact on the evolution of Soviet society. Increasing imports of Western scientific and technical equipment for Soviet laboratories, factories, mines, and oil wells, and of consumer goods from Eastern and Western Europe, exposed millions of Soviet citizens to the qualities of Western products. Scientific and cultural exchanges as well as expanded tourism provided growing opportunities for Soviet citizens to travel abroad, to encounter foreign visitors in the USSR, or to hear of the experiences and impressions of acquaintances who enjoyed such opportunities and who flaunted the products of their privileged travel. Western books and films as well as radio broadcasts supplemented direct personal experience in providing information about, and whetting appetites for, the accoutrements of a Western life style. The emigration during the 1970s of over 300,000 Soviet citizens who maintained close communication with friends and relatives back home added to the flow of information about Western goods and prices. The variety, quality, and sheer quantity of Western goods seen and described established new standards for evaluating Soviet products and services, and invited increasingly negative evaluations of Soviet economic performance.

Even comparisons with an Eastern Europe more accessible and less ideologically suspect to the average Soviet citizen had subversive implications. Between 1960 and 1976 roughly eleven million Soviet tourists visited Eastern Europe, perhaps half of them for the first time, in addition to two and one half million soldiers, and large numbers of East Europeans visited the USSR. The legendary acquisitiveness of Soviet travelers abroad offered ample testimony to both the scarcity and the poor quality of Soviet goods.

The growing tide of criticism gradually extended beyond the realm of consumer goods and services to include even features of the Soviet system once quite highly regarded. Health care is a case in point. Widespread dissatisfaction and criticism of an institution once hailed as one of the system's great achievements is almost commonplace in the press. The survey of attitudes toward living standards and prospects for improvements discussed earlier revealed the greatest disappointment in the area of medical services. Whether the system has actually deteriorated in recent years is the subject of some controversy, but it is clear that medical care, like many other social services, has failed to keep pace with new needs, or with the expectations placed upon it by an increasingly educated and demanding population less tolerant of shortcomings and failures than at earlier stages of Soviet development.

George Feifer, a veteran observer of the Soviet scene returning to Moscow in 1981, after an absence of some ten years, offers especially graphic testimony of a whole array of social changes countless Western observers, emigres, and Soviet sources have reported.[31] Food shortages and disruptions in the supply of other goods and services have generated a preoccupation with procurement that extends from manual workers to senior engineers and that feeds a rapidly growing second economy. Energy is increasingly diverted from work, and from other civic activities, into moonlighting, black-market activities, and the pursuit of desired goods: "It is private enterprise running wild, although the enterprise goes almost entirely into obtaining, rather than into producing, goods and services." The loss of confidence in public distribution, the surge in cheating and bribery have led to disintegration of old restraints and widespread demoralization. As one friend of Feifer's recounted, "The scorn [for official values] has led to the moral emptiness—as demonstrated by mass apathy, lying and cheating—in which we live."

Decline in Civic Morale

This decline in civic morale has three distinct though interrelated elements: loss of optimism, loss of purpose, and disintegration of internal controls and self-discipline. The loss of optimism is associated with a growing sense that the system cannot live up to expectations and that problems associated with a new stage of development have outrun the capacity of existing institutions. A growing feeling is developing within the elite that the problem may be systemic, but there is little sense of viable alternatives and no belief that the United States or any other capitalist system offers a preferable model.

The loss of a sense of purpose is connected with the declining relevance and vitality of official ideology. Khrushchev's effort to revive the utopian, egalitarian, and populist features of Marxism-Leninism as a way of rekindling mass enthusiasm and dedication represented a last gasp of a tradition well on the way to extinction. There is increasing recognition that the values and policies of an earlier era are inadequate to contemporary challenges and require serious rethinking.

Finally, the erosion of social control and individual self-discipline, evident in significant increases in the entire gamut of "anti-social" behavior, from alcoholism to corruption to violations of labor discipline to theft of state property, reflects the limited success at internalizing new social norms and their breakdown under conditions of reduced reliance on coercion and of social relaxation. At an earlier period of Soviet history the leadership could attribute such behavior to capitalist remnants or to strains associated with urbanization and subjecting a peasant population to the discipline of factory life. Two generations later, without a great national crisis to bind the social fabric, traditional explanations ring hollow.

New Values

To attempt to characterize the full range of responses to these trends is a separate undertaking. Broadly speaking, the loss of optimism associated with declining performance has been accompanied by a shift of expectations to the private realm. The decline in the relevance and vitality of ideology has awakened a quest for alternative sources of values and a revival of religious activity. Also, the breakdown in social controls has fueled a nostalgia for greater order and discipline and growing social conservatism.

The shift in expectations and concerns to the private realm is nowhere more powerfully illustrated than in the virtual revolution in Soviet attitudes toward the family that has occurred in recent years. It suffices to evoke the image of the Bolshevik feminist Alexandra Kollontai to recall the critical attitude of revolutionary Marxism-Leninism toward the bourgeois family and the expectation that in the socialist society of the future the traditional economic and social functions of the family, from cooking to housework to child care, would be taken over by communal facilities. While the Stalin period inaugurated a shift away from these expectations, only in recent years has a family-centered value system emerged full-blown. The economic and social policies of the Brezhnev regime supported this trend by assigning the family a central social role, enhancing the resources of income, privacy, and leisure available to it, and strengthening its role in transmitting social status.

Official policy is supplemented by a growing body of literature which virtually glorifies the family as the basis of social stability, the decisive factor in the education, socialization, and moral upbringing of children, and the indispensable provider of necessary social services which the state either cannot or should not supplant. In a striking inversion of revolutionary values, leading Soviet sociologists now maintain that communal arrangements would not permit satisfaction of increasingly diverse and individual needs, tastes, and lifestyles, and that even if society were in a position to assume the burdens of housework and child care, it should refrain from doing so in order to maintain, even artificially, the cohesion of the family as a social unit.

An analogous shift in values is evident in recent discussions of the balance to be struck between public and private consumption. Specialists are now questioning the traditional reliance on social consumption funds as an instrument of income equalization and a symbol of social solidarity. Arguing that the Soviet system need no longer retain social arrangements which originated in the different historical conditions of the 1920s and 1930s, some urge that although a "safety net" should still extend to low-income families, the state should reduce or end its subsidization of housing, medical care, vacations, and other goods and services and should allow and even encourage the use of private incomes for their purchase.

These two examples, though limited to relatively specialized scholarly publications, illustrate the emergence in recent years of an intellectual and moral rationale for the increasing "privatization" of Soviet life, and legitimization of the greater social inequality, as well as diversity, it is bound to generate.

The decline in a sense of purpose, and with it the disappearance of the enthusiasm and zeal which has accompanied, in varying degree, the great campaigns of earlier times from the First Five-Year Plan to the Great Fatherland War to even the Virgin Lands program, and the spread of cynicism and political apathy have also prompted a relatively widespread quest, largely by the intelligentsia, for alternative values and sources of meaning. Heightened interest in religion among younger people, evident in increased church attendance, growing use of religious symbolism, and the affirmation of moral and spiritual values, is a manifestation of this quest. It is associated as well with a revival of interest in national traditions and nostalgia for the past.

While much of this interest focuses on culture and is illustrated by the rapid rise and massive membership of the Society for the Preservation of Historical and Cultural Monuments, the first "grass roots" organization to emerge in the USSR with a reported twelve million members, it extends to the political realm as well. Moreover, this revival is not confined to the Russian past; from the Baltic to Central Asia it has parallels and counterparts among the non-Russian nationalities. To the extent that this quest embodies a critical attitude toward or even rejection of the scientific positivism and materialistic world view associated with official ideology and the "scientific-technological revolution" it so repetitiously extols, it also contains elements of an anti-urban, anti-industrial set of values. The emergence of a Soviet-style environmental movement, the first more or less spontaneous large-scale phenomenon of its kind in the USSR, represents both a concern for the preservation of the natural environment against the ravages of unbridled industrialism and an effort to exert pressure on behalf of a balanced weighing of costs and benefits. Finally, there is the impulse to sheer escapism, whether to other countries in the form of travelogues, to the more intimate universe of personal relations, to the realms of parapsychology, or to the unexplored universe of science fiction.

Widespread anxiety over the erosion of traditional social norms and growing evidence of indiscipline, social disorder, and corruption extending to the highest levels of the political hierarchy, including the Politburo itself, have evoked a growing impulse for restoration of "law and order," greater discipline, and a reassertion of authority. This finds expression in a wide variety of ways, from nostalgia for Stalin, the *krepkii khoziain* (strong boss), to the inchoate yearning expressed in the village prose movement for a return to an idealized patriarchal rural society where male and female roles were more sharply differentiated and "women knew their place and things were in order." The selection of Andropov as Brezhnev's successor might well be a response to this widespread yearning for strong and decisive leadership after the immobilism of the late Brezhnev period.

Anxiety over the erosion of civic morale is also a factor in the extraordinary importance of World War II as a cultural symbol. The search for sources of pride and satisfaction, and heroic causes with which to identify, leads backward rather than forward, to a renewed emphasis on patriotism, a focus on World War II, and the widespread praise of military virtues. World War II offers the single most potent unifying symbol for positive identification; it epitomizes the optimism, clarity of goals, righteousness of purpose, and extremes of self-discipline which the nation had once sustained and which are now felt to be lacking in a society viewed as preoccupied with consumerism and self-gratification and tainted by pacifism. It is, however, far more a focus of nostalgia and comfort than a premonition of future intent; few foreign policy objectives, short of a conflict with China, could generate comparable intensity.

The political consequences of this erosion of civic morale are ambiguous. These trends reflect a growing retreat from, rather than direct challenge to, the political domain, a diversion of energies and ambitions into more rewarding private concerns. They ease the tasks of ruling even as they undermine the mobilization ethos. At the same time, such trends are a source of serious concern to a political elite already worried about declining labor productivity, social discontent, and diminishing respect for authority, and fearful that its own legitimacy will be eroded in the revival of many elements of traditional political culture.

Conclusions

Implications for Domestic Stability

What are the likely political consequences of these broad social trends? These developments point to a widening gap between the leadership's aspirations to shape and channel the direction of social change and its diminishing capacity to do so, the result of a progressive weakening of the three mechanisms of social control traditionally available: coercive, material, and normative.

A diminished reliance on terror, increased predictability in the definition and punishment of violations of Soviet law, and greater use of material and normative incentives to elicit desired social behavior have characterized the period since Stalin. While this shift reflected an assessment that the benefits of such an approach would outweigh costs, particularly in view of the new challenges and opportunities the emergence of an increasingly complex modern society and educated population presents, it also created dilemmas for the system. At an earlier date one could speak of a "revolution from above," with connotations of state domination of a largely passive society. Today the image no longer corresponds to reality. Not only have social forces achieved a certain degree of autonomy, but they actively impinge on the political system in unprecedented ways. The erosion of political control over important sectors of economic life is clearly demonstrated by the evolution of the "second economy," which by its existence subverts centrally established priorities and challenges centralized control over prices, income distribution, and the allocation of resources of manpower as well as capital. The spread of corruption, particularly within the political elite, threatens the organizational integrity and political legitimacy of the party and feeds both the resentment of those excluded from patronage and the hostility of those critical of its existence.

A parallel development is visible in the escape of important dimensions of social behavior from regime control. Families marry, reproduce, and divorce without reference to demographic policy;

populations migrate from north and east to south and west, rather than vice-versa; labor absenteeism and turnover defy repeated calls for strengthening labor discipline; and religious practices continue despite efforts to invigorate atheistic propaganda. A whole spectrum of social pathologies, from rising alcoholism and crime to declining civic morale, dramatize the limits of regime control. While the diminution of terror reduces the costs of such behavior, it remains unclear to what extent reimposition of tighter social controls would in fact resolve these problems. In a complex modern society, successful social policies require a high degree of fine tuning, a strategy of the scalpel rather than of the hammer. While a more authoritarian pattern of political rule might produce greater compliance, it would hardly elicit the initiative, creativity, and motivation which current problems demand.

Having increased its reliance on material incentives and social advancement to elicit greater individual initiative and productivity, the Soviet leadership now faces a situation in which the combination of economic slowdown and diminished social mobility erodes the availability of these incentives as a mechanism of social control. The ties between the political elite and the working class are especially vulnerable. The precarious balance of the existing social compact is threatened by the possibility that the elites may not match declining mass consumption by equivalent sacrifices but will adopt a more energetic defense of established privileges. The combination of deteriorating welfare and growing inequalities could thus enhance the potential for social unrest.

Finally, the weakening of the normative underpinnings of the system of social control are visible in the decline of civic morale. Throughout its history, the Soviet system has successfully mobilized its population on behalf of a succession of political and economic goals, defining a series of large purposes in heroic terms and invoking external and internal enemies to elicit the popular zeal and national unity necessary. This "heroic" period of Soviet history is past. Neither official ideology nor current economic and social policy is capable of eliciting the popular enthusiasm and unity of purpose that characterized an earlier epoch now remembered with nostalgia, and it is not clear that pride in superpower status will continue to offer a sufficiently powerful compensation.

Thus, the cumulative nature of current social difficulties exacerbating the erosion of traditional mechanisms of social control presents the Soviet leadership with unprecedented problems. During the 1980s a new and less experienced leadership will have to address simultaneously economic stagnation, declining prospects for social mobility, unfavorable demographic trends, and the rise of both Russian and non-Russian nationalism, at the time of a major systemic crisis in Poland and a less benign international environment.

While these problems are serious and not easily managed, only a very particular and somewhat remote conjunction of circumstances could endow them with crisis proportions. First, although the gap between expectations and possibilities may be widening, the demands of the Soviet population for material goods, social opportunities, and political freedoms remain modest, not only by comparison with Western societies but even with Eastern Europe. Moreover, unlike the situation in Poland, patriotism strengthens support for the Soviet regime rather than working against it. Given the likelihood that economic difficulties will cause a slowdown in improvements but not an absolute decline in mass welfare, the regime will still have at its disposal resources with which to moderate discontent.

Even were social frustrations to reach considerable proportions, the Soviet system imposes severe constraints on their political expression. The paucity of institutionalized channels for making demands on the system and the numerous barriers to the formation of groups and the articulation of interests make the mobilization of social protest difficult. Moreover, deep cleavages divide Soviet social strata and ethnic groups from each other, preventing the formation of broad social coalitions which might sustain alternative political programs. By contrast with Czechoslovakia in 1968 and Poland in 1980, there have been few efforts in the USSR thus far to link intelligentsia dissent with working class demands. While the force of nationalism might bridge that gap in some non-Russian areas, such as the Baltic republics, the relative success of the regime in coopting local elites reduces the likelihood of such developments. Thus, while the decades ahead are likely to see increased working-class unrest and more frequent though still sporadic outbreaks of strikes and demonstrations, these are likely to be local rather than nationwide, to focus on specific economic grievances, and to submit to a combination of repression and redress.

The Soviet leadership has, moreover, demonstrated considerable skill at conflict-management. It has successfully isolated and managed cultural and political dissent by a combination of repression, bribery, and emigration. At the same time, it has recognized the need for more and better information about social attitudes, trends, and behavior, and has sponsored an increasingly broad and sophisticated program of social research. Virtually every major party organization and industrial complex has its resident or consulting sociologist. Leading Politburo members including Chernenko and Andropov himself have repeatedly called for greater party reliance on opinion surveys as a guide to popular attitudes. The party has not only sought to keep in touch with social trends, but it has also committed considerable resources to policies aimed at improving food supplies, raising living standards, and heading off working class unrest, all with the spectacle of "Polonization" very much in mind. Moreover, it has attempted to coopt both social and national elites by offering a substantial stake in the system and considerable rewards in exchange for loyalty, exploiting both social and ethnic cleavages to undermine the foundations of hostile coalitions.

While it is therefore likely that the Soviet system will evolve in more authoritarian directions and will rely on a greater degree of repression to contain growing social tensions and conflict in the years ahead, it is difficult to imagine circumstances under which current social trends will become unmanageable or provoke a serious political crisis. Indeed, the power and the resolution the leadership has consistently shown and the respect and fear the security police and the other forms of repression still command constitute a convincing demonstration that the regime will not tolerate the expression of serious discontent and will crush any efforts to give it organized form.

Implications for Foreign Policy

How will these internal problems affect Soviet objectives and capabilities in the international environment in the years ahead? Will these accumulating domestic problems have a restraining effect on Soviet behavior abroad, or are they likely on the contrary to evoke a more assertive and expansionist pattern of behavior to compensate for domestic failures?

There is no way to predict confidently the impact of domestic factors on Soviet foreign policy for several reasons. First, social trends will affect foreign policy only indirectly, as they are mediated through the filter of leadership perceptions and perceived reactions. Given our uncertainty concerning the composition of the future Soviet elite, our lack of knowledge of its major concerns and priorities, and the difficulty in anticipating the international environment it is likely to encounter, efforts to anticipate its likely behavior are highly speculative.

Moreover, the feature of Soviet foreign policy making which most distinguishes it from that of the United States is its insulation from domestic social pressures. Control over information and access to the policy making process is even more tightly circumscribed in the case of foreign policy than it is with respect to domestic issues, even within the ruling group. Soviet citizens are notoriously ignorant about the outside world, and they have virtually no exposure to competing points of view about foreign policy. The tradition of rallying around the state against a foreign enemy, especially in circumstances when knowledge of the nature and character of the enemy is limited and gravely distorted, assures the Soviet leadership considerable freedom in formulating and executing its policies toward other states.

Some observers have therefore argued that the Soviet leadership is likely to compensate for domestic failures by pursuing a more aggressively expansionist foreign policy and by calling upon reserves of patriotism, if not outright chauvinism, in support. Such an effort would forge increased national unity in the face of growing social divisiveness, rekindle a fading sense of national purpose, and revive public morale. Its domestic consequences would be strengthened Russian nationalism, an appeal to patriotic and military virtues, increased reliance on the military as a symbol of national power and potent source of legitimation, and repression of domestic dissent.

While such a scenario cannot be excluded, it suffers from several flaws. First, it tends mechanistically to project outward from domestic conditions without adequate consideration of the international environment itself and the kinds of opportunities or challenges it will present to the Soviet leadership in the years ahead. Moreover, there is no historical precedent for the view that the Soviet Union has used external adventures to compensate for domestic difficulties, and much evidence to suggest the contrary. Periods of domestic crisis have usually been accompanied by a partial withdrawal from international involvement. While the achievement of strategic parity may reduce the relevance of historical precedents, it is significant that the treatment of Soviet involvement in Afghanistan in the Soviet press has, if anything, sought to minimize its military dimension and to focus instead on the economic, cultural, and administrative support rendered by Soviet troops. In other cases as well, the leadership has tried to avoid fueling popular resentment at the diversion of resources from domestic needs by minimizing the scale of its foreign commitments in the media. China aside, it is difficult to imagine a foreign policy scenario that would serve as the functional equivalent of World War II in mobilizing the Soviet population on behalf of a popular and unifying national cause.

This does not preclude the possibility that Soviet imperial arrogance will exacerbate the long succession of regional problems and crises which are likely in the years ahead and that competitive demagogy and greater risk taking will contribute to increased international instability. While many factors, and above all the international environment itself, will shape Soviet foreign policy behavior in the 1980s, and while it is as difficult to anticipate the many opportunities and challenges that will arise as it is to predict the outcomes, the Soviet leadership will undoubtedly have accumulating domestic problems and vulnerabilities very much in mind as it weighs the costs and benefits of alternative foreign policies.

NOTES

1. Gertrude Schroeder Greenslade, "Consumption and Income Distribution," in Abram Bergson and Herbert Levine, eds., *The Soviet Economy to the Year 2000* (London: Allen & Unwin, 1982), p. 2. See also her article, "Soviet Living Standards: Achievements and Prospects," in U.S. Congress, Joint Economic Committee, *The Soviet Economy in the 1980s: Problems and Prospects* (Washington, D.C.: USGPO, 1982).

2. For evidence of food shortages and price differentials based on interviews with recent Soviet emigrants, see Radio Free Europe/Radio Liberty, "Food Supply in the USSR: Evidence of Widespread Shortages," AR 2-82, April 1982.

3. *Pravda*, May 25, 1982, p. 1.

4. *Voprosy ekonomiki*, 1978, no. 7, p. 60.

5. V. I. Zorkaltsev, "Anatomiia defitsita: Voprosy bez otveta" [The Anatomy of the Deficit: Questions without an Answer], *Ekonomika i organizatsiia promyshlennogo proizvodstva*, EKO, no. 2, February 1982.

6. Cited in Richard B. Dobson, "Socialism and Social Stratification," in Jerry G. Pankhurst and Michael Paul Sacks, eds., *Contemporary Soviet Society* (New York: Praeger, 1980), p. 97.

7. M. N. Rutkevich, ed., *Zhiznennye plany molodezhi* [Life Plans of Youth] (Sverdlovsk, 1966), p. 35.

8. F. R. Filippov, "The Role of the Higher School in Changing the Social Structure of Soviet Society," *Sotsiologicheskie issledovaniia*, 1977, no. 2, p. 48.

9. M. N. Rutkevich and F. R. Filippov, "Social Sources of Recruitment of the Intelligentsia," in Murray Yanowitch and Wesley A. Fisher, eds., *Social Stratification and Mobility in the USSR* (White Plains, N.Y.: International Arts and Sciences Press, 1973), pp. 256–57.

10. Cited in Richard B. Dobson, "Education and Opportunity," in Pankhurst and Sacks, *Contemporary Soviet Society*, p. 129.

11. *Komsomol'skaia pravda*, January 17, 1975, p. 2.

12. A discussion of discriminatory examination procedures based on interviews with emigres is found in Michael Swafford, "Political Attitudes and Behavior of Soviet University Students," unpublished paper, U.S. International Communications Agency, 1979, pp. 54–60. Extensive documentation of "affirmative action" in admissions to higher education in Uzbekistan is provided by Nancy Lubin, *Labor and Nationality in Soviet Central Asia* (New York: Macmillan, forthcoming). Efforts "not only to eliminate any opportunity for dishonesty but also to convince candidates . . . that all prospective students stand a fair and equal chance of success" were instituted in the three Transcaucasian republics where the intense competition for university admissions encouraged widespread bribery. The measures included radio and TV coverage of the examinations, tape recording of the oral sections, allowing candidates to review the written papers of those who gained higher marks, and allowing friends of candidates to attend oral exams. The Armenian and Georgian party first secretaries also stressed that no university teacher who engages in private tutoring should be appointed to exam committees. See Elizabeth Fuller, "University Admissions in the Transcaucasian Republics," *Radio Liberty Research Bulletin*, 349/81, September 4, 1981.

13. V. Churbanov, "The Young Worker and Uninteresting Labor," *Molodoi kommunist*, 1972, no. 6, pp. 64–71, cited in Dobson, "Socialism and Social Stratification," p. 104.

14. B. Urlanis, *Problemy dinamiki naseleniia SSSR* [The Problems of Population Dynamics in the USSR] (Moscow: Nauka, 1974), p. 283.

15. A leading exponent of this view is V. Perevedentsev; see, for example, his articles in *Literaturnaia gazeta*, March 20, 1968, p. 11, and *Voprosy ekonomiki* 1976, no. 6, pp. 127–33. The recommendation is from E. D. Grazhdannikov, *Prognosticheskie modeli sotsial'no-demograficheskikh protsessov* [Prognostic Models of Socio-Demographic Processes] (Novosibirsk, 1974).

16. Christopher Davis and Murray Feshbach, *Rising Infant Mortality in the USSR* (Washington, D.C.: Department of Commerce, 1980).

17. See, for example, the exaggerated interpretation offered by Nick Eberstadt, "The Health Care Crisis in the USSR," *New York Review of Books*, February 19, 1981, and the exchange with Albert Szymanski in *New York Review of Books*, November 5, 1981, pp. 57–60. Szymanski's critique of Eberstadt, and to a limited extent of Feshbach and Davis, is developed further in an article "On the Uses of Disinformation to Legitimize the Revival of the Cold War: Health in the USSR," *Science and Society* 45, no. 4, Winter 1981/82, pp. 453–74, although Szymanski obscures the problem of male mortality by lumping together male and female life expectancy. See also Murray Feshbach, "Health in Russia: Statistics and Reality," *Wall Street Journal*, September 14, 1981, p. 30.

18. John C. Dutton, "Causes of Soviet Adult Mortality Increases," *Soviet Studies* 33, no. 4, October 1981, pp. 548–59; John C. Dutton, "Changes in Soviet Mortality Patterns, 1959–1977," *Population and Development Review* 5, no. 2, June 1979, pp. 267–91; Murray Feshbach, "Issues in Soviet Health Problems," U.S. Congress, Joint Economic Committee, *Soviet Economy in the 1980s: Problems and Prospects* (Washington, D.C.: USGPO, forthcoming).

19. Tsentral'nyi komitet kommunisticheskoi partii sovetskogo soiuza, *Materialy XXVI s"ezda KPSS* [Materials of the Twenty-sixth Congress of the CPSU] (Moscow: Politizdat, 1981), p. 61.

20. V. Korchagin, "Rol' zdravookhraneniia v vosproizvodstve trudovykh resursov" [The Role of Health Care in the Reproduction of Labor Resources], *Voprosy ekonomiki*, 1981, no. 12, pp. 65–72.

21. A. Ia. Kvasha, *Problemy ekonomiko-demograficheskogo razvitiia SSSR* [Problems of Economic-Demographic Development in the USSR] (Moscow, 1974), pp. 139–40. At a meeting sponsored by the Academy of Sciences in 1975, a participant from Turkmenistan noted that "from the standpoint of economic and social interests, this highly expanded type of population reproduction in Turkmenia and other republics with similar birthrate indices is less than optimal. The present high birthrate makes it virtually impossible for mothers to work." Another contributor urged that the government encourage vocational education for women in Central Asia and that it publicize different methods of contraception more widely. R. Galetskaia, "Sfery demograficheskoi politiki" [Spheres of Demographic Policy], *Voprosy ekonomiki*, 1975, no. 8, pp. 152, 149.

22. For an account of these debates, see Cynthia Weber and Ann Goodman, "The Demographic Policy Debate in the USSR," *Population and Development Review* 7, no. 2, June 1981, pp. 279–95.

23. For one example among many, see A. S. Kadyrszhanova, "O metodologicheskikh problemakh issledovaniia vyravnivaniia urovnei ekonomicheskogo razvitiia sotsialisticheskikh natsii" [On Methodological Problems in the Investigation of Equalization of Levels of Economic Development in Socialist Nations], Akademiia Nauk Kazakhskoi SSR, *Izvestiia; Seriia obshchestvennykh nauk,* 1981, no. 4, pp. 37–43.

24. I. P. Tsamerian, "Vklad XXVI s" ezda KPSS v marksistsko-leninskuiu teoriiu natsional'nykh otnoshenii" [The Contribution of the 26th CPSU Congress to the Marxist-Leninist Theory of National Relations], *Nauchnyi kommunizm*, no. 4, July–August 1981, pp. 63–64.

25. N. Shumikhin, *Krasnaia zvezda*, October 9, 1980.

26. G. I. Litvinova and B. Ts. Urlanis, *Sovetskoe gosudarstvo i pravo*, 1982, no. 3, pp. 38–46.

27. The interesting work of Iu. V. Arutiunian identifies two distinct sources of narrow ethnic orientations. The first is, in effect, traditionalism; the second is associated with the sociooccupational interests of professionals and is rooted in socioeconomic factors: the supply and demand relationship for skilled employees and the opportunities for social and occupational advancement. "Konkretno-sotsiologicheskoe issledovanie natsional'nykh otnoshenii" [Concrete Sociological Research on National Relations], *Voprosy filosofii*, 1969, no. 2, pp. 129–39.

28. *Sovetskaia Kirgiziia* editorial, December 27, 1981, p. 3.

29. Cited in the excellent article by John Bushnell, "The 'New Soviet Man' Turns Pessimist," in Stephen F. Cohen, Alexander Rabinowitch, and Robert Sharlet, eds., *The Soviet Union Since Stalin* (Bloomington: Indiana University Press, 1980), p. 183.

30. V. K. Alekseev, B. Z. Doktorov, and B. M. Firsov, "Izuchenie obshchestvennogo mneniia: Opyt i problemy," *Sotsiologicheskie issledovaniia*, 1979, no. 4, pp. 23–32.

31. George Feifer, "Russian Disorders," *Harper's*, February 1981, pp. 41–55.

5

★

Cultural and Intellectual Life

Maurice Friedberg

Introduction

THOSE INTENT on trying to gauge the sources of a state's conduct quite properly devote primary attention to the political system, military forces, economy, sociological data, and relations with near and distant countries. I submit that cultural and intellectual life are of equal importance, whether the state be authoritarian or democratic. In an authoritarian system, literature and the arts, the mass media, and journals devoted to serious intellectual concerns all provide information of fundamental importance concerning the government's goals, the direction it provides, its strengths and weaknesses, and its relations with all elements of society. Cultural and intellectual life constitutes a mirror of society and provides insight into the government's foundations. It reveals to what degree the government and those who serve the government's effort to direct and control society are successful. High culture, popular culture, and propaganda all serve to illuminate the strains and to identify the issues and elements that constitute problems for the government in its efforts to convert Soviet citizens to its point of view. Cultural life also reveals the degree to which the state reflects popular national goals, as well as the way in which it bends policies to attain the necessary degree of public support. Literature, the media, and the arts provide essential information concerning the level of political knowledge and understanding that various elements of society possess. They reveal the extent to which the government is successful in its efforts to isolate the population from the rest of the world and to restrict the impact of the outside world upon its citizens, especially the various elites. Even changing fads and fashions, particu-

I should like to express my appreciation to John Dunlop, Leopold Labedz, and Sidney Monas for the information and critical comments they provided.

larly those rooted in tradition and/or in quasi-ideological values, are part of a related, cohesive process, not isolated developments.

In short, as scholars and practical politicians have always recognized, cultural and intellectual life serves as a barometer of a society's health and as an indicator of the sources of a government's conduct. The interrelationship of the two is particularly close in the USSR, but the ultimate primacy of politics is never in doubt. As Leszek Kolakowski, the Polish philosopher now living in the West, pointed out some years ago in his memorable essay, "What Is Socialism?" in pseudosocialist societies poets and generals say the same things, but generals always say them first. At the same time, literature and the arts often serve as trial balloons for new ideas, engendering debates in which significant divergences of views are allowed to surface, some of which are later enshrined in official party and state policy.

This chapter examines Soviet cultural and intellectual life and seeks to predict the directions it is likely to take for the remainder of this decade. I believe that the evidence suggests that the Soviet Union will be a politically conservative, nationalistic, and increasingly repressive society. The civilization this culture reflects would thus be inward-looking, permeated by nostalgia for the Russian past, the travail of World War II, and even the country's early heroic revolutionary period. The virtual absence of goals such as those that once inspired the Soviet population and helped it endure hardships and sacrifices serves to intensify obsession with the past and to underscore a pervasive sense of vague dissatisfaction with the seemingly aimless present. All of these trends describe an immobile and aging society at once restless and insecure. The pattern reveals also the authorities' desire to sustain a work ethic, a sense of Soviet patriotism, and a distrust of the outside world, even if this involves accepting a culture more concerned with problems of the individual than with social issues. Above all, this analysis describes a government torn between its determination to control thought and its decision to expand higher education and economic, scientific, and cultural relations with the West, which are necessary for continued economic and military growth. This conflict leads to some confusion and even bafflement as the government wrestles with a dilemma which Nicholas I and other Russian tsars encountered: it wants a fire that will not burn.

Historical Background

Even in rigidly authoritarian societies, intellectual, artistic, and cultural processes and production offer surprisingly significant resistance to politically inspired pressures and outright commands. Simultaneously, in an apparent paradox, they often anticipate these pressures, thus contributing to an ultimate uneasy accommodation. This pattern may help explain the stronger continuities that exist in the cultural sphere than in other areas of Soviet life. Modern Russian history provides some rather striking examples. Thus, revolutionary art and poetry antedated revolutionary political change. Indeed, they helped inspire the upheaval. The abdication of the last Romanov tsar in February 1917, the establishment in Russia of a democratic republic ("the freest country in the world," Lenin called it without intended irony), as well as its destruction a few months later in a Communist *coup d'état,* took place within a context in which revolutionary changes in literature, music, and painting were already an accomplished fact. Symbolist and Futurist Russian poetry, abstract canvases, daring new religious and philosophical treatises, and modernist music were created when monarchy still appeared stable.

Ironically, many of the rebellious cultural and intellectual figures, left the country soon after the revolution, along with the political elite of the *ancien régime* and those who had sought a constitutional and democratic Russia. The new revolutionary rulers proved less tolerant of nonconformist culture than the staunchly conservative monarchs had been. Bolshevik appeals for a revolutionary culture proved little more than self-serving exhortations to shape an art and thought that would adorn their cause, promote it, and impart to it a degree of intellectual respectability and legitimacy. The responses of the political authorities to the demands of writers, painters, theatrical directors, film makers, and other members of the artistic intelligentsia were often unacceptable, creating tensions between political authorities and cultural figures that have persisted for over six decades. In some areas, such as independent philosophy or disciplines outside the pale of tolerated intellectual activity like theology, no accommodation was possible because of Communist doctrinal rigidity. Subsequently, the number of proscribed tendencies in the arts and the sciences multiplied. During Stalin's last years, they included Freudian psychology and abstract painting, cybernetics and *le nouveau roman,* genetics and modernist music.

Stalin's cultural gendarmes exacted outward obedience, but their effectiveness at producing genuine converts was not impressive. The fact that the first rebellious public stirrings in the artistic and cultural world followed Stalin's death in March 1953 by only a few weeks suggests that subterranean cultural ferment had existed for some time. The dictator's demise, a momentous event in Soviet history, did not engender these stirrings. It merely made possible their initial public expression of discontent, a phenomenon that ultimately affected all areas of intellectual, cultural, and artistic life. Once again in Russian history, Marxism was stood on its head. Its political component triggered and intensified upheavals in the intellectual, cultural, and artistic superstructure, with little apparent impact upon the largely immobile economic base.

Censorship and Propaganda

The Communists established censorship of the press and the performing arts within weeks of seizing power in 1917, and state ownership of the means of information and communication has remained a hallmark of the system. The party announced censorship as a temporary measure necessitated by the military dangers facing the young Soviet republic. Yet censorship continues to this day, even though the government denies its existence; one can find the censor's number easily in nearly every Soviet book. In the early 1930s, Soviet authorities liquidated even censored private and cooperative publishing and established the monopoly of government-owned presses as a further means of tightening control of cultural expression. They also established several unions (of writers, painters, etc.) as supplemental instruments for implementing the party's will. Each union wielded a monopoly in its area, and each exercised a degree of positive constructive control that went far beyond the negative tasks of censorship. The unions were to ensure that artists produced films and marching songs, novels and nursery rhymes, paintings and melodramas that would exhort, warn, inspire, and, above all, explain party directives.

All these institutions have survived with their functions essentially unchanged, although some bureaucratic reorganization has taken place, such as the post-Stalin establishment of a committee for publishing which has the status of an autonomous ministry. Because of their relative efficiency and familiarity these institutions appear destined to survive into the late 1980s and beyond. At the same time, "formal" censorship may become increasingly superfluous as the leadership of these creative organizations acquires ever greater political sophistication and ability to discern the proper ways to express current party objectives in the arts. As in Gogol's *Inspector General,* the sergeant's widow will, at long last, master the art of flogging herself without needing assistance from the authorities.

Decades of experience demonstrate that censorship and other control mechanisms prevent mass dissemination of cultural materials found objectionable, although some typescripts continue to circulate surreptitiously. Creation of desirable cultural products is far more problematic. It is easier to appoint a new staff for a government agency or even an entirely new cabinet to implement a new policy than it is to reeducate a country's poets and artists. An authoritarian government can prevent the public appearance of undesirable works by its monopoly of publishing and by state ownership of all film studios, museums, galleries, theaters, and concert halls. It cannot, however, obtain new art and literature without relying upon the very individuals whose lives and thought it seeks to control.

The manufacture of propagandistic journalism, much as that of posters and placards, is simple, and their production is among the more efficient of otherwise sluggish Soviet industries. Moreover, the Soviets skillfully tailor such propaganda to the needs of various audiences, from the intelligentsia to peasants, in scores of languages. One often marvels at the speed, thoroughness, and even imagination with which Soviet foreign and domestic policy goals are translated into the language of journalism and scholarship, films and newspaper cartoons, television soap operas, and more subtle dramatic productions, all carefully orchestrated and catering to various educational, ethnic, and other special audiences.

Soviet propaganda and its oral variant, *agitatsiia,* are resilient, purposeful, and efficient. Every effort will undoubtedly be made to retain those qualities in the future. More problematic is the Soviet authorities' continued ability to point to new goals capable of stirring the public's imagination. Ideological stagnation, already much in evidence, offers no grounds for expectation of spectacular successes in that respect. In the late 1980s and early 1990s, Soviet propaganda may come to resemble a magnificent sound technology that must make do with old-fashioned and dull musical compositions. Incidentally, this paucity of new official goals and ideas also argues for an intolerant attitude in the coming decade toward unofficial ideas, which would be doubly dangerous because they would easily fill an ideological vacuum.

High culture is another matter. The government may encourage it by a wide range of incentives, ranging from appeals to patriotic duty to financial benefits, but "the silence in Soviet culture" which Sir Isaiah Berlin noted a generation ago still prevails. Indeed, the many spectacular defections of musicians of the stature of Mstislav Rostropovich and ballet dancers such as Mikhail Baryshnikov and Rudolf Nureyev bespeak a serious malaise in the Soviet arts that is likely to continue.

The Khrushchev Era

Thirty years have elapsed since Stalin's death. In cultural life, one can divide that span into two periods. The first, which lasted for nearly a decade, was the heady time of great expectations that followed the dictator's demise. The second, almost twice as long, was the era of Brezhnev's rule. In the sphere of intellectual and artistic activity, the Khrushchev period began with a veritable explosion of long-suppressed grievances and proposals for reforms that followed in the wake of Khrushchev's "secret" speech at the Twentieth Communist Party Congress in 1956. Understandably, the most pressing issues were voiced first, such as the self-evident need for honesty and sincerity in literature and the arts. Some of these were too sensitive politically to allow frank discussion, so the authorities developed an intricate code of euphemisms and circumlocutions for events, processes, and persons linked to the crimes of the Stalin era. Thus, Stalin's tyranny became a "cult of personality," crimes of the Stalin era were known as "violations of socialist legality," and victims of Stalin's terror whom the police had murdered were designated "illegally repressed." It was fitting that the first post-Stalin decade ended shortly after the 1962 publication of Alexander Solzhenitsyn's *One Day in the Life of Ivan Denisovich*, with Khrushchev's downfall in 1964 marking the closing of that relatively liberal era.

In retrospect, the achievements and limitations of those years appear in sharp focus. For the country's intellectual life, the decade was above all one of great hopes. Even though many dreams were disappointed, the changes brought about were remarkable, particularly viewed against the gloomy background of oppressive immobility during the last years of Stalin's rule. The reign of terror in science and the humanities was greatly relaxed. Some of the more blatant ideologically inspired falsifications of history were exposed or more or less openly challenged. Degrading genuflections to the infallibility of the current party leader's pronouncements on subjects outside his political expertise ceased to be obligatory. Ludicrous claims to Russian primacy in a bewildering variety of human endeavors were moderated, as was the self-imposed Soviet isolation from Western art and thought.

The opening to the West ranked high among the changes Khrushchev made. The government allowed scholars to resume a modest degree of professional contact with Western colleagues, including foreign travel, and it accepted small numbers of Western scholars, especially in the humanities, for study in the Soviet Union. It also enabled European and American performing artists to visit the USSR. Muscovites enjoyed hearing foreign pianists, violinists, and symphony orchestras, and attending theatrical performances by the Old Vic and La Comédie Française. An American ensemble presented George Gershwin's *Porgy and Bess*.

A major cultural event, one that proved of great long-term importance, was the establishment of a monthly journal, *Inostrannaia literatura* [Foreign Literature], which publishes in each issue some 250 densely printed pages of translated foreign writing, including excerpts and even complete (if slightly censored) texts of contemporary Western writing. Other literary journals began to publish similar fare. In addition to the venerable masterpieces and contemporary left-wing foreign authors printed during the Stalin era, hundreds of West European and American books, some recognized long ago in the West as literary classics, such as the works of Kafka, were published in the USSR for the first time. (On the other hand, the full text of *Ulysses* has yet to appear in Russian, the centennial of Joyce's birth in 1982 notwithstanding.)

The more extreme forms of socialist realism, crudely propagandistic poster-type painting and sculpture, went out of fashion, as did similar music, drama, and films. Above all, literature and literary criticism were allowed to resume their traditional roles, if only to a degree. The first reverted to portrayals of genuine human and social conflicts. The latter became once more an arena where intellectuals passionately debated real, not contrived, ideological issues.

We should remember that the publication of a book or the official release of a film does not indicate even today that either is within reach of the ordinary citizen. Alongside shortages of consumer goods and services, which produce shocking inequalities and privileges, a *de facto* rationing of the privilege of access to cultural products still exists. As the foremost Soviet comedian Arkadi Raikin, aptly noted, "We have everything—but not for everybody." Many films, especially foreign ones, appear at restricted showings with admission by invitation only. Similarly, there exist rigidly hierarchical levels of access to library materials and to special library catalogues for a select elite of readers. Books of questionable ideological content, ostensibly published without overt restrictions, are printed in limited numbers, available only to those with access to special bookstores or, through foreign friends, to bookstores in the West. Naturally, such privileges are status symbols. A similar rationing system exists for information. The state makes available to a small elite of Soviet officials varying amounts of uncensored information in the so-called Red and White bulletins of TASS, the Soviet press agency.

The "liberalization" that ensued in Soviet arts and letters after Khrushchev's speech in 1956 had limits, though the boundaries were never explicitly delineated. Thus, literary works were grudgingly allowed to depict social injustices (for instance impoverished peasants, as in Fedor Abramov's fiction or in the sketches of Valentin Ovechkin), but only on the condition that the authors ascribe them to minor aberrations of the bureaucracy, and not to false basic Soviet values or defective institutions. Writers could depict or at least refer to mass arrests and to Stalin's purges and condemn inhuman treatment of prisoners, provided these portrayals did not suggest that those responsible for such crimes be brought to justice. Outright falsifications of the historical record became rarer, but discreet silences and half-truths often replaced them. Still, progress—moderate progress perhaps, but progress nevertheless—occurred. Surely, the reasoning went, and hope kept it alive, more would follow in time.

The Brezhnev Years

The first post-Stalin decade had been, in retrospect, one of euphoria, social muckraking, and clamor for reforms within the limits of Soviet perceptions and institutions. Dashed hopes characterized the second. Obviously, those wielding political power felt that further relaxation of political vigilance in intellectual life threatened to challenge the party's monopoly of authority. The transition to a less tolerant stance began with Khrushchev's abusive outbursts at abstract painting and sculpture as well as politically unorthodox writing during his visit to an art exhibit in 1963. The tightening of restrictions intensified after his downfall the following year and marked by and large the end of hopes for liberalization in intellectual and artistic life. Disappointed writers, artists, historians, philosophers, and others who felt the need for freedom to express their perceptions suffered from this partial retreat to Stalinist practices.

By the end of the second post-Stalin decade, such liberalization as persisted benefited for the most part only books by Soviet writers long deceased and hitherto consigned to oblivion. Mikhail Bulgakov's satirical novels were the foremost example, though even here the heavy hand of the Stalinist past continued to weigh. Some Bulgakov novels, such as *Master and Margarita,* appeared in censored form, and others not at all. Most important among the latter was *The Heart of a Dog,* a brilliant satirical parable on Communist attempts to create a New Soviet Man. Carefully selected anthologies of prose by long proscribed authors such as Boris Pilnyak and of poets such as Marina Tsvetaeva and Osip Mandelstam also appeared. Tsvetaeva and Mandelstam were not allowed to claim the place of honor to which talent entitled them; their verse was not memorized by school children, as was some traditionally Stalinist doggerel. The publication of writings by these leading twentieth-century Russian authors after decades of prohibition was a transparent gesture to mollify the disappointed liberal intelligentsia. That the authors affected included two who died in Stalin's prisons, Pilnyak and Mandelstam, and another, Tsvetaeva, who committed suicide shortly after her return to the USSR from emigration, was heavy with ironic symbolism. The circumstances brought to mind a ditty from the early 1900s, when a few gestures of accommodation followed another period of high expectations: "Tsar

Nicholas the Second/Proclaimed a Manifesto/The dead were granted freedom/The living were arrested" *(Tsar' Nikolai/Izdal manifest/ Mertvym svobodu/Zhivykh pod arest).*

In contrast to the Stalin era, warnings to the wayward to mend their ways usually preceded police intervention, and even arrests and exile were somewhat less inhuman. Still, the warnings offered a choice among three options, all variants of capitulation. The first was observance of the state's rigid standards of ideological purity and absolute artistic conformity. The second was complete silence. The third, "writing for the drawer," so to speak, rested on hope for a period when dangerous pages of seditious ideas or other subversive art and thought might appear. The modest publication of verse by such long silenced living poets as Boris Pasternak and Anna Akhmatova was among the most exciting cultural events in the USSR and kept hope alive that such a period would one day come for other works that remained suppressed.

Dissidence

The majority of Soviet artists and thinkers resigned themselves to the inevitable. However, a few chose a new path: unauthorized circulation of their writings in crude typewritten form, illegal exhibits of canvases, and increasingly frequent smuggling of manuscripts for publication abroad. For the first time in Soviet history, rebellious writers and intellectuals turned defiantly to *samizdat* and *tamizdat,* "self-publishing" and "publishing out there," that is, in the West.

Andrei Sinyavsky, whose arrest in 1965 and subsequent trial established the precedent of criminal prosecution for publishing one's work abroad (which was not illegal), shrewdly noted that the existence of censorship in the USSR promoted, indeed assured, graphomania, since a rejected manuscript inevitably invited suspicions of political discrimination. Many *samizdat* publications were devoted to a variety of implicitly political causes. Foremost among these was *The Chronicle of Current Events,* a scrupulously dispassionate journal that recorded with admirable restraint and impartiality Soviet violations of human rights. The *Chronicle* was identified with the so-called Democratic Movement, of which the unofficial leader was Andrei Sakharov. *The Political Diary,* copies of which did not reach the West until it suspended publication, was liberal Marxist in orientation. The other end of the political spectrum was occupied by the journal *Veche* (the name of the People's Assembly in medieval Russia), which served for a time as spokesman for a conservative and occasionally xenophobic variety of Great Russian nationalism.

As surrogate for a nonexistent free press, *The Chronicle of Current Events* understandably emphasized issues never mentioned in official Soviet media. One of the most important was systematic ethnic discrimination in the USSR, a charge always indignantly denied by Soviet spokesmen abroad. Another was the persistent harassment of religious believers, which was similarly refuted as a slanderous fabrication. Both were meticulously documented in *The Chronicle,* which carried the texts of signed petitions by representatives of the aggrieved ethnic and religious groups. Let us first examine the latter case.

Officially, there is separation of church and state in the Soviet Union, and this might be assumed to imply the state's nonintervention in religious matters. In the 1960s and 1970s, however, complaints multiplied from groups of religious believers—Pentecostals, dissident Baptists, Roman Catholics, Moslems, and even members of the Russian Orthodox Church. All of these groups were (and still are) subjected to systematic mistreatment by the militantly atheist Soviet state, some more than others and at different times with varying degrees of zeal. All were, and still are, outwardly resigned to the fact that *no* religious believer is allowed to occupy a position of any prominence in the USSR. Often driven to desperation by persistent discriminatory practices, the Soviet Union's religious believers and clergy of all denominations are thus ironically restricted to seeking refuge in Lenin's admonition that the antireligious struggle be waged with a degree of tact, lest crudely offensive tactics ultimately interfere with its effectiveness.

Since the days of the biblical prophets and the Kings of Israel, secular rulers have frequently clashed with religious leaders but have usually avoided mass persecution of the faithful. Curiously, the reverse now is true in the USSR. Since Stalin's *de facto* concordat with the Russian Orthodox Church during World War II, the authorities have harassed the lower clergy and rank-and-file believers but have been quite solicitous of the welfare of the church leaders, the hierarchy of the Russian Orthodox Church above all, but of other church hierarchies too. The Moslem hierarchy, for instance, maintains contacts with coreligionists abroad, as do the "official" Baptists. Thus, the Soviet Union exhibits a curious anomaly: several theological academies function, but not a single parochial or Sunday school provides religious instruction for children of any denomination.

The Soviet government has been quite successful in using religious leaders for advancing Soviet policy objectives abroad through their participation in such bodies as the World Council of Churches and in the various "peace" drives, and through their steadfast denials of any antireligious persecutions or restrictions at home. Soviet propagandistic exploitation of American evangelist Billy Graham's visit to Moscow in 1982 was a telling illustration of this tactic applied to a foreign religious leader.

The two ethnic groups whose complaints have gradually assumed

a mass character since the 1960s are the Jews and the Moslem Crimean Tatars, both victims of Stalin's ire. Stalin had the Crimean
Tatars deported from their ancestral habitat during World War II,
and they live in effect in a Soviet diaspora. After Stalin's death, the
Tatars demanded that they be allowed to return to their native
Crimea. Their efforts were unsuccessful: Slavic settlers had in the
meantime populated their territories.

The Jews, more precisely those who survived the Nazi Holocaust,
were subjected after the war to vicious anti-Semitic persecutions, eu-
phemistically called an "anti-cosmopolitan" campaign, and all their
cultural and educational institutions were closed. Disappointed in the
single concession obtained after the dictator's death—publication of
the Yiddish language literary monthly *Sovetish heimland* (which was
allowed in order to please Soviet sympathizers in the West, as the
Minister of Culture Yekaterina Furtseva admitted in a moment of
candor)—the Soviet Jews demanded reestablishment of Yiddish cultural institutions and the right to be reunited with families separated
during the war. The authorities' failure to meet these modest demands gradually changed the direction of the Jews' efforts. Prodded
by official and popular anti-Semitism and further stimulated by such
Jewish *samizdat* journals as *Iskhod* (the Russian term for Exodus) and
Iton (Hebrew for newspaper), many Jews made emigration their goal.
Observers in the West, including those who took an active part in
efforts on behalf of Soviet Jews, were skeptical of the likelihood of any
large-scale emigration: history offered no precedent. Yet, for a variety of reasons, such mass emigration did occur. During the 1970s
and the early 1980s over a quarter of a million Jews were allowed to
depart, all ostensibly for Israel, though in fact more than half reached
the United States.

The government's desire to rid the country of malcontents or
potential political troublemakers no doubt was among the reasons for
the decision to allow large-scale emigration. This policy was consonant with the overall posture of international goodwill, a consideration that also benefited tens of thousands of Volga Germans
seeking "repatriation" to West Germany and Armenians wishing to
join relatives in the United States. Because of the extremely high
percentage of Jews or persons married to Jews in the Democratic
Movement, the departure of tens of thousands of Jews enabled the
authorities to cripple the Democratic Movement with little resort to
police measures. In effect, the regime's deportation of scores of non-
Jewish dissidents and nonconformist writers, artists, and thinkers,
including even socially recalcitrant Russian Orthodox priests, reveals
that it used emigration to weaken the dissident movement.

The emigres included many leading proponents of unorthodox

ideas debated in the USSR during the first two post-Stalin decades, advocates of close intellectual and artistic ties to the West, and practitioners of experimentation in literature and the arts. The emigres, Jewish or not, included a large number of the "internationalist" intelligentsia. Their departure, which the regime probably thought would weaken and diffuse Zionism, may paradoxically in the long run exacerbate competing nationalisms among the various ethnic minorities and among the Russians themselves. Both the nationalisms of the ethnic minorities, which include a multiplicity of national movements, like the Turkic, Baltic, and others, and the vaguely pan-Slavic nationalism of the Russians are, in part, responses to each other. Each is likely to gain momentum in the competition. One need not subscribe in its entirety to the late Andrei Amalrik's vision of their eventual clash in *Will the Soviet Union Survive to 1984?* (the year is practically upon us!) to anticipate that grave frictions between Russian and non-Russian nationalisms are all but inevitable.

The emigration of many believers notwithstanding, there is every reason to expect that religion will continue to attract large numbers of adherents, including Soviet-educated young men and women. Many factors lead to this, of which the chief are probably a sense of dissatisfaction with a Soviet ideal that no longer inspires and a quest for spiritual values. Thus, Russian Orthodox Christianity can be seen also as a dimension of the Slavic nationalism that will be ascendant through the coming decade. Roman Catholicism will no doubt continue as the Lithuanians' national symbol of opposition to Russification, while Islam will serve as both a religion and a way of life for millions of non-Slavs. Judaism may persist among a handful of adherents, if only because it is the single tolerated form of Jewish expression in the atheist Soviet state. Some religious sects may serve similarly as a means of self-expression for some members of the most oppressed classes in a state that boasts of having abolished social inequality.

The large-scale Soviet emigration of the 1970s has provided immense benefits to the West as earlier immigrants have. At the same time, Soviet losses of men and women of talent have, to be sure, weakened the social protest movement there. Yet this emigration has also deprived the USSR of the originality and experimentalism, the "salt" that all societies require, especially in times of rapid social change further accelerated by technological advances.

The impact of the Soviet emigration of the 1970s, often referred to as the Third Emigration, on Soviet cultural and intellectual life of the early 1980s is already established. The flow of communication between these emigres and their relatives and friends in the Soviet Union has provided their native countrymen with information about the Western societies in which the emigres now live. This new source of information, in turn, has stimulated both the criticisms and the hopes of millions in the Soviet Union who now know someone who actually lives in the West. Western radio broadcasting into the Soviet Union, such as the Voice of America and Radio Liberty, has been able to disseminate this insight into the differences between the Soviet system and other societies to audiences increasingly receptive, because the information and judgments come from men and women deeply familiar with their lives and interests. Some of these emigres will of course carry on this work through their writings and other artistic productions, and a handful have helped significantly to improve the quality of Western radio broadcasts by joining one of the several services that provide knowledge to those the Soviet government tries to isolate within the USSR. Moreover, an ironic consequence of this emigration has been its influence on Western knowledge and understanding of the Soviet system, renewed and invigorated by this flood of highly educated men and women eager to describe the conditions under which they had lived and able to speed their message through relatives, friends, and Western media eager for new information about a country about which reliable information is difficult to obtain.

Russian Nationalism and Other Nationalisms

Russian nationalism received a visible stimulus in 1981, when Soviet scholars and journalists took advantage of the one hundredth anniversary of Dostoevsky's death to recall his hostile comments about Roman Catholicism, the Papacy, Jews, and Poles. This celebration of Russia's beleaguered status and virtues and of the Soviet Union's role as herald of a universalist Marxist Soviet idea was also unavoidably an attack upon Western "cosmopolitan, anti-patriotic, and liberal poison." The power of Russian nationalism is such that few historians and literary critics raised their voices against the shrill anti-Westernism and xenophobic patriotism of the campaign.

Two events will almost certainly have a strong impact on Soviet intellectual and cultural life in the next few years. The first is Brezhnev's recent death. The transfer of power will almost certainly produce a reduced commitment to policies associated with the Brezhnev administration and consequently will lead to modifications in or even drastic departures from the *status quo*.

The second event is the millennium in 1988 of Russia's conversion to Christianity, the importance of which transcends by far its purely religious aspect. Conversion to Byzantine Christianity marked the emergence of Eastern Slavs as an ethnic entity with an identity of their own, the beginning of an East Slavic culture symbolized by acquisition of an alphabet, and the Eastern Slavs' accession to European culture through their new link to Byzantium. Given Soviet sensitivity to anniversaries, it is reasonable to expect that the government will not confine observances of that momentous act and the following one thousand years to the Russian Orthodox Church. Indeed, the jubilee will almost certainly turn into a nationwide celebration of Russia's coming of age, marked on a grand scale in high and popular culture, in the issue of commemorative postage stamps, in scholarship and architectural monuments, in opera, in marching songs, and in art exhibits. In short, it will be a very important occasion. The nationalist flavor of the observances, with some inevitably religious overtones, will be accompanied by lip service to proletarian internationalism, Marxism-Leninism, and other traditional Soviet pieties. The citizenry, however, will almost certainly perceive this as little more than ritualistic etiquette.

A sort of dress rehearsal of the upcoming event occurred in 1980 on the occasion of the six hundredth anniversary of the battle of Kulikovo Field, which marked the beginning of the end to nearly three centuries of the Tatar and Mongol yoke. Observances of the Kulikovo anniversary had strong anti-Oriental and specifically anti-Chinese overtones. We can expect more of this in 1988. The millennium will no doubt become a "positive" celebration of vaguely perceived common Slavic virtues and achievements, in part because of the historical fact that it was Kievan Rus' that was baptized in A.D. 988. This would have the advantage of coopting some Ukrainians and Belorussians for the celebration.

Tensions between various nationalisms within the USSR are strong and are likely to become exacerbated. Moreover, all ethnic groups resent in varying degrees the preeminent role of the Great Russians, which is likely to become even greater with the passage of time. Nationalism in the Baltic republics of Lithuania and Estonia and, to a lesser extent, Latvia as well, is almost as intense as it is in parts of Eastern Europe, which is understandable: all three Baltic republics were independent states until 1940. Nationalism in the Ukraine, particularly in areas annexed from Poland in 1939, as well as in Georgia and in Armenia, is strong, albeit not quite so strong as in the Baltic. In the Ukraine, contacts with thousands of kinsmen in Canada and the United States intensify national feeling, as do similar ties between Armenians and the Armenian diaspora in Europe, the Middle East, and the United States. Nationalism is strong among members of ethnic groups whom the Soviet authorities deported during World War II, such as the Volga Germans and the Crimean Tatars. Many Volga Germans have left for West Germany; the Tatars have not been so fortunate. It is important to remember that Central Asian nationalism is often synonymous with Islam, both as a religious faith and as a way of life. It is thus less noticeable, perhaps, but also more resilient because of the religious camouflage. The spectacular upsurge of Islam across the Soviet borders in the 1970s may act as a serious contributing factor, further enhancing this trend.

In all likelihood, Soviet authorities will concentrate upon trying to present Russian nationalism in terms acceptable to the bulk of assimilated urban Ukrainians and Belorussians, while they seek at the same time to combat manifestations of non-Slavic nationalism. The establishment will view minority religions with suspicion, in particular those without a hierarchy that can be manipulated and also those that unite Soviet believers with adherents of the same denominations outside the USSR, such as Roman Catholics, Pentecostals, and above all Jews. Indeed, Jewish emigration during the 1970s and early 1980s, far from "solving" the Soviet Union's Jewish "problem," has probably served to exacerbate it. The overwhelming majority of the over two million Soviet Jews who remain have friends and relatives abroad, and the government therefore regards them with ever greater distrust. Discrimination in employment and the drastic decline in the percentage of Jews admitted to universities in recent years bear this out. Islam is similarly a cause for grave concern because it serves as a potentially dangerous unifying force for scores of otherwise dissimilar ethnic groups scattered through the Caucasus, Central Asia, and the upper reaches of the Volga, many of whom share religious belief and some ethnic ties with awakening millions outside the Soviet Union.

The government tries to make the struggle against non-Russian nationalisms appear ideologically respectable by presenting it as a campaign directed at vestiges of Islamic and other religious "obscurantism." It refers to Marx's famous dictum about religion as an opiate of the people and just as inevitably does not refer to the fact that it cites Marx's pronouncement out of context: Marx quite rightly observed that religion may be a pain-killer, a source of solace to the suffering masses. Perhaps this particular function of religion explains in part its surprising resilience in the militantly atheist Soviet state.

My predictions of heightened religious and ethnic frictions within a multinational Soviet society that pays lip service to ethnic equality are thoroughly relevant in the 1980s, when Cypriot Greeks and Turks, Iranians and Iraqis, Lebanese Christians and Lebanese Moslems, Arabs and Israelis, and even Irish Catholics and Irish Protestants fight viciously. A Soviet anecdote comes to mind: Leninist friendship of nations may be seen in practice when Latvians and

Turkmen, Belorussians and Kirgiz, Azeris and Lithuanians, Russians and Tatars volunteer to help Georgians beat up Armenians.

The Vestiges of Marxism

Marxism-Leninism in the Soviet Union no longer is a vital source of belief or faith and no longer provides even effective ceremonies. Its empty slogans do not inspire and are not taken seriously within the USSR. Yet this traditional set of formulae and quotations has value, just as the leadership finds useful the continued existence of ecclesiastical hierarchies of various denominations. Its dogma is deeply imbedded in scholarship, and references to its postulates are as obligatory as invocations to the Muses once were in neoclassical odes and just as much a convention largely devoid of meaning. Marxism-Leninism imparts a sense of continuity and legitimacy and a form of respectability. It establishes a general framework through which the leaders view the world and therefore influences attitudes toward foreign policy. It enhances the regime's stability. It justifies many of its practices, if only because the corpus of Marxist-Leninist patristic writings is so vast and varied that knowledgeable and skilled polemicists can easily find appropriate chapter and verse for any argument or policy.

This ideological scholasticism permits Soviet propagandists to designate armed conflicts of its choice as just wars of national liberation, while branding as unjust those it disapproves: Argentina's unsuccessful attempt to seize the Falkland Islands was treated as a war of national liberation. It allows the government and its agents to denounce non-Soviet colonialism, while defending the proposition that its analogous practices are just and progressive. It enables it to differentiate between the old Russian Empire, which Lenin called "a prisonhouse of nations," and the Soviet successor state, which the old Stalinist anthem described as an "inviolable union of free republics rallied forever around great Rus'."

Finally, Marxism-Leninism enables the USSR to claim unquestioned loyalty and doctrinal obedience from the international Communist movement and to reject with protestations of injured innocence insinuations that the movement advances Soviet national interests, positions of visibly decreasing effect upon once blind supporters of all Soviet policies. Indeed, a formula may be devised: Marxist-Leninist incantations are most useful where simple Russian "National Bolshevik" slogans might be most harmful. The leaders emphasize nationalism when appealing to patriotic sentiments of the country's Russian, or, in its expanded sense, Slavic population. They use Marxism-Leninism in warding off charges that the USSR is a modern variant of the old Russian Empire pursuing narrow and selfish imperial aims at the expense of non-Slavs both at home and abroad. In short, they use the doctrine to support any current Soviet policies, without affecting these policies. One may expect that in the ensuing decade Soviet artistic, cultural, and intellectual production aimed primarily for export will continue to avoid emphasis on patriotic Russian themes, seeking out instead Marxist "internationalist" motifs of ethnic equality or economic and social justice.

Conversely, when domestic audiences are the consumers of such cultural productions, the government will emphasize Russian nationalism, though not to the extent that non-Russian Soviet audiences might consider it offensive. Wolfgang Kasack's highly informative annual surveys of translations of recent Soviet writing that appear in West Germany demonstrate that Soviet publishing agencies do not promote the dissemination in West Germany of Soviet novels with wartime settings, because often such works not only are celebrations of Russian nationalism strongly permeated with anti-Nazism, but also are crudely anti-German. On the other hand, many novels of that kind appear in translation in other languages, particularly in East Europe. Occasionally, such considerations extend even to classics of Russian literature. Thus, Nikolai Gogol's *Taras Bulba,* a paean to the bravery of seventeenth-century Ukrainian Cossacks, has not been translated into Polish because of its strongly anti-Polish flavor. Russian nationalist motifs are rarely found in prose and verse printed in the Ukrainian monthly *Dnipro,* the Belorussian *Neman,* or even in Russian-language journals that appear in the non-Russian republics, such as *Literaturnaia Gruziia* or *Literaturnaia Armeniia.* Some journals with a national circulation, such as *Molodaia gvardiia* and *Oktiabr',* print much material with a pronounced Russian nationalist flavor; others, such as *Yunost'* and *Novy mir,* feature little. Provincial literary publications printed within the Russian Federation, such as *Don* or *Sibirskie ogni,* all possess Russian nationalist features. These journals are intended almost exclusively for Russian local readership, and appeals to Russian nationalist sentiments are likely to strike a responsive chord.

Facets of Cultural and Intellectual Life

In the USSR the dictum that history is current politics extended into the past also encompasses historical fiction, drama, and all literary criticism, although such uses of the latter antedate the Soviet regime. With freedom of expression severely restricted, Soviet historians, writers, and literary critics have developed over the years an intricate system of allusions and code words understood at least in part by educated readers, thus making it possible, with the connivance of the authorities, to discuss surreptitiously a wide variety of issues one cannot raise openly because of their politically sensitive nature. Thus, behind the façade of optimism and unanimity, observers voice concerns and fight polemical battles that explain and sometimes also affect government policy. Hidden by long-accepted custom from the public view, such debates are tolerated, within limits, on the condition that decencies of Aesopian language be observed. Thus, Stalin's cruel rule was justified as necessary and beneficial in the long run by suggesting parallels with Peter the Great and Ivan the Terrible.

Occasionally, some discussions of this type suggest rather startling ideas. Thus, a literary critic in the third issue of *Literaturnoe obozrenie* in 1977 referred to the "idiocy of urban life," thus literally contradicting Marx. These often heated exchanges may be quite invisible to a foreigner's untrained eye. A foreigner may not readily detect in an otherwise unremarkable historical treatise or literary essay departures from conventional formulae, omissions of otherwise all but obligatory slogans, or references to persons and historical events that have specific associations for Soviets.

I expect such practices to endure. Soviet historians, writers and literary critics are likely to continue the necessarily inconclusive debate about Russia's unique destiny as a nation at once European and Asian. That polemic, rooted in Peter the Great's momentous eighteenth-century reforms that ultimately transformed a backward state into a European power, is the most central and chronologically the longest single controversy in Russian history. Waged in the nineteenth century by Slavophiles and Westernizers, the debate transcends history, for its present implications are both immediate and real: the legitimacy of the Soviet Union's credentials as a member of the Western community of nations and the compatibility of that membership with its simultaneous claim to status as friend and protector of the Third World are ultimately at stake. As in the past, the debate will ostensibly be confined to such esoteric problems as the Tatar and Mongol invasions centuries ago, or French influences on Russian verse, or the ruinous impact of indiscriminate industrialization in present-day America. That, however, is not likely to deceive experienced Soviet readers, who can decipher that the real issues are Sino-Soviet relations, Eurocommunism, and destruction of traditional Russian villages and village churches in Siberia by bulldozers clearing the taiga for new factories. Historical writing may also reflect political moods in straightforward ways. Thus, Russian nationalist moods may lift a number of long-standing taboos, allowing, for instance, discussion of such subjects as the reign of Nicholas II, Russian nationalist and religious movements of the turn of the century, and such monarchist statesmen as Pyotr Stolypin.

Cultural Isolationism

With a number of exceptions, the Slavophiles in nineteenth-century Russia tended to be political conservatives, while most Westerners were liberal in orientation. Most indications are that political conservatives will predominate in the 1980s. That in turn implies a general tendency toward cultural isolationism from the West. Whatever the explanations ultimately advanced, and some, such as perennial shortages of hard currency may be plausible, the two central components of National Bolshevism, nationalism and political conservatism and consequent fear of foreign influences, are likely to be the decisive reasons for the decline in cultural relations. As the experience of the post-Stalin decade has amply demonstrated, the large-scale influx of Western literature, cinema, and even technology (to say nothing of overtly ideological works in the social sciences) inevitably results in a gradual erosion of traditional Soviet values and corresponding inroads by alien "bourgeois" ideas. At the very least, Western books promote skepticism with regard to hitherto accepted articles of Marxist Soviet faith and hence prepare the soil from which weeds of heresy may soon spring. Hence the prudent desire of the Soviet authorities to minimize the penetration into the USSR of potentially dangerous cultural imports from the West, and a preference for relative cultural isolationism. Since an atmosphere of nationalism and conservatism is not likely to engender writing and other artistic production that Western audiences would find attractive, the declining relationship would also result from a mutual waning of interest.

The Soviet public's unflagging demand for Western books, films, and other material will have little influence on this. Even now Soviet spokesmen regularly complain about an alleged "lack of reciprocity" in cultural "traffic," pointing to large sales of translated Western books in the USSR and the modest success of Soviet books in the West. Allowing for Western publication of Russian authors the Soviets find objectionable, such as Pasternak and Solzhenitsyn, the argument has little merit, but that is another matter. Soviet statistics regularly compare data on all American books, from James Fenimore Cooper, Mark Twain, and Jack London to the present, with figures only on the U.S. publication of post-revolutionary authors, hence excluding Gogol and Tolstoy, Dostoevsky and Chekhov. Ideologically and artistically objectionable cultural imports would, of course, be a major casualty, but it is unlikely that such policies would significantly affect such staples as regular republication of Western classics, theatrical performances of old masterpieces of Western drama, or the already established musical repertory. Newer cultural imports may once again be generally restricted to works by foreign comrades, friends, and ideologically kindred spirits, their contents suggesting that life may be hard in the USSR, but that it is far preferable to the horrors of capitalism. Since such conclusions clash with information other sources provide on the West, the state will increase efforts to emphasize the alleged moral and psychological squalor of life in capitalist Europe and America and, above all, the absence of prospects for improvement.

Restrictions on contacts with the non-Soviet world, the flow of information by print and by radio, and the availability of Western cultural materials (even those from Eastern Europe are likely to be suspect) are nearly certain to engender a feeling of deprivation among the intelligentsia and the young. Technological progress, to be sure, may make these restrictions more difficult to enforce, but the Soviet authorities will exert necessary efforts to achieve their aims. Such feelings of deprivation in turn may encourage reliance on unsanctioned sources of news and entertainment. The black market in foreign books and periodicals, including those in the Russian language, will probably remain of marginal importance in Moscow, Leningrad, and two or three other cities. There is little likelihood of its significant expansion because of the risks involved.

Education and Science

Education is a baffling subject for a student of any society, including one's own, and otherwise intelligent observers probably write more nonsense about higher education, its weaknesses and strengths, than about any other subject except perhaps that of military capabilities. Measuring the quality of a single educational institution is difficult enough; determining that of a country, even one with an educational system as standardized as that of the Soviet Union, is even more so.

The Soviet leaders from the beginning have devoted much attention to education at every level, in part because they consider education, science, and technology keys to the Soviet future, and in part because they have an obsession with control. They seek dominance over every aspect of life and are especially fearful of information and ideas.

The Soviet Union has clearly made considerable progress in education since 1917, building on the small foundation of high quality research and instruction in some fields, especially in the natural and physical sciences and in the arts, and on the broad primary and secondary educational system the tsarist government had begun to build especially after 1905. Soviet achievements in some of the sciences have been impressive, and the emphasis upon fundamentals and upon orderly work throughout the educational system has earned praise from foreign observers. However, Soviet education is handicapped by restrictions on freedom, the lifeblood of research and instruction in any educational system. It suffers greatly from a form of cultural isolation much deeper than that of Western countries, an isolation especially damaging at a time of lively change and growth in every field of study. Education receives inadequate financial support from an economy which cannot meet the demands of the military and other requirements. Finally, Soviet higher education provides narrow training at every level, at a time when the walls between disciplines of study have collapsed.

The percentage of GNP the United States devotes to education is about a third higher than that of the Soviet Union. The percentage of Americans who graduate from high school is about twice that in the Soviet Union, and about twice as many Americans attend college as do Soviets.

Science is especially valued in the USSR, as it was in Russia. Seventy-five percent of all Soviet graduate students are in science and engineering (though this includes also low-level technicians), compared to 20 percent in the United States. The Soviet Union has about three times as many engineers and technicians, and twice as many graduates in physics, the life sciences, and mathematics as the United States, although once more the often inferior quality of many must be borne in mind.

To education (and to science in particular) freedom of inquiry is of paramount importance. One of Khrushchev's most significant changes, one which Soviet citizens and Western observers thought symbolic, effected the relaxation of controls over science. With the passage of time, it has become increasingly clear that purely pragmatic and practical considerations inspired these changes rather than a governmental decision to embrace the principle of academic freedom. Thus, in biology, the government abandoned the Stalinist aberration of Lysenkoism in favor of Western-style genetics, because the former had contributed to the Soviet Union's disastrous performance in agriculture. Similarly, cybernetics, a "pseudoscience" in Stalin's time, received ideological clearance because the leaders thought it conducive to overcoming technological backwardness. Soviet scientists, in short, benefited from the party's rational decision to grant them greater freedom from ideological interference so that they could function more efficiently. (For analogous reasons, not only are scientists given greater creature comforts than ordinary Soviets, but they are also allowed to indulge their tastes in Western music, abstract painting, and, by Soviet standards, even daringly erotic films.) By contrast, scholarship in the humanities and the social sciences remains heavily politicized, though much less so than during the Stalin era.

Yet even the relaxation of interference in science, while impressive under Soviet conditions, has not implied that the exact and natural sciences could hope for its disappearance. Soviet universities continue to train narrow specialists, men and women who are competent and sometimes brilliant in their fields. At the same time, concepts of a liberal education, of critical, independent thought, of a healthy distrust of authority and of conventional wisdom remain alien to Soviet higher education. Indeed, the rulers view these not merely with distrust, but with hostility. Soviet school children are taught facts and respect for authority: Moscow found *Sesame Street,* an otherwise admirable American television series for preschoolers, unacceptable because its boisterous and rather independently minded boys and girls set a bad example for their Soviet counterparts.

Advanced training at the university level and beyond is, in a way, a logical extension of earlier schooling. It aims at professional excellence but does not encourage independence, originality, or least of all, interest in problems outside the scientist's direct and immediate professional concerns. Soviet scientists are not expected to show interest in the social, moral, and political implications of their work. In fact, the party rarely presses scientists to become even nominal party members, except those aspiring to administrative positions.

The party's desire to stifle potentially dangerous moral and political concerns among scientists is tellingly illustrated by the fact that those with access to the American journal *Science* receive copies with some articles removed and their titles erased from the table of contents. The objectionable materials are essays discussing the scientist's social and moral responsibilities for the uses to which his work may be put. Soviet authors who tried to treat such subjects—such as Daniil Granin and the brothers Strugatsky, the latter the country's foremost authors of science fiction—have submitted to severe pressures and abandoned their attempts. By contrast, Soviet publishers disseminate translations of analogous writings by such Western novelists as Ray Bradbury, Isaac Asimov, and the late Mitchell Wilson, who discuss such moral problems and dilemmas in capitalist conditions.

The spirit of critical inquiry mandatory in scientific work also influences, if only to a limited extent, the scientific elite's thought processes. Evidence abounds that Soviet authorities cannot simultaneously promote scientific contacts with the West and rigidly restrict them to purely technical matters. Some social exchanges ensue, and some nonscientific discussions occur. As is frequently the case in other areas of life, the East Europeans, with stronger traditional ties to the

West, often act as catalysts and intermediaries. Western influences reach Soviet scientists as a result of improved communications and access to efficient copying equipment. On a number of occasions American and West European scientists have succeeded in holding unauthorized seminars in the apartments of Soviet scientists barred from laboratories for political reasons. One heroic example towers above all and suggests the fundamental problem science and intellectual life in general pose for the regime. Andrei Sakharov, considered the father of the Soviet hydrogen bomb, is in exile in the provinces, the symbol of embattled democratic dissent. His followers are not many, and only a handful may replace them in the next generation. Still, they demonstrate that the acquisition of Western scientific and technological know-how entails some risk of contamination by Western ideas and values, such as independence of thought, pluralism, and tolerance.

The Youth

The potential threat posed by an alert and politically inquisitive scientific and technical intelligentsia is a problem of the future. Since the early 1960s, however, a domestic strain of another virus has appeared as a clear and present danger among the urban, more affluent, and better educated young. Newspapers report incidents involving not merely old-fashioned drunks, a familiar fixture of the Soviet and pre-Soviet Russian landscape, but long-haired youths clad in foreign jeans, similar to American and Western European hippies. Their partiality both to the English language and to loud rock music is a cause for concern, largely because it reflects frustration, alienation, and even individualism. More ominously, some official observers note that adherents of such fads occasionally express admiration for a supranational youth culture that expresses contempt for all adult values and establishments and defiantly proclaims the slogan of not trusting anyone over the age of thirty, a motto that hardly appeals to the ruling gerontocracy. The government has not been able to control this phenomenon and wavers between attacking it as ideologically subversive and trying to tame it by declaring Soviet modifications of Western fashions respectable.

The Mass Media

The mass media are the general press, radio, and television. As the lowest common denominators among purveyors of information and commentary, which Soviet media routinely blend into a single whole so that separating facts from editorials is a hopeless task, these offer only a modest amount of the former and a simplistic variety of the latter. Precisely because of their simplicity and national circulation, commentaries *cum* news found in the mass media represent the official views of the Soviet leadership. Careful scrutiny of these sources for their bland contents, omissions, and intentional prominence or, conversely, for their inconspicuous manner of presentation, yields much information concealed from an inexperienced observer, because clichés and jargon ingeniously obscure them. Nearly every Soviet newspaper reader, radio listener, or television viewer possesses a modest degree of such skills. Solzhenitsyn's *Cancer Ward* provides a good literary portrayal, showing a party bureaucrat in his hospital bed scrutinizing an issue of *Pravda* for hints of policy shifts after Stalin's death. Another fine illustration of this use of the press is provided by an anecdote. An old woman stops every day at a Moscow newsstand, looks at the headline in the newspaper, and walks away. Finally, the news vendor inquires what it is that she seeks. "An obituary," says the old lady. "But don't you know that obituaries are always printed on the last page?" The old woman replies, "The one I am looking for will be on the front page." The story is an old one told during the Stalin era. It has not lost validity.

In 1980, about 85 percent of all Soviet families had access to a total of 64 million sets, and more than 70 percent of the adult population viewed television primarily as a means of entertainment. These statistics impart considerable importance to the contents of Soviet television programs. Both radio and television are ponderous and heavily didactic. Even mild controversy is rare and discussions are amplifications of information rather than clashes of opinion. According to Genrikh Gabai, a Soviet film specialist now in the United States, one reason for Soviet television's stricter political orthodoxy, compared, for instance, with the cinema is its higher degree of centralization. Another likely reason is the medium's general accessibility. Closed circuit television exists in the USSR, but there is no cable television. Unlike films, which can be shown to selected audiences, television programs are presumably accessible to all owners of television sets in a given area.

Social criticism in Soviet television is and no doubt will remain tame, much like "The Wick," a series of mildly satirical twenty-minute shows popular during the 1970s. This series featured exposés of malfunctions in services, shopping, and the bureaucracy, always making sure that these did not reflect on the system as a whole or on Soviet values. Such fare allows for letting off steam which might otherwise generate "unhealthy" social commentary. According to Gabai, the policy that "The Wick" followed, announced repeatedly by the show's producer, the loyal satirical poet Sergei Mikhalkov, was to describe isolated incidents and avoid at all costs any generalization.

Entertainment offered on Soviet television tends to the soap opera and offers viewers an opportunity to see on the screen, day after day, stories about the consequences of alcoholism, messy divorces and their impact upon children, and so forth. This type of pseudosocial commentary may become more common because it fills a genuine need without involving social costs. Indeed, in the hands of experienced writers and directors the soap opera may offer opportunities for sound "educational" activity.

As in the United States, television in the Soviet Union shows older films, many of which depict World War II. The latter not only portray the nation's travail and heroism but also extol martial virtues and exude a militaristic brand of patriotism that often smacks of xenophobia. In fact, I know of no pacifist films or antiwar expressions in any Soviet art forms. I expect that treatments of war will continue to occupy a prominent place in television programming, as will such fare as Yulian Semenov's serial *Seventeen Moments of Spring,* which in the 1970s related the heroic adventures of a Soviet secret agent abroad.

Film

The similarities between Soviet television and the cinema are numerous and often obvious. For instance, films are shown on television without changes. Many motion pictures released in recent years for mass circulation resemble television programming. Falling in this category, for instance, are Alexander Allov's and Vladimir Naumov's inspirational patriotic films and *Teheran 1943,* a motion picture glorifying Soviet counterintelligence for foiling an alleged assassination plot aimed at Churchill, Roosevelt, and Stalin at their wartime meeting.

Some recent films are genuinely entertaining, like Emil Braginsky's and Eldar Ryazanov's *The Garage,* which depicted intrigues and minor violations of the law when a group of affluent citizens decided to build a cooperative shelter for their privately owned cars. Another attractive motion picture of the late 1970s was *Moscow Does Not Believe in Tears,* which was favorably reviewed in the United States, notwithstanding its sentimentality and its theme, which would certainly have been roundly denounced in an American film as offensive sexism: women, even otherwise successful, can find fulfillment only in marriage; to attract a man, a woman must defer to him and generally make him feel superior. Sentimentality is common in Soviet films dealing with love. Ilya Maslin's *Love and Lies,* which reached these shores in 1982, is blatantly sentimental. Still, Soviet spectators find them preferable to obviously contrived and openly propagandistic films, such as Alexander Gelman's *The Prize,* in which upright Soviet workers refuse to accept extra pay because they believe it is undeserved. In an atmosphere of ideological conservatism with strongly nationalistic overtones, such films would doubtlessly be pushed by the authorities.

More problematic is the future of films such as those that provoked controversy in the recent past. It is unlikely, for instance, that Sergei Bondarchuk's *Peace unto Him Who Enters,* a film charged with engendering pacifist moods, would be shown if revived at all. Its director's unblemished political past may have been one reason why the film was not banned outright. The late Vasili Shukshin's *The Red Guelder Rose* (1974), by contrast, may receive a tentative stamp of approval because of its clear Russian nationalist flavor, despite its strong note of social criticism. Indeed, Shukshin's model may be emulated in years to come. At worst, films of that type may be cleared at first for restricted showings, and later for wider distribution. Their outright prohibition is unlikely.

The fate of Andrei Tarkovsky's *Andrei Rublev* supports this hypothesis. Completed in 1966, this film, probably the most important produced since Stalin's death, has been shown in the USSR with moderate frequency since the early 1970s but was strictly an export commodity before that. The vicissitudes in the picture's fate reflect recent developments in ideological priorities. In the mid-1960s, its portrayal of Russia's great medieval icon painter was unacceptable because the heroic Rublev invited a degree of respect, if not admiration, for religion. Ten years later, that objectionable trait of the film was considered less important than its redeeming value as a paean to Russian nationalism.

The lesson of *Andrei Rublev* becomes clear if one considers its fate in conjunction with that of another hauntingly beautiful motion picture completed at about the same time and that shared in its destiny for several years. Like *Andrei Rublev,* Sergei Paradzhanov's *Shadows of Forgotten Ancestors* was shown abroad, but it has not appeared in the USSR, primarily because of its strong mood of Ukrainian nationalism, of which the government disapproves.

Elem Klimov's *Agony,* a film about Rasputin, the religious charlatan whose influence on Nicholas II was great, remains proscribed, apparently because of its sympathetic treatment of the last tsar. However, the film's director may simply have overestimated the rapidity with which the nationalist trend would become so acceptable that one might portray in a positive light the Russian monarch whom a Communist firing squad executed.

It is also likely that the happy resolution of initial difficulties for *Andrei Rublev* encouraged its creator to produce in 1977 another film with strong religious overtones. Indeed, the early career of *The Mirror* parallels that of *Rublev.* It has elicited high praise abroad, in France in particular, while in the USSR *The Mirror* is, so far, restricted in availability. *The Mirror* may become acceptable in spite of its religious elements and motifs of social protest. If so, the film's eventual "security clearance" will derive in part from its clever pandering to the currently fashionable anti-Chinese bias: a reference to Pushkin's letter to Chaadayev about Russia's role as protector of Christian civilization precedes closeups of stern Soviet soldiers guarding the Sino-Soviet frontier. The white Russians are barring the way to frenzied Chinese carrying countless portraits and statues of Chairman Mao.

Anti-Chinese motifs are prominent also in *Dersu-Uzala*, another film made in the 1970s, based on a minor turn-of-the-century Russian novel. The hero is an officer in the Imperial Russian army engaged in preparing maps of hitherto unexplored areas of the eastern Siberian wilderness. The officer's faithful comrade, whom he treats with both affection and condescension, is an aborigine hunter. The primitive Siberian reciprocates the affection and treats the officer with admiration and respect, in part because the Russians protect the natives from the cruel Chinese, whose atrocities the film shows in graphic detail. *Dersu-Uzala* reminds a Western spectator of Rudyard Kipling and the doctrine of the "white man's burden."

Classics of Russian literature are probably the most important single inspiration for the Soviet cinema of the past decade. These include Sergei Bondarchuk's twelve-hour film of Tolstoy's *War and Peace* (1963–67); Lev Kulidzhanov's version of Dostoevsky's *Crime and Punishment* (1970); Andrei Mikhalkov-Konchalovsky's adaptation of Turgenev's *A Net of Gentlefolk* (1969); and two creations of Nikita Mikhalkov—a screen version of Goncharov's *Oblomov* (1980) and a film based on several tales by Chekhov, *An Unfinished Piece for a Player Piano* (1977). (The title of the latter was probably inspired by Kurt Vonnegut, whose work is widely published in the USSR, albeit in heavily censored form.)

Film versions of classics are highly popular with Soviet moviegoers, and a number have earned high praise and substantial royalties abroad. Many directors, therefore, are eager to produce more. Since such motion pictures also feature loving portrayals of the Russian countryside, old Russian churches, customs, costumes, dances and songs, they evoke moods of patriotic nostalgia. Yet, however attractive such films may be esthetically, however favored by the public and acceptable to the Soviet establishment, emphasis on their production may not be healthy. A robust culture combines respect for and interest in art of the past with an ability to reflect and respond directly to issues that agitate its contemporaries. Undue preoccupation with literature of a bygone era at the expense of modern writing, reflected in the enormous interest in Russian classical literature in

Stalin's time, bespeaks also cultural stagnation and fear. In short, museums are not only repositories of old art. When they begin to dominate society's culture, when they overshadow galleries of contemporary art, they may also serve as a refuge from the present. The warning sounded only four years after the Communist revolution by Yevgeni Zamyatin, author of the novel *We,* which anticipated Orwell's *1984,* remains valid today and is applicable to all artistic and intellectual creation:

> I am afraid that we won't have real literature as long as Russia's citizenry is viewed as a child whose innocence must be protected. I am afraid that we won't have real literature until we recover from a new variety of Catholicism that fears every word of heresy in no lesser measure than the old. And should this affliction prove incurable, I am afraid that Russian literature has but one future—her past.

Literature

While conceding the wider appeal and potentially larger audiences of Soviet television and the cinema, one must not underestimate the impact of modern literature. Ten years ago, the Writers' Union numbered 7,280 members, who wrote in the sixty-four languages spoken in the USSR; literary periodicals were published then in forty-five languages. Some of the approximately ten major Russian literary monthlies have press runs of half a million copies, while one series of paperbacks, *Roman gazeta,* occasionally prints three million copies of a volume. Thus, the potential impact of new writing is great.

At the same time, while the government closely supervises literature at all stages and also subjects it to formal censorship, it nevertheless allows it considerably wider ideological latitude than other art forms and types of intellectual expression. For that reason, foreign correspondents stationed in Moscow learn to observe the literary scene closely for clues of developments that may later affect other areas of life.

Literature also serves as a transmission belt to ordinary citizens for policy decisions the authorities have made. Prose, drama, and, to a lesser extent, verse thus "translate" the abstractions in formal speeches and resolutions into concrete examples for emulation or warning. On occasion, imaginative writing can thus directly or indirectly suggest implications of current priorities for day-to-day informal situations. In a manner of speaking, contemporary writing refines values, moods, apprehensions, and aspirations out of party directives and slogans.

This writer, chastened and exhausted by reading tens of thousands of pages of Soviet literary productions of the late 1970s and early 1980s—works of unequal artistic merit ranging from distinguished writing to middlebrow and to ordinary potboilers—wishes to record that vintage Soviet Socialist Realism is alive, even if not always well, though its health has shown remarkable improvement in recent years.

Traditionally, literature in Russia has been a carrier of ideas with social implications, with the most notable exception the Symbolist era at the turn of the century. Because of the state's ultimate control over publishing and other sources of a writer's livelihood (even Pushkin declared, "I write for myself, but I publish for money"), pressures are strong. Much new Soviet writing disseminates ideas the state finds desirable. Gifted and sophisticated authors do this with subtlety and tend to advance general values and goals. Hacks do it crudely and endorse specific and immediate objectives. At the same time, obviously, literature and other art forms are effective only when they find acceptance. For that reason, Soviet fiction, poetry, and drama reflect also their readers' personal concerns, values, and aspirations. In short, a Soviet author attempts to strike a balance between desires of the state and those of the public. A complete disregard for either is impossible.

"Liberal" periods do occur in which the state is not severe in enforcing its programs. In periods of "freeze," the state's insistence on its goals is so strict that it ignores the public's desires. This posture is self-defeating, because the public possesses a weapon that it can and does use to retaliate: It simply ignores such writing, thus robbing it of all didactic effectiveness. The latter consideration, often ignored during the Stalin era, when contact with such "opportunistic" considerations did not "soil" ideological firmness, now receives careful attention. The tug-of-war one often witnessed in literary periodicals is usually disagreement over the degree to which writing can be politicized, in the broad sense of the term, without endangering its literary integrity and viability. Liberal opponents believe that conservatives tend to overestimate that degree. The liberals, conservatives charge, so underestimate it that they lose sight of the fact that it is not "bourgeois" writing that is at issue, but Soviet writing, and Soviet writing should be different. So it goes, with the debate showing little prospect of abating.

One interesting feature of intellectual and cultural life in recent years has been the proliferation of journals that serve the needs of specialized groups of readers. While satisfying such legitimate interests, journals of this kind offer another advantage to monopolistic publishers. They provide an opportunity for publication on a very restricted scale of materials and views that the authorities do not wish to ban outright but also prefer not to disseminate widely. Though bearing the obligatory number of the censor who authorized their publication, as well as the dates of preliminary and final clearance, the press runs of such materials indicate that they are intended for restricted circulation only. A variety of photo-offset journals and books that provincial universities publish falls into this category. The group also includes scholarly publications that largely, in some cases completely, eschew politics, such as structuralist literary analyses by adherents of the so-called Tartu school, of which Yuri Lotman is the best known exponent. Given the number of university libraries in the USSR and the quantities of each printing destined for foreign readers, such publications are, in effect, "authorized" *samizdat,* and help in some measure to deflect the allure of real *samizdat.* Recently, disquieting signs have appeared that even such moderately liberal practices are falling into disfavor. This apparently successful method of control over the circulation of ideas may once more expand in years to come.

Hypocrisy, La Rochefoucauld notes in his *Maxims,* is the tribute vice pays to virtue. Observers agree that the USSR is among the world's most status-conscious societies, where privilege extends even to rigidly enforced separation in shopping, libraries, and medical service. In literature, however, the pretense of equality persists. Scholarly journals of literary theory and criticism exist, and some of the more interesting clashes of ideas take place in the pages of such staid publications as *Voprosy literatury,* which deals with all literature, and *Russkaia literatura,* which restricts itself to Russian writing, past and present.

Even more interesting is *Literaturnaia gazeta,* a weekly ostensibly devoted to literature, but in reality the liveliest political and social publication in the Soviet Union. Its editor, Alexander Chakovsky, is a prolific author of highly politicized novels of war and diplomatic intrigue, and one of the few Jews in the establishment. While not really "liberal," *Literaturnaia gazeta* is a periodical the intelligentsia favor. Its coverage of foreign affairs, for instance, is much more thorough than that of either *Pravda* or *Izvestiia,* and its press run (1,300,000 in 1971) indicates that the weekly's readership is not restricted to *aficionados* of *belles lettres.*

Among the primarily literary publications, many in the category of "thick" journals of literature and ideas that played such an important role in pre-Soviet Russia (these are usually subtitled "literary and artistic" and "sociopolitical"), the distinctions are implied or simply a matter of common knowledge. Thus, *Yunost'* and *Molodaia gvardiia* are for the young, and their literary contents reflect that. Within the Soviet spectrum, the latter is rather reactionary and "National Bolshevik," while the former, now moderate, was a leading "liberal" publication during the post-Stalin thaw. *Novy mir,* once the rallying banner of "liberal" literary elements, is now politically moderate, but it still considered more "highbrow" than the always conservative *Zvezda* or *Oktiabr'*. Understandably, the literary materials (including critical essays) found in these various publications differ to a significant degree. Those meant for simple audiences are likely to be direct and blunt in their approach, or at least more transparent in their educational purposes. Those aimed at better educated readers are likely to be more sophisticated and the didactic message, if any, indirect. Some may, indeed, become apparent only when one considers the likely cumulative effect of reading such fare. The stories comprising Turgenev's *Sportsman's Sketches,* when read separately more than a century ago, may have seemed innocent. Taken together, they amounted to a powerful denunciation of serfdom. The Russian censor who failed to foresee this fact was fired.

Soviet literary commentators never tire of sneering at pulp literature as typical of the fare that publishing tycoons in the West provide their public. They often emphasize that vast numbers of Soviet citizens read and appreciate distinguished West European and American writing. It is a fact, however, that pulp fiction exists in the Soviet Union and accounts for a very large share of Soviet writing.

Publishing houses produce these volumes in massive quantities, normally after mass circulation periodicals or one of the "thick" journals referred to earlier have introduced them. Professional purveyors of these commodities, most of them recognized members of the Union of Soviet Writers, steadily replenish the assortment of dime novels as well as analogous drama and verse. The literary value of these concoctions may be limited and their existence short-lived, but faithful addicts devour them avidly, much as Americans read Westerns and thrillers, and their influence is no less real than that of highbrow writing.

Western observers know little of this literature because few scholars are interested in writing that has, admittedly, little esthetic merit. Yet, precisely because of its simplistic quality, pulp fiction offers readily discernible outlines of literature's social content and hence also didactic potential and clearly defined traits of its artistic manner. Second- and third-rate artists are better illustrations of tendencies and trends than first-rate writers because they are not "obscured" by artistic individuality. Moreover, in an analysis of literature's social and political implications, popular literature and the arts deserve particularly careful consideration because of their mass appeal. After all, Harriet Beecher Stowe's *Uncle Tom's Cabin,* no literary masterpiece, greatly accelerated the advent of the American Civil War. Highbrow literature, on the other hand, in addition to its immediate appeal to sophisticated readers, is also more likely to be imitated, and the best of it may live for centuries. Of course, popular writing may endure as well. Thus, in 1982, readers in the USSR obtained, at long last, the first Russian translation of Margaret Mitchell's *Gone with the Wind,* America's best seller of half a century ago. Even a study of esthetically significant writing should not disregard popular fiction, including potboilers and various types of subliterary genres, because all leave an impact on the literary process.

In short, highbrow as well as popular literature exist in the USSR, and the line dividing the two is no more blurred than corresponding demarcations in the West. In the USSR, in keeping with pre-Soviet traditions, poetry, prose, and verse often appear in nonliterary publications, where the audience at which the periodical is aimed determines the contents.

Consequently, "highbrow" and popular writing frequently appear to have little in common. Their artistic merit aside, they often differ also in subject matter, settings, plots, protagonists, and even in predilection for specific genres. Nevertheless, I submit that the short-range causes they champion and the long-range political, social, and ethical goals they promote coincide to a remarkable degree. They are not completely identical, because there is no need to extol the virtues of education when addressing primarily the intelligentsia, or, conversely, to warn farmers and factory workers against dangers of assorted ideological heresies.

I shall identify those that were definitely on the upswing in the late 1970s and early 1980s and seem destined to endure in the coming decade. I do so without suggesting that writers produce such literature, as it were, to order. Most authors in the USSR, as elsewhere, produce writing for which genuine demand exists both in the literary marketplace and among the reading public. Of these two factors there can be no doubt. In recent years virtually every issue of the eight leading literary monthlies I examined featured at least one item tackling in some way each of the following themes. Solid reasons exist to believe that these will survive.

The work ethic in its broad sense remains a major concern of Soviet writing. Popular writing fosters this value through collective farm or industrial novels that bear a striking resemblance to similar creations of the Stalin era, though with one important difference. Even the crudest propagandistic potboilers extolling the virtue of selfless labor in fields or factories now include generous doses of human interest motifs. Thus, in these novels even otherwise absolute paragons of Soviet virtues suffer the pangs of unrequited love, episodes of depression, or bouts of alcoholic stupor, disabilities which did not trouble positive heroes of Stalinist fiction. The district Communist Party secretary, the effective collective farm chairman, and the heroic shock worker fearlessly wrestle with personal difficulties, overcome them, and carry out tasks above and beyond the call of duty. Semen Babayevsky, a Stalinist stalwart temporarily in decline during the thaws, continues to produce such fare, as do Anatoli Ananyev, Mikhail Kolesnikov, and prior to his death in 1979, Vil' Lipatov.

In writing apparently aimed at more discriminating readers, values of the work ethic are often fostered by indirect means that blend motifs of scientific progress with tales of adventure, such as Yuri Sbitnev's novella about a geological expedition or Vladimir Sanin's trilogy about the Arctic. Two leading Soviet authors extol human courage in taming nature. Both Yuri Kazakov and Chingiz Aitmatov describe sailors, pilots, and fishermen in a manner strongly reminiscent of Ernest Hemingway's *The Old Man and the Sea,* a work very popular in the USSR in the 1960s.

Patriotism, another central concern of recent Soviet literature, appears in a similar combination of approaches. In popular writing, a wartime setting provided the most frequent vehicle for this theme. Prose, drama, and verse inspired by World War II and memoirs of the war are still written and published in the USSR on a truly massive scale. That memories of the war linger nearly four decades after the end of hostilities is only part of the reason for the phenomenon. After all, such memories must also remain vivid for other countries, such as the Federal Republic of Germany and Japan. Since authors too young to retain any memories of the war write many of the new literary works with wartime settings, one must assume that the subject is one editors and publishers, who reflect the wishes of the authorities, actively encourage. Memories of the war provide opportunities for appeals for vigilance and for voicing Russian patriotic slogans and, occasionally, anti-German and generally antiforeign comments. While some Soviet writing dealing with the war is produced by such gifted authors as Yuri Baklanov and Vasili Bykov (the latter, a Belorussian, often writes in Russian), the bulk is crude and its purpose obvious.

Writing favored by the intelligentsia and hence also the works most frequently translated in the West handle the Russian patriotic theme quite differently. This literature describes situations that probe dilemmas of the human condition with compassion and often much insight and skill against a rich background of Russian lore and customs. Authors associated with this type of writing are known as *derevenshchiki,* a term usually rendered in English as "village prose," though "agrarians" would come closer to reproducing the term's associations, because much of this writing is set in the countryside. Siberia is the favored setting for these novels and short stories, because patriarchal Russian ways are best preserved in distant and sparsely populated areas. Many leading exponents of this school, Valentin Rasputin, Victor Astafyev, and the late Vasili Shukshin, to mention but three, are Siberian themselves.

Rasputin and his colleagues emphasize that this authentic, unspoiled Russia faces destruction in the name of industrial progress. The implied message of these writings is an appeal to avert this calamity, because nothing less than Russian ethnic identity is at stake. Such "agrarian" and Luddite appeals collide with and probably vitiate in part the efforts of other authors who extol industrial progress. Indeed, a number of Soviet critics have noted this contradiction. The government has made no attempt to suppress this politically dubious prose, partly because the "agrarians" contribute to strengthening a sense of Russian ethnic identity, particularly among those who need it the most, the intelligentsia, the social group particularly vulnerable to dangerous "cosmopolitan" influences. A second consideration may be the geographic associations of this prose. The action of Astafyev's *Kingfish,* of Rasputin's *Farewell to Matyora,* and of other works by the "agrarians" unfolds against the background of Eastern Siberia, those parts of Soviet territory that the Chinese allegedly covet. By selecting these regions as the symbol of true Russia, rather than the European part of the country, as was traditional in Tolstoy or Turgenev, the "agrarians" are indirectly refuting insinuations that Siberia may not be an organic part of Russia. Their efforts and those of their colleagues who produce writing concerned with World War II should remain useful through the 1990s.

Until relatively recently, private concerns have been absent from Soviet writing, which cultivates a public, collectivist stance appropriate for work dedicated to the advancement of revolutionary change. Vladimir Mayakovsky's military, declamatory verse was an apt archetype of this type of literature. Authors engrossed in contemplation of self were suspect. Thus, the intimate lyric verse and occasional religious notes of Anna Akhmatova, one of this century's great poets, once provoked a Soviet guardian of ideological purity into dubbing her "half nun and half whore." Over the years the government and its spokesmen have excoriated scores of authors for a major sin of omission, failure to raise "public" social questions with significant ideological implications in their works. This shortcoming, doctrinaire Soviet critics warned, deprived these writings of *ideinost'*, ideological content, which together with *partiinost'* (an overtly militant partisanship that eschews pretense of objectivity) and *narodnost'* (a "popular" quality implying accessibility), constitute the three whales on which the universe of Socialist Realism rests.

Ideinost' and *narodnost'* (though emphatically not *partiinost'*) have a long tradition in Russian literature, which often served as a most active battlefield of ideas. During the Stalin era, it was assumed that the choice and treatment of these ideas could be not merely manipulated (a realistic enough goal, as our discussion of motifs of the work ethic and of patriotism suggests), but actually regulated with absolute mechanical precision. And so they were. Ultimately, such contrived and regimented discussions of ideas vitiated their intent. Artificially conceived and with preordained conclusions, they repelled or at least bored those whom they were meant to instruct and inspire. Stalinist literature inadvertently came to fit Mark Twain's mocking definition of classics as books which everybody wants to have read, and nobody does.

Another consideration may contribute to the *de facto* tolerance of the "private" literature characteristic of the Brezhnev era. As demonstrated by Russian literature of the nineteenth century and confirmed by the liberal "thaws" of the Khrushchev period, even censorship does not offer reliable protection from another danger. That peril is "public" literature's understandable tendency to raise undesirable social issues and then presume to offer unsolicited advice or, worse, to demand concrete reforms. Ingenious use of allusions and hints, the "Aesopian language" that censorship of literature seems to engender, also helps bypass censorship restrictions. Authoritarian regimes of the past may have been wise in restricting literary articulation of their aspirations and goals to a single court poet or ceremonial occasions, encouraging under ordinary circumstances the cultivation in literature of purely personal concerns. In the final analysis, such regimes are not interested in their subjects' praise or, for that matter, any opinion, as long as they are assured of absolute obedience. Perhaps the Brezhnev leadership understood that lesson after Stalinist writing's self-inflicted defeat and the dangerous tremors of the "thaw" that followed.

In any case, Soviet writing of the Brezhnev era has been purged of the social reformism of the period immediately preceding and allowed and encouraged to immerse itself in probing human emotions. These span a wide range and include love and jealousy, loneliness and longing, curiosity and grief, fear and joy. These emotions are frequently portrayed in complex social surroundings. One finds it difficult to escape the impression that Soviet authors often exert every effort to avoid linking the fortunes of their protagonists to specific Soviet policies and institutions, lest some interpret this as a veiled call for social and political reforms. When such connections cannot be avoided, the authors establish links to suprapolitical social customs that antedate the regime and are not restricted to Soviet conditions.

I. Grekova's novellas, such as *The Ladies' Hairdresser* or *The Mis-*

tress of a Hotel, are a good example. The special problems Grekova's heroines face derive from the difficulties of reconciling the demands of a career with the duties of a single mother. The problems are not specifically Soviet, yet Grekova and scores of less gifted authors probing the same subject avoid any intimation of the need for specific measures that would ease her protagonists' plight, such as better child care, for instance, or services, or financial assistance.

It may be that the current decline of the Soviet novel, the most socially oriented literary genre, is in part a result of this trend and not just of the periodic cycle of growth and exhaustion of specific forms of fiction. The same rationale may help explain the converse phenomenon, the popularity of lyric poetry and, above all, of the short story, the novella, and also of drama, traditionally the most neglected of literary species in Russia. In contrast to the bulky novel that almost naturally gravitates toward posing as well as resolving conflicts and dilemmas with social and political repercussions, the shorter genres, if they treat quasi-social issues, need not concern themselves with suggesting possible social solutions. Merely posing the problem should suffice, and often even that can be avoided.

To use an old Soviet locution, it may not be accidental that a number of authors whose works of the 1950s and 1960s dealt with problems of social justice, such as Solzhenitsyn above all but also Vasili Aksyonov, Anatoli Gladilin, Andrei Sinyavsky, Victor Nekrasov, all now are in exile abroad. Writers who remain in the USSR restrict themselves to problems of personal ethics, often probed by protagonists while alone and communing with nature, which imparts to these quests a somewhat abstract quality. Thus, the stories of the recently deceased Yuri Trifonov, particularly his *House on the Embankment* and *The Old Man,* suggest that moral and ethical squalor is somehow a consequence not so much of specific institutions (the antihero of Trifonov was the son of a secret police officer!) but of the general corrupting influence of prosperity and of the city. Some of these stories are so permeated by a sense of hopelessness and despair that they suggest this emphasis on personal concerns may reflect a loss of will. Still other authors, including such former "reformist" firebrands as Yevgeni Yevtushenko and Alexander Kron, now often content themselves with discussing the lowest rung in the hierarchy of "ethical" concerns, that of good manners, of etiquette.

This type of literature is not new to Russian writing. Disapproval of urban sins and the corrupting impact of abstract (never very concrete) rank and privilege, idealization of the purifying and ennobling effects of Man's proximity to Nature, sympathetic accounts of human afflictions and emotional turmoil, and simultaneously steadfast refusal to link these to social processes and institutions are all familiar traits of two major schools of Russian writing. Toward the end of the eighteenth century, they were among the central attributes of Neoclassicism, especially of Sentimentalism. The foremost Russian exponent of Sentimentalism, Nikolai Karamzin, was also the author of the unswervingly conservative *History of the Russian State,* of which Alexander Pushkin wrote that it "dispassionately demonstrates to us the necessity of autocracy and the delights of the whip." The literature that Sentimentalism and Neoclassicism begat, its praise of rustic simplicity and lachrymose compassion for the underdog notwithstanding, was decidedly not sympathetic, let alone conducive, to social change. The conservative society of Brezhnev's successors would find this type of writing to its taste.

Of the three categories of recent writing, that advancing the work ethic, the one fostering a sense of Russian ethnic identity, and that centering on private concerns, the last is quantitatively the most important. One may assume with some confidence that it will retain its place as one of the leading types of Soviet writing. It is therefore significant that the message of social inertia this recent literature contains for the educated public is complemented, as it were, by that found in pulp fiction.

Soviet pulp fiction bears much resemblance to similar prerevolutionary writing, which combined elements of the soap opera and the novel of adventure and whose chief attraction was that it satisfied, or pretended to satisfy, its readers' prurient interest in the life of the "upper crust." In old Russia, as in the West, the protagonists in such writing were often members of high society bearing impressive aristocratic titles. In the USSR, during the last years of the Stalin era, pulp fiction assigned the protagonist's role to factory directors and party bureaucrats, though rarely above the district level. This type of fiction provided only brief glimpses of their immediate superiors at the province or republic level, presumably because this would entail coming dangerously close to *lèse majesté.* As Vera Dunham has pointed out, the accounts of what the high and the mighty eat, how their homes are furnished, and what their families look like titillated Soviet readers.

Analogous post-Stalin fiction differs in one seemingly trivial but important respect. Its protagonists are now not party secretaries, but members of the scientific "jet set" and the artistic intelligentsia, writers, film directors, actors, musicians. As old issues of *Krokodil,* the Soviet Union's lone satirical Russian weekly with a national circulation, demonstrate, the foibles of these groups were among the few subjects left within the province of satire and satirical journalism even during the most repressive years of Stalin's rule. Experienced purveyors of pulp fiction, fully aware of that fact, take advantage of the opportunities it offers. They depict celebrated scientists and famous artists as men and women whose fame and wealth, though fully deserved, of course, do not guarantee moral rectitude or imperviousness to human frailties. Their consecutive marriages are stormy and their love affairs sordid; alcoholism and psychiatric disorders plague them; they dissipate much of their time on petty intrigue and squabbles. The conclusions an ordinary Soviet reader may be expected to draw from all this are simple: money and fame do not bring happiness; aspiring to that station in life is silly. Foreign trinkets, clothes, travel, fancy foods may be very nice, but they are not worth the price that those who have them must pay.

Pulp fiction thus contributes to a lowering of expectations. It puts a damper on the aspirations for social mobility among ordinary folk. Above all, it reinforces a relatively recent motif of Soviet propaganda. Unable to carry out many of its promises of higher living standards, the USSR is now engaged in systematic vilification of yet another evil of capitalism, consumerism. A cause that in the West has definite "democratic" and populist associations, that many Americans view as the little man's defense from the tyranny of big business, has been transformed in the USSR for reasons of internal policy into capitalism's latest sinister incarnation. Since Soviet leadership is not likely to relinquish guns for butter, this particular motif of pulp fiction promises to retain its validity.

Conclusions

Allowing for a relatively high degree of continuity during the Brezhnev succession, an extrapolation from the present state of Soviet cultural and intellectual activity points to a high likelihood of the following trends.

As a result of renewed hunger for uncensored news, interest in Western radio broadcasts, such as the BBC, the Voice of America, and Radio Liberty, all subject to jamming, will remain strong, in part because of easier availability of shortwave receivers. Western radio may also assume greater importance as a source of entertainment. Indeed, more such broadcasts may be illegally disseminated on tape in the near future than in 1982. During the first post-Stalin decade, jazz music was recorded on used X-ray plates, which were supplanted by primitive but reasonably adequate tape recordings within a few years. Similar technological progress is likely in the future. The phenomenon of bootlegged homemade recordings of otherwise unobtainable entertainments, a phenomenon known as *magnitizdat,* will remain alive as long as certain types of recorded music and songs, of the type made famous in the 1960s and 1970s by Vladimir Vysotsky and Alexander Galich, two deceased social satirists, remain unavailable through official channels. Indeed, several Soviet pretenders to the mantle of these two satirists of *magnitizdat* of earlier years were active in 1982.

Samizdat will endure for similar reasons, although it is difficult to predict its precise nature and concerns. Should our prognosis of an essentially conservative, nationalist orientation of policies prove correct, Russian nationalist *samizdat* of the type that *Veche* and *Slovo natsii* made familiar in the 1960s and 1970s will simply lose its *raison d'être* because the Soviet establishment will have coopted it. Russian Orthodox *samizdat* may continue as an expression of socially activist, perhaps liberal tendencies within the country's largest religious denomination. The number of *samizdat* publications of other faiths, the Moslems above all, may increase, and perhaps a successor or two to such liberal journals as the now defunct democratic *Chronicle of Current Events* or the liberal Marxist *Political Diary* or *The Twentieth Century* may come into existence. All in all, however, these are not likely to be either numerous or long-lived, or, for that matter, to enjoy wide circulation. The police appear to have developed efficient methods for ferreting out such unauthorized publications. Moreover, they deal harshly with offenders, who can expect either long prison sentences or semivoluntary deportation. The majority of potential Soviet dissenters may therefore content themselves with attempting to present their views in a modest form through official channels and to explore other possibilities of working within the system.

One *samizdat* genre almost certain to survive is anthologies of literary materials. Such collections of prose and verse may be perfectly innocuous in themselves, but the government will treat them as illegal writings because they, too, will lack official sanction. The authorities are not likely to set a dangerous precedent of tolerating such typewritten materials. Dissident literature will not be allowed much range or exposure, in substance, because this would erode the principle of party control over all publishing.

I foresee little likelihood of significant relaxation in political controls over cultural and intellectual life. There are no grounds to expect that the party might tolerate open dissent from its major policies, although it may allow indirect questioning of the manner in which policies are implemented or disagreement about the implications of a general policy for a specific problem. Indeed, the party must tolerate such disagreements because their implications are largely a matter of subjective political intuition. While the prospects for freedom of speech are dim, a considerable degree of *de facto* freedom of conversation is possible. Oral *samizdat*, rumors, political gossip, and that literary molecule, the anecdote, may flourish in the coming decade, in part at least because of restrictions imposed on more formal expression.

I predict a general atmosphere of social conservatism and Russian nationalism, the latter a response in part to the numerical growth of the Turkic population with its Islamic heritage. This mood would be conducive to the further development of ethnocentric, parochial, and old-fashioned literature and art. Conditions of this sort do not preclude artistic excellence, but they do discourage experimentation. Contacts with the West would be viewed with disfavor as ideologically risky and incompatible with national exclusiveness, the more so because experience of the 1960s and 1970s has demonstrated the West's lack of susceptibility to Soviet ideology, and the alarming responsiveness of the Soviet public to Western fads and fashions. The sense of deprivation thus engendered may, in turn, boost attention to foreign radio broadcasts, and also contribute to the survival of *samizdat*. By contrast, the process of reclamation of Russian history would proceed as conducive to strengthening patriotic moods, and the classics of nineteenth-century literature will almost certainly thrive. Moreover, similar considerations may produce a less hostile stance toward religion, and consequently toward religious motifs in literature, music, painting, historical writing, and film. The government may even make quiet use of the Russian Orthodox Church, especially in campaigns against divorce, abortion, and alcoholism.

The Soviet leadership would probably treat a high degree of preoccupation with the family, personal feelings and values, and abstract ethics and esthetics in literature and the arts with benign neglect, because these interests deflect attention from reformist and potentially political social concerns. Of positive values, art and thought are likely to be concerned most often with Russian patriotism, which it would treat as a forerunner of Soviet Russian patriotism, and with a generalized work ethic. It may not be coincidental that these values recall the motto of *travail, famille, patrie* that Vichy France promulgated forty years ago as more conducive to law and order and stability than the republican *liberté, egalité, fraternité*.

6

★

Eastern Europe

Andrzej Korbonski

Introduction

RELATIONS BETWEEN the Soviet Union and Eastern Europe have occupied the attention of Western policy makers and scholars since the end of World War II. This interest has escalated markedly in the most recent period, stimulated by striking changes taking place within that region and by the changing character of East-West relations, which have brought the issue of interaction between Moscow and its East European allies into sharp focus.[1]

This paper seeks to analyze the effect developments within Eastern Europe will have upon Soviet domestic and especially foreign policy in the 1980s. It tries to assess the role of Eastern Europe as a whole, as well as of the individual countries in the region in influencing Soviet behavior on the international scene, although it does not neglect the impact of Eastern Europe on Soviet internal politics.

It is increasingly difficult to define Eastern Europe accurately. The eight countries—Albania, Bulgaria, Czechoslovakia, East Germany, Hungary, Poland, Romania, and Yugoslavia—not only are located in a well-defined geographical area of Europe but also share several essential features, including political and economic structures and institutions; patterns of socioeconomic changes; except for Albania and Yugoslavia, membership in two important regional organizations, the Warsaw Pact (WTO) and the Council for Mutual Economic Assistance (CMEA); and to a great extent a common historical heritage, especially since World War II.

Some may question the inclusion of Yugoslavia and Albania on the grounds that neither country is currently under Soviet domina-

I should like to express my appreciation to Charles Gati, Sarah Terry, and Jiri Valenta for the information and critical comments they provided.

tion. Nonetheless, Yugoslavia has long been an attractive target for Soviet policy, if only because of its strategic location, its position before 1948, its role in the camp of neutral and nonaligned countries, where it has frequently criticized Soviet policy, and its persisting economic and social problems, which affect its political stability. Moreover, as the only East European country where Communist rule has achieved considerable legitimacy, Yugoslavia challenges the USSR as an alternative model for other countries in the region. Albania is also strategically located and was closely associated with the Soviet Union even longer than was Yugoslavia. At the present time it exhibits considerable hostility toward the Soviet Union, but internal developments, including a likely succession crisis, offer Moscow renewed opportunity for direct involvement in Albania's affairs in the 1980s.

With the exception of Albania and Yugoslavia, these countries share a substantial economic dependence on the Soviet Union, although the degree and dimensions vary from country to country, a profound political dependence characterized by a need to keep their international and domestic policies within limits Moscow establishes, and a direct military vulnerability based on geography, recent history, and Soviet military power. While, on balance, systemic similarities seem to outweigh the differences, the presence of persisting and even growing differences among the individual states makes Eastern Europe a fascinating yet frustrating focus of research, and, above all, a central factor for Soviet policy.

The differences among the individual countries are less easily observable. On the one hand, they derive from many deeply rooted cultural and socioeconomic phenomena that have created national political cultures which continue to influence the respective countries' foreign and domestic policies, even after more than three decades of Communist efforts to eradicate or weaken them. On the other hand, the differences relate to the way the particular states have faced various developmental and systemic crises.

Our analysis rests on the premise that developments in Eastern Europe directly affect Soviet foreign policy decision making. The relationship between the Soviet Union and Eastern Europe therefore represents an interaction of a special kind, qualitatively different from the relationship between the USSR and other regions and countries throughout the world, both Communist and noncommunist. Moscow's special stake in Eastern Europe in turn gives rise to a variety of particular interests and objectives for the Kremlin. This does not mean, however, that Soviet leaders view control of Eastern Europe as an end in itself. Their policies toward the region have been closely linked to their domestic needs and the broader international environment. Thus, the Kremlin has always considered Eastern Europe an important area whose resources it must harness and utilize to achieve its domestic and international objectives.

While our main task is to investigate the influence Eastern Europe will exert upon Soviet foreign policy in the 1980s, we shall also examine the conduct and pattern of Soviet behavior toward the region, with special emphasis on major objectives and determinants of that policy. These issues or perspectives are not easily separable and, in fact, represent two sides of the same coin. Hence, one of our objectives will be to identify and investigate the linkages between the USSR and the East European states.

Before attempting to analyze East European influences on Soviet policy, we must settle a number of conceptual and methodological questions. The first concerns the current state of Soviet–East European relations, more difficult to define than earlier. In the early postwar period, relations between the USSR and the smaller countries were characterized by what Zbigniew Brzezinski called "domesticism," legitimized to a large degree by the doctrine of "many roads to socialism."[2] Then Stalin established a monolithic Soviet empire, replaced after his death by a more loosely structured alliance that in the early 1960s acquired the name, "socialist commonwealth." Following Soviet intervention in Czechoslovakia, Moscow tightened its controls again, although it did not return to the classical Stalinist model. Toward the end of the 1970s indications appeared that Soviet domination of the region might relax, but the crisis in Poland dampened that process.

In the 1970s, Western images of Soviet hegemony in Eastern Europe ranged from the belief that it was a multinational colonial empire run by the Kremlin to a minority view that a more conventional type of a military, political, and economic alliance had replaced the Stalinist *imperium*. Some perceived the Soviet Union and Eastern Europe as a hierarchical regional system which "conveys some sense of the distinct limits on the behavior of the small states, while still allowing for some independent behavior on the part of all the states in the system."[3] Still others viewed the relationship as a kind of *dependencia* which enabled the USSR to extract resources and political conformity from its client-states in Eastern Europe.

Defining clearly the Soviet–East European relationship is not just a matter of intellectual curiosity, for it determines our perception of Soviet objectives, interests, and expectations concerning the region, as well as the character of the mutual interaction between the Soviet hegemon and its junior allies. In 1982 it is safe to discard the notion of the relationship as a conventional alliance of sovereign states: one cannot and should not compare the Warsaw Pact or the Council for Mutual Economic Assistance to a politico-military alliance such as

NATO or to economic integration schemes akin to the European Economic Community. Donna Bahry and Cal Clark have demonstrated that Eastern Europe may have been a *dependencia* under Stalin because of his almost exclusive focus on economic exploitation, but that the concept was no longer relevant in the 1970s and probably will not be so in the 1980s.[4] Thus, our choice lies between the imperial and the hierarchical models. In the foreseeable future, I believe that Soviet–East European relations will represent a synthesis of the characteristic features of both systems, with an increasing emphasis on Soviet control.

Although most East European countries are perceived as Soviet satellites, clients, or allies, they remain nominally sovereign entities. From some points of view the USSR benefits from the existence of a group of seemingly independent states which support its position in a variety of international fora and generally enhance the legitimacy of its status as a great power and its claims to represent the shape of things to come. Thus, the Soviet-dominated, military-economic alliance system in Eastern Europe increasingly provides a framework for establishing close ties with Moscow's new client states in other parts of the globe, such as Cuba and Vietnam.

On the other hand, the special nature of the relationship between the USSR and Eastern Europe suggests that the Kremlin in many respects perceives Eastern Europe as a vital, indeed indispensable domestic factor. Its importance varies with time and country, and from one policy area to another, and is the result of historical, geopolitical, and ideological perspectives. Moreover, Eastern Europe is an "internal" factor not only because Moscow treats it in certain respects as a regional outpost of the Soviet system, but also because the Kremlin believes deviations in Eastern Europe have a potential impact on the Soviet homeland as well as on the rest of the region.

Thus, in substance Moscow treats Eastern Europe as an "internal" problem and as an extension of the Soviet state but in some contexts chooses to consider the individual states as semi-independent actors granted a degree of autonomy, especially in domestic affairs. Hence, in the area of military security as Moscow defines it, there is not much difference between the German Democratic Republic and the Ukraine, whereas in the economic realm Hungary clearly has more room for maneuver than, say, Estonia. These differences help illuminate the inconsistencies, ambiguities, and conflicts in Soviet policy toward the region. They also throw some light on why the USSR has treated some junior partners differently from others, how Soviet policy toward the individual countries has changed over time, and what the nature of Soviet–East European interaction is in specific areas, such as economics, politics, and ideology.

Assuming that the Soviet–East European relationship contains elements of a regional hierarchical system raises the issue of linkages between the hegemon and its clients, in particular the question of the influence the USSR exerts on Eastern Europe and vice versa. I take as axiomatic that such transmission will not only continue but also probably expand in the future. I shall discuss the different types of linkages and influences, trace the manner in which they act as determinants of Soviet and East European behavior on the domestic and international scene, and speculate on how they are likely to evolve in the 1980s.

Finally, predicting the future is a hazardous exercise, especially difficult because we are investigating a highly volatile and heterogeneous area. Moreover, since we are dealing with essentially closed systems, we know relatively little about the decision-making processes and have to rely on their policy outputs as guides to future actions.

The Western record of predicting events in Eastern Europe in the 1960s and 1970s has not been impressive, except for judging that Soviet control over the region would remain unimpaired. Few Western scholars forecast Romania's maverick stance in the early 1960s, the "Prague Spring" of 1968, or the Polish internal crises of the 1970s, not to mention the explosion of summer 1980. On the other hand, the basic conclusion of Western scholars that the Soviet Union faces enormous, perhaps intractable, difficulties in trying to control and then to transform the peoples and cultures of Eastern Europe has proved correct.

Soviet Objectives in Eastern Europe

Eastern Europe's influence on Soviet foreign policy decision making cannot be readily divorced from Soviet objectives in the region. The same factors that have an impact on Moscow's behavior in the international arena determine to a large extent Soviet policy toward a country or countries and set in motion the process of influence transmission. Soviet objectives in an East European country which the Kremlin considers important for the attainment of its foreign or domestic policy goals will obviously differ from Soviet objectives in a country whose relevance to Moscow's international aspirations is marginal.

In examining the impact of Eastern Europe on Soviet decision making, the following questions need to be addressed:

(1) How do problems faced by Eastern Europe—political instability, social tensions, or economic difficulties—influence Soviet foreign policy goals, priorities, and performance?

(2) To what extent do the East European countries contribute to

the achievement of Soviet foreign policy goals as proxies vis-à-vis international Communism, the West, and the Third World, as purveyors of arms, providers of economic aid, links to deviating Communist parties, and promoters of East-West detente?

(3) How do East European countries inhibit Soviet behavior by failing, for one reason or another, to meet Soviet expectations, or by presenting Moscow with serious problems which force the Kremlin to modify its policies elsewhere?

To put it differently, Moscow's objectives in Eastern Europe have been conditioned by these problems. Its aims remain a function of Soviet domestic policy requirements as well as of perceived Soviet goals toward a global environment. The Kremlin has always had a "wish list" or a set of expectations concerning the role Eastern Europe should play in attaining Soviet policy goals. Thus, Eastern Europe has influenced the broader spectrum of Soviet foreign and domestic policy to the extent it has met, or failed to meet, Moscow's expectations in the past. It is bound to do so in the future.

Moscow's "wish list" for Eastern Europe has several dimensions— security, political, ideological, and economic—each of which has both defensive and offensive elements. The importance the Soviet leaders attach to these dimensions shifts over time, as does the balance between defensive and assertive thrusts. Moreover, these dimensions are often in conflict with one another. For example, the Soviet Union cannot easily expect to achieve both ideological-political conformity and economic viability. These conflicts, inherent in the USSR's multiple expectations of Eastern Europe's role and performance, are likely to be the source of the region's potential instability and volatility in the 1980s, which are bound to be augmented by growing nationalism and the continuing influence of Western Europe and the United States.

Throughout the postwar period the impact that Eastern Europe has had on Soviet foreign policy decision making has been shifting. The same was true for Moscow's expectations and manipulation of that impact, successful or not.

Historically, the Stalinist period represented one extreme: the overall thrust of Soviet foreign policy and of Stalin's expectations of Eastern Europe was basically defensive, although the outside world understandably considered it offensive. Eastern Europe was to serve as a *cordon sanitaire,* or buffer zone, and as a source of economic reconstruction. It was also to validate the universality of the Soviet system and of Soviet doctrine. Moreover, the scope and reach of Soviet policy was limited then and focused largely on the USSR's periphery, especially on Europe, although even then Eastern Europe was expected to contribute to the Korean War effort and to aid the development of Communist China.

At the other end of the spectrum were Soviet expectations in the 1970s and possibly their long-range hopes for the 1980s. The greater assertiveness and scope of Soviet foreign policy in these years obviously affected Moscow's expectations concerning East European contributions, with the goal not so much security in the traditional sense as promotion of Soviet interests throughout the world. By the 1970s the Kremlin had succeeded in establishing an apparent division of labor among East European countries for promoting diverse Soviet interests, providing military and economic assistance to Third World countries, promoting East-West detente and/or weakening the Western alliances, opposing anti-Soviet factions in the international Communist movement, and others.

The in-between period, which coincided roughly with Khrushchev's rule in the USSR, was characterized by Soviet efforts to reestablish its hegemony in Eastern Europe, a hegemony weakened by the revolution in Hungary and the regime change in Poland. There is little doubt that developments in the region in the aftermath of de-Stalinization, accompanied by the defection of Albania from the Soviet to the Chinese orbit and by the escalation of the Sino-Soviet conflict, forced Moscow to turn inward and to assume a defensive stance which persisted until Brezhnev's assumption of power in 1964.

One important factor until the beginning of the 1980s was that Eastern Europe was no longer the primary target of Soviet interests and that its centrality to the Kremlin gradually declined. This is not to say that the region was no longer important for the USSR: it only means that as Soviet interests and capabilities expanded, Eastern Europe diminished in relative importance. The strategic weapons buildup, the development of a blue water navy, and the creation of a long-range airlift capacity have made the Soviet Union into a global military power whose interests ranged far beyond its immediate periphery.

Probably the most important consequence of the Polish crisis has been the return of Eastern Europe to its earlier status as Moscow's most vital possession and an indispensable part of the Soviet empire. The upheaval in Poland must have convinced the Soviet leaders that they made a serious mistake in failing to pay sufficient attention to internal developments throughout the region or misunderstanding them. As a result, Eastern Europe has once again become the primary focus of Soviet foreign policy, and its centrality in Soviet decision making remains indisputable in the 1980s.

Apart from conventional military security considerations, the Kremlin must have concluded that if it is unable to maintain full control over the region, its image as a global power and its ability to validate the universal applicability of its own brand of Communism by ensuring the perpetuation of Communist rule in its sphere of influence will be tarnished. Eastern Europe has become an important legitimizing device for the USSR and any diminution of Soviet hegemony in the region, not to mention possible defection from Moscow's orbit, would have a most serious impact on Soviet domestic and foreign policy. Thus, in the eyes of the Kremlin, Eastern Europe is a highly valuable asset whose future status is simply nonnegotiable.

The centrality of Eastern Europe will further increase in the 1980s for two additional reasons. As will be shown below, Eastern Europe has played a major role in achieving detente between East and West, especially in supporting rapprochement between the USSR and Western Europe. In light of the deterioration of U.S.-Soviet relations, Western Europe will become a principal target of Soviet foreign policy in the near future as Moscow seeks to drive a wedge between Europe and America. The success or failure of Soviet initiative will greatly depend on the situation in Eastern Europe, which is of keen interest to West Europeans long concerned with the fate of their brethren east of the Elbe. Thus, if the Kremlin is truly interested in maintaining and improving its relations with Western Europe, it must make sure that conditions in Eastern Europe do not hinder Moscow's rapprochement with Western Europe at the expense of the United States. It may be taken for granted that if another Polish-type crisis erupts in Eastern Europe or if the Polish situation remains unsettled, forcing the Soviet Union to intervene, the chances of decoupling Western Europe from the United States will be badly hurt, if not destroyed. Thus, Eastern Europe holds the key to the success of a crucial Soviet diplomatic offensive directed at Western Europe.

Another reason for the increased centrality of Eastern Europe in the 1980s is the growing importance of the region in Soviet domestic policy, especially in the economic realm. In the course of the coming decade the USSR will be faced with the need for some systemic reforms, and Eastern Europe can serve as a model or a testing ground for economic experiments that might eventually be introduced in the Soviet Union. Brezhnev's praise of East European economic reforms delivered at the Twenty-sixth Congress of the Soviet Communist Party in 1981 illustrates renewed Soviet interest in the area.

Hence, the 1980s will witness Eastern Europe's elevation to the central focus of Soviet foreign policy. The rise in importance of Eastern Europe will influence the price the USSR is willing to pay to maintain its control of the region and is also bound to affect Moscow's expectations of Eastern Europe's contribution to the pursuit of Soviet goals in different parts of the world, Cuba, Angola, Vietnam, or Western Europe.

In dissecting future Soviet priorities and options with respect to the Kremlin's behavior toward Eastern Europe, we shall be dealing, in essence, with the Soviet hierarchy's perceptions of the region. A variety of factors and forces, such as Russian political culture and history, attitudes and behavior of East European and other countries toward the USSR, and personal idiosyncrasies of Soviet leaders influence these perceptions, especially with regard to individual countries. East European perceptions of the Soviet Union also vary sharply from country to country. Historical circumstances determined most of them, although geography and such factors as religion also continue to play important roles. Moscow's perceptions of the individual East European countries cannot be easily separated from those countries' attitudes toward the USSR, and both tend to reinforce each other.

Thus, there is little doubt that the Kremlin must regard Poland as a complicated and frustrating case. It may be argued that in 1983, despite a host of problems, Moscow still considers Poland a military-strategic asset, especially as long as Soviet forces remain in East Germany. In every other respect, however, the country appears mostly a liability, even though it is relatively well endowed with natural resources and has a well-developed transportation network and heavy industry production, especially in arms. In the past two decades Poland has undergone four major political crises, March 1968, December 1970, June 1976, and July–August 1980, which could hardly have pleased the Kremlin. Yet, instead of using its powerful economic and political leverage to enforce conformity and eliminate growing political opposition to the successive Polish regimes, Moscow chose to prop up the Polish ruling oligarchy by providing substantial economic aid to the beleaguered leaders.

At the same time Poland has been and is clearly most hostile to the USSR. Throughout history Russia has been one of Poland's fiercest enemies. The crass Soviet involvement in the postwar seizure of power, the Soviet role in Polish political life, and Soviet control of the country have deepened this popular attitude. The events of 1980–81 have shown that anti-Soviet sentiment in Poland remains strong after more than thirty-five years of incessant official campaigning to eradicate it. Indeed, it may now be more powerful than ever.

The main focus of Soviet attention in 1982 is likely to be East Germany, for some time the lynchpin of the Soviet control system in Eastern Europe. It has been and remains strategically the most exposed of all Warsaw Pact members, serving as a base for some twenty Soviet divisions and also making an important contribution to the military and economic power of the alliance. It has been a major supplier of sophisticated machinery and equipment to the USSR and other CMEA countries and an important conduit for Western know-how and technology, by virtue of its close economic links with West Germany and, *ipso facto*, with the European Economic Community.

Historically, the Russo-German relationship has been one of love-hate on both sides. On the one hand, the Germans tend to be contemptuous of the backward Russians. On the other hand, Russia, because of its sheer size and military-economic potential, appears to many Germans an attractive market for German capital and commodity exports and a valuable ally against common enemies such as Poland. Germany's defeat in World War II, followed by the country's division, exacerbated anti-Soviet feelings in both parts of Germany. However, the increasing prestige and relative prosperity of the German Democratic Republic have helped reduce enmity there toward the USSR.

Soviet perception of Hungary is complex. In the ideological realm Hungary has undergone a striking metamorphosis from being close to a Soviet ideological liability to becoming an asset in the 1970s, when the Kadar regime appeared to have acquired considerable popularity, having instituted innovative economic reforms that made Hungary a rather unique member of CMEA. The Hungarian economic experiment was accepted and legitimized by Moscow which, in fact, could point with some pride to Hungary as an example of a reformed Communist system that has worked but that also stayed within the pale, demonstrating thereby Soviet readiness to tolerate a considerable degree of diversity within the Warsaw alliance.

The attitude of Hungary toward the Soviet Union is similar to that of Poland. This is not surprising, since the two countries are very much alike in many respects. Moreover, Russia's leadership in partitioning Poland at the end of the eighteenth century was matched by its suppression of the Hungarian Revolution of 1848–49, while the Polish-Soviet War of 1919–20 followed by only a few weeks Bela Kun's abortive Hungarian Soviet Republic. The harsh Stalinist rule culminating in Moscow's suppression of the 1956 Hungarian uprising further increased hostility toward the USSR.

If Hungary is perceived by the Soviet Union as a major asset or at least as a useful ally, Romania is most likely regarded as a liability. This again is not particularly surprising, since Romania's relationship with the USSR in the past two decades has been checkered. In contrast to the other CMEA members, Romania's economic relations with the Soviet Union have been rather stormy, starting in the early 1960s when Bucharest openly challenged Moscow's ideas about closer economic integration and specialization under CMEA aegis. Militarily, the Kremlin sees Romania increasingly as a major liability and its behavior on the international scene as detrimental to Soviet interests. It is only in the politico-ideological context that Romania's perform-ance must give the Soviet leaders little cause for complaint.

It is not surprising, then, that next to Poland and Hungary Romania is the third most strongly anti-Soviet country in the region. It has had a long-standing territorial dispute over Bessarabia with the Soviet Union, strong enough to lead Romania to join Nazi Germany in attacking the USSR in June 1941. Romania's enmity surfaced again in the early 1960s. For the past twenty years Bucharest has not at-tempted to hide its hostility toward Moscow and has paid only lip service to Soviet leadership of WTO and CMEA.

The Soviet leaders most likely perceive Czechoslovakia as an im-portant ally from both the strategic-military and economic points of view, despite the debacle of 1968. It and East Germany are the only Warsaw Pact countries bordering on West Germany, and it serves as a base for five Soviet divisions. Even though Czechoslovakia has been replaced by East Germany as the chief supplier of technologically advanced goods to the USSR and the rest of CMEA, its contribution to the Soviet economic potential has been considerable and will re-main so. The country has also been active in the Third World, chiefly as a purveyor of weapons, thus reinforcing Soviet initiatives in various parts of the globe.

Whereas Poland, East Germany, and Czechoslovakia form the so-called Iron Triangle the Kremlin views as the strategic core of the Warsaw Pact, the strategic-military value of the remaining countries— Albania, Bulgaria, and Yugoslavia—is clearly important in Soviet eyes as well. For various reasons Albania is a tempting target for Moscow, although not nearly so attractive as Yugoslavia. Bulgaria has tradi-tionally been Moscow's most faithful ally in Eastern Europe since the Communist takeover, and no evidence exists of any serious deviation from the Soviet model or of any diminution of its devotion to the USSR, which explains Kremlin willingness to grant Bulgaria substan-tial economic aid.

The perceptions of the Soviet Union held by Bulgaria, Czecho-slovakia, and Yugoslavia are complex. Historically, all have had tradi-tionally warm feelings toward Russia, which in the late 1870s liberated Bulgaria from the Turkish yoke and raised the banner of Panslavism as protector of all, but particularly of Balkan Slavs, Serbs, Macedo-nians, Montenegrins, and Bulgarians. The historic links were in some cases reinforced by the existence of close linguistic and religious ties with Russia. However, both the heavy-handed postwar policy toward Yugoslavia, which led to the Stalin-Tito conflict in 1948, and the Soviet suppression of the "Prague Spring" in 1968 have radically changed the previously warm feelings toward the USSR. Consequently, only Bulgaria sees the Soviet Union as its historical friend and protector. How the Albanian people perceive the USSR is anybody's guess. Official statements emanating from Tirana are deeply anti-Soviet, but whether the tirades of the Hoxha regime reflect popular attitudes is impossible to say.

One cannot exaggerate the importance of perceptions and misperceptions in the context of Soviet-East European relations. Postwar history is replete with examples of mutual misperceptions and misplaced inferences. Thus, in 1948 Stalin believed that Yugoslavia would not resist and would eventually collapse and surrender to Soviet demands, while Tito remained convinced for several years after the break with Moscow that it was all a misunderstanding that would soon clear up, with Yugoslavia again welcome in the camp. Dubček in 1968 believed that the Kremlin would accept "socialism with a human face," while Brezhnev apparently expected that a new pro-Soviet government would welcome Soviet troops. Most recently, the "Solidarity" leaders in Poland seemed to believe that the Soviet Union had become reconciled to independent trade unionism in a Communist state, while the Soviet leadership clearly misjudged the ability of the Polish Communist party and later of the Polish military to stabilize the country.

Over the years both the Soviet Union and the East European countries have presumably learned lessons and drawn inferences from the past in the attempt to achieve a correct perception of each other's objectives and attitudes. Insofar as Eastern Europe as a whole is concerned, the key problem has been to determine the threshold of its autonomy vis-à-vis the USSR, a difficult task since the rules of the game are fuzzy, frequently changed, or nonexistent. The leaders of individual countries faced the responsibility of estimating the margin of freedom at their disposal to conduct foreign and/or domestic policies that might depart to a greater or lesser degree from the norm the Kremlin specified. The striking differences that developed in this respect among the various countries testify to the continuing and growing differentiation of the region.

This process may not continue into the 1980s and is likely to be replaced by a policy of consolidation and *Gleichschaltung* directed by the Kremlin, as Moscow becomes increasingly concerned about possible loss of control over the area.

Eastern Europe as a Determinant of Soviet Foreign Policy Making

Whether the relationship between the Soviet Union and Eastern Europe is a dependency or interdependence, whether the USSR considers itself the undisputed leader of a Communist camp or of a political-military-economic alliance, whether the relationship may be called "organic" or "inorganic," developments in the various East European countries have influenced Soviet policies, both external and internal.

As stated at the outset, our emphasis will be on Soviet foreign policies. Postwar history shows that while major systemic crises and other developments in the individual East European countries have had a considerable impact on their immediate neighbors in the region, they have generated relatively little spillover into Soviet domestic politics.[5] Soviet decision makers were certainly more adept at defusing outside influences than their counterparts in the smaller East European countries, who found it difficult to neutralize the "demonstration effect" of changes occurring in other countries in the region.

However, while Soviet society has remained largely insulated from Eastern Europe, Soviet domestic policy has been affected to a degree by developments in Eastern Europe. The Soviet elites do derive lessons from East European experiences in various fields, both positive and negative. On the positive side, some Soviet elites look to Eastern Europe for intellectual input and support of policies intended to reform the Soviet system. On the negative side, crises in Eastern Europe alert the Soviet leadership to the existence of social tensions and prompt it to take prophylactic actions at home.

Thus, the Czechoslovak crisis of 1968 contributed to the final defeat of the 1965 Soviet economic reform, which had both domestic and foreign policy implications. The Polish upheaval of 1970 spurred increased Soviet attention to consumer needs and carried with it important implications for the allocation of resources. The recent crisis in Poland provided an impetus for tightening controls, yet, at the same time, it led to an enhancement of the trade unions' role and to renewed emphasis on improving the performance of Soviet agriculture.

Moreover, the fragility of the East European political and economic systems represents a drain on the Soviet economy in several respects. On one hand, it increases the need for emergency Soviet economic aid to the country in crisis. On the other, it also creates an obstacle to economic reforms in the Soviet Union for fear that these reforms, if emulated in Eastern Europe, might spill over from the economic to the political realm, as illustrated by the example of Czechoslovakia in the mid-1960s. Hence the vulnerability of Eastern Europe to systemic crises exerts a conservative influence on the USSR, with serious domestic and foreign policy implications.

In discussing the role of Eastern Europe as a determinant of

Soviet foreign policy making we must differentiate conceptually between two major sets of issues: we must clearly define Soviet foreign policy interests in Eastern Europe and in the rest of the world; at the same time, we must examine the ways in which Eastern Europe contributes to the achievement of Soviet foreign policy objectives.

Soviet stakes and interests in Eastern Europe can be subsumed under two broad headings, cohesion and viability.[6] Cohesion implies the general conformity of East European domestic and foreign policies to Soviet prescriptions and the identity of institutional arrangements between Eastern Europe and the Soviet Union. Viability suggests the presence of confident, credible, efficient, and legitimate regimes in Eastern Europe that obviate the need for continuous Soviet preoccupation with, and intervention in, the region.

The main conflict facing Moscow is that between cohesion and viability. Historically, relations between the Soviet Union and Eastern Europe reflect unsuccessful Soviet attempts to achieve a balance between them. Stalin was clearly concerned with cohesion and paid little attention to viability. Khrushchev was more interested in viability but without losing sight of the need for cohesion. Brezhnev, especially after the crisis in Czechoslovakia, became concerned with reestablishing cohesion and, except for a relatively brief period in the mid-1970s, continued to emphasize its necessity. The crisis in Poland obviously underscored the need for greater Soviet vigilance and closer cohesion.

The two broad Soviet interests can be further subdivided for the sake of convenience into four categories: security, political, ideological, and economic. The dividing line between the four rubrics is arbitrary and imprecise, and I shall use the various labels mostly to achieve a sharp focus on key developments and policies in Eastern Europe and on their impact on Soviet policy. The four sets of Moscow's interests are not independent; in fact, they are closely intertwined. They are frequently incompatible, generating tensions and forcing the Kremlin to make choices among its competing objectives in Eastern Europe.

The issue of Eastern Europe's influence on Soviet foreign policy also has several dimensions. One concerns the way in which Eastern Europe has enhanced or inhibited Soviet foreign policy, in response to changing Soviet goals and expectations. Another factor is the contemporary situation in Eastern Europe and the sources of political stability or instability, which are correlated with political changes, economic trends, and social tensions. The third element involves the question of the likely impact Eastern Europe will exert on Soviet foreign policy in the 1980s, taking into account both the past relationship and the current situation in the region. This framework should provide a better understanding of the interaction and tensions among the four basic dimensions of Soviet interests in Eastern Europe.

Security Interests

Throughout most of the postwar period and certainly since the emergence of East-West detente, most observers have agreed that the most important Soviet interest in Eastern Europe has been that of security. The reason for this is twofold. First, the USSR no longer derived tangible benefits from its economic interaction with the smaller East European states, and indeed, the relationship was proving increasingly costly to Moscow. Second, the "end of ideology" has also infected Soviet foreign policy, which, as a result, has become more pragmatic than before. It followed that since Soviet policy toward Eastern Europe could not be guided by either economic or ideological considerations, all that was left was Soviet security concerns as perceived and interpreted by the Kremlin.

While this view is not without merit, it raises the question of what "security" means to Moscow. Is it comparable to the traditional Western concept of military or physical security, or does it represent something different? It may be argued, especially in the wake of the Polish crisis, that the Soviet concept of security is far broader than the conventional Western one. To the extent that Poland in 1980–81 was not about to leave the Warsaw Pact, developments there did not threaten Soviet security in the Western sense of the word, as developments in Hungary did in 1956 and possibly did in Czechoslovakia in 1968. While martial law in Poland showed that Moscow's idea of security extends beyond conventional boundaries, the concept itself is difficult to define since it tends to change over time.

Hence, I argue that the Soviet notion of security in the East European context entails the traditional military aspect as well as political, ideological, and economic components. Soviet security in the region, therefore, requires two buffer zones, one narrowly defined in terms of physical or military security, and the other conceptualized more broadly in terms of Soviet political and ideological concerns. In this part of the essay we shall focus on the former aspect and will discuss separately the political, ideological, and economic interests.

Although in the missile age geography has become a much less important strategic factor than formerly, one may assume that the Kremlin still views Eastern Europe today as a valuable piece of real estate that it is prepared to protect against foreign incursions and influences and that, in turn, will continue to afford protection to the USSR. This also means that Moscow will resist any attempt either by an external power or by domestic political forces to undermine Soviet military and political hegemony in both the short and the long run.

There is little doubt that the "Northern Tier" of the region, composed of Czechoslovakia, East Germany, and Poland, will attract most attention from Soviet military planners in the 1980s. The reasons are obvious: geography, economic and military potential, and, perhaps most importantly, the history of domestic instability, especially in Poland but in Czechoslovakia as well. The "Southern Tier," Bulgaria, Romania, and Hungary, is geographically, economically, and strategically of lesser importance to the Kremlin than its Northern counterpart, although that area has also experienced political instability and, therefore, is bound to occupy Moscow's attention.

The two countries outside the Warsaw Pact, Albania and Yugoslavia, represent tempting military targets for the USSR, if only because of their strategic location. The Soviet Union remains eager to reestablish a foothold on the Adriatic, from which it was ousted in the early 1960s when Albania switched its allegiance from Moscow to Beijing. While the chances of a Soviet return to either Albania or Yugoslavia appear highly problematical in the foreseeable future, one can expect renewed efforts by the Kremlin to seek naval facilities and other bases in both countries that would permit the Soviets to challenge NATO's southern flank.

In the eyes of the Kremlin, the Warsaw Pact, which will celebrate its thirtieth anniversary in 1985, has over the years played three separate albeit interrelated roles: as a security or military alliance; as a diplomatic actor on the international scene; and as an instrument of political integration in Eastern Europe.[7] In each case the Treaty was a handmaiden of Moscow, which the Soviet leaders used and manipulated for their own purposes.

From a purely military security standpoint, the accomplishments of the Warsaw Pact since it began have been mixed, especially when contrasted with the initial expectations of the Soviet Union, which was responsible for its creation. In other words, the Pact seemed a sensible instrument as a military alliance in the mid-1950s when its signatories thought it strengthened their security vis-à-vis West Germany and NATO. The Western threat, real or imaginary, practically disappeared with East-West detente in the early 1970s, symbolized in official Western recognition of East Germany, settlement of the Berlin issue, the treaties between Bonn and Moscow and Warsaw, the still inconclusive Vienna talks on Mutually Balanced Force Reductions (MBFR), the Conference on Security and Cooperation in Europe (CSCE) in Helsinki, increased East-West trade, and the flood of Western loans. Moreover, while detente began to show signs of wear and tear in the late 1970s and its deterioration accelerated in the wake of the Soviet intervention in Afghanistan and the events in Poland, West Germany, the villain of the 1950s, has assumed the role of an East-

West intermediary, a stance the Kremlin and its junior allies could hardly consider a serious threat. Thus, the Warsaw Pact has lost a good deal of its *raison d'être,* at least insofar as its military security aspect is concerned.

Nonetheless, in 1982 the Treaty represented, at least on paper, a formidable fighting force. Whether it will remain so in the coming decade is open to question. One of the problems facing the Kremlin is the member states' degree of commitment to the alliance, which one can view from two different perspectives. One aspect concerns the willingness of the junior partners fully to participate in the Treaty's activities, including joint maneuvers, weapon standardization, and combined military operations. Here the most visible maverick has been Romania, which for some time has shown strong aversion to involvement in the Pact's activities Apart from its refusal to participate in joint military exercises, Bucharest has initiated its own defense doctrine, patterned closely after the Yugoslav concept of the "People's War," and has frequently called for the dissolution of military alliances in Europe. This suggests that in an East-West confrontation Moscow could not rely on Romania as a reliable WTO member ready to fight to defend Soviet interests. Barring some unexpected developments on the Romanian political scene, such as the replacement of President Ceausescu by a pro-Moscow leader or leaders, it may be assumed that Bucharest will maintain its independent stance in the coming years.

It may also be expected that, other things being equal, no other member country is likely to follow Romania's example and declare its *désintéressement* in the Pact, not to mention its intention to leave the alliance. The memories of Hungary of 1956 are still fresh not only in the minds of East European decision makers but also among the actual or potential opposition leaders, who accept membership in the Treaty as a necessary evil, as the Polish case illustrates. While we anticipate no defections from the Pact, an outside chance exists that Albania may decide after the death of Enver Hoxha to rejoin the alliance which it formally left in 1968.

The other aspect of the Pact that occupies the Kremlin's attention is the reliability of the Treaty members' national military establishments. Evaluating the reliability of combat troops is a difficult task. Nevertheless, the emergence of new political and military elites, characterized by often virulent nationalism, has raised the question of whether the Soviets still consider the Pact forces dependable fighting forces in any future conflict in Europe and elsewhere. Recent attempts at estimating the reliability of the East European armies concluded that the only army that the Soviets could count upon to participate in military operations, both offensive and defensive, was that of East Germany. None of the others is entirely reliable.[8]

On the other hand, the recent crisis in Poland illustrated that the armed forces can be a reliable instrument of internal coercion and control, although the fact that the crackdown on "Solidarity" protests after the imposition of martial law was conducted *not* by the Polish military but by the police and internal security troops suggests that there were serious doubts in Moscow's mind about the allegiance of Polish troops.

The imposition of martial law in Poland in December 1981 did not enhance the Soviet security position in the region. It checked the open challenge to the political system at least for the time being, making direct Soviet intervention unnecessary. However, the military regime in Poland has effectively removed Polish armed forces from active participation in the Warsaw Pact for an indefinite period of time, thus weakening the fabric of the alliance. Since the new Polish regime is unlikely to make much progress toward economic recovery without the help of the USSR and other East European countries and may not recover even with outside aid, Poland is likely to remain the "sick man" of Eastern Europe for many years to come, further weakening the strength and cohesion of the alliance, diminishing its value as a Soviet buffer zone, reducing Soviet capabilities for actions elsewhere in the world, and, of course, staining the image of Communism as the wave of the future.

It is now generally recognized that the Soviet security interests the Warsaw Treaty symbolizes are both defensive and offensive and the West should view Eastern Europe both as a potential launching pad for Soviet aggression against Western Europe and as a defense glacis against possible Western attack on the USSR. Stalin's policy in Eastern Europe was decidedly more defensive than Brezhnev's, largely out of necessity because of Western military superiority. Even in 1955, which marked the formation of WTO, Khrushchev was clearly concerned over West Germany's integration into NATO and the possibility that the Federal Republic might acquire nuclear weapons. However, WTO has undergone a conventional and nuclear buildup that no one except the Kremlin ascribes primarily to defensive motives. Nonetheless, one can still consider WTO's presence in Eastern Europe as a defensive measure, especially if the term "defensive" covers resistance to domestic upheavals intended to undermine or overthrow the existing Communist regime.

One of the most important aspects of WTO's contribution to Soviet offensive capabilities and interests has been the willingness of some WTO members to play an increasing role as Soviet proxies or surrogates in other parts of the globe, especially in the Third World. Soviet ability to mobilize its junior allies in Europe and elsewhere to act as surrogates in Africa, Central America, and the Middle East has been one of the most successful accomplishments of the Brezhnev regime. If the East European states can resolve their economic problems we may expect growing use of these countries as Soviet proxies, especially now that the USSR has become widely recognized as a global power willing to challenge the West and, to a lesser degree, China in the Third World. While the junior members have presumably insisted that the Warsaw alliance applies only to Europe and over the years have successfully resisted Soviet requests to deploy units of their national armies outside Europe, primarily on the Sino-Soviet border, in Vietnam and, most recently, in Afghanistan, most member states appear willing to follow Moscow's orders to act as Soviet proxies in such African countries as Angola, Ethiopia, Libya, Mozambique, and Zimbabwe, as well as in the Middle East (Syria and South Yemen) and more recently in Central America (Nicaragua and El Salvador).

Czechoslovakia and East Germany have been most active in shipping arms and advisers to the different countries, while Bulgaria, Hungary, and Poland have offered extensive training facilities to military personnel from the Third World countries. As will be shown below, the various East European states were willing to follow Moscow's orders to act as Soviet proxies in the Third World because of pressure exerted on them by the Kremlin, which used powerful economic leverage to force the smaller countries into supplying weapons and other scarce commodities to Soviet clients in different regions of the world.

However, the deteriorating economic situation throughout Eastern Europe may prevent these countries from continuing such aid without increasing tensions at home. The Soviet Union will therefore face a difficult choice. Either it can press its East European allies to continue supplying military and economic aid, regardless of domestic political consequences, or, by using economic leverage, it can reward the willing proxies and punish those countries that refuse to act as surrogates. The choice will depend on the overall international climate and on the general thrust of Soviet policy. Since Eastern Europe is likely to become again the central focus of Soviet policy in the 1980s, the Soviet Union may be forced to curtail its expansionist activities in the less-developed world in order to pay closer attention to Eastern Europe. This would suggest that the role of the East European countries as Soviet proxies in the Third World will decline in the coming decade.

What about the future role of the Warsaw Pact as an instrument of Soviet diplomacy? One of the reasons for creation of the Treaty was Moscow's desire to establish a NATO-like organization as a counterbalance to the Atlantic Alliance in various East-West negotiations. The Soviets are known to be sensitive about preserving parity in East-West relations and attach great importance to maintaining this image.

Apart from the question of parity, the Pact could always be used as an important bargaining chip, and its possible dissolution would certainly involve some concessions by NATO and the United States.

So far, however, the Treaty's role as a tool of Soviet diplomacy has proved limited in scope and character. The two most important areas of diplomatic activity directly or indirectly involving the Warsaw Pact have been East-West negotiations on arms control and disarmament and creation of an all-European collective security pact. The most visible example of the former was the previously mentioned MBFR negotiations, which began in October 1972 and have continued without reaching agreement.

In view of the prolonged impasse, one can question whether Moscow has been or is seriously interested in force reduction in Europe. On the one hand, the USSR may be sincerely concerned with reducing its defense burden and thus willing to discuss troop reduction in Central Europe. Furthermore, the Kremlin might also view the MBFR talks as a way of driving a wedge between the United States and the rest of NATO. On the other hand, an equally plausible argument suggests that the Soviet leadership is not interested in changing the balance of conventional forces in Europe and that it is, in fact, committed to maintenance of the status quo.

Whatever the Soviet position, the junior WTO members, with the possible exception of East Germany, strongly favor troop reduction in Central Europe, including Soviet forces stationed on their territory. Moreover, such a reduction would most likely revive East-West detente, which the East European countries favor.

The Warsaw Pact granted creation of an all-European collective security system a prominent place. The importance the Soviet Union attached to such a pact was clearly expressed in the charter, which tied the continued existence of the Warsaw alliance to the European security treaty by explicitly offering to disband the alliance in the event of the signing of the treaty. It is for this reason that the Kremlin pushed very hard for the Conference on Security and Cooperation in Europe (CSCE), which convened in Helsinki and concluded with a Final Act signed on August 1, 1975. Thus, while Soviet intentions with regard to MBFR were, to say the least, ambivalent, this was not true in the case of CSCE. Moscow was most eager to reach an understanding with the West that would ratify Soviet hegemony east of the Elbe. In order to achieve this goal the Kremlin was apparently willing to accept the provisions of Basket Three of CSCE and of Article Six of the Final Act, with their emphasis on human rights.

Although observers initially viewed the signing of the Helsinki Final Act as a major Soviet gain, it soon became obvious that it was at best a Pyrrhic victory. With relatively little attention paid to Baskets

One and Two, the world's attention soon focused on the human rights provisions of Basket Three, to the discomfort and surprise of the Kremlin. While the Soviet Union hoped to derive some tangible benefits from CSCE, the major achievement of the Final Act was to endow dissident movements in a number of WTO countries with international legitimacy.

It is, therefore, not surprising that the two CSCE Follow-Up meetings at Belgrade (1977–78) and Madrid (1980–82) accomplished next to nothing, apart from focusing again on the violations of human rights in the USSR and some of its junior allies. Moscow has now lost most of its initial interest in CSCE. The same is not true for the smaller East European countries, among which only Czechoslovakia and East Germany continue steadfastly to follow the Soviet line. The remaining states support the "Helsinki process" as one of the few concrete remnants of East-West detente that underscore their traditional ties to Western Europe.

To sum up, it is clear that the accomplishments of the Warsaw Treaty as a bargaining tool and an instrument of Soviet diplomacy have not been impressive. On paper the alliance appeared a useful regional international actor Soviet policy makers could manipulate in order to advance Soviet interests and obtain concessions from the West. In reality, however, its utility proved quite limited. Ultimately, all the major East-West decisions were made outside the framework of the Treaty, usually as a result of an agreement between the United States and the Soviet Union or among the USSR and the Western Big Three of Britain, France, and the United States. This remains true today.

The Warsaw Treaty's most important task has been serving as Moscow's tool of political integration of Eastern Europe. This particular objective was implicit in the Treaty's creation in 1955, when Khrushchev decided to replace the discredited Stalinist system of multiple informal controls with a more formal and structured organization to ensure Soviet hegemony. This aspect of the Treaty received a powerful boost in the aftermath of the intervention in Czechoslovakia in 1968 with the proclamation of the so-called Brezhnev Doctrine, by virtue of which the Soviet Union assumed the role of guardian of the alliance, responsible for its security and integrity. Any attacks from the outside or changes from within that threatened the "socialist achievements" of any member country were to be considered as attacks on the Treaty as a whole, triggering an automatic response by the USSR and the rest of the membership. The proclamation of the "Brezhnev Doctrine" represented a reassertion of Moscow's traditional role in Eastern Europe (minus Yugoslavia and Albania), underscoring the fact that the Kremlin considered Eastern Europe *de facto* a Soviet internal rather than an external matter.

The message that the new doctrine was intended to convey was not lost on the membership, including Romania, the only country that has been able to defy the Treaty with relative impunity. For the next twelve years the alliance enjoyed considerable tranquility, even though Romania resumed its independent stance in the mid-1970s. It was only in the course of the Polish crisis that the half-forgotten Soviet pronouncements and tactics came into play once again.

Having defined the nature and scope of Soviet security interests in Eastern Europe, the question arises how the current situation in the region is likely to affect Moscow's military security in the 1980s. Here, as in other cases, the recent crisis in Poland provides a convenient starting point for our analysis.

There is no doubt that the Kremlin will make every effort to limit and then repair the damage caused by the crisis in Poland and to tighten its military control over Eastern Europe, following the example of a similar tightening in the wake of the Czechoslovak crisis of 1968. In this, it will most likely use as an instrument the Warsaw Pact, which had been showing signs of drifting in the 1970s. Among the many lessons of the Polish upheaval the Kremlin has presumably learned, one of the most important concerns the obvious loss of Treaty cohesion and the need to strengthen Soviet control. The Polish crisis revealed obvious fissures in the fabric of the alliance. How can the Soviets improve the dependability of the Warsaw Pact in the future?

Leaving aside the possibility of resurrecting the Western threat as a catalyst of great coordination and cohesion within the Pact, the Kremlin may choose a combination of carrot and stick policies. On the one hand, Soviet leaders may initiate institutional changes in the Treaty's structure that would enhance the role of the junior members, at least formally. The changes in the Treaty's command structure announced in 1969 were intended to meet at least partly the criticism of Soviet monopoly of the High Command. Judging by the continuing dissatisfaction with the Treaty that Romania voiced at a summit meeting in Moscow in 1978, the changes have not produced a radical departure from past practice, and for all practical purposes the Unified Command remains an appendix to the Soviet General Staff. Thus, Moscow may expand its allies' participation in military decision making, at least symbolically. The chances, however, are slim.

On the other hand, it is more than likely that the Kremlin may decide to tighten its control over the Treaty, especially in the aftermath of the Polish upheaval. This may take the form of greater penetration of national military establishments by Soviet officers, more frequent joint exercises, such as those held at the height of the Polish crisis, stronger insistence on ideological indoctrination, closer standardization of weapons and training manuals, and so on. The most plausible outcome may be a synthesis of both approaches, combining formally greater access to decision making for the smaller East European countries with additional selective Soviet controls.

The state of East-West relations in the 1980s will surely exert some influence on these Soviet problems and policies. If Soviet intervention in Afghanistan and the Polish crisis spelled the end of East-West detente and a return to the Cold War for an indefinite period, these alone would provide a "justification" for strengthening and reorganizing the alliance. However, if Soviet policy in the wake of the invasion of Czechoslovakia offers any clue, it is possible that in the near future we may witness a concerted effort by Moscow to seek renewed rapprochement with the West, especially with Western Europe, which assumed a rather benign stance toward the crisis in Poland. If this is the case, the Kremlin might be willing to engage in another round of East-West negotiations in an effort to erase the impact of the Polish events and ingratiate itself with the West European governments and public opinion. This might mean a postponement of Warsaw Pact reorganization in favor of maintaining the status quo.

Thus, on the eve of the 1980s, the Kremlin faced again the perennial dilemma of cohesion versus viability. It has presumably decided to emphasize the former at the expense of the latter, at least in the short run. The task of restoring cohesion will surely be more difficult than in the 1950s and 1960s. As long as the Warsaw Pact was confronted with an outside threat in the form of NATO, West Germany, or the United States, the traditional national animosities within the alliance were suppressed. The gradual disappearance of the Western threat has revived historical antagonisms. The crisis in Poland, which brought to the surface hitherto largely submerged hostility between Poland and East Germany and Czechoslovakia, not to mention the Soviet Union itself, accentuated these hostilities. Whatever the ultimate resolution of the Polish problem, the various conflicts, to which should be added the old rift between Hungary and Romania, are not likely to disappear overnight. Their presence will obviously affect the cohesion of the alliance.

What can the Soviet Union do to reestablish that cohesion in the 1980s? As suggested earlier, one option is to invoke again the presence of an outside threat. Whether such a threat will appear credible to the East Europeans is difficult to say. On the one hand, Moscow has received unexpected help from Washington, where the Reagan administration has been engaging in rhetoric, to the discomfort of its NATO allies. On the other hand, the much more relaxed attitude of Western Europe toward events in Poland and its obvious yearning for the return of detente make the utility of a resurrected Western threat highly questionable. Probably the most compelling and credible way for the Kremlin to strengthen the unity of the Warsaw alliance would be to use Soviet economic leverage, which appears most formidable today and which is likely to grow in importance in the near future in light of the deteriorating economic situation in Eastern Europe.

There remains the question of continuing Soviet use of the East European countries as Moscow's proxies in the Third World. The Kremlin has derived considerable benefit from Eastern Europe's providing substantial military and economic aid to selected Third World countries, and the USSR may insist that such assistance should not only continue but expand in the 1980s. The problem is that the worsening economic situation in most European countries may make it impossible to continue providing increasing amounts of aid without generating political opposition at home.

Political Interests

The principal Soviet objectives in establishing Communist power in Eastern Europe after World War II were to deny control of the region to countries hostile to the USSR and potentially threatening to its security and to ensure that control of the political systems in the area would remain in the hands of elements friendly to Moscow. The latter goal meant in practice the perpetuation of party monopoly of political power in the individual East Europen countries. Today, this means that the USSR is certain, sooner or later, to respond to any challenge it perceives as threatening that monopoly. Thus, the chief Soviet political interest in Eastern Europe focuses on maintenance of viable Communist regimes which accept the general line of Soviet foreign and domestic policy and support unquestioningly attainment of Moscow's multiple policy objectives.

The Kremlin's main political concern, in contrast with its security interests, is to ensure that the individual East European regimes are in full control of their political, economic, and social systems. For that reason, Moscow has over the years created a set of linkages that enables Soviet leaders to exercise a high degree of control over internal developments in their client states. Some of the links, such as the Warsaw Pact and the Council for Mutual Economic Assistance, represent a set of formal institutional linkages augmented by a variety of informal linkages, all of which form a rather formidable network of controls that permits the Kremlin to maintain an impressive degree of authority over its East European domain.

It is clear that the Soviet Union has not succeeded in achieving the balance between cohesion and viability that has been its major objective in Eastern Europe. This is not surprising since Moscow was saddled with an impossible task; the proper mix of cohesion and viability requires the presence of preconditions, some of which do not exist in Eastern Europe. While by now most if not all East European countries have become reconciled to their fate and generally accept Soviet hegemony in the region, and although there is probably a high degree of harmony and understanding between the Soviet and East European ruling elites, the key requirement, legitimacy of Communist rule, is nearly totally absent in the region.

There is no doubt that after being in power for more than thirty-five years, the East European regimes, with the possible exception of Albania and Yugoslavia, are still perceived as illegitimate by their populations, which view them as intruders forcibly imposed on the region by the Soviet Union. The recent Polish crisis illustrates that various official efforts to acquire legitimacy, such as the encouragement of nationalism and "consumerism," the emphasis on social mobility, advancement and equality, and the attempts to increase the level of political participation, have failed dismally in generating popular support for the existing regimes. All East European countries are currently experiencing a crisis of legitimacy, although its intensity varies from country to country.

Faced with the areawide crisis of legitimacy, Moscow has no choice but to emphasize cohesion at the expense of viability. Since the USSR regards Eastern Europe as an extension of its own system, the Kremlin simply cannot allow the continuing crisis of confidence in the local Communist regimes to spill over into the Soviet Union itself.

The different political problems and dilemmas the Kremlin faces in Eastern Europe surfaced with full force in the Polish crisis of 1980–81. The impact of developments in Poland on the rest of Eastern Europe and the Soviet Union has had two basic dimensions, political and economic. From the political viewpoint, by far the most crucial element in the complex matrix of relations within the region was the possibility that the Polish crisis might spill over into the other countries, by no means an idle fear. The Kremlin and ruling oligarchies throughout Eastern Europe certainly remembered the "Titoist heresy" of 1948, the Hungarian Revolution of 1956, and the "Prague Spring" of 1968, and their effect on the rest of the region. The Polish crisis appeared even more dangerous than the previous three. The Tito-Stalin quarrel and the Hungarian revolt occurred during the Cold War period, and Moscow succeeded in limiting the damage by isolating them rather quickly. The "Prague Spring" did affect neighboring countries but its impact was limited, perhaps because the Czechoslovak reform movement represented in essence a revolution "from above" rather than "from below." The Prague reformers did not challenge the political monopoly of power exercised by the ruling party: they wanted mostly to liberalize Communist rule and build "Socialism with a human face."

The challenge posed by the Polish workers is far more serious because it goes straight to the control issue by denying legitimacy of the Communist rule. "Solidarity" was above all a grassroots mass movement, much more powerful than the previous attempts to democratize the political systems staged by groups within the ruling elites, disenchanted and disillusioned with the Marxist-Leninist creed. As the 1981 "Solidarity" congress indicated, the Polish workers, after initial hesitation, decided finally to dismantle the traditional Communist political system by calling for free elections, political pluralism, elimination of censorship, virtual abolition of central planning, and a number of other changes, all of which would ultimately result in creation of a political system radically different from those in existence throughout Eastern Europe.

The reaction throughout the region varied from country to country. Predictably, the only sympathetic response to Polish events came from Yugoslavia, long a critic of Soviet hegemony in Eastern Europe and an advocate of a more relaxed brand of Communism. During most of the crisis Hungary, although officially silent or mildly critical, informally indicated sympathy to the Poles. Romania tended to blow hot and cold, criticizing some developments but also stressing its support for Poland's right to settle its own affairs without outside interference. The two smallest countries, Albania and Bulgaria, remained largely silent. As expected, the sharpest negative reactions, in some instances even more critical than those of Moscow, originated in Czechoslovakia and East Germany.

The factors that influenced the reactions of the individual governments ranged from historical national antagonisms to the paranoia exhibited by some East European regimes who believed themselves particularly vulnerable to, and threatened by, the Polish crisis. The critical reaction from both Czechoslovakia and East Germany stemmed largely from the character of their regimes, clearly the least secure and legitimate in the region. The Husak regime in Prague was especially afraid of anything resembling the "Prague Spring," as its harsh treatment of local dissidents illustrated. The Honecker regime in East Berlin was equally vulnerable: after more than thirty years, twenty Soviet divisions and a highly developed system of internal coercion remain necessary to protect the continuing existence of the German Democratic Republic.

In contrast, the Kadar regime in Hungary and the post-Tito government in Yugoslavia possess a considerable degree of legitimacy, which makes them relatively immune to the "Polish disease." The ambivalent attitude of Romania reflected the peculiarity of that country's situation. On the one hand, Bucharest has for some time asserted the right of every East European country to settle its internal problems without Soviet interference. On the other hand, the Polish working class's frontal attack on the Communist monopoly of power must have irked the Romanian regime, one of the most oppressive in the region and one which has experienced recent serious labor problems. The two small Balkan countries remained outside the mainstream of criticism, if only for reasons of geography, although ultimately both criticized events in Poland for somewhat different reasons: Albania as probably the only truly Stalinist country today, and Bulgaria as Moscow's trusted and faithful ally.

Another consideration reinforced the purely political concerns of the various countries. It was the fear that unless the Polish crisis was settled peacefully, it would lead to Soviet military intervention, the impact of which could have only negative consequences for Eastern Europe, including tightening of Soviet controls and further deterioration in East-West relations. Neither prospect appeared attractive to the East Europeans.

In these circumstances it is not surprising that the impact of the Polish crisis on domestic politics in Eastern Europe has been insignificant. To be sure, spurred by events in Poland, individual regimes began to pay lip service to greater workers' participation, promising to enhance the status and authority of the labor unions, which until now have been essentially stooges of the party. Growing concern was also expressed for raising the standard of living, especially for increasing the supply of basic foodstuffs and consumer goods. These policies, intended to defuse popular discontent and forestall possible replication of the Polish strikes, were counterbalanced by escalation of the anti-dissident campaign and appeals for greater ideological vigilance. Other than that, at least on the surface, the effects of the Polish upheaval have been almost nil.

The main reason for the character of the Polish explosion's impact on the rest of Eastern Europe may be that other East Europeans perceive Poland as an economic disaster, hardly an attractive model. Although there may have been a strong undercurrent of sympathy for the efforts of the Polish workers to emancipate themselves, the highly negative example of the Polish economic catastrophe and a fear of economic and political disturbances more than offset it. However, if "Solidarity" and the Polish government had succeeded in implementing far-reaching economic reforms and pulled the country out of the economic morass, Poland would have become a much more attractive society, combining political liberalization with economic efficiency and thus presenting a model which would have appealed to large segments of the population throughout Eastern Europe.

Still, the fact that the Warsaw Pact countries remained immune to the Polish crisis provides a testimony to the strength of Communist regimes. To some extent this is not surprising or unexpected. During more than thirty-five years, the various regimes have, by and large, managed to create and develop institutions, mechanisms, and policies they could use to deter and neutralize internal challenge to their rule. Even in Poland in 1981, when it appeared that the ruling party and the government were on the verge of total disintegration, the Warsaw government, admittedly with Soviet blessing, succeeded in staving off impending collapse and reasserting its authority at least temporarily. Thus, the East European regimes today may be stronger than they appear: They have developed an impressive capacity for survival and immunity to internal and external shocks.

Much of the credit for this achievement should go to individual Communist parties and their leaders. Political stability in the respective countries is largely a function of the character and cohesion of the party, especially the strength of its leadership and bureaucracy and their control over the instruments of coercion, the security police, and the military. The Polish events provided a good illustration of this basic truth: while the party's rank and file and its local leadership were in considerable disarray, the *apparat* remained practically untouched and ultimately was able to make a comeback. The absence of an efficient bureaucracy may be offset by the presence of a popular leader, but the record shows that a well-trained *apparat* is a *sine qua non* of an effectively functioning political system.

In at least three East European countries the ruling Communist party clearly faces no difficulties. This is certainly true for Hungary, where the party and its leadership have been in full control of the political and economic system for more than a quarter of a century. All available evidence suggests that both the Bulgarian and East German parties have also been successful in retaining and exercising authority. The situation in the remaining countries is more complex. There are signs, for example, that the Romanian party may be on the verge of a crisis. It has not been able to cope with deteriorating economic conditions, and the rapid and increasingly frequent turnover at the top echelons indicates growing disagreement regarding future remedial policies. Until recently, Ceausescu's *ersatz* charisma and control of the‚levers of power succeeded in holding the party together, but there are signs that his skill in handling the various crises may be coming to an end. On the surface, the situation in the Czechoslovak party appears relatively calm, yet the worsening economic situation may take its toll in the form of growing rifts and divisions in the party leadership.

More than a year after the imposition of martial law, the Polish party has not recovered from the trauma of 1980–81, and it is clear that the process of recovery will consume years. In fact, reconstruction may take decades. Not only has the party lost many of its members but, in addition, its leadership is sharply divided, creating inertia and impotence in facing the country's pressing problems. Moreover, since December 1981 the "ruling" party has been overshadowed by the military.

Outside the Warsaw Pact, the situation in Albania and Yugoslavia appears uncertain. The recent bizarre incidents in Albania reflect a ferment in the ruling oligarchy in anticipation of the impending departure from the scene of Hoxha who has ruled without interruption since 1945. In Yugoslavia the remarkably smooth and uneventful post-Tito transition period has persuaded many observers that the League of Communists of Yugoslavia remains united and fully in control. This judgment, however, may be premature; the official and popular reaction to the Kosovo riots in the spring of 1981 and to galloping inflation reflect the presence of a lingering dissatisfaction with the existing situation.

The political landscape in Eastern Europe will become more complex in the near future since five of the countries will face succession problems in the 1980s: in addition to Albania, where Hoxha turned 74 this year, the Bulgarian, Czechoslovak, East German, and Hungarian parties will have new leaders replacing Zhivkov (71), Husak (69), Honecker (70), and Kadar (70). Thus far, the collective leadership in Yugoslavia appears to hold its own; barring some dramatic deterioration in the country's economic situation or a sudden revival of nationalist strife, there is no reason why the present leadership could not continue in the foreseeable future.

As pointed out by John Campbell, the East European leaders play a key role in Moscow's calculations with respect to the region.[9] Once the Kremlin has decided not to exercise its rule directly, it relies on individual leaders to maintain stability in their respective countries and to fulfill Moscow's requirements and expectations. Hence, the Kremlin is vitally interested in East European succession problems. Although since 1956 Moscow has tried, by and large, to remain aloof from internal party conflicts in Eastern Europe, it has presumably retained a veto power in the leadership selection process.

In general, the Soviet Union has assumed a rather pragmatic stance on the transfer of authority. For example, it made no attempt to save discredited or unpopular leaders from being ousted: this was the case with Novotny in 1968, Gomulka in 1970, and Gierek in 1980. Similarly, the Kremlin tended to accept the East European parties' choices of new leaders, Ceausescu in 1965, Dubček in 1968, Gierek in 1970, Kania in 1980, and Jaruzelski in 1981. In the past decade or so, so far as we know, Moscow has intervened directly in the leadership selection only once, when Ulbricht was forced in 1971 to surrender the leadership of the East German party in favor of Honecker.

This rather relaxed attitude is likely to change in the 1980s. One of the repercussions of the Polish crisis will be much greater Soviet insistence on East Europe's cohesion at the expense of viability. Experiences in Czechoslovakia, Poland, and Romania must have convinced the Kremlin that the East European leadership selection process is too important to be left to the spontaneous interplay of political forces and groupings and that Moscow should become closely involved, especially in those cases where, for various reasons, no consensus exists regarding the succession or where the party's choice might displease the Soviets. The timing and form of Soviet involvement are hard to predict.

The USSR probably will not be greatly concerned with the changeover in Bulgaria and Hungary or the succession in Czechoslovakia and East Germany. The Kremlin views these countries as reliable and faithful allies and has every expectation that the new generation of leaders will continue following the Soviet line in foreign and domestic policies, or at least will not engage in excessive economic experimentation, especially in the case of Hungary. Insofar as Albania is concerned, the impending departure of Hoxha presents the Soviet Union with an opportunity for bringing Tirana back into the Warsaw Pact, but the Byzantine domestic politics of Albania make any prediction highly suspect. While we anticipate that an early change of leadership in Romania is not likely, the Kremlin would be happy to see Ceausescu's star tarnished still further. The same is true to some extent for Yugoslavia; floundering on the part of the collective leadership will provide the Kremlin a chance to reestablish its influence in Yugoslav politics. As for Poland, the Soviet leadership is likely to adopt a "wait and see" attitude: if Jaruzelski succeeds in stabilizing the country and in returning rule to the party, Moscow may accept him; if he fails, there is an excellent chance that it will replace him with someone in the ruling oligarchy willing to take drastic measures and more attuned to Soviet wishes.

The Soviet Union itself faced a succession decision in November 1982. The choice of Andropov to replace Brezhnev will influence Moscow's attitude toward Eastern Europe. As former Soviet ambassador to Hungary (1954–57) and Central Committee Secretary responsible for the liaison with "fraternal" parties (1957–62), Andropov is much better acquainted with conditions in Eastern Europe than any of his erstwhile competitors or, for that matter, Brezhnev himself. The question remains whether his knowledge of Eastern Europe will persuade him to stress closer conformity or whether he will be willing to relax Soviet control in favor of political and economic innovation *à la hongroise*. It is interesting to note that Andropov, prior to his elevation to full membership of the Soviet Politburo and Secretariat, headed the KGB for fifteen years (1968–82). This means that he may take advantage of his experience and improve the connection between the Soviet and East European internal security networks.

The relationship between the East European internal security establishments and Moscow remains an object of intense speculation. Ample evidence shows that during the Stalinist period the extensive secret police network in the region was closely supervised by Beria and his colleagues. Following the latter's demise and the general downgrading of discredited police methods, the network presumably was weakened. The close contacts between the Czechoslovak and Soviet secret police prior to the intervention in August 1968 show that it did not disappear, and developments in Poland before and after imposition of martial law in December 1981 suggest that the Soviet secret police cooperated closely with Polish internal security forces. Thus we may assume that close liaison between the Soviet KGB and its equivalents in Eastern Europe has continued and perhaps will be strengthened, especially if Moscow decides to tighten its grip on the region.

How will Soviet political interests in Eastern Europe be affected by developments in the region, and how will potential political changes influence the conduct of Soviet foreign policy in the coming decade?

Here again, the crisis in Poland is bound to dominate Soviet behavior toward the region. The utter collapse of the Polish party and its replacement by a military regime have created a shock in Moscow, leading to reassessment of overall policy toward Eastern Europe. The "agonizing reappraisal" is likely to focus on whether Poland in 1980–81 was an aberration or a promise of things to come in the rest of the region. One consolation to Moscow must have been the absence of significant spillover from Poland to the other East European countries. This might suggest that the Polish upheaval was an exception and that it was avoidable rather than inevitable. The failure of the "Polish disease" to spread throughout the region must have reassured Soviet leaders that the Communist systems outside of Poland were reasonably well entrenched and able to withstand outside shocks. This would imply that no major political and/or ideological tightening is necessary at this time.

In other words, the ways and means of achieving Soviet political objectives in Eastern Europe in the 1980s will depend to a large extent on the Kremlin's perception and interpretation of the Polish upheaval. If it views the crisis in Poland as an isolated phenomenon, the Soviet response may be relatively mild. However, if it perceives the crisis as a reflection of a general malaise that may sooner or later infect the other countries, one may anticipate a major Moscow-directed campaign aimed at restoring political cohesion and ideological orthodoxy.

What is the likely impact of greater political consolidation in Eastern Europe on Soviet foreign policy in the 1980s? Here the Kremlin may assign top priority to the settlement of the Polish crisis, especially to an early return to civilian rule in Warsaw, one of the chief demands voiced by the United States and Western Europe. There is no doubt that the continued presence of martial law in Poland hamstrings Soviet foreign policy by restricting the room for maneuver available to Moscow and forcing it to adopt a defensive stance.

Moscow's insistence on tighter political cohesion in Eastern Europe is not likely to have a major impact on the conduct of Soviet foreign policy in the 1980s, unless its attempts to reestablish control meet with resistance which would necessitate the use of stern measures. Any sign of continuing political instability in the region may make it more difficult for the USSR to seek improved relations with Western Europe, which is particularly sensitive to developments in Eastern Europe. Thus, Moscow will try to reestablish its authority in the region gradually, using informal rather than formal channels so as not to antagonize key West European countries, such as West Germany or France. The same will be true for Soviet involvement in the leadership selection process in Eastern Europe, including Yugoslavia.

Although the Kremlin should be satisfied by the international behavior of its allies, the next few years may see an effort at even greater coordination in foreign policy and international relations. In addition to bringing Romania back in line, Moscow may want to reestablish closer control over Eastern Europe's foreign economic policy because of the rapid growth of the region's hard currency indebtedness and its increased dependence on trade with the West. While the Soviet Union is not likely to curtail East-West trade sharply, it is conceivable that the essentially uncontrolled growth in trade and credit relations between Eastern Europe and the West will give way to a much more rigid and structured policy coordinated by Moscow. Whether closer supervision and control will also apply to the individual countries' membership in such international institutions as the International Monetary Fund and the World Bank remains to be seen. The fact that both Hungary and Poland applied for membership in 1981, presumably with Soviet approval, may encourage Bulgaria and East Germany, the remaining nonmembers in the region, to follow suit. If they do, this may signify Moscow's realization that Eastern Europe's membership in both IMF and the World Bank may prove beneficial to the USSR by relieving it of at least some burden of helping its clients.

Ideological Interests

The Soviet Union's ideological stake in Eastern Europe rests on the success or failure of a Communist polity to become firmly embedded in a given East European society, thus validating if not

legitimizing the Soviet-type brand of Marxism-Leninism as the potentially universal model. It does not mean total adoption of all Soviet
institutions and policies, but rather a basic adherence to such essential
principles as the Leninist conception of the party's role, nationaliza-
tion and control of key sectors of the economy, media censorship,
party control over instruments of coercion, the military and police,
and belief in proletarian internationalism.

Eastern Europe performs two additional functions for the Kremlin. Since the mid-1950s it has acted as an ideological *cordon sanitaire*
or a barrier against political, ideological, and cultural influences
emanating from the West or, for that matter, from other Communist
states and parties not always willing to adhere to policies initiated and
implemented by Moscow. The Soviet Union expects Eastern Europe
to provide the first line of defense against the penetration of revisionist ideas aimed at challenging Soviet hegemony in the region and at its
domination of international Communism. In many cases individual
East European countries are much better suited than the USSR to
deal with ideological offensives mounted from the outside. In recent
years, however, the defenses have proved increasingly porous, reducing Eastern Europe's value as an ideological barrier.

The other important task performed by Eastern Europe is to act
as a testing ground for various systemic reforms and innovations,
especially in the political and economic realms. Despite its extreme
sensitivity to changes in Eastern Europe, there is no doubt that Moscow's attitude toward developments there has not been entirely rigid
and dogmatic. Faced with a plethora of economic and social problems, the Kremlin looks to its junior allies for clues to possible solutions, particularly in economics.

Still, from the ideological point of view Eastern Europe's primary
value to the USSR has been and is its role in legitimizing the Soviet
system, not only in the eyes of Soviet elites and masses but also in the
minds of outsiders, both in Eastern Europe and beyond. The fact that
for close to four decades eight countries in the heart of Europe have
developed under Communist rule provides impressive testimony for
the Kremlin in support of its claim that Marxism-Leninism is a viable
and dynamic doctrine that has universal applicability. That two of the
eight countries, Albania and Yugoslavia, are not under direct Soviet
control does not weaken greatly Moscow's belief that Communism
represents the wave of the future.

Although the USSR must derive considerable satisfaction from
the fact that Communist rule in Eastern Europe has remained relatively unimpaired since the end of World War II, it is equally clear
that past and present leadership in the Kremlin has been and is
greatly concerned with the viability of that rule. Events in Hungary in

1956, in Czechoslovakia in 1968, and in Poland in 1956, 1970, and 1976 provided clear signals that Communist rule in those countries was fragile and that the political systems have been unsuccessful in achieving popular support. For that reason the Soviet Union has from the beginning seen itself as the guardian of Communist orthodoxy responsible for close adherence to the Soviet model.

Despite its obvious concern for ideological conformity, Moscow has seldom spelled out its parameters exactly. Even the "Brezhnev Doctrine," proclaimed after the Soviet intervention in Czechoslovakia, only reserved the Soviet Union the right to determine what was or was not ideologically correct and acceptable, without establishing the threshold which the East European countries could not cross. Thus, the "Brezhnev Doctrine" simply reaffirmed the principle of Soviet ideological supremacy and its role as the ultimate arbiter of doctrinal orthodoxy.

Recent history shows that Moscow's ideological stance with regard to Eastern Europe has been full of contradictions and inconsistencies, illustrating again the perennial Soviet dilemma with regard to its policy toward the region, that of viability versus cohesion. The Kremlin must have realized that conditions for political stability and economic efficiency do not necessarily coincide with requirements for ideological conformity and cohesion. As a result Soviet policy toward Eastern Europe has vacillated over the years, and Moscow's attitude toward developments in the region has been characterized by a mixture of relative relaxation and recompression.

The 1970s provide a good illustration of ambiguous and contradictory Soviet behavior. There is little doubt that Moscow has been aware of the various political and socioeconomic processes and tendencies occurring in Eastern Europe. In the course of the decade it adopted a rather benign attitude toward the growth of dissident movements and did not object to economic reforms and expanded economic relations with the West. Apparently the Kremlin did not even oppose visits by American presidents and other high-ranking U.S. officials to Poland, Hungary, and Romania, although it vehemently criticized Chairman Hua Kuo-feng's tour of Romania and Yugoslavia in 1978. Occasionally Moscow even propped up faltering regimes with substantial economic aid, as in Poland in 1976. Several reasons explain this rather relaxed posture. One was East-West detente, which did not begin to fall apart until the Soviet intervention in Afghanistan. As long as detente held firm, it was obviously important for Moscow to project an image of Eastern Europe free from Soviet interference and able to pursue its own course in foreign and domestic politics. The Kremlin apparently believed that the Communist parties in the individual East European countries were fully in control and that there was no need to intervene, especially when such intervention, whether overt or covert, would affect the climate of detente which the Soviets were eager to maintain.

The official Soviet attitude toward developments in Hungary, Poland, and Romania testifies to Moscow's confidence that the local parties maintained control. Thus the Kremlin tolerated the continuing process of "Kadarization" in Hungary and even praised some reforms undertaken in Hungarian agriculture. Despite many signs that the Polish party was losing its grip, like the workers' riots in June 1976, the emergence of a dynamic dissident movement, and the growing assertiveness of the Catholic church, there is no evidence that the Soviet Union put pressure on the Gierek regime to toughen its policies. Finally, despite Ceausescu's persistent challenges to Soviet hegemony, whether in the course of the Helsinki negotiations or during various Warsaw Pact summit meetings, no visible deterioration in relations occurred between Bucharest and Moscow.

To be sure, the Kremlin has kept a watchful eye on the changing situation in Eastern Europe. If they allowed further economic experimentation in Hungary, it was because Soviet leaders were convinced that Kadar had learned a lesson from Czechoslovakia and would not allow any spillover from the economic to the political arena. If they continued to support Gierek, it was probably largely because the Polish leader persuaded them that he was indispensable and because he managed to gain the confidence of two key West European leaders, President Giscard d'Estaing and Chancellor Schmidt, and thus was clearly useful as an intermediary between the USSR and Western Europe. As long as Ceausescu continues to rule Romania with an iron hand, the Kremlin apparently views him as a nuisance rather than a serious threat.

Because of these experiences in the 1970s, the upheaval in Poland in the 1980s must have shocked Moscow, which was clearly caught by surprise, as was just about every other capital, East and West. As events in Poland unfolded over eighteen months, the Soviets must have been pleased with the absence of any significant spillover into the rest of Eastern Europe but they must have also been concerned about the possible occurrence of similar crises in other countries, including their own, particularly in light of the deteriorating socioeconomic situation throughout the region.

As the Polish crisis revealed, the two grave problems facing Eastern Europe on the eve of the 1980s were the lack and/or decline in regime legitimacy and growing economic difficulties, both of which generated popular discontent and contributed to the decrease in the bloc's ideological conformity and cohesion. In some countries the economic failures, resulting in nonfulfillment of promises the ruling elites made earlier, have produced widespread alienation of the working class, which also became the victim of a slowdown in social mobility that had guaranteed its members and their children progress up the social and economic ladder. The professional and creative intelligentsia, although less than pleased with the lack of significant progress on the economic front, has probably been even more disappointed by the absence of channels for meaningful participation. In some countries it began to organize formal or informal opposition groups which articulated demands and questioned the legitimacy of the regimes simultaneously. One of the major weaknesses of the dissident movement throughout the region has been the fragmented character and nature of the opposition, with the workers seemingly less interested in political freedoms and more in improving their economic well-being, and the intellectuals showing reverse preferences. The events in Poland in the summer of 1980 demonstrated a striking change in attitudes; the workers' joining the intellectuals in demanding, among other things, establishment of independent labor unions and the end of censorship augured a new era in the domestic politics not only of Poland but of Eastern Europe as a whole.

The demand for recognition of free labor unions stemmed from the fact that the Communist regime in Poland succeeded in the early "revolutionary" period in harnessing the population to accomplish a variety of tasks associated with building the foundations of socialist order but failed to provide adequate outlets for the mobilized masses, especially the workers, to express preferences and articulate demands. The institutional arrangements the ruling party erected during the thirty-five years of its rule played a one-sided role, serving as vehicles for penetrating and manipulating Polish society and generating conformity and support rather than channels of communication and interest articulation. As a result, a wide gap emerged between the rulers and the ruled, a gap which grew because of the presence of a powerful Catholic church that proved much more successful than the regime in representing Polish society and obtaining its allegiance.

Demands for greater participation were not confined to Poland. At least two other countries in the region managed to defuse demands by providing access to decision making for some key groups. In Hungary both the party and the official interest groups, such as the labor unions, professional organizations, and collective farm associations, have served not only as instruments of support but also as articulators of demands. Several of them took part in the process of initiating and implementing the New Economic Mechanism (NEM), which represents the most comprehensive economic reform in Eastern Europe. In Yugoslavia the workers' councils have played a similar role, endowing the workers with considerable power of decision making, especially in the economic sphere.

Elsewhere in the region demands for greater participation were either muted or nonexistent, in part because of the regimes' ability to neutralize disaffected groups through a policy of "consumerism." The ruling oligarchies realized the close correlation between legitimacy and economic well-being and attempted to raise the level of the latter by introducing economic reforms, raising the share of GNP going to consumption, or increasing import of consumer goods. Hungary achieved the most notable success in this respect, while Poland and Romania failed signally on all fronts.

In the context of Soviet ideological concerns in Eastern Europe, the upheaval in Poland raises two questions of relevance for the 1980s:

(1) What is the likelihood of Moscow's ordering certain political and ideological tightening? Judging from the tenor of Soviet statements during the eighteen-month crisis, the Kremlin above all blamed the Polish Communist leadership for letting the situation drift. This would imply that the USSR may insist throughout the 1980s on strengthening the "leading role" of the party in the individual countries, while at the same time increasing Soviet authority in these parties and urging major purges in order to make the ruling parties ideologically more vigilant yet sophisticated.

(2) In line with the above, can we expect a renewed Soviet emphasis on ideological orthodoxy? Soviet leaders are likely to blame failure of the system in Poland on the mistakes of the Polish ruling oligarchy, not on ideology. On the contrary, they may interpret the absence of sympathetic response to events in Poland to mean that close adherence to ideology was the strongest bulwark against counterrevolutionary activities. Thus, one may assume that Moscow in the 1980s will stress the continued importance and relevance of Marxism-Leninism and urge renewed vigilance against the encroachment of Western ideas, regardless of the state of East-West relations.

From the Soviet vantage point the Polish events emphasized at least two points: the importance of consumer well-being and the need to provide the masses with some form of popular participation. Thus, one may expect Soviet policy to stress the importance of economic factors in achieving some degree of legitimacy for the Communist regimes and, in the same vein, to emphasize the necessity of upgrading existing "transmission belts," thus providing an outlet for the most dissatisfied segments of society. Hence, in the 1980s the Kremlin may encourage East European governments to experiment with economic reforms and some forms of *ersatz* participation.

Leaving aside for the time being the impact of global economic disturbances on Eastern Europe, it is obvious that the only way to improve economic performance would be to engage in radical, across-the-board, systemic reforms. Such reforms, however, would once again bring to the surface the old Soviet dilemma of cohesion versus viability, which may prove insoluble for the Kremlin, at least in the short run. While Moscow has given its blessing to the Hungarian NEM, the Hungarian reforms could not be easily replicated elsewhere in the region. Apart from the fact that the trauma of 1956 made the country more amenable to reforms, the character of the Hungarian leadership and the party made the reforms not only successful but also acceptable to Moscow.

With the possible exception of Bulgaria, such conditions do not now exist in the remaining East European countries. In all CMEA countries the chief obstacle to meaningful reforms is the presence of a well-entrenched party and government bureaucracy dead set against comprehensive restructuring of the economic systems in the direction of decentralization and marketization. While any reform would cost some bureaucrats their jobs, their main excuse for opposing changes is fear they will affect the political system. They also argue that innovations should not be undertaken in times of economic stringency and that any tampering with the existing system should be postponed until a significant improvement in the economic situation has occurred.

The only way to overcome these obstacles and clear the way for change would be for the Kremlin to put sufficient pressure on its clients to break down bureaucratic resistance. The probability of such a move on the part of Moscow is very low; not only is the Kremlin, still shocked by the Polish crisis, unlikely to tamper with local party hierarchies, but also Moscow may fear a potential spread of reformism from Eastern Europe to the USSR. Above all, of course, the Soviet leadership has been and remains opposed to these changes in the Soviet Union. It is one thing to praise experiments in Hungarian agriculture and another to urge East Europeans to proceed with a wholesale reform program. Hence, at least in the immediate future, we may assume that the Soviet Union will opt in favor of the "muddling through" solution, allowing the East Europeans to cope with economic difficulties as best they can, without introducing radical changes, even at the risk of causing some popular discontent.

Growing popular disaffection is only a matter of time. Apart from Poland and Romania, which are in a class by themselves, all the remaining East European countries will face economic hardships in the 1980s, with Czechoslovakia, East Germany, and possibly Yugoslavia most likely suffering more than Bulgaria and Hungary. All will be affected by a declining rate of growth, reduced standard of living, decreased investment, and foreign trade difficulties. Social implications of the slowdown should not be underestimated: declining rate of growth spells lower consumption, growing unemployment, and reduced social mobility. It reflects the regime's failure to fulfill popular expectations, exposing inherent weaknesses of the socialist order, which has prided itself on securing full employment, improving living standards, and ensuring social advance better than the capitalist system. While the USSR so far has been relatively successful in insulating its society from the "demonstration effect" emanating from Eastern Europe and in defusing mass discontent, this may prove more difficult in the 1980s, forcing the Soviet regime to make some hard political choices.

These choices will focus attention on leadership selection in several countries. The Kremlin's disappointment with such leaders as Dubček, Gierek, and Kania suggests greater future Soviet preoccupation with East European leadership questions. Considering the fact that the region in the 1980s is likely to experience mounting economic and social problems, the selection of new leaders will be crucial for Moscow, especially if it also insists on closer political and ideological conformity with the Soviet model.

It follows that Moscow will also place renewed emphasis on the principle of the "leading role" of the party, which was badly weakened in the course of the Polish crisis. Not only was the Polish party largely overshadowed by "Solidarity," but in the final analysis the military had to rescue it, an act which could hardly have pleased Soviet ideologues, for whom the specter of Bonapartism remains a cardinal sin. Moreover, the far-reaching economic crisis that for the first time since the war affects all East European countries simultaneously is bound to increase popular discontent. This in turn will call not only for great vigilance and discipline but also for great political and ideological sophistication. The 1980s may also witness the return of the so-called twenty-year crisis in many East European parties, in which a new generation of younger functionaries may begin to assume leading positions in the party *apparat*.[10] All this would suggest further need for the Soviet leadership to watch developments in the East European parties.

As for Eastern Europe's role in the international Communist movement, that task is likely to be much less important than in the past, when the Soviet Union was able to mobilize the East European parties against Titoism, Maoism, and Eurocommunism. For all practical purposes Titoism has ceased to have much impact, even though Yugoslavia has continued to assert its independence of the Kremlin.

The Sino-Soviet conflict has become muted, especially at the ideological level, and Eurocommunism has become a reduced threat to Soviet hegemony. Nonetheless, it is likely that Moscow will insist on preserving the fiction of an essentially united Communist camp and that Eastern Europe will be expected to play its part in helping to maintain that unity and in resisting any attempts challenging Soviet leadership, such as the recent criticism of the USSR voiced by the Communist parties of Italy and Japan.

The impact of ideological retrenchment in Eastern Europe on Soviet foreign policy decision making in the 1980s is likely to reinforce the influence exerted by greater political consolidation in the region. The key issues are solution of the continuing Polish crisis and revival of detente with Western Europe. If the political and economic situation in Poland is stabilized satisfactorily and if political and ideological cohesion in the bloc is tightened without arousing the ire of the outside world, the chances of resuming detente with Western Europe, clearly high on Moscow's list of priorities, will be greatly strengthened. That the process of ideological tightening may further alienate some foreign Communist parties is a risk the Kremlin is prepared to bear in the coming decade.

Economic Interests

Unlike Soviet security, political, and ideological concerns, Moscow's economic interests in Eastern Europe have undergone significant change since the Communist seizure of power after World War II. It is generally agreed that one Soviet objective in the early postwar period was to utilize the resources of Eastern Europe for aiding the USSR's economic recovery and development. As a result, the Cold War period witnessed a massive transfer of resources from Eastern Europe to the Soviet Union, which engaged in a large-scale economic exploitation of the region. Moreover, individual East European countries were forced by the Kremlin to divert scarce resources from civilian to military uses in order to create an impressive armaments industry to strengthen Soviet defense potential.

The crude Soviet economic exploitation of Eastern Europe came to an end with the death of Stalin. Faced with growing popular discontent in the region, manifested in the Polish and Hungarian upheavals of 1956, Stalin's successors apparently concluded that, at least for the time being, they should give priority to the political and economic viability of East European regimes over ideological cohesion. This meant that individual East European countries were allowed greater autonomy in the conduct of economic policy. To be sure, the Kremlin did not relinquish its control over the economies of Eastern

Europe; the resurrected Council for Mutual Economic Assistance was given the task of coordinating economic policies of the member states under Moscow's supervision.

The 1960s witnessed the first significant downturn in East European economic performance, which had two important consequences. On the one hand, several countries initiated reforms of their economic systems. On the other, the USSR decided to continue supplying its clients with increasing quantities of raw materials at favorable prices. Both decisions illustrated Soviet concern with the economic viability of East European economies as a precondition of political stability of the region. Moreover, East European economies benefited the Soviet Union in at least two additional ways: as suppliers of scarce ("hard") commodities and as conduits for technologically advanced goods imported from the West for transshipment to the USSR.

Despite the reforms the East European economies continued to falter during the 1970s. The different regimes tried to counteract the decline in economic performance by modernizing their industrial base with the help of Western credits, but the emerging worldwide energy crisis, economic recession in the West, incompetence, and unwise decisions resulted in the accumulation of a huge hard currency debt without corresponding improvement in the economic performance of individual East European countries.

In the meantime, the Kremlin reasserted its economic priorities in Eastern Europe. The crisis in Czechoslovakia in 1968 persuaded Moscow to revise its earlier benign attitude with regard to East European economic reforms and to insist on stricter political controls of economic experiments. More importantly, the Soviet Union decided to use its growing economic leverage in order to extract East European conformity to Moscow's political and economic goals. With the Soviet rise to globalism, the Kremlin began increasingly to utilize individual East European countries as proxies in different parts of the world and to use its economic leverage, especially oil, to reward its clients in Eastern Europe for their support of Soviet foreign policy objectives. Moreover, Moscow forced the various countries to contribute resources, such as labor and capital, for development of new sources of raw materials on Soviet territory in the form of joint investment projects. Here again the continuing deliveries of scarce materials, principally oil, were tied to East European contribution to these projects. Whenever necessary, the Kremlin also used its leverage to assist regimes faced with economic difficulties and popular discontent, as illustrated by emergency aid to the Gierek regime in Poland in the fall of 1976.

The principal form of Soviet economic leverage on Eastern Europe has been and is "implicit trade subsidies," whereby the USSR supplies Eastern Europe with raw materials at below–world market prices and purchases East European manufactured goods at above–world market prices. The Soviet Union is willing to subsidize Eastern Europe in return for what Michael Marrese and Jan Vaňous call "unconventional gains from trade," defined as comprising various East European contributions to Soviet security and defense, such as military bases, transportation facilities, military manpower, defense industries, continued support of Soviet policy goals elsewhere, and a host of other forms of political and ideological support.[11] From 1960 to 1980 the chief recipients of Soviet largesse were East Germany, Czechoslovakia, and Poland, while Romania received virtually no benefits. The per capita figures, which show Bulgaria first, followed by East Germany, Czechoslovakia, and Hungary, with Poland and Romania at the bottom, are even more revealing. Although the findings of Marrese and Vaňous are open to questions on methodological and other grounds, the rankings of the individual countries correspond roughly to what we know of Soviet perceptions of the particular states' relative contributions to Soviet policy goals.

One of the contributions that has recently come to light has been growing use of East European countries as providers of "aid" and/or "loans" to Soviet Third World clients, such as Angola, Cuba, Syria, and Vietnam, in the form of foreign trade surpluses. While the available data are difficult to attain and equally difficult to interpret, the general trend appears unmistakable. Moreover, the upward trend and the overall magnitude of East European subsidies to Third World countries may be understated, since the East European countries, like the Soviet Union, offer concessionary prices for their exports and/or pay above–world market prices for their imports.

As was pointed out above, the economic situation has been deteriorating throughout Eastern Europe in the past few years. This is the most volatile problem that the Soviet Union will have to face in the coming decade. In addition to the inherent weaknesses of centrally planned economies, which are singularly inept at coping with economic difficulties, the East European countries are now paying the price for the failure of their economic strategy in the 1970s, which had two major objectives: rapidly expanding East-West trade, including technology transfer, as substitutes for comprehensive economic reforms, and increasing regime legitimacy by raising living standards. By the early 1980s it became clear that neither objective would be fulfilled: the rapid expansion in East-West trade succeeded mostly in generating huge hard currency debts that most countries have difficulty repaying, and the absence of economic reforms contributed to a stagnation rather than an increase in living standards, reducing rather than augmenting regime legitimacy. Moreover, deterioration of terms of trade vis-à-vis both the USSR and the West was an important factor in the economic slowdown in several East European countries in the late 1970s, notably in Czechoslovakia, East Germany, and Hungary.

A brief country-by-country survey shows that all East European states are suffering from declining growth rates and their consequences. If one takes into account population growth and the fact that official East European statistics tend to exaggerate production data, it is likely that several countries in the region are now in recession.

The Bulgarian economy seems to have suffered relatively little, at least thus far. The official data indicate a fairly dynamic growth in the past few years, but the plan for 1981–85 suggests more modest growth, compared with the 1976–80 period. Even though the various official data are open to suspicion, there is little doubt that in contrast to other countries Bulgaria has generally been successful.

This is certainly not the case with Czechoslovakia, where evidence abounds that the economy has been faltering in the last few years. While Czechoslovakia has undoubtedly been more affected by the Polish crisis, particularly by Poland's failure to deliver coal and other raw materials, as well as by the shortfalls of energy deliveries from Romania, the preeminent reason for Czechoslovak economic difficulties has been the failure of the post-1968 economic strategy of "normalization," a failure Czechoslovak economists now admit freely.

The East German economy is clearly the healthiest in the region, but it is apparently headed for serious strains in the coming years, although probably not so serious as elsewhere in Eastern Europe. While the recent official data most likely overstate progress, the country's economic performance has been rather impressive. The danger signals include a large planned increase in productivity that appears quite unrealistic, a cutback in Soviet oil deliveries, and a high planned expansion in foreign trade, presumably to allow East Germany to begin closing the gap in its hard currency accounts and repaying its foreign debt. This means that further improvement in the living standard is highly unlikely in the near future.

There are indications that the Hungarian economy has shown little if any progress in the past few years and that the immediate future does not appear much brighter. The critical problem facing Hungary and most other countries in the region is the escalating cost of energy and raw materials, imported primarily from the USSR, which must be offset by an ever larger volume of exports, resulting in a serious drain on the country's economy. Together with Czechoslovakia and East Germany, Hungary was subjected to a 10 percent reduction in Soviet oil deliveries in 1982, which will not make the overall economic situation easier.[12]

Much has been written about Poland's shattered economy, and only some of its highlights need mention. Thus, the country's national income is now approximately 20 percent below the peak level attained in 1978. If the projected decline for 1982 holds true, national income will drop to slightly less than two-thirds of the 1978 level.[13] With the possible exception of agriculture, all sectors and activities, such as industrial output, capital investment, household consumption, and foreign trade, show steep declines, with little improvement in sight.

Poland aside, Romania has the shakiest economy in Eastern Europe. Romanian industry and agriculture are performing poorly and suffer greatly from a growing shortage of energy and raw materials. As in the case of some other countries, Romania projects a steep increase in exports, which is unquestionably related to the escalating burden of the country's hard currency debt. This is bound to have a serious impact on Romania's domestic consumption, already thought to be the lowest on a per capita basis in the region, even assuming that such an expansion of exports could be easily achieved or achieved at all in the current world economic environment, which is doubtful.

Yugoslavia has also been encountering serious difficulties, not unlike those faced by the CMEA members. For the first time in many years there are shortages of basic consumer goods and foodstuffs, and Yugoslavia suffers from one of the highest inflation rates in Europe, East or West. The country has also felt the impact of the worldwide energy crisis and of the growing burden of its hard currency debt, which on a per capita basis is close to that of Poland. Here again the prospects of an early turnaround do not appear bright.

There is no doubt that the economic situation in Eastern Europe has exerted considerable impact on Soviet domestic and foreign policy. The Soviets have long been concerned with the viability and legitimacy of Communist regimes in the region. They are aware of the close correlation between economic well being and regime legitimacy and of the latter's crucial role in the attainment of Moscow's security, political, and ideological objectives not only in Eastern Europe but in the world at large. The Kremlin realizes that an economically healthy and efficient Eastern Europe is indispensable for validation of its cherished claim of the universality of the Soviet model. The latter's implications for Soviet foreign policy toward the Third World and Western Europe are obvious. This is one reason why Moscow has been willing to subsidize Eastern Europe's economies, despite the fact that the standard of living in many countries in the region is markedly higher than that in the Soviet Union.

Soviet options for absorbing, deflecting, ignoring, or otherwise coping with their allies' economic troubles in the 1980s can be divided roughly into five categories:

(a) *"Business as usual."* This implies continuing Soviet subsidies (if gradually declining) for Eastern Europe's purchases of energy and other raw materials and continuing Soviet overpayment for imports of East European machinery and equipment.

How long is the Soviet Union prepared to continue subsidizing the East European economies? It has been clear for some time that the Kremlin has been intent on reducing and eventually eliminating the subsidies, which must annoy some elements of the Soviet elite, not to mention the Soviet population, which has been very much aware of the generally higher standard of living in Eastern Europe compared with the USSR. Even though the substantial Soviet economic aid to Poland since the beginning of the crisis in the summer of 1980 would suggest that the Soviet Union was greatly concerned with Poland's possible economic collapse and its political repercussions and that it was willing to pay a heavy price to stave off disintegration of the Polish economy, Moscow's economic aid to Warsaw was somewhat restrained, implying a limit to the Kremlin's readiness to underwrite its clients indefinitely.

Another indication that the Soviet Union has recently become reluctant to bail out its ailing East European allies has been the apparent failure of the so-called umbrella theory. Western creditors have been convinced that there was no serious danger of any East European debtor's defaulting on its obligations, since the USSR was standing by, ready to extend its financial "umbrella" to help out its delinquent East European clients to maintain CMEA solvency and credibility and to attract further Western credits. This has not happened, even though both Poland and Romania have been in technical default on their debts. As a result, the West has become most reluctant to grant further credits not only to those countries in obvious trouble but also to countries such as East Germany and Hungary whose repayment record thus far has been largely unblemished. So far, Moscow has shown no sign of being willing to extend its "umbrella," which may mean that it was disenchanted with its allies' record and performance, that it was prepared to leave the East European countries to fend for themselves, and that it believed the West would not allow these economies to collapse.

To some extent the question of future Soviet subsidies may answer itself if world market prices of oil and other raw materials remain constant or even show a decline, which was the case in 1981–82. This would narrow the differential between world market prices and prices charged by the USSR, and hence reduce if not eliminate the subsidies. Another possibility may be a Soviet decision to raise prices to the level of world market prices. Finally, Moscow may divert some of its exports earmarked for Eastern Europe, which would also diminish the amount of subsidies. This happened in early 1982, when the Soviet oil shipments at intra-CMEA prices intended for Czechoslovakia, East Germany, and Hungary were cut 10 percent, supposedly to increase Soviet deliveries to Poland and Western Europe. While the USSR cannot easily influence the level of world market prices of its exports, it obviously can reduce its shipments to CMEA and increase the flow of Soviet oil and natural gas to the West, especially if its economic situation requires increased amounts of hard currency imports. The rather dismal performance of the Soviet economy suggests that the USSR may be forced in the near future to expand its imports from the West to the detriment of Eastern Europe.

A reduction of Soviet subsidies would not mean that the Kremlin would agree to a modification of the "business as usual" equation and would revise its expectations regarding Eastern Europe's obligation to advance the "socialist cause," whether through the strengthening of the Warsaw Pact, the proliferation of CMEA joint investment projects on Soviet territory, or economic and/or military assistance to Soviet clients in the Third World.

(b) *Greater tolerance or even encouragement of economic reforms.* Here the goal would be to promote more efficient use of resources and improved productivity and quality of production in order to boost the competitiveness and self-sufficiency of the East European economies. This would imply a willingness on Moscow's part to countenance the region's progressive interdependence with world markets as a way of easing the burden that those countries impose on the Soviet economy. As mentioned earlier, the USSR raised no objection to extension of the Hungarian NEM in 1979 and more recently allowed Bulgaria to embark on a highly touted economic reform. There was also no indication of Soviet opposition to a package of reforms approved by the Polish parliament in February 1982, which at least on paper is designed to move the Polish economy along Hungarian lines.

However, any inference that these developments signal a meaningful shift in Soviet attitudes toward genuine economic reforms in Eastern Europe is at best premature, if not unfounded, for at least two reasons. One, discussed above, concerns Moscow's fear of potential political repercussions of reforms and its refusal to break down bureaucratic resistance at a time when the USSR is putting a high premium on stability and cohesion.

The other reason is that innovations sufficiently comprehensive to generate measurable improvement in economic performance and efficiency across the board would entail a reorientation of priorities in favor of domestic consumer and service sectors at the expense of investment and heavy industry. Moreover, genuine changes would also include a massive price reform, as well as the introduction of rational criteria for estimating efficiency and profitability. All such measures would be in direct conflict with Soviet expectations of the role the East European economies should play within CMEA, which is likely to become increasingly important as a tool of Moscow-directed closer economic integration of the region. While the Kremlin is presumably interested in greater economic efficiency in Eastern Europe, it is even more concerned with securing East European contributions to solving Soviet problems and to providing aid to Soviet Third World clients. The two objectives are not easily reconcilable.

(c) *Diversion of additional Soviet resources to Eastern Europe.* This is the least likely of all options over the long run, not only because the USSR feels that it has been exploited by the individual East European countries but also because Moscow's own economic problems are so serious. It is clear that the Kremlin would be willing to divert scarce resources from either domestic or foreign uses only in times of dire emergency, such as the recent Polish crisis, but even then it would put a ceiling on the amount of support it would grant. It should be noted that Soviet attempts to persuade CMEA members to shore up the Polish economy in 1981 proved unsuccessful.

(d) *Expansion of Eastern Europe's trade with the Third World.* The Soviet Union as a global power, stymied in its quest for influence in the developed world, may turn to and become more assertive in the less developed regions of the world. In addition to challenging Western influence, the Kremlin may contemplate establishing closer links between Eastern Europe and the Third World in order to harness the resources of the latter for the purpose of alleviating the economic hardships faced by the former.

This may take different forms: some key oil-producing states that already have close ties to the USSR, such as Libya and Iraq, might be persuaded to join CMEA; a joint Soviet-East European effort might be made to bring additional countries producing raw materials, such as Iran, into Moscow's orbit. This remains the most speculative of all the options, yet the combination of Soviet and East European economic strains and both historical and current policy objectives may have considerable appeal to some factions in the Kremlin, for which such an option would accomplish two goals: helping Eastern Europe without putting additional burden on Soviet resources and, at the same time, reducing Western influence in the Third World.

(e) *Rejuvenating CMEA.* Throughout the 1970s CMEA has been floundering, despite the introduction of new programs intended to strengthen economic cooperation, such as the Long-Term Target Program. Despite official commitment to expanding intra-CMEA trade, the member countries were primarily if not solely interested in maintaining close bilateral trade relations with the Soviet Union in order to ensure a steady (and growing) supply of raw materials. As a result, frequent interruptions or reductions occurred in mutually agreed deliveries of key commodities within CMEA. This had a highly negative impact on economic performance, especially of those member-countries which relied on an uninterrupted flow of imports from the other CMEA members for fulfillment of their plans. The difficulties Czechoslovakia and East Germany faced because of reduced shipments of coal and energy from Poland and Romania are a good illustration of the problems plaguing CMEA.

One may speculate that looking for ways to alleviate the pervasive economic crisis in Eastern Europe might lead the Kremlin to consider rejuvenating and strengthening CMEA through a combination of new incentives and tougher sanctions. What form these may take is not clear, but the circumstances for the introduction of new measures appear highly favorable. The growing difficulties in obtaining new Western credits will force most countries in the region to reduce their imports from the West. They will have little choice but to turn inwards and attempt to obtain the necessary goods from their CMEA partners, even though such a "turning inward" strategy may prove exceedingly difficult to implement. Another possible option, namely an increase in trade between Eastern Europe and the Asian Communist countries, particularly China, offers some opportunities, but its future is highly uncertain, to say the least.

The above five options may be entertained by a Kremlin increasingly concerned with the potential political reverberations of the economic difficulties its East European allies encounter and willing to help them out in some fashion in order to prevent repetition of another societal crisis in the region. However, one should not exclude the possibility that a new Soviet leadership might assume a diametrically different stance toward Eastern Europe. Conceivably, the new occupants of the Kremlin may be less apprehensive about the political repercussions of economic troubles in the region and may even be eager to utilize the resources of Eastern Europe to prop up the faltering Soviet economy.

The latter option would not necessarily mean a return to the old methods of crass and open economic exploitation that characterized Soviet-East European economic relations during the Stalinist period. It may instead mean utilizing Soviet economic leverage to extract additional resources from CMEA members, by demanding higher contributions to joint investment projects located in the Soviet Union, by charging higher prices for Soviet exports, or by introducing new forms of bilateral or multilateral cooperation.

The East European CMEA members are already making a substantial contribution to joint investment projects. Faced with a critical shortage of key raw materials, they may be forced to provide additional contributions in the form of manpower, capital goods, or hard currency loans. Some East European countries have been complaining that the use of "transferable rubles" as means of payment in intra-CMEA trade has provided the USSR a convenient tool to exploit its partners. If this is true, Moscow may further manipulate the ruble exchange rates for its benefit. The Kremlin may also decide to accelerate the increase in Soviet prices of raw materials and to utilize the two CMEA banks for its own purposes. A recent move by the Soviets to "lease" Polish plants to produce for the Soviet economy provides an example of a new form of bilateral cooperation. The Polish side will supply plant, capital, and labor, while the Soviet side will provide all or most of the essential materials. The details of this arrangement have not been publicized, which may imply that its major benefit will accrue to the Soviet Union.

Whether Moscow will adopt the "get tough with Eastern Europe" alternative at the expense of a "softer" approach is anybody's guess. Until now the USSR has been rather selective in utilizing its economic leverage to extract resources or impose political and ideological conformity in the region. Even at the height of the Polish crisis only one instance was reported of Soviet economic pressure on the Warsaw regime to force it to take stronger measures against "Solidarity."[14] However, it may be assumed that, especially since the energy price explosion in 1973, Moscow has fairly routinely used veiled or implicit threats to reduce deliveries of Soviet oil and other materials to achieve political or economic goals. If the Kremlin opts in favor of a tougher economic policy toward Eastern Europe, it will most likely resist the temptation to use the most drastic measures in favor of less visible manipulative devices.

Ultimately the choice between "hard" and "soft" policies will be determined by the Kremlin's perception of the overall political and economic situation in the region, as well as of its own political, economic, and security requirements, not to mention the state of East-West relations and the general international atmosphere. Over the years Moscow has become better informed about conditions in Eastern Europe and more aware of the complex character of the situation in individual countries. As a result, its policy toward the region has become more sophisticated than in the past. Hence we may assume that the Soviet leadership will decide its policies only after considerable soul-searching and thorough examination of available options and their potential consequences. The ambivalent and hesitant Soviet posture during the crisis in Poland illustrates this point.

Thus, if the Kremlin concludes that it was the rather relaxed Soviet stance on developments in Eastern Europe in the 1970s which led directly or indirectly to the Polish upheaval, Moscow may opt for political and ideological cohesion instead of economic viability. If this is the case, we may expect tougher Soviet policies on all fronts, including the economic one. This choice will be made easier if East-West relations continue to worsen, forcing the USSR to adopt a more defensive posture and tighten its controls over its East European allies.

Conclusion

The purpose of this essay was to examine and analyze developments in Eastern Europe and the influence they are likely to have on Soviet foreign and domestic policies in the 1980s. Since I concluded at the outset that events in Eastern Europe have had only a marginal impact on Soviet domestic politics, the focus of the essay is on Eastern Europe as an input or a determinant of Soviet behavior on the international scene. Since one cannot divorce the region's influence on the foreign policy of the USSR from Moscow's attitudes, interests, and objectives concerning Eastern Europe, I have also investigated Soviet policies toward the region and hypothesized about their future course.

In discussing the East European inputs into Soviet foreign policy decision making as well as Soviet goals and policies in the area, I had to settle first the fundamental question likely to determine Soviet–East European relations in the 1980s, namely, whether Moscow considered Eastern Europe, except for Albania and Yugoslavia, an "internal" or an "external" matter. Settling this crucial issue obviously influenced my judgment and perception of both East European policy inputs and Soviet policy objectives and interests.

I concluded that over the years the Soviet Union has increasingly regarded Eastern Europe as an internal matter and that this perception is bound to condition the Soviet–East European relationship in the foreseeable future. This also means that on one hand, the USSR will be highly sensitive to developments and processes in Eastern Europe that may threaten the status quo, and on the other hand, Soviet interests in the region are qualitatively different from Moscow's concerns with regard to Communist clients in other parts of the world. This, in turn, suggests that Soviet interests, which for the sake of convenience we divided into four major categories, security, political, ideological, and economic, have a much broader meaning than their "Western" equivalents. Thus, the Soviet notion of security not only comprises conventional strategic-military concerns but spills over into political and economic realms. The same is true for the other three categories: Moscow's economic objectives are closely related to important security, ideological, and political issues, and Soviet polit-

ical concerns have equally important ideological, economic, and security aspects.

On the strength of our examination of past and present Soviet–
East European relations, I come to the conclusion that their future
course, at least in the short run, is likely to be characterized by greater
Soviet assertiveness, aimed at reinforcing its domination of the region
and at preventing repetition of Polish-type crises. This may take different forms. One is likely to be a strengthening of the Warsaw Pact,
which would include greater East European contribution to its modernization and also greater involvement of the individual countries as
Soviet military proxies around the world. On the political level, the
Kremlin is bound to pay greater attention to the leadership selection
processes, especially in the 1980s, when several East European parties
are destined to choose new leaders. In the realm of ideology, the
Soviets are likely to put greater emphasis on the principle of the
"leading role" of the ruling parties in the respective countries. Finally,
in the economic sphere we may expect a decline in the level of Soviet
economic support for East European allies, Moscow's aid being reserved only for emergency situations. We may witness also rejuvena-
tion of the hitherto largely moribund CMEA and, last but not least,
greater Soviet insistence on larger East European contributions to
easing Moscow's economic and defense burdens.

Altogether, I strongly believe that the Soviet Union will retain its
hold on Eastern Europe, regardless of its mounting cost. In this respect I fully agree with Zvi Gitelman, who stated some time ago:

> Politically, Eastern Europe has been a mixed blessing to the USSR. The
> existence of socialist systems in the area has increased the size, and hence
> the prestige and quantitative power, of the socialist camp led by the
> Soviet Union, but the political instability of the area . . . has imposed on
> the USSR the role of policeman. . . . But even if the costs of association
> with Eastern Europe along present lines become very high in economic
> and political terms, the costs of dissociation might well be higher.[15]

In this overall context, the Kremlin is likely to treat different East
European countries differently, and in turn the individual countries
in the region will exert a differential impact on the USSR. It may be
taken for granted that Moscow does not and will not view all East
European countries in the same light: militarily and politically some
Soviet allies are and will be perceived as more important than others.
From the economic standpoint, a clear-cut division of labor exists
among CMEA members, based on their size and population, resource
base, and industrial profile. A good illustration of the Soviet ranking
of the importance of the individual countries is the previously mentioned estimate of absolute and relative Soviet implicit trade subsidies

granted to each of them in the past twenty years. This ranking is not likely to change in the immediate future.

Finally, in attempting to chart the future course of Soviet-East European relations we must recognize the presence of two unknowns that strongly affect our prognosis. One concerns domestic developments in various East European countries. The other is the state of East-West relations, especially the relationship between the Soviet Union and the United States.

The conclusion that emerges from analysis of internal situations in the individual East European countries suggests that the region is bound to face increasing difficulties at home. The economic situation is likely to deteriorate in the 1980s, contributing to an escalation of social tensions. The growing economic difficulties may result in imposition of tighter controls rather than the introduction of comprehensive reforms. The problems individual countries face will be compounded by the impending leadership change in several states, which is likely to bring a new generation of leaders more attuned and responsive to Soviet wishes. This, in turn, will give rise to growing popular dissatisfaction and potential political destabilization, which, for once, may affect the region as a whole rather than a single country.

Insofar as East-West relations are concerned, the demise of East-West detente, accelerated by Soviet intervention in Afghanistan, the crisis in Poland, and the change in the White House in 1980, has had a very serious impact on Eastern Europe and its relations with the Soviet Union. The key factor was obviously the rapid cooling of relations between Washington and Moscow and the adoption of a tough course vis-à-vis the Kremlin by the Reagan administration, especially after the imposition of martial law in Poland in December 1981. This is not the place to discuss the rationale for American policy, but it is clear that while its main target is and will be the Soviet Union, the main victim is likely to be Eastern Europe. At least a few U.S. policy makers who for the past twenty years or so have engaged in a dual-track policy of "peaceful engagement" in, and "bridge building" to, Eastern Europe and who until the most recent period raised no objection to granting large volumes of American and West European credits to individual East European countries have now become converted to the view that it was all a mistake. Some policy makers have also concluded that Western credit largesse represented a gross miscalculation and that not the West but the Soviet Union should bail out its allies in their hour of need. This would put the burden of supporting Eastern Europe squarely on Moscow's shoulders, force the Kremlin to divert scarce resources from its defense sector, and thus automatically reduce the Soviet potential for waging war. If worsen-

ing economic conditions in Eastern Europe lead eventually to outbreaks of Polish-type crises resulting in Soviet military intervention,
this would also benefit the United States by weakening the Soviet
defense posture.

Thus, there is little doubt that developments in Poland and in the
rest of Eastern Europe are bound to influence Soviet foreign policy
vis-à-vis the United States. Washington is on record stipulating that
the lifting of martial law in Poland, including release of political prisoners and recognition of "Solidarity," is a precondition for removal of
sanctions and "normalization" of relations with Poland and the USSR.
Moscow must decide whether an improvement in U.S.-Soviet relations is worth risking the return to pre–martial law conditions in
Poland. In light of the far-reaching consequences of the Polish crisis
for the rest of Eastern Europe, the Kremlin is not likely to risk
another conflagration in Poland in the 1980s.

While the Soviet Union may not seek better relations with the
United States, it is clearly interested in a renewed rapprochement
with Western Europe, especially now that the NATO alliance shows
signs of considerable strain. The Kremlin must be aware of the fact
that its intervention in Afghanistan did not overly disturb the West
Europeans, but that the Polish crisis has had a much greater impact.
Still, Western Europe's reaction to the imposition of martial law in
Poland has been less critical than that of the United States, and Moscow may take this opportunity to drive another wedge between Washington and the rest of NATO. Western Europe is clearly interested in
the resumption of a dialogue with the USSR, but not at any price.
Here again the situation in Poland and in the rest of Eastern Europe
plays an important part. While such key West European countries as
West Germany, France, and Italy do not insist on the return to the
status quo prior to December 1981, they do expect some relaxation of
martial law by the Warsaw regime as a condition of renewed detente
with the Soviet Union. Hence, the Kremlin must decide whether putting pressure on the Polish leaders to loosen military rule will be more
than compensated by the benefit of improved relations with Western
Europe. The possibility of detaching Western Europe from the
United States, thus weakening NATO, perhaps mortally, must be
very tempting for Moscow, particularly during the sensitive TNF
negotiations at Geneva, and one cannot exclude the possibility of such
a move on the part of the USSR.

What about Eastern Europe's influence on the conduct of Soviet
foreign policy in other parts of the globe? Greater Soviet emphasis on
closer cohesion and conformity in Eastern Europe is likely to be wel-
comed by such Communist countries as Cuba, which has been
strongly critical of what Havana has considered a relaxation of Soviet

control over Eastern Europe and the negative consequences this implied for the future of the Communist camp. There is evidence that China has also been uneasy about developments in Poland. Reassertion of Soviet authority in the bloc cannot help restoring the image of the USSR as a resolute world power that intends to maintain its grip on Eastern Europe. Whether it will help Moscow in its efforts to normalize relations with Beijing is difficult to predict, but such a possibility cannot be excluded.

It is also likely that many Soviet clients in the Third World will be pleased with the Kremlin's determination to reassert its control of Eastern Europe. For years these countries have benefited from military aid and economic subsidies provided by the East European states acting as Soviet surrogates, and they want this arrangement to continue in the 1980s.

The above illustrates the dilemma faced by the Kremlin, which has to choose between possible enhancement of its foreign policy and imposing tighter control over its domain in Eastern Europe. The presence of a stable and cohesive Eastern Europe is likely to improve the image and prestige of the Soviet Union and reinforce its policy toward the Third World, but at the same time it will inhibit Moscow's relations with the United States and, possibly, Western Europe. The continuation of what Fritz Ermarth calls the "troubles of empire" is likely to have the opposite effect. It will weaken the Soviet stance toward the Communist camp outside Europe and toward Moscow's Third World clients, but it may contribute to an improvement in U.S.-Soviet relations and to a return of detente between the USSR and Western Europe. Faced with that choice, the Kremlin will opt in favor of maintaining a tight grip on Eastern Europe. Hence relations between the Soviet Union and the West are not likely to show significant improvement in the 1980s.

NOTES

1. See, for example, Morris Bornstein, Zvi Gitelman, and William Zimmerman, eds., *East-West Relations and the Future of Eastern Europe* (London: George Allen & Unwin, 1981); Karen Dawisha and Philip Hanson, eds., *Soviet-East European Dilemmas* (London: Heinemann, 1981); Paul Marer, "The Economies of Eastern Europe and Soviet Foreign Policy," and Andrzej Korbonski, "Eastern Europe as an Internal Determinant of Soviet Foreign Policy," in Seweryn Bialer, ed., *The Domestic Context of Soviet Foreign Policy* (Boulder, Colo.: Westview Press, 1981), pp. 271–332; Ronald H. Linden, ed., *The Foreign Policies of Eastern Europe* (New York: Praeger, 1980); and Sarah M. Terry, ed., *Soviet Policies in Eastern Europe* (forthcoming).

2. Zbigniew Brzezinski, *The Soviet Bloc*, revised and enlarged edition (Cambridge, Mass.: Harvard University Press, 1967), pp. 51–58.

3. William Zimmerman, "Soviet–East European Relations in the 1980s and the Changing International System," in Bornstein et al., *East-West Relations and the Future of Eastern Europe,* p. 91.

4. Donna Bahry and Cal Clark, "Political Conformity and Economic Dependence in Eastern Europe: The Impact of Trade with the West," in Linden, *The Foreign Policies of Eastern Europe,* pp. 135–58.

5. For an interesting discussion of this issue, see Zvi Gitelman, "The Impact on the Soviet Union of the East European Experience in Modernization," in Charles Gati, ed., *The Politics of Modernization in Eastern Europe* (New York: Praeger, 1974), pp. 256–74.

6. James F. Brown first drew attention to the inherent incompatibility of Soviet goals of cohesion and viability in Eastern Europe. For details, see his "Relations Between the Soviet Union and Its Eastern European Allies: A Survey," *RAND Report R-1742-PR,* 1975, *passim.*

7. The literature on the Warsaw Pact is by now quite extensive. For the most recent studies, see A. Ross Johnson, "The Warsaw Pact: Soviet Military Policy in Eastern Europe," *RAND Paper P-6583,* July 1981; Christopher D. Jones, *Soviet Influence in Eastern Europe: Political Autonomy and the Warsaw Pact* (New York: Praeger, 1981); and Andrzej Korbonski, "The Warsaw Treaty After Twenty-five Years: An Entangling Alliance or an Empty Shell?" in Robert W. Clawson and Lawrence S. Kaplan, eds., *The Warsaw Pact: Political Purposes and Military Means* (Wilmington, Del.: Scholarly Resources, 1982), pp. 3–25.

8. For details, see Dale R. Herspring and Ivan Volgyes, "Political Reliability in the Eastern European Warsaw Pact Armies," *Armed Forces and Society,* VI, no. 2, Winter 1980, pp. 270–96.

9. John C. Campbell, "Soviet Policy in Eastern Europe: An Overview," in Terry, *The Soviet Union and Eastern Europe.*

10. Zygmunt Bauman, "Twenty Years After: The Crisis of Soviet-Type Societies," *Problems of Communism,* XX, no. 6, November-December 1971, pp. 45–53.

11. Michael Marrese and Jan Vaňous, *Implicit Subsidies and Non-Market Benefits in Soviet Trade with Eastern Europe* (Berkeley, Calif.: University of California Institute of International Studies, forthcoming).

12. David Brand and Steve Mufson, "Oil-Price Slump Puts Pressure on the Soviets to Raise Export Levels," *Wall Street Journal,* May 11, 1982.

13. "Gospodarka w 1981 roku," *Zycie Gospodarcze* (Warsaw), no. 3, February 2, 1982, and Andrzej Olechowski, "Katastrofa i ratunek," *Polityka-Eksport-Import* (Warsaw), no. 1, March 1982.

14. John Darnton, "Polish Aide Says Soviet May Cut Key Supplies," *New York Times,* September 23, 1982.

15. Gitelman, "The Impact on the Soviet Union of the East European Experience in Modernization," pp. 270–71.

7

★

The World Outside

Adam B. Ulam

The Anatomy of Soviet Policy Making

General Considerations

CONTEMPLATING THE vast quantity of Kremlinology produced in this country since World War II, a layman might well paraphrase Marx's famous thesis on Feuerbach and complain that various experts have only interpreted the Soviet Union in different ways, while the urgent need is to find out how its policies can be changed. There have been many prescriptions as to how this country might influence the USSR through its own policies to alter what for most Americans has been a most disquieting pattern of Soviet behavior on the world scene.

But before trying to formulate such prescriptions, we must first of all try to understand the process of Soviet policy making. To repeat what this author wrote in another study, "The student of Soviet affairs has as his first task to be neither hopeful nor pessimistic, but simply to state the facts and tendencies of Russian politics. It is when he begins to see in certain political trends the inevitabilities of the future and when he superimposes upon them his own conclusions about the desirable policies of America towards the USSR that he is courting trouble."[1] American policy making ought to profit by, but cannot be a substitute for, a dispassionate analysis of Soviet motivations and actions.

Having identified the fulcrum of the Soviet political system, the twenty-odd full and alternate members of the Politburo and those Central Committee secretaries who are outside it, we still need to know more about how this group operates and about its relationship to the wider Soviet political elite and to the people at large. For our

I should like to express my appreciation to David E. Albright, Raymond W. Baker, Gerrit Gong, Angela Stent, and Rebecca Strode.

purposes, it is especially important to establish some analytical guidelines about how the inner ruling group arrives at its decisions on foreign policy and to what extent it is susceptible to changes in the international environment.

Elitist and secretive as the process of Soviet decision making is in general, it is especially so when it comes to foreign policy. One may find occasionally in the Soviet press and in the utterances of lower officials fairly far-reaching criticisms, e.g., of the country's economic system and performance. It is almost inconceivable for such public discussion to take place in connection with any major aspect of the Soviet stand on international affairs. This taboo is also observed concerning past foreign policies of the USSR.

Those who see the Soviet system moving toward pluralism or who hypothesize about the growing influence of the military in decision making thus disregard the exclusive prerogative of decision making to which the inner ruling group, especially in the Brezhnev era, has held with such tenacity. Even Khrushchev, who intermittently attempted to enlarge his political base by using the Central Committee to curb his fellow oligarchs, jealously guarded the party's monopoly of power. He could speak slightingly in the presence of foreigners about Andrei Gromyko, then "only" minister of foreign affairs, but not yet a member of the charmed circle; and he dismissed Marshal Zhukov largely because the marshal had helped him in his 1957 scrap with the Molotov faction, and it was intolerable that in the future a professional soldier should be allowed to interfere in settling disputes on the Soviet Olympus.

In their turn, Brezhnev and his colleagues have been especially insistent not only on preserving the party's role as the only source of political power, but on recouping the narrower oligarchy's prerogative of being the final arbiter in policy making. There is a Soviet equivalent of our National Security Council, but it is presided over *ex officio* by the General Secretary, and nothing entitles us to believe that it is more than an advisory body to the Politburo. Since 1964 the Central Committee has been relegated again to a forum where decisions of the top leadership are announced and perhaps explained in greater detail than they are to the public at large, but not debated. Emperor Paul I once told a foreign ambassador that the only important public figures in Russia were those to whom he talked, and even their influence disappeared once they were no longer in conversation with the sovereign. The only participants in the decision-making process in the USSR, outside the twenty-odd members of the inner circle, are those whom it chooses to consult, and only while it does so. Unless he is simultaneously a member of the Politburo, the status of the head of an important government branch—the armed forces, security, foreign ministry, or economic planning—is similar to that of a high civil servant in the West, rather than a minister and policy maker.

Because of its very rigidity, and in view of the average age of the ruling oligarchy, the pattern we just sketched is likely to become exposed to increasing strains in the future and might break down, at least temporarily, during a succession struggle or a situation like that in 1956–57 and the early 1960s. Then the inner group split into hostile factions and, especially on the latter occasion, the leader found himself increasingly out of tune with his senior colleagues.

For the present and immediate future we must assume, however, that the USSR will continue to be governed under a system where policy options and moves are freely discussed by and fully known only to some twenty-five people, and the ultimate decisions are made by an even smaller group—the thirteen or fifteen full members of the Politburo.

This being so, we have little reason to expect basic changes in the Soviet philosophy of foreign relations. The present leaders and their prospective successors have seen the Soviet Union develop from the backward, militarily and industrially weak state of the early 1920s to one of the two superpowers of the post-1945 world. They have been brought up in the belief that the Soviet Union's connection with the worldwide Communist movement has been a source of strength to their country, and only recently have they had occasion to have doubts on that score. Their formative years witnessed the Soviet system's survival of the ravages of terror and the tremendous human and material losses of World War II. As rising bureaucrats in the immediate postwar period, the people of the Politburo could observe how Soviet diplomacy managed to offset the Soviet Union's industrial and military inferiority vis-à-vis the principal capitalist state. Even when the country's resources had to be devoted mainly to the task of recovery from the war, the USSR still managed to advance its power and influence in the world at large.

In brief, very little in their experience or in the international picture as it has evolved during the past twenty years or so could have persuaded the Kremlin that its basic guidelines for dealing with the outside world need drastic revision. It has increasingly been the external power and influence of the USSR that has been used by propaganda addressed at the home front to demonstrate the viability and dynamism of the Soviet system and its historical legitimacy. Granted the essentially conservative approach of the present Soviet leadership toward international affairs, one could hardly imagine it responding to a specific internal emergency by contriving a dangerous international crisis. But the Kremlin still persists in seeking to impress upon its people the paradoxical dichotomy of world politics: the imperialist threat remains as great as ever, and yet the USSR is steadily growing more powerful. Both beliefs are seen as essential in preserving the cohesion of Soviet society. The average citizen is never to be dissuaded from seeing the capitalist world and especially its main power as a source of potential danger to his country and its allies. By the same token, he must not lose faith in the ability of his government and its armed forces to repel this threat and to ensure even in this nuclear age the security and greatness of the USSR and of the entire "socialist camp." It would take an extraordinary combination of domestic political, social, and economic pressures to form a critical mass capable of impelling the regime to change its outlook on world politics.

It is virtually impossible to conceive of the Soviet system's survival in its present form were its rulers to abandon explicitly, or even implicitly, the main premises behind their foreign policy. Practically every feature of Russian authoritarianism is ultimately rationalized in terms of the alleged foreign danger inherent in the existence of the "two struggling camps," one headed by the USSR and the other, the capitalist one, by America. Writing at the most hopeful period of detente and painting a very rosy picture of the future of Soviet-American relations, Georgi Arbatov still had to add the caveat, "There can be no question as to whether the struggle between the two systems would or would not continue. That struggle is historically unavoidable."[2] If the struggle continues, the Soviet citizen must be made to believe that his side is steadily forging ahead on the world stage. Otherwise, what can compensate him psychologically for his perception—increasingly unsuppressible—that life is freer and materially more abundant in the West?

To be sure, this official rationale of Soviet foreign policy becomes vulnerable in cases where its ideological premises cannot be readily reconciled with the nationalist ones, and it is mainly on that count that one can foresee the possibility of popular reactions at home affecting the course of foreign policy. Tito's apostasy could be dismissed by the Kremlin as being in itself not of great significance. The burdens inherent in standing armed guard over East Europe or in suppressing the Afghan insurgency have been explained in the official media by the necessity of warding off the class enemy and, less explicitly, in terms of Russia's historical mission and interests antedating the Revolution. All these developments could be interpreted as still not disproving the thesis that Communism is a natural ally and an obedient servant of the Soviet national interest.

However, the Sino-Soviet conflict has struck at the very heart of the ideology-national interest *Weltanschauung* of Soviet foreign policy. In his *Letter to the Soviet Leaders*, Solzhenitsyn formulated very cogently the essential dilemma that has confronted the Kremlin in public since the eruption of the dispute, in fact since Mao's forces conquered the mainland. It is another Communist state—and precisely because it is Communist, writes Solzhenitsyn—which has posed the greatest threat to Russia's future. Thus, even when it comes to the outside world, he charges, one can readily see how this false ideology has had disastrous consequences for the true interests and security of the Russian people and threatens it eventually with having to fight for survival. This is not the isolated opinion of a writer and dissident who abhors every aspect of Communism. Fear of China on account of its enormous size, vast industrial-military potential, and the nature of its regime and ruling philosophy is probably the most visceral reaction of the average Russian insofar as his outlook on world affairs is concerned. No other aspect of the regime's policy has had as wide approval among the Soviet population at large as its efforts to contain and isolate the other great Communist state.

It is important to note that even this problem has not been allowed to affect the official rationale of Soviet foreign policy. This rationale is still couched in terms inherited from the era when the world Communist movement was monolithic in its subservience to Moscow. When it first erupted in public, the Sino-Soviet dispute might have prompted a foreign observer to prophesy that its implications were bound to change not only the Kremlin's actual policies, but its whole approach to international situations. The confrontation between ideology and reality inherent in the clash ought to have led to a thorough reevaluation of the former, not merely as a justification, but also as an operating principle for foreign policies. The USSR should have abandoned even the pretense that what it was doing in Africa, the Near East, and other areas was in the furtherance of socialism.

Yet, in fact, such secularization of Soviet foreign policy has not taken place. One might object that the USSR has tried to cope with the Chinese problem without any ideological inhibitions. It has attempted to enlist the United States in a joint effort to stop or delay China's nuclear development. It has encouraged India to attack and fragment China's only major ally in Asia. The Kremlin viewed with equanimity the massacre of the pro-Beijing Indonesian Communist party, and it encouraged and helped Vietnam in its open defiance of its huge neighbor. Ideological kinship has not restrained the Soviet Union from hinting at times that it might have to resort to a preemptive strike against China.

Yet, for all such unsentimental measures and attitudes, the Soviet leadership has refused to draw what an outsider would consider the logical deductions of its predicament with China. The doctrine of the two camps is still as stoutly maintained as when the two great Communist powers were linked "by unshakeable friendship" and alliance against a potential capitalist aggressor. China's departure from the straight and narrow path of "proletarian internationalism" has been explained in official Soviet rhetoric as a temporary lapse, while even at the most hopeful periods of peaceful coexistence, the conflict with the capitalist world has been presented as an unavoidable and permanent feature of world politics. There have been fairly serious armed clashes along the Sino-Soviet border, and a sizable proportion of the Soviet armed forces is deployed along the frontier. However, those Russian military manuals accessible to the public discuss at length the dangers and various scenarios of conventional and nuclear warfare between the USSR and the capitalist powers, without even alluding to the possibility of war with another Communist power.

This bizarre pattern of behavior cannot be ascribed solely to the Soviet leaders' cynicism and ability to divorce their actions entirely from their words. Nor can it be attributed to some lingering ideological scruples. Given a truth serum, a Soviet statesman would readily confess that barring something very unexpected, the danger of unprovoked capitalist aggression against the USSR is virtually nil, while the possibility of China's some day advancing territorial and other claims on his country is very real indeed. The "immobilisme" of Soviet foreign policy doctrine finds its roots in the nature of the political system as a whole. The thirteen or so men at the apex of the Soviet power structure have to think of themselves not only as rulers of a national state, but also as high priests of a world cult, which in turn is the source of legitimacy for the system as a whole and for their own power in particular. Could that legitimacy and with it the present political structure of the Soviet Union endure, were its rulers to renounce one of the most basic operating tenets of Communist political philosophy?

To a Westerner it might appear that the regime could greatly strengthen itself by curtailing its expansionist policies abroad and by concentrating on raising the living standards of the Soviet people. It would gain in popularity, the argument would continue, by being more explicit about the real dimension of the problem the USSR faces in relation to China and putting in proper perspective the alleged threat from the West. But it is most unlikely that the present generation of leaders would or feels it could afford to heed such arguments. They remember how even Nikita Khrushchev's modest and clumsy attempts at domestic liberalization and at relieving the siege mentality of his countrymen had most unsettling effects on the party and society. Without a continuing sense of danger from abroad, economic improvement at home, far from being an effective remedy for political dissent, is in fact likely to make it more widespread. For the diehards within the elite, even some of the side effects of detente, such as increased contacts with and knowledge of the West, must have appeared potentially harmful, because they brought in their wake ideological pollution and threatened the stability and cohesion of Soviet society.

History has played an unkind trick on the masters of the USSR. Probably no other ruling oligarchy in modern times has been as pragmatically minded and power-oriented as the current Soviet one. (Compared to them, even Nikita Khrushchev, who joined the party in 1918 during the Civil War, showed some characteristics of a true believer.) Ironically, it is precisely because of power considerations that the rulers cannot disregard ideological constraints on their policies.

A superficial view of Soviet politics would lead us to believe that a Soviet statesman enjoys much greater freedom of action, especially in foreign affairs, than his Western counterpart. He can order and direct rather than having to plead or campaign for his program. If he has to persuade others, it is a small group rather than an unruly electorate or a partisan legislature. The Politburo's decisions are not hammered out in the full glare of publicity or subjected to immediate public debate and criticisms. Whatever the fears, hesitations, and divisions among the rulers, they seldom become known outside the precincts of the Kremlin. Hence how can a democracy avoid finding itself at a disadvantage when negotiating with the Kremlin? Neither budgetary constraints nor fear of public opinion can deflect Andropov and Company from a weapons policy or an action abroad which they believe necessary for their purposes and for the prestige and power of the USSR.

This picture, while correct in several details, is greatly misleading overall. The structure of the decision-making process in the USSR enables the Kremlin to be free from many constraints under which nonauthoritarian governments must operate. Yet the nature of the Soviet political system creates its own imperatives that the leaders must heed and that may make their choice among foreign policy options more difficult and cumbersome than is the case in a democracy. Superbly equipped as it is for moving rapidly and effectively on several fronts, the Soviet political mechanism has not shown equal capacity during the last twenty years for effectively braking the momentum of its policies once launched. Whether the Soviet political mechanism can develop such braking devices must be of special interest to any student or practitioner of international affairs.

The immediate background of Soviet policies in the 1980s lies in the series of agreements and understandings reached between the USSR and the United States, as well as other states of the Western bloc, which set up the foundations of what has come to be known as detente. It would be a gross oversimplification on our part to view detente simply as an attempt by the Kremlin to deceive the West or, conversely, as a definitive change in Moscow's philosophy of international affairs. Soviet leaders sought a temporary accommodation with the West and a consequent lowering of international tension for reasons inherent in their interpretation of the world scene as of 1970.

Even if undertaken solely as a tactical maneuver, detente was not cost-free for the Soviets. Domestically it gave more resonance to the voices of dissent and placed the government under the obligation of relaxing restrictions on Jewish emigration, a concession that would have been unthinkable a few years earlier. Abroad, it was bound to raise doubts and suspicions in the minds of Soviet clients and friends. Only a few weeks after the Nixon-Brezhnev summit, Anwar Sadat ordered some 20,000 Soviet military personnel out of Egypt, a step largely motivated by his conviction that his country's foreign policy now had to be more balanced between the two superpowers.

The Soviet policy makers' usual skill at having their cake and eating it too was thus put to a severe test. The 1972–73 period offers a convincing example of the Soviet Union's sensitivity to its antagonists' policies and of the importance it places on its perception of the overall condition of the noncommunist world. In 1972 the economy of the West as a whole was still flourishing and expanding. Political stability appeared to be returning to the United States. With his recent successes in the international field, Nixon was virtually sure of reelection. This political and economic strength of the West, as well as several other international developments, added up to compelling reasons for the Soviets to pull in their horns.

How long this restraint would have prevailed in the councils of the Kremlin and whether there was any possibility of a more fundamental alteration in Soviet foreign policy is something we shall never know. Within a year and a half of the inauguration of detente, the premises on which the Soviets' restraint had been based began to crumble. By the end of 1974 Moscow was bound to conclude that the West was not nearly so stable and strong politically or economically as it had appeared in 1972.

Beginning in 1974, the USSR became much less concerned about American reactions to its policies abroad, even those openly directed at undermining the influence and interests of the United States and its friends. Unlike the case of the 1973 Middle Eastern conflict, Soviet actions in Angola, Ethiopia, and South Yemen betrayed little hesitation or fear that they might bring effective American countermeasures, or even seriously damage overall Soviet-U.S. relations, thus bringing an end to the benefits the USSR was deriving from detente. To be sure, the Soviets have always been aware of how sensitive the United States is to what happens in the Middle East, and in comparison the average American knows little and cares less about Angola or South Yemen. However, what should have been the cause of alarm to American policy makers was not so much the targets but the character of Soviet activities in Africa.

Such activities were not merely another example of Soviet skill at scavenging amidst the debris of Western colonialism, and through ideological appeal or an alliance with the local dictator or oligarchy, wresting yet another country from its nonaligned or pro-Western position. Angola was the testing ground for a new technique of Soviet imperial expansion. The experiment was allowed to succeed and thus became a precedent for further employment of this technique. Nonnative, up to now Cuban, troops would be used to establish Soviet presence in the country and to maintain the pro-Soviet regime in power. Thus, wars of "national liberation" could be carried out and won by the pro-Soviet faction, because it was helped not only by Soviet arms and advisers, but also by massive infusion of Communist bloc troops! Had the general international situation remained similar to that of 1972–73, it is unlikely that the conservative-minded Brezhnev regime would have attempted such a daring innovation as projecting Soviet power into areas thousands of miles away from the USSR.

The reasons for the Kremlin's confidence that this innovative form of international mischief-making was not unduly risky were probably very similar to those that persuaded North Vietnam about the same time to launch a massive invasion and to occupy the south. A North Vietnamese general spelled out candidly the rationale of his government's actions and why it was certain the United States would not interfere. "The internal contradictions within the U.S. administration and among U.S. political parties had intensified. The Watergate scandal had seriously affected the entire United States. . . . It faced economic recession, mounting inflation, serious unemployment and an oil crisis."[3]

This revealing statement illustrates well the hard-boiled pragmatism of the Soviets and their disciples and how free they can be of the dogmas of their ideology in their socioeconomic evaluations of a given situation. According to classical Marxist-Leninist doctrine, an internal crisis impels the capitalists to act more aggressively and to seek a remedy for economic troubles, as well as to distract the attention of the masses through imperialist adventures. Here we had quite a realistic analysis of the reasons for this country's acquiescence in North Vietnam's flagrant violation of the agreement it had signed only two years before, and of the debilitating effects of domestic crises on a democratic country's foreign policies. The statement demonstrates once again how in their calculus of potential risks and gains in world politics, the Soviets tend to go beyond the arithmetic of nuclear missiles, tanks, and ships and pay even closer attention to the psychopolitical ingredients of a given situation. It did require a degree of sensitivity to U.S. politics to perceive how seriously American foreign policy was harmed by reopening the wounds of Vietnam and by pitting Congress against the Executive. The Watergate affair had crippled America's capacity to act effectively abroad, especially when it came to meeting the Soviet and/or Communist challenge in the Third World.

It was less remarkable for the Kremlin to draw the proper lesson from the energy crisis which gripped the West's economy. If the world's leading industrial nations were incapable of synchronizing their policies to counteract or soften the OPEC blow, more serious in its implications to the West than anything done by the Soviet Union since World War II, how could they be expected to mount concerted action to deal with Soviet expansion in Africa or outright invasion of a neighboring country?

The effect of the Soviets' redefinition of detente in light of the economic crisis in the West weakened American leadership, and the fissiparous tendencies within the Atlantic alliance could be observed at the 1979 Vienna Brezhnev-Carter summit. Anxious as the Soviets were to seal SALT II and to prevent relations between the two countries from deteriorating, there was little at Vienna of that studied courting of the Americans that had characterized the 1972 Moscow conference. This time there were no grandiloquent declarations about both countries' scrupulously respecting each other's broad policy interests throughout the world. Instead, Brezhnev chose to lecture Carter and his entourage in public on the impermissibility and uselessness of trying to link the fate of SALT II and detente to Soviet restraint in foreign policy. "Attempts also continue to portray social processes taking place in one or another country or the struggles of the peoples for liberation as 'Moscow's plots or intrigues.' Naturally, the Soviet people are in sympathy with the liberation struggle of various nations. . . . We believe that every people has the right to determine its own destiny. Why then pin on the Soviet Union the responsibility for the objective course of history, or what is more, use this as a pretext for worsening our relations?"[4] With the worldwide configuration of forces much more in their favor than it had been in 1972, it was probably genuinely incomprehensible to the Soviet leaders that anyone could expect them to abide by the same obligations and cautions they had pledged to observe on the earlier occasion.

Choices and Projections

Their actions in the recent past and present offer a suggestive guide to the Soviet leaders' choices and decisions in the future. While it is of little use to try to divide the Kremlin decision makers into "hawks" and "doves" or to try to divine who might represent the "hard" or "soft" factions, there is a considerable division of opinion within the Politburo and its affiliates when it comes to foreign policy. These differences, however, are not found in any permanent groupings or factions, but in the fluctuation between two main tendencies present in the mind of the leadership as a whole.

One such approach might be likened to that of the rentier. This view holds that the USSR can afford to be patient and circumspect in its foreign policies, eschew risky ventures abroad, and continue to collect the dividends of its past successes and the inherent and worsening afflictions of the capitalist world. The rentier's attitude is based not so much on the policies and certitudes of Marxism as on deductions from the historical experiences of the Soviet state, especially since World War II, when the United States has been its only real rival for worldwide power and influence. The Americans have been unable to oppose effectively the Soviets' advance, and they are unlikely to do so in the future. The cumbersome procedure of American foreign policy making and the unruly democratic setting in which it operates will always place the United States at a disadvantage vis-à-vis the flexible and unconstrained apparatus of Soviet diplomacy. Hence, it is unwise to provoke the Americans and risk a confrontation when the U.S. position is bound to grow weaker and that of the USSR stronger in the natural course of events.

The rentier puts the "imperialist danger" in a pragmatic perspective. It *does* exist as a general tendency within the capitalist world, but with proper caution on Moscow's part, it will not assume the form of a concrete menace. The United States was not able to threaten the USSR at the time of greatest American superiority. It is not likely to do so now, when there is general awareness in the West of what a nuclear war might mean. The Reagan administration's early rhetoric has already been blunted by the realization that the Soviet Union cannot be intimidated and that both economic realities and those of European politics will not permit the United States to regain superiority in strategic weapons or to match quantitatively those of the USSR.

The rentier then would urge that the Soviets moderate the pace of their nuclear arms buildup and be prepared to offer timely concessions in the course of negotiations. The USSR has already gained great political advantages from having surpassed the United States in several categories of these weapons and would compound the gains by making what the world at large (if not the Pentagon) would hail as a magnanimous gesture, say, stopping the production of the Backfire bomber. Piling up arms eventually becomes politically counter-productive. The goal is to disarm the West psychologically and pre-vent it from regaining the momentum toward political integration; Soviet military intimidation, if kept up for too long, is bound to have the opposite effect.

The same reasoning would apply to the general guidelines of Soviet policies throughout the world. Having established bridgeheads in Africa and the Caribbean, the Soviet Union would err by trying to expand them too blatantly. The problems facing the United States in those areas are essentially intractable, and it is much better for Mos-cow to wait upon events in the Third World than to attempt to give history a push, for example, in South Africa. The USSR must refrain from any action likely to touch on a raw nerve of American politics, such as identifying itself with the extreme Arab position on Israel, or reaching too obviously for control of the oil routes. In most of these areas of contention, time is essentially working for the Soviet Union, and precipitate actions by the Soviets might tend to reverse the trend.

The rentier's case on this last point becomes most debatable when Politburo discussions turn to East Europe and China. But even there, the rentier instinct would plead for a conservative approach. Soviet bloc countries can always be handled, though preferably not by mili-tary means. In China, it is true, time does not seem to work in the Soviets' favor. But for the balance of the 1980s and probably con-siderably beyond that, China can be contained, provided that the West and Japan do not launch a massive effort to help Beijing moder-nize its economy and become a major industrial, and hence military power. Therefore, the need to contain China makes it all the more important to exercise restraint and blend firmness with conciliatory gestures in their approach toward the West.

The other side of the Soviet leadership's split personality might be called that of the speculator. For him the "imperialist danger" is not merely a doctrinal or propaganda phrase. It is not that he believes any more than the rentier that the United States is about to attack the USSR or engineer a revolution in East Germany or Poland. But only the constant growth in power by the Soviet Union and its avowed readiness to contemplate nuclear war have kept the West off balance and have prevented it from more explicit attempts to undermine the socialist camp. The USSR, therefore, must not desist from active and aggressive exploitation of the weaknesses and vulnerabilities of the world capitalist system, even where it involves the possibility of a major clash with the United States. Such "brinksmanship" becomes especially important for the immediate future, because any lessening in the Soviets' militancy would be read by Washington as a vindication of tough American rhetoric, would encourage the United States to play the China card to the hilt, and could embolden the West Europeans to heed American pleas to join in applying economic pressures upon the Soviet Union.

The speculator would not desist from trying to enhance and exploit whatever military advantages the USSR has already secured over the United States. To give up any of those advantages would be a grave mistake politically even more than militarily. Awe of Soviet military might has kept the United States from interfering in the Czechoslovak and Polish crises, made the Europeans fearful about offending Moscow by imposing effective economic sanctions, and in fact makes them ever more eager to propitiate the Soviet colossus with trade and credits. Any slackening in the arms buildup would thus be taken in the West as confirmation of the thesis that internal economic and other problems have made the USSR more malleable on defense and international issues and that consequently one can pressure the Soviets to alter not only their military and foreign policies, but also the domestic ones. One has to negotiate with the United States and NATO on tactical and strategic nuclear arms, but to offer any one-sided concessions, even if not substantive, would be most damaging for the USSR's image and bargaining position.

The speculator would not only stress the necessity of militancy from the angle of relations with the West. In the years ahead some Third World leaders might well be tempted to imitate Sadat's gambit and exploit the USSR for their own purposes, only to switch to the other side once the Soviet connection had been fully exploited. In retrospect it may have been a mistake to make Egypt the fulcrum of Soviet policies in the Middle East and to pour so much money and effort into buttressing its regime without obtaining a firmer grasp on its internal politics. Future Soviet ventures in the Third World must not only lead to a temporary discomfiture for the West but also result in firm Soviet ideological and military control over the new client.

Analysts in the West and even some figures within the Soviet establishment keep pointing to Afghanistan as an illustration of the dangers of overt and precipitate Russian aggression. In fact Afghanistan, for all its troublesome aspects, served as a salutary lesson to those of Moscow's protégés who might contemplate following Egypt's example and try to reap the benefits of Soviet political and economic support while maneuvering between the two camps. For all the initial indignation, the Afghanistan coup served to strengthen the respect or fear in which the USSR is held in the Moslem world. When a mob tried to attack the Soviet embassy in Tehran, it was (unlike the embassy of another power) protected by the forces of that very fundamentalist Moslem regime. Direct Soviet military intervention is not something to be used too often, but once in a long while it serves as a useful reminder that the USSR is not to be trifled with.

Similar considerations indicate that the Soviet Union cannot afford to be a passive observer or just assist occasionally and indirectly in the erosion of U.S. influence in Latin America or that of the West in general in Africa. In fact it is doubtful whether this process can continue to benefit the Soviet Union's interests, unless the latter promotes it energetically with more than just rhetoric and military supplies. All radical and liberation movements are inherently unstable and volatile in their political allegiance. If rebuffed in their pleas for more active Soviet help, they may turn to others or tend to disintegrate. It would thus be a mistake for Moscow to stand apart, if and when armed struggle erupts in South Africa, or in the case of a violent confrontation between the forces of left and right in a major Latin American country.

Our speculator tends to question, not explicitly of course, the thesis that "the objective course of history" must favor the Soviet cause. Where would the USSR be today if it had allowed "objective factors" to determine the fate of East Europe? In Latin America, Africa, and Asia one ought not to confuse the emotional residue of anticolonialism and local radicalism with a secular tendency toward Communism or with automatic gravitation of the new and developing societies toward the Soviet model. Anticapitalism and perhaps anti-Western sentiments may be the common denominator of most radical and liberation movements in the non-Western world. But once in power, if they feel they can afford it, such movements tend to seek freedom from any foreign tutelage. Their leaders have grown sophisticated enough to understand the complexities of the international scene and, if left to themselves, would prefer to be genuinely nonaligned and able to play one side against the other.

It is not by patiently waiting upon events but by bold coups that Soviet power and influence have been projected into all areas of the globe, and it is not the "inherent logic of economic and social development" but the greatly expanded naval and airlift capabilities that have maintained and enlarged those enclaves of influence. And so for the balance of the 1980s, "the objective course of history" must continue to be carved out by strenuous Soviet efforts including, when necessary, the use of military force.

Political and economic stability is a natural ally of the capitalist world. The USSR, therefore, can have no interest, except in special cases, in a general U.S.-Soviet understanding that would lessen the intensity of political ferment in the troubled areas of the world or reduce appreciably the present level of international tension. The speculator rejects the practicality or desirability of any long-term accommodation between the USSR and America. Even if it pursues the most peaceful policies, the United States will always represent a standing danger to the Soviet system and the socialist camp simply by what it is. Close relations with the democracies lead inevitably to ideological pollution at home and to weakening that combination of political vigilance and social discipline that is the sine qua non of a Communist regime.

The rentier and the speculator would disagree most violently concerning the degree of urgency of the Chinese problem. The activist rejects emphatically the notion that the USSR can afford to sit and watch while China's economy is modernized and its stockpile of nuclear weapons grows. Some efficacious solution of the problem must be found during the next few years. Perhaps the intra-faction struggle which has been going on in China since the Cultural Revolution might assume the proportions of a civil war. Barring that rather slim hope, the USSR would have to take some measures beyond just trying to contain China. Perhaps Beijing could still be enticed to paper over its dispute with the Russians and be pushed again into a collision course with the United States. Conversely, a moment might come when the Soviets will have sufficiently intimidated the West to compel it to leave them a free hand for even the most drastic resolution of their Chinese dilemma. Ever since the heating up of the Sino-Soviet dispute, and even when relations between Washington and Beijing were at their worst, America's nuclear power has been a key factor in restraining the Soviets from trying to resolve the conflict by force.

Neither of the two impulses currently coexisting in the minds of the Politburo is likely to achieve complete mastery during the balance of the decade. Ascendancy of the rentier mentality would clearly make the Soviet Union much less of a destabilizing force in the world arena and in the long run could open up prospects of a major change in the Soviet philosophy of international relations. The speculator motif, if dominant, would greatly increase the danger of an all-out war. For the immediate future the Soviet leaders can be expected to seek a middle course between the two approaches, the benefits and risks of either weighed in their minds by their perceptions of the strengths and weaknesses of the noncommunist world.

Areas of Opportunity

Sub-Saharan Africa

That rather imprecise and misleading term, "The Third World," or its equally unsatisfactory and nearly synonymous phrase, "underdeveloped countries," still assumes a fairly concrete meaning within the conceptual framework of Soviet foreign policy. For Lenin and his generation of Soviet leaders, the colonial and semicolonial dependencies of the West appeared the crucial future battlegrounds of the struggle between the worlds of socialism and capitalism. The current, much less doctrinal leadership of the Soviet Union continues to stress its historical mission in the same areas and affirms the natural affinity of interests and goals between the Fatherland of Socialism and the nations of the Third World. As Brezhnev said, "We know very well, and we shall not forget, that the nations of Asia, Africa, and Latin America form, together with those of the socialist camp, a mighty detachment of the forces for peace in international relations. Working together we have already accomplished quite a lot. And we are firmly convinced that in the future, too, our paths will not diverge."[5]

Among Third World areas, Africa was the last to engage active Soviet interest. From the practical point of view, until the post–World War II period, the USSR had neither power nor other effective means of projecting its influence to a continent then almost entirely dominated by the Western countries. Ideologically, the difficulties of propagating Communism were equally insuperable. Sub-Saharan Africa was almost completely devoid of the industrial proletariat and of the "national bourgeoisie," the two traditional targets of Leninist tactics. South Africa was the only partial exception in the generally unpromising socioeconomic and political picture of the region. Even there, while the seeds of Communism could be implanted, racial divisions in the country condemned militant Marxism to virtual insignificance as a revolutionary or anti-imperialist force. When Lenin and Trotsky spoke of anti-imperialism's becoming the catalyst of the world revolution, they had before their eyes Shanghai and Calcutta, not Johannesburg or Lagos. The Communist parties of the colonial powers had to carry on the missionary work for what then seemed the very distant day of revolutionary struggle in Africa, and they did so mainly by recruiting converts among the few Africans studying or settled in West.

This bleak picture was transformed drastically by the postwar "winds of change," which within two decades overturned the major colonial systems in Africa and led to creation of a multitude of independent states. Only the weakest of the colonial powers, Portugal, clung ever more precariously to its African possessions. In Rhodesia, a tiny white majority began its foredoomed experiment in preserving a quasi-colonial system. South Africa remained the only strong enclave of white domination in the whole vast area, but it was increasingly isolated internationally and subjected to mounting pressures internally.

The Soviet and/or Communist contribution to this initial, most decisive phase of decolonization was virtually nil. It is more than an exaggeration for a Soviet author to assert that "The alliance between world socialism and the national-liberation forces . . . has played a key role in bringing about the collapse of the colonial empires."[6] Insofar as Africa was concerned, it was precisely and ironically the collapse of Western imperialism that enabled the USSR to influence the course of politics on the continent and to adopt the posture of supporter of national liberation movements after national liberation had already been accomplished in most cases.

Superficially, numerous factors should have favored the spread of Soviet influence in the new states, such as lingering anti-Western feelings among the population and the radical, often Marxist, leanings of the new ruling elites. Also, the "Soviet model of development" was attractive for many Africans of all political persuasions, who shared the misconception (not unknown in the West) that it was under and because of Communism that backward Russia had grown into the second greatest industrial power in the world.

On the other hand, the very instability and volatility of the political situation in the wake of rapid decolonization often frustrated Soviet efforts to win a firm political foothold in the new nations. Political leaders or parties they cultivated would fall prey to the usually turbulent political climate or would suddenly be compelled to shift their political orientation. In helping the new states economically, the USSR could not as yet compete with the West. Knowledge of local conditions among Soviet diplomats and technical advisers (whether the real ones or those combining their technical qualifications with KGB membership) was often rudimentary.

The Soviets' greatest asset in competing with the West has been their unsqueamish attitude about the hard facts of politics in lands which had little or no tradition of representative institutions or political pluralism, not to speak of democracy. Recipients of American economic aid and other forms of assistance could expect intermittent admonitions from the U.S. government or from visiting Congressional delegations about the inadmissability of putting aid to uses other than economic development and raising the standard of living, about the wickedness of political repression, and, conversely, about the virtues of parliamentary institutions and an independent judiciary. Free from such scruples, the Soviets could court unabashedly and gain political leverage with local leaders such as Kwame Nkrumah in Ghana and Sékou Touré in Guinea.

However, this influence could seldom be translated into a solid basis for Soviet presence in the given country. The local leader would be overthrown, as in Nkrumah's case, or grow suspicious and disenchanted with the Soviets, as has happened intermittently in Ghana and Mali. In the former British and especially the French colonies, the Soviets had to deal with ruling elites that had imbibed cultural and political traditions of their former imperial masters and were therefore resistant to Soviet blandishments. In brief, for all their theoretical advantages over the West in recruiting clients among African elites and rulers, the Soviets were usually bested in that competition until well into the 1970s.

The first major Soviet foray to achieve a political hold over an African country came in the former Belgian Congo, today's Zaire. Unlike the British and the French in most of their colonies, the Belgians had neglected laying down even rudimentary foundations for the territory's future self-rule. The resultant chaos following the proclamation of independence in 1960 enabled Moscow to make a serious bid for dominant influence by establishing close links to Prime Minister Patrice Lumumba and helping him fight a secessionist movement in the Katanga province. After his overthrow, the Soviets sponsored a number of insurrectionary forces claiming to be legatees of the martyred Lumumba.

Failure of this initial major effort at securing a foothold in the heart of Africa gave the Soviets some lessons they undoubtedly remembered when readjusting their African policies in recent years. First, the influence of the Western nations within the United Nations proved still strong enough to make the latter take effective steps to preserve Zaire's territorial integrity and to hold at bay Soviet-supported forces. Second, the Soviet efforts in Zaire had to be improvised: there had been no opportunity before independence to groom a pro-Soviet faction to bid for power when the Belgians left. Third, and most fundamentally, the Soviets still lacked adequate logistic capabilities to project power thousands of miles away from their borders, nor would they have used surrogate troops to secure victory for their side in an African civil war, even if they had had them available at that time.

Some of the lessons drawn by the Soviets from their first serious immersion in African politics were reflected in Khrushchev's founding of the Patrice Lumumba University in Moscow, intended to train pro-Soviet cadres among the future intelligentsia of African and other Third World nations.[7] He also paid an unwitting tribute to the United Nations' effectiveness in having kept the Congo from complete anarchy by pressing that the Secretary General's functions be divided among three people, one to be chosen from the Communist bloc. Such a proposal would have made the world organization virtually impotent to stave off future Soviet attempts to exploit similar crises.

How drastically the situation in Africa changed in the Soviets' favor and to the West's disadvantage within the next decade! The

U.N. had become so enfeebled that it could not intervene in crises such as that following the collapse of the Portuguese empire. It has proved incapable of preventing territorial disputes between African states from erupting into wars, as in the Somali-Ethiopian struggle over Ogaden in 1977–78. One of the main assumptions of those in the West, especially in the United States, who urged speedy emancipation of colonial areas, even those ill-prepared for self-rule, had been that the United Nations would smooth the new nations' path to political stability and seal them off from the East-West conflict. This not entirely altruistic hope (for it implied the persistence of Western influence) foundered upon the realities of African politics in the 1970s. Nor has any other supranational entity such as the Organization of African Unity (OAU) been able to prevent growing political fragmentation and instability both within the individual states and in the region as a whole.

In some countries a charismatic leader such as Kenya's Kenyatta or Senegal's Senghor has been able to assure a degree of political continuity and national unity. Several Francophone African countries have maintained close links with France. In Kenya and Tanzania, the imprint of British political and administrative institutions and traditions has not yet been entirely eroded. But as the first post-independence generation passes from the scene, even those enclaves of relative political calm are becoming subject to the same pressures and ailments that afflict the majority of African states. *Coups d'état,* periods of military rule, and internal struggle between ethnic and tribal factions, at times assuming the proportions of a civil war, have become increasingly frequent on the African scene.

Against the background of political troubles lie the stark facts of the African economy. The majority of countries in the area are among the poorest and least economically developed in the world. Only three or four black sub-Saharan states currently have a major industrial capacity. In 1979 the gross national income per capita for twenty-eight countries was $350 or less; for another twelve, the figure was between $350 and $700. Only seven states in the area had a per capita income over $700.[8] In the white-dominated areas, South Africa, Namibia, and, until recently, Rhodesia-Zimbabwe, there has been a great disparity between the standard of living of the dominant race and that of the black majority.

Rudimentary modernization has tended in general to compound rather than to ameliorate the distressing economic conditions. Indeed such modernization, unless accompanied by vigorous industrial and agricultural development, contributes to the stagnation or actual lowering of the average standard of living. Thus, Nigeria, with its great oil earnings, should have one of the highest GNPs per capita, but given its over eighty million people, the actual figure for per capita income was but $330. More than half the sub-Saharan states had a per capita GNP growth rate during 1970–77 of less than 2 percent, with seventeen registering no growth or an actual decline.[9] By building upon their mineral resources and nationalizing their agriculture, individual states may achieve a much higher growth rate, and/or develop effective population control programs. But as a whole, sub-Saharan Africa is unlikely to improve significantly its economic position during the balance of the decade. Only massive foreign aid, on a scale that does not seem realistic to expect, could alter this bleak prospect.

Ostensibly, Africa might appear an area of limitless opportunity and of almost irresistible temptation for the spread of Soviet influence. By the same token, the West's opportunity to maneuver successfully in the morass of African politics is subject to severe limitations. The usual instruments of Western influence and thereby of countering the Soviet one—parliamentary institutions, a middle class imbued with liberal values, a strong sense of nationhood—are either missing or weak and vulnerable. The persistence of white domination in South Africa and, for the immediate future, in Namibia and of the economically privileged position of European minorities in Zimbabwe, Kenya, as well as of smaller groups of such expatriates in other states, is yet another element of fundamental importance in the Western dilemma in Africa. The complexity of the racial problem inherent in the survival of the white-dominated regimes and the virtual impossibility of a both democratic and nonviolent solution not only affect Western policies on the continent but also find their reverberations in domestic politics in the United States and Great Britain. Add to it the considerable economic and strategic stake of the democratic world in Africa, e.g., U.S. dependence on a number of important minerals found mainly in the southern part of Africa, and one begins to realize the full extent of the West's predicament and of the Soviet Union's opportunity.

On the face of it, in no other major area of the world could the USSR expect to score such substantial successes with so little effort and risk as in Africa. In urging the wisdom of waiting upon events rather than advancing Soviet goals by precipitate actions, the rentier argument would appear most persuasive when pointing to predictable tendencies within African politics. The racial tension in South Africa is bound to heat up, provoking civil disobedience, possibly mass violence, even civil war by the end of the decade. Any position taken by the West in that struggle is likely to be deleterious to its interests, to antagonize both sides, and to have profound and negative effects on the United States and its allies. The USSR can watch this struggle, whatever character it assumes, with equanimity. Uninhibited by the prospects of bloodshed, the Kremlin does not have to assume an overt role in the crisis or its resolution to see South Africa lapsing into complete chaos or becoming fragmented. Its anti-imperialist rhetoric and covert help to one of the contending factions are likely to be sufficient to keep the situation from cooling off and to prevent the West from advancing a compromise solution acceptable to both sides.

The same attitude of patiently waiting for fresh crises to fall in the Soviets' lap seems sensible almost everywhere else on the continent. Superficially, Zaire might appear a solid bastion of Western influence in the area, and the intermittent forays from Angola (sanctioned if not sponsored by Moscow) by forces opposed to the Zaire regime have to date been frustrated. Yet, in the very nature of things, the Mobutu regime will sooner or later fall of its own weight. The usual Western panacea for securing political stability—economic development, assisted by large credits from the International Monetary Fund and Western banks—has worked no better in Zaire than in most other African countries. For inefficient and corrupt regimes such as Mobutu's, foreign economic aid, unless its use is strictly monitored, tends to aggravate the country's economic and social problems, as the Soviets themselves have learned in Indonesia and, most recently, in Poland. Instead of leading to the development of a middle class with appropriate (i.e., Western) values, U.S. and European economic assistance to shaky Third World regimes is expended on spectacular development projects having little relevance to the most pressing problems of the local economy or leads to proliferation of parasitic bureaucracies and enrichment of the ruling clique. Frustrated, "the revolution of rising expectations" then gives rise to real revolutionary strivings among an educated class already predisposed to think in quasi–Marxist-Leninist terms.

It is unlikely that the West can continue indefinitely to prop up the Mobutu regime. Its army has been barely adequate for the purpose of internal repression and was unable on its own to repulse the secessionist movements in 1977 and 1978, even though they were poorly led and armed. With the collapse of the regime, the country may again fragment along tribal-provincial lines. Or, if a central authority does emerge, it might decide to eschew undue dependence on the West in view of its predecessor's fate. Either case would open interesting possibilities for the USSR, which then might have recourse to friendly forces across the Angolan border.

If such pleasing prospects can be anticipated in a large African state that the United States and its allies have been especially solicitous to preserve and build into a mainstay of influence, the Soviets have even rosier expectations elsewhere. The temper and attention span of democratic politics acts against the American or the French governments' being able to monitor continuously and to react instantaneously to political crises in some forty-seven African states, most of them remote from the average citizen's awareness. Will the French, increasingly weary of what remains of their formal imperial role, send their paratroops to little, oil-rich Gabon in case of a pro-Soviet insurgency there, as they sent them to Zaire in 1978? Could American public opinion tolerate any administration's embarking on a policy of the El Salvador type in a little-known African state? Even to ask such questions makes one realize how the cards in the African game appear stacked in the Soviet Union's favor.

On the other hand, there are cogent reasons to believe that the problems facing the USSR in Africa are much more complex and difficult than hitherto implied.

We first encounter the natural reluctance of African leaders to exchange one form of foreign tutelage for another, a reluctance all the stronger because of their awareness of the fragility of their countries' political and social fabric. African intellectuals' and politicians' original attraction to Moscow was based mainly on their scanty knowledge of Soviet politics and life. The actual Soviet presence in Africa, the exposure of many thousands of blacks to the conditions of Soviet society, so different from what they had been led to expect from propaganda tracts, and the thinly veiled undertones of xenophobia and racism in the Soviets' attitude have contributed to considerable disenchantment with the Soviet "model of development" and even with the image of the USSR as staunch enemy of imperialism and as advocate of the cause of all oppressed peoples.

The politicians have had ample opportunities to observe the manipulative quality of the Soviets' approach to Africa's problems and the superficiality of their professions of disinterested and genuine engagement in the cause of national liberation. Even in a tract designed for propaganda use, a Soviet author cannot avoid a tone of condescension when speaking of "liberation" and similar movements that Moscow usually exalts and courts so strenuously: "A typical feature of most of the ideological concepts used by the revolutionary democrats is that they do not possess a well developed theoretical basis. . . . They are largely inconsistent and contradictory."[10]

One may then question whether further radicalization of African politics must automatically rebound to the Soviets' advantage. Quite a few African radical movements and regimes have tended to profess greater affinity with China than with the senior Communist power. In terms of material support to the revolutionary forces and self-proclaimed revolutionary regimes, Beijing has until now been in no position to compete with Moscow. This has been vividly demonstrated during the civil wars in Nigeria and Angola. But even the very fact of

China's appearance on the scene must have produced very choleric reactions within the Kremlin. Beijing's involvement in African politics definitely ended the USSR's monopoly as the only alleged external champion of anti-imperialism and racial oppression. China's influence was significant in the resolution of the Rhodesia-Zimbabwe conflict, where the Soviets backed what until now has been the wrong horse, the Joshua Nkomo faction among the guerrilla forces. This backing might explain the Mugabe government's initial hesitation to enter upon full-fledged diplomatic relations with the USSR.

But if stymied or bested in their struggle for "men's hearts and minds," the Soviets do not and will not scorn more direct methods of achieving their goals. There are few governments in the area that a few thousand well-trained soldiers could not overthrow or, conversely, maintain in power in the face of widespread popular discontent. In that sense, the Cuban gambit in Angola was both a fundamental innovation in Soviet methods of political penetration and a probe of both Western and African reactions to this new way of furthering the cause of "national liberation." On both counts the test proved highly successful. The OAU, after some internal dispute, finally decided to recognize the regime installed with the help of the Cubans, allegedly because a competing faction had sought South African aid, but also in all probability because of the feeling that it seemed unwise to provoke the USSR, a power that can conjure up thousands of troops to assist its friends in other African countries. How far the Soviet-Cuban arrangement has now been accepted as a fact of African political life can be judged from the fact that one argument used in the West to urge a speedy settlement of the Zimbabwe question was that unless the conflict was brought to a close, that country too might experience a large-scale Cuban military intervention.

Having once established their political grip on a given state, it is more than problematic that the Soviets would relinquish it and pull out the surrogate troops, even if the pretext for military intervention had passed. It is sometimes argued that the MPLA regime in Angola would be eager to get rid of its Cuban guests once the internal situation stabilized and Namibia became independent, thus eliminating the danger of South African intrusions. But the Soviets may feel that the Luanda government would need the comforting presence of their foreign helpers for a long time. Even if Namibia became independent, the Cubans would be needed to help "build socialism" in Angola and to protect it from its internal enemies. It would be logical to lend Cubans to Namibia too, to fend off South African designs on its independence and to advance the "national liberation" struggle in South Africa proper.

Similar considerations would make Moscow extremely unwilling to lift its military presence from Ethiopia. There the surrogate troops' technique received a further twist with Soviet officers' assuming command over joint Cuban-Ethiopian operations, both in fighting local insurrections and in the war against Somalia. The USSR must feel that it has made considerable sacrifices to enable the bloodstained Mengistu regime to hold on to power and to prevent Ethiopia's territorial disintegration. In addition to its generous help with arms and experts and to the expense incurred in transporting and arming the Cubans, the USSR had also to give up, at least temporarily, its friendship with Somalia and, what is more important, its naval and air facilities in that country.

It is inconceivable that after Ethiopia had received so much Soviet "selfless help," Moscow would heed a suggestion by Mengistu or a successor that Soviet benevolence, or at least its military presence in his country, is no longer needed. The Soviets presumably have learned a lesson from their bitter experience with Egypt. If they can help it, they will not let it be repeated in a country that they must consider much easier to handle in a no-nonsense fashion than Egypt or Afghanistan.

This last point raises again the question of whether the volatile flux of African politics can be dammed and harnessed to Soviet goals. Soviet policies have traditionally fed upon racial, ethnic, and national conflicts, yet the multiplicity and complexity of such conflicts in Africa tend to create situations that the Kremlin finds difficult to handle to its advantage or lead to successes in one area having unfavorable repercussions for Soviet influence and interests in another. No African leader could have missed this object lesson of Soviet Machiavellianism when, with the bigger prize of Ethiopia in sight, Moscow suddenly and unceremoniously dropped its support not only for Somalia but also for the Eritrean rebels and hastened to provide the Addis Ababa regime the means for defeating and repressing the USSR's erstwhile friends.

Conscious of such inherent difficulties, the USSR has tried and will undoubtedly intensify such efforts in the future to build more solid foundations for its bridgeheads on the continent. In both Angola and Ethiopia, it has urged the local regimes to transform the rather amorphous movements that brought them into power into something closer to the Marxist-Leninist model of a political party. The USSR would like to see both countries integrated ideologically and economically into the Soviet bloc. It remains to be seen whether and to what extent such experiments can succeed and whether they will justify Moscow's hopes or help create varieties of African Titoism.

In any case, Africa is bound to remain one of the principal targets of Soviet efforts at expansion and at gaining advantages over the

West. How intensive these efforts will be and how much the USSR will be willing to risk would depend, however, on political developments outside the continent. It was not only the Kremlin's assessment of the Angolan political scene in 1974–75 but also the strange consequences of a janitor's discovery in a Washington apartment complex some years before that emboldened the Soviets to embark on a new technique of expansion in Africa. As before and as elsewhere, what the Soviets try to do in Africa will depend heavily on their reading of the West.

The Eastern Areas of the Moslem World

Unlike those of Africa, problems associated with the world of Islam have been of long-standing and direct importance to the USSR internally, as well as in the international field. Historically, the Russian state was forged in an almost constant struggle with the Moslem states and tribes south and east of its nucleus. The absorption of its former Mongol and Turkic conquerors was followed in the nineteenth century by the conquest of Central Asia and subjugation of the Moslem tribes of North Caucasus. Russian expansion at the expense of the Moslem world has had a long tradition. Only the rivalry with the British empire prevented the tsars from wresting further territories from the Ottoman and Persian empires and allowed Afghanistan to preserve its very shaky independence.

Communist Russia abjured officially its imperial predecessor's policy toward the Moslem world, and indeed Moscow attempted to employ both the religious and the nationalist dynamism of the awakening Islamic world for undermining the still surviving colonial systems, principally the British. The religious motif, rather theatrically presented at the Baku Congress of the Peoples of the East in 1920, could not long be sustained by a power that in its own territory proceeded to wage war upon all religious institutions and beliefs, Islam included. Still, Leninist tactics in the 1920s were a preview of those followed by the USSR once it became a world power and could promote its interests in the Moslem areas by more than anti-imperialist rhetoric. It sought special ties with those oriental countries that had entered or tried to enter the path of modernization, such as Ataturk's Turkey and Amanullah's Afghanistan. In these cases, the interests of local Communism or other radical movements were already considered secondary to those of the Soviet state. There were also abortive attempts at promoting outright pro-Soviet regimes when conditions for such developments were judged favorable, as in Northern Persia.

The post–World War II scene found the Soviets' attention still focused on the traditional targets of Russian imperial expansion:

Turkey and Iran. Stalin pressed for Soviet naval bases on Turkish territory, and Soviet territorial demands on Ankara kept relations between the two countries at a high level of tension until 1953. There were more overt attempts to carve out Russian satellite states from Iran by prolonging Soviet military occupation of its northern part beyond the time limit agreed upon in 1943 at the Big Three Tehran conference, but they collapsed because of determined American-British opposition. The USSR did not yet feel strong enough to challenge the Western powers in an area of secondary importance, compared with East Europe and the Far East. Stalin was a man with a firm set of priorities, and even the clear signs of forthcoming turbulence in the Arab world were not allowed to divert the attention of the Kremlin away from Berlin and Prague and toward Cairo or Algiers.

With the collapse of the British and French presence in the Middle East coming much sooner than they had expected, the Soviets were still prompt to adjust their policies toward this new area of Western vulnerability and hence of fresh opportunities for the USSR. In 1948 they supported the foundation of the Israeli state and were the first to recognize it *de jure*. Moscow realized that this new element in Middle Eastern politics would raise almost insuperable difficulties to any lasting accommodation between the Arab world and the West. It could already be foreseen that with Britain and France bound to surrender the enclaves of their power in the region, the United States would have to try to be the balancing factor in Middle East politics. This task, in view of America's special relationship with Israel, was bound to incur difficulties and costs that would immeasurably increase the burden of this country's foreign policy.

Again the Soviets may have originally intended to draw only indirect benefits from the West's travails in liquidating another part of its imperial legacy. America's self-proclaimed mission as champion of the colonial peoples' independence was likely to appear unconvincing to the Arabs in view of the special American relationship with Britain and France, as well as with Israel. At the same time, Washington's pressure on London and Paris to emancipate their colonies and liquidate their special rights in the Arab lands more expeditiously lest the latter turn toward the Communist world was bound to throw a spoke in the wheels of the Atlantic alliance.[11] The Soviets, therefore, could afford a certain detachment from the conflicts in the Middle East. Diplomatic relations with Israel, which were broken off in 1952 more because of Stalin's anti-Jewish obsession than of foreign policy considerations, were quickly restored by his successors, who also proceeded to mend Soviet-Turkish relations. The first stages of the Algerian rebellion did not find vociferous support on the part of the USSR. Until 1956, Soviet policies in the Middle East were attuned to the priority of their European goals, which were to weaken NATO,

prevent West European political intergration, and secure formal recognition of the division of Germany.

Khrushchev's adventurist itch, the first indication of the Chinese
bid to lead militant forces in the Third World, and the almost irresistible temptation to exploit the ill-fated Suez affair combined to impart
to Soviet policy in the Middle East that activist bent it has exhibited
ever since 1956.

Paradoxically, this direct and intense engagement of the Soviet
Union in the politics of the area has for the most part contributed to
weakening the appeal and influence of the Communist parties in most
Arab countries. The Soviets' ostensible posture became one of cham-
pioning Arab nationalism in its struggle against the remnants of Western imperialism and Israel. The USSR has had to soft-pedal the
ideological motif and watch with equanimity when the Arab regimes it
befriended dealt unceremoniously with local Communists. Occasionally this inherent conflict within Soviet policies between their ideological and *realpolitik* elements would surface and provide a preview of
the Kremlim's future troubles. The overthrow of the Hashemite
monarchy in Iraq in 1958 brought to power the regime of General
Kassim, in which initially the Communists played an important role.
This aroused considerable anxiety on the part of Moscow's recent
protégé, Colonel Nasser. The Egyptian leader became vociferous
about the danger of Communism in the Arab world and dealt severely with its adherents in what was then the United Arab Republic.
Central as Egypt had already become to the Soviets, Khrushchev
could not suppress entirely his Marxist-Leninist side. He tactlessly
chided Nasser as a "hot-headed young man" and demonstratively
praised the new regime in Iraq for pursuing the kind of progressive
policies that the other Arab states should emulate. Kassim's flirtation
with the Communists was not to last long, and his own rule and life
came to a violent end not much later. The USSR and Egypt reverted
to that close though occasionally troubled friendship that was to
characterize their relations until Nasser's death.[12]

The initial premise of Kremlin strategy in the Middle East and
the Mediterranean area was that the Soviets should build most effectively upon exploitation of the anti-Western and anti-Israeli sentiments of already existing regimes and "liberation movements," rather
than by trying to create enclaves of direct Soviet domination. Eventually, Nasser might grow into a facsimile of Castro, and "Arab socialism," finding itself unable to cope with the multifarious social and
economic problems of the region, would have to give way to the real,
scientific one. To begin, however, by trying to create a Middle Eastern
"People's Republic" would harm, perhaps fatally, the image of the
USSR as a disinterested champion of the Arab cause.

Yet, as always, the Soviets have not been able to resist the temptation to hedge their bets. While maintaining an official and decorous liaison with the powers that be in Egypt, Syria, or Iraq, Moscow has not desisted from exploring the possibilities and preparing the ground for a more intimate relationship with those who might offer an alternative. This dialectical or duplicitous pattern of Soviet policies has perhaps been more evident in the Middle East than in other major areas of conflict. It has on occasion created serious embarrassments for the USSR and in one case rendered a serious blow to its position in the region as a whole, with reverberations that are likely to affect increasingly the general trend of Soviet policies in the entire Third World.

The abortive Communist coup in the Sudan in 1971 was followed within a few months by President Sadat's purge of the Sabri faction from the Egyptian regime. The Soviet Union's reaction to both developments reflected the relative weight of the two countries in the Kremlin's calculations. The Egyptian leader had good reasons to suspect that Sabri's machinations were foreign-inspired. His group consisted of "all those senior Egyptian officials whom the Russians had come to know best, and so to regard as their friends."[13] But such friends were expendable when it came to the Soviets' retaining close links with the key country of the Arab world. Sadat, the USSR believed, was propitiated by the Kremlin's agreeing to a formal treaty of alliance signed in the same year.

In the case of the Sudan, Moscow reacted sharply to the regime's mass execution of the Communist plotters and their associates and broke off diplomatic relations. It is unlikely that this action was dictated by purely ideological or sentimental considerations. To act otherwise, especially toward a country that was not of great importance in the Soviet scheme of things, would have damaged even further the already low morale of Arab Communists.[14]

The 1971 contretemps in Cairo and the Sudan crisis were no doubt instrumental in persuading Sadat to take the first steps on the road to Jerusalem and Camp David and in making Egypt the most important and spectacular case of Soviet failure in the Third World. No conceivable modification of the late president's stand on international issues by his successors is likely to erase the far-reaching significance and implications of this defeat for Soviet diplomacy in a country that has been the object of Moscow's courtship more than any other in the Third World. Soviet leaders may have convinced themselves that at least on two occasions they had risked for Egypt's sake a direct confrontation with the United States and thus saved the ungrateful country from utter disaster. As a reward the perfidious Egyptians, having fully exploited the USSR, proceeded to switch to the U.S. camp.

Sadat's "betrayal" has undercut much of the Soviets' efforts, pursued strenuously for over a quarter of a century, to keep the Middle East in that state of turmoil judged essential by Moscow for securing a Soviet presence in the area. It is not surprising that upon announcing his intention of seeking a settlement with Israel, the Egyptian states-man was subjected to a barrage of personal vituperation such as, with the possible exception of Mao, has never before been released by the Soviet press against the head of a state with which the USSR has continued to maintain diplomatic relations.

The Soviets' experience in Egypt goes to the very heart of the speculator/rentier argument about the future direction of Soviet policies, and not only in the Moslem world. The rentier would argue that the character and extent of Soviet involvement with the Egyp-tians and the willingness to give *carte blanche* to Egypt's rulers from the beginning had been unreasonable and excessive. The basic aims of the Soviet Union in the area could have been served by a less close relationship, not only with Cairo, but also with other "progressive" Arab regimes. In fact, by the early 1960s the USSR had already drawn the maximum possible benefits from its active advocacy of the Arab cause. Western domination had ended, and U.S. influence was being eroded, with the Eisenhower doctrine a thing of the past. The Israeli-Palestinian question has made it impossible for the United States to fill the vacuum the crumbling of the British and French imperial position caused. This question can be depended upon to continue to poison American-Arab relations and thus render superfluous a too-active Soviet involvement in the Middle Eastern conflict, an involvement that someday might lead, even accidentally, to an armed clash be-tween the two superpowers.

Who in fact struck the greatest blow at the interests of the United States and its allies, not only regionally but on a worldwide scale? This blow, the rentier would point out, came not as a consequence of anything done by pampered "progressive" Arab regimes into which the USSR had poured billions in military aid and other forms of assistance. It came as the result of OPEC's actions in 1973–74, even though most of the members were conservative Moslem regimes, de-pendent on the West in many ways.

OPEC's exactions are a principal cause of the most serious eco-nomic crisis the capitalist world has experienced since World War II, with all that crisis has meant for the political stability of the West and for its willingness and/or ability to maintain a high level of military expenditures. How could the benefits secured by the USSR through the actions of such unwitting helpers as the Saudi princes, the late Shah, and petty sheikhs be compared to those meager dividends ac-crued through the expensive and risk-laden sponsorship of rulers like Nasser and Kassim?

Iran, the rentier's case continues, provides another conclusive example of how much to be preferred, how much more prudent, it is to wait patiently upon what the "objective course of history" will bring, rather than to try to give history a push. It would be a mistake to hint at the possibility of Soviet military action in Iran or blatantly encourage the separatist and radical elements in that country. In fact one ought to discourage any premature attempt by the left to seize power in Tehran.

Similar cautions, so this argument would continue, should be observed in regard to such other non-Arab Moslem states as Turkey and Pakistan. There, too, the general trend of social and political development works against the West, and the military regimes cannot indefinitely contain radicalism, whether of the political or religious variety. Turkey's ties with the West have already been strained by skillful Soviet exploitation of the Cyprus problem, and it is by further cultivation of the opportunities offered to it by the Turkish-Greek dispute that Moscow can work most effectively to detach both countries from NATO. Similarly, friendship with India offers the most effective leverage for dealing with Pakistan and for discouraging active support for the Afghani rebels or its seeking to draw close to Beijing.

The more activist-minded members of the Politburo would quarrel not so much with the rentier's conclusion as with his premises. All developments in the Moslem world that have been favorable to the Soviet Union and harmful to Western interests have not come of themselves. The USSR has been the catalyst of this new Arab revolution that has attenuated Western power and influence throughout the region and that has enabled the Moslem world to persist in its opposition to Israel and its support of the Palestinian cause. It is naive to think that without the USSR's playing an active role in the area, without fear of Soviet action always present in the minds of Washington policy makers, the capitalists would have reacted so meekly to OPEC's economic blackmail or would not have taken some vigorous measures to prevent the collapse of the Shah's regime in Iran. As elsewhere, any precipitate slackening of Soviet interest in the area would embolden the United States to try to contain and even to roll back Soviet power in the Moslem world and to encourage other "hard line" Arab regimes to follow the example of Egypt.

The Soviets must have concluded that it was a mistake to have their position in Egypt based on nothing more substantial than its rulers' goodwill and the assumption that the Israeli-Palestinian problem would always keep them apart from the United States. What to the rentier is an illustration of the dangers of Soviet overcommitment on behalf of a Moslem country is from the opposite point of view a reason for urging that the USSR should seek a firmer grip on the internal politics of its allies. The Soviets' motives in licensing and then protecting the 1978 Communist coup in Afghanistan and their prompt and drastic action in South Yemen, when its government in the same year showed signs of trying to emancipate itself from them, both followed and were influenced by their experience with Sadat. Cuban, or in an extreme case, Soviet soldiers, plus the appropriate ideological bent of the given regime, are more efficacious safeguards of its continued reliability than mere treaties of alliance or mutual interest in combating neo-imperialism and Zionism.

On the other hand the Soviets' Afghan venture could hardly be qualified as a resounding success. The 1979 military intervention in Afghanistan, which most Western observers have viewed as a grave miscalculation on the Kremlin's part, was probably considered by even the most cautious Politburo member as a practical necessity: having once authorized a Communist coup and put their seal of approval on the revolutionary regime, the Soviets could not afford to let it disintegrate or be overthrown by a popular revolt. Some Soviet leaders must have felt instead that their error had been in authorizing the 1978 experiment in the first place, the old Kabul regime having been quite amenable to Moscow's wishes.

In any case, Afghanistan cannot serve any more than Egypt as a promising model for future Soviet efforts at making and retaining friends and expanding their influence in the Moslem world. Nor is it reasonable to see recent Soviet moves as part of a deliberate long-run strategy to secure direct control over the oil-producing countries of the area or to cut off the oil supply routes to the West and Japan. Not even the most insistent proponent of the speculator approach within the Soviet leadership could endorse such strategies, unless prepared to accept an all-out war with the United States. If ever such an argument might be made, it would not be in the context of the Middle Eastern situation, or because of the depletion of the Soviets' own energy sources.

The Kremlin is aware that in the Middle East, more than in any other area of the world outside the Soviet bloc, it has allowed its prestige to be engaged to the point that it has almost lost control over the situation on several occasions. Occasionally, actions by a client state threatened to draw the Soviet Union into a conflict it did not seek. A Soviet analyst undoubtedly had this region principally in mind when he wrote, "In a world where international tension is the rule, where there exist smouldering military conflicts in many places, states may be drawn quite unintentionally into a sequence of events where eventually they lose control over the situation and it becomes impossible to prevent a catastrophe."[15]

But have Soviet calculations about the area and the Moslem

world in general reached the point where a marginal gain in Western discomfiture is not worth the increment of risk involved for the USSR? We run again into the split personality of the Soviet foreign policy-making establishment. No blueprint in some Kremlin safe contains detailed plans for the USSR's achieving mastery of the Mediterranean's southern littoral or of the Persian Gulf. On the other hand, if the Politburo were to state its true goals for the whole vast region, it would most likely echo an American labor union leader's definition of what his constituents wanted: more. Even that would not be a complete answer, for on occasion the Soviets have sought to undermine the interests of the West even in a situation where such actions were not likely to bring concrete benefits for themselves. Both the competitive impulse of the Soviets' foreign policy and their lack of experience in techniques of retrenchment make it almost inconceivable that the present generation of leaders should seek to moderate Soviet imperial expansion in a region full of opportunities.

There is, on the other hand, a dawning realization that recent developments in the Moslem world might make a degree of Soviet disengagement from its problems and conflicts not only prudent but necessary. Moscow greeted the Khomeini revolution in Iran with obvious and understandable satisfaction. Many a Soviet Oriental expert, as well as those who still take their Marxism seriously, must have winced at the official appraisal of the social implications of this outburst of religious fanaticism: "The peculiarity of the Iranian situation consists in the fact that the majority of the population there is under the influence of the Shiite branch of Islam, whose slogans under the given circumstances have a progressive character."[16] But under most circumstances Moslem fundamentalism cannot be a friend of the Soviet cause. Unlike Khaddafi, Khomeini and his followers have not exempted the Soviets from their bitterly hostile attitude toward anything that smacks of modernization and European influence.

The present politico-religious ferment in the Islamic world is bound to assume forms and lead to situations that impinge not only on Western, but also Soviet interests. This has already been demonstrated in Afghanistan, and what is happening in that country, as well as stirrings of religious fanaticism elsewhere in the Orient, could find reverberations among the Soviet Union's Moslem population, especially in Central Asia. A time may come when the Soviets find it impractical to try to manipulate the political and social turmoil of the Moslem world and impossible to steer it into a "safe," e.g., predominantly anti-Western, direction.

As much as it runs against the grain, the Soviets then might seek to establish a pattern of cooperation with the West in order to keep this turmoil from leading to a situation threatening both sides. It may be an oversimplification to assert that "the Soviets have consistently acted as though they preferred a U.S.-USSR general agreement that extended to the Moslem world over a hazardous confrontation there."[17] For the most part, as we have seen, Moscow has been confident that it could both poach on American interests there and avoid "a hazardous confrontation." In a crisis situation, it has usually communicated rather than cooperated with Washington, as in urging the latter to restrain its friends, usually Israel, in return for Soviet intimations, not always truthful, that it has tried to exert a moderating influence on its own protégés.

How likely is it that this pattern of trying to prevent fires from turning into conflagrations rather than mounting joint efforts to eliminate the combustible materials could change in the years to come?

Much of the answer will depend on the policies of Israel. "The reach of Israeli power in the early 1980s was breathtaking, and the consequences of its uninhibited display (the raids on Lebanon, the strike against the Iraqi reactor, and the overflights of Saudi territory) quite stunning from a regional perspective. . . . Further, Israeli power threatened to be an important catalyst for fundamental alteration in the character of at least Lebanon, quite possibly Syria, and perhaps Jordan."[18] The events of June 1982, with Israeli armies surging to the outskirts of Beirut, add poignancy to the above passage.

The Soviet Union could not abandon its support for the PLO, its vociferous advocacy of Palestinians' rights, and its association with and military assistance to the hard-line Arab states without virtually terminating its role in Middle Eastern politics and incurring grave damage to its prestige and influence throughout the rest of the Moslem world. But the continued credibility of Moscow's position on all those points will henceforth depend on more than just rhetoric and supplying friends with arms. The Soviet Union's reliability as an ally and protector will be judged increasingly by the Arabs according to its readiness and ability to curb the explosion of Israeli power.

Somewhat ironically, then, the focus of Soviet maneuvers in the Middle East may shift to efforts to impress the United States with the urgent need of curbing Israel, possibly coupling the plea with more or less explicit warnings that continued Israeli forays would make it necessary for the USSR to introduce its own land- and air-combat forces into the area.

This picture warrants the conclusion that if the USSR intends to preserve major influence on the course of events, it would have to accept military commitments going considerably beyond those it undertook in 1969–70, when it helped to protect Egypt from Israeli air raids with some 12,000 Soviet troops manning Egyptian missile sites and Soviet pilots flying combat missions. Except for a probable bluff during the 1973 conflict, the USSR has eschewed such commitments since then, and it must be remembered that the Soviet combat role in the Egypt-Israeli air duel over the Suez Canal took place before detente and during the most burdensome phase of America's involvement in Southeast Asia.

Alternatively, Moscow may decide to cut its losses in the Middle East, yet save its prestige with the Arabs by securing for them some tangible gains through strenuous diplomatic efforts. Officially it has always clung to the position that a lasting settlement of the Arab-Israeli dispute must include guarantees of the sovereignty and security of all concerned states and that Israel return to its pre-1967 borders. Despite Soviet propaganda on the theme of sinister Zionist influences determining Washington's policies, the Kremlin must have noted that Israeli policies on the occupied territories have been the subject of mounting criticism in some circles in the United States and even more so in Western Europe. The Camp David process having come at least temporarily to a halt, the Soviets may count on eventual American assistance to procure Israeli withdrawal to the pre-1967 borders. The USSR then could pose as the godfather of the Palestinian state, comprising the West Bank and Gaza. If that happened, or even if the Soviets could point to tangible progress in achieving such a solution, they could look with confidence, even if with somewhat diminished expectations, to their future standing in the Middle East. The Palestinian state, they could claim, was brought into being mainly through their unremitting efforts in the face of Israel's opposition and America's obstruction.

There would still remain a number of thorny questions, such as the exact boundaries of the new state, the status of Jerusalem, the nature of guarantees for Israel, and even the problem of the latter's Arab minority, that would intermittently heat up the situation and allow the USSR to play a new hand. For the foreseeable future it would take a miracle for real peace to come to the unfortunate nations of the area, and the Soviets do not believe in miracles.

Traditionally the USSR has reacted to its policies' being thwarted in one area by making more vigorous attempts to penetrate and increase its influence in another. Were the Israeli-Arab conflict alleviated, the Kremlin would look more intently elsewhere in the Arab world and employ other techniques in order to make friends and establish its presence. If logic were an infallible guide to political behavior, one might hope that the Moslem politicians have learned the lesson of what happens when they allow themselves to be ensnared in great powers' rivalries, especially when they respond too eagerly to Moscow's blandishments. But recent history does not offer many examples of such lessons' having always been effective.

The USSR has many strings to its bow, and in the future it may stress one it has hitherto muted: ideology. The wave of Moslem fundamentalism may eventually recede, leaving behind soil favorable to the growth of radical movements of the secular variety. Few outside observers would credit regimes such as those of Morocco or Tunisia with the ability to repress political dissent and social ferment in their countries indefinitely. Much as they find it convenient to maintain a kind of liaison with Libya, the Soviets can have no illusions about the durability of its present eccentric ruler and would not be sorry to have a more reliable partner. The Soviets' Mediterranean fleet does not cruise just to show the flag. Today, with the United States expanding its bases in the area and developing a rapid deployment force, it is unlikely that the Soviets would use their naval force to assist a coup aimed at the overthrow of an existing Moslem regime or to protect one friendly to them from being toppled. But such an intervention, especially under the latter conditions, is not inconceivable. The Soviets must be wondering, not just out of curiosity, how long the feudal structure of the Arab Peninsula states can withstand the pressures of modernity, and whether those expensive military baubles that the Saudis have been accumulating can help prolong the survival of the antiquated social and political structure of their society.

If the United States ever finds itself constrained to prop up a conservative Moslem regime by more direct means than it employed in the case of Iran, that would give the USSR a fresh opportunity to fan anti-Western sentiments in the Arab world and recoup much of the credit lost through the setbacks and frustrations it has experienced by attuning its policies primarily to the Arab-Israeli struggle. Moscow then would presumably try to infuse new life into the rather comatose body of Arab Communism and shift its emphasis from the nationalist to the ideological motif as the main instrument for undermining Western interests and promoting its own in the Moslem world.

Latin America

Were Lenin resurrected and apprised of present Soviet policies in various areas of the world, there is little doubt that he would feel most comfortable with those currently pursued in Latin America. In principle, he could not oppose those temporary alliances with local dictators, anti-Western military regimes, etc., that Moscow has entered upon in Asia and Africa, nor even perhaps its courtship of the "progressive" mullahs in Iran. But it is in Latin America that the ideological ingredient of Soviet policies has been most in evidence, and more here than elsewhere (except perhaps in the Far East, and with what sad results!) the Soviets have based their bid for global power on the purported ideological mission of the Soviet state. The revolutionary struggle fomented or assisted by the USSR in the Western hemisphere has been closely related to the real economic and social blights of Latin American countries, and it is not a mere propaganda phrase to describe what is going on in some of them as the class war. And since he had always been more of a revolutionary than a Marxist, Vladimir Ilich would also have been gratified that the advance of Communist influence in Latin America is being pursued more through armed insurrections than through diplomatic maneuvers, arms deals with various local potentates, certifying tribal uprisings as *bona fide* movements of "national liberation," or wooing such dubious characters as Idi Amin, Khaddafi, or Mengistu.

Also, Lenin would note with approval the fact that, largely on account of Latin America's cultural roots and links with the West, one finds there real Marxist-Leninists, not some ideological illiterates advertising their questionable wares as "African" or "Arab" socialism. True, the main hero of the Latin American revolutionary movement has been a rather late adherent to Communism who is reputed to have confessed that he had never gotten beyond page 300 of Marx's *Capital.* But in many ways, Castro could be described as an instinctive Marxist-Leninist, and he has imparted militant tone and revolutionary impatience to a movement that had been stagnating until his appearance on the scene.

However, the current Soviet leadership has not been invariably happy with Castro, nor quite convinced of the desirability of revolutionary and political tactics associated with Castroism. Something bohemian and unprofessional about the man himself tends to make him a bit suspect to people of Andropov and Co.'s age and temper. Even now, after all the services he has rendered to the USSR, Castro must appear an outsider to Moscow, compared with a Zhivkov or a Husak (heads, respectively, of the Bulgarian and Czechoslovak Communist parties). In the past he and "Che" Guevara (who as late as 1960 had the impudence to visit Beijing) were thought not immune to the Chinese disease, their itch to set up guerrilla activities all over the continent, whatever the local conditions, making them suspect as carriers of "left-wing sectarianism" and "dogmatism." Such adventurist policies were frequently out of tune with Moscow's overall aims. The Kremlin's displeasure and suspicions about certain features of Castroism have been reflected in what old-line Latin Communist party leaders had occasionally said about him while in the Soviet Union. At the Twenty-third Party Congress in 1966, Argentina's Victorio Codavilla was unmistakably referring to Castro when he complained that some Communists in the hemisphere would take the path of adventurism rather than concentrating on building a mass base for the revolutionary party: "We oppose the anti-Leninist views of certain bourgeois ideologists who attempt to reject or minimize the role of the Party."[19]

The passage of time has soothed such concerns, and Castro has regularized his relations with Communism, removed those party old-timers who tried (conceivably with some very discreet encouragement from the Soviets) to create trouble for him, and been careful to observe proper reverence for the Fatherland of Socialism. His attitude toward China and his public pronouncements on Soviet military intervention in Czechoslovakia and Afghanistan could not be faulted. After the initial fiasco in 1962, Soviet investments in Cuba have begun to pay dividends in Africa, Nicaragua, and El Salvador. What may have been considered Khrushchev's folly by his more cautious colleagues has apparently turned into one of the most solid bastions of the worldwide system of Soviet domination and influence.

Still, one senses a certain ambivalence in the Kremlin's evaluation of Castro and his policies. The Soviet leadership does not feel at ease in dealing with another Communist country it cannot fully control and whose politics is so much dominated by one man and his "cult of personality." Until Castro plopped in their laps, the Soviets' policy vis-à-vis Latin America was one of restraint. They recognized that the region's chronic political instability and the social and political problems many of its countries faced offered great opportunities for revolutionary actions. At the same time, one had to weigh such opportunities against the risk of trying to exploit them too overtly. Latin America was within the U.S. sphere of influence, and American public and governmental opinion was very sensitive to political developments there. It would have been incautious on the part of the USSR and harmful to its interests elsewhere to goad the United States by trying to establish a bridgehead in the Western hemisphere. Latin America was a U.S. preserve, and the dangers of poaching there were incommensurate with any potential gains for the USSR. The Guatemalan episode in the 1950s seemed to confirm that Washington would not tolerate anything smacking of Communism or Moscow's influence on the continent.

It was undoubtedly the coincidence of several factors—the calming of the winds of the Cold War, the widespread belief in the alleged missile gap, but mostly Washington's initial uncertainty about the political orientation of the Cuban rebels' movement (connected perhaps with its leader's initial confusion on the subject)—that contributed to U.S. acquiescence in Castro's victory. Only after the first steps in the rapprochement between Fidelismo and Moscow did the United

States government initiate that series of clumsy, clandestine operations that culminated in the Bay of Pigs.

Castro's victory broke the charm. Latin America would no longer
be a backwater insofar as Soviet foreign policy was concerned. At both
the official and the unofficial level the Soviet Union's contacts with the
area have multiplied prodigiously. "The Soviet Union had only three
embassies in Latin America and the Caribbean in 1960. . . . By the end
of the 1970s it had diplomatic relations with nineteen countries in the
region. Soviet trade with Latin America and the Caribbean, aside
from Cuba, has multiplied fifteen-fold since 1960, from $70 million in
that year to over $1 billion in 1980; trade with Latin America has not
only grown, but diversified; trade with Argentina and Brazil had
accounted for 94 percent of Soviet exports to Latin America, that
figure was down to 60 percent by 1969. Soviet bloc credits to Latin
America also grew importantly during the 1960s and 1970s, from 5
percent of total Soviet bloc credits to developing countries in 1968 to
above 15 percent in the late 1970s. Cultural exchange has also multiplied; by 1980, 5,010 Latin American and Caribbean students were
studying in Soviet bloc countries, up from virtually zero before
1960."[20]

This opening and widening of communications between the
USSR and Latin America has coincided with a polarization of politics
in many of its countries. It would be a gross oversimplification to see
any direct connection between the two. Many factors have combined
to bring about the downfall or weakening of democratic institutions
and political pluralism existing, or on the point of emerging, in several countries some twenty years ago. Only one element, by no means
the most important one, has been Cuba, both as an example and as a
propagator of revolution.

Latin America has been first of all a victim of that "cultural revolution" which struck the entire Western world in the 1960s. The revolution's most prominent features have been the weakening of most
traditional institutions and conventions, radicalization of the intelligentsia, especially the young, and growing skepticism about the
durability and universal applicability of liberal values. In the United
States and Western Europe, where those values had been more firmly
rooted, this revolution has receded, at least in terms of its direct
impact on politics. In Latin America, which has always suffered from
political instability and endemic poverty, and where the West's usual
repository of liberal values—the middle class—was almost nonexistent
or weak, this revolution has continued in full force.

No amount of economic or sociological data could in themselves
fully explain why Chile and Argentina, with all the objective condi-

tions for becoming highly prosperous and politically stable societies on the continent, have in fact fallen prey to a continuous economic crisis, terrorism from both extremes of the political spectrum, and a particularly inept and adventurist kind of authoritarianism. Nor could such data explain why Argentina, for so long the region's model of orderly political and economic development, should first come close to emulating the Cuban example and then fall prey to military coup and junta rule. Military rule in several underdeveloped countries has served as temporary cure for political extremism and at times has been a catalyst for social and economic reform. This has not been so in Latin America, except in Peru. Elsewhere, rule by the armed forces has contributed to political polarization and fragmentation and has aggravated rather than improved the socioeconomic situation.

Revolution has not prevailed, but democracy has suffered a severe setback over most of Latin America. Thus, in practically every country on the continent a leftist coalition similar to that of Allende's in Chile could become a viable contender for power, following the overthrow or resignation of the current regime.

The sociopolitical condition of the vast area represents a serious burden for the United States and will continue to offer potential advantages to the USSR in the worldwide superpower rivalry. America's inability to transplant or strengthen democratic institutions in the countries with which it has been linked by geography and many other ties has been seen by much of the world and of Latin America itself as reflecting Washington's failure to practice what it preaches. In a sense, the U.S. plight might be compared to that faced by the USSR in Eastern Europe, the major difference being that Washington cannot impose its values and institutions on the states to the south, though much of the world refuses to believe it cannot.

The United States has placed itself in an equivocal position through its relations with quasi-fascist regimes and extreme right-wing forces in Latin America and in a tragicomic one by its constant quest for a political force or regime combining just the right proportions of anti-Communism and social reformism. This produces the unenviable predicament of having to support some rather unsavory regimes as a lesser evil to what the alternative might be, while at the same time undermining and antagonizing the very same government by intermittent criticisms of its repressive policies and constant pressure to mend its ways.

In an interview he gave to Harold Stassen in 1947, Stalin, among other musings on the world situation, suggested that America was fortunate in having as its neighbors such "weak" states as Canada and Mexico, "so you need not be afraid of them."[21] The late despot would undoubtedly be amused by the problems this country has encountered in recent years in dealing with those allegedly docile neighbors: Canada's economic nationalism, effects of the Mexican population explosion on the demographic problems in the United States, etc. But Mexico is a good example of how a Latin American government genuinely sympathetic to the main goals of United States foreign policies and quite alert to the danger of Communist subversion at home still feels it necessary to put a certain distance between its own stand and that of the United States on important issues of hemispheric politics. Mexico has found it expedient to strike a posture of cordiality toward Castro's Cuba, and it has disagreed emphatically with Washington's policies in Central America.

Few among the most pro-U.S. circles in Latin America would refrain from placing much of the onus for their countries' political and economic troubles on the United States' past and present sins of omission and commission. Even such spectacular concessions by the United States as relinquishing the Canal Zone to Panama are seen by much of Latin America as belated and insufficient attempts to undo the harm done by this country's past hegemonist practices. Though the United States is often held to be entirely alien to the mainstream of Latin American political culture and problems, at the same time Latin America expects the United States to act in an exemplary Pan-American fashion, indeed as a kind of imperial protector of the area, whenever the interests of its states appear to be threatened by an outside power. Not only in Argentina did the Falkland conflict give rise to the accusation that the United States has betrayed its hemispheric obligations and has ranged itself on the side of a colonial power against a sister American nation, in line with its past imperialist practices.

In surveying the Latin American scene, the Soviets must note with satisfaction the profusion and variety of forces and influences creating an environment favorable both for revolutionary activism and for further erosion of American interests there.

The authors of a Soviet compendium on Latin American politics have good words to say about Peru's military regime: "The attempt of the military leaders to link the influence of general revolutionary thought with the ideology of the Peruvian revolution and with the concept of 'Western civilization' offers firm evidence of their [the military leaders] having been influenced by the ideas of scientific socialism."[22] Similar praise is bestowed on the left Catholics, increasingly an important feature of the region's political landscape: "The nationalism of the left Catholics . . . is considerably different from all other varieties of Christian-nationalist reformism. It stands out among them in virtue of its revolutionary elan, its emphasis on the struggle against capitalism and for the liquidation of all forms of oppression, the creation of a just, classless society."[23]

As seen by the Soviets, virtually all major radical and nationalist movements in the area are actual and potential allies of revolution and Communism. Argentina's Communists have for long courted and maintained contacts with the left wing of the Peronist movement. It remains to be seen whether such an alliance could be fully consummated and whether it would become a serious contender in the struggle for power if the junta eventually collapses.

Perhaps to a greater degree than in other Third World areas, the Soviets' criteria in assessing a Latin American regime or political movement depend on its attitude toward the United States. One would expect a Soviet publication to be ultracritical of a movement whose ideology bears a clear imprint of "leftist sectarianism and dogmatism," which is critical of the USSR for its alleged "refusal to propagate revolution through violent means," and which condemns detente as a deal between two "rich" nations at the expense of the revolutionary interests of the Third World. Yet while chiding the organization in question for its ideological errors, the Soviet author approves of "the positive character of its stand against the domination by the United States, as well as the uncompromising thrust of its social protest."[24] Being anti-American excuses many sins, including, in this case, a basic revolutionary philosophy derived from the ideas of the late Mao and Lin Biao rather than the preachments of Suslov or Ponomarev.

One might conclude that Latin America will become of even more intense interest to the Kremlin and that the latter would try to expand its active role in penetrating the region's affairs. The first part of such a prognosis is quite justified, the latter much less so. Here is one area concerning which the rentier and the speculator in the Soviet leaders' mind would probably come closest to agreeing on what actual Soviet policies should be. Precisely because the region is so fertile with revolutionary situations and opportunities and because here, above all, the "objective course of history" seems to point in a direction promising further troubles for the United States and its allies, the USSR should eschew direct or ostentatious intervention in Latin American politics.

Such direct attempts would be both risky and counterproductive, especially given the plain evidence that it has been by indirect help, by its links with and protection of Cuba, that the USSR has been able to assist most effectively in the development of the Latin American revolution. By allowing Castro and his friends not only to receive the credit for but also to run the Latin American revolutionary show to a large extent the USSR eschews direct responsibility for its troubles and potential setbacks and can deny the imputations that events in Nicaragua, El Salvador, and elsewhere are yet another manifestation of Soviet imperial expansion.

Furthermore, anything that puts in question the purely native roots, dynamics, and directions of the Latin American revolution weakens the appeal of that revolution and undercuts the potential of Castro's Cuba as the Communist piedmont of Latin America. The USSR will go as far as standing by its Cuban coreligionists or occasionally supplying arms and sympathy to those who are or will be fighting for social justice in Central America and elsewhere, but beyond that an identification of the revolutionary cause with the policies of the Soviet Union would harm the interests of both.

We might then expect to see the USSR persist in its posture of sympathetic observer of the Latin American scene, ready to discharge its obligations to support the forces fighting for social justice morally and occasionally with more tangible assistance, but willing to be friends with regimes of all political complexions. Special circumstances, as the case of Chile, may call for exceptions to this latitudinarian attitude on the Soviets' part. However, they have had no scruples in preserving very correct relations with the Argentine regime, though its ruling junta could hardly be thought preferable to its Chilean counterpart, whether on ideological or humanitarian grounds. Such broadmindedness has already been rewarded by the Argentine generals' increasing substantially their wheat sales to the USSR and thus helping offset the effects of the grain embargo imposed by the United States after the invasion of Afghanistan. If the consequences of the Falklands crisis should warrant, the Kremlin would undoubtedly be prepared for much closer Soviet-Argentine relations.

The Kremlin's Latin American game must be expected to continue to emphasize adding to U.S. burdens and troubles in the hemisphere, rather than securing new clients for the USSR and thus incurring direct commitments. Marxist and quasi-Marxist regimes that embarrass the United States but do not openly profess loyalty to the USSR would serve the Soviet Union's purposes much better than a Latin American Bulgaria or Ethiopia. The advantages of this approach can best be illustrated by the case of El Salvador. The civil war in that tiny country has not only absorbed an inordinate amount of attention and effort from the current U.S. administration, but also brought it criticism from the more progressive countries of the region and from America's European allies as well. Insofar as its divisive influence on U.S. domestic politics has been concerned, El Salvador has become a sort of miniature replica of the Vietnam issue. Why should the USSR seek more direct means of combating America's influence and power in the hemisphere when the El Salvador approach serves it so well? This is a classic example of the Soviet Union tossing out, so to speak, a few matches (and not with its own hands) and making the United States rush in with expensive and cumbersome fire-fighting equipment, thus hampering its capabilities of fighting a serious conflagration elsewhere.

At the same time, the Soviets may flatter themselves that what happened in Cuba and has been happening in Central America offers a gratifying example of the persistent appeal of militant Marxism here. Alas, such examples cannot be duplicated in many other parts of the world. Whatever the Soviet leaders' inner convictions (and it is unlikely that what they have been reciting for years has not left some residue in the minds of the most cynical), they must treasure such examples of the continued vitality of the Leninist legacy, which is important to them for the purposes of foreign and domestic politics and propaganda.

In that context, Cuba has been of crucial importance, just as it remains the fulcrum of Soviet policies in much more than the Caribbean region. Any future projections of Soviet-Cuban relations must take into account the fact that while Castro has not been a mere puppet, he is not, nor is he likely to become, an entirely free agent. His relations with the USSR are not based merely on common ideological values and a temporary political alliance. As some American analysts have noted, "Cuba's desire for some degree of autonomy from the USSR might be greater than is generally recognized,"[25] but the statement would undoubtedly be true of the majority of leaders of Soviet bloc countries. Castro's original commitment to the Soviet camp was motivated not only by his strong anti-Yankee sentiments, but also by his ambition to cast a world figure and become a Latin American Lenin. He cannot be pleased that his country has been used as a cat's-paw of Soviet imperialism in Africa and elsewhere, nor be unmindful of the relative niggardliness of Soviet economic help.

Castro has obviously resented those periods of Soviet-American detente that made Moscow restrain the Cubans' propagation of revolution in other Latin American countries. The official line that the Angolan venture was undertaken at Havana's initiative may well be true, insofar as Castro's initial willingness to help the revolutionary cause there was concerned. But he could hardly have anticipated or wished for what in proportion to Cuba's population has been massive use of its armed forces in places like Ethiopia. There they have been employed to suppress what by his definition have been revolutionary and "national liberation" movements.

To be sure, the on and off Cuban intimations of establishing better relations with the United States might well be in line with the overall Soviet scheme of things for Latin America and, thus, a testimony to Moscow's confidence in its hold over Castro rather than evidence of the Cubans' straining at the leash. Stingy as they are themselves, the Russians would not begrudge Cuba an infusion of economic help from the West, any more than they have in the case of their East European friends. The North Vietnamese have also on occasion suggested that they might deign to accept American economic assistance in order to lessen their dependence on the Kremlin.

The Cubans' willingness, as indicated to a group of Americans who visited Havana in April 1982, to consider a negotiated settlement in El Salvador may also fit the general pattern of Soviet political strategy for Central America. Washington's current determination to deny the left a military victory in El Salvador suggests the radical forces should seek a temporary settlement through negotiations and coalition arrangements. Then, after a passage of time, with the United States weary and inattentive to the problems of the area, these forces might well make a bid for total power.

It is in America's interest to explore every option for a peaceful solution of the Salvadoran mess, to give the Nicaraguan regime the benefit of the doubt, and to keep testing Havana's flexibility on a number of issues. But such efforts can be productive only if the other side can really be persuaded that it cannot manipulate negotiations to achieve what it had previously pursued through violent means. To secure tangible concessions through negotiations with a regime such as Castro's requires more tenacity of purpose and patience than either American diplomacy or public opinion have been able to display.

It is not in Moscow's, or especially Havana's, interest that the United States should lose its patience in the wrong way. The accretion of American discomfitures and setbacks in Latin America should be gradual, never reaching the proportions that would spark a crisis like that of 1962.

For Castro himself or any likely successor, the difficulties of disengaging Cuba from the Soviets' embrace would be almost insuperable. Almost as much as in the case of Bulgaria or Czechoslovakia, it is the shadow of Soviet power that protects the Communist government in Cuba, not only from a potential external enemy, but from its own people. For all of Castro's charisma and the revolutionary elan of the ruling elite, it is unlikely that his regime currently holds the loyalty of the majority of Cubans. The statistics of those who have chosen to leave the island within the last two decades tell their own tale. Military ventures abroad could not have improved the Communist government's image among the masses: ". . . widespread unhappiness among the Cuban people concerning compulsory military service was equally obvious. Now [in 1975 with the Cubans in Angola] it became clear that even ordinary people found it disagreeable and thought it coercive."[26]

Unlikely as it seems that Castro would succeed or even try to sever his links to Moscow, the Soviets, bearing in mind what happened with such zealous revolutionaries as Tito and Mao, are unlikely to leave anything to chance. The size of the Soviets' military and civilian presence in Cuba and their intermittent efforts (in contravention of the 1962 Soviet-American understanding) to sneak in a naval base can be understood in terms of exploiting fully the strategic and intelligence gathering potential of an area so close to the United States. But such activities serve also as a constant irritant to Washington and stand in the way of any meaningful effort by Castro to reach an accommodation with this country.

Such then is the mosaic of Soviet policies, aims, hopes, and apprehensions concerning Latin America. Their sum total, as in the other two areas of the Third World, still does not add up to one of the absolute priorities for the Kremlin in the years immediately ahead. In any of the three it is possible to envisage a situation arising out of U.S.-Soviet rivalry that could escalate into a confrontation and beyond. But in the natural course of events, Soviet policies in these regions should continue to reflect much less the local conditions and whatever they might offer for Russian expansion, and much more what happens in the three focal areas of the Kremlin's world view: China, Western Europe, and the United States.

Areas of Decision

China

If one considers the political premises of the two systems and the realities of the international situation, then the Sino-Soviet conflict is not, in the long run, susceptible to a peaceful resolution. But Soviet leaders heed Keynes's dictum that "in the long run we shall all be dead." Their concern must be centered on the opportunities, options, and dangers inherent in the Chinese situation within the next few years. It would be too cynical to suggest that this approach is conditioned mainly by the average age of the present Kremlin team. Rather, for all their *realpolitik* attitudes, they have not entirely lost the belief that ideological miracles, at times, do happen. Perhaps the international situation of the 1990s would open some unseen new opportunities that might solve or alleviate this most agonizing dilemma of Soviet foreign relations. What are the factors that make the long-run prospects so unpromising, and how could they be affected by the developments of the next few years?

On the Chinese side, the main answer lies in nationalism and in the Chinese historical experience with Russia, going back long before the Revolution. Shared ideology helped at first to dispel much of the traditional distrust between the two nations, but actual exposure to

Soviet policies since the birth of the People's Republic in 1949 served to revive and even to intensify the bitter suspicion of the past. The Chinese fear the Russians, because they realize that the latter fear them. Since common ideology has not been able to overcome the Russians' xenophobia and its racist undertones, the nationalist motif in Beijing's hostility toward the USSR has been strengthened by an ideological one: the Soviets have betrayed and perverted Communism.

Details of China's ideological indictment of the Kremlin have changed in accordance with the vicissitudes of Chinese domestic politics. At one time the Soviets were seen as having abandoned the egalitarian and populist elements of the cult and having entered upon the path of revisionism, with its bureaucratic and bourgeois excrescences. At another time, Beijing was at pains to present Moscow as standing for a white and developed country's brand of Communism, and hence scornful of the needs and revolutionary aspirations of the great majority of mankind.

In both cases the Chinese used the ideological argument not only to score debating points against Moscow, but also to pressure it into a more uncompromising posture vis-à-vis the West, thus making it more difficult, if not impossible, for the Soviets to strike a deal at China's expense with the United States. This eventuality was Beijing's nightmare in the 1950s and 1960s and has not entirely disappeared from its leaders' minds up to now.

The paradoxical and ironic situation that prevailed well into the 1970s and may yet recur was that even though the Soviets could see perfectly well through Beijing's game, China's vituperation and accusations *did* affect their foreign policy. Even after the 1960 break, when they no longer had to pretend to be friends with China, the Soviets, because of insolent Chinese kibitzing of their policies, found themselves unable to be more explicit about seeking detente with the United States or about cooling off those revolutionary situations throughout the world that were harmful to Soviet interests. Moscow increasingly saw China's revolutionary rhetoric and its advocacy of the most militant tactics in the Third World as designed not only to keep the two superpowers apart, but also to embroil them in continuous conflicts, not precluding the possibility of their leading to a nuclear war. Mao's famous apothegm, "The current international situation is excellent; there is great disorder under heaven,"[27] could not be treated by the Kremlin in a jocular vein, since it epitomized the Chinese leaders' deliberate attempt to throw the international situation into a turmoil that could not be controlled even through joint superpower efforts. It was a variation in the nuclear age of the old Chinese maxim about using one set of barbarians to fight another.

In some ways China's shift toward accommodation with the United States did have some redeeming features from the Soviet point of view. It cleared the air; "Beijing's leaders" could now be denounced uninhibitedly, as direct allies of imperialism. China's prestige among the more militant Communist parties and "liberation movements" declined, and it would no longer be able to cause the USSR major embarrassments on that count. Finally, that undesirable but rational act on the part of the Chinese leaders probably removed the Kremlin's lurking suspicion that Mao really meant what he said and just might succeed in plunging the world into a nuclear holocaust. The People's Republic now would try to play the same tricks from the other side, i.e., to set the West against the USSR. But Beijing would discover how hard it is to push the democracies into anything resembling a bellicose stand or to make them choose an alliance with a still weak and backward China over propitiating the military colossus of the USSR. In any case, as practical politicians rather than fanatics, the Chinese would probably be easier to deal with. They would abandon their feigned nonchalance about nuclear war and understand the implicit warning contained in the concentration of Soviet troops on their northern border. They would have to take full measure of the economic mess into which they had plunged their country through various "great leaps" and "cultural revolutions." In a few years one might begin to talk business with China, with neither side likely to have any illusions about the other, but with the Chinese having lost most of those they had about world Communism and about the benefits of their liaison with the West.

As of 1982 such expectations have failed to materialize, as have some of Moscow's other hopes of how "their" Chinese problem might be resolved: factional strife after Mao's death reaching the proportions of a civil war, a miraculous rebirth of proletarian internationalism within the post-Mao leadership, etc. The ideological part of the Chinese Communists' case against the Soviets has become attenuated but not disappeared. Forced to resort to many policies they once denounced as revisionism, maintaining wide contacts with the capitalist world, and trying to undo the damage done by past fanatical zeal, the Chinese Communists still retain something of the neophytes' ideological fervor. The present phase in China's development may yet become something parallel to the Soviet NEP of the 1920s, rather than a definite divorce between ideology and practical politics. It is at least premature to say that "In fact nationalism has triumphed over all else, as was true earlier in the Soviet Union."[28] The People's Republic is still assailing the USSR for having prostituted the ideals of Communism and for practicing imperialism under the cover of revolutionary slogans.

Yet, in the future ideological elements may prove to be a factor in lessening the tensions between the two Communist powers, but not in the positive sense of restoring the political collaboration and "unshakable friendship of the fraternal peoples" maintained in outward appearances until the late 1950s. Rather it is a negative factor: the residue of revolutionary radicalism in Chinese Communism acting as a barrier against a too close rapprochement between the People's Republic and the West. The Chinese leadership has not apparently resolved the conflict between those who see Western credits and technology as necessary for the country to get out of its present economic morass and achieve rapid growth and modernization and the more ideological members of the elite, for whom such extensive contacts with the capitalist world spell danger to the socialist ethos. "Especially important in this regard is the radicals' insistence that although the social and political imperatives of certain moderate policies may be conducive to successful economic development, they actually threaten the long-run objectives of China's socialist revolution."[29]

It is safe to say that intimate ties with the USSR will never be reestablished. But for domestic and foreign considerations, the Beijing government might decide to accept the Soviets' repeated pleas that the two countries normalize their state-to-state relations, settle their territorial disputes (minor in themselves), and expand trade and cultural links. The People's Republic would thus be signaling that while emphatically not in the Soviet camp, it proposes also to keep some distance from the capitalist West. Such a posture might have advantages also for those who place economic growth at the top of their priorities: the West would be less inclined to take China's anti-Sovietism for granted and therefore more forthcoming with economic aid.

The Soviets wish for a formal rapprochement for exactly the opposite reasons. According to Moscow's calculations, it should dampen the Americans' enthusiasm for playing the "China card" and, by the same token, reinforce Washington's reluctance to disinterest itself completely in the fate of Taiwan. The mere fact of the two Communist powers' desisting from mutual vituperation and signing a treaty of nonaggression would have a positive result on the Soviet Union's somewhat strained relations with North Korea and the Japanese Communists, as well as on the morale of Communist parties all over the world.

Yet, when in a more skeptical mood, the Soviets must ponder whether a nonaggression treaty and other cosmetic adjustments would really help, even in the short run. As in the other two main areas of their attention, it is China's present and future power rather than its actual and prospective policies that are of main concern to the

Kremlin. In the 1990s an unfriendly and sullen China but one that is still far from a first-rate industrial and military power would be preferable to a Beijing with the most proper relations with Moscow but a high rate of economic growth, a burgeoning industry, and a respectable stockpile of nuclear and conventional arms. For all their seeming reluctance, perhaps all those wily Dengs, etc., really desire a patching up of Sino-Soviet relations to gain a breathing spell that would enable them to rebuild their shattered economy and erect a modern military establishment. Once they achieve those goals, would they not revert to the incredible brazenness that characterized Mao's tone when in 1954 he demanded that the USSR acknowledge China's suzerainty over Mongolia or when in September 1964 he informed the whole world that China had never forgotten or acquiesced in the loss of all those vast territories the Russians had wrested from the Manchu Empire in the nineteenth century? China has never explicitly repudiated the intimations that sometime it might reopen the question of Mongolia and of the legitimacy of those "unequal treaties" that had secured imperial Russia more than a million and a half square kilometers of territory, now an integral part of the USSR. The Soviet leaders must reflect at their low moments that their Chinese counterparts are unlikely to be fooled or deflected from their goals ("They are really like ourselves in that respect," is a thought that may occur to a member of the Politburo), and so no treaty or papering over of the dispute can relieve the Kremlin from the need for constant vigilance over China and keeping in mind the horrendous possibilities and ramifications of the problem in every area of its foreign relations.

In the Soviet view, Beijing's potential to cause mischief on a large scale is not precluded even by its current condition of overall industrial and military weakness. Here is how a Soviet author fills in the disturbing details: "Chinese leaders spend approximately 40 percent of their budget on military purposes, and have been rapidly developing China's nuclear, as well as conventional [military] potential. The People's Republic has through the middle of 1978 carried out twenty-three atmospheric tests. It has accumulated . . . several hundred warheads (both atomic and hydrogen), has deployed about forty intermediate missile launchers, and tested intercontinental missiles (with up to a 13,000 kilometer range). It has [constructed] a diesel submarine with missile tubes, and begun the development of ballistic missiles with solid fuel."[30] Of course it would be an act of utter, suicidal irrationality for the Chinese to stage a nuclear strike at Soviet territory, and the Kremlin is no longer as nervous on that count as it had appeared during the Cultural Revolution. Still, the Soviets, once frightened, never completely discard their suspicions. The following nightmarish scenario, sketched some years ago by a leading Soviet authority on international affairs, is still very likely in the back of their minds, but with China to be inserted where the author mentions West Germany: "The Federal Republic, having received nuclear weapons, could, while *keeping it secret from the United States,* equip one of its vessels with a nuclear missile . . . then it might send it close to the U.S. shores to carry out a nuclear strike against its territory in a manner suggesting that the attack came from a Soviet ship or submarine. The U.S. government, which would have to decide upon retaliation within minutes, might then order a nuclear strike against the USSR. Be it even . . . a single missile, striking one city . . . the USSR would have to retaliate. The adventurer's goal to provoke a major nuclear war would thus have been achieved."[31]

China's as yet modest nuclear arsenal must have already brought a qualitative change in the Kremlin's thinking of military options vis-à-vis China. In view of the frightful devastation that even a single nuclear missile can achieve, the USSR would not consider massive use of military force against China unless under extreme circumstances. Border skirmishes are one thing. But even the most speculator-minded member of the Politburo would hesitate to advocate, short of a very unusual situation, a large-scale invasion of Chinese territory or Soviet military intervention in a hypothetical civil war in China. Only a Chinese invasion of the USSR or an outright alliance between the United States and China (probabilities on a par with the introduction of a multiparty system in the Soviet Union) could change that situation.

Yet, the Soviet leadership may well feel there is no reason to feel unduly depressed in the immediate future by the repercussions of the Chinese problem. There are encouraging signs that the People's Republic's internal problems, which stem mainly from economic trouble but inevitably affect the political and social picture, will increasingly preoccupy the leadership's attention and substantially decrease its ability to promote and encourage anti-Soviet mischief throughout the world. In retrospect, that "left-wing sectarianism and dogmatism" that the Kremlin had so strenuously denounced in the Chinese comrades have turned out to have been of great indirect help to the USSR. The attempt to pull themselves up by their own bootstraps, their rigid egalitarianism and other doctrinaire policies, compounded by the ultimate folly of the Cultural Revolution, have cost the Chinese dearly. It has set the country back by a whole generation insofar as its economic growth and modernization are concerned. The ambitious plan of the post-Mao leadership to make China a first-rate industrial and military power by the end of the century through the "Four Modernizations" (in industry, agriculture, science, and the military complex) would obviously have to give way to much more modest goals and expectations. Beijing's initial confidence that modernization and socialism could be achieved through its own efforts has given way to the recognition that even modest progress requires foreign, i.e., capitalist, help. "By early 1978, however, the Chinese were negotiating for large-scale syndicated loans from Western and Japanese banking groups. . . .[A government official] explicitly stated that China would accept foreign government loans."[32]

A similar retreat from Communist fundamentalism has taken place in agriculture. Once proud of having gone far beyond the Soviets insofar as the communal organization of rural life was concerned, the Chinese have been constrained to reintroduce material incentives and stress the role of the individual farmer in order to cope with the desperate problem of feeding a population of one billion that keeps increasing (despite all drastic population control measures) at a rate of something like 2 percent per year.

Domestic problems of a Communist regime, rather than setting constraints on its foreign policies, often tend to make it more adventurous and expansion-minded in its activities on the international scene. But in the case of the People's Republic, its socioeconomic problems are of a magnitude that would seem to set limits to playing an ambitious international role. The regime has of late been constrained to reduce its expenditures on the military (even after the Chinese army's lamentable performance in the brief war with Vietnam) and to invest more in light industry. For the time being, progress toward industrialization, the key condition of modernization and of becoming a military power, has slowed down. Even according to official statistics, heavy industry's output actually decreased during the first half of 1981 by 8.2 percent, and the state enterprise's profits during the same period had fallen by 12.3 percent.[33] It would require simply enormous investments over the next decade to speed up significantly the pace of China's industrialization, estimates ranging from $250 to $600 billion. It is beyond the People's Republic's internal resources to generate anything approaching such amounts or to pay for credits of similar magnitude with its export earnings.

Such statistics must be read with grim satisfaction by the Soviet "China hands." Those with a sense of humor might reflect that perhaps it was not such a monumental folly for the USSR to help the Chinese Communists conquer all of the mainland. What if the Kuomintang had prevailed and all of China had emulated the pattern of development in Taiwan? On a more serious level, mere statistics cannot assuage completely the Soviets' fears. Their own economic troubles, though not nearly so serious, have not kept them from cutting quite a figure in world affairs. There is an unpleasant possibility that the West might embark on a massive Marshall Plan–type aid program to enable China to overcome current difficulties and become a more effective potential threat to the USSR. The USSR has hinted that it might consider such a plan of assistance to China a hostile act directed against Soviet interests. "The Beijing leaders aim to transform China by the end of the twentieth century into a 'superpower,' and above all through expanding and modernizing its military potential. They count on active assistance of the imperialist powers. . . . It is difficult to exaggerate the dangerous character of such maneuvers: the Beijing leaders continually repeat that a new world war is 'inevitable,' advance territorial demands on the neighboring states, provoke border conflicts and indulge in aggressive raids. . . ."[34]

As for direct Soviet attempts to influence the course of domestic Chinese politics, they would appear to be doomed to failure. In his paper on China in the 1980s Gerrit Gong has drawn attention to some possible pro-Soviet or at least anti-Western stirrings within the Chinese military. A clandestine radio station, "Eight-one," evidently located on Soviet territory, has been broadcasting messages and programs aimed at those within the Chinese military establishment who have resented Deng's recent policies, especially rapprochement with the United States and the reduction of military expenditures: "The radio broadcasts show great sophistication and detailed 'inside' knowledge of the workings of the People's Liberation Army."[35] It must be remembered that Lin Biao, once Mao's designated successor, was alleged to have met his death while fleeing in a plane to the USSR.

It is quite likely that there should be considerable disaffection within military circles after the less than brilliant showing of the People's Liberation Army in the clash with Vietnam, a fiasco probably blamed on the regime's political leadership. It would also be surprising if the Soviets had not succeeded in planting Soviet agents and sympathizers within the officer corps and scientific and administrative apparatus of the People's Republic during the period of close USSR-China collaboration. Still, given the fierce nationalism of the Chinese Communists and people in general, the notion of a *sizable* pro-Moscow faction within the military or political establishment appears unrealistic. There are obviously influential groups both in the army and elsewhere who would like the country's international stand to be less explicitly anti-Soviet than it has been for almost a generation. Some might wish to exploit the "Soviet card" to press the United States harder on Taiwan and to secure more American aid. But short of a complete fragmentation of Chinese politics, it is almost inconceivable that a pro-Soviet faction might play a significant role in the struggle for power. Everything is possible in the strange world of contemporary international politics, but a Beijing regime ready to discard its distrust and to seek again close ties with the USSR would be perhaps the most amazing eventuality of all.

One cannot develop an entirely convincing pattern of prognosti-
cation about China's domestic development and especially about the
course of Sino-Soviet relations during the next few years. In view of
the Chinese experience with Vietnam, who would have predicted that
the PRC would cut down on military expenditures and put defense in
last place among the "Four Modernizations"? And again, what on the
face of it ought to be reassuring to the Soviets is, in view of their
mentality, very likely to lead to increased apprehensions about
China's long-term goals. Beijing has evidently decided that the volun-
taristic approach does not work any better in the defense sector than
in other policy areas. It is impossible to have an efficient, modern
defense establishment without first developing a firm industrial base
for the country as a whole.

What at first might seem a sign of Beijing's moderation appears
on second thought an indication to the Soviets that it proposes to
pursue its old goals, but in a more rational and deliberate manner.
Far from reassuring the Soviets, such modernization is likely to increase apprehensions about China's long-term goals. The Chinese
have given up the childish idea of "punishing" Vietnam by relying
mostly on their vast manpower, but they are obviously biding their
time until ready to administer such lessons to Soviet friends in a more
professional and convincing manner. If China's economy and hence
military capabilities should, against all the odds, show some spectacular gains by the end of the decade, might not Vietnam decide to hedge
its bets and once again seek friendship with a Communist power to
which it had once felt much closer than it did to Moscow? The logic of
the geographic situation makes Mongolia undoubtedly the most
genuinely loyal of the Soviet Union's satellites at the present time. But
would it remain so when and if China becomes much stronger?

In trying to dissuade China from developing its own nuclear
deterrent, Khrushchev expostulated with Beijing that it should devote its efforts "to the development of the national economy . . .
improving the well-being of the Chinese people rather than wasting
money on such expensive baubles."[36] The USSR was protecting
China with its own nuclear might, so what purpose could be served by
the People's Republic acquiring its own necessarily modest stockpile
of atomic weapons? The argument was specious, and the Chinese
disdainfully made an appropriate retort. But in the future, a variant
of Khrushchev's argument may well be convincing to Beijing and a
source of anxiety to the Kremlin. Some in China's highest councils
probably feel that the United States is protecting it from a preemptive
Soviet strike. Therefore, now that national pride has been satisfied by
demonstrations that the People's Republic is capable of developing
the hydrogen bomb and the intercontinental ballistic missile, it would
be counterproductive to continue a race in which China could not

hope to catch up with the superpowers for decades. Why not concentrate instead on developing and modernizing conventional forces, thus exploiting China's unmatched manpower asset?

At present the condition of these forces is lamentable. "The list of China's needs for conventional military equipment is long. The PRC still does not have an all-weather fighter, advanced airborne radar, modern bombers or helicopters. It lacks anti-tank missiles, air-to-air missiles, and modern naval and airborne guns. Its battle tanks possess limited fire power. Its air transport capabilities are very inadequate."[37] The Vietnamese war also demonstrated the obsolescence of the People's Army's tactics and logistics, which were essentially the same as those it followed thirty years before in the Korean war.

Unlike its backwardness in nuclear weapons, China's conventional arms and technology could be considerably modernized within a relatively short time. There are no legal barriers, such as those imposed by the Non-Proliferation Treaty, which would prevent the United States, Britain, or France from furnishing the People's Republic with modern conventional weapons and technology. One of the highest priorities of Soviet diplomacy is to try to interdict such Western aid to China.

Even a relatively modest improvement in China's conventional military capabilities would open up some rather alarming perspectives for Moscow. In a few years Beijing's leaders might conclude that their own nuclear weapons provide a sufficient deterrent against a Soviet invasion, while the uncertainty of what America might do would inhibit the Kremlin from a more drastic nuclear attack upon China. There would be then a considerable temptation for the leadership of the People's Republic to engage in more active forms of curbing the Soviet Union's hegemonism. Is it entirely inconceivable to visualize Chinese soldiers fighting alongside the rebels in Afghanistan?

Even to envisage such a possibility leads to appreciation of another facet of the Kremlin's worries. China may and probably will eschew such "brinksmanship" in the immediate years ahead. But the mere fact of the People's Republic's growing strength could translate into the gradual erosion of Soviet influence in Asia: the USSR's allies and protégés could no longer be sure that it would be ready to protect them against the Chinese colossus should the need arise. Even the past China-Vietnam clash, though it ended in virtual defeat for the PRC, was hardly a victory for the Soviet Union. Though its ally had been attacked, Moscow confined itself mostly to ominous warnings, and many Asians must have wondered what, if anything, the Soviets would have done had Chinese troops penetrated deep into Vietnam.

Alongside of other actual or tentative attempts to deal with the

Chinese problem, the Kremlin has intermittently employed tactics bearing a marked resemblance to U.S. policies in the immediate post–World War II period for trying to cope with what America perceived as the Soviet threat. George Kennan in his celebrated essay defined one element of containment as requiring the West "to confront the Russians with unalterable counterforce at every point where they show signs of encroaching upon the interests of a peaceful and stable world."[38] With a few appropriate alterations this phrase could be a description of what the Soviet Union has been trying to do to contain China through a system of alliances and understandings with the latter's neighbors, and by its own impressive array of military power along the Sino-Soviet border: thus, any threat to the interests of the Soviets or their allies could be met with "unalterable counterforce."

The Soviet version of containment does not promise to prove any more effective than its American prototype had been. Even under Khrushchev the Kremlin gave serious thought to the possibility of India's becoming a counterweight to China in Asian politics. The 1971 Soviet-Indian treaty of friendship and cooperation gave New Delhi a green light to embark on something it had hitherto not dared, largely because of its fear of possible Chinese reactions—a full-scale war against Pakistan in order to enable the Bengali nationalists to obtain independence. The whole affair was undoubtedly a severe blow to Beijing's prestige in Asia. It remained on the sidelines while India, to the Soviets' plaudits, defeated and dismembered Pakistan, until then China's staunchest friend among the noncommunist nations. However, it seems unlikely that any New Delhi regime, even one as friendly to the USSR as Indira Gandhi's, would wish to transgress certain bounds of caution in its attitude toward the People's Republic for the immediate future. It would require a very unusual set of circumstances for India to join an anti-Beijing coalition on any issue not touching directly on the affairs of the subcontinent or of such neighbors as Burma and Nepal. Mao's successors have been careful to emphasize that their country has no territorial claims on its smaller neighbors who are not directly linked with the Soviet bloc. They have also become much less strident in their support of national liberation movements and Communist parties in the neighboring areas.

In Indochina the USSR has indeed gone beyond containment and has assisted and applauded Vietnam's "rollback" of Chinese influence. However, other Southeastern Asian countries, whatever their apprehensions about China's ultimate aims and about tensions from their own sizable Chinese communities, have been reassured for the immediate future by Beijing's change of course in its foreign policies and its friendly relations with the West. For some years the Kremlin has propagated the idea of an Asian security pact. While understandably vague on details, the Soviet goal has been obviously to erect some kind of *cordon sanitaire* around China. Yet the idea has found few takers among Asia's statesmen. Though still apprehensive of China, most of them may be even more afraid of any kind of Soviet protection or "guarantees."

The most conspicuous case of Soviet diplomatic failure in Asia has been in its relations with Japan. Apart from much else this gross error has cost the USSR, it has condemned to futility any Kremlin dreams of isolating China within the Asian community, at least for the present. Instead, the Soviet leadership must live with a nightmare: China's vast manpower and natural resources becoming linked to Japan's prodigious industrial power and technology. It is as if history were repeating itself, not as tragedy turning into comedy, but as a slogan for conquest becoming a signpost for peaceful cooperation. The possibility of an "East Asian co-prosperity sphere" might materialize as a genuine description of relations between the two Far Eastern powers.

Although eager to draw Japan out of the American orbit and to enlist its capital and industrial skills in developing Siberia (thus incidentally erecting another barrier against Beijing's possible future claims on the Soviet Far East), the USSR has still balked at returning to Tokyo the four southernmost Kurile Islands Moscow seized with other territorial loot in 1945. This insistence on retaining perhaps the *least* important Soviet territorial acquisition in World War II has offended Japanese public opinion and prevented a Soviet-Japanese treaty, by now a formality but of great psychological importance for Moscow-Tokyo relations. Perhaps the real reason for this fundamental blunder in the Kremlin's usually pragmatic and skillful diplomacy is in itself connected with the Soviets' visceral reaction to their Chinese predicament: any territorial concession in *Asia* might embolden Beijing's leaders to become more strident about "unequal treaties" and more brazen about reclaiming some of the territories Russia had wrested from China.

In any case Moscow's hard line with Japan, epitomized by Brezhnev's statement at the Twenty-fifth Party Congress, played directly into Beijing's hands. The Soviet leader said revealingly: "There are people in Japan, obviously inspired by some outsiders, who in connection with the peace settlement are trying to make completely groundless and illegal claims upon the USSR."[39] Those "outsiders" have profited by the Soviets' unwillingness to part with a few fishing villages. The Sino-Japanese Peace and Friendship Treaty was concluded despite Moscow's warnings to Tokyo. Both signatories joined in condemning "hegemonism," a code word that now stands for Soviet imperialism to much of the world.

Moscow may yet try to undo its error in relation to Japan. Conversely, it might attempt to use more forceful arguments to dissuade Tokyo from underwriting China's industrial development. But should it go too far in pressuring the Japanese, they might in turn abandon their hitherto frugal approach to defense and proceed to build a military establishment more compatible with their industrial might.

The Chinese problem thus does not yield itself easily to any single ingenious stratagem, or even a combination of them. Some of the Soviets' efforts to probe for possible solutions have verged on the ludicrous, like the occasional hints of possible collusion with Taiwan. There have even been occasional hints in Soviet literature about the disaffection among China's minorities, especially those in the northern region, who are ethnically and culturally close to their kinsmen across the Soviet border. Such hints only remind the Chinese of the humiliation they must have felt during negotiations with Stalin's Russia in 1949–50, when the Soviet press stressed that Moscow was hosting special representatives of the Manchurian and Sinkiang regional regimes, along with the delegation of the People's Republic headed by Mao.

There are factors mitigating the Soviets' immediate concerns on account of China. Perhaps some in the Politburo may hope against hope that when and if China emerges from its present disarray, the USSR will be in a worldwide position so strong that the danger coming from that quarter will become quite distant. But in his more sober moments, whether leaning toward the rentier or the speculator position, a Soviet leader must feel a bit like the sorcerer's apprentice in the famous fable: there is as yet no formula capable of propitiating the Chinese colossus or making him heed the Kremlin's wishes. For the rest of the decade the Kremlin will anxiously search for such a formula, and this quest will affect all areas of its foreign and perhaps its domestic policies.

Western Europe

If China's unity and the determined if erratic strivings of its leaders to build their country into a great power fill the Kremlin with forebodings, then it can view Western Europe's condition as of 1982 with a certain equanimity. It is still politically fragmented; the political leadership, heads of states that dominated the world stage not so long ago, have apparently foresworn any ambition for a European role analogous to that of the United States or the USSR.

The momentum for European political integration had spent itself by the mid-1960s. Even before, one could note the melancholy fact, possibly unique in modern history, that the region's economic flowering and industrial growth, which was on a scale that no one in

1945 would have dared to predict, had not been accompanied by a corresponding increase in its political power. On the contrary, as the GNP indices of West Germany, France, Britain, etc., rose at a rapid pace, their relative importance in world affairs steadily declined. Throwing off the incubus of colonialism might have been expected to strengthen the West; it has certainly given the lie to the Leninist doctrine that the workers' high standard of living in industrial nations is dependent on their countries' domination of the Third World. But casting off the imperial burden had not enabled Western Europe to become more of an arbiter of its own fate.

For all the enormous agglomeration of industrial and potential military strength that the European community represents, its influence on world affairs has been much smaller than that of the United States or the USSR, and even the security of the continent itself depends more on decisions made in Moscow and Washington than those made in Paris or Bonn. In 1980 the European community's share of the world Gross National Product stood at 22.6 percent, against that of 22.1 for the United States and 11.5 for the USSR. The combined population of the community equaled that of the Soviet Union and surpassed the United States'.[40] Because all that strength is not being translated into adequate political and military power, Europe's security against Soviet aggression, whether carried out with conventional or other weapons, depends ultimately (so at least the official NATO view has held ever since its inception) on America's readiness to defend its allies and on the Kremlin's realization of such readiness.

The reasons for this paradoxical situation are not merely of historical interest. The West's past attitudes and policies concerning the defense of Europe have left their imprint on the Soviets, and they will continue to influence the Kremlin's own strategy and tactics in dealing with Western Europe.

Thus, a Soviet analyst (and a future historian might well agree) could make a convincing case that the Marshall Plan aid fulfilled its purpose either too well or not well enough. It led to a generation of unprecedented economic prosperity, but that very prosperity made the individual European states lose sight of one of the main premises of the Plan—the need for political integration of the West. Europe's consumer- and social welfare-oriented societies have failed to realize that economic strength and even military alliances cannot be effective substitutes for political unity in an age of superpowers and nuclear weapons. Unless Europe becomes a superpower in its own right, it cannot by itself resist Soviet pressures, not to mention an actual invasion, and it cannot even protect its interests and values in other parts of the world.

Another major sin of omission in the West's overall strategy vis-à-vis the Soviets has been the almost invariably bad timing of its policies. When NATO was being formed in 1949 it appeared imperative (although in fact it was not so) that the United States maintain sizable land and air forces in Europe. It was widely believed that the USSR might at any moment unleash its army upon the West and that Soviet troops could be at the Channel before America's SAC could be put effectively into play. NATO's European members were still recovering from the effects of the war, and they could not be expected to match the Soviets man-for-man and tank-for-tank. The U.S. military presence in Europe was supposed to act as a tripwire activating America's strategic force in the case of a Russian attack. The USSR could not hope to make a bid for conquest without realizing that it would bring nuclear retaliation against their own territory.

Whatever the soundness of the original premise (and it is most doubtful that the Soviet Union, itself recovering from the ravages of war, would have attacked had there been no NATO in 1949), it had lost its validity by the 1960s. By then the European members of NATO (fortified by the accession of West Germany and Italy) should have been in a position to match the Warsaw Pact's conventional forces in both manpower and economic strength. There was no reason to persist in the assumption that NATO would not be able on its own to discourage a Soviet land invasion and that the security of Europe against such an attack must still be found ultimately in America's nuclear power. Yet, no adjustment of the Atlantic Alliance's strategy took place. The United States was preoccupied by the Vietnam conflict, and the Europeans had grown used to the idea that the U.S. nuclear umbrella rather than more troops and tanks must ultimately guarantee their security.

It was a rude awakening for Europe when it realized that the USSR was catching up with America in the nuclear race and that the "nuclear umbrella" was becoming increasingly porous.

Instead of strengthening their common defense, the Europeans responded to the new situation with a variety of separate approaches, including individual states' efforts to reach an accommodation with the USSR. There was the mirage of De Gaulle's "Europe from the Channel to the Urals," while simultaneously France proceeded to build its own *force de frappe*. Bonn embarked on its *Ostpolitik*, thus formally acquiescing in the division of Germany and in Poland's western borders as set at Potsdam, and renounced its nuclear pretensions by adhering to the Non-Proliferation Treaty. What Stalin had not been able to obtain through the Berlin blockade and Khrushchev through his madcap ultimata and threats was now achieved at no expense and risk through the Soviets' patient diplomacy of the late 1960s and early 1970s.

The SALT I agreement seriously undermined the Europeans'

faith in the viability of the nuclear deterrent insofar as their own security was concerned. SALT II, though not ratified, has in fact had the same effect. To an expert the quantitative elements of SALT I did not appear too significant in view of the U.S. lead in nuclear weapon technology. But the average German could be excused for worrying: the U.S. now had many fewer ICBMs than the USSR; should Soviet tanks roll into Hamburg, would the United States really stand by its obligations and use its nuclear weapons on the USSR in full knowledge of what fearful retaliation it might expect?

It is in Western Europe that the USSR has drawn the greatest benefits from detente. The average European's (and to some extent his government's) reaction to detente was relief, since it signified that the Soviets were really bent upon peaceful coexistence, extensive trade, and cultural intercourse with the West. Perhaps the USSR might even loosen its reins on Eastern Europe, an especially important point for the Germans in view of their hopes concerning the GDR. At the same time, a German or Dutchman was bound to feel that should the Soviets be provoked or change their attitude, Europe would be in a much more exposed and dangerous position than before detente, because the Soviets were much stronger, the Americans now weaker, and U.S. readiness to come to Europe's aid had become at least problematic if it meant risking a Soviet nuclear strike against American territory.

Detente's psychological impact on the Europeans was far from unwelcome from the Soviet point of view. Observing the Kremlin's policies over the last decade, one gets a strong impression that they have been attuned to the perpetuation and strengthening of that dichotomous image of the USSR: peaceable and desirous of all forms of cooperation, yet extremely dangerous should Western Europe allow itself to be pushed into policies that seriously threaten the Soviets' interests. The Soviet Union has already declared that one such policy could be the installation of intermediate nuclear weapons and cruise missiles proposed by the NATO council in December 1979. In the future the list of such policies considered as hostile to the USSR and pregnant with dangerous consequences for Western Europeans could be greatly enlarged. They might include proposals for massive economic assistance from individual states or the European community as a whole to China or going beyond certain limits in furnishing the People's Republic with modern weapons and technology.

The USSR does not need to make its threats explicit. In actual polemics it prefers quite astutely to present Western Europe as an unwilling accomplice of the United States, when it comes to policies to which it objects. The Soviets for the most part have relied on the silent persuasiveness of military statistics. "By 1980 NATO had 7000 battle tanks on the Central Front (in Europe) compared to Warsaw Pact's 20,500, 13,500 of which were Soviet. . . . Soviet plans for rapid rates of advance, if successful, would overwhelm NATO's forces more quickly than they could be reinforced."[41] Soviet deployment of SS-20s has also served the same purpose. It is a gross oversimplification to see the Soviets' maneuvers and arms buildup as a clear indication that they contemplate offensive action against NATO, just as it is naive to wonder why Warsaw Pact forces are being expanded and equipped far beyond the defensive needs of the Soviet bloc. The Soviets hope all these arms and troops will continue to provide them with solid political dividends.

There are economic dividends as well. Quite apart from the actual benefits of expanded trade with the USSR during a recession, the Europeans see such trade as a psychological reassurance against the possibility of Soviet aggression. Surely the Soviet Union would not be negotiating and concluding various long-term joint economic ventures with Western Europe if the Kremlin were preparing to pounce upon it or even if it proposed to revert to old threats and harassments, such as another blockade of West Berlin, etc.? Furthermore, by bolstering the faltering Soviet economy (as well as those of the Soviet bloc) with technology transfers and credits at a low rate of interest, many in European political and business circles feel that they are domesticating the Soviets and reinforcing those within the Kremlin leadership who urge that it is more profitable to cooperate with the capitalists than to pursue goals of conquest and expansion at their expense. Thus, it would be unwise to yield to America's pleas and respond with drastic sanctions each time the USSR misbehaves, e.g., in Afghanistan. Nor should Europe follow Washington's hints and encourage centrifugal tendencies within the Soviet bloc. On the contrary, the democracies' real interests lie in preserving a degree of stability in the Soviet bloc, even though many in the United States obstinately refuse to recognize this. Dramatic challenges to the Soviet domination of Eastern Europe, such as the one inherent in the Polish crisis, may drive them into a corner and thus make them really dangerous. One key to European security lies in gradual evolution toward liberalization within the individual Communist states and toward greater autonomy in their relations with the Soviet Union, an evolution that can be advanced best by maintaining commercial and cultural links with them rather than by treating them as mere satrapies of Moscow.

It would be unfair to describe such attitudes as dominant in the thinking of either governments or people at large within the European community. Yet, it is this kind of attitude that Soviet policies are likely to try to foster in order to loosen ties between the United States

and its European allies on the one hand and in order to keep the
European community from achieving a degree of meaningful political unity on the other.

In her paper on Western Europe, Dr. Angela Stent has identified
five major areas of interest for the USSR insofar as Europe is concerned: (1) the determination that Germany must never again become a military threat and the resolve to maintain the current division
of that country; (2) the encouragement and deepening of fissures
within the Atlantic Alliance, especially those between West Germany
and the United States; (3) the maintenance of a fragmented Western
Europe, since once united it could resist Soviet pressures much more
effectively and could exert unhealthy influence on the Soviets' satellites in the East; (4) the Soviets' links with West European Communism; (5) Moscow's continuing and growing economic interest in
Western Europe, trade that the USSR hopes will prop up the Soviets'
own faltering economy and earn it hard currency for exports of
Soviet raw materials.[42]

For the balance of the decade we might safely scratch number
four from that list of top Soviet priorities. From being an obedient
tool of Soviet foreign policy before 1953 and a staunch pro-Soviet
lobby in their respective countries for quite a while thereafter, the
West's Communist parties have recently become something of an embarrassment to the USSR. The current leadership of the Italian and
Spanish Communists is a source of irritation and an ideological burden to the Kremlin. Their general anti-U.S. orientation does not compensate for the harm done, for example, by the Italian party's
criticisms of Soviet policies in Poland or Afghanistan or even of the
Kremlin's domestic practices. Such criticisms damage the Soviet Union's anti-imperialist and pro-national liberation image in the Third
World, find occasional reverberations within the Soviet bloc, and provide further evidence of the growing incompatibility between Russia's
national interest (as currently interpreted by the Kremlin) and that of
the worldwide movement to which it has given birth.

At the same time the fragrance of Moscow still clings to even the
most independently minded Communist party, and that by itself complicates the Soviet game of exploiting French, German, or Italian
nationalism against U.S. influence in those countries. Though unimportant and generally servile to the USSR the French Communist
party still gets in the way of those closer relations the Kremlin would
like to establish with Paris. In the last French presidential elections the
Soviets obviously preferred Giscard d'Estaing to the candidate of the
Socialist-Communist bloc, and their relations with the Mitterand regime have been notably cooler than those with its predecessor.

The Kremlin has not entirely given up on Western European

Communism. The Berlinguers and Carillos may eventually give way to people more in sympathy with "proletarian internationalism" and more tolerant of the Soviet Union's foreign and domestic peccadilloes. Western Communism remains a potentially valuable resource for the USSR, and as such it will neither be left to its own devices nor disappear entirely from Moscow's calculations.

Points two and three on Stent's list present something of a dilemma to the Soviet policy makers. Would they really wish the fissures in the Atlantic Alliance to become so serious that the United States withdraws or greatly reduces its land forces under NATO? The shock of America's partial (it could never be complete) disengagement from European defense might prove strong enough to revive the impetus for European unity or to make the Federal Republic reconsider its renunciation of nuclear weapons, or have other unpleasant consequences.

The present not very harmonious state of U.S.-Western Europe relations offers certain benefits to the USSR. America's European allies, especially West Germany, act as a moderating influence on Washington's anti-Soviet attitudes and initiatives, especially with an administration such as the current one. It is largely because of European pressures that the Reagan administration has felt constrained to reopen the nuclear arms limitation talks with the USSR. Europe's reluctance, or more bluntly, Germany's and France's refusal to cut down on their trade with the Eastern bloc, makes it more difficult for the United States to withhold its high technology, not to speak of grain, from the USSR and its clients. Insofar as the Soviet Union is concerned, the most desirable pattern of relations between this country and Europe for the immediate future would be that of a less than happy marriage, with both partners continuously squabbling rather than deciding on a trial separation. Such a separation might well make each strive to be more self-dependent vis-à-vis the third party or end up by bringing them together in a much firmer alliance than before.

U.S.-West European squabbles have greatly helped the USSR to enhance its military superiority in Europe, with all the consequent political and even economic advantages for Moscow. Given the incredible tenacity with which Moscow holds on to a position of advantage, the Soviets would fight tooth and nail to retain that superiority and to block the deployment of 108 Pershing II IRBMs and 464 ground-launched cruise missiles proposed by NATO in 1979. Even in their deepest apprehensions the Soviets could not envisage NATO as likely to provoke a war. But anything that makes Western Europe feel more secure and removes the specter of nuclear war on its territory deprives the USSR of its most potent means of psychological pressure

on the West. Therefore, in a remarkable tour de force, Soviet propaganda has apparently convinced many in Europe and in this country
that the present imbalance in tactical nuclear weapons between the
U.S. and USSR is conducive to peace and that any attempt to right
this balance threatens war. Careless rhetoric in Washington, coupled
with the constant (sometimes justified) refrain that the Americans do
not understand the Russians, has given the Soviets an opening to
exploit European fears. Opening the campaign for a nuclear freeze,
Brezhnev said at the Twenty-sixth Party Congress: "A 'limited war,'
say in Europe, would mean in its very beginning the absolute end of
European civilization." And then: "We propose an immediate
moratorium on the deployment by NATO and the USSR of new
missiles of intermediate range; that is, a freeze both quantitative and
qualitative on such weapons."[43]

The mills of Soviet propaganda will grind relentlessly in the years
to come, preventing Western Europe from achieving a position of
military preparedness that would strengthen its defenses and hence
make it less anxious to propitiate the Russians. There are so many
disparate elements upon which the "peace" movement, the nuclear
freeze initiative, and anti-Americanism can feed: the Green party and
the left wing of the SPD in Germany, the unilateral disarmament
sentiments within the British Labor party, the skepticism of countries
such as the Netherlands and Norway as to whether the whole military
game makes much sense for small states like themselves. One could
not place more than even odds on the NATO 1979 decision's being
put into effect. Even a partial success on that score is very likely to
make the Soviets more obdurate in any strategic arms negotiations,
the sum total of such developments being Western Europe's continued feeling of insecurity and inferiority when dealing with Moscow
and of irritation over its relations with the United States.

In many ways Western Europe remains *the* decisive area of world
politics. The current situation there provides perhaps the strongest
case for the rentier type of argument within the Politburo. What
possible Soviet gain elsewhere can compensate for the potential damage done to the Soviets' interests by Western Europe becoming
stronger and/or more united? There are a number of issues on which
the Europeans remain indifferent or divided. They are unlikely to
become unduly perturbed by the spread of Castro-like regimes in
Latin America. Europe remains largely critical and fearful of what it
regards as America's excessive support of Israeli policies, hence somewhat oblivious of the danger inherent in the Soviet connection with
hard-line Arab states. But a threat to its oil supplies or a too overt
Soviet intrusion in any future struggle in South Africa would be a
signal for West Europeans to close ranks and become more responsive to Washington's urgings.

The rentier would wonder also whether the Soviet venture in Afghanistan has been worth the damage it has done to detente. Wouldn't another Afghanistan or a military intervention in Poland play directly into the hands of Washington "hawks" by causing Western Europe to lose its delusions about detente and pushing it to translate its economic strength into political and military power?

The speculator would counter such arguments by pointing out that Europe's present disarray and somewhat ambivalent position in the Soviet-American duel is based not so much on appreciation of the Soviet Union's peaceful intentions as on a shrewd suspicion that the USSR may not be so peacefully inclined after all. It is desirable to do everything possible to make the Europeans more friendly toward Moscow, provided they do not lose entirely that salutary fear of Soviet power. It is an intricate but necessary game the USSR has to play in Europe of balancing friendly assurances with intimidation. For example, wasn't the initial West German reaction to the Polish crisis colored by fear that the USSR in its wrath over Poland might do something unpleasant to the West, e.g., making trouble over Berlin? But suppose the USSR had let the scandalous state of affairs in Poland continue. Would not the West Germans have acquired some dangerous notions of what might happen in the GDR and become more tough-minded in their dealings with the East Germans and even the Russians? It would be a mistake to tip the balance of the Soviets' European policy too much in favor of conciliation. The best policy is to keep the Europeans apprehensive but not panicky. The USSR must continue to emphasize that the real danger to Europe comes from the United States. If America continues to provoke Moscow and keeps trying to regain nuclear superiority, then the consequences of such malevolence might have to be suffered also by Europe.

The original Western concept of detente was premised on the carrot-and-stick simile, among others. As things have developed, especially insofar as Europe is concerned, one sees the Soviets munching the carrots vigorously, with the Western stick nowhere in sight. The West Europeans' somewhat shamefaced arguments in justification of this are the well-known refrains: "Economic sanctions never work," "trade has helped to liberalize East European regimes," etc. With much greater justification, Bonn or Paris could ask why they should be called upon to make economic sacrifices when the United States, for all the tough rhetoric of the Reagan administration, has hastened to lift the grain embargo.

West-East trade has flourished, that of West Germany with the USSR having increased eightfold from 1969 to 1981.[44] Afghanistan and the proclamation of martial law in Poland did not slacken the flow. The Mitterand regime has indulged in some strong anti-Soviet rhetoric; but it joined in the consortium for the construction of the

West Siberian natural gas pipeline, and in February 1981, barely a month and a half after the Polish coup, it extended $140 million in credit to the USSR. The pipeline project indeed opens up the prospect of the USSR's obtaining the carrots and to some extent being able to wield its *own* stick over Europe. Once the pipeline is completed, Germany and France will depend on the Soviet Union for one-third of their natural gas consumption,[45] with eight other European nations also importing substantial amounts of Soviet natural gas. The USSR also would appreciably increase its hard currency earnings.

It is often argued that despite the increase of Soviet trade with the West, it still does not loom very large against the size of the Soviet GNP, and one should not exaggerate the benefits Moscow has derived from it. Yet in view of the parlous state of the Soviet economy, of the worse plight of several other Eastern bloc countries, and of the crucial technological importance of many items acquired by the USSR and its client states, one must conclude that the West has relieved the Soviet Union of some burdens of its imperialist policies. Total indebtedness of the Soviet bloc to the West by the end of 1980 passed $70 billion.

The case of Poland illustrates the danger inherent in a Communist regime's becoming addicted to capitalist largesse, something that Stalin was mindful of when he spurned the Marshall Plan and told the Czechs and the Poles to beware of capitalists bearing grants and low interest loans. Despite the lessons of virtual bankruptcy in Poland and Romania, Western, especially European, willingness to lend to the Communists has not entirely abated. The Soviet Union's credit rating is still good, and Western bankers have thus far been willing to keep rescheduling Poland's debts. Some people in Western government and business circles have even greeted the imposition of martial law by the Warsaw regime with a degree of relief. For all the sympathy felt for the Polish people in their tragic predicament, many European politicians would be secretly pleased to see Gen. Jaruzelski and his fellow satraps succeed in restoring the Communist version of law and order in Poland. The Russian bear must not become incensed, for the consequences of its wrath might spill far beyond Poland's borders.

Much of the West European ambivalence can be traced to West Germany and its crucial role within both the European community and the Atlantic Alliance. More sensitive to the Soviet threat than any other European state (Helmut Schmidt's government stoutly supported the NATO decision to deploy intermediate missiles), the Federal Republic has been at the same time the most reluctant to antagonize the USSR on trade, East European politics, or other issues. Psychologically this ambivalence is quite understandable: detente has meant for Bonn the hope (which it has been reluctant to admit has increasingly turned into a mirage) of German reunification. West

Berlin, for all the Soviets' 1972 pledges and guarantees, continues to remain a hostage within the Communist camp. It would take a dramatic development in West Germany's attitudes and political climate to change that current immobilism of Western Europe in world politics: allied with the United States yet unwilling to synchronize its policies with the United States except on issues that affect directly Europe's military security, conscious of the damage done to Europe's interests through its fragmentation yet unable to move toward effective political unity.

The Soviet Union's immediate objectives in the area must be aimed at preserving that immobilism. Beyond that, the Kremlin would be pleased to see Western Europe move toward what has been dubbed "Finlandization." But the Soviets realize that their foreign policy in Europe must be more finely tuned than anywhere else. In areas like Africa or the Moslem world, the USSR could suffer reverses and decide to cut its losses without too much damage to its overall world position. China represents a clear but not yet present danger. But any Soviet move that might unwittingly become the catalyst of Europe's unity could overnight transform the entire international scene. Nor could the USSR look with equanimity on any American initiatives that would restore the momentum toward unity of the Atlantic community as a whole. Keeping Europe divided must remain the cardinal objective of the Kremlin's policies.

The United States

We have already discussed various themes in the Soviets' thinking about the United States. The most obvious touches on America's role as the main capitalist power that must always be viewed as a constant rival and a direct military threat to the USSR.

At the other extreme of the analytical spectrum, within the Politburo's image of the United States there is a tendency to downgrade it, whether as a direct threat or a worldwide rival. At times the Soviets act on the unspoken premise that by itself the U.S. cannot compete effectively with the Soviet Union. Its political structure makes its foreign policy unwieldy and incapable of matching Moscow's moves. At the time of their greatest military and industrial power, when they had complete monopoly and later crushing superiority in nuclear weapons, the Americans were still unable to check Soviet expansion or threaten the Soviet system and empire, then so fragile, especially in the first years after Stalin's death. No matter what those sinister voices in the Pentagon and elsewhere might urge, the political ethos of American society makes it virtually impossible for the United States to initiate an all-out war against the USSR.

While accepting much of the historical validity of the preceding argument, a variant Soviet view would still point out the danger of such a complacent view of the United States. Whatever the natural inclinations of the Americans and the structure of the political system that makes it difficult for the country to play a world role, let alone aim at a world empire, the United States has always been and will continue to be a threat to the USSR through its power and resources. In the past, Americans, while by themselves little inclined to adopt a menacing stand vis-à-vis Moscow, have often been pushed in that direction by outsiders. The Churchills and Adenauers succeeded in stirring American democracy into a course leading to direct confrontations with the Soviets. In the future Beijing might well attempt a similar role. While the mutual threats and military alerts over the 1973 Arab-Israeli war were largely theatrics, someday a similar crisis, whether in the Middle East or elsewhere, might escalate to the point of a horrifying clash.

Even if one admits privately that the American people and even for the most part their rulers are peacefully inclined, one still cannot ignore the dangerously volatile nature of American reactions to foreign affairs, those extreme and seemingly irrational swings of the pendulum in public opinion about the USSR. Thus American democracy's usual mood of weariness with foreign affairs and of subdued irritation with the Soviets' behavior is intermittently punctuated by violent spasms of anxiety and anger at some developments that are far from extraordinary by Moscow's standards. Having desisted from any serious attempt to overthrow Castro after the Bay of Pigs, Americans became dangerously overexcited over what should have been viewed as a logical sequence of the Soviet-Cuban liaison. Compare the excitement over the missiles in Cuba with the fact that the Russians had for some time lived with the knowledge of American bases in Turkey without making much fuss. If it is Soviet expansionism that Americans really mind, why was Washington calm over the 1978 Communist coup in Afghanistan, only to go into convulsions when the Russians felt it necessary to straighten out a few troubles in what was already their satellite?

By the Kremlin's lights, this irrationality of the Americans' approach to foreign policy makes it very difficult to deal in a businesslike fashion with Washington, whether over the differences separating the two powers or over an issue where both sides could profit by mutual understanding and cooperation. The United States at one time had a strong interest in containing China. Most Americans have forgotten that the massive U.S. involvement in Vietnam was mainly prompted by the desire to teach China, then considered the more bellicose and dangerous of the two Communist powers, that the wars of "national liberation" could not succeed. The prospect of Beijing's acquiring nuclear weapons caused more apprehension in Washington in the 1950s and early 1960s than the Soviet Union's already quite extensive stockpile. Yet Khrushchev's attempts to raise the problem of China with the United States were either misunderstood or categorically rebuffed by American officials.

The same obtuseness, the Kremlin probably believes, has characterized Washington's current attitude on China. Of what use has the "China card" been so far for the United States? The Americans simply cannot understand that Beijing is playing its own game, and that game is ultimately as dangerous for the United States as for the Soviet Union. Any lessening of United States-Soviet tension and hence a more peaceful atmosphere in the world has been and will be opposed by the Chinese Communist leaders. Yet one could not approach the United States with any suggestion of a sensible way of coping with the problem, one that would be really in the interests of both powers and that might lead to their fruitful collaboration in other areas. The Americans would treat such a Soviet approach (just as in the past they had treated mere hints on the subject) as an indication of Moscow's alarm and a vindication of their present policy on China. Furthermore, they would trumpet the Soviets' confidences to the whole world, discretion not being an outstanding characteristic of American policy makers.

Another difficulty in dealing with these exasperating people is the legalistic quality of the American political mind. Many in the United States have somehow failed to grasp the fact that Brezhnev's signature on the Helsinki Final Act, with all its "baskets," could not have meant that the general secretary and the Politburo of the Communist party had given their assent to the dissolution of the Soviet system or to its gradual transformation into a pluralistic society. For their own part, the Soviet leaders must feel that they have made a considerable sacrifice and incurred political risks in letting some dissidents and thousands of Jews and ethnic Germans leave the USSR. Such steps are not cost-free insofar as they erode some of that awe of the regime and of the average citizen's political passivity on which the security of the Soviet system ultimately rests. Why didn't the United States, then infinitely more powerful, address pleas concerning human rights to Stalin? How illogical to make a big fuss about what happens to Dissident X or the case of Refusenik Y when it has not objected too vigorously to entire nations' being subjugated by the USSR and has been notably silent when it comes to human rights in China?

At times, one gets the strong impression that the Soviets would feel less disturbed about the human rights issue if they considered it a purely contrived propaganda effort on the part of the United States.

•

It is the illogical premise of the whole campaign (as they see it) and the undoubted blow to the *amour propre* of the leadership that makes the West's admonitions on the subject a source of anxiety and irritation to Moscow.

The leadership must feel a certain sense of exasperation about the possibility of ever reaching an accommodation with people who never cease sticking their nose in the USSR's domestic affairs. It must enhance the Kremlin's suspicion that the West by its very being constitutes a standing threat to the Soviet Union, to its internal cohesion and that of the Soviet bloc as a whole. No agreement on outstanding world issues could eliminate the insidious danger of Western ideas, values, and "lifestyles" permeating Soviet society. What is described by the leadership as the "impermissibility of ideological coexistence" has little to do with the fear of alien ideologies undermining the average Soviets' alleged devotion to the ideals of Marxism-Leninism. The phrase reflects the Kremlin's sense of insecurity about the whole framework of official mythology, propaganda, and coercion that constitutes the foundation of the system. In many ways the Soviets must feel it would be easier to deal with an authoritarian America than with the kind of rambunctious democracy it represents.

To impute to the Soviets hurt *amour propre* is not to see them as endowed with excessive delicacy. But the present generation of Soviet leaders would not be human if they did not feel pride in having been able to abolish the most horrendous features of Stalinism. It probably credits itself with great generosity toward the dissenters and those ethnic groups that do not appreciate the blessings of life in the Fatherland of Socialism. It deeply offends the Kremlin's sense of propriety that foreign government officials presume to criticize Soviet domestic politics instead of appreciating such generosity. No other American political leader, not even the late Mr. Dulles, had ever been subjected by the Soviet press to such venomous vituperation as was Mr. Carter after his outburst about the invasion of Afghanistan, largely because of his previous outspokenness in connection with human rights. Moscow's animosity toward Mr. Carter did not abate even when the Republican right-wing candidate emerged as his chief rival and prospective president. For all of Mr. Reagan's anti-Soviet rhetoric, his victory was greeted by the Soviet press with an equanimity bordering on satisfaction.

Mr. Carter epitomized for the Kremlin that besetting sin of American politics, one that makes it so difficult for it to gauge and cope with Washington's policies—unpredictability. As *Pravda* put it: "It is not without reason that the term 'unpredictable' has been appearing in the newspapers more and more when U.S. policy is discussed. . . . And isn't 'unpredictability' in the actions of the head of a state like the U.S. too dangerous in the age of nuclear missiles?"[46]

These attitudes are not irrelevant or incidental to current and future Soviet policies. Insofar as we can judge, they pervade the thinking of that small group of men whose image of America influences their decisions on the size of the Soviet defense budget or the risks inherent in a fresh Soviet move in Africa or a military intervention in Poland. It is largely by gauging what element in that composite picture is currently dominant or likely to become so that the Politburo will shape its tactics in arms control negotiations and decide how far the USSR may go in trying to interdict intermediate nuclear missiles for NATO.

The recent past must guide the Politburo in trying to answer the fundamental question for the immediate future: does the Reagan administration's stand mark the beginning of a long-term shift in U.S. policies toward the USSR? Is this another Washington administration beginning its term of office by producing a magic formula of "how to deal with the Russians," only to have time, budgetary stringencies, and the allies' pleas rob the prescription of magic and novelty and push U.S. policy back to its hesitant and vacillating course?

In the last two decades American concerns about the USSR centered mainly on its strategic nuclear force and the question of whether the Kremlin considers all-out war a viable political option. In human terms, such an approach is only too understandable. No danger, no fear can equal that of nuclear devastation. No task, no policy can come close to the urgency of offering credible deterrence to a Soviet nuclear strike and in a broader sense precluding or minimizing the possibility of all-out war between the superpowers. Yet in pursuing the elusive goal of credible deterrence, a democracy finds itself at a fearful disadvantage when dealing with a political system like the Soviet one. American fears, hopes, and calculations concerning nuclear weapons and their use must become public knowledge. Discussion of the issue arouses such deep emotions that at times a rational dialogue concerning national policy on nuclear arms in relation to overall priorities in foreign policies is virtually impossible.

The mere existence of nuclear weapons tends inexorably to confer an automatic advantage on an authoritarian power over a democratic state whenever they grapple in the international arena and whatever the issue. One might make a plausible case that the USSR was a beneficiary of the atom bomb even before it acquired a single one of its own: the knowledge that the Soviet Union would someday acquire the weapon inhibited American policies toward the USSR more than America's actual possession of the bomb did those of the Soviets. Stalin could very effectively feign complete indifference to the bomb as a factor in international politics. Though Khrushchev's attitude on the subject was much less nonchalant, he tried to exploit his limited nuclear arsenal in ways that the United States with its much greater power simply could not match. The average Russian is undoubtedly as terrified of the prospect of nuclear war as an American, and it is unlikely that official Soviet propaganda or civil defense preparations do much to relieve that fear. But as on other foreign policy issues, Soviet society is anesthetized. Whatever the Soviets' real hopes, fears, and calculations concerning nuclear policies options, they are discussed and decided within a small circle of Kremlin policy makers, and it is unlikely that any but the highest members of the Soviet military and scientific establishment have a voice in the deliberations.

While the Soviet psychological advantage because of the existence of nuclear weapons can never be entirely eliminated, it has been within the power of the United States to reduce it considerably. In the first place, the technical aspect of nuclear weaponry should never have obscured its political significance. One hopes nuclear war will never be fought, but it is obvious that international conflicts could and would be decided by nuclear weapons, even though not a single atomic bomb or missile is used. For a democracy the quantitative aspect of the strategic weapons question could never be considered secondary. A technically superior American strategic force, though inferior in numbers and megatonnage, might be an adequate deterrent against a possible Soviet attack upon this country. But to allow the USSR to get ahead in numbers risked a political defeat and, to paraphrase Churchill, opened up a possibility for the Soviet Union to gather the fruits of wars without having to fight for them.

In fact America's strategic arms doctrine has long appeared oblivious to the political dimension of the problem. The United States has traditionally considered nuclear arms the ultimate *defensive* weapons and never a bargaining chip. When it comes to actual threats of using the weapon, one could argue with some difficulty that it was implicit in the American stand in the Cuban missile crisis. We have obscure hints in some presidential memoirs and recollections that their writers did issue more or less explicit warnings, but one must respectfully question the accuracy of such recollections.

Between 1968 (when the SALT talks were supposed to start) and 1979, the U.S. approach to the damnable weapons became somewhat bifurcated. Military experts continued to rivet their attention on the technical security aspect of the strategic balance to ensure that the Soviets should have no illusions about crippling America's retaliatory power with a Soviet first strike. Superior American technology would take care of that and more than compensate for the Soviets' superiority in ICBMs and in overall megatonnage. Reassured on the military side, American statesmen sought to take the curse off the problem and appease growing popular anxiety by negotiating strategic arms limitations pacts with the USSR. In this country and *at first* in Western Europe, these agreements had a profoundly soothing effect; any agreement between the two powers made the specter of a nuclear holocaust recede further from one's consciousness. It was a somewhat illogical, if understandable feeling. Unless set within the framework of a general political agreement between the two superpowers, however, no conceivable SALT or START treaty could make the possibility of a nuclear war between the two powers appreciably smaller or greater. No one in this country loses much sleep over the fact that Britain's nuclear force, puny as it is compared to ours or the Soviets', could cause millions of casualties if released against America. It is the political character of the East-West conflict that threatens us all with a nuclear calamity, and it would even if the nuclear arsenals on both sides were reduced to a fraction of their present numbers.

It is clear why the Soviets have followed the dual policy of trying to exploit to the fullest their quantitative advantage in several categories of strategic and tactical nuclear weapons while remaining eager to keep the SALT process going. The first provides them with solid political and economic advantages in Western Europe. The second, the Soviets hope, acts as a tranquilizer on the West and permits the Kremlin to control the level of international tension. Moscow hopes to navigate between the Scylla and the Charybdis of international situations: the West must never entirely lose its fear of the Soviets' intentions nor become so alarmed about them as to put up impregnable barriers against Soviet expansion.

Has Mr. Reagan's proposed arms buildup shaken Moscow's confidence on both points? The USSR still remains to be convinced that the vagaries of American politics, budget stringencies, etc., will allow the program to go through. Many of the rationales for Mr. Reagan's defense policies have come from the belated American reaction to SALT I, the "discovery" that the American ICBMs have become vulnerable to a hypothetical Soviet strike, the fear of the celebrated "window of vulnerability" opening up some time in the 1980s, and the conclusion by some analysts that the Soviets believe that they could carry out and win a nuclear war.[47] The debate must have created mixed feelings in Moscow. From the psychopolitical point of view it was desirable that the Americans should compound their initial errors by emphasizing and exaggerating the importance of the quantitative factor in the overall nuclear picture. On the other hand, the Americans might react to that discovery in a typically irrational and dangerous way.

When it comes to America, the speculator motif in the thinking of the Politburo translates into considerable equanimity about what the Americans might actually do, while the rentier viewpoint expresses itself in the apprehension that they would do something quite dangerous. The first would draw attention to the fact that for all of the Reagan administration's warnings, its grandiose weapons projections, etc., it has not done anything in contravention of SALT II provisions, and it has considerably toned down its rhetoric on the USSR in two years in office. The nuclear freeze movement in the United States is doing quite well. What is usually a nuisance in dealing with the United States might on the arms issue prove to be beneficial to Moscow: presidential elections are held every four years, and preparatory politicking is just around the corner. In many ways the current administration has been as inconsistent in its suggestions on how to meet the alleged Soviet challenge as was its predecessor. It has already broached the subject of a summit and has sought to ease general apprehension over the enhanced Soviet-American tension its own careless rhetoric had stirred up. In any case, any new weapons and systems would not become operational before the 1990s, so by their own admission the Americans are not likely to feel too secure and cocky vis-à-vis the USSR for quite a few years to come.

There is no imperative reason for the Soviets to make any substantive and one-sided concessions on strategic arms or any other major area of the dispute. In any such negotiations the pressure is inevitably on the party that must negotiate with all its cards on the table and to the cacophony of public opinion. It would be prudent to avoid for the foreseeable future anything that might give Washington hardliners an argument for breaking off the negotiations. But by the mere fact of engaging in them, Washington has already signified its "forgiveness" of Moscow for Afghanistan and martial law in Poland, so it would be ludicrous to display any signs of contrition over what the USSR has been doing.

The rentier would criticize the above argument as greatly oversimplifying the problem of Soviet-American relations during the coming years. Much more than just the nuclear arms balance and related problems is at issue. One may be confronted with a basic shift in American thinking about the Soviet Union on the scale of the advent of the Cold War and the later acceptance of detente. The Americans are again viewing the Soviet Union not merely as their rival in world politics, but as a force determined to destroy any remaining vestiges of the international order. As Reagan's speech to the British Parliament suggested, this feeling is compounded by a much more acute perception of the Soviet Union's internal weaknesses and vulnerabilities. Even so, the administration's policies are criticized in some influential American circles as having been "soft on the Russians." Hence it behooves the USSR to do everything possible before some dangerous tendencies crystalize into actual policies, and a new version of the Cold War and containment takes over in Washington. A hard position vis-à-vis the United States and refusal to meet it halfway on strategic arms and NATO's tactical weapons in Europe would be dangerous and threaten the long-run interests of the USSR and its allies.

One can perceive neither attitude as currently dominant in the Kremlin's councils. This is perhaps natural in view of the leadership change and of the insufficient evidence on how long Washington will persevere in its "hard" stance. Do Soviet fears extend to the possibility of actual war being initiated by some action on the "imperialists'" part? Recent attitudes reflect the realization that the Soviets may have overdone their act of appearing ready to chance a nuclear exchange, which in turn led to changes in the American strategic doctrine that pose real dangers. The Schlesinger Doctrine, PD 59, etc., have quite disturbing implications, and some Soviet political leaders must use them as examples of what happens when you let your marshals and civil defense specialists shoot off their mouths.

Therefore, the Kremlin will spare no effort in promoting its current "war is hell and we know it" line, as opposed to its former feigned confidence that it could sustain and win a nuclear shootout. At the same time the Soviets are political hypochondriacs. The Americans are prone to change their minds when it comes to policies, but once a technical idea or contrivance gets hold of their imagination, they often carry it out. The "open skies" notion and the U-2 are ancient history, but suppose some scientists achieve a breakthrough in laser technology? "War-mongering circles" in Washington might become emboldened to the point of actually threatening the USSR over a new crisis in Eastern Europe or some other contingency. Although the Soviets generally feel reassured that the other superpower happens to be a disorderly democracy, the Kremlin must occasionally experience pangs of anxiety on that count: how dangerous in this age to have great issues of world policy influenced by sudden gusts of popular emotion, rather than decided entirely according to the rational criteria of a small and experienced group of men the way it is done in the USSR.

The variety and volatility of current American policy trends are likely to continue disturbing the Kremlin, even though in the past it has often taken advantage of what it perceived as the unsteadiness of purpose behind U.S. policies. Kremlin leaders lack that confidence in being able to gauge American reactions that characterized Stalin, and, until 1962, Khrushchev. For the present they appear to feel that the main priority must be to lower the present level of tension between the two superpowers, hence Brezhnev's declaration that the USSR would not be first to use nuclear weapons. Aside from its propaganda

element, the late Soviet leader's statement is good evidence of what
the Soviets consider the most crucial area of American foreign policy.
It is not what Washington says and does in direct relations with the
USSR that is Moscow's main concern (except for the extreme and
horrible possibilities). Barring a war, the most important factor in
world politics during the next few years will be the success or failure
of U.S. policies in Western Europe.

In a recent article, four distinguished American public figures
made a cogent argument that "the time has come for careful study of
ways and means of moving to a new Alliance policy and doctrine: that
nuclear weapons will not be used unless an aggressor should use them
first."[48] We shall not examine their argument, except to note that if
indeed accepted formally by NATO, the policy they recommend
might lead, after the initial reaction of relief, to a greater feeling of
insecurity on the part of the West Europeans. It is U.S. policy on
Western Europe that the USSR will watch with the greatest attention.
In his celebrated essay, Mr. Kennan argued that desirable changes in
Soviet foreign policy would come only if the USSR became convinced
of the strength and durability of the democratic world. "For no mysti-
cal Messianic movement, and particularly not that of the Kremlin, can
face frustration indefinitely without adjusting itself in one way or
another to the logic of that state of affairs."[49] On the basis of the
thirty-five years since the essay was written, one might envisage a
Soviet official arguing that Mr. Kennan got his parties and adjectives
wrong. It has been the United States, impelled by a Messianic impulse, that sought to promote democracy and a free market economy
throughout the world, while the USSR has followed realistic and
pragmatic policies to aggrandize its power. As of now, America has
still not adjusted itself to "the logic of that state of affairs." But there is
one form of adjustment that would render this country's strivings
more realistic. Building even the rudiments of a new world order is
clearly beyond the resources of a single power, and people stopped
talking about the "American century" long ago. America's present
posture is predicated upon the assumption that because of internal
and/or external factors, the USSR will turn toward cultivating its own
garden and stop reaching for those belonging to others. But such a
change is unlikely to occur under the present conditions. Even if by
some miracle the USSR turned most of its attention to domestic affairs, that in itself would not cure the anarchy of current international
relations. Such a cure or a dramatic change in the configuration of
world forces could come only as the result of the emergence of Western Europe as a superpower in its own right, and it is only then that
the Kremlin will be constrained to rethink the basic premises of its
foreign policy.

NOTES

1. Henry L. Stimson and McGeorge Bundy, *On Active Service in War and Peace* (New York: Octagon, 1947), p. 644.

2. Georgi Arbatov, "Soviet-American Relations," in *The Communist* (Moscow: February, 1973), p. 110.

3. Fox Butterfield, "Hanoi General Was Surprised at Speed of Saigon's Collapse," *New York Times*, April 26, 1976.

4. Quoted in *State Department Bulletin*, no. 2028 (Washington, D.C.: USGPO, July 1979), p. 51.

5. Quoted in *Pravda*, August 30, 1973.

6. K. Brutents, *The Present Stage of the Liberation Struggle of the Asian and African Peoples and Revolutionary Democracy* (Moscow, 1977), p. 6.

7. Though it remains debatable whether a prolonged exposure to Russian life is an equally effective way of fostering pro-Soviet sentiments in those young men and women as their being subjected to Marxist influence in some Western academic milieu.

8. These statistics are drawn from David Albright, "Sub-Saharan Africa and Soviet Foreign Policy in the 1980s," an unpublished paper prepared for this project, p. 8.

9. Data from Colin Legum et al., *Africa in the 1980s* (New York: McGraw-Hill, 1979), pp. 75–79.

10. Brutents, *Present Stage of the Liberation Struggle*, p. 64.

11. Indeed, though it was de Gaulle himself who presided eventually over the liquidation of the French Empire, undoubtedly the memory of the American importunities on that count contributed to his estrangement from the United States and the "Anglo-Saxons" in general. (He also remembered bitterly how the British had pushed the French out of Syria during the latter phase of his rule.)

12. Adam B. Ulam, *Expansion and Coexistence: History of Soviet Foreign Policy, 1917–73* (New York: Praeger, 1974), p. 622.

13. Mohamed Heikal, *Sphinx and Commissar* (London: Collins, 1978), p. 225.

14. Is it not just possible, though on the face of it it may seem incongruous, that the rebirth and intensity of Islamic fundamentalism have profited from the political and psychological plight of Communism over so much of the Moslem world? Compromised by the Soviets' apparent indifference to the fortunes of their coreligionists and by Moscow's own transparently imperialist actions, Communism has become less attractive as a vehicle for the social and anti-imperialist protest; those sentiments, especially among the young, now being channelled not into a political, but a more traditional variety of faith.

15. Arbatov, "Soviet-American Relations," p. 110.

16. *Pravda*, January 24, 1979.

17. Quoted from Raymond Baker, "The Soviet Union and the Moslem World," an unpublished paper prepared for this project, p. 2.

18. Ibid., p. 23.

19. *Twenty-third Congress of the Communist Party of the Soviet Union, Stenographic Report* (Moscow, 1966), p. 315.

20. The Institute of the Academy of Sciences of the USSR, *Intra-State Relations in Latin America*, ed. A. N. Glinkin (Moscow, 1977), p. 6.

21. From Abraham F. Lowenthal, "Latin America in the 1980s: Opportunities for Expanding Soviet Influence," an unpublished paper prepared for this project, p. 8.

22. *Nationalism in Latin America: Political and Ideological Currents,* ed. A. F. Shulgovski (Moscow, 1976), p. 7.

23. Ibid., p. 219.

24. Ibid., p. 170.

25. Ibid., p. 175.

26. Seweryn Bialer and Alfred Stepon, "Cuba, the U.S. and the Central American Mess," in *New York Review of Books,* May 27, 1982.

27. Allen S. Whiting and Robert F. Dernberger, *China's Future* (New York: McGraw-Hill, 1978), p. 40.

28. Robert Scalapino, "Chinese Foreign Policy in 1979," in *China Briefing, 1980,* ed. Robert B. Oxnam and Richard C. Bush (Boulder, Colo.:Westview Press, 1980, p. 84.

29. Whiting and Dernberger, *China's Future,* p. 185.

30. *The Global Strategy of the United States Under the Conditions of the Scientific and Technological Revolution,* eds. Georgi Arbatov et al. (Moscow, 1979), p. 75. In *China's Future,* Whiting and Dernberger offer a more modest estimate of China's nuclear arsenal (p. 55), but their book was published in 1978.

31. H. A. Trofimenko, *The Strategy of Global War* (Moscow, 1968), p. 229. My Italics.

32. A. Doak Barnett, *China's Economy in Global Perspective* (Washington, D.C.: Brookings Institution, 1981), p. 144.

33. Kazuo Yamanouchi, "The Chinese Economy, 1981," in *China Newsletter,* no. 37, March-April 1982, p. 2.

34. Arbatov et al., eds., *Global Strategy,* p. 76.

35. From Gerrit W. Gong, "China in the 1980s," an unpublished paper prepared for this project.

36. Quoted in William E. Griffith, *The Sino-Soviet Rift* (Cambridge, Mass.: M.I.T. Press, 1964), p. 351.

37. From Rebecca V. Strode, "External Factors Affecting Soviet Policy for the 1980s: The Military Dimension," an unpublished paper prepared for this project, p. 28.

38. George F. Kennan, "The Sources of Soviet Conduct," in *American Diplomacy, 1900–1950* (Chicago: University of Chicago Press, 1960), p. 121.

39. Quoted in L. I. Brezhnev, *Following in Lenin's Path* (Moscow, 1976), p. 471.

40. CIA, National Foreign Assessment Center, *Handbook of Economic Statistics, 1981* (Washington, D.C.: USGPO, 1982), p. 1.

41. Strode, "External Factors Affecting Soviet Foreign Policy," p. 19.

42. From Angela Stent, "The USSR and Western Europe in the 1980s," an unpublished paper prepared for this project, pp. 1–6.

43. *The Twenty-sixth Congress of the Communist Party* (Moscow, 1981), pp. 38–39.

44. Stent, "USSR and Western Europe," p. 10.

45. Ibid., p. 54.

46. Yuli Yakhontov, *Pravda,* April 27, 1980.

47. The classical argument in support of this thesis is developed in Richard Pipes, "Why the Soviet Union Thinks It Could Win a Nuclear War," *US-Soviet Relations in the Era of Detente* (Boulder, Colo.: Westview Press, 1981), pp. 135–68.

48. McGeorge Bundy et al., "Nuclear Weapons and the Atlantic Alliance," *Foreign Affairs,* Spring 1982.

49. Kennan, *American Diplomacy,* p. 13.

8

★

Critical Choices in the 1980s

Robert F. Byrnes

A CENTRAL THEME of this book is that Soviet leaders face increasingly acute challenges to undertake changes in their system and in certain of its policies. These challenges have been generated by the regime's successes in modernizing a traditional society, in impelling vigorous and long-sustained economic growth, and in making a more powerful place for itself in the world of nations. Having successfully transformed the old society, the leaders must decide, probably during the decade of the 1980s, whether and how they can adapt and alter the political order in ways necessary to make the new society work effectively. The basic question is: can a narrowly constituted political elite, comfortable in the security of its achievements and power and reluctant to face the hazards of change, generate the will to move innovatively to meet potential threats of stagnation, instability, and decline? Can it choose wisely between the disagreeable and the intolerable?

The Converging Dilemmas in the 1980s
　　The Soviet leaders' central problem derives from the convergence in the 1980s of several basic dilemmas, all coming to a critical point at about the same time; all cumulative, complicated, and closely and irrevocably interrelated; and all demanding hard policy choices that will greatly affect the Soviet system and its role in world politics for years ahead. These years promise to be as crucial as the late 1920s, when the Soviet leaders debated the policies that they should adopt after they had consolidated Communist rule and completed reconstruction from war and revolution.
　　None of these quandaries is new. All are fundamental and reflect long-term developments. The Soviet leaders have long been aware of them and have been struggling to evade them or to resolve them in a piecemeal way. Above all, the problems have become crucial at a time when the Soviet Union must complete the transfer of its highly centralized authority from Brezhnev to Andropov and then to a new

generation. These are delicate and even hazardous undertakings in a political structure in which contending interest groups can be ruthless.

Changing a Conservative System and Society

The Soviet Union is an authoritarian state ruled by a stable, aged oligarchy determined to preserve full party authority and deeply committed to the status quo within the Soviet Union. The Soviet population is generally patriotic and at least outwardly submissive to whatever policies the leadership adopts, although apathy and discontent are widespread, especially among non-Russians; some areas of social life remain outside effective government control; and the Soviet peoples have shown shrewd skills in circumventing official policies they do not approve. The government and the country have benefited from three decades of economic growth, rising standards of living, steadily increasing military strength and prestige, and success in world politics, but this period has recently come to an end. Like all countries at all times, the Soviet Union faces a number of serious issues. These threaten to become acute in the 1980s.

Introducing fundamental transformations into any complex modern society is difficult, but it is especially so for a system that has become immobile and even frozen and is tied to an outmoded and perhaps irrelevant philosophy, allegedly revolutionary and internationalist but actually conservative and nationalist.

Ironically, the Soviet Union faces a new set of demanding choices in part because of its successes. By moving peasants into the urban world and providing two or three generations of workers the opportunity to move up and to assist their children to reach even higher class status, the leaders have fostered the creation of skills and knowledge, aspirations and appetites that the system would find increasingly difficult to satisfy, even if its economy were booming and opportunities for higher education and advancement were not declining. Soviet emphasis upon science, education, status, and the rights of workers and peasants has made the issue of social mobility especially acute. Like Count Witte in the 1890s, and indeed all Russian rulers since Peter the Great, Soviet leaders from Lenin through Brezhnev have appreciated that education in unprogressive societies leads to revolution, but that ignorance produces defeat. Careful Soviet monitoring of education has prevented the accumulation of violent pressures for change, but the provision of training and education to millions has enlarged pressures for upward mobility and created skepticism in a society based on faith.

The growth of nationalisms in this multinational state, that of the Russians as well as those of the minorities, has intensified the issue of governance. This phenomenon is related to the growth of national consciousness and the establishment of national states elsewhere in the world, but it is also a consequence of Communist fostering of minority cultures within the Soviet Union.

Russian nationalism has a longer history than most of the other Soviet nationalisms. It has blossomed because of the prominent role Russians play throughout the Soviet system and because of their visible contribution to the rise of the Soviet Union as a world power. The burgeoning thrust of Russian nationalism inevitably collides with the interests of the other ethnic groups, who are increasingly self-assertive and who seek higher status, increased freedom from Russian rule, and greater access to the instruments of authority. These hostilities are sharpened by economic, social, and religious discontent, especially in the Baltic republics, Ukraine, and Central Asia, and by the visible flattening of Slavic population growth at a time when most of the increase in the Soviet population comes from Moslem non-Russians in Central Asia.

Regime efforts to base itself on Russian national tradition as a means of stimulating support among the Russians and other Slavs naturally alienate the non-Russian half of the Soviet population. The party's simultaneous efforts to emphasize Soviet patriotism and to suppress extreme Russian nationalism have turned some Russian nationalists, Communists as well as noncommunists, against the system. In short, the rise of competing nationalisms is creating a bundle of annoying, increasingly serious strains that may constitute a powder keg in another generation or two.

The many varieties of dissident movements that keep coming up like flowers through cracks in concrete are another assertion of values that differ from those of the state, particularly because these attitudes now appear among the professional elite, a crucial class in any authoritarian society. Dissidence is a reflection of stubborn human nature. It expresses individualism against authority, old traditions and religious beliefs against the official state creed, and the eternal problems any dictatorship faces as its seeks to enforce total discipline in a modernizing society at a time when its coercive, material, and normative methods of social control are slowly losing effectiveness.

Marxist-Leninist faith and revolutionary enthusiasm among the population died long ago and left a vacuum, and the heroic period of Soviet history has ended. Evidence from party programs to pulp literature reflects disillusionment, pessimism, decline of the work ethic, and evaporation of civic morale.

The general rejection of official values and a turning away from a sense of national purpose toward nostalgia and the cultivation of private interests have led to widespread corruption, the decline of self-discipline, absenteeism, the second or unofficial economy, consumerism, and cynicism. Alcoholism has become a serious social curse. This is not the kind of society Lenin had in mind in 1917.

Many of these problems are similar to those in Western societies, but they are especially corrosive to a Communist system that seeks full control and imposition of its values. The visible conflict between the leaders' determination to preserve the system and the inexorable flowering of social, national, and spiritual forces that demand change creates one of the most serious dilemmas the rulers face and one closely related to their other challenges.

The Changing World:
Technology, Especially Communications

Preserving an established authoritarian system is becoming increasingly difficult because the Soviet Union cannot isolate itself from a world going through changes of every kind at an ever more rapid and increasingly universal pace. These transformations of values, customs, habits, dress, economies, means of communication, and every aspect of human life have spread to every part of the globe. Even "the winds of freedom" that helped destroy the old empires have invaded the Soviet Union.

Some Russian rulers, such as Peter the Great, and Soviet leaders—Stalin in the first Five-Year Plan and at an increasingly rapid pace Khrushchev and Brezhnev—in a gingerly way established relationships with the West. The expansion of economic and cultural ties with the most advanced countries has introduced forces for change, beginning with the elites, those most involved, and then seeping slowly down through society. Louis XIV declared that nations touch only at the top, but this century's revolutions of transportation and communications have destroyed that old truism, even in an age of censorship and jamming. Contact with other countries through acquisition of scientific ideas and technical products, cooperative economic programs, participation in international conferences, exchange of scholars and graduate students, increasing access to foreign technical literature and selected belles lettres weakens authority at home. The Soviet government seeks a fire that will not burn. It wishes to be in the world, but not of it. It is struggling, as the tsars did, with the eternal problem of Western influence, trying to borrow on the one hand and to keep infection away on the other, but its participation in the affairs of the world has increased at an ever greater rate in the last two decades and therefore the choice has become ever more painful.

Soviet participation in the world market under Brezhnev illustrates this change and the problems it raises. In the late 1960s and throughout the 1970s, Soviet and Eastern European leaders increased trade with the West and borrowed heavily to evade the hard decisions concerning decentralization of the economy and the reallocation of resources among the military, capital investment, and the consumer. The Communist leaders hoped these injections would modernize their economies, increase the supply of satisfactory consumer goods, and resolve basic economic problems. Far from eliminating the need for innovation, this approach created an enlarged set of problems, thus making the need more urgent. Economic involvement with the West introduced more external influences, including inflation and recession; increased consumer appetites; softened the popular view of Western Europe; helped bring about systemic crisis in Poland; and at the same time exhausted the Western cornucopia as a *deus ex machina*.

The dilemma that contact with the West raises is especially visible and acute because a new era, the age of information, is transforming the West even more rapidly than the steam and jet engines did. Knowledge is becoming the world's most important product, as agricultural research, atomic weapons and energy, medical science, and discoveries affecting every aspect of life demonstrate. The age of the university, miniature electronics, automatic machinery, computers, and satellites is inevitably a worldwide age. The production of information and the development and manufacture of the equipment which produces knowledge and distributes it quickly are transforming all societies.

The countries that recognize this transformation, join the world, and contribute are becoming stronger. They also develop closer relations with other states and peoples, export their political systems and values, open themselves up to ideas, and become increasingly interdependent. A country that restricts this flow, controls the number and use of Xerox machines, prevents automatic dial telephoning between its own cities, reduces telephonic and other communications with other states, and tries to isolate itself inevitably slips toward decline. It forces itself into an eternally unsuccessful effort at "catching up," hampered by restraints of its own creation.

The Soviet leaders must soon make a hard choice concerning this challenge by defining their relations with this new technology and changing world because the transformations in the outside world that technology creates will not wait. The options are all hazardous, particularly because Soviet leaders cannot isolate the choices in the field of information from decisions they must make about other problems. Withdrawal from contact with the world is virtually impossible and would be costly even in the short run. Maintaining a wall with carefully monitored turnstiles is difficult, ineffective, and in a perverse way increases fascination with the outside world. Moreover, tightening restrictions is more difficult than earlier and would weaken further the vitality of national life, make the Soviet Union technologically more backward, and reduce its effectiveness in the competition for influence abroad. On the other hand, reducing or eliminating barriers would be fatal to control, first in Eastern Europe and then in the Soviet Union itself.

Most observers agree that the most likely response to this series of options will be increased repression and cultural isolation, combined with a determined effort to obtain the fruits of Western advance without the infections, basically an impossible task and one that will make the dilemma ever more acute.

The Slowing Economy:
"Swollen State, Spent Society"

The economy of the USSR, having grown consistently since 1890, except during the two world wars, is the second largest in the world. It benefits from abundant natural resources, a large population, a vast industrial base, and potential for continued growth. During the 1970s, it profited from a windfall in foreign trade; its exports of oil and gas at sharply rising world prices enabled it considerably to expand imports of Western science, technology, and food products. At the same time, the economy displays grave systemic weaknesses.

The most visible determinant of Soviet policy in the 1980s and the most complicated, far-reaching, and difficult policy decisions are the consequences of the slowing rate of economic growth and unprecedented conditions of resource stringency. Years of economic growth at a constantly diminishing rate, from seven percent in the 1950s to five percent in the sixties, to four and then three percent in the seventies, enabled the Soviet leaders simultaneously to increase investment, the size and quality of the armed forces, and the standard of living. However, they now face a period in which the annual rate of growth will at best average 2 or 2.5 percent and may decline to one percent and virtual stagnation. The declining rate of growth reduces funds available for investment just when aging plant demands new equipment and when new needs arise.

In addition, the growth of labor supply will decelerate in the years ahead, falling to about 0.4 percent per year in the 1980s. Most of the increase will be among non-Russians in Central Asia, a population far from the most advanced infrastructure and main sources of raw materials, less skilled than the Russians, and generally unwilling to leave their homes or their region. On the other hand, bringing industry to areas where population is increasing would have very high capital costs and would intensify problems among ethnic groups.

Labor productivity will continue to decline: it is now zero or even negative because of insufficient capital investment, poor organization, failure to innovate, restrictions on labor mobility, and the government's continued inability to provide sufficient consumer goods as material incentives for an apathetic working class that has large savings accounts but nothing to purchase.

Most embarrassingly, agriculture remains an expensive problem. In spite of massive investments over the last twenty years (about one-third of all Soviet investment), greatly increased attention from government, and an annual increase of two percent in agricultural production, Soviet agriculture proves less and less capable of meeting consumer demands for more and better food. Even in 1982, Soviet citizens ate only two-thirds as much meat as Poles did. The cost of imported grain in 1981 was about $16 billion in hard currencies. American specialists estimate that the Soviet Union will import 25 to 40 million tons of grain annually throughout the 1980s (it imported 44 million tons of grain in 1981–82), and that other agricultural imports, including meat, will remain at the high levels of 1975–82. These massive purchases have riddled the hope that the Soviet Union could become self-sufficient with regard to food and have weakened the myth that the Soviet Union was or could become a model for other developing countries to emulate. Above all, they make the Soviet Union to some degree dependent upon the United States and other grain growers and therefore affect the conduct of Soviet policy.

Government policies designed to keep food prices low for workers have created a structure in which the consumer's market price is about one-half the cost of the produce to the state. The food subsidy in 1980 was about $50 billion and about $70 billion in 1982, 8 or 9 percent of Soviet GNP. The annual per capita cost of food subsidies then was about 195 rubles, somewhat more than an industrial worker's monthly wages and fifty percent more than the combined per capita expenditures for health and education. However, the Soviet government remains unwilling to introduce reality into pricing.

Soviet agriculture suffers bouts of poor weather, but its problems lie deep in the system and its operating procedures. Collectivization and the dead hand of centralized control of planning and management share responsibility. Government by a city-based apparatus since 1917 has neglected and penalized the rural folk. The basic backwardness of rural life, from mud roads to dreadful housing, poor schools, and grossly inadequate consumer goods, the exodus of the young to the cities, and the aging of the agricultural labor force have led to low productivity of farm labor.

The basic trouble is that central control and direction of the economy are an essential part of the political system. Major changes in the economy, which many Soviet specialists recognize as necessary, would undermine the controls party leaders consider crucial. Making or tolerating major innovations therefore strikes at the system itself.

Within this central dilemma, other equally awkward perplexities persist. Thus, the declining rate of growth makes the choices on allocation of resources among the military forces, capital investment, and the consumer both decisive and painful. Reducing or even freezing the level of military spending to free resources for investment or the consumer would require a heroic effort by the rulers and create serious political strains. Most Soviet leaders would consider such a step strategically dangerous, especially if the reductions affected R and D and production of new weapons at a time when they believed the United States was leaping ahead with new technology. Indeed, only a solidly entrenched leadership convinced that the need for innovation is desperate would decide to limit military expenditures, a course that many outside observers consider vital.

Increasing investment to stimulate growth, unleash new energy resources, develop new territorial complexes, and replace aging machinery would force the leaders to reduce or freeze military spending or consumer goods production or both. Similarly, increased attention to the consumer sector would directly affect the resources available for the military and investment.

Changing allocations of resources is particularly difficult because the immediate interests of central institutions and elites and of millions of Soviet citizens are so visibly engaged and because this conundrum is so tightly related to others, to potential ideological quarrels among the leaders, and to the character of the system. Party and bureaucratic opposition to relaxing familiar controls is great. Many workers oppose innovations because change would threaten job security, create sharp wage differentials to increase incentives, and raise prices by ending subsidies. All those benefiting from the system fear, justifiably, that changes in the economy would lead to ever greater pressures for further innovations. In addition, significant changes within the Soviet economy would encourage pressures for innovation in Eastern Europe, which would threaten stability, especially in Poland.

Most Western observers and many Soviet economists recognize the need for specific changes in the management of industry, especially for relaxation of the connections between the planner and the manager and between the manager and the consumer, and for a turn toward market socialism. They also recognize the need for changes in agriculture, including decentralization of control from Moscow, encouragement of private plots, vast improvements in rural life, the phased end of food subsidies, and perhaps even a return to the New Economic Policy of the 1920s. They agree that increased production and improved quality of consumer goods are now a prerequisite for Soviet economic growth. They also recognize that reducing production of consumer goods and the standard of living would affect in a negative way every aspect of Soviet life, beginning with productivity. Most Soviet citizens, accustomed to steady improvement in living standards, have visibly higher expectations than earlier and are aware of the gap between their own levels and standards of living elsewhere, even in Eastern Europe; the Soviet standard of living is about one-third the American. Keeping the Russian worker reasonably satisfied may provide the regime its greatest challenge. In fact, the situation is so grave that skilled observers conclude that the system must somehow meet consumer demands for such basic elements as food, housing, and health care to assure continuing stability.

In short, great pressures for changes in the Soviet economic system exist, ideas are abundant, and the potential for dramatic change and improvement is high. On the other hand, the political hazards and bureaucratic inertia are equally strong. Prospects for change are therefore problematic. Most outside observers believe that military expenditures will remain at least at the same absolute level, even if the Soviet Union and the United States reach effective arms control and reduction agreements. In sum, reform or innovation is risky and disagreeable. On the other hand, stagnation is intolerable. Sooner or later, Soviet leaders must make hard choices. Most observers believe that the Soviet government will seek to stimulate recovery by tinkering with the economy, especially through "organizational" and "mobilizational" changes aimed at increasing production of consumer goods.

Eastern Europe

The Soviet Union dominates the regimes and the policies of Poland, East Germany, Czechoslovakia, Hungary, Bulgaria, and to some extent Romania. These countries greatly enhance the USSR's power position because of their geographical location, natural resources, population, and productive capabilities. Stalin saw Eastern Europe as a barrier against the West and as the first step beyond the Soviet frontiers toward universal Communism. His successors see it as a vital part of the Soviet empire, one which ensures that the Soviet Union is a great European power. A Communist Eastern Europe provides a point of pressure against Western Europe. The Warsaw Pact constitutes a useful military alliance and diplomatic instrument. Different East European countries serve in a variety of ways as Soviet proxies in foreign areas, as purveyors of arms and economic aid to revolutionary movements in various parts of the world, and as links to Communist parties and to international front movements. The Soviet presence maintains Communist rule in those countries, serves as a barrier against the West, and helps to legitimize the Soviet system in Soviet eyes. Above all, rule by Communists loyal to or subservient to Moscow strengthens faith among Communists everywhere and creates fear among others that a Soviet Eastern Europe represents a permanent step toward Communist world power. A reversal of this situation would lead to unraveling of this central doctrine in the Communist faith.

Eastern Europe as a whole remains visibly unstable, even though Communist rule seems solid, except in Poland. Much of this instability derives from a history that thirty or forty years cannot overcome, for these peoples have created instabilities for all their conquerors. Soviet rule has revived East European nationalisms, aimed now against the Soviet effort to transform their cultures. The peoples resent Communism because it violates their histories and traditions, because the Soviets imposed it, and because the usurped authority of their rulers rests on Soviet power.

The social and cultural tensions that have developed in the Soviet Union have bubbled in Eastern Europe, too, only with greater visibility and effect. East European economic rates of growth have slowed greatly; in Poland they have been negative since 1978, and in most countries, especially Czechoslovakia, they are stagnant or declining. Prospects for improvement in the 1980s, except for Hungary, are dismal. Each state also faces the delicate problem of transferring authority to another set of rulers at some point in the 1980s.

Soviet rule under Stalin in particular exploited these peoples mercilessly, but they have been an expensive dependency and growing economic drain since about 1970, tieing down vast numbers of Soviet manpower and enormous Soviet resources. The Soviet Union granted these countries subsidies of $20 billion in one form or another in 1980, and the dependency is likely to remain high, particularly in oil and gas.

Poland is the heart of the Soviet empire, as it was of the Russian empire a century ago. In the 1980s it plays the central role in Soviet relations with the West that it has often played before. The collapse of the Polish party and economy illuminates the serious instabilities that wrack this potentially explosive area and the way in which the major hard choices converge and affect each other. The situation in Poland places an additional heavy strain upon the Soviet economy, and those contemplating the introduction of innovations into the Soviet economy must consider the ultimate effects of such changes in Poland and elsewhere in Eastern Europe.

As the consequence of national history and of a crisis which has matured over two decades, the great bulk of the Polish nation has rejected not just particular leaders, policies, incompetence, and corruption but the Communist system itself in a genuine, unplanned, if abortive, revolution from below. As far as one can tell, all Polish youth have rejected the system. Only the sense of responsibility that Poles have learned in crises since 1956, deserved fear of Soviet military intervention, and the dependence of the Polish Central Committee, military leaders, and security apparatus on the Soviets have prevented civil war, Soviet invasion, and international crisis. Poland is a cancer that the Soviets may freeze into temporary remission but one for which even a miraculous economic recovery would provide no certain cure.

The choices in Poland are even more troubling than those the Soviet economy offers, and Soviet leaders possess few if any options. Tinkering or palliatives would at best slow economic decline and perhaps prevent violent outbreaks: the gap between policy and reality is too wide, and the Communists have squandered too many years. Salvation from now-cautious Western bankers is most unlikely, with or without default and bankruptcy.

If the Polish regime could bring itself to honor its 1980 agreements concerning trade union and other rights—and if it could win Soviet approval for such a stunning reversal—the Polish appetite for sweeping reforms would grow. A government attempt to regain direct but discreet control of restored popular forces, even if the church restrained them, while it maneuvered between the vigilant Soviet Union and a watchful West, would require political skill a weak and divided party could hardly sustain. Moreover, such innovations in Poland would signal pressures for comparable changes elsewhere in Eastern Europe and in the Soviet Union's western regions. The inevitable reaction of the great mass of conservatives in the Soviet government, especially in the armed forces, to proposals that threaten to weaken the Soviet grip on the main approach to Germany and Europe would clearly prevent such a policy.

Another Soviet option, the most likely one, is that of reasserting Soviet authority over its East European empire, particularly Poland. This choice would mean supporting the military junta, or an even more reactionary group if Jaruzelski is not successful; strengthening those instruments that retained Poland for the Communists (the party apparatus, the military forces, and the security police); tightening all controls; relying on the presence or proximity of Soviet forces to ensure submission; and intervening directly if that should prove necessary. This is not an inviting prospect, but one to which the failures of the last thirty-five years have brought them. Such a policy would involve paying great attention to the transfers of authority throughout Eastern Europe in the 1980s. The Soviets would also seek to strengthen and tighten the Warsaw Pact and to provide limited economic assistance in dire crises, just as they provided $8 billion to Poland in 1981–82. At the same time, they would press these regimes to reduce the Soviet subsidy by raising the price of energy supplies, organizing new bilateral and multilateral trading agreements under the Council for Mutual Economic Assistance (CMEA), and arranging that these states help build Soviet pipelines and other capital enterprises.

All this would only reiterate the unsuccessful policies of the past three decades. The effect would increase apathy in the Polish economy and resentment against the Soviet Union. Restricting access to the West to carefully monitored turnstiles would increase alienation of the intellectuals and the youth already disaffected and simultaneously heighten the West's attraction to the entire population. The impact upon Western Europe, the Middle East and the Mediterranean states, the United States, and indeed most of the world would constitute a serious blow to Soviet prospects and adversely affect Soviet options on the other converging dilemmas. Indeed, some Soviet leaders must worry about the high cost of maintaining empire, the way in which its unraveling might begin with any loss of control over Poland, and the high cost of intervention and open Soviet occupation of Poland. But they cannot now escape.

A century ago Russian leaders recognized that no solution existed for "the Polish problem." The situation in Poland was a millstone around all efforts to introduce political, economic, or social reform into the Russian Empire: "The Poles, like the poor, we will always have with us." The Polish issue also divided Russia from the West European states, as it does again. Holding on to Warsaw cost Russia Constantinople a hundred years ago, and Warsaw bears a heavy price a century later. Poland and its economy remain major touchstones of Soviet policy and reveal the complicated and difficult nature of the hard choices Soviet leaders face. The Polish situation is so grave and the instabilities of some of its neighbors of such concern to Soviet leaders that maintaining the vigilant grip on the territory and people and returning Poland to some kind of "normal" Communist rule will constitute a main determinant of Soviet policy throughout the 1980s.

Opportunities Abroad

Events beyond the Soviet empire's frontiers, including developments in which the Soviets play no direct role, affect Soviet conduct and also raise policy dilemmas. Such developments demonstrate that Soviet leaders must take into consideration the complexities of an ever-shrinking and more interdependent world in reaching decisions. Some occurrences raise concerns for Soviet security. Others promise bright opportunities for Soviet advantage through meddling or scavenging but at the same time create problems because Soviet actions would affect other complicated and interrelated problems. In the 1980s, these factors and the presumed revival of American strength and resolution will force Soviet leaders to choose between taking advantage of tempting lures of expansion elsewhere in the world and maintaining the positive kinds of relations with the West that will enable the USSR to face its domestic dilemmas and to achieve its main goals in Western Europe. Relations with the People's Republic of China complicate foreign policy choices greatly because the Soviets see the Chinese as rivals for influence among radical and revolutionary forces.

In sum, the Soviet Union has limited ability to maneuver in its foreign policy, as it does in its domestic problems, and it faces a series of hard choices. Ironically, these dilemmas reflect in part Soviet foreign policy achievements in the 1970s, when the Soviet Union construed detente as a one-way street requiring no Soviet restraint. These policies ended the SALT process and provoked a massive military effort in the United States, alienated much of the Third World, and produced a negative effect on Soviet economic relations with the West. Both the successes and the costs of these policies sharpen the dilemmas the political system faces in the 1980s.

The Soviet leaders' main concern is to help prevent a nuclear war by preparing for such a war and using fear of war outside the Soviet Union to weaken resolution in other societies.

The United States is the principal Soviet adversary, a powerful country with strong military forces, an enormously productive and inventive economy, and such vitality that both its high and its low culture have gained permanent influence in much of the world. In fact, comparison of the vigor of American culture and the moribundity of Soviet culture and of their relative impact everywhere in the world, even in Eastern Europe, illustrates the weakness of the Soviet Union in all fields of competition except military.

However, the United States suffers, as does most of the world, from a numbing recession that as yet has no end in sight. The apparent, perhaps temporary, decline of American confidence and resolution, the social and intellectual fissures that disturb its serenity, its economic problems, and the perpetual uncertainties of American foreign policy weaken its role in the West. Leading an alliance of countries, particularly democratic ones, over a prolonged period of time has always proved difficult. Even so, Soviet leaders must keep the United States and its policies in mind whenever they make decisions on modifying the Soviet political structure, entering the era of information, resolving domestic economic issues, choosing alternatives in Poland, and considering actions anywhere in the world.

Even though it is underdeveloped and weak, and will remain so for at least another generation, the People's Republic of China also exerts a visible influence on Soviet conduct. The Soviet leaders and people have a deep irrational fear of the Chinese. The Soviet leaders still see themselves as the high priests of the international Communist movement and regard China as a keen rival for that movement's tattered flag. Beyond these ideological ambitions and quarrels lie ancient and deep national hostilities and conflicts of national interest, represented in the 1980s by Chinese opposition to the Soviet role in Vietnam and to the Soviet invasion of Afghanistan. Soviet maintenance of massive military forces on the Chinese borders at the expense of long-term economic growth demonstrates the depth of the Soviet preoccupation with China. Soviet options with regard to China are limited by reluctance to abandon positions in Southeast Asia and Afghanistan or to revise relationships with India, by the visible clash of Soviet and Chinese national interests as neighboring states, and to a lesser degree by ideology. However, the major Soviet concern is not so much the China of 1982 or even of 1990, but that American and Japanese aid may help increase Chinese economic and military power so that China may one day become a serious and unrelenting threat. The greatest fear, of course, is that the United States, Japan, and China, and possibly a unified Western Europe, will one day encircle the Soviet Union.

The Soviet leaders see Western Europe as a crucial area in which Soviet influence and leverage can grow. In spite of its remarkable political and economic recovery since 1945, cooperative efforts unthinkable as recently as forty years ago, and construction of bases for increased cooperation and even unity among democratic states, Western Europe lacks confidence and self-assurance. The area is vulnerable to outside pressures and no longer feels certain of the American guarantee of security and peace. Skillful Soviet diplomatic and psychological use of their huge military forces; disagreements between the United States and its allies over Soviet power and policy, strategies, trade, and the division of responsibilities and costs; and the effects of the so-called peace campaign have enriched the culture of appeasement and fueled neutralist and even pacifist movements that will bedevil Western policy makers throughout the decade. Those movements will probably reach one of their peaks in the controversy over theater nuclear weapons, and 1983 may therefore witness an impressive Soviet "peace" campaign, based on attractive Soviet arms proposals, just when the West Germans especially are reaching decisions about the installation of weapons to counter the long-established SS20s.

Western Europe represents no military threat to the Soviets. However, its existence, its freedoms, and its prosperity exert a continuing powerful appeal throughout Eastern Europe and the Soviet Union. Western Europe is therefore both a source of infection and an area of opportunity, one in which Soviet leaders see an important role for patient, opportunistic diplomacy, but one in which they must approach their limited options with immense skill and tact, using both the carrot and the stick and somehow conducting themselves at home and in Poland in such a way as not to strengthen West European fears.

Areas further afield are less attractive than Western Europe but nevertheless influence Soviet conduct. The more than one hundred new Third World countries and some older ones vary greatly one from another, but many are fragile constructs and suffer from serious maladies: insecure new institutions; internal discord; dreadful poverty side by side with spectacular new wealth; generally rising popular expectations; ethnic, religious, and social divisions; resentment of their former imperial rulers; and powerful anti-Americanism. Many have ambitious radical leaders who seek quickly to transform their countries and make them important in world politics. They invite Soviet interest and support, and Soviet achievements and authoritarianism attract some leaders.

In many of these countries, previous performance, distance, Soviet inability to compete with the United States and Western Europe in providing economic assistance, and the sorry economic performance of all Communist states in recent years hamper Soviet prospects. The Soviets' need to take sides in sensitive conflicts (such as between Iran and Iraq) and Soviet policy on Afghanistan and on religion hampers them in many areas, especially in the Moslem world.

Even so, Soviet leaders must conclude that a number of opportunities to advance Soviet interests in several different areas of a chaotic and even anarchic world will appear in the 1980s. In some cases, they may be able without significant cost or hazard to increase anarchy and disorder in regional and world politics, undermine Western influence, and create conditions from which they may benefit openly, merely by providing direct or indirect support through proxies, such as Cuba, radical and revolutionary movements, terrorism, and disruptive countries, such as Libya.

In other cases, countries in several different parts of the world will on some occasion offer attractive opportunities for meddling or scavenging, as Angola, South Yemen, and Ethiopia did in the 1970s.

Soviet choices in each case would presumably reflect careful calculation of benefits and costs and of the effect upon the other complicated
and interrelated problems for which they seek solutions.

Latin America, especially Central America, offers an especially attractive area for a carefully calibrated Soviet policy, combining the
skills of the sympathetic observer and the speculator, of the nationalist and the Communist. The Soviets can profit from the deep fissures
within each state and the disagreements among them, the strength of
anti-Americanism, and Cuba as an instrument. On the other hand,
Soviet leaders appreciate the sensitive concern with which the American public and any American government would face any expansion
of Cuban and/or Soviet influence in Central America.

Finally, the Soviet leaders' decisions and conduct in the Middle
East will reflect their alert and keen interest in the enormous potential
benefits a deeply divided Iran could provide. Their choices here
would represent the other interrelated concerns, the kinds of openings or opportunities which arise, timing, and Soviet evaluation of
American firmness in defending American national interests, and
that of other countries, in that part of the world. When considering all
these attractive opportunities, the Soviet leaders must recognize that
their ability to act is sharply limited by the other hard choices they
face.

Conclusion

The new leadership that will one day emerge into power after
Andropov, like that associated with him, has been carefully selected,
trained and monitored. As far as outsiders can tell, the members of
the younger generation (those now in their fifties and sixties) apparently share the values of present leaders, embrace and benefit from
the party-state system, and view the Soviet Union, Eastern Europe,
and the world in much the same way as their elders do. They entered
political life after Stalin's death, and they are probably eager to set
aside those who have ruled for such a long time. They seem more
aware of the grave character of Soviet problems and more eager to
"get the country going" than their elders have been. The failures of
the system, the convergence of a number of critical problems, and the
centrality of these rites of passage suggest that internal affairs will
attract the bulk of their interest. The speed and skill with which
Andropov moves this new generation into some share of power will
greatly affect Soviet policy over the next decade and long into the
future.

Most outside observers consider that resolute and far-reaching
internal changes within a decade are necessary to prevent the erosion
of Soviet power, future instabilities of a serious character within the

Soviet empire, and perhaps as a consequence aggressive diplomatic and other forceful actions outside the empire. At the same time, these observers generally agree that the immobile character of the system, the absence of a reform mechanism, the thorny nature of the problems, and the ways the issues are interrelated limit the likelihood of major changes. They also conclude that the Andropov generation and those close to it will originally at least emphasize more law and order, labor discipline, Soviet nationalism, and moderately tighter police measures and negative incentives to increase productivity. Such a series of policies would produce stagnation, or even some decline in the Soviet economy, but not an immediate decline in military power or collapse, because both the system and the Soviet people are stubborn and adaptable.

In short, most observers see muddling through or muddling down as one likely choice within the Soviet Union and in Eastern Europe and in Soviet policy in the world at large. Such an option, common among political leaders everywhere, would delay fundamental decisions until the 1990s.

Under Andropov, the debate over policy choices may sharpen. Candidates jostling for place and power may advocate changes primarily to advance the interest of their bureaucratic or territorial constituencies or simply to amass power. Policy disagreements may arise within the leadership, and some candidates may adopt demagogic postures for change merely to strengthen their positions in the leadership. However, the problems are such that intense concerns will almost surely break through the now dominant apparent unanimity and that some members of the elite will advocate fundamental changes. No one can forecast whether or when such debates or disagreements will become acute or how the leadership will resolve them.

Whether Andropov and his colleagues, or their successors, would have the authority, resolution, and skill to carry through such transformations is a great unknown, because the oppositions to innovation are strong and entrenched. However, the death of Brezhnev and other senior Politburo officials does raise the possibility that the new leaders will act upon the recognized need for changes.

I believe that some present and probable future leaders, as well as many members of the Soviet elite, recognize the need for structured changes in the system and for major policy changes after sixteen years of immobility. Andropov and his colleagues may therefore attempt and somehow carry out important changes, beginning with a peace campaign with genuine arms reduction proposals as the centerpiece. But resistance to change is powerful and determined.

Outside actors, including the United States, can have little or no direct influence on how the Soviet Union chooses to manage its internal affairs. The United States and its allies should at least recognize the character of the challenge the Soviet Union presents and should be prepared to use their considerable strengths at appropriate times to contain Soviet power. The West should appreciate that the contest will be a long one, that it is at heart a political struggle, not a military one, that managing or controlling the competition will remain crucial, and that no quick solutions or early answers are likely. The struggle is a test of two civilizations, two cultures, each with its own strengths and weaknesses. If the United States and its allies should succeed in improving the quality of life in their societies and establishing consistency and coordination in their foreign policies, they may be able to nudge the Soviet Union into policies that make the system more tolerable for its citizens and less threatening to the world. But if the world outside the Soviet empire descends further into economic and political disarray, the incentives for the Soviet leaders to reform their internal system and to moderate their ambitions abroad will correspondingly decline.

Bibliography

This bibliography includes, in addition to sources cited in the text, a selected list of books and articles for further reading, topically arranged.

The Political System

Bialer, Seweryn. *Stalin's Successors: Leadership, Stability, and Change in the Soviet Union.* Cambridge: Cambridge University Press, 1980.

————, ed. *The Domestic Context of Soviet Foreign Policy.* Boulder, Colo.: Westview Press, 1981.

Breslauer, George W. *Khrushchev and Brezhnev as Leaders: Building Authority in Soviet Politics.* London: Allen & Unwin, 1982.

Brown, A. H., and Jack Gray, eds. *Political Culture and Political Change in Communist States.* London: Macmillan, 1977.

Brown, Archie, and Michael Kaser, eds. *Soviet Policy for the 1980s.* Bloomington: Indiana University Press, 1983.

Brown, Archie, et al., eds. *The Cambridge Encyclopedia of Russia and the Soviet Union.* Cambridge: Cambridge University Press, 1982.

Bunce, Valerie. *Do New Leaders Make a Difference? Executive Succession and Public Policy Under Capitalism and Socialism.* Princeton, N.J.: Princeton University Press, 1981.

Cocks, Paul, Robert V. Daniels, and Nancy Heer, eds. *The Dynamics Of Soviet Politics.* Cambridge, Mass.: Harvard University Press, 1976.

Cohen, Stephen F., Alexander Rabinowitch, and Robert Sharlet, eds. *The Soviet Union since Stalin.* Bloomington: Indiana University Press, 1980.

Fainsod, Merle. *Smolensk under Soviet Rule.* New York: Vintage Books, 1963.

Griffith, William E., ed. *The Soviet Empire: Expansion and Detente.* Lexington, Mass.: D. C. Heath & Co., 1976.

Gustafson, Thane. *Reform in Soviet Politics: The Lessons of Recent Policies on Land and Water.* New York: Cambridge University Press, 1981.

Heclo, Hugh, and Aaron Wildavsky. *The Private Governance of Public Money.* London: Macmillan, 1974.

Hough, Jerry. "The Evolution of the Soviet World View." *World Politics,* July 1980, pp. 509–30.

————. *Soviet Leadership in Transition.* Washington, D.C.: Brookings, 1980.

————, and Merle Fainsod. *How the Soviet Union Is Governed.* Cambridge, Mass.: Harvard University Press, 1979.

Kaiser, Robert G. *Russia: The People and the Power.* New York: Atheneum, 1976.

Osborn, Robert J. *The Evolution of Soviet Politics.* Homewood, Ill.: Dorsey Press, 1974.

Powell, David E. "In Pursuit of Interest Groups in the USSR." *Soviet Union,* vol. 6, part 1, 1979, pp. 99–124.

Rush, Myron. *How Communist States Change Their Rulers.* Ithaca, N.Y.: Cornell University Press, 1974.

Schwartz, Morton. *The Foreign Policy of the USSR: Domestic Factors.* Encino, Calif.: Dickinson Publication Co., 1975.

Simes, Dimitri and associates. *Soviet Succession: Leadership in Transition.* The Washington Papers, no. 59. Beverly Hills-London: Sage Publications, 1979.

Skilling, H. Gordon, and Franklyn Griffiths, eds. *Interest Groups in Soviet Politics.* Princeton, N.J.: Princeton University Press, 1971.

Smith, Hedrick. *The Russians.* New York: Quadrangle, 1976.

Wesson, Robert G. *The Aging of Communism.* New York: Praeger, 1980.

———. *The Soviet Union: Looking to the 1980s.* Stanford, Calif.: Hoover Institution Press, 1980.

White, Stephen. *Political Culture and Soviet Politics.* London: Macmillan, 1979.

Yanov, Alexander. *The Russian New Right: Right-Wing Ideologies in the Contemporary USSR.* Berkeley: University of California, Institute of International Studies, 1978.

The Economy

Amann, Ronald, and Julian Cooper, eds. *Industrial Innovation in the Soviet Union.* New Haven, Conn.: Yale University Press, 1982.

Amann, Ronald, Julian Cooper, and R. W. Davies, eds. *The Technological Level of Soviet Industry.* New Haven, Conn.: Yale University Press, 1977.

Arbatov, Georgii. *Ideologicheskaia bor'ba v sovremennykh mezhdunarodnykh otnosheniiakh.* Moscow: Politizdat, 1970.

Baibakov, N. K. *Gosudarstvennyi piatiletnyi plan razvitiia narodnogo khoziaistva SSSR 1971–75 gody.* Moscow, 1972.

Becker, Abraham S. *Soviet Military Outlays since 1955.* Santa Monica, Calif.: Rand Corporation, RM-3886-PR, January 1963.

———. *CIA Estimates of Soviet Military Expenditure.* Santa Monica, Calif.: Rand Corporation, P-6534, August 1980.

———. *The Burden of Soviet Defense.* Santa Monica, Calif.: Rand Corporation. October 1981.

Bergson, Abram. *Productivity and the Social System: The USSR and the West.* Cambridge, Mass.: Harvard University Press, 1978.

———. *The Real National Income of Soviet Russia since 1928.* Cambridge, Mass.: Harvard University Press, 1961.

Bergson, Abram, and Herbert Levine, eds. *The Soviet Economy to the Year 2000.* London: Allen & Unwin, 1982.

Berliner, Joseph S. *The Innovation Decision in Soviet Industry.* Cambridge, Mass.: MIT Press, 1976.

Bornstein, Morris, ed. *Comparative Economic Systems: Models and Cases.* Homewood, Ill.: Richard D. Irwin, Inc., 1979.

———. *The Soviet Economy: Continuity and Change.* Boulder, Colo.: Westview Press, 1981.

Bornstein, Morris, and Daniel R. Fusfeld, eds. *The Soviet Economy: A Book of Readings.* Homewood, Ill.: Richard D. Irwin, Inc., 1972.

Bush, Keith "Unofficial Soviet Estimates of the Soviet Defense Burden." *Radio Liberty Research Report,* CRD 197/72, Munich, August 3, 1977.

Campbell, Robert W. *Accounting in Soviet Planning and Management.* Cambridge, Mass.: Harvard University Press, 1963.

———. *Economics in the Soviet Oil and Gas Industry.* Baltimore, Md.: Johns Hopkins University Press, 1968.

———. *Soviet Energy Technologies: Planning, Policy, Research and Development.* Bloomington: Indiana University Press, 1981.

———. *Soviet Technology Imports: The Gas Pipeline Case.* California Seminar on International Security and Foreign Policy, Discussion Paper No. 91, Santa Monica, Calif.: Rand Corporation, 1981.

———. *The Soviet-Type Economies.* New York: Houghton Mifflin, 1974.

Central Intelligence Agency. *Estimates of Soviet Defense Spending.* Hearings before the Subcommittee on Oversight of the Permanent Select Committee on Intelligence. House of Representatives, September 3, 1980. Washington, D.C.: USGPO, 1980.

———. *Soviet and U.S. Defense Activities, 1971–80: A Dollar Cost Comparison.* Washington, D.C.: USGPO, January 1981.

———, Net Foreign Assessment Center. *Handbook of Economic Statistics, 1980.* Washington, D.C.: USGPO, October 1980.

Checinski, Michael. "The Cost of Armament Production and the Profitability of Armament Exports in COMECON Countries." *Osteuropa Wirtschaft* 20, no. 2, June 1975.

Cohn, Stanley. *Economic Development in the Soviet Union.* Lexington, Mass.: D. C. Heath & Co., 1970.

Dienes, Leslie, and Theodore Shabad. *The Soviet Energy System.* Washington, D.C.: V. H. Winston & Sons, 1979.

Economic Commission for Europe. *Review of the Agricultural Situation in Europe at the End of 1980.* New York: United Nations, 1981.

Erickson, John. *Regional Development in the USSR: Trends and Prospects.* Newtonville, Mass.: Oriental Research Partners, 1979.

Field, Mark G., ed. *Social Consequences of Modernization in Communist Societies.* Baltimore, Md.: Johns Hopkins University Press, 1976.

Friesen, Connie M. *The Political Economics of East-West Trade.* New York: Praeger, 1976.

Green, Donald W., and Christopher I. Higgins. *SOVMOD I: A Macroeconometric Model of the Soviet Union.* New York: Academic Press, 1977.

Hanson, Philip. *Trade and Technology in Soviet-Western Relations.* New York: Columbia University Press, 1981.

Hayami, Yujuo, and Vernon Ruttan. *Agricultural Development: An International Perspective.* Baltimore, Md.: Johns Hopkins University Press, 1971.

Johnson, D. Gale, ed. *The Politics of Food: Producing and Distributing the World's Food Supply.* Chicago: Chicago Council on Foreign Relations, 1980.

Johnson, D. Gale, and Karen McConnell Brooks. *Prospects for Soviet Agriculture in the 1980s.* Bloomington: Indiana University Press, 1983.

Loebl, Eugene. "Russia's Economy: The Impossible Prediction." *Interplay*, 4:2, February 1971, pp. 18–24.

Nimitz, Nancy. *The July 1979 Decree and Soviet Economic Reform.* Santa Monica, Calif.: Rand Corporation, 1982.

Ofer, Gur. *The Opportunity Cost of the Nonmonetary Advantages of the Soviet Military R & D Effort.* Santa Monica, Calif.: Rand Corporation, R-1741-DDRE, August 1975.

———. *The Relative Efficiency of Military Research and Development in the Soviet Union: Systems Approach.* Santa Monica, Calif.: Rand Corporation, R-2522-AF, November 1980.

Rapawy, Stephen. *Estimates and Projections of the Labor Force and Civilian Employment in the USSR, 1950–1990.* Foreign Economic Report no. 10, U.S. Department of Commerce, September 1976.

Sutton, Anthony. *Western Technology and Soviet Economic Developments,* vols. 1-3. Stanford, Calif.: Stanford University Press, 1968–73.

Treml, Vladimir, and Barry Kostinsky. *The Domestic Value of Soviet Foreign Trade: Exports and Imports in the 1972 Input-Output Table.* Washington, D.C.: Report for the Foreign Demographic Analysis Division, U.S. Bureau of the Census, August 1981.

Tsentral'noe statisticheskoe upravlenie, *Narodnoe khoziaistvo SSSR.* Moscow, for successive years.

U.S. Arms Control and Disarmament Agency. *World Military Expenditures and Arms Transfers, 1970–79.* Washington, D.C., 1982.

U.S. Bureau of the Census. *Population Projections by Age and Sex for the Republics and Major Economic Regions of the USSR, 1970–2000.* International Population Series, P-91, No. 26. Washington, D.C.: USGPO, 1979.

U.S. Congress, House Committee on Science and Technology, 96th Congress, 1st Session, 1979. *Key Issues in U.S.–USSR Scientific Exchanges and Technology Transfer.*

U.S. Congress, Joint Economic Committee. *Soviet Economy in a Time of Change,* vol. 2. Washington, D.C.: USGPO, 1979.

———. *Consumption in the USSR: An International Comparison.* Washington, D.C.: USGPO, 1981.

———. *Soviet Economy in the 1980s: Problems and Prospects,* Washington, D.C.: USGPO, 1982.

———. *Allocation of Resources in the Soviet Union and China.* Washington, D.C.: USGPO, 1974, 1975, 1977.

———. *USSR: Measures of Economic Growth and Development, 1950–1980.* Washington, D.C.: USGPO, 1982.

U.S. Department of Agriculture. *Agricultural Statistics, 1981.* Washington, D.C.: USGPO, 1982.

———. *USSR: Review of Agriculture in 1981 and Outlook for 1982.* Washington, D.C.: USGPO, 1982.

USSR in Figures, 1980, The. Moscow: Statistika Publishers, 1981.

Zaleski, Eugene, and Helgard Weinert. *Technology Transfer Between East and West.* Paris: Organization for Economic Cooperation and Development, 1980.

Military Forces

Adomeit, Hannes. *Soviet Risk Taking and Crisis Behavior, from Confrontation to Coexistence.* Adelphi Paper no. 101. London: International Institute for Strategic Studies, 1973.

Alexander, Arthur J. *Decision-Making in Soviet Weapons Procurement.* Adelphi Paper no. 147/48. London: International Institute for Strategic Studies, Winter 1978–79.

Alexander, Arthur J., Abraham S. Becker, and William Hoehn, Jr. *The Significance of Divergent U.S.-USSR Military Expenditure.* Santa Monica, Calif.: Rand Corporation, N-1000-AF, February 1979.

Arnett, Robert L. "Soviet Attitudes Toward Nuclear War: Do They Really Think They Can Win?" *Journal of Strategic Studies,* September 1979, pp. 172–91.

Bertram, Christoph, ed. *Prospects of Soviet Power in the 1980s.* London: Archon Books, 1980.

Booth, Ken. *The Military Instrument in Soviet Foreign Policy, 1917–1972.* London: Royal, 1973.

Caldwell, Lawrence T. "The Warsaw Pact: Directions of Change." *Problems of Communism,* September-October 1975, pp. 1–19.

Clawson, Robert W., and Lawrence S. Kaplan, eds. *The Warsaw Pact; Political Purpose and Military Means.* Wilmington, Del.: Scholarly Resources, Inc., 1982.

Collins, John M. *American and Soviet Military Trends since the Cuban Missile Crisis.* Washington, D.C.: Center for Strategic and International Studies, 1978.

———. *U.S.-Soviet Military Balance.* New York: McGraw-Hill, 1981.

Colton, Timothy. *Commissars, Commanders and Civilian Authority: The Structure of Soviet Military Politics.* Cambridge, Mass.: Harvard University Press, 1979.

Deane, Michael J. *Political Control of the Soviet Armed Forces.* New York: Crane, Russak & Co., 1977.

Defense Intelligence Agency. *Handbook of the Soviet Armed Forces.* Washington, D.C.: USGPO, 1978.

Douglass, Joseph D. *Soviet Military Strategy in Europe.* New York: Pergamon, 1980.

———. *The Soviet Theater Nuclear Offensive.* Washington, D.C.: USGPO, 1976.

———. *Conventional War and Escalation: The Soviet View.* New York: Crane, Russak & Co., 1981.

Dziak, John J. *Soviet Perceptions of Military Power: The Interaction of Theory and Practice.* New York: Crane, Russak & Co., 1981.

Erickson, John. "The Ground Forces in Soviet Military Policy." *Strategic Review,* vol. 6, Winter 1978, pp. 64–79.

———. "Trends in the Soviet Combined-Arms Concept." *Strategic Review,* vol. 5, Winter 1977, pp. 38–53.

———. *Soviet Military Power.* London: Royal Institute, 1971.

Ermarth, Fritz W. "Contrasts in American and Soviet Strategic Thought." *International Security,* no. 2, Fall 1978, pp. 138–55.

Garthoff, Raymond L. *Soviet Military Policy: An Historical Analysis.* New York: Praeger, 1966.

———. "Mutual Deterrence and Strategic Arms Limitation in Soviet Policy." *International Security,* Summer 1978, pp. 112–47.

———. "The Meaning of the Missiles." *Washington Quarterly,* Fall 1982, pp. 76–82.

Gray, Colin S. *The Geopolitics of the Nuclear Era: Heartland, Rimlands, and the Technological Revolution.* New York: Crane, Russak & Co., 1977.

Gray, Colin S., and Rebecca Strode. "The Imperial Dimension of Soviet Military Power." *Problems of Communism,* November-December 1981, pp. 1–15.

Grechko, Marshal A. A. "Rukovodiashchaia rol' KPSS v stroitel'stve armii razvitogo sotsialisticheskogo obshchestva." *Voprosy istorii KPSS,* 1974, no. 5.

———. *Vooruzhennye sily sovetskogo gosudarstva.* Second edition. Moscow: Voenizdat, 1975.

Herspring, Dale R., and Ivan Volgyes, eds. *Civil-Military Relations in Communist Systems.* Boulder, Colo.: Westview Press, 1978.

Holloway, David. *Technology Management and the Soviet Military Establishment.* Adelphi Paper, no. 26. London: International Institute for Strategic Studies, 1971.

———. *The Soviet Union and the Arms Race.* New Haven: Yale University Press, 1983.

Holzman, Franklyn D. "Soviet Military Spending: Assessing the Numbers Game." *International Security,* Spring 1982, pp. 78–101.

Horelick, Arnold L., and Myron Rush. *Strategic Power and Soviet Foreign Policy.* Chicago, 1966.
International Institute for Strategic Studies. *The Military Balance, 1981–82,* London, 1981.
———. "Strategic Survey 1979." *Strategic Survey,* 1980, pp. 38–41, 99–107.
Jacobsen, Carl G. *Soviet Strategy-Soviet Foreign Policy: Military Considerations Affecting Soviet Policy-Making.* Glasglow: Robert Maclehose, 1972.
———. *Soviet Influence in Eastern Europe.* New York: Praeger, 1981.
Johnson, A. Ross, Robert W. Dean, and Alexander Alexiev. *East European Military Establishments: The Warsaw Pact Northern Tier.* New York: Crane, Russak & Co., 1982.
Jones, Christopher D. "Just Wars and Limited Wars: Restraints on the Use of the Soviet Armed Forces." *World Politics,* 28:1, October 1975, pp. 44–68.
Kaplan, Stephen S. *Diplomacy of Power: Soviet Armed Forces as a Political Instrument.* Washington, D.C.: Brookings, 1981.
Kolko, Gabriel. *The Politics of War.* New York: Random House, 1968.
Kolkowicz, Roman. *The Soviet Military and the Communist Party.* Princeton, N.J.: Princeton University Press, 1967.
Lafeber, Walter. *America, Russia and the Cold War, 1945–1980.* New York: Wiley, 1980.
Lambeth, Benjamin. *Soviet Strategic Conduct and the Prospects for Stability.* Santa Monica, Calif.: Rand Corporation, R-2579-AF, December 1980.
———. *How To Think About Soviet Military Doctrine.* Santa Monica, Calif.: Rand Corporation, 1978.
Lee, William T. *The Estimation of Soviet Defense Expenditures 1955–75: An Unconventional Approach.* New York: Praeger, 1977.
Legvold, Robert. "The Nature of Soviet Power." *Foreign Affairs,* Fall 1977, pp. 49–71.
MccGwire, M., K. Booth, and J. McDonnell, eds. *Soviet Naval Policy, Objectives and Constraints.* New York: Praeger, 1975.
Nolan, Gerald A. *The USSR: The Unity and Integration of Soviet Political, Military, and Defense Industry Leadership.* Defense Intelligence Agency, ODI-2250-17-77. Washington, D.C., March 1977.
Odom, William E. "Who Controls Whom in Moscow?" *Foreign Policy,* no. 14, Summer 1975, pp. 109–23.
———. "The Party Connection." *Problems of Communism,* September–October, 1973.
Perry, William. "The Nature of the Defense Problem in the 1980s and the Role of Defense Technologies in Meeting the Challenge." In *The Role of Technology in Meeting the Defense Challenges of the 1980s.* A Special Report of the Arms Control and Disarmament Program. Stanford, Calif.: Arms Control and Disarmament Program, 1981.
Pipes, Richard. "Why the Soviet Union Thinks It Can Fight and Win a Nuclear War." *Commentary,* July 1977, pp. 21–34.
———. "Militarism and the Soviet State." *Daedalus,* Fall 1980, pp. 1–12.
Record, Jeffrey. *Sizing Up the Soviet Army.* Washington, D.C.: Brookings, 1975.
Rositzke, Harry. *The KGB: The Eyes of Russia.* Garden City, N.J.: Doubleday, 1981.
Ross, Dennis. *Risk Aversion in Soviet Defense Decisionmaking.* Los Angeles, Calif.: UCLA Center for International and Strategic Affairs, August 1980.
Scott, Harriet Fast, and William F. Scott. *The Armed Forces of the USSR.* Boulder, Colo.: Westview Press, 1979.
Sokolovsky, V. A. *Soviet Military Strategy.* Third edition, Harriet Fast Scott, ed. New York: Crane, Russak & Co., 1975.

Spielmann, Karl. *Prospects for a Soviet Strategy of Controlled Nuclear War: An Assessment of Some Key Indicators.* Institute for Defense Analysis, P-1236. March, 1976.

U.S. Department of Defense. *Soviet Military Power.* Washington, D.C.: USGPO, 1981.

Vigor, Peter. *The Soviet Views of War, Peace and Neutrality.* Boston: Routledge & Kegan Paul, 1975.

Warner, Edward L., III. *The Military in Contemporary Soviet Politics: An Institutional Analysis.* New York: Praeger, 1977.

Wolfe, Thomas W. *Soviet Power and Europe, 1945–70.* Baltimore, Md.: Johns Hopkins University Press, 1970.

————. *The Military Dimension in the Making of Soviet Foreign and Defense Policy.* Santa Monica, Calif.: Rand Corporation, 1977.

Social Trends

Atkinson, Dorothy, Alexander Dallin, and Gail Warshofsky Lapidus, eds. *Women in Russia.* Stanford: Stanford University Press, 1977.

Breslauer, George. *Five Images of the Soviet Future: A Critical Review and Synthesis.* Berkeley, Calif.: Institute of International Studies, 1978.

Connor, Walter D. *Socialism, Politics, and Equality: Hierarchy and Change in Eastern Europe and the USSR.* New York: Columbia University Press, 1977.

Davis, Christopher, and Murray Feshbach. *Rising Infant Mortality in the USSR.* Washington, D.C.: U.S. Department of Commerce, 1980.

Feifer, George. "Russian Disorders." *Harper's,* February 1981.

Kahan, Arcadius, and Blair A. Ruble. *Industrial Labor in the USSR.* New York: Pergamon, 1979.

Lane, David. *The End of Social Inequality: Class, Status, and Power under State Socialism.* London: Allen and Unwin, 1982.

Lapidus, Gail W. *Women in Soviet Society: Equality, Development, and Social Change.* Berkeley: University of California Press, 1978.

————, ed. *Women, Work, and Family in the USSR.* Armonk, N.Y.: M.E. Sharpe, 1982.

McAuley, Alastair. *Economic Welfare in the Soviet Union: Poverty, Living Standards, and Inequality.* London: Allen & Unwin, 1978.

Matthews, Mervin. *Privilege in the Soviet Union.* London: Allen & Unwin, 1978.

Pankhurst, Jerry G., and Michael Sacks, eds. *Contemporary Soviet Society.* New York: Praeger, 1980.

Parkin, Frank. *Class Inequality and Political Order.* London: MacGibbon and Kee, 1971.

————, ed. *The Social Analysis of Class Structure.* London: Tavistock, 1974.

Pond, Elizabeth. *From the Yaroslavsky Station: Russia Perceived.* New York: Universe Publishing, 1981.

Simis, Konstantin M. *USSR: The Corrupt Society.* New York: Simon and Schuster, 1982.

Yanowitch, Murray. *Social and Economic Inequality in the Soviet Union: Six Studies.* Armonk, N.Y.: M. E. Sharpe, 1977.

Yanowitch, Murray, and Wesley A. Fisher, eds. *Social Stratification and Mobility in the USSR.* Armonk, N.Y.: M. E. Sharpe, 1978.

Cultural and Intellectual Life .

Aksenov, Vasilii P. *Colleagues.* Translated by Margaret Wettlin. Moscow: Foreign Languages Publishing House, n.d.

————. *The Steel Bird and Other Stories.* Translated by Rae Slonek et al. Ann Arbor, Mich.: Ardis, 1979.

Brown, Deming. *Soviet Russian Literature since Stalin.* New York: Cambridge University Press, 1978.

Brown, Edward J. *Russian Literature since the Revolution.* Revised and enlarged edition. Cambridge, Mass.: Harvard University Press, 1982.

Dunham, Vera. *In Stalin's Time: Middle-Class Values in Soviet Fiction.* Cambridge: Cambridge University Press, 1976.

Dunlop, John B. *The New Russian Revolutionaries.* Belmont, Mass.: Nordland, 1976.

Fletcher, William C. *The Russian Church Underground.* Oxford: Oxford University Press, 1973.

Friedberg, Maurice. *A Decade of Euphoria.* Bloomington: Indiana University Press, 1977.

————. *Western Classics in Soviet Jackets.* New York: Columbia University Press, 1962.

Hosking, Geoffrey. *Beyond Socialist Realism: Soviet Fiction since Ivan Denisovich.* New York: Holmes & Meier, 1980.

Kasack, Wolfgang. *Lexikon der russischen Literatur ab 1917.* Stuttgart: Kroner Verlag, 1976.

Labedz, Leopold, ed. *Solzhenitsyn: A Documentary Record.* New York: Harper & Row, 1971.

Medvedev, Zhores A. *Soviet Science.* Oxford: Oxford University Press, 1979.

Segel, Harold B. *Twentieth-Century Russian Drama: From Gorky to the Present.* New York: Columbia University Press, 1979.

Shneidman, N. N. *Soviet Literature in the 1970s: Artistic Diversity and Ideological Conformity.* Toronto: University of Toronto Press, 1979.

Shukshin, Vasili M. *Snowball Berry and Other Stories.* Edited by Donald M. Fiene, with translations by Donald M. Fiene et al. Ann Arbor, Mich.: Ardis, 1979.

Sinyavsky, Andrei D. *For Freedom of Information.* Translation and introduction by Laszlo Tikos and Murray Peppard. New York: Holt, Rinehart & Winston, 1971.

————. *On Trial: The Soviet State versus "Abram Tertz" and "Nikolai Arzhak."* Translated, edited, and with an introduction by Max Hayward. New York: Harper & Row, 1966.

————. *A Voice from the Chorus.* Translated by Kyril FitzLyon and Max Hayward, with an introduction by Max Hayward. New York: Farrar, Straus & Giroux, 1976.

Svirskii, Grigorii. *Na lobnom meste: Literatura nravstvennogo soprotivleniia (1946–76).* London: Overseas Publications Interchange, 1979.

Trifonov, Yuri V. *The Long Goodbye: Three Novellas.* Translated by Helen P. Burlingame and Ellendea Proffer. New York: Harper & Row, 1978.

Voinovich, Vladimir. *The Ivankiad: Or, the Tale of the Writer Voinovich's Installation in His New Apartment.* Translated by David Lapeza. New York: Farrar, Straus & Giroux, 1977.

————. *The Life and Extraordinary Adventures of Private Ivan Chonkin.* Translated by Richard Lourie. New York: Farrar, Straus & Giroux, 1977.

————. *Pretender to the Throne: The Further Adventures of Private Ivan Chonkin.* Translated by Richard Lourie. New York: Farrar, Straus & Giroux, 1981.

Vorontsov, Yuri, and Igor Rachuk. *The Phenomenon of the Soviet Cinema.* Moscow: Progress Publishers, 1980.

Eastern Europe

Bornstein, Morris, Zvi Gitelman, and William Zimmerman, eds. *East-West Relations and the Future of Eastern Europe: Politics and Economics.* London: Allen & Unwin, 1981.

Brown, James F. "Relations Between the Soviet Union and Its Eastern European Allies: A Survey." Santa Monica, Calif.: Rand Corporation, 1975.

Brzezinski, Zbigniew. *The Soviet Bloc.* Revised and enlarged edition. Cambridge, Mass.: Harvard University Press, 1967.

Clawson, Robert W., and Lawrence S. Kaplan, eds. *The Warsaw Pact: Political Purposes and Military Means.* Wilmington, Del.: Scholarly Resources, Inc., 1982.

Dawisha, Karen, and Philip Hanson, eds. *Soviet-East European Dilemmas: Coercion, Competition and Consent.* New York: Holmes & Meier, 1981.

Drachkovitch, Milorad M., ed. *East Central Europe: Yesterday-Today-Tomorrow.* Stanford, Calif.: Hoover Institution Press, 1982.

Gati, Charles, ed. *The International Politics of Eastern Europe.* New York: Praeger, 1976.

———. *The Politics of Modernization in Eastern Europe.* New York: Praeger, 1974.

Johnson, A. Ross. "The Warsaw Pact: Soviet Military Policy in Eastern Europe," Santa Monica, Calif.: Rand Corporation, 1981.

Johnson, A. Ross, Robert W. Dean, and Alexander Alexiev. *East European Military Establishments: The Warsaw Pact Northern Tier.* New York: Crane, Russak & Co., 1982.

Jones, Christopher D. *Soviet Influence in Eastern Europe: Political Autonomy and the Warsaw Pact.* New York: Praeger, 1981.

Korbonski, Andrzej. "Eastern Europe as an Internal Determinant of Soviet Foreign Policy." In *The Domestic Context of Soviet Foreign Policy,* ed. Seweryn Bialer. Boulder, Colo.: Westview Press, 1981.

Linden, Ronald H., ed. *The Foreign Policies of Eastern Europe.* New York: Praeger, 1980.

Marer, Paul. "The Economies of Eastern Europe and Soviet Foreign Policy." In *The Domestic Context of Soviet Foreign Policy,* ed. Seweryn Bialer. Boulder, Colo.: Westview Press, 1981.

Marrese, Michael, and Jan Vaňous. *Implicit Subsidies and Non-Market Benefits in Soviet Trade with Eastern Europe.* Berkeley: University of California, Institute of International Studies, 1983.

Rakowska-Harmstone, Teresa, and Andrew Gyorgy, eds. *Communism in Eastern Europe.* Bloomington: Indiana University Press, 1979.

Terry, Sarah M., ed. *Soviet Policy in Eastern Europe* (forthcoming).

The World Outside

Adomeit, Hannes. "Soviet Foreign Policy Making: The Internal Mechanism of Global Commitment." In Hannes Adomeit and Robert Boardman, eds., *Foreign Policy Making in Communist Countries.* England: Saxon House, 1979.

Albright, David. "Sub-Saharan African and Soviet Foreign Policy in the 1980s." Paper prepared for the Center for Strategic and International Studies, Washington, D.C., 1982.

Arbatov, G. et al., eds. *The Global Strategy of the United States under the Conditions of the Scientific and Technological Revolution.* Moscow, 1979.

Baker, Raymond. "The Soviet Union and the Moslem World." Paper prepared for the Center for Strategic and International Studies, Washington, D.C., 1982.

Barnett, A. Doak. *China's Economy in Global Perspective*. Washington, D.C.: Brookings, 1981.

Bialer, Seweryn, and Alfred Stepon. "Cuba, the U.S., and the Central American Mess." *New York Review of Books*, May 27, 1982.

Brezhnev, L. I. *Following in Lenin's Path*, vol. 5. Moscow, 1976.

Brudents, K. *The Present State of the Liberation Struggle of the Asian and African Peoples and Revolutionary Democracy*. Moscow, 1977.

Bundy, McGeorge, George F. Kennan, Robert McNamara, and Gerard Smith. "Nuclear Weapons and the Atlantic Alliance." *Foreign Affairs*, Spring 1982, pp. 753–68.

Caldwell, L. T. *Soviet Attitudes toward SALT*. London: Institute for Strategic Studies, 1971.

Central Intelligence Agency, National Foreign Assessment Center. *The Handbook of Economic Statistics*. Washington, D.C.: USGPO, 1981.

Dawisha, Adeed, and Karen Dawisha, eds. *The Soviet Union in the Middle East*. London: Heinemann, 1982.

Dominguez, Jorge I. *Cuba, Order and Revolution*. Cambridge, Mass.: Harvard University Press, 1978.

Duncan, Raymond W., ed. *Soviet Policy in the Third World*. New York: Pergamon Press, 1980.

Glinken, A. N., ed. *Intra-State Relations in Latin America*. Moscow: USSR Academy of Sciences, 1977.

Gong, Gerrit W. "China in the 1980s." Paper prepared for the Center for Strategic and International Studies, Washington, D.C., 1982.

Griffith, William E. *The Sino-Soviet Rift*. Cambridge: MIT Press, 1964.

Heikal, Mohamed. *The Road to Ramadan*. New York, 1975.

———. *Sphinx and Commissar*. London: Collins, 1978.

Hoffmann, Erik P., and Frederic Fleron, Jr., eds. *The Conduct of Soviet Foreign Policy*. Chicago: Aldine-Atherton, 1977.

Kennan, George F. *The Nuclear Delusion: Soviet-American Relations in the Atomic Age*. New York: Pantheon, 1982.

———. *Soviet Foreign Policy, 1917–1941*. Princeton: Van Nostrand, 1960.

Kohler, Foy D., et al. *Soviet Strategy for the Seventies: From Cold War to Peaceful Coexistence*. Coral Gables, Fla.: Center for Advanced International Studies, 1973.

Legum, Colin et al. *Africa in the 1980s*. New York: McGraw-Hill, 1979.

Lowenthal, Abraham F. "Latin America in the 1980s: Opportunities for Expanding Soviet Influence." Paper prepared for the Center for Strategic and International Studies, Washington, D.C., 1982.

Mlynar, Zdenek. *Night Frost in Prague*. New York: Karz, 1980.

Pipes, Richard. *U.S.-Soviet Relations in the Era of Detente*. Boulder, Colo.: Westview Press, 1981.

Royal Institute of International Affairs. *Documents on International Affairs, 1947–48*. London, 1952.

Scalapino, Robert. "Chinese Foreign Policy in 1979." In *China Briefing 1980*, Robert B. Oxnam and Richard Bush, eds. Boulder, Colo.: Westview Press, 1980.

Schwartz, Morton. *Soviet Perceptions of the United States*. Berkeley: University of California Press, 1978.

Sergeichuk, S. *Through Russian Eyes: American-Chinese Relations.* Arlington, Va.: International Library, 1975.

Shulgovski, A. F., ed. *Nationalism in Latin America: Political and Ideological Currents.* Moscow, 1976.

Shulman, Marshall. *Stalin's Foreign Policy Reappraised.* Cambridge, Mass.: Harvard University Press, 1963.

Solomon, Richard, ed. *The China Factor: Sino-Soviet Relations and the Global Scene.* Englewood Cliffs, N.J.: Prentice-Hall, 1981.

Stebbins, Richard, and Elaine May. *American Foreign Relations, 1972 Documents.* Washington, D.C.: USGPO, 1976.

Stent, Angela. "The USSR and Western Europe in the 1980s." Paper prepared for the Center for Strategic and International Studies, Washington, D.C., 1982.

Stimson, Henry L., and McGeorge Bundy. *On Active Service in War and Peace.* New York: Octagon, 1947.

Strode, Rebecca V. "External Factors Affecting Soviet Foreign Policy for the 1980s: The Military Dimension." Paper prepared for the Center for Strategic and International Studies, Washington, D.C., 1982.

Trofimenko, Henry A. *The Strategy of Global War.* Moscow, 1968.

Twenty-second Congress of the CPSU, Stenographic Report, II. Moscow, 1961.

Twenty-sixth Congress of the CPSU, Stenographic Report, I. Moscow, 1981.

Twenty-third Congress of the CPSU, Stenographic Report, I. Moscow, 1966.

Ulam, Adam. *Dangerous Relations: The Soviet Union in World Politics.* New York: Oxford University Press, 1983.

———. *Expansion and Coexistence: History of Soviet Foreign Policy, 1917–73.* New York: Praeger, 1974.

Whiting, Allen S., and Robert Dernberger. *China's Future.* New York: McGraw-Hill, 1978.

Yamonouchi, Kazuo. "The Chinese Economy, 1981." *China Newsletter,* No. 37, Tokyo, March-April, 1982.

Zagoria, Donald, ed. *The Soviet Union and Asia.* New Haven, Conn.: Yale University Press, 1982.

Index